Theory of Financial Decision Making

Rowman & Littlefield Studies in Financial Economics
Jonathan E. Ingersoll, Jr., General Editor

forthcoming:

Frontiers of Modern Financial Theory
Sudipto Bhattacharya and George Constantinides

Theory of Financial Decision Making

Jonathan E. Ingersoll, Jr.
Yale University

Rowman & Littlefield
PUBLISHERS

ROWMAN & LITTLEFIELD

Published in the United States of America in 1987
by Rowman & Littlefield, Publishers
(a division of Littlefield, Adams & Company)
81 Adams Drive, Totowa, New Jersey 07512

Library of Congress Cataloging-in-Publication Data

Ingersoll, Jonathan E.
Theory of financial decision making.

(Rowman & Littlefield studies in financial economics)
Bibliography: p. 449
1. Finance — Mathematical models. I. Title.
II. Series.
HG173.I54 1987 332.6′0724 86–1907
ISBN 0-8476-7359-6

89 88 87
10 9 8 7 6 5 4 3 2

Printed in the United States of America

Contents

List of Tables

List of Figures

Preface

In the past twenty years the quantity of new and exciting research in finance has been large, and a sizable body of basic material now lies at the core of our area of study. It is the purpose of this book to present this core in a systematic and thorough fashion. The notes for this book have been the primary text for various doctoral-level courses in financial theory that I have taught over the past eight years at the University of Chicago and Yale University. In all the courses these notes have been supplemented with readings selected from journals. Reading original journal articles is an integral part of learning an academic field, since it serves to introduce the students to the ongoing process of research, including its mis-steps and controversies. In my opinion any program of study would be amiss not to convey this continuing growth.

This book is structured in four parts. The first part, Chapters 1–3, provides an introduction to utility theory, arbitrage, portfolio formation, and efficient markets. Chapter 1 provides some necessary background in microeconomics. Consumer choice is reviewed, and expected utility maximization is introduced. Risk aversion and its measurement are also covered.

Chapter 2 introduces the concept of arbitrage. The absence of arbitrage is one of the most convincing and, therefore, farthest-reaching arguments made in financial economics. Arbitrage reasoning is the basis for the arbitrage pricing theory, one of the leading models purporting to explain the cross-sectional difference in asset returns. Perhaps more important, the absence of arbitrage is the key in the development of the Black-Scholes option pricing model and its various derivatives, which have been used to value a wide variety of claims both in theory and in practice.

Chapter 3 begins the study of single-period portfolio problems. It also introduces the student to the theory of efficient markets: the premise that asset prices fully reflect all information available to the market. The theory of efficient (or rational) markets is one of the cornerstones of modern finance; it permeates almost all current financial research and has found wide acceptance among practitioners, as well.

In the second main section, Chapters 4–9 cover single-period equilibrium models. Chapter 4 covers mean-variance analysis and the capital asset pricing model — a model which has found many supporters and widespread applications. Chapters 5 through 7 expand on Chapter 4. The first two cover generalized measures of risk and additional mutual fund theorems. The latter treats linear factor models and the arbitrage pricing theory, probably the key competitor of the CAPM.

Chapter 8 offers an alternative equilibrium view based on complete markets theory. This theory was originally noted for its elegant treatment of general equilibrium as in the models of Arrow and Debreu and was considered to be primarily of theoretical interest. More recently it and the related concept of spanning have found many practical applications in contingent-claims pricing.

Chapter 9 reviews single-period finance with an overview of how the various models complement one another. It also provides a second view of the efficient markets hypothesis in light of the developed equilibrium models.

Chapter 10, which begins the third main section on multiperiod models, introduces models set in more than one period. It reviews briefly the concept of discounting, with which it is assumed the reader is already acquainted, and reintroduces efficient markets theory in this context. Chapters 11 and 13 examine the multiperiod portfolio problem. Chapter 11 introduces dynamic programming and the induced or derived single-period portfolio problem inherent in the intertemporal problem. After some necessary mathematical background provided in Chapter 12, Chapter 13 tackles the same problem in a continuous-time setting using the mean-variance tools of Chapter 4. Merton's intertemporal capital asset pricing model is derived, and the desire of investors to hedge is examined.

Chapter 14 covers option pricing. Using arbitrage reasoning it develops distribution-free and preference-free restrictions on the valuation of options and other derivative assets. It culminates in the development of the Black-Scholes option pricing model. Chapter 15 summarizes multiperiod models and provides a view of how they complement one another and the single-period models. It also discusses the role of complete markets and spanning in a multiperiod context and develops the consumption-based asset pricing model.

In the final main section, Chapter 16 is a second mathematical interruption—this time to introduce the Ito calculus. Chapter 17 explores advanced topics in option pricing using Ito calculus. Chapter 18 examines the term structure of interest rates using both option techniques and multiperiod portfolio analysis. Chapter 19 considers questions of corporate capital structure. Chapter 19 demonstrates many of the applications of the Black-Scholes model to the pricing of various corporate contracts.

The mathematical prerequisites of this book have been kept as simple as practicable. A knowledge of calculus, probability and statistics, and basic linear algebra is assumed. The Mathematical Introduction collects some required concepts from these areas. Advanced topics in stochastic processes and Ito calculus are developed heuristically, where needed, because they have become so important in finance. Chapter 12 provides an introduction to the stochastic processes used in continuous-time finance. Chapter 16 is an introduction to Ito calculus. Other advanced mathematical topics, such as measure theory, are avoided. This choice, of course, requires that rigor or generality sometimes be sacrificed to intuition and understanding. Major points are always presented verbally as well as mathematically. These presentations are usually accompanied by graphical illustrations and numerical examples.

To emphasize the theoretical framework of finance, many topics have been left uncovered. There is virtually no description of the actual operation of financial markets or of the various institutions that play vital roles. Also missing is a discussion of empirical tests of the various theories. Empirical research in finance is perhaps more extensive than theoretical, and any adequate review would require a complete book itself. The effects of market imperfections are also not treated. In the first place, theoretical results in this area have not yet been fully developed. In addition the predictions of the perfect market models seem to be surprisingly robust despite the necessary simplifying assumptions. In any case an understanding of the workings of perfect markets is obviously a precursor to studying market imperfections.

The material in this book (together with journal supplements) is designed for a full year's study. Shorter courses can also be designed to suit individual tastes and prerequisites. For example, the study of multiperiod models could commence immediately after Chapter 4. Much of the material on option pricing and contingent claims (except for parts of Chapter 18 on the term structure of interest rates) does not depend on the equilibrium models and could be studied immediately after Chapter 3.

This book is a text and not a treatise. To avoid constant interruptions and footnotes, outside references and other citations have been kept to a minimum. An extended chapter-by-chapter bibliography is provided, and my debt to the authors represented there should be obvious to anyone familiar with the development of finance. It is my hope that any student in the area also will come to learn of this indebtedness.

I am also indebted to many colleagues and students who have read, or in some cases taught from, earlier drafts of this book. Their advice, suggestions, and examples have all helped to improve this product, and their continuing requests for the latest revision have encouraged me to make it available in book form.

Jonathan Ingersoll, Jr.

New Haven
November 1986

Glossary of Commonly Used Symbols

a — Often the parameter of the exponential utility function $u(Z) = -\exp(-aZ)$.

B — The factor loading matrix in the linear model.

b — Often the parameter of the quadratic utility function $u(Z) = Z - bZ^2/2$.

b_i^k — $= \mathrm{Cov}(\tilde{z}_i, \tilde{Z}_e^k)/(\mathrm{Cov}(\tilde{z}_e^k, \tilde{Z}_e^k)$. A measure of systematic risk for the ith asset with respect to the kth efficient portfolio. Also the loading of the ith asset on the kth factor, the measure of systematic risk in the factor model.

C — Consumption.

E — The expectation operator. Expectations are also often denoted with an overbar $\bar{\ }$.

e — The base for natural logarithms and the exponential function. $e \approx 2.71828$.

$\tilde{f}$ — A factor in the linear factor model.

I — The identity matrix.

i — As a subscript it usually denotes the ith asset.

J — A derived utility of wealth function in intertemporal portfolio models.

j — As a subscript it usually denotes the jth asset.

K — The call price on a callable contingent claim.

k — As a subscript or superscript it usually denotes the kth investor.

L — Usually a Lagrangian expression.

m — As a subscript or superscript it usually denotes the market portfolio.

N — The number of assets.

$N(\cdot)$ — The cumulative normal distribution function.

$n(\cdot)$ The standard normal density function.

$O(\cdot)$ Asymptotic order symbol. Function is of the same as or smaller order than its argument.

$o(\cdot)$ Asymptotic order symbol. Function is of smaller order than its agrument.

$\mathbf{p}$ The supporting state price vector.

q Usually denotes a probability.

R The riskless return (the interest rate plus one).

r The interest rate. $r \equiv R - 1$.

S In single-period models, the number of states. In intertemporal models, the price of a share of stock.

s As a subscript or superscript it usually denotes state s.

T Some fixed time, often the maturity date of an asset.

t Current time.

$\mathbf{t}$ The tangency portfolio in the mean-variance portfolio problem.

U A utility of consumption function.

u A utility of return function.

V A derived utility function.

$\mathbf{v}$ The values of the assets.

W Wealth.

$W(S, \tau)$ The Black–Scholes call option pricing function on a stock with price S and time to maturity of τ.

$\mathbf{w}$ A vector of portfolio weights. w_i is the fraction of wealth in the ith asset.

X The exercise price for an option.

$\mathbf{Y}$ The state space tableau of payoffs. Y_{si} is the payoff in state s on asset i.

$\mathbf{Z}$ The state space tableau of returns. Z_{si} is the return in state s on asset i.

$\tilde{Z}_{\mathbf{w}}$ The return on portfolio $\mathbf{w}$.

z As a subscript it denotes the zero beta portfolio.

$\tilde{\mathbf{z}}$ The random returns on the assets.

$\bar{\mathbf{z}}$ The expected returns on the assets.

$\mathbf{0}$ A vector or matrix whose elements are 0.

$\mathbf{1}$ A vector whose elements are 1.

$>$ As a vector inequality each element of the left-hand vector is greater than the corresponding element of the right-hand vector. $<$ is similarly defined.

$\geqslant$ As a vector inequality each element of the left-hand vector is greater than or equal to the corresponding element of the right-hand vector, and at least one element is strictly greater. $\leqslant$ is similarly defined.

$\geqq$ As a vector inequality each element of the left-hand vector is greater than or equal to the corresponding element of the right-hand vector. $\leqq$ is similarly defined.

α The expected, instantaneous rate of return on an asset.

β $\equiv \text{Cov}(\tilde{z}, \tilde{Z}_m)$. The beta of an asset.

γ Often the parameter of the power utility function $u(Z) = Z^{\gamma}/\gamma$.

Δ A first difference.

$\tilde{\varepsilon}$ The residual portion of an asset's return.

$\boldsymbol{\eta}$ A portfolio commitment of funds not nomalized.

Θ A martingale pricing measure.

$\boldsymbol{\iota}_j$ The jth column of the identity matrix.

$\tilde{\Lambda}$ The state price per unit probability; a martingale pricing measure.

λ Usually a Lagrange multiplier.

$\boldsymbol{\lambda}$ The factor risk premiums in the APT.

$\boldsymbol{\nu}$ A portfolio of Arrow–Debreu securities. ν_s is the number of state s securities held.

$\boldsymbol{\pi}$ The vector of state probabilities.

ρ A correlation coefficient.

$\boldsymbol{\Sigma}$ The variance-covariance matrix of returns.

σ A standard deviation, usually of the return on an asset.

τ The time left until maturity of a contract.

Φ Public information.

ϕ_k Private information of investor k.

$\boldsymbol{\omega}$ An arbitrage portfolio commitment of funds $(\mathbf{1}'\boldsymbol{\omega} = 0)$.

ω A Gauss–Wiener process. $d\omega$ is the increment to a Gauss–Wiener process.

Theory of Financial Decision Making

Mathematical Introduction

DEFINITIONS AND NOTATION

Unless otherwise noted, all quantities represent real values. In this book derivatives are often denoted in the usual fashion by $'$, $''$, and so forth. Higher-order derivatives are denoted by $f^{(n)}$ for the nth derivative. Partial derivatives are often denoted by subscripts. For example,

$$F_1(x, y) \equiv F_x(x, y) \equiv \frac{\partial F(x, y)}{\partial x},$$
$$F_{12}(x, y) \equiv F_{xy}(x, y) \equiv \frac{\partial F(x, y)}{\partial x \, \partial y}. \tag{1}$$

Closed intervals are denoted by brackets, open intervals by parentheses. For example,

$$x \in [a, b] \quad \text{means} \quad \text{all } x \text{ such that } a \leqslant x \leqslant b,$$
$$x \in [a, b) \quad \text{means} \quad \text{all } x \text{ such that } a \leqslant x < b, \tag{2}$$

The greatest and least values of a set are denoted by Max($\cdot$) and Min($\cdot$), respectively. For example, if $x > y$, then

$$\text{Min}(x, y) = y \qquad \text{and} \qquad \text{Max}(x, y) = x. \tag{3}$$

The relative importance of terms is denoted by the asymptotic order symbols:

$$f(x) = o(x^n) \quad \text{means} \quad \lim_{x\to 0} \frac{f(x)}{x^n} = 0;$$
$$f(x) = O(x^n) \quad \text{means} \quad \lim_{x\to 0} \frac{f(x)}{x^{n+\varepsilon}} = 0 \quad \text{for all } \varepsilon > 0. \tag{4}$$

Dirac delta function

The Dirac delta function $\delta(x)$ is defined by its properties:

$$\delta(x) = \begin{cases} 0, & x \neq 0, \\ \infty, & x = 0, \end{cases} \tag{5}$$

$$\int_{-a}^{a} \delta(x)\,dx = 1 \qquad \text{for any } a > 0.$$

The delta function may be considered as the limit of a mean zero density function as the dispersion goes to zero. For example, for the normal density

$$\delta(x) = \lim_{\sigma\to 0} (2\pi\sigma^2)^{-1/2} \exp\left(\frac{-x^2}{2\sigma^2}\right). \tag{6}$$

In the limit all the probability mass is concentrated at the origin, but the total mass is still unity.

The Dirac delta function is most often used in formal mathematical manipulations. The following property is useful:

$$\int_{a}^{b} \delta(x - x_0) f(x)\,dx = f(x_0) \qquad \text{if } a \leqslant x_0 \leqslant b. \tag{7}$$

Unit step function

The unit step function is the formal integral of the Dirac delta function and is given by

$$u(x) = \begin{cases} 1, & x > 0, \\ \frac{1}{2}, & x = 0, \\ 0, & x < 0. \end{cases} \tag{8}$$

Taylor Series

If f and all its derivatives exist in the region $[x, x + h]$, then

$$f(x + h) = f(x) + f'(x)h + \tfrac{1}{2}f''(x)h^2 + \cdots + \frac{1}{n!}f^{(n)}(x)h^n + \cdots. \tag{9}$$

If f and all its derivatives up to order n exist in the region $[x, x + h]$, then it can be represented by a Taylor series with Lagrange remainder

$$\begin{aligned} f(x + h) = f(x) + f'(x)h + \cdots + \frac{1}{(n-1)!}f^{(n-1)}(x)h^{n-1} \\ + \frac{1}{n!}f^{(n)}(x^*)h^n, \end{aligned} \tag{10}$$

where x^* is in $[x, x + h]$. For a function of two or more arguments the extension is obvious:

$$F(x + h, y + k) = F(x, y) + F_1(x, y)h + F_2(x, y)k$$

$$+ \tfrac{1}{2}F_{11}(x, y)h^2 + \tfrac{1}{2}F_{22}(x, y)k^2 + F_{12}(x, y)hk \tag{11}$$

$$+ \cdots + \frac{1}{n!}\left(h\frac{\partial}{\partial x} + k\frac{\partial}{\partial y}\right)^n f(x, y) + \cdots.$$

Mean Value Theorem

The mean value theorem is simply the two-term form of the exact Taylor series with Lagrange remainder:

$$f(x + h) = f(x) + f'(x + \alpha h)h \tag{12}$$

for some α in $[0, 1]$. The mean value theorem is also often stated in integral form. If $f(x)$ is a continuous function in (a, b), then

$$\int_a^b f(x)\,dx = (b - a)f(x^*) \tag{13}$$

for some x^* in (a, b).

Implicit Function Theorem

Consider all points (x, y) on the curve with $F(x, y) = a$. Along this curve the derivative of y with respect to x is

$$\left.\frac{dy}{dx}\right|_{F=a} = -\frac{\partial F/\partial x}{\partial F/\partial y}. \tag{14}$$

To see this, note that

$$dF = \frac{\partial F}{\partial x}dx + \frac{\partial F}{\partial y}dy.$$

Setting $dF = 0$ and solving for dy/dx gives the desired result.

Differentiation of Integrals: Leibniz's Rule

Let $F(x) \equiv \int_{A(x)}^{B(x)} f(x, t)\,dt$ and assume that f and $\partial f/\partial x$ are continuous in t in $[A, B]$ and x in $[a, b]$. Then

$$F'(x) = \int_A^B f_1(x, t)\,dt + f(x, B)B'(x) - f(x, A)A'(x) \tag{15}$$

for all x in $[a, b]$. If $F(x)$ is defined by an improper integral ($A = -\infty$ and/or $B = \infty$), then Leibniz's rule can be employed if $|f_2(x, t)| \leqslant M(t)$ for all x in $[a, b]$ and all t in $[A, B]$, and the integral $\int M(t)\,dt$ converges in $[A, B]$.

Homotheticity and Homogeneity

A function $F(\mathbf{x})$ of a vector $\mathbf{x}$ is said to be *homogeneous of degree k to the point* $\mathbf{x}_0$ if

$$F(\lambda(\mathbf{x} - \mathbf{x}_0)) = \lambda^k F(\mathbf{x} - \mathbf{x}_0). \tag{16}$$

If no reference is made to the point of homogeneity, it is generally assumed to be $\mathbf{0}$. For $k = 1$ the function is said to be linearly homogeneous. This does not, of course, imply that $F(\cdot)$ is linear.

All partial derivatives of a homogeneous function are homogeneous of one smaller degree. That is, let $f(\mathbf{x}) \equiv \partial F(\mathbf{x})/\partial x_i$. Then $f(\lambda\mathbf{x}) = \lambda^{k-1}f(\mathbf{x})$. To prove this, take the partial derivative of both sides of (16) with respect to x_i:

$$\frac{\partial F(\lambda\mathbf{x})}{\partial x_i} = \lambda F_i(\lambda\mathbf{x}) \qquad \text{and} \qquad \frac{\partial \lambda^k F(\mathbf{x})}{\partial x_i} = \lambda^k F_i(x). \tag{17}$$

Then

$$f(\lambda\mathbf{x}) = \lambda^{k-1} f(\mathbf{x}).$$

Similarly, all nth-order partial derivatives of $F(\cdot)$ are homogeneous of degree $k - n$.

Euler's theorem states that the following condition is satisfied by homogeneous functions:

$$\sum x_i \frac{\partial F(\mathbf{x})}{\partial x_i} = kF(\mathbf{x}). \tag{18}$$

To prove (18), differentiate (16) with respect to λ:

$$\frac{\partial}{\partial\lambda} F(\lambda\mathbf{x}) = \sum x_i \frac{\partial F(\lambda\mathbf{x})}{\partial x_i} = k\lambda^{k-1}F(\mathbf{x}). \tag{19}$$

Now substitute $\lambda = 1$.

A function $F(\mathbf{x})$ is said to be *homothetic* if it can be written as

$$F(\mathbf{x}) = h(g(\mathbf{x})), \tag{20}$$

where g is homogeneous and h is continuous, nondecreasing, and positive.

MATRICES AND LINEAR ALGEBRA

It is assumed that the reader is familiar with the basic notions of matrix manipulations. We write vectors as boldface lowercase letters and matrices as boldface uppercase letters. $\mathbf{I}$ denotes the identity matrix. $\mathbf{0}$

denotes the null vector or null matrix as appropriate. **1** is a vector whose elements are unity. $\boldsymbol{\iota}_n$ is a vector with zeros for all elements except the nth, which is unity. Transposes are denoted by $'$. Vectors are, unless otherwise specified, column vectors. Transposed vectors are row vectors. The inverse of a square matrix $\mathbf{A}$ is denoted by $\mathbf{A}^{-1}$.

Some of the more advanced matrix operations that will be useful are outlined next.

Vector Equalities and Inequalities

Two vectors are equal, $\mathbf{x} = \mathbf{z}$, if every pair of components is equal: $x_i = z_i$. Two vectors cannot be equal unless they have the same dimension. We adopt the following inequality conventions:

$$\mathbf{x} \geqq \mathbf{z} \quad \text{if} \quad x_i \geq z_i \qquad \text{for all } i, \tag{21a}$$

$$\mathbf{x} \geq \mathbf{z} \quad \text{if} \quad x_i \geq z_i \qquad \text{for all } i \text{ and } x_i > z_i \text{ for some } i, \tag{21b}$$

$$\mathbf{x} > \mathbf{z} \quad \text{if} \quad x_i > z_i \qquad \text{for all } i. \tag{22c}$$

For these three cases $\mathbf{x} - \mathbf{z}$ is said to be nonnegative, semipositive, and positive, respectively.

Orthogonal Matrices

A square matrix $\mathbf{A}$ is *orthogonal* if

$$\mathbf{A}'\mathbf{A} = \mathbf{A}\mathbf{A}' = \mathbf{I}. \tag{22}$$

The vectors making up the rows (or columns) of an orthogonal matrix form an orthonormal set. That is, if we denote the ith row (column) by $\mathbf{a}_i$, then

$$\mathbf{a}_i'\mathbf{a}_j = \begin{cases} 1, & i = j, \\ 0, & i \neq j. \end{cases} \tag{23}$$

Each vector is normalized to have unit length and is orthogonal to all others.

Generalized (Conditional) Inverses

Only nonsingular (square) matrices possess inverses; however, all matrices have generalized or conditional inverses. The conditional inverse $\mathbf{A}^c$ of a matrix $\mathbf{A}$ is any matrix satisfying

$$\mathbf{A}\mathbf{A}^c\mathbf{A} = \mathbf{A}. \tag{24}$$

If $\mathbf{A}$ is $m \times n$, then $\mathbf{A}^c$ is $n \times m$. The conditional inverse of a matrix always exists, but it need not be unique. If the matrix is nonsingular, then $\mathbf{A}^{-1}$ is a conditional inverse.

The Moore–Penrose generalized inverse $\mathbf{A}^{-}$ is a conditional inverse satisfying the additional conditions

$$\mathbf{A}^{-}\mathbf{A}\mathbf{A}^{-} = \mathbf{A}^{-}, \tag{25}$$

and both $\mathbf{A}^{-}\mathbf{A}$ and $\mathbf{A}\mathbf{A}^{-}$ are symmetric. The Moore–Penrose inverse of any matrix exists and is unique. These inverses have the following properties:

$$(\mathbf{A}')^{-} = (\mathbf{A}^{-})', \tag{26a}$$

$$(\mathbf{A}^{-})^{-} = \mathbf{A}, \tag{26b}$$

$$\operatorname{rank}(\mathbf{A}^{-}) = \operatorname{rank}(\mathbf{A}), \tag{26c}$$

$$(\mathbf{A}'\mathbf{A})^{-} = \mathbf{A}^{-}\mathbf{A}'^{-}, \tag{26d}$$

$$(\mathbf{A}\mathbf{A}^{-})^{-} = \mathbf{A}\mathbf{A}^{-}, \tag{26e}$$

$$(\mathbf{A}^{-}\mathbf{A})^{-} = \mathbf{A}^{-}\mathbf{A}. \tag{26f}$$

Also $\mathbf{A}\mathbf{A}^{-}$, $\mathbf{A}^{-}\mathbf{A}$, $\mathbf{I} - \mathbf{A}\mathbf{A}^{-}$, and $\mathbf{I} - \mathbf{A}^{-}\mathbf{A}$ are all symmetric and idempotent.

If $\mathbf{A}$ is an $m \times n$ matrix of rank m, then $\mathbf{A}^{-} = \mathbf{A}'(\mathbf{A}\mathbf{A}')^{-1}$ is the *right inverse* of $\mathbf{A}$ (i.e., $\mathbf{A}\mathbf{A}^{-} = \mathbf{I}$). Similarly, if the rank of $\mathbf{A}$ is n, then $\mathbf{A}^{-} = (\mathbf{A}'\mathbf{A})^{-1}\mathbf{A}'$ is the left inverse.

Vector and Matrix Norms

A norm is a single nonnegative number assigned to a matrix or vector as a measure of its magnitude. It is similar to the absolute value of a real number or the modulus of a complex number. A convenient, and the most common, vector norm is the Euclidean norm (or length) of the vector $\|\mathbf{x}\|$:

$$\|\mathbf{x}\| \equiv \sqrt{\mathbf{x}'\mathbf{x}} \equiv (\textstyle\sum x_i^2)^{1/2}. \tag{27}$$

For nonnegative vectors the linear norm is also often used

$$L(\mathbf{x}) \equiv \mathbf{1}'\mathbf{x} \equiv \textstyle\sum x_i. \tag{28}$$

The Euclidean norm of a matrix is defined similarly:

$$\|\mathbf{A}\|_E \equiv (\textstyle\sum\sum a_{ij}^2)^{1/2}. \tag{29}$$

The Euclidean matrix norm should not be confused with the spectral norm, which is induced by the Euclidean vector norm

$$\|A\| \equiv \sup_{\mathbf{x}\neq\mathbf{0}} \frac{\|\mathbf{A}\mathbf{x}\|}{\|\mathbf{x}\|}. \tag{30}$$

The spectral norm is the largest eigenvalue of $\mathbf{A}'\mathbf{A}$.

Other types of norms are possible. For example, the Hölder norm is defined as

$$h_n(\mathbf{x}) \equiv (\Sigma|x_i|^n)^{1/n}, \qquad 1 \leqslant n, \tag{31}$$

and similarly for matrices, with the additional requirement that $n \leqslant 2$. $\rho(\mathbf{x}) \equiv \max|x_i|$ and $M(\mathbf{A}) \equiv \max|a_{ij}|$ for an $n \times n$ matrix are also norms.

All norms have the following properties ($\mathbf{A}$ denotes a vector or matrix):

$$\|\mathbf{A}\| \geqslant 0, \tag{32a}$$

$$\|\mathbf{A}\| = 0 \quad \text{iff} \quad \mathbf{A} = \mathbf{0}, \tag{32b}$$

$$\|c\mathbf{A}\| = |c|\ \|\mathbf{A}\|, \tag{32c}$$

$$\|\mathbf{A} + \mathbf{B}\| \leqslant \|\mathbf{A}\| + \|\mathbf{B}\|, \tag{32d}$$

$$\|\mathbf{AB}\| \leqslant \|\mathbf{A}\|\ \|\mathbf{B}\|, \tag{32e}$$

$$\|\mathbf{A} - \mathbf{B}\| \geqslant |\|\mathbf{A}\| - \|\mathbf{B}\||, \tag{32f}$$

$$\|\mathbf{A}^{-1}\| \geqslant \|\mathbf{A}\|^{-1} \qquad \text{(square matrices)}. \tag{32g}$$

Properties (32d) and (32f) apply only to matrices or vectors of the same order: (32d) is known as the triangle inequality; (32f) shows that norms are smooth functions. That is, whenever $|\|\mathbf{A}\| - \|\mathbf{B}\|| < \varepsilon$, then $\mathbf{A}$ and $\mathbf{B}$ are similar in the sense that $|a_{ij} - b_{ij}| < \delta$ for all i and j.

Vector Differentiation

Let $f(\mathbf{x})$ be a function of a vector $\mathbf{x}$. Then the gradient of f is

$$\nabla f \equiv \frac{\partial f}{\partial \mathbf{x}} = \left(\frac{\partial f}{\partial x_1}, \frac{\partial f}{\partial x_2}, \ldots, \frac{\partial f}{\partial x_n}\right)'. \tag{33}$$

The Hessian matrix is the $n \times n$ matrix of second partial derivatives

$$\mathbf{H}f \equiv \frac{\partial^2 f}{\partial \mathbf{x}\,\partial \mathbf{x}'} = \begin{pmatrix} \dfrac{\partial^2 f}{\partial x_1^2} & \dfrac{\partial^2 f}{\partial x_1 \partial x_2} & \cdots & \dfrac{\partial^2 f}{\partial x_1 \partial x_n} \\ \dfrac{\partial^2 f}{\partial x_2 \partial x_1} & \dfrac{\partial^2 f}{\partial x_2^2} & \cdots & \dfrac{\partial^2 f}{\partial x_2 \partial x_n} \\ \vdots & & & \vdots \\ \dfrac{\partial^2 f}{\partial x_n \partial x_1} & & \cdots & \dfrac{\partial^2 f}{\partial x_n^2} \end{pmatrix}. \tag{34}$$

The derivative of the linear form $\mathbf{a}'\mathbf{x}$ is

$$\frac{\partial(\mathbf{a}'\mathbf{x})}{\partial\mathbf{x}} = \mathbf{a}. \tag{35}$$

The derivatives of the quadratic form $\mathbf{x}'\mathbf{A}\mathbf{x}$ are

$$\begin{aligned} \frac{\partial(\mathbf{x}'\mathbf{A}\mathbf{x})}{\partial\mathbf{x}} &= (\mathbf{A} + \mathbf{A}')\mathbf{x}, \\ \frac{\partial^2(\mathbf{x}'\mathbf{A}\mathbf{x})}{\partial\mathbf{x}\partial\mathbf{x}'} &= (\mathbf{A} + \mathbf{A}'). \end{aligned} \tag{36}$$

Note that if $\mathbf{A}$ is symmetric, then the above look like the standard results from calculus: $\partial ax^2/\partial x = 2ax$, $\partial^2 ax^2/\partial x^2 = 2a$.

CONSTRAINED OPTIMIZATION

The conditions for an unconstrained strong local maximum of a function of several variables are that the gradient vector and Hessian matrix with respect to the decision variables be zero and negative definite:

$$\nabla f = \mathbf{0}, \qquad \mathbf{z}'(\mathbf{H}f)\mathbf{z} > 0 \quad \text{all nonzero } z. \tag{37}$$

(For an unconstrained strong local minimum, the Hessian matrix must be positive definite.)

The Method of Lagrange

For maximization (or minimization) of a function subject to an equality constraint, we use Lagrangian methods. For example, to solve the problem Max $f(\mathbf{x})$ subject to $g(\mathbf{x}) = a$, we define the Lagrangian

$$L(\mathbf{x}, \lambda) \equiv f(\mathbf{x}) - \lambda(g(\mathbf{x}) - a) \tag{38}$$

and maximize with respect to $\mathbf{x}$ and λ:

$$\nabla f - \lambda \nabla g = \mathbf{0}, \qquad g(\mathbf{x}) - a = 0. \tag{39}$$

The solution to (39) gives for $\mathbf{x}^*$ the maximizing arguments and for λ^* the marginal cost of the constraint. That is,

$$\frac{df(\mathbf{x}^*)}{da} = \sum \frac{\partial f(x^*)}{\partial x_i} \frac{dx_i^*}{da} = \lambda. \tag{40}$$

The second-order condition for this constrained optimization can be stated with the bordered Hessian

$$H^{\mathrm{B}} \equiv \begin{pmatrix} \mathbf{H}f & \nabla g \\ (\nabla g)' & 0 \end{pmatrix}. \tag{41}$$

(iv) Both primal and dual are feasible. $p = d$ and $|p| < \infty$. The optimal vectors have all finite elements.

THEOREM *For any feasible* $\mathbf{x}$ *and* $\mathbf{z}$, $p(\mathbf{x}) - d(\mathbf{z}) \geq 0$.

THEOREM *(of complementary slackness) For the optimal controls, either* $x_{1i}^* = 0$ *or the* i^{th} *row of (47b) is exactly equal. Also, either* $z_{1i}^* = 0$ or the ith *row of (46b) is exactly equal.*

Each dual variable can be interpreted as the shadow price of the associated constraint in the primal. That is, the optimal value of a dual variable gives the change in the objective function for a unit increase in the right-hand side constraint (provided that the optimal basis does not change).

PROBABILITY

Central and Noncentral Moments

The moments of a random variable $\tilde{x}$ about some value a are defined as

$$\mu_n'(a) \equiv \int_{-\infty}^{\infty} (x - a)^n f(x)\, dx \tag{48}$$

provided the integral exists. If a is taken as the mean of $\tilde{x}$, then the moments are called central moments and are conventionally written without the prime. For any other a the moments are noncentral moments. The most common alternative is $a = 0$.

Central and noncentral moments are related by

$$\mu_n' = \sum_{i=0}^{n} \binom{n}{i} \mu_{n-i}(\mu_1')^i, \qquad \mu_n = \sum_{i=0}^{n} \binom{n}{i} \mu_{n-i}'(-\mu_1')^i. \tag{49}$$

Characteristic Function and Related Functions

The characteristic function for the density function $f(x)$ is

$$\phi(t) \equiv E[e^{it\tilde{x}}] \equiv \int_{-\infty}^{\infty} e^{itx} f(x)\, dx \qquad \text{where } i \equiv \sqrt{-1}. \tag{50}$$

The nth noncentral moment of $f(x)$ about the origin is related to the characteristic function by

$$\mu_n' \equiv E[\tilde{x}^n] = i^{-n}\phi^{(n)}(0). \tag{51}$$

This property is easily verified by differentiating (50). Using Leibniz's rule (15) gives

$$\frac{\partial^n \phi(t)}{\partial t^n} = \int_{-\infty}^{\infty} (ix)^n e^{itx} f(x)\,dx,$$
$$\frac{\partial^n \phi(0)}{\partial t^n} = i^n \int_{-\infty}^{\infty} x^n f(x)\,dx = i^n \mu_n'. \tag{52}$$

The moment generating function

$$M(q) \equiv \int_{-\infty}^{\infty} e^{qx} f(x)\,dx = \phi(-iq) \tag{53}$$

is a related real-valued function which is also useful in determining the moments of a distribution, $M^{(n)}(0) = \mu_n'$. The characteristic function of a distribution is always defined and uniquely determines the distribution. The moment generating function is undefined if the integral in (53) diverges. It exists if and only if moments of all orders are finite.

For strictly nonnegative random variables, the Laplace transform $L(r) = M(-r) = \phi(ir)$ is often used. The Laplace transform is defined for all piecewise continuous density functions of nonnegative random variables.

Chebyshev's Inequality

If the mean and variance, μ and σ^2, of a distribution exist, then for all $t > 0$,

$$\text{Prob}[|\tilde{x} - \mu| \geqslant t\sigma] \leqslant t^{-2}. \tag{54}$$

Normal Density

If x is a normally distributed random variable with mean μ and variance σ^2, its density function and characteristic function are

$$f(x) = (2\pi\sigma^2)^{-1/2} \exp\left(-\frac{(x-\mu)^2}{2\sigma^2}\right),$$
$$\phi(t) = \exp\left(i\mu t - \frac{\sigma^2 t^2}{2}\right). \tag{55}$$

The higher central moments of a normal random variable are

$$\mu_n \equiv E[(\tilde{x} - \mu)^n] = \begin{cases} 0, & n \text{ odd}, \\ (n-1)(n-3)\cdots 3\cdot 1\cdot \sigma^n, & n \text{ even}. \end{cases} \tag{56}$$

If $\tilde{x}$ is a normal random variable with mean zero and variance one, it is said to be a standard normal deviate. The density and distribution functions of a standard normal deviate are often denoted by $n(x)$ and $N(x)$.

Probability Limit Theorems

Let $\tilde{x}_i$ represent a sequence of independent random variables. If the $\tilde{x}_i$ are identically distributed and have finite expectation μ, then for any constant $\varepsilon > 0$,

$$\lim_{n\to\infty} \text{Prob}\left(\left|\frac{1}{n}\sum_{i=1}^{n}\tilde{x}_i - \mu\right| < \varepsilon\right) = 1. \tag{57}$$

This relation can also be expressed as

$$\text{plim}\left(\frac{1}{n}\sum_{i=1}^{n}\tilde{x}_i\right) = \mu. \tag{58}$$

If the $\tilde{x}_i$ are not identically distributed, but each has finite expectation μ_i and finite variance, then a similar relation holds:

$$\text{plim}\left(\frac{1}{n}\left(\sum_{i=1}^{n}\tilde{x}_i - \sum_{i=1}^{n}\mu_i\right)\right) = 0. \tag{59}$$

These results are two different forms of the weak law of large numbers. If the $\tilde{x}_i$ are identically distributed with common finite expectation μ and variance σ^2, then the central limit theorem applies. This theorem indicates that the approach to the limits above is asymptotically normal; that is, the sample mean of the $\tilde{x}_i$ is approximately normal with mean μ and variance σ^2/n, or

$$\lim_{n\to\infty} \text{Prob}\left(a < \frac{\sqrt{n}}{\sigma}\left(\frac{1}{n}\sum_{i=1}^{n}\tilde{x}_i - \mu\right) < b\right) = N(b) - N(a). \tag{60}$$

Bivariate Normal Variables

Let $\tilde{x}_1$ and $\tilde{x}_2$ be bivariate normal random variables with means μ_i, variances σ_i^2, and covariance σ_{12}. The weighted sum $w_1\tilde{x}_1 + w_2\tilde{x}_2$ is normal with mean and variance

$$\mu = w_1\mu_1 + w_2\mu_2, \qquad \sigma^2 = w_1^2\sigma_1^2 + 2w_1w_2\sigma_{12} + w_2^2\sigma_2^2. \tag{61}$$

For such $\tilde{x}_1$ and $\tilde{x}_2$ and for a differentiable function $h(x)$,

$$\text{Cov}[\tilde{x}_1, h(\tilde{x}_2)] = E[h'(\tilde{x}_2)]\sigma_{12}. \tag{62}$$

This property can be proved as follows. If $\tilde{x}_1$ and $\tilde{x}_2$ are bivariate normals, then from our understanding of regression relationships we may write

$$\tilde{x}_1 = a + b\tilde{x}_2 + \tilde{e}, \tag{63}$$

where $b \equiv \sigma_{12}/\sigma_2^2$ and $\tilde{e}$ is independent of $\tilde{x}_2$. Therefore

$$\begin{aligned}\operatorname{Cov}[\tilde{x}_1, h(\tilde{x}_2)] &= \operatorname{Cov}[a + b\tilde{x}_2 + \tilde{e}, h(\tilde{x}_2)] \\ &= b \operatorname{Cov}[\tilde{x}_2, h(\tilde{x}_2)] \\ &= b\, E[(\tilde{x}_2 - \mu_2)h(\tilde{x}_2)] \\ &= b\int_{-\infty}^{\infty} (x_2 - \mu_2)h(x_2)f(x_2)\, dx_2,\end{aligned} \tag{64}$$

where $f(x_2)$ is the univariate normal density defined in (55). Now

$$\frac{df(x_2)}{dx_2} = -\frac{x_2 - \mu_2}{\sigma_2^2} f(x_2), \tag{65}$$

so the last line in (64) may be rewritten as

$$\begin{aligned}\operatorname{Cov}[\tilde{x}_1, h(\tilde{x}_2)] &= -b\sigma_2^2 \int_{-\infty}^{\infty} h(x_2)\, df(x_2) \\ &= -b\sigma_2^2 h(x_2) f(x_2)\Big|_{-\infty}^{\infty} + b\sigma_2^2 \int_{-\infty}^{\infty} h'(x_2) f(x_2)\, dx_2\end{aligned} \tag{66}$$

upon integrating by parts. Then if $h(x_2) = o(\exp(x_2^2))$, the first term vanishes at both limits, and the remaining term is just $E[h'(\tilde{x}_2)]\sigma_{12}$.

Lognormal Variables

If $\tilde{x}$ is normally distributed, then $\tilde{z} \equiv e^{\tilde{x}}$ is said to be *lognormal*. The lognormal density function is

$$f(z) = (\sqrt{2\pi}\, \sigma z)^{-1} \exp\left[-\frac{(\ln z - \mu)^2}{2\sigma^2}\right]. \tag{67}$$

The moments are

$$\begin{aligned}\mu_n' &= \exp\left(n\mu + \frac{n^2\sigma^2}{2}\right), \\ \bar{z} &= \exp\left(\mu + \frac{\sigma^2}{2}\right), \\ \operatorname{Var}(z) &= \exp(2\mu + \sigma^2)(\exp(\sigma^2) - 1).\end{aligned} \tag{68}$$

The values of μ_n' can be derived by setting $it = n$ in the characteristic function for a normal random variable (55). A quantity that is very useful to know in some financial models is the truncated mean $E(z;\, z > a)$:

$$\int_a^{\infty} zf(z)\, dz = \exp\left(\mu + \frac{\sigma^2}{2}\right) N\left[\frac{\mu - \ln a}{\sigma} + \sigma\right]. \tag{69}$$

To verify (69), make the substitutions $z = e^x$ and $dz = z\, dx$ to obtain

$$\begin{aligned}\int_a^\infty zf(z)\,dz &= (2\pi\sigma^2)^{-1/2}\int_{\ln a}^\infty e^x \exp\left[\frac{-(x-\mu)^2}{2\sigma^2}\right]dx \\ &= (2\pi\sigma^2)^{-1/2}\int_{\ln a}^\infty \exp\left[\frac{-(x-(\mu+\sigma^2))^2}{2\sigma^2}\right] \\ &\quad\times \exp\left(\frac{2\mu\sigma^2+\sigma^4}{2\sigma^2}\right)dx \\ &= \exp\left(\mu+\frac{\sigma^2}{2}\right)\int_{\ln a}^\infty n\left(\frac{x-\mu-\sigma^2}{\sigma}\right)dx.\end{aligned} \tag{70}$$

Evaluating the integral confirms (69).

"Fair Games"

If the conditional mean of one random variable does not depend on the realization of another, then the first random variable is said to be *conditionally independent* of the second. That is, $\tilde{x}$ is conditionally independent of $\tilde{y}$ if $E[\tilde{x}|y] = E[\tilde{x}]$ for all realizations y. If, in addition, the first random variable has a zero mean, then it is said to be *noise* or a *fair game* with respect to the second, $E[\tilde{x}|y] = 0$.

The name "conditional independence" is applied because this statistical property is intermediate between independence and zero correlation, as we now show. $\tilde{x}$ and $\tilde{y}$ are uncorrelated if $\text{Cov}(\tilde{x}, \tilde{y}) = 0$; they are independent if $\text{Cov}[f(\tilde{x}), g(\tilde{y})] = 0$ for all pairs of functions f and g. Under mild regularity conditions $\tilde{x}$ is conditionally independent of $\tilde{y}$ if and only if $\text{Cov}[\tilde{x}, g(\tilde{y})] = 0$ for all functions $g(\tilde{y})$.

To prove necessity, assume $E[\tilde{x}|y] = \bar{x}$. Then

$$\begin{aligned}\text{Cov}[\tilde{x}, g(\tilde{y})] &= E[\tilde{x}g(\tilde{y})] - E[g(\tilde{y})]E[\tilde{x}] \\ &= E[E[\tilde{x}g(\tilde{y})|y]] - E[g(\tilde{y})]\bar{x} \\ &= E[g(\tilde{y})E[\tilde{x}|y]] - E[g(y)]\bar{x} = 0.\end{aligned} \tag{71}$$

The second line follows from the law of iterated conditional expectations. In the third line $g(y)$ can be removed from the expectation conditional on y, and the last equality follows from the assumption that the conditional expectation of x is independent of y.

In proving sufficiency we assume that $\tilde{y}$ is a discrete random variable taking on n outcomes y_i with probabilities π_i. Define the conditional excess mean $m(y) \equiv E[\tilde{x}|y] - E[\tilde{x}]$. Then for any function $g(y)$,

$$\begin{aligned}\text{Cov}[\tilde{x}, g(\tilde{y})] &= E[(\tilde{x} - \bar{x})g(\tilde{y})] \\ &= E[E(\tilde{x} - \bar{x}|y)g(\tilde{y})]\end{aligned} \tag{72}$$

$$= \sum_{i=1}^{n} \pi_i m(y_i) g(y_i) = 0$$

by assumption. Now consider the set of n functions defined as $g(y; k) = i^k$ when $y = y_i$ for $k = 1, \ldots, n$. For these n functions the last line in (72) may be written as

$$\mathbf{\Pi G m} = \mathbf{0}, \tag{73}$$

where $\mathbf{\Pi}$ is a diagonal matrix with $\Pi_{ii} = \pi_i$, $\mathbf{G}$ is a matrix with $G_{ki} = i^k$, and $\mathbf{m}$ is a vector with $m_i = m(y_i)$. Since $\mathbf{\Pi}$ is diagonal (and $\pi_i > 0$), it is nonsingular. $\mathbf{G}$ is nonsingular by construction. Thus the only solution to (73) is $m = 0$ or $E(\tilde{x}|y) = E(\tilde{x})$.

If y is continuous, then under mild regularity conditions the same result is true. Note that the functions used were all monotone. Thus a stronger sufficient condition for conditional independence is that $\text{Cov}[x, g(y)] = 0$ for all increasing functions.

A special case of this theorem is *$\tilde{x}$ is a fair game with respect to $\tilde{y}$ if and only if $E(\tilde{x}) = 0$ and $\text{Cov}[\tilde{x}, g(\tilde{y})] = 0$ for all functions $g(y)$.* Also equivalent is the statement that $E[\tilde{x}g(\tilde{y})] = 0$ for all functions $g(y)$.

Jensen's Inequality

If $\tilde{x}$ is a random variable with positive dispersion and density function $f(x)$ and G is a concave function of x, $G''(x) < 0$, then

$$E[G(x)] < G[E(x)]. \tag{74}$$

To prove this inequality, we use Taylor's series (10) to write

$$G(x) = G(\overline{x}) + (x - \overline{x})G'(\overline{x}) + \tfrac{1}{2}(x - \overline{x})^2 G''(x^*(x)). \tag{75}$$

Then

$$\begin{aligned} E[G(x)] &\equiv \int G(x) f(x)\, dx \\ &= G(\overline{x}) \int f(x)\, dx + G'(\overline{x}) \int (x - \overline{x}) f(x)\, dx \\ &\quad + \tfrac{1}{2} \int G''(x^*(x))(x - \overline{x})^2 f(x)\, dx \\ &= G(\overline{x}) + \tfrac{1}{2} \int G''(x^*(x))(x - \overline{x})^2 f(x)\, dx \\ &< G(\overline{x}). \end{aligned} \tag{76}$$

The last line follows since the integrand is uniformly negative.

Stochastic Processes

A *stochastic process* is a time series of random variables $\tilde{X}_0, \tilde{X}_1, \ldots, \tilde{X}_N$ with realizations $x_0, x_1, \ldots, x_N$. Usually the random variables in a stochastic process are related in some fashion, and we can write the probability density function of $\tilde{X}_n$ as measured after observing the ith outcome as $f_n^i(X_n; x_0, x_1, \ldots, x_i)$.

One example of a stochastic process is the random walk with drift

$$\tilde{X}_n = \mu + x_{n-1} + \tilde{\varepsilon}_n, \tag{77}$$

where the $\tilde{\varepsilon}_n$ are independent and identically distributed. μ, which is the expected change per period, is called the *drift*. Another stochastic process is the autoregressive process

$$\tilde{X}_n = (1 - a)\mu + ax_{n-1} + \tilde{\varepsilon}_n, \tag{78}$$

where again the error terms are independent and identically distributed.

Markov Processes

A *Markov process* is a stochastic process for which everything that we know about its future is summarized by its current value; that is, the distribution of X_n is

$$f_n^i(X_n; x_0, x_1, \ldots, x_i) = g_n^i(X_n; x_i). \tag{79}$$

Both the random walk in (77) and the autoregressive process in (78) are examples of Markov processes.

Martingales

A *martingale* is a stochastic process with the properties

$$E[|\tilde{X}_n|] < \infty, \tag{80a}$$

$$E[\tilde{X}_{n+1} | x_0, x_1, \ldots, x_n] = x_n. \tag{80b}$$

The random walk in (77) with zero drift ($\mu = 0$) and the autoregressive process with $a = 1$ are special cases of martingales.

More generally, the stochastic process $\{\tilde{X}_n\}_0^N$ is a martingale with respect to the the information in the stochastic process $\{\tilde{Y}_n\}_0^N$ if, in addition to (80a),

$$E[\tilde{X}_{n+1} | y_0, y_1, \ldots, y_n] = x_n. \tag{81}$$

It is clear from (81) that x_n is a function of $y_0, \ldots, y_n$. (In particular, it is the expected value of $\tilde{X}_{n+1}$.) Thus, (81) is a generalization of (80b).

The martingale property can also be stated as $\tilde{X}_{n+1} - \tilde{X}_n$ is a fair game with respect to $\{\tilde{Y}_i\}_0^n$.

A time series of updated conditional expectations is alwayse a martingale in this generalized sense (provided that the expectations are finite). That is, let $\tilde{X}$ be a random variable, and let $\{\tilde{Y}\}_0^N$ be any stochastic process. Then

$$x_n \equiv E[\tilde{X} \mid y_0, y_1, \ldots, y_n] \tag{82}$$

are the realizations of a martingale. To prove this proposition, note that by the law of iterated expectations

$$\begin{aligned} &E[\tilde{X}_{n+1} \mid y_0, y_1, \ldots, y_n] \\ &\quad = E[E[\tilde{X}_{n+1} \mid \tilde{Y}_0, \tilde{Y}_1, \ldots, \tilde{Y}_{n+1}] \mid y_0, y_1, \ldots, y_n]. \end{aligned} \tag{83}$$

But $\tilde{X}_{n+1}$ is a function of $y_0, \ldots, y_{n+1}$ (that is, it is not random), so the inner expectation is just the realization x_{n+1}, which is also, by definition, $E[\tilde{X} \mid y_0, \ldots, y_{n+1}]$. Therefore, the right-hand side of (83) is

$$\begin{aligned} &E[E[\tilde{X} \mid y_0, y_1, \ldots, y_{n+1}] \mid y_0, y_1, \ldots, y_n] \\ &\quad = E[\tilde{X} \mid y_0, y_1, \ldots, y_n] \equiv x_n. \end{aligned} \tag{84}$$

Now equating (83) and (84) verifies the martingale property (81).

One important property of martingales is that there is no expected change in the level over *any* interval. This is obviously true for a single period from the definition in (81). Over longer intervals this can be proven as follows. Take the unconditional expectation of both sides of (81). Then

$$E[\tilde{X}_{n+1}] = E[E[\tilde{X}_{n+1} \mid \tilde{Y}_0, \tilde{Y}_1, \ldots, \tilde{Y}_n]] = E[\tilde{X}_n]. \tag{85}$$

Then by induction $E[\tilde{X}_{n+m}] = E[\tilde{X}_n]$ for all $m > 0$.

1

Utility Theory

It is not the purpose here to develop the concept of utility completely or with the most generality. Nor are the results derived from the most primitive set of assumptions. All of this can be found in standard textbooks on microeconomics or game theory. Here rigor is tempered with an eye for simplicity of presentation.

UTILITY FUNCTIONS AND PREFERENCE ORDERINGS

A utility function is not presumed as a primitive in economic theory. What is assumed is that each consumer can "value" various possible bundles of consumption goods in terms of his own subjective preferences.

For concreteness it is assumed that there are n goods. Exactly what the "goods" are or what distinguishes separate goods is irrelevant for the development. The reader should have some general idea that will suffice to convey the intuition of the development. Typically, goods are different consumption items such as wheat or corn. Formally, we often label as distinct goods the consumption of the same physical good at different times or in different states of nature. Usually, in finance we lump all physical goods together into a single consumption commodity distinguished only by the time and state of nature when it is consumed. Quite often this latter distinction is also ignored. This assumption does little damage to the effects of concern in finance, namely, the tradeoffs over time and risk. The n vector $\mathbf{x}$ denotes a particular bundle or *complex* of x_i units of good i. Each consumer selects his consumption $\mathbf{x}$ from a particular set $\mathscr{X}$. We shall always take this set to be convex and closed.

Preferences are described by the preordering relation $\succsim$. The statement

$$\mathbf{x} \succsim \mathbf{z} \tag{1}$$

is read "$\mathbf{x}$ is weakly preferred to $\mathbf{z}$" or "$\mathbf{z}$ is as good as $\mathbf{z}$." This preordering also induces the related concepts of strict preference $\succ$ and indifference $\sim$, which are defined as

$$\mathbf{x} \succ \mathbf{z} \quad \text{if} \quad \mathbf{x} \succsim \mathbf{z} \quad \text{but not} \quad \mathbf{z} \succsim \mathbf{x},$$
$$\mathbf{x} \sim \mathbf{z} \quad \text{if} \quad \mathbf{x} \succsim \mathbf{z} \quad \text{and} \quad \mathbf{z} \succsim \mathbf{x}, \tag{2}$$

and read as "**x** is (strictly) preferred to **z**" and "**x** is equivalent to **z**."

The following properties of the preordering are assumed.

AXIOM 1 (COMPLETENESS) *For every pair of vectors* $\mathbf{x} \in \mathscr{X}$ *and* $\mathbf{z} \in \mathscr{X}$ *either* $\mathbf{x} \succsim \mathbf{z}$ or $\mathbf{z} \succsim \mathbf{x}$.

AXIOM 2 (REFLEXIVITY) *For every vector* $\mathbf{x} \in \mathscr{X}$, $\mathbf{x} \succsim \mathbf{x}$.

AXIOM 3 (TRANSITIVITY) *If* $\mathbf{x} \succsim \mathbf{y}$ *and* $\mathbf{y} \succsim \mathbf{z}$, *then* $\mathbf{x} \succsim \mathbf{z}$.

Axioms are supposed to be self-evident truths. The reflexivity axiom certainly is. The completeness axiom would also appear to be; however, when choices are made under uncertainty, many commonly used preference functions do not provide complete orderings over all possible choices. (See, for example, the discussion of the St. Petersburg paradox later in this chapter.) The transitivity axiom also seems intuitive, although among certain choices, each with many distinct attributes, we could imagine comparisons that were not transitive, as illustrated by Arrow's famous voter paradox. This issue does not loom large in finance, where comparisons are most often one dimensional.

Unfortunately, these three axioms are insufficient to guarantee the existence of an *ordinal utility function*, which describes the preferences in the preordering relation. An ordinal utility function is a function Υ from $\mathscr{X}$ into the real numbers with the properties

$$\Upsilon(\mathbf{x}) > \Upsilon(\mathbf{z}) \Leftrightarrow \mathbf{x} \succ \mathbf{z}, \tag{3a}$$

$$\Upsilon(\mathbf{x}) = \Upsilon(\mathbf{z}) \Leftrightarrow \mathbf{x} \sim \mathbf{z}. \tag{3b}$$

Examples of a preording satisfying these three axioms but which do not admit to representation by ordinal utility functions are the *lexicographic* preorderings. Under these preferences the relative importance of certain goods is immeasurable. For example, for $n = 2$ a lexicographic preordering is $\mathbf{x} \succ \mathbf{z}$ if either $x_1 > z_1$ or $x_1 = z_1$ and $x_2 > z_2$. The complexes **x** and **z** are equivalent only if $\mathbf{x} = \mathbf{z}$. In this case the first good is immeasurably more important than the second, since no amount of the latter can make up for a shortfall in the former.

To guarantee the existence of a utility function, we require a fourth axiom. The one generally adopted is the continuity axiom because it also guarantees that the utility function is continuous.

AXIOM 4 (CONTINUITY) *For every* $\mathbf{x} \in \mathscr{X}$, *the two subsets of all strictly preferred and all strictly worse complexes are both open.*

The lexicographic preordering does not satisfy this axiom because the set of complexes strictly preferred to (x_1^*, x_2^*) includes the boundary points when $x_1 > x_1^*$ and $x_2 = x_2^*$.

Continuity of the utility function is guaranteed by Axiom 4 because the openness of the preferred and inferior sets requires that it take on all values close to $\Upsilon(\mathbf{x}^*)$ in a neighborhood of $\mathbf{x}^*$.

With just these four axioms the existence of a continuous ordinal utility function over $\mathcal{X}$ consistent with the preordering can be demonstrated. Here we simply state the result. The interested reader is referred to texts such as *Introduction to Equilibrium Analysis* by Hildenbrand and Kirman and *Games and Decisions* by Luce and Raiffa.

THEOREM 1 *For any preordering satisfying Axioms 1–4 defined over a closed, convex set of complexes $\mathcal{X}$, there exists a continuous utility function Υ mapping $\mathcal{X}$ into the real line with the property in (3).*

PROPERTIES OF ORDINAL UTILITY FUNCTIONS

The derived utility function is an ordinal one and, apart from continuity guaranteed by the closure axiom, contains no more information than the preordering relation as indicated in (3). No meaning can be attached to the utility level other than that inherent in the "greater than" relation in arithmetic. It is not correct to say $\mathbf{x}$ is twice as good as $\mathbf{z}$ if $\Upsilon(\mathbf{x}) = 2\Upsilon(\mathbf{z})$. Likewise, the conclusion that $\mathbf{x}$ is more of an improvement over $\mathbf{y}$ than the latter is over $\mathbf{z}$ because $\Upsilon(\mathbf{x}) - \Upsilon(\mathbf{y}) > \Upsilon(\mathbf{y}) - \Upsilon(\mathbf{z})$ is also faulty.

In this respect if a particular utility function $\Upsilon(\mathbf{x})$ is a valid representation of some preordering, then so is $\Phi(\mathbf{x}) \equiv \theta[\Upsilon(\mathbf{x})]$, where $\theta(\cdot)$ is any strictly increasing function. We shall later introduce cardinal utility functions for which this is not true.

To proceed further to the development of consumer demand theory, we now assume that

ASSUMPTION 1 *The function $\Upsilon(\mathbf{x})$ is twice differentiable, increasing, and strictly concave.*

This assumption guarantees that all of the first partial derivatives are positive everywhere, except possibly at the upper boundaries of the feasible set. Therefore, a marginal increase in income can always be profitably spent on any good to increase utility. The assumption of strict concavity guarantees that the indifference surfaces, defined later, are strictly concave upwards. That is, the set of all complexes preferred to a given complex must be strictly convex. This property is used is showing that a consumer's optimal choice is unique.

The differentiability assumption is again one of technical convenience. It does forbid, for example, the strict complementarity utility function $\Upsilon(x_1, x_2) = \mathrm{Min}(x_1, x_2)$, which is not differentiable whenever $x_1 = x_2$. (See Figure 1.2.) On the other hand, it allows us to employ the very useful concept of marginal utility.

A utility function can be characterized by its indifference surfaces (see Figures 1.1 and 1.2). These capture all that is relevant in a given preordering but are invariant to any strictly increasing transformation. An indifference surface is the set of all complexes of equal utility; that is, $\{\mathbf{x} \in \mathscr{X} | \mathbf{x} \sim \mathbf{x}^{\mathrm{o}}\}$ or $\{\mathbf{x} \in \mathscr{X} | \Upsilon(\mathbf{x}) = \Upsilon^{\mathrm{o}}\}$. The directional slopes of the indifference surface are given by the marginal rates of (commodity) substitution. Using the implicit function theorem gives

$$-\left.\frac{dx_i}{dx_j}\right|_{\Upsilon} = \frac{\partial\Upsilon/\partial x_j}{\partial\Upsilon/\partial x_i} \equiv \frac{\Upsilon_j}{\Upsilon_i}. \tag{4}$$

For the equivalent utility function $\Phi = \theta[\Upsilon]$ the indifference surfaces are the same since

$$-\left.\frac{dx_i}{dx_j}\right|_{\Phi} = \frac{\theta'\Upsilon_j}{\theta'\Upsilon_i} = -\left.\frac{dx_i}{dx_j}\right|_{\Upsilon}. \tag{5}$$

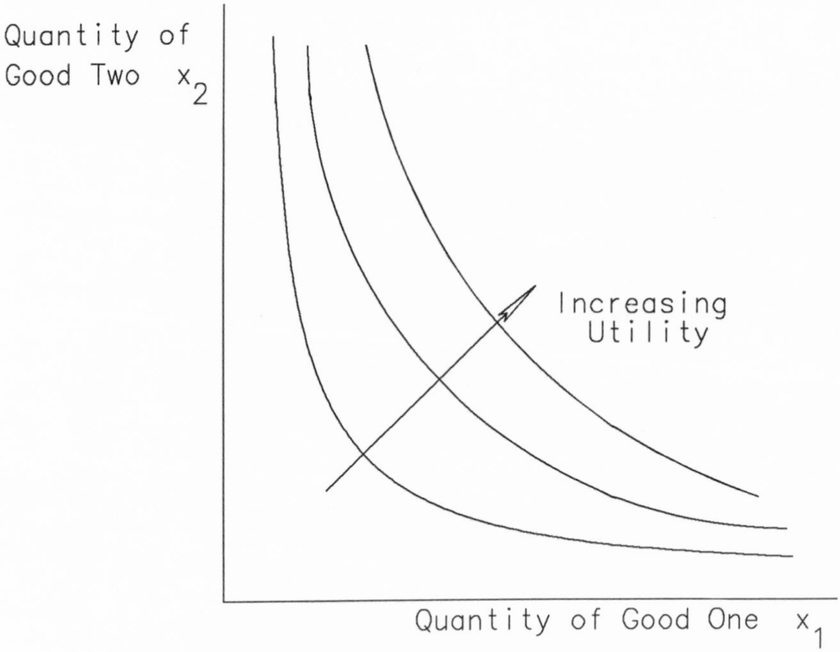

Figure 1.1 Indifference Curves

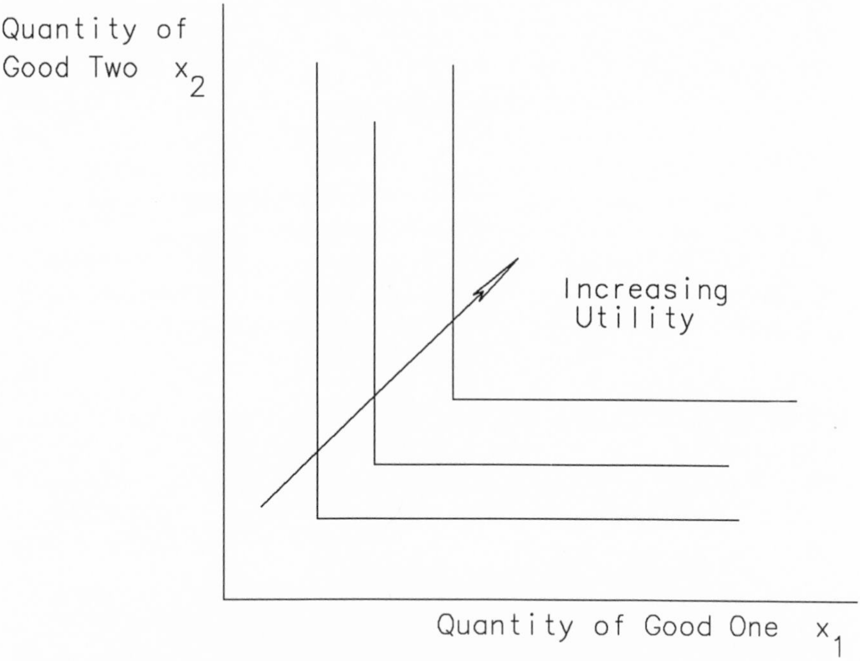

Figure 1.2 Strict Complements

PROPERTIES OF SOME COMMONLY USED ORDINAL UTILITY FUNCTIONS

An important simplifying property of utility is *preferential independence*. Two subsets of goods are preferentially independent of their complements if the conditional preference ordering when varying the amounts of the goods in each subset does not depend on the allocation in the complement. In other words, for **x** partitioned as (**y**, **z**),

$$[(\mathbf{y}_1, \mathbf{z}_0) \succsim (\mathbf{y}_2, \mathbf{z}_0)] \Rightarrow [(\mathbf{y}_1, \mathbf{z}) \succsim (\mathbf{y}_2, \mathbf{z})] \quad \text{for all } \mathbf{y}_1, \mathbf{y}_2, \mathbf{z}, \tag{6a}$$

$$(\mathbf{y}_0, \mathbf{z}_1) \succsim (\mathbf{y}_0, \mathbf{z}_2) \Rightarrow (\mathbf{y}, \mathbf{z}_1) \succsim (\mathbf{y}, \mathbf{z}_2) \quad \text{for all } \mathbf{y}, \mathbf{z}_1, \mathbf{z}_2. \tag{6b}$$

Preferential independence can also be stated in terms of marginal rates of substitution. Two subsets with more than one good each are preferentially independent if the marginal rates of substitution within the each subset (and the indifference curves) do not depend upon the allocation in the complement.

A preferentially independent utility function can be written as a monotone transform of an additive form

$$\Upsilon(\mathbf{x}) = \theta[a(\mathbf{y}) + b(\mathbf{z})] \tag{7}$$

since marginal rates of substitution are

$$-\left.\frac{dy_i}{dy_j}\right|_{\Upsilon} = \frac{\theta(\cdot)\partial a/\partial y_j}{\theta(\cdot)\partial a/\partial y_i}, \tag{8}$$

which are independent of **z**; we can write a similar expression for the marginal rates of substitution within the subset **z**.

If a utility function over three or more goods is mutually preferentially independent (all subsets are preferentially independent), then the utility function has a completely additively separable or additive form

$$\Upsilon(\mathbf{x}) = \sum \upsilon_i(x_i). \tag{9}$$

Mutual preferential independence is obviously a necessary condition for additivity as well.

One commonly used form of additive utility function is a sum of power functions. These utility functions can all be written as

$$\Upsilon(\mathbf{x}) = \frac{\sum a_i x_i^{\gamma}}{\gamma}. \tag{10}$$

These include linear $\gamma = 1$ and log-linear $\gamma = 0$, $(\mathbf{x}) = \Sigma a_i \log(x_i)$, as limiting cases. An equivalent representation for the log-linear utility function is

$$\Phi(\mathbf{x}) = \exp[\Upsilon(\mathbf{x})] = \prod x_i^{a_i}. \tag{11}$$

This is the commonly employed Cobb–Douglas utility function.

Each of these utility functions is *homothetic* as well as additive. That is, the marginal rates of substitution depend only on the relative allocation among the goods. For linear utility the marginal rates of substitution are constant.

$$-\left.\frac{dx_i}{dx_j}\right|_{\Upsilon} = \frac{a_j}{a_i}. \tag{12}$$

Log-linear utility is characterized by constant proportionate rates of substitution

$$-\left.\frac{dx_i/x_i}{dx_j/x_j}\right|_{\Upsilon} = \frac{a_j}{a_i}. \tag{13}$$

In general, the marginal rates of substitution are

$$-\left.\frac{dx_i}{dx_j}\right|_{\Upsilon} = \frac{a_j}{a_i}\left(\frac{x_j}{x_i}\right)^{\gamma-1}, \tag{14}$$

which depends only on the ratio of consumption of the two goods.

For $\gamma = 1$ the goods are perfect substitutes, and the indifference curves are straight lines. Another special case is $\gamma \to -\infty$, in which the marginal rate of substitution $-dx_i/dx_j$ is infinite if $x_i > x_j$ and zero for $x_i < x_j$. This is the strict complementarity utility function mentioned earlier.

In the intermediate case $\gamma < 0$, the indifference surfaces are bounded away from the axes. For a level of utility Υ^0 the indifference surface is asymptotic to $x_i = (\Upsilon^0/a_i)^{1/\gamma}$. Thus, a limit on the availability of any single good places an upper bound on utility. For $0 < \gamma < 1$ the indifference surfaces cut each axis at the point $x_i = \Upsilon^0 \, a_i^{-1/\gamma}$, and for $\gamma = 0$ the indifference surfaces are asymptotic to the axes so no single good can limit utility.

THE CONSUMER'S ALLOCATION PROBLEM

The standard problem of consumer choice is for consumers to choose the most preferred complex in the feasible set. In terms of utility functions they are to maximize utility subject to their budget constraints. Formally, for a fixed vector $\mathbf{p}$ of prices and a given feasible set, the consumer with wealth W and utility function Υ solves the problem

$$\text{Max}\, \Upsilon(\mathbf{x}) \quad \text{subject to } \mathbf{p}'\mathbf{x} \le W. \tag{15}$$

In analyzing this problem we assume that the feasible set satisfies the following description.

ASSUMPTION 2 *The set $\mathcal{X}$ is closed, convex, and bounded below by $\mathbf{x}^l$. It is unbounded above, so that if $\mathbf{x}^0 \in \mathcal{X}$, then $\mathbf{x} \in \mathcal{X}$ when $\mathbf{x} \ge \mathbf{x}^0$. $\mathcal{X}$ contains the null vector.*

Because $\mathcal{X}$ contains the null vector a feasible solution to (15) exists for $\mathbf{p} > \mathbf{0}$ and $W > 0$. Since it is unbounded above, the optimum will not be constrained by the scarcity of any good, and since it is bounded below the consumer cannot sell unlimited quantities of certain "goods" (e.g., labor services) to finance unlimited purchases of other goods.

THEOREM 2 *Under Assumptions 1 and 2 the consumer's allocation problem possesses a unique, slack-free solution $\mathbf{x}^*$ for any positive price vector, $\mathbf{p} > \mathbf{0}$, and positive wealth.*

Proof. The existence of a solution is guaranteed because the physically available set $\mathcal{X}$ is closed and bounded below by assumption $x_i \ge x_i^l$. The set $\mathcal{E}$ of economically feasible complexes is bounded above. (Each $x_i \le (W - \Sigma_{j \ne i} x_j^l p_j)/p_i$.) Thus, the set of feasible complexes $\mathcal{F}$, the intersection of $\mathcal{X}$ and $\mathcal{E}$, is closed and bounded; that is, it is compact. Furthermore, it is not empty since $\mathbf{x} = \mathbf{0}$ is an element. But since $\Upsilon(\mathbf{x})$ is continuous, it must attain a maximum on the set $\mathcal{F}$. If the solution is not slack free, $\mathbf{p}'\mathbf{x}^* < W$, then the slack $s \equiv W - \mathbf{p}'\mathbf{x}^*$ can be allocated in a new complex $\mathbf{x} \equiv \mathbf{x}^* + \boldsymbol{\delta}$, where $\delta_i = s/np_i > 0$. This new complex is feasible since $\mathbf{p}'\mathbf{x} = W$, and it must be preferred to $\mathbf{x}^*$ (since $\mathbf{x} > \mathbf{x}^*$), so $\mathbf{x}^*$ cannot be the optimum. Now suppose that the optimum is not unique. If there is a second optimum $\mathbf{x}^0 \neq \mathbf{x}^*$, then $\Upsilon(\mathbf{x}^0) = \Upsilon(\mathbf{x}^*)$. But $\mathcal{F}$ is convex since $\mathcal{X}$ is, so $\mathbf{x} = (\mathbf{x}^0 + \mathbf{x}^*)/2$ is in $\mathcal{F}$, and, by strict concavity, $\Upsilon(\mathbf{x}) > \Upsilon(\mathbf{x}^*)$, which is a violation. Q.E.D.

Note that existence did not require Assumption 1 apart from continuity of Υ, which can be derived from the axioms. The absence of slack required the utility function to be increasing. Uniqueness used, in addition, the strict concavity.

To determine the solution to the consumer's problem we form the Lagrangian $L \equiv \Upsilon(\mathbf{x}) + \lambda(W - \mathbf{p}'\mathbf{x})$. Since we know the optimal solution has no slack we can impose an equality constraint. The first-order conditions are

$$\frac{\partial L}{\partial \mathbf{x}} = \frac{\partial \Upsilon}{\partial \mathbf{x}} - \lambda \mathbf{p} = \mathbf{0}, \tag{16a}$$

$$\frac{\partial L}{\partial \lambda} = W - \mathbf{p}'\mathbf{x} = 0. \tag{16b}$$

The second-order conditions on the bordered Hessian are satisfied since Υ is concave. The result in (16a) can be reexpressed as

$$\frac{\partial \Upsilon/\partial x_i}{\partial \Upsilon/\partial x_j} = \frac{p_i}{p_j}, \tag{17}$$

or, from (4), the marginal rates of substitution are equal to the negative of the price ratio.

This optimum is illustrated in Figure 1.3. The consumer holds that combination of goods that places him on his highest indifference curve and is affordable (on his budget line).

ANALYZING CONSUMER DEMAND

The solution to the consumer's allocation problem can be expressed as a series of demand functions, which together make up the demand correspondence.

$$x_i^* = \phi_i(\mathbf{p}, W). \tag{18}$$

Under the assumption that the utility function is twice differentiable, the demand functions can be analyzed as follows.

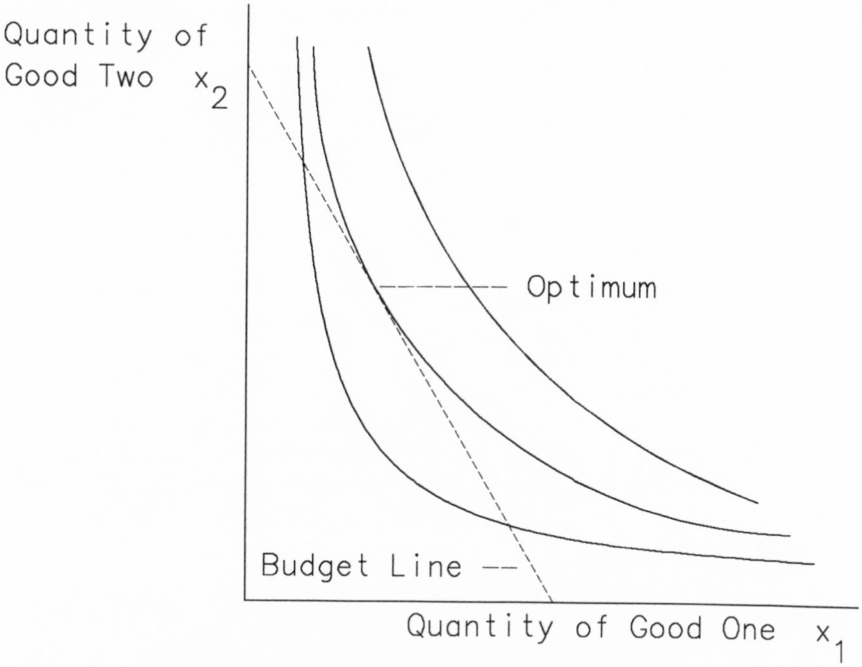

Figure 1.3 Consumer's Maximization Problem

Take the total differential of the system in (16) with respect to **x**, **p**, λ, and W:

$$\mathbf{0} = \frac{\partial^2}{\partial \mathbf{x}\,\partial \mathbf{x}'}\,d\mathbf{x} - \mathbf{p}\,d\lambda - \lambda\,d\mathbf{p}, \tag{19a}$$

$$0 = dW - \mathbf{p}'\,d\mathbf{x} - d\mathbf{p}'\mathbf{x}. \tag{19b}$$

This can be written as

$$\begin{pmatrix} \mathbf{H}(\Upsilon) & -\mathbf{p} \\ -\mathbf{p}' & 0 \end{pmatrix} \begin{pmatrix} d\mathbf{x}^* \\ d\lambda \end{pmatrix} = \begin{pmatrix} \lambda\,d\mathbf{p} \\ -dW + d\mathbf{p}'\mathbf{x}^* \end{pmatrix}. \tag{20}$$

The matrix on the left-hand side of (20) will be recognized as the bordered Hessian of the maximization problem. Since Υ is concave, we know that we have a maximum and the second-order condition is met, so the determinant of the bordered Hessian is negative. Therefore, it has an inverse which is

$$\begin{pmatrix} \mathbf{H}^{-1}(\mathbf{I} - \eta\mathbf{p}\mathbf{p}'\mathbf{H}^{-1}) & -\eta\mathbf{H}^{-1}\mathbf{p} \\ -\eta\mathbf{p}'\mathbf{H}^{-1} & -\eta \end{pmatrix}, \tag{21}$$

where $\eta \equiv (\mathbf{p}'\mathbf{H}^{-1}\mathbf{p})^{-1}$.

The solution to (20) is

$$d\mathbf{x}^* = \lambda\mathbf{H}^{-1}(\mathbf{I} - \eta\mathbf{p}\mathbf{p}'\mathbf{H}^{-1})\,d\mathbf{p} + \eta\mathbf{H}^{-1}\mathbf{p}(dW - d\mathbf{p}'\mathbf{x}^*), \tag{22}$$

so the partial derivatives can be expressed as

$$\left.\frac{\partial\mathbf{x}^*}{\partial p_i}\right|_W = [\lambda\mathbf{H}^{-1}(\mathbf{I} - \eta\mathbf{p}\mathbf{p}'\mathbf{H}^{-1}) - \eta\mathbf{H}^{-1}\mathbf{p}\mathbf{x}^{*\prime}]\boldsymbol{\iota}_i, \tag{23a}$$

$$\left.\frac{\partial\mathbf{x}^*}{\partial W}\right|_{\mathbf{p}} = \eta\mathbf{H}^{-1}\mathbf{p}, \tag{23b}$$

where $\boldsymbol{\iota}_i$ is the ith column of the identity matrix. Substituting (23b) into (23a) gives

$$\left.\frac{\partial\mathbf{x}^*}{\partial p_i}\right|_W = \lambda\mathbf{H}^{-1}(\mathbf{I} - \eta\mathbf{p}\mathbf{p}'\mathbf{H}^{-1})\boldsymbol{\iota}_i - x_i^*\frac{\partial\mathbf{x}^*}{\partial W}. \tag{24}$$

Equation (24) is the Slutsky equation. The first term measures the substitution effect, and the second term is the income effect. The former can be given the following interpretation. Consider a simultaneous change in p_i and W to leave utility unchanged. Then

$$0 = d\Upsilon = \frac{\partial\Upsilon}{\partial\mathbf{x}'}\,d\mathbf{x} = \lambda\mathbf{p}'\,d\mathbf{x}, \tag{25}$$

where the last equality follows from (16a). Substituting (25) into (19b) gives $dW = d\mathbf{p}'\mathbf{x}$, which, when substituted into (22), gives

$$\left.\frac{\partial\mathbf{x}^*}{\partial p_i}\right|_\Upsilon = \lambda\mathbf{H}^{-1}(\mathbf{I} - \eta\mathbf{p}\mathbf{p}'\mathbf{H}^{-1})\boldsymbol{\iota}_i, \tag{26}$$

the first term in (24). The Slutsky equation can now be written in its standard form

$$\left.\frac{\partial\mathbf{x}^*}{\partial p_i}\right|_W = \left.\frac{\partial\mathbf{x}^*}{\partial p_i}\right|_\Upsilon - x_i^*\left.\frac{\partial\mathbf{x}^*}{\partial W}\right|_{\mathbf{p}}. \tag{27}$$

The direct substitution effect $\partial x_i^*/\partial p_i|_\Upsilon$ must be negative because the bordered Hessian and, hence, its inverse are negative definite. The income effect can be of either sign. If $\partial x_i^*/\partial W < 0$, then good i is an *inferior* good and the income effect is positive. If the good is sufficiently inferior so that the income effect dominates the substitution effect and $\partial x_i^*/\partial p_i > 0$, holding W fixed, then i is a *Giffen* good. If the cross substitution effect, $\partial x_i^*/\partial p_j$ holding Υ constant, is positive, the goods are substitutes. Otherwise they are complements.

The income and substitution effects are illustrated in Figure 1.4. An increase in the price of good 1 from p_1 to p_1' will rotate the budget line clockwise. The substitution effect, a movement from points A to B, involves increased consumption of good 2 and decreased consumption of good 1 at the same utility. The income effect is the movement from points

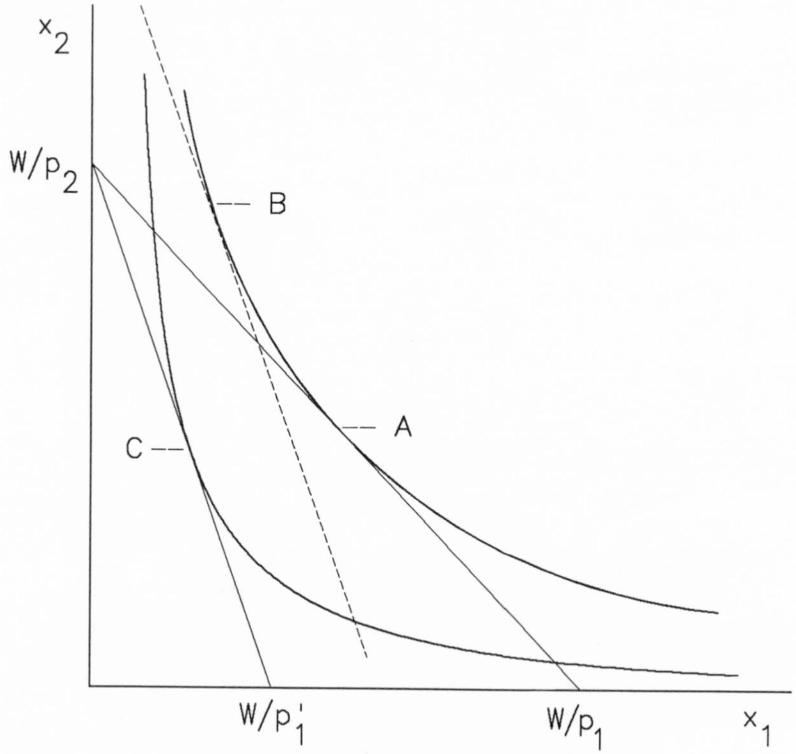

Figure 1.4 Income and Substitution Effects

B to C. In the illustrated case, good 1 is a normal good, and its consumption decreases.

SOLVING A SPECIFIC PROBLEM

Consider an investor with the log-linear utility function $\Upsilon(x, z) = \alpha \log(x) + (1 - \alpha)\log(z)$. The first order conditions from (16a) are

$$\frac{\alpha}{x} = \lambda p_x, \qquad \frac{1-\alpha}{z} = \lambda p_z \tag{28}$$

with solutions

$$x^* = \frac{\alpha W}{p_x}, \qquad z^* = \frac{(1-\alpha)W}{p_z}. \tag{29}$$

The income effect is

$$\frac{\partial x^*}{\partial W} = \frac{\alpha}{p_x} > 0. \tag{30}$$

The substitution effect is

$$\left.\frac{\partial x^*}{\partial p_x}\right|_W + x^* \left.\frac{\partial x^*}{\partial W}\right|_{\mathbf{p}} = \frac{x^*}{p_x}(\alpha - 1) < 0. \tag{31}$$

The cross substitution effect is

$$\left.\frac{\partial x^*}{\partial p_z}\right|_W + z^* \left.\frac{\partial x^*}{\partial W}\right|_{\mathbf{p}} = \frac{\alpha z^*}{p_x} > 0. \tag{32}$$

Similar results hold for z^*.

EXPECTED UTILITY MAXIMIZATION

We now extended the concept of utility maximization to cover situations involving risk. We assume throughout the discussion that the economic agents making the decisions know the true objective probabilities of the relevant events. This is not in the tradition of using subjective probabilities but will suffice for our purposes. The consumers will now be choosing among "lotteries" described generically by their payoffs $(\mathbf{x}_1, \ldots, \mathbf{x}_m)$ and respective probabilities $\boldsymbol{\pi} = (\pi_1, \ldots, \pi_m)'$.

Axioms 1–4 are still to be considered as governing choices among the various payoffs. We also now assume that there is a preordering on the set of lotteries that satisfies the following axioms:

AXIOM 1A (COMPLETENESS) *For every pair of lotteries either $L_1 \succsim L_2$ or $L_2 \succsim L_1$. (The strict preference and indifference relations are defined as before.)*

AXIOM 2A (REFLEXIVITY) *For every lottery $L \succsim L$.*

AXIOM 3A (TRANSITIVITY) *If $L_1 \succsim L_2$ and $L_2 \succsim L_3$, then $L_1 \succsim L_3$.*

These axioms are equivalent to those used before and have the same intuition. With them it can be demonstrated that each agent's choices are consistent with an ordinal utility function defined over lotteries or an ordinal utility functional defined over probability distributions of payoffs. The next three axioms are used to develop the concept of choice through the maximization of the expectation of a *cardinal* utility function over payoff complexes.

AXIOM 5 (INDEPENDENCE) *Let $L_1 = \{(\mathbf{x}_1, \ldots, \mathbf{x}_v, \ldots, \mathbf{x}_m), \boldsymbol{\pi}\}$ and*

$L_2 = \{(\mathbf{x}_1, \ldots, z, \ldots, \mathbf{x}_m), \boldsymbol{\pi}\}$. *If* $\mathbf{x}_\nu \sim z$, *then* $L_1 \sim L_2$. *z may be either a complex or another lottery. If z is a lottery* $z = \{(\mathbf{x}_1^\nu, \mathbf{x}_2^\nu, \ldots \mathbf{x}_n^\nu), \boldsymbol{\pi}^\nu\}$, then

$$L_1 \sim L_2 \sim \{(\mathbf{x}_1, \ldots, \mathbf{x}_{\nu-1}, \mathbf{x}_1^\nu, \ldots, \mathbf{x}_n^\nu, \mathbf{x}_{\nu+1}, \ldots, \mathbf{x}_m), (\pi_1, \ldots, \pi_{\nu-1}, \pi_\nu\pi_1^\nu, \ldots, \pi_\nu\pi_n^\nu, \pi_{\nu+1}, \ldots, \pi_m)'\}.$$

In Axiom 5 it is important that the probabilities be interpreted correctly. π_i^ν is the probability of getting $\mathbf{x}_i^\nu$ conditional on outcome ν having been selected by the first lottery. $\pi_\nu\pi_i^\nu$ is the unconditional probability of getting $\mathbf{x}_i^\nu$. This axiom asserts that only the utility of the final payoff matters. The exact mechanism for its award is irrelevant. If two complexes (or subsequent lotteries) are equally satisfying, then they are also considered equivalent as lottery prices. In addition, there is no thrill or aversion towards suspense or gambling per se. The importance of this axiom is discussed later.

AXIOM 6 (CONTINUITY) *If* $\mathbf{x}_1 \gtrsim \mathbf{x}_2 \gtrsim \mathbf{x}_3$, *then there exists a probability* π, $0 \leq \pi \leq 1$, *such that* $\mathbf{x}_2 \sim \{(\mathbf{x}_1, \mathbf{x}_3), (\pi, 1 - \pi)'\}$. *The probability is unique unless* $\mathbf{x}_1 \sim \mathbf{x}_3$.

AXIOM 7 (DOMINANCE) *Let* $L_1 = \{(\mathbf{x}_1, \mathbf{x}_2), (\pi_1, 1 - \pi_1)'\}$ *and* $L_2 = \{(\mathbf{x}_1, \mathbf{x}_2), (\pi_2, 1 - \pi_2)'\}$. *If* $\mathbf{x}_1 > \mathbf{x}_2$, *then* $L_1 > L_2$ *if and only if* $\pi_1 > \pi_2$.

THEOREM 3 *Under Axioms 1–7 the choice made by a decision maker faced with selecting between two (or more) lotteries will be the one with the higher (highest) expected utility. That is, the choice maximizes* $\Sigma\pi_i\Psi(\mathbf{x}_i)$, *where* Ψ *is a* particular *cardinal utility function.*

Proof. (We show only the proof for two alternatives.) Let the two lotteries be $L_1 = \{(\mathbf{x}_1^1, \ldots, \mathbf{x}_m^1), \boldsymbol{\pi}^1\}$ and $L_2 = \{(\mathbf{x}_1^2, \ldots, \mathbf{x}_\nu^2), \boldsymbol{\pi}^2\}$ and suppose the prizes are ordered so that $\mathbf{x}_1^i \gtrsim \cdots \gtrsim \mathbf{x}_m^i$. Choose $\mathbf{x}^h$ so that it is preferred to both $\mathbf{x}_1^1$ and $\mathbf{x}_1^2$ and choose $\mathbf{x}^l$ so that both $\mathbf{x}_m^1$ and $\mathbf{x}_\nu^2$ are preferred to it. For each $\mathbf{x}_j^i$ compute q_j^i such that $\mathbf{x}_j^i \sim \{(\mathbf{x}^h, \mathbf{x}^l), (q_j^i, 1 - q_j^i)'\}$. This can be done by Axiom 6. By Axiom 5, $L_i \sim \{(\mathbf{x}^h, \mathbf{x}^l), (Q_i, 1 - Q_i)'\}$, where $Q_i \equiv \Sigma q_j^i\pi_j^i$. By Axiom 7, $L_1 > L_2$ if and only if $Q_1 > Q_2$. The only thing remaining is to show that q_j^i is a valid utility measure for $\mathbf{x}_j^i$. This is so because, by Axiom 7, $\mathbf{x}_j^i > \mathbf{x}_k^i$ if and only if $q_j^i > q_k^i$, so q is increasing, and, by Axiom 6, it is continuous. Q.E.D.

The utility function just introduced is usually called a von Neumann–Morgenstern utility function, after its originators. It has the properties of any ordinal utility function, but, in addition, it is a "cardinal" measure. That is, unlike ordinal utility the numerical value of utility has a precise meaning (up to a scaling) beyond the simple rank of the numbers.

This can be easily demonstrated as follows. Suppose there is a single good. Now compare a lottery paying 0 or 9 units with equal probability to one giving 4 units for sure. Under the utility function $\Upsilon(x) = x$, the former, with an expected utility of 4.5, would be preferred. But if we apply the increasing transformation $\theta(s) = \sqrt{s}$, the lottery has an expected utility of 1.5, whereas the certain payoff's utility is 2. These two rankings are contradictory, so arbitrary monotone transformations of cardinal utility functions do not preserve ordering over lotteries.

Cardinality has been introduced primarily by Axioms 6 and 7. Suppose $\mathbf{x}^h$ and $\mathbf{x}^l$ are assigned utilities of 1 and 0. By Axiom 6 any other intermediate payoff $\mathbf{x}$ is equivalent in utility to some simple lottery paying $\mathbf{x}^h$ or $\mathbf{x}^l$. This lottery has expected utility of $q \cdot 1 + 0 = q$. But, by Axiom 7, q ranks outcomes; that is, it is at least an ordinal utility function. Finally, by construction, $\Psi(\mathbf{x}) = q$; no other value is possible. Thus, a von Neumann–Morgenstern utility function has only two degrees of freedom: the numbers assigned to $\Psi(\mathbf{x}^h)$ and $\Psi(\mathbf{x}^l)$. All other numerical values are determined. Alternatively, we can say that utility is determined up to a positive linear transformation. $\Psi(\mathbf{x})$ and $a + b\Psi(\mathbf{x})$, with $b > 0$, are equivalent utility functions.

Von Neumann–Morgenstern utility functions are often called measurable rather than cardinal. Neither use is precise from a mathematician's viewpoint.

CARDINAL AND ORDINAL UTILITY

Each cardinal utility function embodies a specific ordinal utility function. Since the latter are distinct only up to a monotone transformation, two very different cardinal utility functions may have the same ordinal properties. Thus, two consumers who always make the same choice under certainty may choose among lotteries differently.

For example, the two Cobb–Douglas utility functions $\Psi_1(x, z) = \sqrt{xz}$ and $\Psi_2 = -1/xz$ are equivalent for ordinal purposes since $\Psi_2 = -\Psi_1^{-2}$. Faced by choosing between (2, 2) for sure or a 50–50 chance at (4, 4) or (1, 1), the first consumer will select the lottery with an expected utility of $\frac{5}{2}$ over the sure thing with utility of 2. In the same situation the second consumer will select the safe alternative with utility $-\frac{1}{4}$ over the lottery with expected utility $-17/32$.

As mentioned previously, preferences can still be expressed by using ordinal utility; however, the domain of the ordinal utility functional is the set of lotteries. Let $\pi(\mathbf{x})$ denote the probability density for a particular lottery, and let $\Psi(\mathbf{x})$ be the cardinal utility function of a consumer. Then his ordinal utility functional over lotteries is

$$Q[\pi(\mathbf{x})] = E[\Psi(\mathbf{x})] \equiv \int \Psi(\mathbf{x})\pi(\mathbf{x})\, d\mathbf{x}, \tag{33}$$

When all lottery payoffs come from some common family of distributions, it is often possible to express this ordinal functional for lotteries as an ordinal utility function defined over parameters of the distributions of the lotteries. For example, if there is a single good, the consumer's cardinal utility function is $\Psi(x) = x^\gamma/\gamma$, and the payoff from each lottery is lognormally distributed [i.e., $\ln(x)$ is $N(\mu, \sigma^2)$], then

$$Q[\pi_i(x)] = \frac{1}{\gamma}\exp\left[\gamma\mu_i + \frac{\gamma^2\sigma_i^2}{2}\right] \equiv \Upsilon(\mu_i, \sigma_i), \tag{34}$$

where μ_i and σ_i now are the "goods." Since this is an ordinal utility function, choices can be expressed equivalently by

$$\Phi(\mu, \sigma) \equiv \frac{\ln[\gamma\Upsilon(\mu, \sigma)]}{\gamma} = \mu + \frac{\gamma\sigma^2}{2}. \tag{35}$$

Utility functions like this are often called derived utility functions. As discussed in Chapter 4, derived mean-variance utility functions have an important role in finance.

THE INDEPENDENCE AXIOM

Axiom 5 is called the independence axiom because it asserts that the utility of a lottery is independent of the mechanism of its award. The independence asserted here is a form of preferential independence, a concept discussed previously. It should not be confused with utility independence (for cardinal utility functions), introduced later.

To see the relation to preferential independence, consider a simple lottery with two outcomes $\mathbf{x}_1$ and $\mathbf{x}_2$ with probabilities π_1 and π_2. Now consider a set $\mathcal{Y}$ of $2n$ "goods." Goods y_1 through y_n denote quantities of goods x_1 through x_n under outcome 1, and goods y_{n+1} through y_{2n} denote quantities of goods x_1 through x_n under outcome 2. The lottery payoffs are $\mathbf{y}_1' = (\mathbf{x}_1', \mathbf{0}')$ and $\mathbf{y}_2' = (\mathbf{0}', \mathbf{x}_2')$. The expected utility of this lottery is

$$E[\Psi(\tilde{\mathbf{x}})] = \pi_1\Psi(\mathbf{x}_1) + \pi_2\Psi(\mathbf{x}_2) = \upsilon_1(\mathbf{y}_1) + \upsilon_2(\mathbf{y}_2) \equiv \Upsilon(\mathbf{y}). \tag{36}$$

In this latter form it is clear that the ordinal representation displays additivity, which guarantees preferential independence [see Equation (9)].

In the formulation just described, the ordinal utility functions υ_i depend on the lottery (through its probabilities). It is possible to express choices in a general fashion by using a utility functional as outlined in the previous section. Only the additive (integral) representation (or monotone transformations) displays preferential independence. It is possible to construct other functionals which satisfy the other six axioms. These, of course, are not representable as expectations of cardinal utility functions.

Consider a set of lotteries, with payoffs in a single good, described by the density functions $\pi_i(x)$. The functional

$$Q[\pi(x)] \equiv \tfrac{1}{2}\int x\pi(x)\,dx + \tfrac{1}{2}\left[\int \sqrt{x}\,\pi(x)\,dx\right]^2$$
$$= \tfrac{1}{2}E[x] + \tfrac{1}{2}E^2[\sqrt{x}] \tag{37}$$

defines a unique number for any lottery (provided only that its payoffs are nonnegative and its mean payoff exists), and therefore Axioms 1a, 2a, and 3a are clearly satisfied. Axioms 6 and 7 are also satisfied, since for any lottery with only two distinct payoffs (at fixed levels) the functional Q is continuously increasing in the probability of the higher payoff.

Axiom 5 is not valid. Note first that the utility value for a sure thing is numerically equal to its payoff $Q[\delta(x - x_o)] = x_0$. Now consider three lotteries: L_1, equal chances at 4 or 0; L_2, equal chances at 32/3 and 0; and L_3, a one-fourth chance at 32/3 and a three-fourths chance at 0. Using (37) gives

$$Q[L_1] = \frac{1}{2}2 + \frac{1}{2}\left[\frac{1}{2}\sqrt{4}\right]^2 = \frac{3}{2},$$
$$Q[L_2] = \frac{1}{2}\frac{32}{6} + \frac{1}{2}\left[\frac{1}{2}\sqrt{\frac{32}{2}}\right]^2 = 4, \tag{38}$$
$$Q[L_3] = \frac{1}{2}\frac{8}{3} + \frac{1}{2}\left[\frac{1}{4}\sqrt{\frac{32}{3}}\right]^2 = \frac{5}{3}.$$

Thus, L_3 is preferred to L_1. But if Axiom 5 were valid, the first lottery would be equivalent to $\{L_2, 0; \frac{1}{2}, \frac{1}{2}\}$. Furthermore, this last lottery would be equivalent to $\{\frac{32}{3}, 0; \frac{1}{4}, \frac{3}{4}\}$. But this is just lottery 3, which we know to be preferred. Therefore Axiom 5 cannot be valid, and a payoff cannot be assigned a cardinal level of utility which is independent of the mechanism of its determination.

Machina has demonstrated that utility functionals of this type have most of the properties of von Neumann–Morgenstern utility functions. Many of the properties of the single-period investment problems examined in this book hold with "Machina" preferences that do not satisfy the independence axiom. Multiperiod problems will have different properties.

UTILITY INDEPENDENCE

As with ordinal utility, independence of some choices is an important simplifying property for expected utility maximization as well. A subset of goods is *utility independent* of its complement subset when the conditional preference ordering over all lotteries with fixed payoffs of the complement goods does not depend on this fixed payoff.

If the subset $\mathbf{y}$ of goods is utility independent of its complement $\mathbf{z}$, then the cardinal utility function has the form

$$\Psi(\mathbf{y}, \mathbf{z}) = a(\mathbf{z}) + b(\mathbf{z})c(\mathbf{y}). \tag{39}$$

Note that this form is identical to that given in (7) for preferential independence; however, in (7) ordinal utility was described so any monotone transformation would be permitted. Thus, the utility function $\psi(\mathbf{y}, \mathbf{z}) = \theta[a(\mathbf{z}) + b(\mathbf{z})c(\mathbf{y})]$ displays preferential independence but not utility independence for any nonlinear function θ.

As with preferential independence, utility independence is not symmetric. If symmetry is imposed and it is assumed that the goods are mutually utility independent, then it can be shown that the utility function can be represented as

$$\Psi(\mathbf{x}) = k^{-1}(\exp[k\textstyle\sum k_i\psi_i(x_i)] - 1) \tag{40}$$

with the restriction $k_i > 0 \cdot \psi_i$ is a valid (univariate) cardinal utility function for marginal decisions involving good i alone. An alternative representation is

$$\Psi(\mathbf{x}) = \textstyle\sum k_i\psi_i(x_j), \tag{41a}$$

$$\Psi(\mathbf{x}) = \textstyle\prod\phi_i(x_i), \tag{41b}$$

$$\Psi(\mathbf{x}) = -\textstyle\prod[-\phi_i(x_i)], \tag{41c}$$

corresponding to zero, positive, or negative k. Again the ϕ_i are univarite utility functions related to the functions ψ_i. In (41b), ϕ_i are uniformly positive, and in (41c), ϕ_i are uniformly negative.

If the utility function has the additive form, then the preference ordering among lotteries depends only on the marginal probability distributions of the goods. The converse is also true. For multiplicative utility this simple result does not hold. As an illustration consider the lotteries $L_1 = \{(x_h, z_h)', (x_l, z_l)', (.5, .5)'\}$ and $L_2 = \{(x_h, z_l)', (x_l, z_h)', (.5, .5)'\}$. For additive utility functions both lotteries have the same expected utility.

$$E\Psi = .5(\psi_1(x_h) + \psi_1(x_l) + \psi_2(z_h) + \psi_2(z_l)). \tag{42}$$

For the multiplicative form, expected utilities are not equal:

$$.5[\phi_1(x_h)\phi_2(z_h) + \phi_1(x_l)\phi_2(z_l)] \neq .5[\phi_1(x_h)\phi_2(z_l) + \phi_1(x_l)\phi_2(z_h)]. \tag{43}$$

UTILITY OF WEALTH

Thus far we have measured outcomes in terms of a bundle of consumption goods. In financial problems it is more common to express outcomes

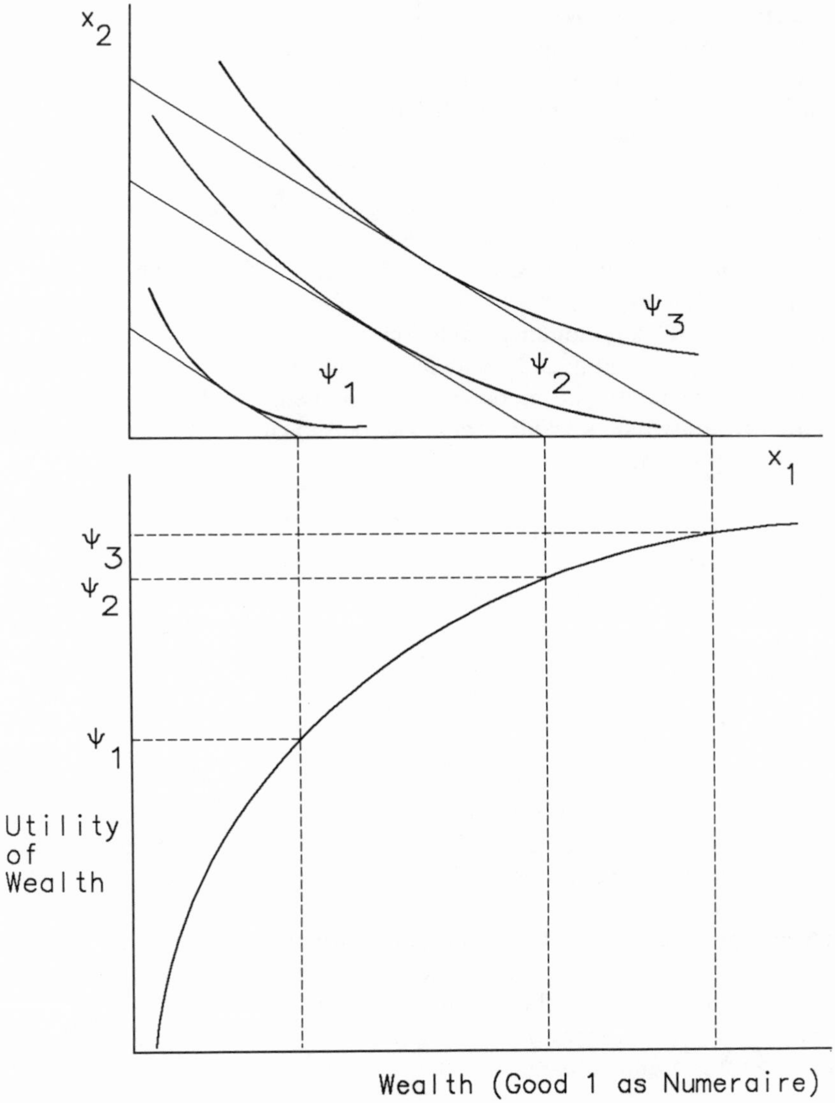

Figure 1.5 Derived Utility of Wealth Function

in monetary values with utility measuring the satisfaction associated with a particular level of wealth. If there is a single consumption good, then this can be the numeraire for wealth, and the preceding analysis is valid. If there are a number of consumption goods, then utility can be expressed as a function of wealth and the vector of consumption good prices as

$$U(W; \mathbf{p}) = \text{Max}\{\Psi(\mathbf{x}); \text{ subject to } \mathbf{p}'\mathbf{x} = W\}. \tag{44}$$

This construction is illustrated in Figure 1.5, where good 1 is used as numeraire. If the utility function depends only on wealth (and not on relative prices), then utility of wealth is said to be state independent. Otherwise it is state dependent.

If the utility function $\Psi(\mathbf{x})$ is increasing and $\mathbf{p} > \mathbf{0}$, then the utility of wealth is strictly increasing. And, if differentiable, $U'(W) > 0$.

RISK AVERSION

The aversion to risk on the part of economic decision makers is a common assumption and one that we shall adopt throughout this book unless explicitly stated otherwise. What exactly do we mean by risk aversion? The answer to this question depends on its context.

A decision maker with a von Neumann–Morgenstern utility function is said to be *risk averse* (at a particular wealth level) if he is unwilling to accept every actuarially fair and immediately resolved gamble with only wealth consequences, that is, those that leave consumption good prices unchanged. If the decision maker is risk averse at all (relevant) wealth levels, he is globally risk averse.

For state-independent utility of wealth, the utility function is risk averse at W if $U(W) > EU(W + \tilde{\varepsilon})$ for all gambles with $E(\tilde{\varepsilon}) = 0$ and positive dispersion. If this relation holds at all levels of wealth, the utility function is globally risk averse.

THEOREM 4 *A decision maker is (globally) risk averse, as just defined, if and only if his von Neumann–Morgenstern utility function of wealth is strictly concave at the relevant (all) wealth levels.*

Proof. Let $\tilde{\varepsilon}$ denote the outcome of a generic gamble. If it is actuarially fair, then $E(\tilde{\varepsilon}) = 0$. By Jensen's inequality, if $U(\cdot)$ is strictly concave at W, then

$$E[U(W + \tilde{\varepsilon})] < U(E[W + \tilde{\varepsilon}]) = U(W). \tag{45}$$

Thus, higher expected utility results from avoiding every gamble.

To prove necessity, consider the simple gamble $\varepsilon = \lambda a$ with probability $1 - \lambda$ and $\varepsilon = -(1 - \lambda)\, a$ with probability λ. This gamble is fair, so by assumption it is disliked:

$$U(W) > \lambda U[W - (1 - \lambda)a] + (1 - \lambda)U(W + \lambda a). \tag{46}$$

Equation (46) must hold for all pairs a and λ (provided $0 \leq \lambda \leq 1$ and both outcomes are in the domain of U), but since $W = \lambda[W - (1 - \lambda)a] +$

$(1 - \lambda)(W + \lambda a)$ for any a and λ, U is concave.

The proof for global risk aversion is the same, point by point. Q.E.D.

If a utility function is twice differentiable, then it is concave, representing risk-averse choices, if and only if $U''(W) < 0$.

To induce a risk-averse individual to undertake a fair gamble, a compensatory risk premium would have to be offered, making the package actuarially favorable. Similarly, to avoid a present gamble a risk-averse individual would be willing to pay an insurance risk premium. These two premiums are closely related but not identical. They are the solutions to

$$E[U(W + \Pi_c + \tilde{\varepsilon})] = U(W), \tag{47a}$$

$$E[U(W + \tilde{\varepsilon})] = U(W - \Pi_i). \tag{47b}$$

The latter risk premium is the one more commonly used in economic analysis. It corresponds in an obvious way to a casualty or liability insurance premium. In financial problems, however, the compensatory risk premium is more useful. It corresponds to the "extra" return expected on riskier assets. The quantity $W - \Pi_i$ is also known as the certainty equivalent of the gamble $W + \tilde{\varepsilon}$, since it is that certain amount which provides the same expected utility.

If the risk is small and the utility function is sufficiently smooth, the two risk premiums are nearly equal. When these assumptions are met, the risk premium can be determined approximately as follows. Using Taylor expansions with Lagrange remainders for (47b) gives

$$\begin{aligned} E[U(W) + \tilde{\varepsilon}U'(W) + \tfrac{1}{2}\tilde{\varepsilon}^2 U''(W) + \tfrac{1}{6}\tilde{\varepsilon}^3 U'''(W + \alpha\tilde{\varepsilon})] \\ = U(W) - \Pi_i U'(W) + \tfrac{1}{2}\Pi_i^2 U''(W - \beta\Pi_i) \\ \tfrac{1}{2}\operatorname{var}(\tilde{\varepsilon})U''(W) \approx -\Pi_i U'(W) \\ \Pi_i \approx -\frac{1}{2}\left[\frac{U''(W)}{U'(W)}\right]\operatorname{var}(\tilde{\varepsilon}). \end{aligned} \tag{48}$$

Sufficient conditions for this approximation to be accurate are that U''' and the support of $\tilde{\varepsilon}$ are bounded.

From (48) it is clear that the term in brackets is an appropriate measure of infinitesimal or local risk aversion. It is known as the Arrow–Pratt absolute risk-aversion function. This measure incorporates everything important in a utility function but is free from the arbitrary scaling factors. To recover the utility function, we note that $A(W) = -d[\log U'(W)]/dW$, so integrating twice gives

$$\int^W \exp\left[-\int^z A(x)\,dx\right]dz = a + bU(W) \tag{49}$$

with $b > 0$.

Two related measures are the risk-tolerance function and the relative (or proportional) risk-aversion function

$$T(W) \equiv \frac{1}{A(W)}, \qquad R(W) \equiv WA(W) \tag{50}$$

The latter is useful in analyzing risks expressed as a proportion of the gamble for example investment rates of return.

SOME USEFUL UTILITY FUNCTIONS

The HARA (hyperbolic absolute risk aversion) or LRT (linear risk tolerance) class of utility functions is most commonly used. Utility functions in this class are

$$U(W) = \frac{1-\gamma}{\gamma}\left(\frac{aW}{1-\gamma} + b\right)^{\gamma}, \qquad b > 0. \tag{51}$$

This utility function is defined over the domain $b + aW/(1 - \gamma) > 0$. That is, there is a lower bound for $\gamma < 1$ and an upper bound for $\gamma > 1$. (Note that for integer γ's greater than 1 the function would be defined for wealth levels above the upper bound, but marginal utility would be negative.) The absolute risk-tolerance function is

$$T(W) = \frac{1}{A(W)} = \frac{W}{1-\gamma} + \frac{b}{a}, \tag{52}$$

which is linear, as the name suggests. Risk tolerance is obviously increasing or decreasing as $\gamma < 1$ or $\gamma > 1$. Risk aversion is therefore decreasing for $\gamma < 1$ and increasing for $\gamma > 1$.

Special cases of LRT utility are linear (risk neutral) with $\gamma = 1$, quadratic with $\gamma = 2$, negative exponential utility with $\gamma = -\infty$ and $b = 1$, isoelastic or power utility with $b = 0$ and $\gamma < 1$, and logarithmic with $b = \gamma = 0$.

The negative exponential utility functions

$$U(W) = -e^{-aW} \tag{53}$$

have constant absolute risk aversion $A(W) = a$. The power utility functions

$$U(W) = \frac{W^{\gamma}}{\gamma} \tag{54}$$

have constant relative risk aversion $R(W) = 1 - \gamma$ and, therefore, decreasing absolute risk aversion.

Log utility also displays constant relative risk aversion; specifically, $R(W) = 1$. It obviously corresponds to $\gamma = 0$ in (54) in this respect. This can be verified for the equivalent utility function $(W^\gamma - 1)/\gamma$. For $\gamma = 0$ this function is not defined, but using L′ Hospital's rule gives

$$\lim_{\gamma\to 0}\frac{W^\gamma - 1}{\gamma} = \lim_{\gamma\to 0}\frac{W^\gamma \log W}{1} = \log W. \tag{55}$$

COMPARING RISK AVERSION

If one individual is more hesitant to take on risk than another, then it is natural to say that he is more risk averse. To be more precise, one investor is clearly more risk averse than another if he always chooses a safe investment whenever the other does. Theorem 5 gives four equivalent definitions of greater risk aversion.

THEOREM 5 The following four conditions are equivalent:

$$A_k(W) > A_j(W) \quad \text{all } W, \tag{56a}$$

$$\exists G \text{ with } G' > 0,\ G'' < 0 \text{ such that } U_k(W) = G[U_j(W)], \tag{56b}$$

$$\Pi_k > \Pi_j \quad \text{all } W \text{ and all gambles}, \tag{56c}$$

$$U_k[U_j^{-1}(t)] \quad \text{is concave.} \tag{56d}$$

Proof. (a) ⇒ (b) Since both U_k and U_j are strictly increasing and twice differentiable, there exists a function G with positive first derivative such that $U_k = G(U_j)$. Differentiating twice gives

$$U_k' = G'U_j', \qquad U_k'' = G'U_j'' + G''(U_j')^2. \tag{57}$$

Combining and solving for G'' gives

$$G'' = -\frac{G'}{U_j'}(A_k - A_j) < 0. \tag{58}$$

(b) ⇒ (c) Using Jensen's inequality, we get

$$\begin{aligned} U_k(W - \Pi_k) &\equiv E[U_k(W + \tilde{\varepsilon})] = E(G[U_j(W + \tilde{\varepsilon})]) \\ &< G(E[U_j(W + \tilde{\varepsilon})]) \equiv G[U_j(W - \Pi_j)] \equiv U_k(W - \Pi_j). \end{aligned} \tag{59}$$

Now $\Pi_k > \Pi_j$ since U_k is strictly increasing.

(c) ⇒ (a) Consider the simple gamble $\tilde{\varepsilon} = \pm x$ with equal probability. In the limit for small x,

$$\Pi_i \approx \frac{A_i(W)x^2}{2}. \tag{60}$$

Therefore if $\Pi_k > \Pi_j$, then $A_k > A_j$.

(a) $\Leftrightarrow$ (d) Define $f(t) \equiv U_k[U_j^{-1}(t)]$. Differentiating twice gives (recall that for $x = g^{-1}(z)$, $dg^{-1}(z)/dz = 1/g'(x)$)

$$f''(t) = (U_j')^{-2}U_k'\left(\frac{U_k''}{U_k'} - \frac{U_j''}{U_j'}\right) = (U_j')^{-2}U_k'(A_j - A_k). \tag{61}$$

Therefore, f is strictly concave if and only if $A_k > A_j$. Q.E.D.

A similar theorem is true if the relative risk-aversion function is used in (56a). A proof is immediate since $A_k(W) > A_j(W)$ if and only if $R_k(W) > R_j(W)$.

If an individual is more (less) absolutely or relatively risk averse at higher wealth levels, then he or she displays increasing (decreasing) absolute or relative risk aversion. For any utility function $U(W)$ define a related utility function $\hat{U}(W; x) \equiv U(W + x)$. Then for $x > 0$, U is increasingly risk averse if $\hat{A}(W) > A(W)$.

HIGHER-ORDER DERIVATIVES OF THE UTILITY FUNCTION

If an individual is decreasingly risk averse, then $U''' > 0$. Since

$$A' = -(U')^2[U'U''' - (U'')^2], \tag{62}$$

A' can only be negative if $U''' > 0$. Usually, no further assumptions about derivatives of the utility function are made, and even this last assumption is not common. However, if investors are consistent in their first m preferences (each of the first m derivatives of U is uniformly positive, negative, or zero) over an unbounded positive domain of W, then the derivatives must alternate in sign; that is,

$$(-1)^i U^{(i)}(W) < 0, \qquad i = 1, \ldots, m. \tag{63}$$

We prove this result by induction. Define $f_n(W) \equiv (-1)^n U^{(n)}(W)$ and assume that $f_i(W) < 0$ for $i = 1, \ldots, n$. Using the mean value theorem gives

$$\begin{aligned} f_{n-1}(W_2) &= f_{n-1}(W_1) + f_{n-1}'(W^*)(W_2 - W_1) \\ &= f_{n-1}(W_1) - f_n(W^*)(W_2 - W_1) \end{aligned} \tag{64}$$

for some W^* in $[W_1, W_2]$. Now assume (63) is false for $n + 1$; that is, $f_{n+1}(\cdot) = -f_n'(\cdot) \geq 0$. Then $f_n(W^*) \leq f_n(W_1)$, and, in (64),

$$f_{n-1}(W_2) \geq f_{n-1}(W_1) - f_n(W_1)(W_2 - W_1). \tag{65}$$

Now choose $W_2 > W_1 + f_{n-1}(W_1)/f_n(W_1)$. This choice is possible since the ratio is positive and the domain of interest is unbounded above. Substituting into (65) gives

$$f_{n-1}(W_2) > f_{n-1}(W_1) - f_n(W_1)\frac{f_{n-1}(W_1)}{f_n(W_1)} = 0, \tag{66}$$

which contradicts our previous assumption.

THE BOUNDEDNESS DEBATE: SOME HISTORY OF ECONOMIC THOUGHT

It is often assumed that utility is bounded or at least bounded above. The reason for this assumption is that in its absence it is possible to construct lotteries which cannot be ordered by their expected utility even in cases when one of the lotteries strictly dominates another. This point was made originally by Karl Menger, who constructed a "super St. Petersburg paradox."

The (ordinary) St. Petersburg paradox involves the evaluation of a gamble designed to pay 2^n dollars if the first occurrence of a "head" is on the nth toss of a fair coin. The expected payoff is infinite:

$$\sum_{n=1}^{\infty} 2^{-n}2^n = \sum 1 = \infty. \tag{67}$$

For any risk-averse utility function, however, expected utility is finite. For example, for log utility expected utility is

$$\sum_{n=1}^{\infty} 2^{-n}\log(2^n) = .5\log(2) \approx .346. \tag{68}$$

For any unbounded (from above) utility function, there exists for every n a solution W_n to $U(W) = 2^n$. If we construct a super St. Petersburg gamble with payoffs $W_n = U^{-1}(2^n)$ when the first occurrence of a head is on the nth toss, the expected utility is infinite:

$$\sum_{n=1}^{\infty} 2^{-n}U[U^{-1}(2^n)] = \infty. \tag{69}$$

For our example of log utility the payoffs would be $W_n = \exp(2^n)$.

The problem with unbounded utility is not per se that expected utility can be infinite, but that obviously preference-orderable gambles cannot be ranked by expected utility. For example, a gamble offering payoffs of $U^{-1}(3^n)$ is clearly preferable but also has infinite utility. In addition, a gamble offering $U^{-1}(3^n)$ for n even and 0 for n odd also has infinite expected utility. This last gamble is clearly worse than the second but might be better or worse than the first. Expected utility offers no clue.

With a bounded utility function this problem can never arise. For example, for $U(W) = a - 1/W$, utility can never rise above a, so we cannot find the solutions W_n for any $n > \log_2 a$.

There is, of course, a clear bankruptcy problem embedded in these paradoxes. The large prizes beyond some bound could never be awarded in a finite economy. Since the game could never be feasible, we should be safe in ignoring it. We are also safe on a purely theoretical basis. If we circumvent the bankruptcy problem (by defining negative wealth in a meaningful fashion for example), then the two participants will be taking exactly opposite positions in the gamble. But only one side can be better than actuarially fair, so whoever is offered the other side would definitely refuse to participate. Therefore, such lotteries will never need to be evaluated.

MULTIPERIOD UTILITY FUNCTIONS

In finance we are often concerned with a consumer's intertemporal allocation of his wealth to consumption. All of the mechanics required to handle this problem have already been developed. Good i at each point of time is considered as distinct for the purpose of measuring utility. So with n goods and T time periods, the ordinal or cardinal utility functions have n times T arguments. All of the previous analysis remains valid.

For simplicity we shall often work with a multiperiod utility of consumption function. This is justified if there is but a single good. More generally, we can consider it a derived utility function as in (44):

$$\hat{U}(C_1, C_2, \ldots, W_T; \mathbf{p}_1, \ldots, \mathbf{p}_n) = \text{Max}\{\Psi(\mathbf{x}_1, \ldots, \mathbf{x}_T); \text{ subject to } \mathbf{p}_t'\mathbf{x}_t = C_t\}. \tag{70}$$

Here W_T represents remaining wealth left as a legacy. If there is no motive for bequest, $\partial\hat{U}/\partial W_T = 0$.

Throughout this book we shall typically assume that intertemporal choices are made without regard to (are utility independent of) past consumption; that is, $(C_t, C_{t+1}, \ldots, W_T)$ is utility independent of $(C_0, C_1, \ldots, C_{t-1})$ for all t. Also, decisions affecting lifetime consumption are utility independent of bequest. These two conditions are sufficient for mutual utility independence, so the utility of lifetime consumption function can be written as in (40):

$$\hat{U}(\mathbf{C}) = k^{-1}(\exp[k\textstyle\sum k_t U_t(C_t)] - 1). \tag{71}$$

If we further assume that lotteries to be resolved immediately and paid off contemporaneously in consumption are evaluated the same at all points of time, then the univariate utility functions are all the same, $U_t \equiv U$. The static absolute risk-aversion function $A(C_t) \equiv -U''(C_t)/U'(C_t)$ is sufficient information for choosing among single-period gambles.

The parameters k_t measure the impatience to consume or time preference. The marginal rate of substitution of period t goods for period τ goods is

$$-\frac{dC_t}{dC_\tau} = \frac{\partial\hat{U}/\partial C_\tau}{\partial\hat{U}/\partial C_t} = \frac{k_\tau U'(C_\tau)}{k_t U'(C_t)}. \tag{72}$$

If consumption is currently at the same level, substitution is measured completely by k_t and k_τ. If the consumer displays impatience, as is commonly assumed, then $k_\tau < k_t$ for $\tau > t$, and one unit now is valued more than one unit later. Often a constant rate of time preference is assumed, with $k_t = \delta^t$. In this case substitution between periods depends only on the interval of time and not specifically on the date.

The final parameter, k, measures temporal risk aversion, the dislike of gambles with lengthy consequences. The smaller or more negative is k the more temporally risk averse is the consumer. For $k = 0$, corresponding to additive utility, the consumer is temporally risk neutral. For positive or negative k, the consumer is temporally risk preferring or risk averse, respectively.

Temporal risk aversion can be defined as follows. Consider the single-period lottery with payoffs C_h or C_l and certainty equivalent C_1^*. Now consider the lottery which is resolved now but whose level payoffs C_h or C_l continue for T periods. If the certainty equivalent level stream C^* is greater (less) than C_1^*, the consumer is temporally risk averse (preferring). For two periods another explanation of temporal risk aversion is that the lottery with equal chances of paying (C_h, C_l) or (C_l, C_h) is preferred to the lotery with equal chances of paying (C_h, C_h) or (C_l, C_l).

To explore temporal risk aversion, let us define a utility function for level streams:

$$\lambda(C) \equiv \hat{U}(C\mathbf{1}) = k^{-1}(\exp[k\alpha U(C)] - 1), \tag{73}$$

where $\alpha \equiv \Sigma k_t > 0$. The absolute risk-aversion function for this utility function is

$$a(C) \equiv -\frac{\lambda''(C)}{\lambda'(C)} = -\frac{U''(C)}{U'(C)} - k\alpha U'(C). \tag{74}$$

Since the lead term in (74) is the static risk-aversion function, $a(C)$ is greater (less) than $A(C)$ and the consumer is temporally risk averse (preferring) if k is negative (positive).

2

Arbitrage and Pricing: The Basics

The factors that affect an investor's utility at a particular point of time are many and varied. Some, such as the quantities consumed of the various goods, are largely under the investor's current control. Others, such as the current level of wealth, are not currently controllable but are to a large part determined by previous decisions. Still others, such as the prices of various goods and assets or investment opportunities ávailable, can be affected little or not at all by individual investors. In general, an investor attempting to maximize expected utility would have to take into consideration all of these factors. On the other hand, investors control over their realized utility can be no finer than the control variables available to them.

In a standard consumption–investment problem investors have two types of controls available. In the first period they can invest their (after consumption) wealth in investment assets. In the second period they sell these assets to buy the various consumption goods (or further investment assets in a multiperiod problem). That is, the investment decision consists of forming a portfolio that "transfers" wealth from one period to the next. The consumption decision allocates this wealth among the various goods (and the amount set aside for further investment).

If each of the consumption goods, or claims to them, such as futures contracts, can be purchased as investments in the first period, then both of these allcoations can be made simultaneously in the first period. If some of the goods cannot be directly purchased, then the decision making does take place in two parts as outlined. In this latter case it is natural to think of the consumption allocation in the second period as specifying a derived utility of wealth function as described in the previous chapter. The first-period investment decision, then, seeks to maximize the expectation of this utility function. Since the one-step decision can also be considered in two parts, this is the formulation we shall adopt. In addition to being more general, it permits us to concentrate on the investment decision.

In making an investment decision an investor has "control" only over those outcomes of nature which can be distinguished by different patterns of prices (cum dividends) of the investment assets. We shall refer to distinct outcomes as *states* (*of nature*). For purposes of the investment decisions two or more distinguishable outcomes of nature with the same pattern of prices for the investment assets must be grouped into a single state. The states are mutually exclusive and collectively exhaustive, so that exactly one state always occurs.

NOTATION

Let the number of outcome states and assets be finite. (We will commonly deal with a continuum of states as well; however, the proofs of many propositions are much simpler in the finite case, and the intuition is the same.) States are indexed by s ($s = 1, \ldots, S$) and assets by i ($i = 1, \ldots, N$).

The one-period investment problem is characterized by the tableau of cum dividend end-of-period prices on the N assets in the S states:

$$\mathbf{Y}' = (\mathbf{y}_1, \ldots, \mathbf{y}_S). \tag{1}$$

The investor will choose a portfolio represented by the vector $\mathbf{n}$, where n_i is the number of units (shares) held of asset i. The current values of the assets are $\mathbf{v}$, and the budget constraint is $\mathbf{n}'\mathbf{v} = W_0$.

For many purposes it will be convenient to deal in asset returns. The realized return (one plus the rate of return) on the ith asset in state s is $Z_{si} = Y_{si}/v_i$. The state space tableau of returns is

$$\mathbf{Z} = \mathbf{Y}\mathbf{D}_{\mathbf{v}}^{-1}, \tag{2}$$

where $\mathbf{D}_{\mathbf{v}}$ is a diagonal matrix with i^{th} element v_i. $\mathbf{Z}$ can also be considered as the payoff tableau in an economy where the number of shares has been adjusted to set all initial prices to unity. The vector $\mathbf{z}_{\cdot i}$ is the ith column of $\mathbf{Z}$ and represents the S possible returns on asset i. Similarly, the sth row of $\mathbf{Z}$, $\mathbf{z}'_{s\cdot}$, represents the returns on the N assets in state s. We shall also adopt the convention of writing $\tilde{\mathbf{z}}$ for the random returns on the N assets. That is, $\tilde{\mathbf{z}}$ is a random vector with realization $\mathbf{z}_{s\cdot}$; $\tilde{z}_i$ is a scalar random variable which is the ith element of $\tilde{\mathbf{z}}$. (This notation is most convenient when the returns on the various assets are continuous, so there are a "continuum" of rows to $\mathbf{Z}$.)

The construction of the returns tableau from the payoffs assumes that each asset's current price is nonzero. If any asset has a nonzero price, then other assets with prices of zero pose no problem. For example, assume $v_i \neq 0$ and $v_j = 0$. We can construct in place of asset j a new asset $\hat{j}$ with payoffs $Y_{s\hat{j}} = Y_{si} + Y_{sj}$ and price $v_{\hat{j}} = v_i + v_j \neq 0$ and return vector $z_{\cdot\hat{j}} = \{Y_{s\hat{j}}/v_{\hat{j}}\}$. Using returns as our basic structure can cause a problem, therefore, only if all prices are currently zero. We shall assume that this is not the case and that any zero prices have been "corrected" as outlined. Note that negative prices do not cause any problems.

For most applications, of course, asset prices will be positive. One common assumption that will ensure this is *limited liability*. An asset has limited liability if there is no possibility of its requiring any additional payments subsequent to its purchase. That is, $\mathbf{y}_i \geqslant \mathbf{0}$. (We do not write $\geqq \mathbf{0}$ to exclude a meaningless asset which is always worth zero.) As we shall see, the absence of arbitrage will assure that an asset with limited liability has a positive price $v_i > 0$ so that $\mathbf{z}_{i\cdot} > \mathbf{0}$.

In returns space, investments can be characterized by a vector $\boldsymbol{\eta}$ of commitments to the various assets. η_i is the commitment to asset i and is proportional to the dollar amount invested in the ith asset: $\eta_i \propto n_i v_i$. If the investment involves a total net commitment of $W_0 > 0$, then we usually normalize η_i to $w_i \equiv n_i v_i / W_0$. In this case the investment is a *portfolio*, and $\mathbf{w}$ is the vector of *portfolio weights*. This normalization imposes the *budget constraint* $\mathbf{1}'\mathbf{w} = 1$. Since $v_i \neq 0$ by assumption, the portfolio weights $\mathbf{w}$ contain all the information that $\mathbf{n}$ does.

If $w_i < 0$ ($\eta_i < 0$), then asset i has been sold short. The exact mechanism of a short sale is not important. Essentially, when an asset is shorted, the investor is exchanging a current receipt equal in value to the asset's price for the promise to make payments matching those on the asset until the short sale is closed by a final repayment equal in value to the then prevailing price. A *no-short-sales restriction* $\mathbf{w} \geqslant \mathbf{0}$ is often applied in portfolio problems, although we generally shall not do so here.

Capital letters are used to denote the random returns on portfolios to distinguish them from the returns on assets. For example, $\tilde{Z}_{\mathbf{w}} \equiv \mathbf{w}'\tilde{\mathbf{z}}$ or $\tilde{Z}_1 \equiv \mathbf{w}_1'\tilde{\mathbf{z}}$.

As an example, consider this economy with two assets and three states:

$$\mathbf{Z} = \begin{pmatrix} 1 & 3 \\ 2 & 1 \\ 3 & 2 \end{pmatrix}. \tag{3}$$

An investment commitment of $\boldsymbol{\eta} = (1, 3)'$ would have state-by-state outcomes of $\mathbf{Z}\boldsymbol{\eta} = (1{\cdot}1 + 3{\cdot}3,\ 2{\cdot}1 + 1{\cdot}3,\ 3{\cdot}1 + 2{\cdot}3)' = (10, 5, 9)'$ and an original commitment of 4. The corresponding portfolio would be $\mathbf{w} = (\frac{1}{4}, \frac{3}{4})'$ with returns $\mathbf{Zw} = (2.5, 1.25, 2.25)'$.

An *arbitrage portfolio* is defined as a vector of commitments summing to zero. To distinguish arbitrage portfolios, we shall denote them by $\boldsymbol{\omega}$ with $\mathbf{1}'\boldsymbol{\omega} = 0$. An arbitrage portfolio should not be confused with an *arbitrage opportunity*, which is defined later. Arbitrage profits can be created with arbitrage portfolios but are by no means guaranteed. The latter, which should perhaps more properly be called *zero-investment* portfolios, are simply characterized by how they are financed. The money received from the short sales is used in the purchase of the long positions. We shall always assume that arbitrage portfolios are nontrivial: $\boldsymbol{\omega} \neq \mathbf{0}$. That is, there is at least one long position and one short position. Note that arbitrage portfolios are scale free; that is, if $\boldsymbol{\omega}$ is an arbitrage portfolio, then so is $\gamma\boldsymbol{\omega}$ for any scalar γ.

A *riskless portfolio* (or asset) is a portfolio with the same return in every state. In other words, a riskless portfolio is the solution to

$$\mathbf{Zw} = R\mathbf{1}, \qquad \mathbf{1'w} = 1. \tag{4}$$

R is the riskless return and $R - 1$ is the *risk-free rate* or the *interest rate*. If $R = 1$, the riskless asset is "costless storage."

If no riskless portfolio exists, then there will be a *shadow* riskless rate whose value will depend on other details of the economy not yet specified, such as investors' preferences. The shadow riskless return takes the place of the actual riskless return in various pricing formulas. One well-known example of a shadow riskless return is the *zero-beta return* in the Black version of the CAPM (see Chapter 4).

The shadow riskless return is bounded below by the largest return that can be guaranteed with *some* portfolio (5a) and bounded above by the largest return that is possible for *every* portfolio (5b):

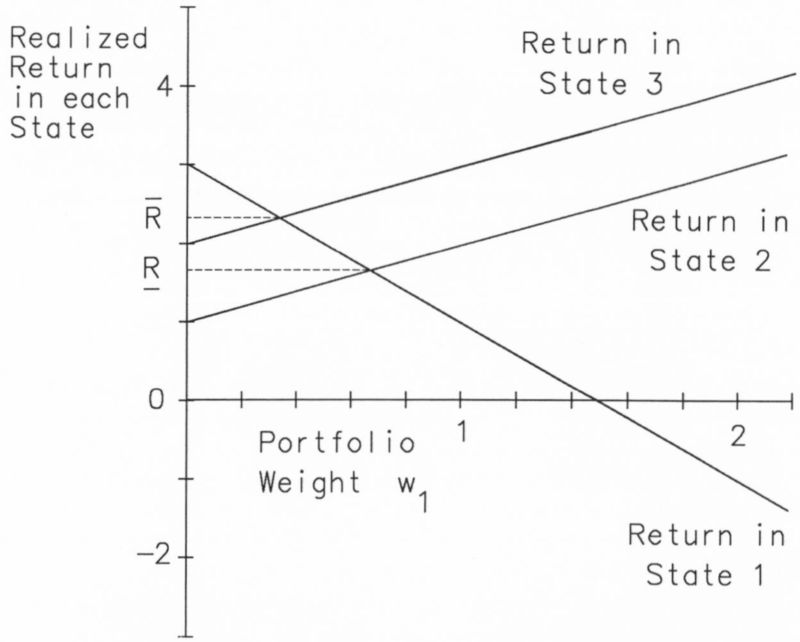

Figure 2.1 State Returns as a Function of w

$$\underline{R} \equiv \underset{\mathbf{w}}{Max}\ [\underset{s}{\text{Min}}(\mathbf{Zw})], \tag{5a}$$

$$\overline{R} \equiv \underset{\mathbf{w}}{Min}\ [\underset{s}{\text{Max}}(\mathbf{Zw})]. \tag{5b}$$

In general, these *maximin* and *minimax* problems are solved by converting them to linear programming problems. For example, in the economy described in Equation (3), the solution to (5a) is $\underline{R} = \frac{5}{3}$ when $w_1 = \frac{2}{3}$, and the solution to (5b) is $\overline{R} = \frac{7}{3}$ when $w_1 = \frac{1}{3}$.

These solutions can be most easily illustrated by the graph in Figure 2.1. The three lines give the return realized in each state as a function of the proportion invested in the first asset. These are $Z_1 = w + 3(1 - w) = 3 - 2w$, $Z_2 = 2w + (1 - w) = 1 + w$, and $Z_3 = 3w + 2(1 - w) = 2 + w$. For $w < \frac{2}{3}$ the lowest return occurs for state 2, where $Z_L(w) = 1 + w$. For $w > \frac{2}{3}$, the lowest return is in state 1, where $Z_L(w) = 3 - 2w$. The former function is increasing in w while the latter is decreasing. The maximum, therefore, occurs at $w = \frac{2}{3}$ with $\underline{R} = Z_L(\frac{2}{3}) = 1 + \frac{2}{3} = 3 - \frac{4}{3} = \frac{5}{3}$. The solution to (5b) can be similarly determined.

REDUNDANT ASSETS

Let $\mathbf{w}_1$ denote a specific portfolio. This portfolio is *duplicable* if there exists some other distinct portfolio $\mathbf{w}_2 \neq \mathbf{w}_1$ such that $\mathbf{Zw}_2 = \mathbf{Zw}_1$. That is, there is a different portfolio with exactly the same state-by-state returns. Note that the portfolio $\mathbf{w}_2$ is also duplicable.

Duplicability is clearly a property of the set of returns as a whole. If there is a single pair of duplicable portfolios, $\mathbf{w}_1$ and $\mathbf{w}_2$, then any portfolio $\mathbf{w}$ is duplicable because $\mathbf{w} + \mathbf{w}_1 - \mathbf{w}_2$ matches it. Duplicability is consequently usually expressed as a redundancy in the primitive assets (columns of $\mathbf{Z}$).

A *redundant* (primitive) asset is one of the assets that contributes to the duplicability just described. From the original definition of duplicability, it follows that one or more of the primitive assets in $\mathbf{Z}$ is redundant if there is a nontrivial arbitrage portfolio with a return of exactly zero:

$$\mathbf{Z}\boldsymbol{\omega} = \mathbf{0}, \qquad \mathbf{1}'\boldsymbol{\omega} = 0, \qquad \boldsymbol{\omega} \neq \mathbf{0}. \tag{6}$$

If we define the *augmented returns tableau matrix* as $\hat{\mathbf{Z}}' \equiv (\mathbf{Z}', \mathbf{1})$, then an equivalent statement is that $\mathbf{Z}$ includes redundant assets if the rank of the augmented returns tableau matrix is less than N, the number of securities. If this rank condition is not met, then any of the primitive assets is duplicable; however, the redundant assets are only from among those contributing to the collinearity. For example, in the economy

$$\hat{\mathbf{Z}} = \begin{pmatrix} 0 & 2 & 1 & 2 \\ 1 & 3 & 2 & 1 \\ 1 & 1 & 1 & 1 \end{pmatrix}, \tag{7}$$

the fourth asset is not redundant. Any one of the first three is since $\hat{\mathbf{z}}_{\cdot 3} = \hat{\mathbf{z}}_{\cdot 1} + \hat{\mathbf{z}}_{\cdot 2})/2$.

The row of ones in $\hat{\mathbf{Z}}$ is important. For example, in the economy

$$\mathbf{Z} = \begin{pmatrix} 0 & 0 & 1 \\ 1 & 2 & 0 \end{pmatrix} \tag{8}$$

none of the three assets is redundant because $|\hat{\mathbf{Z}}| = -1$, so the augmented tableau matrix has full rank of three. $\mathbf{z}_{\cdot 1}$ and $\mathbf{z}_{\cdot 2}$ are linearly dependent, but $\hat{\mathbf{z}}_{\cdot 1}$ and $\hat{\mathbf{z}}_{\cdot 2}$ are not. Although the first asset appears "useless" here when compared to the second, it is not redundant. In fact, as we shall see shortly, it is quite useful.

We shall generally assume that redundant assets have been eliminated from the tableau. In this case the augmented tableau matrix has full column rank N, although $\mathbf{Z}$ may only have rank $N - 1$.

CONTINGENT CLAIMS AND DERIVATIVE ASSETS

A *contingent claim* or *derivative asset* is one whose end-of-period payoff is exactly determined by the payoffs on one or more of the other assets, sometimes distinguished by the name *primitive assets*. Common types of derivative assets are put and call options, warrants, rights offerings, futures and forward contracts, and convertible or more exotic types of bonds.

Contingent claims will be examined in detail in Chapters 14, 17, and 19. Here we describe only the contracts of the most common types.

A (one-period) *forward contract* represents the obligation to purchase at the end of the period a set nubmer of units (shares) of a particular primitive asset at a price specified at the beginning of the period. We usually "normalize" all forward contracts so that they are claims against a single unit of the primitive asset. The payoff on a forward contract, $\tilde{y}_f$, with specified purchase price X is

$$\tilde{y}_f = \tilde{y} - X. \tag{9}$$

A short position in a forward contract is the reciprocal obligation — namely, a commitment to sell the underlying primitive asset.

A (single-period) *call option* represents the right, but *not* the obligation, to purchase at the end of the period a set number of units (shares) of a particular primitive asset at a price specified at the beginning of the period. This price is known as the *striking price* or *exercise price*. As with forward contracts, options will be normalized to be claims on one share. Obviously, an investor will exercise a call option only if it is in-the-money; that is, the price of the primitive asset exceeds the exercise price. The payoff to a call with exercise price X is

$$\tilde{y}_c = \mathrm{Max}(\tilde{y} - X, 0). \tag{10}$$

Unlike a long position, a short position in a call option represents an obligation.

A *put option* is like a call option, but it represents the right to sell. The holder of a put will exercise only if the price of the primitive asset is less than the exercise price. The payoff to a put with exercise price X is

$$\tilde{y}_p = \mathrm{Max}(X - \tilde{y}, 0). \tag{11}$$

As with a call, a short position in a put represents an obligation.

INSURABLE STATES

If it is possible to construct a portfolio which pays off only in one particular state, then this state is called *insurable*. This name is applied because this portfolio can provide insurance against the occurrence of this state.

According to the definition just given, state s is insurable if there exists a solution $\boldsymbol{\eta}$ to

$$\mathbf{Z}\boldsymbol{\eta} = \boldsymbol{\iota}_s. \tag{12}$$

$\boldsymbol{\iota}_s$ is the sth column of the identity matrix, a vector with all zeros except for a one in the sth spot. Retaining the same analogy, we get that $\mathbf{1}'\boldsymbol{\eta}$ is the cost per dollar of the insurance policy against the occurrence of state s.

THEOREM 1 *A state is insurable if and only if the asset returns in this state are linearly independent of the returns on the assets in the other states. ($\mathbf{z}_{s\cdot}$ is not collinear with $\mathbf{z}_{1\cdot}, \ldots, \mathbf{z}_{s-1,\cdot}, \mathbf{z}_{s+1,\cdot}, \ldots, \mathbf{z}_{S\cdot}$).*

Proof. If $\mathbf{z}_{s.}$ is linearly dependent on the other state return vectors, then

$$\mathbf{z}_{s.} = \sum_{\sigma \neq s} \lambda_\sigma \mathbf{z}_{\sigma.}. \tag{13}$$

Thus *for all* $\boldsymbol{\eta}$,

$$\mathbf{z}'_{s.}\boldsymbol{\eta} = \sum_{\sigma \neq s} \lambda_\sigma \mathbf{z}'_{\sigma.}\boldsymbol{\eta}. \tag{14}$$

But if state s is insurable, then there is an $\boldsymbol{\eta}$ which satisfies (12), and for this vector this sum is zero term by term and cannot equal 1 as required.

If $\mathbf{z}'_{s\cdot}$ is not linearly dependent on the other rows, then rank $(\mathbf{Z}, \boldsymbol{\iota}_s)$ = rank $(\mathbf{Z})$. But by the *rule of rank* a solution to (12) then exists. Q.E.D.

As an example of insurability, consider the economy

$$\mathbf{Z} = \begin{pmatrix} 3 & 2 \\ 1 & 2 \\ 2 & 4 \end{pmatrix}. \tag{15}$$

The portfolio (2, −1) has a return pattern (4, 0, 0), so insurance against the first state is possible at a cost of $\frac{1}{4}$. The returns in the second and third states are obviously collinear, so insurance is not available for either.

DOMINANCE AND ARBITRAGE

One portfolio, $\mathbf{w}_1$, is said to *dominate* another, $\mathbf{w}_2$, if

$$\mathbf{Zw}_1 \geqslant \mathbf{Zw}_2. \tag{16}$$

(Recall that the $\geqslant$ inequality is strict for at least one component.) Since the dominated portfolio never outperforms the dominating one, every investor would avoid holding it in favor of the other. Note that this is true regardless of our having made no assumptions about the single- or multi-period nature of the problem or the possibility of different beliefs about the state probabilities. All that is required for the first portfolio to be strictly preferred to the second is that an investor strictly prefer more wealth to less wealth.

Although it is obvious that no rational (and nonsatiated) investor would ever hold a dominated portfolio when the dominating one was available, it is also true that the mere existence of a dominated portfolio means that no unbounded optimal portfolio exists for any investor — even one who would consider neither the dominating nor dominated portfolios. To demonstrate this proposition, let $\mathbf{w}_1$ be a portfolio that dominates $\mathbf{w}_2$ and define $\mathbf{x} \equiv \mathbf{Z}(\mathbf{w}_1 - \mathbf{w}_2)$. From (16), $\mathbf{x} \geqslant \mathbf{0}$. Now any portfolio $\mathbf{w}$ is dominated by $\mathbf{w} + \gamma(\mathbf{w}_1 - \mathbf{w}_2)$ for any $\gamma > 0$. To prove this proposition, note first that $\mathbf{1}'[\mathbf{w} + \gamma(\mathbf{w}_1 - \mathbf{w}_2)] = \mathbf{1}'\mathbf{w} + \gamma\mathbf{0} = 1$, so it is a portfolio. Also,

$$\begin{aligned} \mathbf{Z}[\mathbf{w} + \gamma(\mathbf{w}_1 - \mathbf{w}_2)] &= \mathbf{Zw} + \gamma\mathbf{Z}(\mathbf{w}_1 - \mathbf{w}_2) \\ &= \mathbf{Zw} + \gamma\mathbf{x} \geqslant \mathbf{Zw} \end{aligned} \tag{17}$$

since $\mathbf{x} \geqslant \mathbf{0}$, and the dominance is verified. Furthermore, the dominance is unlimited because $\mathbf{w} + \gamma_1(\mathbf{w}_1 - \mathbf{w}_2)$ also dominates $\mathbf{w} + \gamma_2(\mathbf{w}_1 - \mathbf{w}_2)$ for $\gamma_1 > \gamma_2$. Thus, investors will never be satisfied with any portfolio but would always wish to push their portfolio by additional net purchases of $\mathbf{w}_1 - \mathbf{w}_2$.

The absence of dominance can also be stated thus: There exists no investment which is the solution to

$$\mathbf{1}'\boldsymbol{\eta} \leqslant 0, \tag{18a}$$

$$\mathbf{Z}\boldsymbol{\eta} \geqslant \mathbf{0}. \tag{18b}$$

(Recall that the second inequality has at least one strictly positive component.) If a solution to (18) exists, we call that solution an *arbitrage opportunity of the first type*. Often (18a) will be an equality. In this case $\boldsymbol{\eta}$ is an arbitrage portfolio creating a zero investment arbitrage opportunity.

A negative investment arbitrage or an *arbitrage opportunity of the second type* exists if there is a solution to

$$\mathbf{1}'\boldsymbol{\eta} < 0, \tag{19a}$$

$$\mathbf{Z}\boldsymbol{\eta} \geqq \mathbf{0}. \tag{19b}$$

(Note that in (19b) $\mathbf{Z}\boldsymbol{\eta} = \mathbf{0}$ is permitted, and $\boldsymbol{\eta}$ must have negative total weight and cannot be an arbitrage portfolio.)

Arbitrage opportunities of the first type are limited liability investments with no current commitment and a possibility of a profit. Arbitrage opportunities of the second type are limited liability investments with a current *negative* commitment. These two types of arbitrages are distinct, as the following examples show.

An economy in which there are arbitrage opportunities only of the second type is

$$\mathbf{Z} = \begin{pmatrix} 5 & 2 \\ -5 & -2 \end{pmatrix}. \tag{20}$$

Clearly, no investment $\boldsymbol{\eta}' \equiv (\eta_1, \eta_2)$ satisfies (18) since

$$\mathbf{Z}\boldsymbol{\eta} = \begin{pmatrix} (5\eta_1 + 2\eta_2) \\ -(5\eta_1 + 2\eta_2) \end{pmatrix} \tag{21}$$

cannot be nonnegative unless it is identically zero. However, the investment $\boldsymbol{\eta}' = (2, -5)$ is an arbitrage opportunity satisfying (19) since

$$\mathbf{1}'\boldsymbol{\eta} = -3, \qquad \mathbf{Z}\boldsymbol{\eta} = \begin{pmatrix} 0 \\ 0 \end{pmatrix}. \tag{22}$$

An economy with arbitrage opportunities only of the first type is

$$\mathbf{Z} = \begin{pmatrix} 1 & 0 \\ -1 & -1 \\ 1 & 1 \end{pmatrix}. \tag{23}$$

The payoff vector for any investment $\boldsymbol{\eta}' = (\eta_1, \eta_2)$ is $(\eta_1, -\eta_1 - \eta_2, \eta_1 + \eta_2)$. Clearly, this is nonnegative only if $\eta_1 + \eta_2 = 0$. Thus, any arbitrage portfolio $(\boldsymbol{\omega}, -\boldsymbol{\omega})$ with $\boldsymbol{\omega} > 0$ satisfies (18), creating an arbitrage of the first type; however, there is no way to set up an arbitrage of the second type with a current negative commitment of funds.

A sufficient condition for an arbitrage opportunity of the second type to guarantee the existence of an arbitrage opportunity of the first type is the existence of a (positive investment) portfolio with a semipositive return; that is, $\mathbf{Zw} \geqslant \mathbf{0}$. (For example, an asset with limited liability.) To demonstrate this proposition, assume that $\boldsymbol{\eta}$ is an arbitrage opportunity of the second type with $\mathbf{1}'\boldsymbol{\eta} = -a < 0$, and that $\mathbf{w}$ is the portfolio with semipositive return and positive return in state s: $\mathbf{z}'_{s\cdot}\mathbf{w} = b > 0$. Then $\boldsymbol{\eta} + a\mathbf{w}$ is an arbitrage opportunity of the first type since

$$\begin{aligned} &\mathbf{1}'(\boldsymbol{\eta} + a\mathbf{w}) = -a + a = 0, \\ &\mathbf{Z}(\boldsymbol{\eta} + a\mathbf{w}) \geqslant \mathbf{0} \quad \text{with } \mathbf{z}'_{s\cdot}(\boldsymbol{\eta} + a\mathbf{w}) \geqslant a\mathbf{z}'_{s\cdot}\mathbf{w} = ab > 0. \end{aligned} \tag{24}$$

If any asset has limited liability (and its payoff is not identically zero), then this condition is met. Since this will typically be true, we will be concerned primarily with (the absence of) arbitrage opportunities of the second type, which then guarantees (the absence of) arbitrage opportunities of the first type.

PRICING IN THE ABSENCE OF ARBITRAGE

Whenever arbitrage opportunities are available, then as was previously demonstrated, no investor will be satisfied with any unbounded portfolio, and no equilibrium can obtain. On the other hand, if there are no arbitrage opportunities in the set of returns, then these returns can be supported in some equilibrium. This proposition will not be proved until later. Here we prove the important preliminary result that in the absence of arbitrage, there is a linear pricing relation among the returns.

DEFINITION A vector $\mathbf{p}$ is said to be a pricing vector supporting the economy $\mathbf{Z}$ if $\mathbf{Z}'\mathbf{p} = \mathbf{1}$.

The more usual way of writing this result is in terms of payoffs and current values: $\mathbf{Y}'\mathbf{p} = \mathbf{v}$. Note that this is the same pricing vector; the former result is transformed to the latter by premultiplying by diag($\mathbf{v}$).

Typically some supporting pricing vector will exist. Often it will not be unique. We will be concerned with the conditions under which a *positive* pricing vector exists. The reason for this concern is illustrated in the following example.

Consider the economy

$$\mathbf{Z} = \begin{pmatrix} z_{11} & z_{12} \\ 0 & z_{22} \end{pmatrix}. \tag{25}$$

Clearly, only pricing vectors with $p_1 = 1/z_{11}$ can support this economy. So if p_1 is negative, z_{11} must be as well. In this case just shorting the first asset is an arbitrage (of the second type). In a simple situation like this p_1

is the cost today of getting one dollar in state 1 at the end of the period (and no dollars in every other state). Therefore, a negative (zero) price indicates an arbitrage opportunity of the second (first) type. Similarly, a portfolio investing the fraction $w_1 = z_{12}/(z_{12} - z_{11})$ in the first asset would have a nonzero return only in the second state. Its return in state 2 is $-z_{22}z_{11}/(z_{12} - z_{11})$, so $p_2 = (z_{11} - z_{12})/z_{22}z_{11}$ also must be positive, or this portfolio is an arbitrage opportunity. The connection between positive state prices and the lack of arbitrage is valid in general.

THEOREM 2 *There exists a* nonnegative *pricing vector* **p** *which supports the returns tableau of an economy if and only if there are no arbitrage opportunities of the second type.*

Proof. Consider the linear programming problem

$$\text{Minimize } \mathbf{1}'\boldsymbol{\eta} \qquad \text{Subject to } \mathbf{Z}\boldsymbol{\eta} \geqq \mathbf{0}. \tag{26}$$

Clearly, the objective can be reduced at least to zero since $\boldsymbol{\eta} = \mathbf{0}$ accomplishes this. If there are no arbitrage opportunities of the second type, then by (19) zero is the minimum objective possible as well. Now from the theorem of duality (see Mathematical Background) a finite objective minimum for a primal linear programming problem guarantees that the dual is also feasible. The dual of (26) is

$$\begin{aligned} &\text{Maximize} \quad \mathbf{0}'\mathbf{p} \\ &\text{Subject to} \quad \mathbf{Z}'\mathbf{p} = \mathbf{1} \\ &\qquad\qquad\qquad \mathbf{p} \geqq 0. \end{aligned} \tag{27}$$

The two constraints form the linear pricing result desired, so the sufficiency of no arbitrage is proved.

Conversely, if there is a nonnegative pricing support vector, then the dual problem in (27) is feasible. By necessity its objective is zero. Again by the theorem of duality, the primal problem in (26) has a minimal objective of zero. Thus, no arbitrage opportunities exist. Q.E.D.

This theorem requires the existence of some nonnegative pricing vector. It does not prohibit the existence of other pricing vectors with some negative prices. For example, for the economy described in (3) the pricing support equations are

$$\begin{aligned} p_1 + 2p_2 + 3p_3 &= 1, \\ 3p_1 + p_2 + 2p_3 &= 1 \end{aligned} \tag{28}$$

with solutions

$$p_1 = .2 - .2p_3,$$

$$p_2 = .4 - 1.4p_3. \tag{29}$$

p_1 is positive if $p_3 < 1$, and p_2 is positive for $p_3 < \frac{2}{7}$. Thus, any value of p_3 between 0 and $\frac{2}{7}$ results in all three state prices being positive [e.g., $p_3 = .1$ and $\mathbf{p}' = (.18, .26, .1)$] and shows that no arbitrage opportunities (of the second type) are available. Nevertheless, the pricing vector $(.1, -.3, .5)$ with a negative component also supports the economy.

As a second example consider the economy in (15) where state 1 is insurable. The pricing support equations are

$$\begin{aligned} 3p_1 + \ \ p_2 + 2p_3 &= 1, \\ 2p_1 + 2p_2 + 4p_3 &= 1 \end{aligned} \tag{30}$$

with solutions

$$\begin{aligned} p_1 &= .25, \\ p_2 &= .25 - 2p_3. \end{aligned} \tag{31}$$

Thus, p_1 is fixed, and $p_2 > 0$ for $p_3 < \frac{1}{8}$. Again there is no arbitrage.

For the economy in (20) the pricing support equations are

$$\begin{aligned} 5p_1 - 5p_2 &= 1, \\ 2p_1 - 2p_2 &= 1. \end{aligned} \tag{32}$$

There are obviously no solutions to this set of equations and, a fortiori, no positive solutions. Therefore, we know that arbitrage of the second type is possible as previously demonstrated.

For the economy

$$\mathbf{Z} = \begin{pmatrix} 5 & 2 \\ 3 & 1 \\ 2 & 1 \end{pmatrix}. \tag{33}$$

the solutions to the pricing support equations are

$$\begin{aligned} p_1 &= 2 - p_3, \\ p_2 &= -3 + p_3. \end{aligned} \tag{34}$$

In this case there are solutions for the pricing vector, but clearly p_1 and p_2 cannot both be nonnegative. In this case, also, arbitrage of the second type is possible.

In some cases there is a nonnegative pricing support vector, but one or more its components must be zero. For example, consider the economy in (23). For the two assets the pricing support equations are

$$\begin{aligned} p_1 - p_2 + p_3 &= 1, \\ -p_2 + p_3 &= 1. \end{aligned} \tag{35}$$

Clearly, the only solutions have $p_1 = 0$. As we have already seen, this economy has an arbitrage opportunity of the first type. The next theorem shows that to ensure that the pricing vector is strictly positive we must assume that there are no arbitrage opportunities of the second *or first* types.

THEOREM 3 *There exists a* positive *pricing vector* **p** *which supports the returns tableau of an economy if and only if there are no arbitrage opportunities of the first or second types.*

Proof. (Only the proof of necessity is given here. Sufficiency is demonstrated in the next chapter.) Assume that $\boldsymbol{\eta}$ is an arbitrage opportunity of the first type. Then $\mathbf{Z}\boldsymbol{\eta} \geqslant \mathbf{0}$ [condition (18b)] and $\mathbf{p} > \mathbf{0}$ imply

$$\mathbf{p}'\mathbf{Z}\boldsymbol{\eta} > 0. \tag{36}$$

But, by assumption, $\mathbf{p}$ is a pricing support vector, so $\mathbf{p}'\mathbf{Z} = \mathbf{1}'$ and (36) then imply

$$\mathbf{1}'\boldsymbol{\eta} > 0, \tag{37}$$

which contradicts (18a). Thus, $\boldsymbol{\eta}$ cannot be an arbitrage opportunity as was assumed.

Now assume that $\boldsymbol{\eta}$ is an arbitrage opportunity of the second type. Then $\mathbf{Z}\boldsymbol{\eta} \geqq \mathbf{0}$ [condition (19b)] and $\mathbf{p} > \mathbf{0}$ imply

$$\mathbf{p}'\mathbf{Z}\boldsymbol{\eta} \geqslant 0. \tag{38}$$

As before, $\mathbf{p}$ is a pricing support vector, so $\mathbf{p}'\mathbf{Z} = \mathbf{1}'$ and (38) then imply

$$\mathbf{1}'\boldsymbol{\eta} \geqslant 0, \tag{39}$$

which violates (19a). So again $\boldsymbol{\eta}$ cannot be an arbitrage opportunity as was assumed. Q.E.D.

The two important features of these two theorems are the positivity of the pricing vector and the linearity of the pricing result. Positive state prices assure the absence of arbitrage while linearity guarantees the absence of any monopoly power in the financial market.

The first statement has already been discussed. p_s is the price today of one dollar next period if state s occurs. If any of these prices are zero or negative, then this valuable claim can be obtained at no (or negative) cost.

The linearity of the pricing result guarantees that a payment of two dollars in any state is worth twice as much as a payment of one dollar; that is, there are no scale effects. In addition, the incremental value of one dollar in state s does not depend on the other states' payoffs; that is, there are no scope effects. If the pricing relation were not linear, then it would be profitable to combine assets into particular packages worth more than the parts or to split assets into parts worth more than the whole.

MORE ON THE RISKLESS RETURN

Typically, state prices are not unique. In fact, if there are N assets and $S > N$ states (with no redundant assets), then the absence of arbitrage alone places only N linear restrictions on the vector of state prices, leaving $S - N$ "degrees of freedom."

In later chapters we develop some restrictions on the state prices which are not based solely on arbitrage. Here we only note the following two useful properties.

If there is a riskless asset or portfolio with return R, then (in the absence of arbitrage) the sum of the state prices of any valid supporting pricing vector is equal to $1/R$. To prove this proposition, note that, by assumption, there exists a portfolio $\mathbf{w}_1$ with $\mathbf{1}'\mathbf{w}_1 = 1$ and $\mathbf{Z}\mathbf{w}_1 = R\mathbf{1}$. Then for all valid supporting price vectors

$$\begin{aligned} \mathbf{p}'(\mathbf{Z}\mathbf{w}_1) &= (\mathbf{p}'\mathbf{Z})\mathbf{w}_1, \\ \mathbf{p}'\mathbf{1}R &= \mathbf{1}'\mathbf{w}_1 = 1, \\ \sum p_s &= \frac{1}{R}. \end{aligned} \tag{40}$$

If there is no way to construct a riskless portfolio, then the sum of the state prices is bounded below by $1/\bar{R}$ and above by $1/\underline{R}$, where $\bar{R}$ and $\underline{R}$ are defined in (5b) and (5a). To prove this proposition, note first that, by the definition of $\bar{R}$, there exists a portfolio $\mathbf{w}_1$ such that $\mathbf{Z}\mathbf{w}_1 \leqslant \mathbf{1}\bar{R}$. Since $\mathbf{p}'\mathbf{Z} = \mathbf{1}'$ for any valid pricing vector,

$$\begin{aligned} \mathbf{p}'(\mathbf{1}\bar{R}) &\geqslant \mathbf{p}'(\mathbf{Z}\mathbf{w}_1) = (\mathbf{p}'\mathbf{Z})\mathbf{w}_1 = \mathbf{1}'\mathbf{w}_1 = 1, \\ \sum p_s &\geqslant \frac{1}{\bar{R}}. \end{aligned} \tag{41}$$

Similarly, by the definition of $\underline{R}$, there exists a portfolio $\mathbf{w}_2$ such that $\mathbf{Z}\mathbf{w}_2 \geqslant \mathbf{1}\underline{R}$. Again, since $\mathbf{p}'\mathbf{Z} = \mathbf{1}'$ for any valid pricing vector,

$$\begin{aligned} \mathbf{p}'(\mathbf{1}\underline{R}) &\leqslant \mathbf{p}'(\mathbf{Z}\mathbf{w}_2) = (\mathbf{p}'\mathbf{Z})\mathbf{w}_2 = \mathbf{1}'\mathbf{w}_2 = 1, \\ \sum p_s &\leqslant \frac{1}{\underline{R}}. \end{aligned} \tag{42}$$

The bounds given above are generally tight. That is, there are valid pricing vectors whose elements sum to any value in the open interval $(1/\bar{R}, 1/\underline{R})$. As an example, consider the economy in (3). The two equations representing the pricing constraints are

$$\begin{aligned} p_1 + 2p_2 + 3p_3 &= 1, \\ 3p_1 + p_2 + 2p_3 &= 1. \end{aligned} \tag{43}$$

Solving these equations in terms of p_2 gives

$$p_1 = \tfrac{1}{7} + \tfrac{1}{7}p_2, \qquad p_3 = \tfrac{2}{7} - \tfrac{5}{7}p_2. \tag{44}$$

Therefore, any value of p_2 between 0 and $\frac{2}{5}$ (which sets p_3 to zero) gives a valid pricing vector.

The sum of the state prices is, in terms of p_2.

$$\sum p_s = \tfrac{3}{7} + \tfrac{3}{7}p_2. \tag{45}$$

As p_2 takes on all permissible values (those between 0 and $\frac{2}{5}$), the sum of the state prices takes on all values between $\frac{3}{5}$ and $\frac{3}{7}$ which are the reciprocals of $\underline{R}$ and $\bar{R}$, as given below Equation (5).

RISKLESS ARBITRAGE AND THE "SINGLE PRICE LAW OF MARKETS"

The two previous "no arbitrage" pricing theorems should not be confused with the proposition which has come to be known as *the single price law of markets*. This proposition states that two investments with the same payoff in every state must have the same current value. That is, if $\mathbf{n}_1$ and $\mathbf{n}_2$ are two vectors of asset holdings and $\mathbf{Yn}_1 = \mathbf{Yn}_2$, then $\mathbf{v}'\mathbf{n}_1 = \mathbf{v}'\mathbf{n}_2$. If we define $\mathbf{m} \equiv \mathbf{n}_1 - \mathbf{n}_2$, this result can also be stated as

$$\mathbf{Ym} = \mathbf{0} \quad \text{implies} \quad \mathbf{v}'\mathbf{m} = 0. \tag{46}$$

Using portfolio returns, we can rewrite (46) as

$$(\mathbf{YD}_v^{-1})(\mathbf{D}_v\mathbf{m}) \equiv \mathbf{Z}\boldsymbol{\eta} = \mathbf{0} \quad \text{implies} \quad (\mathbf{v}'\mathbf{D}_v^{-1})(\mathbf{D}_v\mathbf{m}) \equiv \mathbf{1}'\boldsymbol{\eta} = 0, \tag{47}$$

where $\boldsymbol{\eta} \equiv \mathbf{D}_v\mathbf{m}$, and $\mathbf{D}_v$ is a diagonal matrix with $D_{ii} = v_i$.

Any violation of (47) guarantees the existence of an arbitrage opportunity of the second type. (Note that if $\mathbf{1}'\boldsymbol{\eta} > 0$, then $\mathbf{1}'(-\boldsymbol{\eta}) < 0$.) Thus, the single price law of markets covers only a subset of the cases of Theorem 2; it does not cover situations when $\mathbf{Z}\boldsymbol{\eta} \geqslant \mathbf{0}$.

The single price law of markets guarantees the existence of a pricing support vector, but it need not be nonnegative. The proof of this proposition is almost identical to the proof of Theorem 2. In this case the constraints in the primal problem are equalities, so the dual variables, the state prices, are unconstrained.

A related "partial" result deals with the absence of riskless arbitrage. A *riskless arbitrage opportunity* is a nonpositive investment with a constant, positive profit. That is, $\boldsymbol{\eta}$ is a riskless arbitrage opportunity if it is the solution to

$$\mathbf{1}'\boldsymbol{\eta} \leqslant 0, \tag{48a}$$

$$\mathbf{Z}\boldsymbol{\eta} = \mathbf{1}. \tag{48b}$$

The absence of riskless arbitrage opportunities does not by itself guarantee a supporting pricing vector, since it may be impossible to create any riskless investments. For example, there are no riskless arbitrage opportunities in the economy in (20) [as demonstrated in (21)]. Nevertheless, there is no supporting pricing vector either since

$$\mathbf{p}'\begin{pmatrix} 5 & 2 \\ -5 & -2 \end{pmatrix} = (1,\ 1) \tag{49}$$

has no solution. However, provided that (48b) is feasible—that is, some constant positive return investment can be formed—supporting state prices exist. Again they can be positive or negative since the primal constraint is an equality.

Two final comments are in order on riskless arbitrage. Riskless arbitrage need not imply the existence of a riskless asset (a riskless investment with a positive commitment). For example, the economy

$$\mathbf{Z} = \begin{pmatrix} 1 & 2 \\ -1 & 0 \end{pmatrix} \tag{50}$$

has a riskless arbitrage, namely, $\boldsymbol{\omega}' = (-1,\ 1)$, but no riskless asset. If a riskless asset is available in an economy with riskless arbitrage, then it is possible to construct a riskless portfolio with any desired risk-free rate.

To prove this proposition, let $\mathbf{w}$ be a riskless asset with $\mathbf{Zw} = R\mathbf{1}$, and let $\boldsymbol{\omega}$ be a riskless arbitrage opportunity with $\mathbf{Z}\boldsymbol{\omega} = k\mathbf{1}$. Then $\mathbf{w} + \gamma\boldsymbol{\omega}$ is a riskless asset with return $R + \gamma k$.

Conversely, a riskless arbitrage opportunity exists whenever there is a solution to

$$\mathbf{1}'\mathbf{w} = 1, \qquad \mathbf{Zw} = k\mathbf{1} > R\mathbf{1}. \tag{51}$$

POSSIBILITIES AND PROBABILITIES

All of the discussion thus far has been concerned only with possibilities. The probabilities of the various states have not mattered. An arbitrage opportunity will be viewed as such by all investors regardless of their subjective probabilities for the various states. The only requirement about beliefs is that each investor view each state as possible. If a particular investor thought a state was impossible, he or she should be willing to sell for zero an asset that had a positive payoff in that state and a zero payoff in all other states. A second investor who thought that state possible would view this "gift" as an arbitrage opportunity.

We denote investor k's subjective probabilities of the states by ${}_k\boldsymbol{\pi}$ and assume that all agree about possibilities; that is, ${}_k\boldsymbol{\pi} > \mathbf{0}$ for all k. ${}_kE$ denotes the expectations operator with respect to the probabilities ${}_k\boldsymbol{\pi}$. The vector of mean returns and the variance-covariance matrix are

$$
\begin{aligned}
{}_k\bar{\mathbf{z}} &\equiv {}_kE(\tilde{\mathbf{z}}) = \mathbf{Z}'{}_k\boldsymbol{\pi}, \\
{}_k\boldsymbol{\Sigma} &\equiv {}_kE[(\tilde{\mathbf{z}} - {}_k\bar{\mathbf{z}})(\tilde{\mathbf{z}} - {}_k\bar{\mathbf{z}})'] \\
&= \mathbf{Z}'\mathrm{diag}({}_k\boldsymbol{\pi})\mathbf{Z} - \mathbf{Z}'{}_k\boldsymbol{\pi}\,{}_k\boldsymbol{\pi}'\mathbf{Z}.
\end{aligned}
\tag{52}
$$

The mean and variance of a given portfolio $\mathbf{w}$ are

$$ {}_k\bar{Z}_{\mathbf{w}} = \mathbf{w}'{}_k\bar{\mathbf{z}}, \tag{53a} $$

$$ {}_k\sigma^2_{\mathbf{w}} = \mathbf{w}'{}_k\boldsymbol{\Sigma}\mathbf{w}. \tag{53b} $$

All investors regardless of their beliefs (provided only that ${}_k\boldsymbol{\pi} > \mathbf{0}$) believe the covariance matrix to have the same rank. Assuming that there are no riskless arbitrage opportunities and no redundant assets, we see that the covariance matrix has full rank N or rank $N - 1$, depending on whether or not a riskless asset is available. When a riskless asset is available, we usually denote it as the 0th asset and let $\bar{\mathbf{z}}$ and $\boldsymbol{\Sigma}$ refer only to the risky assets. $\boldsymbol{\Sigma}$ will then be positive definite. The portfolio $\mathbf{w}$ of investments in the risky assets will also be unconstrained since the riskless asset will take up the slack; $w_0 = 1 - \mathbf{1}'\mathbf{w}$.

Throughout most of this book we assume that all investors share the same (correct) beliefs. That is, their subjective probabilities are objective probabilities as well. In this case the subscript k will be dropped.

"RISK-NEUTRAL" PRICING

Every investor believes, by definition, that the subjective expected rate of return on each asset is the appropriate discount rate; that is,

$$ v_i = \frac{{}_kE(\tilde{y}_i)}{{}_k\bar{z}_i}. \tag{54} $$

Every investor must also agree that assets can be priced in a "risk-neutral" manner if the subjective probabilities are suitably adjusted. Furthermore, they all must agree on these adjusted probabilities, or, to the extent that the probabilities are not unique, they must agree on the possible sets.

We know from Theorems 2 and 3 that a positive pricing vector exists and that all investors regardless of beliefs agree on these prices or possible sets of prices. Choose a particular pricing vector $\mathbf{p}$ and define

$$\hat{\boldsymbol{\pi}} \equiv \mathbf{p}\hat{R}, \qquad \hat{R} \equiv (\mathbf{1}'\mathbf{p})^{-1}. \tag{55}$$

Since $\mathbf{v} = \mathbf{Y}'\mathbf{p}$, we have

$$\mathbf{v} = \frac{\mathbf{Y}'\hat{\boldsymbol{\pi}}}{\hat{R}} \quad \text{or} \quad v_i = \frac{\hat{E}(\tilde{Y}_i)}{\hat{R}}, \tag{56}$$

where $\hat{E}$ is the expectations operator with respect to the "probabilities" $\hat{\boldsymbol{\pi}}$. The elements of $\hat{\boldsymbol{\pi}}$ are called the *risk-neutral probabilities*. (They are also referred to as *martingale probabilities*.) $\hat{R}$ is the corresponding risk-neutralized risk-free rate. Note that $\hat{\boldsymbol{\pi}} > \mathbf{0}$ (since $\mathbf{p} > \mathbf{0}$), and $\mathbf{1}'\hat{\boldsymbol{\pi}} = 1$. This result can also be expressed as

$$\hat{E}(\tilde{\mathbf{z}}) \equiv \mathbf{Z}'\hat{\boldsymbol{\pi}} = \hat{R}\mathbf{1}; \tag{57}$$

that is, under the risk-neutral probabilities the expected rate of return on each asset is the (risk-neutralized) risk-free rate.

Because all investors agree on the possible pricing vectors, they must also agree on the possible sets of risk-neutral probabilities; however, to the extent that $\mathbf{p}$ is not unique, the risk-neutral probabilities are not either. If a riskless asset exists, then $\hat{R}$ must equal R for any choice of risk-neutral probabilities since, as shown in (40), all valid pricing vectors must price the riskless asset correctly; that is, $\mathbf{p}'(R\mathbf{1}) = 1$. In this case (56) and (57) can also be written as

$$\frac{\hat{E}(\tilde{\mathbf{y}})}{R} \equiv \frac{\mathbf{Y}'\hat{\boldsymbol{\pi}}}{R} = \mathbf{v}, \tag{58a}$$

$$\hat{E}(\tilde{\mathbf{z}}) \equiv \mathbf{Z}'\hat{\boldsymbol{\pi}} = R\mathbf{1}. \tag{58b}$$

Equation (58a) can also be interpreted as a "certainty equivalent" approach to pricing. $\hat{E}(\tilde{\mathbf{y}})$ computes the market-adjusted certainty equivalent of the payoff $\tilde{y}$. Typically, different utility functions would assign different certainty equivalents to the same risk. In this case, however, the certainty equivalent is being assigned in a market context where only the marginal impact on risk is relevant. Because this is a certainty equivalent, it is discounted to the present at the riskless rate.

For now these last results are only tautological with the absence of arbitrage and may not appear relevant or useful. We shall see, however, tht they are very useful in certain applications, such as the valuation of options and other contingent claims.

The pricing result can also be expressed as follows: Define the state price per unit probability: $\Lambda_s \equiv p_s/\pi_s$. Then

$$v_i = \sum \pi_s \Lambda_s Y_{si} = E(\tilde{\Lambda}\tilde{y}_i) \tag{59a}$$

or

$$1 = E(\tilde{\Lambda}\tilde{z}_i) \qquad \text{for all } i. \tag{59b}$$

The result in (59b) can also be expressed as

$$E(\tilde{z}_i) = \frac{1 - \text{Cov}(\tilde{z}_i, \tilde{\Lambda})}{E[\tilde{\Lambda}]} \tag{60a}$$

$$= R - R\,\text{Cov}(\tilde{z}_i, \tilde{\Lambda}). \tag{60b}$$

The representation in (60b) is valid provided there is a riskless asset, because (59b) must hold for it as well, implying $R = 1/E[\tilde{\Lambda}]$. Again the importance of this result will only become clear later.

ECONOMIES WITH A CONTINUUM OF STATES

In many problems it is important or convenient to assume that the assets' returns can take on a continuum of outcomes in a bounded or unbounded range. The capital asset pricing model (Chapter 4), for example, is often based on multivariate normality of returns.

With a continuum of states it is convenient to index the outcomes by a single random variable $\tilde{s}$. The assets' realized returns are a vector-valued function of this variable, $\tilde{\mathbf{z}} = \mathbf{z}(\tilde{s})$. We assume for convenience that s possesses a probability density function $\pi(s)$. (If no probability density exists, then most of the following results still obtain if the integrals are interpreted as Stieltjes integrals.)

Adopting previous definitions to the continuum case, we get that portfolio $\mathbf{w}_1$ dominates portfolio $\mathbf{w}_2$ if

$$\tilde{Z}_2 \equiv \tilde{\mathbf{z}}'\mathbf{w}_2 = \tilde{Z}_1 + \tilde{\xi}, \tag{61}$$

where $\tilde{\xi}$ is a nonpositive random variable with a strictly positive probability of being negative. Arbitrage opportunities of the first and second types are random variables $\tilde{Z}_{\boldsymbol{\eta}} \equiv \tilde{\mathbf{z}}'\boldsymbol{\eta}$ satisfying

$$\mathbf{1}'\boldsymbol{\eta} \leqslant 0, \quad \tilde{Z}_{\boldsymbol{\eta}} \geqslant 0, \quad \text{Prob}(\tilde{Z}_{\boldsymbol{\eta}} > 0) > 0, \tag{62}$$

and

$$\mathbf{1}'\boldsymbol{\eta} < 0, \qquad \tilde{Z}_{\boldsymbol{\eta}} \geqslant 0, \tag{63}$$

respectively. Under suitable regularity conditions the absence of arbitrage will guarantee the existence of a state price density $p(s)$ satisfying

$$p(s) > 0, \qquad \int \mathbf{z}(s)p(s)\,ds = \mathbf{1}. \tag{64}$$

From the state price density a risk-neutralized probability density $\hat{\pi}(s) \equiv p(s)[\int p(s)\,ds]^{-1}$ can be derived with the property

$$\mathbf{1} = \hat{R}^{-1}\int \mathbf{z}(s)\hat{\pi}(s)\,ds = \hat{R}^{-1}\hat{E}(\tilde{\mathbf{z}}),$$

$$\hat{R}^{-1} \equiv \int p(s)\,ds. \tag{65}$$

Similarly, the state price per unit probability $\Lambda(s) \equiv p(s)/\pi(s)$ satisfies

$$\mathbf{1} = E[\Lambda(\tilde{s})\mathbf{z}(\tilde{s})], \tag{66a}$$

$$E[\mathbf{z}(\tilde{s})] = R\mathbf{1} - R\,\mathrm{Cov}[\mathbf{z}(\tilde{s}),\ \Lambda(\tilde{s})]. \tag{66b}$$

3

The Portfolio Problem

In the previous chapter we were introduced to the basics of portfolio formation and pricing by (the absence of) arbitrage. In this chapter we begin our study of the portfolio problem in more detail.

THE CANONICAL PORTFOLIO PROBLEM

The general single-period portfolio problem facing an investor is

$$\text{Max } E[\Psi(C_0, C_s; s)] \tag{1}$$
$$\text{Subject to } \quad C_s = \mathbf{z}_s' . \mathbf{w}(W_0 - C_0)$$
$$\mathbf{1}'\mathbf{w} = 1.$$

C_0 and C_s denote current consumption and period-1 consumption (wealth) in state s. We denote the vector (C_s) by $\mathbf{c}$.

To solve this problem, we form the Lagrangian

$$L \equiv E\Psi - \boldsymbol{\lambda}'[\mathbf{c} - \mathbf{Z}\mathbf{w}(W_0 - C_0)] + \lambda_0(1 - \mathbf{1}'\mathbf{w}). \tag{2}$$

The first-order conditions are

$$\frac{\partial L}{\partial C_0} = E[\Psi_1(\cdot)] - \boldsymbol{\lambda}'\mathbf{Z}\mathbf{w} = 0, \tag{3a}$$

$$\frac{\partial L}{\partial C_s} = E[\Psi_2(C_s)] - \lambda_s = 0, \tag{3b}$$

$$\frac{\partial L}{\partial w} = \mathbf{Z}'\boldsymbol{\lambda}(W_0 - C_0) - \lambda_0\mathbf{1} = 0, \tag{3c}$$

$$\frac{\partial L}{\partial \boldsymbol{\lambda}} = \mathbf{c} - \mathbf{Z}\mathbf{w}(W_0 - C_0) = \mathbf{0}, \tag{3d}$$

$$\frac{\partial L}{\partial \lambda_0} = 1 - \mathbf{1}'\mathbf{w} = 0. \tag{3e}$$

The second-order necessary conditions are met if Ψ is concave.

In Equation (3b) λ_s is identified as the expected marginal utility of wealth in state s. If (3c) is premultiplied by $\mathbf{w}'$ and (3a) is substituted, we obtain

$$\lambda_0 = E[\Psi_1(\cdot)](W_0 - C_0). \tag{4}$$

This formulation allows for the possibility of state-dependent utility. Generally, we assume that utility of consumption in period 1 is state independent, and we write utility as $U(C_0, W)$. In this case it is often more convenient to substitute out the constraint in (3d) and express the portfolio problem as

$$\begin{aligned} &\text{Max } E\{U[C_0, (W_0 - C_0)\mathbf{w}'\tilde{\mathbf{z}}]\} \\ &\text{Subject to} \quad \mathbf{1}'\mathbf{w} = 1. \end{aligned} \tag{5}$$

To solve this problem, we form the Lagrangian $L \equiv EU + \lambda(1 - \mathbf{1}'\mathbf{w})$ and differentiate, which gives the first-order conditions

$$\frac{\partial L}{\partial C_0} = E[U_1(\cdot) - U_2(\cdot)\mathbf{w}'\tilde{\mathbf{z}}] = 0, \tag{6a}$$

$$\frac{\partial L}{\partial \mathbf{w}} = E[U_2(\cdot)(W_0 - C_0)\tilde{\mathbf{z}}] - \lambda\mathbf{1} = \mathbf{0}, \tag{6b}$$

$$\frac{\partial L}{\partial \lambda} = 1 - \mathbf{1}'\mathbf{w} = 0. \tag{6c}$$

If (6b) is premultiplied by $\mathbf{w}'$, we identify λ as the expected marginal utility of wealth. As before, using (6a), λ is also proportional to marginal utility of current consumption.

The consumption investment problem can now be described in the following intuitive fashion. The investor consumes from wealth until the expected marginal utilities of consumption and savings are equal (6a). Then the savings are allocated among the assets until each gives an equal contribution to expected marginal utility (6b).

In finance the primary concern is usually with the portfolio problem as stated in (6b). In this regard we can define a utility function over returns as $u(Z; W_0, C_0) \equiv U(C_0, W)$. Then, since $W = Z(W_0 - C_0)$, $u'(Z) = \partial U/\partial Z = (W_0 - C_0)U_2$, and Equation (6b) becomes

$$E[u'(\mathbf{w}'\tilde{\mathbf{z}})\tilde{\mathbf{z}}] = \lambda\mathbf{1}. \tag{7}$$

Since $u'' = (W_0 - C_0)^2 U_{22}$, utility over return displays risk aversion whenever utility of consumption and wealth is concave in its second argument. (Two notes: First, this is true even if it is meaningful and optimal for investors to consume more than their current wealth in the first period and invest a negative amount. Second, this requirement is somewhat weaker than the second-order condition of the problem in (2). In addition to concavity in each argument, the latter requires that $U_{11}U_{22} - U_{12}^2 > 0$.) Therefore, u is a well-defined risk-averse utility function.

For determining the optimal portfolio we need examine only the utility function of return, u. Two investors with identical (up to an affine transformation) utility functions u (and homogeneous beliefs) will hold the same portfolio even if their direct utility functions $U(\cdot)$ differ. One example of this situation is $U^1(\cdot) = C^\gamma + W^\gamma$ and $U^2(\cdot) = C^\gamma W^\gamma$. In each case $u(Z) = aZ^\gamma$.

The portfolio problem can also be stated in terms of the derived utility function for the portfolio weights $V(\mathbf{w}) \equiv Eu(\mathbf{w}'\tilde{\mathbf{z}})$. In this case the problem is

$$\text{Max } V(\mathbf{w}) \qquad \text{Subject to } \mathbf{1}'\mathbf{w} = 1. \tag{8}$$

Like the direct utility function, $V(\cdot)$ is concave since

$$\begin{aligned} V[\lambda\mathbf{w}_1 + (1-\lambda)\mathbf{w}_2] &\equiv Eu[\lambda\mathbf{w}_1'\tilde{\mathbf{z}} + (1-\lambda)\mathbf{w}_2'\tilde{\mathbf{z}}] \\ &> E[\lambda u(\mathbf{w}_1'\tilde{\mathbf{z}}) + (1-\lambda)u(\mathbf{w}_2'\tilde{\mathbf{z}})] \\ &= \lambda Eu(\mathbf{w}_1'\tilde{\mathbf{z}}) + (1-\lambda)Eu(\mathbf{w}_2'\tilde{\mathbf{z}}) \\ &= \lambda V(\mathbf{w}_1) + (1-\lambda)V(\mathbf{w}_2). \end{aligned} \tag{9}$$

Note that V need not be an increasing function even though u is. In fact, since the portfolio weights are constrained to sum to one, it is not really meaningful to consider this property at all.

OPTIMAL PORTFOLIOS AND PRICING

We can now show that the following three conditions are equivalent: (i) There are no arbitrage opportunities of the first or second types. (ii) There exists some strictly increasingly, twice differentiable utility function for which the solution to the portfolio problem in (1) or (5) is *interior*. (iii) There exists a *positive* pricing vector supporting the economy $\mathbf{Z}$.

The partial proof of Theorem 3 in the previous chapter demonstrated that condition (iii) implies condition (i). Demonstrations that (i) implies (ii) and that (ii) implies (iii) will complete the proof.

Proof. The proof that (i) implies (ii) is straightforward. The absence of arbitrage opportunities means that consumption at time zero or in any of the time period-1 states can only be increased by decreasing that in another state. This coupled with the concavity of the utility function guarantees by standard convex programming analysis that an interior maximum is achieved for any utility function like $-e^{-aZ}$ with $u'(-\infty) = \infty$ and $u'(\infty) = 0$.

To prove that (ii) implies (iii), we use the first-order conditions in (3). From (3c) $\mathbf{Z}'\boldsymbol{\lambda}(W_0 - C_0) = \lambda_0\mathbf{1}$, and from (4) $\lambda_0 = E\Psi_1(\cdot)(W_0 - C_0)$. Substituting the latter into the former gives

$$\mathbf{Z}'[\boldsymbol{\lambda}[E\Psi_1(\cdot)]^{-1}] = 1. \tag{10}$$

$E\Psi_1$ must be positive since marginal utility is everywhere positive. Similarly, from (3b) each element of $\boldsymbol{\lambda}$ is the expectation of marginal utility and, therefore, must also be positive. Thus, every component of the vector in brackets is positive, so this vector can serve as a pricing support vector. Q.E.D.

As shown in the previous chapter, it is clear that arbitrage opportunities will make impossible any solution to the optimal portfolio problem. For example, assume that there is a riskless asset with return R and a risky asset with return R with probability $\frac{1}{2}$ and return $R + a$ with probability $\frac{1}{2}$. In this case expected utility is

$$Eu[w\tilde{z} + (1 - w)R] = \tfrac{1}{2}u(R + wa) + \tfrac{1}{2}u(R), \tag{11}$$

which is clearly strictly increasing in the fraction of wealth invested in the risky asset. Therefore, no finite optimum obtains.

PROPERTIES OF SOME SIMPLE PORTFOLIOS

As a first example of the portfolio problems to come, we consider the case of a riskless asset and a single risky asset. To simplify the notation, let $\tilde{x}$ be *the excess return* on the risky asset $\tilde{x} \equiv \tilde{z} - R$. w will denote the fraction of wealth invested in the risky asset. Note that w is unconstrained; $w < 0$ indicates a short sale of the risky asset, and $w > 1$ indicates a levered portfolio, the purchase of the risky asset on margin.

The first property that we examine is the demand for the risky asset. Since

$$\begin{aligned} V'(0) &\equiv \frac{\partial}{\partial w} E[u(R + w\tilde{x})]\bigg|_{w=0} \\ &= E[\tilde{x}u'(R) + 0\cdot\tilde{x}] = u'(R)E[\tilde{x}] \\ &\gtrless 0 \quad \text{as } E[\tilde{x}] \gtrless 0, \end{aligned} \tag{12}$$

and V is concave, it follows that $V'(w) = 0$ (that is, the optimum occurs) at a positive or negative value of w for $E[\tilde{x}] \gtrless 0$, respectively. Thus, all investors have a demand for the risky asset of the same sign. In the rest of this section we assume that $E[\tilde{z}] > R$, so that the risky asset is held in positive amount by the investing public.

To examine the general effect of risk aversion, let u_k and u_j be two utility functions with the former more risk averse. Recall from Theorem 5 in Chapter 1 that $u_k = G[u_j]$ for some function G with $G' > 0$ and $G'' < 0$. Then

$$\begin{aligned} V_k'(w_j^*) &\equiv \frac{\partial}{\partial w} Eu_k(R + w\tilde{x})\bigg|_{w=w_j^*} = E[u_k'(R + w_j^*\tilde{x})\tilde{x}] \\ &= E\{G'[u_j(\cdot)]u_j'(R + w_j^*\tilde{x})\tilde{x}\}. \end{aligned} \tag{13}$$

w_j^* satisfies the first-order condition for the utility function u_j, so if G' were constant this last expectation would be zero. However, u_j is an increasing function and G' is a decreasing function, as shown in Chapter 1. Therefore, the expectation in (13) puts relatively more weight on the negative values of $\tilde{x}$ than does this first-order condition. Consequently, $V_k'(w_j^*) \equiv \partial Eu_k(R + w_j^*\tilde{x})/\partial w < 0$, and since $V_k' < 0$, $w_k^* < w_j^*$. In other words, just as our intuition would suggest, a more risk-averse investor holds a smaller proportion of wealth in the risky asset than does a less risk-averse investor.

We now consider the effects of changes in the returns of the two assets. We might suspect that an increase in the interest rate would increase demand for the safe asset. Similarly, an increase in the expected return on the risky asset might be presumed to icnrease the demand for it.

As we shall see, the results are not this simple. Changes in the returns on the two assets have two sometimes opposing types of effects. The one just described is similar to the *substitution effect* in standard demand theory—namely, the demand for a good increases as its price falls. But there is also an effect equivalent to the *income effect*. An increase in the interest rate or the expected rate of return on the risky asset improves the opportunities available. This increase in "income" can also cause shifts in demand.

We consider first a comparative static change in the interest rate, leaving the distribution of the *excess* return constant. Using the implicit function theorem on the first-order condition gives

$$\frac{\partial w^*}{\partial R}\bigg|_{\tilde{x}} = -\frac{E[u''(R + w^*\tilde{x})\tilde{x}]}{E[u''(R + w^*\tilde{x})\tilde{x}^2]} = \frac{E[A(\cdot)u'(\cdot)\tilde{x}]}{E[u''(R + w^*\tilde{x})\tilde{x}^2]}, \tag{14}$$

where $A(\cdot)$ is the absolute risk-aversion function. The denominator is negative since $\tilde{x}^2$ is positive and u'' is negative. As in (13), the numerator is positive or negative as $A(\cdot)$ is increasing or decreasing. Since decreasing absolute risk aversion is typically assumed, an increase in the interest rate will typically cause a shift in demand into the risky asset.

In this case we can consider $1/R$ as the price of saving and $\tilde{x}$ as the reward for bearing risk. Then a decrease in the price of saving (an increase in R) while holding the reward for risk constant causes a shift out of the safe asset. That is, the "income effect" dominates the "substitution effect."

Now suppose that the distribution of the raw return $\tilde{z}$, rather than the distribution of the excess return, is held fixed. In this case

$$\begin{aligned}\left.\frac{\partial w^*}{\partial R}\right|_{\tilde{z}} &= -\frac{E\{u''[R(1-w^*)+w^*\tilde{z}](\tilde{z}-R)\}(1-w^*)-E[u'(\cdot)]}{E[u''(R+w^*\tilde{x})\tilde{x}^2]} \\ &= \frac{E[A(\cdot)u'(\cdot)\tilde{x}](1-w^*)+E[u'(\cdot)]}{E[u''(R+w^*\tilde{x})\tilde{x}^2]} \\ &= (1-w^*)\left.\frac{\partial w^*}{\partial R}\right|_{\tilde{x}} + \text{a negative term.}\end{aligned} \tag{15}$$

Now decrease in the price of saving (an increase in R) also decreases the reward for bearing risk, so investors will be more likely to avoid the risky asset. In fact, there is no simple sufficient condition for $\partial w^*/\partial R|_z$ to be positive. Sufficient conditions for an increase in the interest rate to decrease demand for the risky asset are increasing absolute risk aversion and $w^* \leqslant 1$.

To consider a comparative static change in the expected return on the risky asset, we must keep its distribution fixed. Let us replace the raw return by $\tilde{z} = R + \mu + \tilde{x}$ and consider the effect of a change in μ away from zero.

$$\left.\frac{\partial w^*}{\partial \mu}\right|_R = -\frac{E\{u''[R+w^*(\tilde{x}+\mu)](\tilde{x}+\mu)+u'[R+w^*(\tilde{x}+\mu)]\}}{E\{u''[R+w^*(\tilde{x}+\mu)](\tilde{x}+\mu)^2\}}. \tag{16}$$

Evaluating this at $\mu = 0$ gives

$$\left.\frac{\partial w^*}{\partial \mu}\right|_R = \frac{E[A(\cdot)u'(\cdot)\tilde{x}w^* - u'(\cdot)]}{E[u''(R+w^*\tilde{x})\tilde{x}^2]}. \tag{17}$$

Since $w^* > 0$, the first term of the numerator in the expectation is negative iff absolute risk aversion is decreasing. The second term and the denominator are always negative, so decreasing absolute risk aversion is a sufficient condition for an increase in the expected return on the risky asset to cause an increase in the demand for the risky asset.

To consider wealth effects, we must use the direct utility function $U(\cdot)$. To simplify the notation, we write U as a function of the second-period wealth alone and use primes to denote derivatives. We also define *invested wealth* as $I \equiv W_0 - C$. The first-order condition of the portfolio problem is

$$E\{U'[I(R+w^*\tilde{x})]\tilde{x}\} = 0. \tag{18}$$

Using the implicit function rule gives

$$\frac{\partial w^*}{\partial I} = -\frac{E[U''(\cdot)\tilde{x}(R + w^*\tilde{x})]}{E[I\tilde{x}^2 U''(\cdot)]} = \frac{E[\tilde{x}U'(\cdot)\mathrm{R}(\cdot)]}{I^2 E[\tilde{x}^2 U''(\cdot)]}, \tag{19}$$

where $\mathrm{R}(\cdot)$ is the relative risk-aversion function. Comparing this to (14), we see that this derivative is positive or negative as relative risk aversion is decreasing or increasing. Again this result is exactly what would be expected. The portfolio weight measures a fraction of the investor's wealth placed at risk. If relative risk aversion is decreasing, then the investor is less (relatively) risk averse at higher levels of wealth and should be willing to commit more funds to the risky asset.

In the same fashion the effect of a change in wealth on the dollar amount invested in the risky asset is

$$\frac{\partial(Iw^*)}{\partial I} = -\frac{E[R\tilde{x}U''(\cdot)]}{E[I\tilde{x}^2 U''(\cdot)]} = \frac{RE[A(\cdot)U'(\cdot)\tilde{x}]}{IE[\tilde{x}^2 U''(\cdot)]}, \tag{20}$$

where $A(\cdot)$ is the absolute risk-aversion function. As before, the denominator is negative and the numerator is negative or positive if absolute risk aversion is decreasing or increasing.

STOCHASTIC DOMINANCE

As discussed previously, the existence of a dominated asset or portfolio cannot be maintained in the presence of investors who are unconstrained in their actions (and prefer more to less). The absence of dominance (or arbitrage opportunities) is therefore a particularly compelling argument in establishing bounds on asset prices. The requirements for the existence of dominance are so strict, however, that it could seldom arise except in certainty models or when very similar assets are compared. Examples of its application are the APT (Chapter 7), option pricing (Chapters 14, 17), and contingent claims valuation (Chapter 19).

First-order stochastic dominance is a weaker comparison that partially overcomes this limitation. One portfolio (or asset) dominates another if it *always* (weakly) outperforms the other. To stochastically dominate a second portfolio, the first portfolio need not always outperform, but the first portfolio's probability of exceeding any given level of return must be higher than that of the second portfolio.

If $\pi_1(\tilde{Z}_1)$ and $\pi_2(\tilde{Z}_2)$ are the marginal density functions for the returns on portfolios 1 and 2, then the first (weakly) stochastically dominates the second if

$$\int_{-\infty}^{x} \pi_1(t)\,dt \leqslant \int_{-\infty}^{x} \pi_2(t)\,dt \qquad \text{for all } x. \tag{21}$$

The dominance is strict if the inequality is strict for some x. This relation can also be stated as follows: The graph of the cumulative distribution function of returns on the second asset is never below that of the first.

In terms of random variables the stochastic dominance of portfolio 1 over-portfolio 2 can be expressed as

$$\tilde{Z}_2 \overset{d}{=} \tilde{Z}_1 + \tilde{\xi}, \tag{22}$$

where $\tilde{\xi}$ is a nonpositive random variable. The dominance is strict unless $\tilde{\xi} \equiv 0$. The symbol $\overset{d}{=}$ means *equal in distribution*. By comparing (12) to (58) of Chapter 2, we can see the relative weakness of stochastic dominance when compared to dominance. The former only requires an equality of the distributions of $\tilde{Z}_2$ and $\tilde{Z}_1 + \tilde{\xi}$, wheres the latter requires an outcome-by-outcome equality of these random variables.

One important distinction between dominance and stochastic dominance is that the state probabilities are irrelevant in the former. In the latter the probabilities are crucial, although the states themselves are not. For example, consider two assets with returns (1, 3) and (1, 2). If $\text{Prob}(\tilde{z}_1 = 1) \geqslant \text{Prob}(\tilde{z}_2 = 1)$ [and, therefore, $\text{Prob}(\tilde{z}_1 = 2) \leqslant \text{Prob}(\tilde{z}_2 = 3)$], then the first stochastically dominates the second. It dominates the second, however, only if $z_1 = 3$ and $z_2 = 2$ occur as the same state and the tableau is

$$\mathbf{Z} = \begin{pmatrix} 3 & 2 \\ 1 & 1 \end{pmatrix} \tag{23}$$

(or the reverse). In this case the probability restrictions are met as equalities, so stochastic dominance also obtains.

If the returns tableau is

$$\mathbf{Z} = \begin{pmatrix} 3 & 1 \\ 1 & 2 \end{pmatrix}, \tag{24}$$

then there is no dominance, but there is stochastic dominance provided $\pi_1 \geqslant .5$. Note that if two investors have different expectations, with only one believing that $\pi_1 < .5$, then they can disagree about the presence of stochastically dominated assets. Investors can never disagree about dominance, however, provided that each views every state as possible.

No nonsatiated investor (with state-independent utility) would ever hold a stochastically dominated portfolio. The proof of this proposition is quite easy. Since $\tilde{Z}_2$ and $\tilde{Z}_1 + \tilde{\xi}$ have the same distribution,

$$Eu(\tilde{Z}_2) = Eu(\tilde{Z}_1 + \tilde{\xi}) < Eu(\tilde{Z}_1). \tag{25}$$

The inequality follows from the nonpositivity of $\tilde{\xi}$ and the strict monotonicity of u.

This proposition does not rule out the existence of stochastically dominated assets or portfolios. It says simply that no investors would choose to invest *all* their wealth in one. They might hold a stochastically dominated asset as a part of a portfolio with other assets, as the example below illustrates.

Consider the economy tableau in (24) with equal state probabilities. Asset 1 stochastically dominates asset 2. ($\tilde{\xi}$ is a random variable equal to -1 or 0 with equal probabilities.) Recall that the random variables $\tilde{z}_2$ and $\tilde{z}_1 + \tilde{\xi}$ must only have the same distribution and need not be equal state by state. Both assets are useful, however. For example an investor with log utility would invest one-quarter of his or her wealth in asset 2. This would give a portfolio with returns of (2.5, 1.25). We can see that this is the optimum by using (10)

$$\frac{1}{2}\frac{3}{2.5} + \frac{1}{2}\frac{1}{1.25} = 1 = \frac{1}{2}\frac{1}{2.5} + \frac{1}{2}\frac{2}{1.25}. \tag{26}$$

Were the outcomes for assets 1 or 2 switched, then asset 1 would dominate asset 2, and any investor would have an unlimited demand for the former.

To summarize: Dominated assets or portfolio cannot exist or investors could make unlimited arbitrage profits. Stochastically dominated assets or portfolios may exist, although not as optimal holdings for any investors.

THE THEORY OF EFFICIENT MARKETS

The concept of an *efficient market* is very important in the area of finance. An efficient market is one in which information is processed in an efficient and rational manner. In an efficient market each investor's expectations about security returns are (correctly) based on all information available to that investor. This is usually stated as follows: In an efficient market, (equilibrium) prices "fully reflect" available information.

The theory and empirical evidence of efficient markets is usually stated in terms of the behavior of prices over time and of the adjustments of the equilibrium prices to the release of "new" information. As such, much of the treatment of efficient markets must be postponed until the models of equilibrium have been developed. Nevertheless, the concept of market efficiency is so important and so basic to finance that its introduction belongs here.

The history of the theory of efficient markets dates back at least to the turn of the century when Louis Bachelier, in *Theorie de la Speculation* (1900), described security prices by using the equations of Brownian motion. (In fact, this description of the equations of Brownian motion predates that of Albert Einstein's development of them in the physical sciences.) The recent interest in efficient markets which has led to the substantial literature on *rational expectations*, among other things, was kindled by the study of security prices during the late 1950s and early 1960s.

The importance of the theory of efficient markets comes from its predictions about the aggregation and revelation of the information embodied in the equilibrium prices. That is, in an efficient market, investors can learn information that they did not already know by observing the prices of marketed assets. As is usual in economics, we assume that no trading takes place out of equilibrium. That is, investors observe the equilibrium prices prior to being committed to their trade contracts. (The mechanism usually assumed to achieve the equilibrium is the Tatonnement, or "price-contingent," auction described in most introductory economics texts.)

This learning can be illustrated most clearly in a riskless economy. There is, however, a drawback to this approach. Although much of the intuition for efficiency can be gained by looking at riskless economies, a market is efficient in a riskless economy only if there are no arbitrage opportunities. Therefore, in this case, the lack of efficiency has an overly dramatic appearance.

EFFICIENT MARKETS IN A "RISKLESS" ECONOMY

If a market is considered riskless by all investors, then, in each of their opinions, all expected returns must be equal for an equilibrium to occur. For example, if the payoffs on the assets available in the economy are

$$\mathbf{Y} = \begin{pmatrix} 1 & 1 \\ 1 & 0 \end{pmatrix} \tag{27}$$

and all investors consider state 2 to be impossible, then there will be an equilibrium only when the prices on the two assets are equal. The different returns in the impossible second state are irrelevant.

Consider the same economy when only some of the investors view the second state as impossible, based on their private information (prior to observing the equilibrium prices). These investors will be at an equilibrium only if the prices of the two assets are equal. If the price of one asset were less than that of the other asset, then any of these investors would be willing to sell an unlimited amount of the higher-priced asset to finance purchases of the lower-priced one. Conversely, the other investors who view state 2 as possible will believe that asset 1 dominates asset 2 if their prices are the same. Thus, based on the privately held views, no equilibrium can be reached.

This stalemate can be broken when the determined offering of the second asset and demand for the first at the same prices by this second group of investors convinces the first group that state 2 is indeed possible.

Alternatively, an equilibrium can be reached with equal prices only when the unlimited demand for the lower-priced asset by the first group of investors convinces the second group that state 2 will never occur. Which of these two equilibria occurs cannot be predicted by the theory of efficient markets. But when an equilibrium does occur, one or both of the groups of investors must have altered their private opinions about returns. That is, the prices, and therefore the returns, available in equilibrium will reflect both groups' private information.

INFORMATION AGGREGATION AND REVELATION IN EFFICIENT MARKETS: THE GENERAL CASE

When investors hold such firm convictions that they disagree about which outcomes are possible, there is a strong necessity for learning about these divergent beliefs. Without learning, one or both groups of investors would continue to believe that arbitrage is possible. As we shall see, equilibrium prices also reveal private information, even in cases where it is not so extreme.

The basic result of the theory of efficient markets in a *purely speculative* market is that the only equilibrium will result in no trading. The extreme nature of this result is due to our consideration of only a purely speculative market—one in which each of the risky assets is in zero net supply. In a purely speculative market there is no motive on the part of any investor to trade for any reason other than to make a profit on private information. (For example, there are no risk return tradeoff considerations and no advantages to diversification.) We shall return to efficient markets and expand on this result for more general markets after developing the equilibrium models in the next several chapters.

Before presenting a detailed analysis of this proposition, it is useful to provide the intuition as to why all investors would refrain from trading. Consider the case of a single risky asset. As shown in (12) investors will have a positive (negative) demand for the risky asset only if they believe that its expected return is greater (less) than the riskless return. However, the market is a purely speculative one with a zero net supply of the risky asset. Thus, one investor can be long only if some other investor is short, and an investor knows that the desired long (short) position can be purchased only if some other investor believes the opposite—that the expected return on the risky asset is less (greater) than the riskless return. This mutual understanding causes both investors to revise their opinions until they each believe that the expected return equals the riskless return, at which point they no longer have any interest in trading.

To examine the proposition in detail, we use the following market setting. There are N risky assets each in zero net supply and a safe asset, number 0, in positive supply. The safe asset is the numeraire with initial price of 1. The return on the safe asset (and its end-of-period value) is R per share. The initial and end-of-period values of the risky assets are denoted by the vectors $\mathbf{v}$ and $\tilde{\mathbf{y}}$, respectively.

There are K investors. Investor k's initial wealth is $W_{0k} > 0$, consisting of this number of shares of the riskless asset. The chosen portfolio is denoted by $\mathbf{n}_k$, which includes n_{ik} shares of asset i. End-of-period wealth is

$$\tilde{W}_k - \mathbf{n}_k'\tilde{\mathbf{y}} + (W_{0k} - \mathbf{n}_k'\mathbf{v})R = W_{0k}R + \mathbf{n}_k'(\tilde{\mathbf{y}} - R\mathbf{v}). \tag{28}$$

Each investor is strictly risk averse with utility of terminal wealth $U_k(\cdot)$. ϕ_k denotes the private information that investor k has. This is often called investor k's signal. Φ is the common information that all investors have after observing the market price. It includes their common prior, any common information in their signals, and, most importantly, any information that they can deduce from prices or other investors' public behavior (e.g., desire to purchase or sell).

The equilibrium in this market will be that set of prices $\mathbf{v}$ for which net demand of each of the risky assets equals supply; that is, $\Sigma\,\mathbf{n}_k = \mathbf{0}$.

THEOREM 1 *In the market environment just described the equilibrium market prices satisfy* $\mathbf{v} = E[\tilde{\mathbf{y}}|\phi_k, \Phi]/R = E[\tilde{\mathbf{y}}|\Phi]/R$ *for all* k, *and every investor refrains from trading the risky assets.*

Proof. Let $\mathbf{n}_k^*$, $\tilde{Z}_k^*$, and $\tilde{W}_k^*$ denote the kth investor's optimal portfolio, its return, and the resulting wealth. Since each investor has the option of not trading, we must have

$$E[U_k(\tilde{W}_k^*)|\phi_k, \Phi] \geqslant U_k(W_{0k}R) \tag{29}$$

for all ϕ_k and Φ. Furthermore, since each investor is strictly risk averse, (29) implies that

$$E[\tilde{W}_k^*|\phi_k, \Phi] \geqslant W_{0k}R \quad \text{or} \quad E[\tilde{Z}_k^* - R|\phi_k, \Phi] \geqslant 0 \tag{30}$$

for all ϕ_k and Φ, with equality holding only if $\tilde{Z}_k^* \equiv R$, that is, only when investor k does not trade. Now take the conditional expectation of both sides of (30) with respect to just the public information Φ:

$$E[E[\tilde{Z}_k^* - R|\phi_k, \Phi]|\Phi] \equiv E[\tilde{Z}_k^* - R|\Phi] \geqslant 0. \tag{31}$$

Since the net supply of each risky asset is zero, the economy as a whole faces no risk. That is, the market clearing condition guarantees that

$$R\sum_{k=1}^{K} W_{0k} \equiv \sum_{k=1}^{K} \tilde{W}_k \quad \text{or} \quad \sum_{k=1}^{K} W_{0k}(\tilde{Z}_k^* - R) = 0. \tag{32}$$

As all investors know that this condition must be met, this knowledge is, by definition, public and, therefore

$$0 = E\left[\sum_{k=1}^{K} W_{0k}(\tilde{Z}_k^* - R)|\Phi\right]$$
$$= \sum_{k=1}^{K} W_{0k}E[(\tilde{Z}_k^* - R)|\Phi]. \tag{33}$$

From (31) each term in this last sum is nonnegative. Therefore, the sum itself can be zero only if each term is zero. $E[\tilde{Z}_k^* - R|\Phi] = 0$ for each k. That is, the "market" assesses that each investor has an expected gain of trading equal to zero.

Using the same reasoning, we can now show that (30) must also be satisfied as an equality. From (30) the excess return on each investor's portfolio has a nonnegative expected value conditional on the public information and any realization of the investor's private information. But as (31) has now been demonstrated to hold as an equality, the excess return on each investor's portfolio has an expected value of zero conditional on just the public information. This expectation, with information set Φ, is just a weighted average of the the expectations with information sets Φ plus ϕ_k. But from (30) each of these latter expectations is nonnegative, so the former can be zero only if each of its nonnegative components are zero. Thus,

$$E[\tilde{Z}_k^* - R|\phi_k, \Phi] = 0 \tag{34}$$

for all ϕ_k and Φ, and every investor refrains from trading. Q.E.D

Note that this theorem does not require that any investor know specifically which other investors have different information and therefore might be interested in trading. Nor do investors need to know about other investors' wealths or utility functions (except that each has positive wealth and is risk averse). If *any* other investor is willing to trade, this cause them both to update their beliefs until they both agree that there is no longer any incentive for trade. Also notice that it is not necessary that the equilibrium reveal all of the private information that an investor has. It need only reveal enough so that this status of no trading is achieved.

SIMPLE EXAMPLES OF INFORMATION REVELATION IN AN EFFICIENT MARKET

The mechanism of information revelation can be illustrated by the following example. The opportunities available include riskless storage, $R = 1$, and a single risky asset which is worth 8 in state 1 and 0 in state 2. Each investor will wish to take a long (short) position in the risky asset if and only if he or she assesses that the probability of state 1 exceeds (is less than) one-eighth of the current price v. In this case the expected return $\pi_1 \cdot 8/v$ is greater (less) than $R(= 1)$. That is, each investor's reservation (purchase) price is equal to eight times the assessed probability of state 1.

Before making this assessment, each investor receives one of three signals $\phi_1 = (a, b, c)$ and $\phi_2 = \{\alpha, \beta, \gamma\}$. The possible events, consisting of signal pairs and state outcomes, and their probabilities are

		Signal pairs:				
		(a, α)	(a, β)	(b, β)	(b, γ)	(c, γ)
States:	1	.15	.05	.10	.15	.05
	2	.05	.15	.10	.05	.15

Prior to receiving any signal, each investor believes that the probability of state 1 is .15 + .05 + .10 + .15 + .05 = 0.50. Thus, if the price of the risky asset were 4, both investors would agree that the expected excess return on the risky asset is zero, and no trading would take place. At any lower (higher) price both investors would like to take a long (short) position, so no equilibrium could obtain.

Now suppose that a pair of "naive" investors receives signals of the indicated type. If investor 1 observes that $\phi_1 = a$, she concludes that the probability of state 1 is

$$\pi_1(a) = \frac{.15 + .05}{.15 + .05 + .05 + .15} = \frac{1}{2}. \tag{35}$$

Therefore she would buy (some amount) of the risky asset at any price below 4 and sell at any price above 4. Similarly, the assessed probabilities and reservation prices for the other signals are $\pi_1(b) = \frac{5}{8}$, $\hat{v}(b) = 5$; $\pi_1(c) = \frac{1}{4}$, $\hat{v}(c) = 2$; $\pi_1(\alpha) = \frac{3}{4}$, $\hat{v}(\alpha) = 6$; $\pi_1(\beta) = \frac{3}{8}$, $\hat{v}(\beta) = 3$; and $\pi_1(\gamma) = \frac{1}{2}$, $\hat{v}(\gamma) = 4$.

The five possible signal pairs lead to the reservation price pairs listed in the following table. The reservation price of the first investor is listed first. The price that would result if both investors had received both signals is also listed.

	Signal pairs:				
	(a, α)	(a, β)	(b, β)	(b, γ)	(c, γ)
Reservation prices	(4, 6)	(4, 3)	(5, 3)	(5, 4)	(2, 4)
Full information price	6	2	4	6	2

Thus, if the investors receive signals a and α, trading will ensue with investor 1 selling and investor 2 buying at some price between 4 and 6. The actual price that prevails in equilibrium will depend on the investors' wealths and utility functions. For the other signal pairs the equilibrium price will also be in the indicated ranges, with the investor with the lower reservation price purchasing from the other investor.

It is not obvious how the price, by itself, would convey information in general. For example, a price of 4.5 is consistent with both signal pairs (b, β) and (b, γ). So if investor 1 received the signal b and then observed an equilibrium price of 4.5, she could not immediately deduce investor 2's information. In fact, an outside observer, who received no signal but saw only the price, could not even conclude that investor 1 had received signal b because the signal pair (a, α) is also consistent with a price of 4.5.

Note that there is a "full information" equilibrium. If the equilibrium price were somehow always equal to the one given in the second row, then each investor would learn the other's signal from the price and at the same time be content not to trade at this price, so the market would clear. To illustrate this, suppose that investor 1 receives the signal a and the price is 2. Then she knows that investor 2 has received the signal β rather than α since the price is not 6. On the other hand, investor 2 also knows that investor 1 has received the signal a rather than b since the price is 2 and not 4. Each of them then concludes that the probability of state 1 is $.05/(.05 + .15) = \frac{1}{4}$ and that the price should be $\frac{8}{4} = 2$, which it is. Similar reasoning is true for all other signal pairs.

Note also that outside observers would not necessarily be fully informed by the price. A price of 2 might mean that either of the signal pairs (a, β) or (c, γ) had been received. Of course, in either case the probability of state 1 is $\frac{1}{4}$, and if this is all that is really relevant to the outside observers, they are in a sense fully informed.

The mere existence of a fully informative equilibrium does not mean that it must obtain in practice because there might be others. Neither does it answer the more puzzling question of how the information gets into the price in the first place. In this example, the fully informative equilibrium is the only possible one between rational investors. Demonstrating this will also demonstrate how the information influences the price.

Now consider somewhat "more sophisticated" investors. For expositional convenience we assume that they are each risk neutral.

Suppose that investor 2 receives the signal α. In this case he can learn nothing additional from the equilibrium price or investor 1's actions. He knows that investor 1 must have received the signal a and that the probability of state 1 must be $\frac{3}{4}$. Being risk neutral he will be willing to purchase (sell) any amount at any price below (above) 6.

Now assume that investor 1 receives the signal a. She knows that investor 2 must have received signal α or β. In the former case, the equilibrium price will be driven to 6 as just explained. Therefore, if the price is not 6, she can conclude that investor 2 must have received the signal β. But now she is fully informed of both signals and will conclude that the probability of state 1 is $.05/(.05 + .15) = \frac{1}{4}$. Also being risk neutral, she will force the price to 2.

The same resoning applies to investor 1's receipt of the signal c and investor 2's conclusions upon receiving signal γ. The fully informed equilibrium price must obtain.

The only remaining case is when investor 1 receives the signal b and investor 2 receives β. Seeing a signal of b and any price other than 6 investor one will conclude that investor 2 did not receive the signal γ and know that he must have received β. Similarly, if the price is not 2, investor 2 will know that investor 1 did not receive the signal a. Thus, they will each know both signals and, therefore, that the probability of state 1 is $\frac{1}{2}$. A price of 4 must then result.

If the investors were not risk neutral, then the same equilibrium prices would result in each case. We know that this is true since, in the end, the investors end up bearing no risk, so their risk aversions cannot affect the equilibrium price.

What is important is that the investors be competitors and the Tatonnement price auction be honest. To illustrate this point, suppose that investor 2 received the signal α and tried to deceive investor 1 by initially offering to sell at any price above 3. Investor 1 would think that he had received the signal β and conclude that the equilibrium price should be 2. Of course, investor 2 would be happy to purchase at this price (knowing the true value is 6) and might then offer to buy at 2.5. However, if investor 1 were a little more sophisticated she would realize that investor two would do this only if he had been trying to deceive her with his earlier offer and would refuse this new one. In fact, any kind of deception would fail since all investors know by the reasoning in Theorem 1 to avoid any trading.

As stated earlier, it is not necessary that the equilibrium resulting under Theorem 1 be fully informative. All that is required is that sufficient information come out of the price so that no investor wishes to trade. We illustrate this by the following simple example. Suppose there is a single risky asset with possible values next year of $\mathbf{y}' = (1, 2, 4, 5)$ and a riskless asset with a return of 1. Investor 1 receives a signal which indicates that these four states are equally likely. Investor 2 receives a signal that states 1 and 4 have probability $\frac{1}{8}$ and states 2 and 3 have probability $\frac{3}{8}$. Each investor would therefore compute an expected value of 3 and refrain from trading only at this price. Thus, a price of 3 will obviously prevail, but it will not convey any further information to either investor.

COMMON KNOWLEDGE

The type of information described in the previous section, where A has information with a particular structure and B knows that A has information with this structure and A knows that B knows that A has information with this structure, and so on, is called *common knowledge*. (In the problem above these three iterations are sufficient. In general, common knowledge might have to be described by an infinite sequence of "A knows.") At first it might appear that this structuring is very important for the result and perhaps unrealistic. This, however, is mostly an illusion.

Theorem 1 mentions no particular information structure, and what few assumptions it does make about information appear to be innocuous. In fact, the entire "common knowledge" assumption is "hidden" in the presumption that investors have a common prior. If investors did not have a common prior, then their expectations conditional on the public information would not necessarily be the same. In other words, the public information would properly also be subscripted as Φ_k—not because the information differs across investors, but because its interpretation does.

In this case the proof breaks down. Consider the problem from the viewpoint of investor k. Inequality (30) is still valid ($E[\tilde{Z}_k^* - R|\phi_k, \Phi_k] \geqslant 0$), but $E[E[\tilde{Z}_j^* - R|\phi_j, \Phi_j]|\Phi_k]$ can be of either sign because all of the information in Φ_k is not necessarily contained in ϕ_j and Φ_j. Equation (32) still obtains, but now the aggregation of expectations with respect to Φ_k in (33) does not have only nonnegative terms, so we cannot conclude that each must be zero. In the end each investor can expect to make a profit (although each must then expect that some other investors will realize losses).

This theorem would also be false if the risky assets were in positive supply and the investors were endowed with shares. In this case some investors might be willing to enter into trades in which they had expected losses in order to reduce the risk of their endowed wealth.

The latter problem will be handled in Chapter 9 after we have developed portfolio models which deal with risk. The former problem cannot be corrected. Nevertheless, the question as to why priors should differ must then be answered. It is insufficient to argue that differing beliefs are more general. In this case an investor's priors are based on (idiosyncratic) information. Any information that is not common can be considered to be part of the signal. Therefore, differences in priors must come from inherent differences in the investors.

4

Mean-Variance Portfolio Analysis

As a first example of a portfolio problem, we consider standard mean-variance optimization. Historically this was one of the earliest problems considered. It is important because mean-variance analysis provides a basis for the derivation of the equilibrium model known variously as the capital asset pricing model (CAPM), Sharpe–Lintner model, Black model, and two-factor model.

Mean-variance analysis is fully consistent with expected utility maximization only under special circumstances. The required assumptions will be discussed later.

THE STANDARD MEAN-VARIANCE PORTFOLIO PROBLEM

We assume for now that the investors' preferences can be represented by a (derived) utility function defined over the mean and the variance of a portfolio's return, $V(\bar{Z}, \sigma^2)$. Using the notation in Chapter 2, we obtain that the expected return and variance on a portfolio are

$$\bar{Z} = \mathbf{w}'\bar{\mathbf{z}} + w_0 R = \sum_{i=0}^{N} w_i \bar{z}_i, \tag{1a}$$

$$\sigma^2 = \mathbf{w}'\mathbf{\Sigma}\mathbf{w} = \sum_{i=1}^{N}\sum_{j=1}^{N} w_i w_j \sigma_{ij}. \tag{1b}$$

The standard assumption is that preferences induce the favoring of higher means $V_1 > 0$ and smaller variances $V_2 < 0$. Under this assumption the class of potentially optimal portfolios for such investors are therefore those with the greatest expected return for a given level of variance and, simultaneously, the smallest variance for a given expected return. (If short sales are unrestricted, the first condition alone is an adequate description.) Such portfolios are termed *mean-variance* efficient. Here we shall work with the larger class of *minimum-variance* portfolios. This is the set that includes the single portfolio with the smallest variance at every level of expected return. All mean-variance efficient portfolios are also minimum-variance portfolios, but the converse is not true. These sets

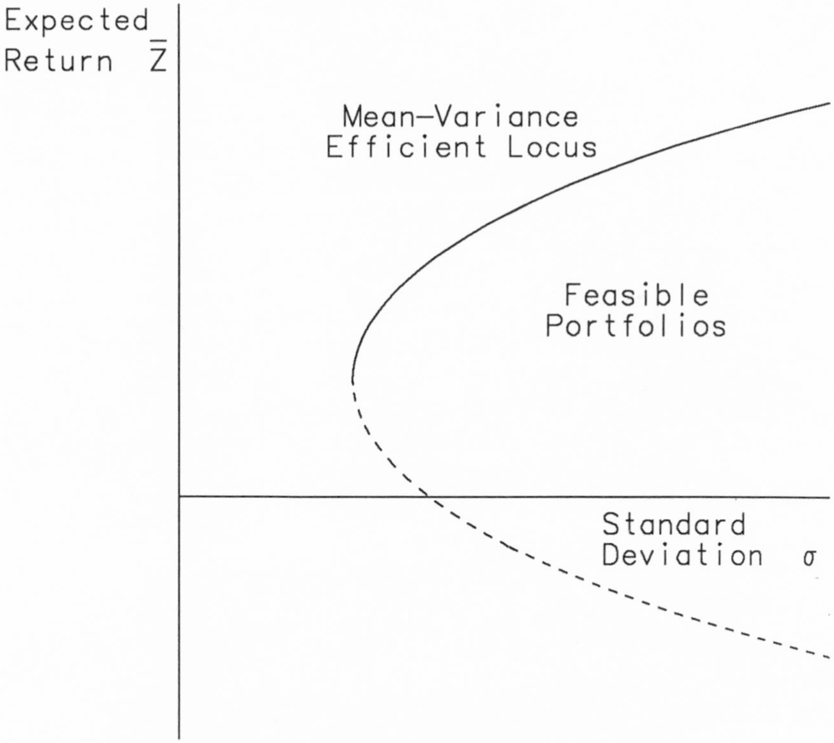

Figure 4.1 Mean-Variance Efficient Portfolios

are illustrated in Figures 4.1 and 4.2. (Not only is the latter class easier to characterize and work with analytically, but also under certain asymmetric distributions V_1 is ambiguous in sign even for investors who strictly prefer more to less. Thus, in general, all minimum-variance portfolios must be included in the optimal set. Whenever mean-variance analysis is consistent with expected utility maximization by a risk-averse investor, however, V_2 must be negative.)

We first find the minimum-variance portfolios in the absence of a riskless asset. The minimum-variance portfolio with expected return μ is the solution $\mathbf{w}(\mu)$ to

$$\text{Min } \tfrac{1}{2}\mathbf{w}'\boldsymbol{\Sigma}\mathbf{w} \tag{2a}$$

$$\text{Subject to } \quad \mathbf{1}'\mathbf{w} = 1, \tag{2b}$$

$$\bar{\mathbf{z}}'\mathbf{w} = \mu. \tag{2c}$$

We have not imposed any positivity constraints of the form $w_i \geq 0$, so unrestricted short sales are permitted.

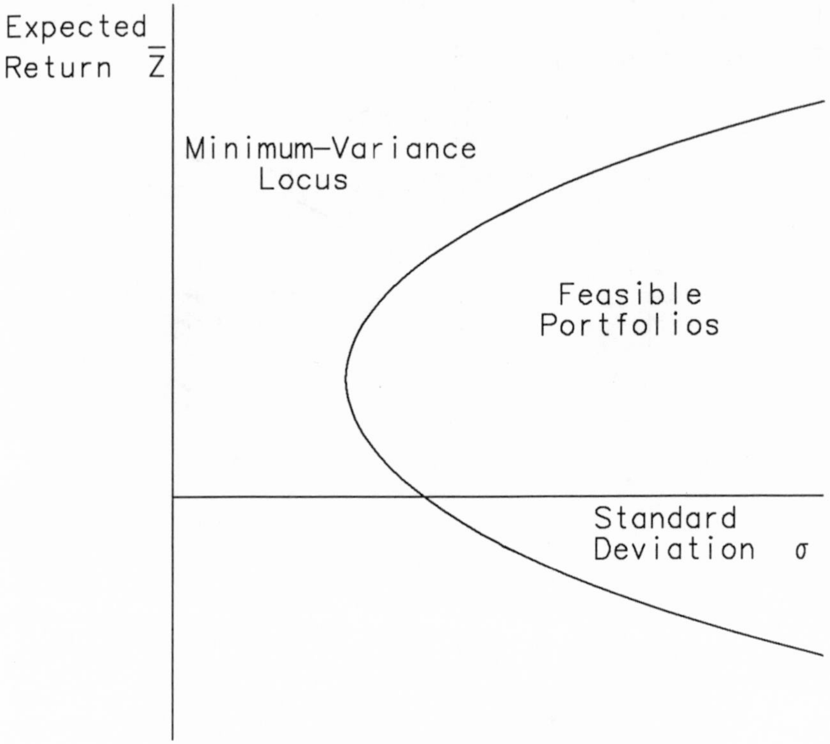

Figure 4.2 Minimum-Variance Portfolios

Forming the Lagrangian $L \equiv \mathbf{w}'\mathbf{\Sigma}\mathbf{w}/2 + \lambda(1 - \mathbf{1}'\mathbf{w}) + \gamma(\mu - \bar{\mathbf{z}}'\mathbf{w})$ and differentiating give the first-order conditions

$$\mathbf{0} = \frac{\partial L}{\partial \mathbf{w}} = \mathbf{\Sigma}\mathbf{w} - \lambda\mathbf{1} - \gamma\bar{\mathbf{z}} \tag{3}$$

and (2b) and (2c). The solution set is

$$\begin{aligned} \mathbf{w}^* &= \lambda\mathbf{\Sigma}^{-1}\mathbf{1} + \gamma\mathbf{\Sigma}^{-1}\bar{\mathbf{z}}, \\ w_i^* &= \lambda\sum_{j=1}^{N} v_{ij} + \gamma\sum_{j=1}^{N} v_{ij}\bar{z}_j. \end{aligned} \tag{4}$$

λ and γ can be determined from the constraints (2b) and (2c):

$$\begin{aligned} \lambda &= \frac{C - \mu B}{\Delta}, \qquad \gamma = \frac{\mu A - B}{\Delta}, \\ A &\equiv \mathbf{1}'\mathbf{\Sigma}^{-1}\mathbf{1} > 0, \quad B \equiv \mathbf{1}'\mathbf{\Sigma}^{-1}\bar{\mathbf{z}}, \\ C &\equiv \bar{\mathbf{z}}'\mathbf{\Sigma}^{-1}\bar{\mathbf{z}} > 0, \quad \Delta \equiv AC - B^2 > 0. \end{aligned} \tag{5}$$

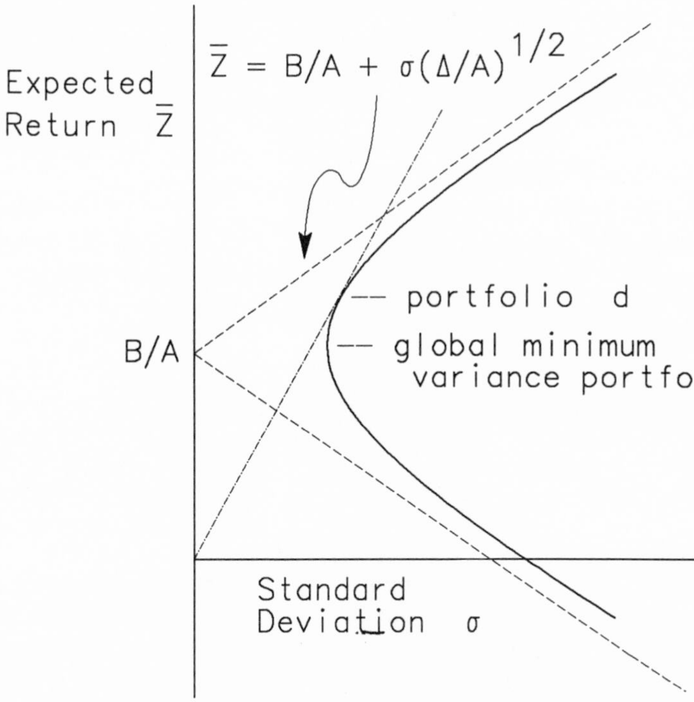

Figure 4.3 Risky-Asset-Only Minimum-Variance Set

(*Note:* $\Delta > 0$ by the Cauchy–Schwarz inequality since we have assumed that $\boldsymbol{\Sigma}$ is nonsingular and all assets do not have the same mean, $\bar{\mathbf{z}} \neq k\mathbf{1}$. If all means were the same, then $\Delta = 0$, and this problem has no solution except when $\mu = k$.) The equation of the minimum-variance set is, from (4), (2b), (2c), and (5),

$$\begin{aligned}\sigma^2 &= \mathbf{w}'\boldsymbol{\Sigma}\mathbf{w} = \mathbf{w}'\boldsymbol{\Sigma}(\lambda\boldsymbol{\Sigma}^{-1}\mathbf{1} + \gamma\boldsymbol{\Sigma}^{-1}\bar{\mathbf{z}}) \\ &= \lambda\mathbf{w}'\mathbf{1} + \gamma\mathbf{w}'\bar{\mathbf{z}} = \lambda + \gamma\mu \\ &= \frac{A\mu^2 - 2B\mu + C}{\Delta}.\end{aligned} \tag{6}$$

This is the equation of a parabola. In mean-standard deviation space the curve is a hyperbola, as illustrated in Figure 4.3.

The global minimum variance portfolio is located by

$$0 = \frac{d\sigma^2}{d\mu} = \frac{2A\mu - 2B}{\Delta}. \tag{7}$$

That is, it has an expected return of B/A and, from (6), a variance of $1/A$. Substituting for μ in (5) gives $\lambda = 1/A$ and $\gamma = 0$, so the global minimum-variance portfolio is

$$\mathbf{w}_g = \frac{\boldsymbol{\Sigma}^{-1}\mathbf{1}}{A} = \frac{\boldsymbol{\Sigma}^{-1}\mathbf{1}}{\mathbf{1}'\boldsymbol{\Sigma}^{-1}\mathbf{1}}. \tag{8}$$

This can also be determined by setting γ, the Lagrange multiplier associated with the mean constraint, to zero in (4). With $\gamma = 0$ the constraint is not binding, and the global minimum-variance portfolio is found.

The slopes of the asymptotes can be computed from $d\mu/d\sigma$ as μ approaches $\pm\infty$.

$$\begin{gathered}\frac{d\mu}{d\sigma} = \frac{d\mu}{d\sigma^2}\frac{d\sigma^2}{d\sigma} = \frac{\Delta}{2A\mu - 2B}2\sigma = \frac{\sqrt{\Delta}}{A\mu - B}\sqrt{A\mu^2 - 2B\mu + C}, \\ \lim_{\mu\to\pm\infty}\frac{d\mu}{d\sigma} = \pm\sqrt{\frac{\Delta}{A}}.\end{gathered} \tag{9}$$

The second and third equalities follow from (7) and (6), respectively.

From (4) we can see that all minimum-variance portfolios are portfolio combinations of only two distinct portfolios. Since the global minimum-variance portfolio corresponds to the first term in (4), we choose, for simplicity, the portfolio corresponding to the second term as the second diversified portfolio. Assuming $B \neq 0$, we define $\mathbf{w}_d \equiv \boldsymbol{\Sigma}^{-1}\bar{\mathbf{z}}/B = \boldsymbol{\Sigma}^{-1}\bar{\mathbf{z}}/\mathbf{1}'\boldsymbol{\Sigma}^{-1}\bar{\mathbf{z}}$, and we can write (4) as

$$\mathbf{w}^* = (\lambda A)\mathbf{w}_g + (\gamma B)\mathbf{w}_d. \tag{10}$$

Since $\lambda A + \gamma B = 1$ [see (5)], we have verified this proposition.

As indicated, portfolio g is the global minimum-variance portfolio at the apex of the hyperbola in Figure 4.3. We can locate the other as follows. The difference in expected returns is

$$\bar{Z}_d - \bar{Z}_g = \frac{C}{B} - \frac{B}{A} = \frac{\Delta}{AB}. \tag{11}$$

As noted previously, $\Delta > 0$. A is also positive since it is a quadratic form. In principal, B can have either sign; however, if the expected return on the global minimum-variance portfolio is positive, then $B > 0$. We take this as the typical case, so $\mathbf{w}_d$ will be on the upper limb of the hyperbola. (*Note*: Even limited liability of the assets is no guarantee of a positive B because the global minimum-variance portfolio may be short in some assets.)

The result we have derived is an example of a separation or mutual fund theorem because all investors who choose portfolios by examining only mean and variance can be satisfied by holding different combinations of only a few, in this case two, mutual funds regardless of their preferences. All of the original assets, therefore, can be purchased by just two mutual funds, and the investors can then just buy these. Separation theorems are very important in finance. We shall see many further examples.

Any two distinct minimum-variance portfolios will serve in place of $\mathbf{w}_g$ and $\mathbf{w}_d$. For example, if $\mathbf{w}_a$ and $\mathbf{w}_b$ are two minimum-variance portfolios, then, from (10), $\mathbf{w}_a = (1 - a)\mathbf{w}_g + a\mathbf{w}_d$ and similarly for portfolio b. Thus

$$\mathbf{w}^* = \frac{\lambda A + b - 1}{b - a}\mathbf{w}_a + \frac{1 - a - \lambda A}{b - a}\mathbf{w}_b. \tag{12}$$

These coefficients also sum to unity so the proposition is proved.

The portfolio weight of any asset is linear in μ along the minimum-variance frontier. Substituting (5) into (10) gives

$$w_i^*(\mu) = w_{ig} + \frac{(A\mu - B)B(w_{id} - w_{ig})}{\Delta}. \tag{13}$$

In the typical case, $B > 0$, assets represented more (less) heavily in $\mathbf{w}_d$ than $\mathbf{w}_g$ will be held in greater amounts in the minimum-variance portfolios with high (low) expected returns. For each asset there is one minimum-variance portfolio in which it has a weight of zero. In all portfolios below (above) this one the asset is sold short.

COVARIANCE PROPERTIES OF THE MINIMUM-VARIANCE PORTFOLIOS

As we shall see, the covariance properties of the portfolios in the minimum-variance set are of particular importance. We will examine some of them.

The global minimum-variance portfolio possesses the peculiar property that its covariance with any asset or portfolio is always $1/A$.

$$\text{Cov}(\tilde{Z}_g, \tilde{Z}_p) = \mathbf{w}_g'\mathbf{\Sigma}\mathbf{w}_p = \frac{\mathbf{1}'\mathbf{\Sigma}^{-1}\mathbf{\Sigma}\mathbf{w}_p}{A} = \frac{1}{A}. \tag{14}$$

For every other minimum-variance portfolio the range of possible covariances is $(-\infty, \infty)$.

Let $\mathbf{w}_a \equiv (1 - a)\mathbf{w}_g + a\mathbf{w}_d$ denote a minimum-variance portfolio. For two such portfolios

$$\begin{aligned}\text{Cov}(\tilde{Z}_a, \tilde{Z}_b) &= (1 - a)(1 - b)\sigma_g^2 + ab\sigma_d^2 + [a(1 - b) + b(1 - a)]\sigma_{dg} \\ &= \frac{(1 - a)(1 - b)}{A} + \frac{ab\,C}{B^2} + \frac{a + b - 2ab}{A} \\ &= \frac{1}{A} + \frac{ab\Delta}{AB^2}.\end{aligned} \tag{15}$$

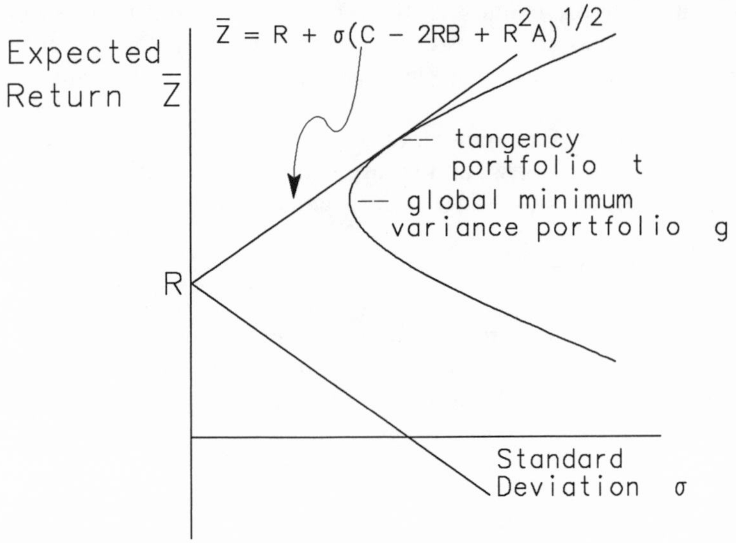

Figure 4.4 Minimum-Variance Set

For a fixed portfolio a on the upper limb of the hyperbola, $a > 0$, this covariance increases from $-\infty$ to ∞ as b is increased; that is, portfolio b is moved up the hyperbola in the standard case. The portfolio uncorrelated with a is on the lower limb. For a fixed portfolio a on the lower limb, the opposite is true. This will be proved later.

Again for a fixed portfolio a on the upper limb, the correlation coefficient increases from $-a/(B^2/\Delta + a^2)^{1/2}$ to 1 as b increases from $-\infty$ to a. It then falls off to $a/(B^2/\Delta + a^2)^{1/2}$ as b goes to ∞.

THE MEAN-VARIANCE PROBLEM WITH A RISKLESS ASSET

When a riskless asset is available, the portfolio problem is changed in two ways. First, there is no budget constraint on the risky assets corresponding to (2b). A position in the riskless asset makes up the residual, or, if negative, finances the risky asset purchases. Second, the constraint on the mean return must be expressed in excess return form

$$(\bar{\mathbf{z}} - R\mathbf{1})'\mathbf{w} = \mu - R. \tag{2c$'$}$$

The resulting maximization yields a solution

$$\mathbf{w}^* = \gamma\mathbf{\Sigma}^{-1}(\bar{\mathbf{z}} - R\mathbf{1}), \qquad w_0^* = 1 - \mathbf{1}'\mathbf{w}^*. \tag{16}$$

γ can be obtained from (2c′) and (16) as the solution to

$$\mu - R = \gamma(\bar{\mathbf{z}} - R\mathbf{1})'\mathbf{\Sigma}^{-1}(\bar{\mathbf{z}} - R\mathbf{1}) = \gamma[C - 2RB + R^2A]. \tag{17}$$

The equation of the minimum-variance set is, from (16), (2c′), and (17),

$$\sigma^2 = (\mu - R)^2[C - 2RB + R^2A]^{-1}. \tag{18}$$

Again, this is a parabola; however, this time in mean-standard deviation space the locus is a pair of rays with common intercepts at R and slopes of $\pm(C - 2RB + R^2A)^{1/2}$. This is illustrated in Figure 4.4.

As before, all minimum-variance portfolios are combinations of only two distinct portfolios. Again, any two minimum-variance portfolios will span the set. In this case, however, there is a natural choice of funds—namely, the riskless asset and that portfolio with none of the riskless asset, the "tangency" portfolio

$$w_{0t} = 0, \qquad \mathbf{w}_t = \frac{\mathbf{\Sigma}^{-1}(\bar{\mathbf{z}} - R\mathbf{1})}{B - AR}. \tag{19}$$

The mean and variance of this portfolio are

$$\begin{aligned} \bar{Z}_t &= \bar{\mathbf{z}}'\mathbf{w}_t = \frac{C - BR}{B - AR}, \\ \sigma_t^2 &= \mathbf{w}_t'\mathbf{\Sigma}\mathbf{w}_t = \frac{C - 2RB + R^2A}{(B - AR)^2}. \end{aligned} \tag{20}$$

Portfolio t is a member of the original risky-asset-only minimum-variance set. This can be easily verified by showing that $\bar{Z}_t$ and σ_t^2 satisfy Equation (6); however, it is also obvious from the geometry in Figure 4.4. Portfolio t is at the tangency point of the hyperbola and a line passing through R. This can be proved by calculating the slope of the hyperbola at this point, but again Figure 4.4 should be sufficient. The case illustrated shows this tangency portfolio on the upper limb of the hyperbola; however, a lower tangency is possible instead. The upper (lower) tangency occurs if the riskless return is less (greater) than the expected return on the (risky-asset-only) global minimum-variance portfolio. That is, either $\bar{Z}_t > B/A > R$ or the reverse ordering is correct. To prove this proposition, we compute

$$\begin{aligned} \left(\bar{Z}_t - \frac{B}{A}\right)\left(\frac{B}{A} - R\right) &= \left[\frac{C - BR}{B - AR} - \frac{B}{A}\right]\frac{B - AR}{A} \\ &= \frac{C - BR}{A} - \frac{B^2}{A^2} + \frac{BR}{A} = \frac{CA - B^2}{A} = \frac{\Delta}{A} > 0. \end{aligned} \tag{21}$$

Therefore, both differences must be of the same sign. (*Note*: In the singular case $B/A = R$ there is no finite point of tangency, and the minimum-variance locus coincides with the asymptotes of the risky-asset-only hyperbola.)

EXPECTED RETURNS RELATIONS

The expected excess return on any asset is proportional to its covariance with the return on Z_t. Let $\boldsymbol{\sigma}_t$ denote the vector of these covariances. Then since the covariance of a random variable with a weighted sum of random variables is the weighted sum of the individual covariances, we have, from (19),

$$\boldsymbol{\sigma}_t = \boldsymbol{\Sigma}\mathbf{w}_t = \frac{\bar{\mathbf{z}} - R\mathbf{1}}{B - AR}. \tag{22}$$

Premultiplying (22) by $\mathbf{w}_t$ gives

$$\sigma_t^2 = \mathbf{w}_t'\boldsymbol{\sigma}_t = \frac{\bar{Z}_t - R}{B - AR}. \tag{23}$$

Combining (22) and (23) gives

$$\bar{\mathbf{z}} - R\mathbf{1} = \boldsymbol{\sigma}_t\frac{\bar{Z}_t - R}{\sigma_t^2} \equiv \boldsymbol{\beta}_t(\bar{Z}_t - R). \tag{24}$$

Because all other portfolios in the minimum variance set are perfectly correlated with the tangency portfolio, exactly the same result holds for them.

All expected returns can also be written in terms of portfolio $\mathbf{w}_d$. If $\boldsymbol{\sigma}_d$ is the vector of covariances with this portfolio, then, from the definition of $\mathbf{w}_d$,

$$\boldsymbol{\sigma}_d = \boldsymbol{\Sigma}\mathbf{w}_d = \frac{\bar{\mathbf{z}}}{B}, \qquad \bar{\mathbf{z}} = \left(\frac{\boldsymbol{\sigma}_d}{\sigma_d^2}\right)\bar{Z}_d \equiv \boldsymbol{\beta}_d\bar{Z}_d. \tag{25}$$

This relation holds only for portfolio d and not for any of the other hyperbola portfolios. For other hyperbola portfolios we can express returns by using a second portfolio. Let $\mathbf{w}_a \equiv (1 - a)\mathbf{w}_g + a\mathbf{w}_d$ ($a \neq 0$, $a \neq 1$) be a risky-asset-only minimum-variance portfolio. Then

$$\boldsymbol{\sigma}_a \equiv \boldsymbol{\Sigma}\mathbf{w}_a = \left(\frac{1 - a}{A}\right)\mathbf{1} + \left(\frac{a}{B}\right)\bar{\mathbf{z}}. \tag{26}$$

Now let $\mathbf{w}_p$ be *any* other risky-asset-only portfolio. Then we can derive from (26) the system of equations

$$\sigma_a^2 = \frac{1 - a}{A} + \frac{\bar{Z}_a a}{B}, \qquad \sigma_{pa} = \frac{1 - a}{A} + \frac{\bar{Z}_p a}{B}, \tag{27}$$

which can be solved for $(1 - a)/A$ and a/B. Substituting these into (26) and rearranging terms give

$$\bar{\mathbf{z}} = \frac{\bar{Z}_p\sigma_a^2 - \bar{Z}_a\sigma_{ap}}{\sigma_a^2 - \sigma_{ap}}\mathbf{1} + \frac{\bar{Z}_a - \bar{Z}_p}{\sigma_a^2 - \sigma_{ap}}\boldsymbol{\sigma}_a. \tag{28}$$

If we choose as portfolio p a portfolio Z_z which has a zero beta with (is uncorrelated with) portfolio a, then (28) simplifies to

$$\bar{\mathbf{z}} = \bar{Z}_z\mathbf{1} + (\bar{Z}_a - \bar{Z}_z)\boldsymbol{\beta}_a. \tag{29}$$

Although (29) is generally true, it is particularly useful when no riskless asset is available. Comparing (29) to (24), we can see that all of the portfolios that are uncorrelated with a particular minimum-variance portfolio have an expected return equal to the intercept on the $\bar{Z}$ axis of a line drawn tangent to the (risky-asset-only) efficient hyperbola at the particular minimum-variance portfolio. From Figure 4.4 or (21), the zero beta portfolio of a minimum-variance portfolio on the upper (lower) limb of the hyperbola must be on the lower (upper) limb.

This linearity property of expected returns and beta holds only if the bench-mark portfolio is in the minimum-variance set. To prove this converse proposition, assume that

$$\bar{\mathbf{z}} = \alpha\mathbf{1} + \gamma\boldsymbol{\sigma}_p = \alpha\mathbf{1} + \gamma\boldsymbol{\Sigma}\mathbf{w}_p \tag{30}$$

for some portfolio p. Then

$$\mathbf{w}_p = \frac{1}{\gamma}\boldsymbol{\Sigma}^{-1}\bar{\mathbf{z}} - \frac{\alpha}{\gamma}\boldsymbol{\Sigma}^{-1}\mathbf{1} = \delta\mathbf{w}_d + \eta\mathbf{w}_g. \tag{31}$$

Furthermore, since $\mathbf{1}'\mathbf{w}_p = 1$, $\delta + \eta = 1$, so portfolio p is a portfolio combination of portfolios g and d and must lie in the minimum-variance set.

The relation between the expected return on any portfolio and its variance can now be expressed as follows. For any portfolio $\mathbf{w}_p$ let $\mathbf{w}_m$ be the minimum-variance portfolio with the same expected return. Then $\mathbf{w}_p$ is

$$\begin{aligned}\mathbf{w}_p &= \mathbf{w}_g + (\mathbf{w}_m - \mathbf{w}_g) + (\mathbf{w}_p - \mathbf{w}_m) \\ &= \mathbf{w}_g + \boldsymbol{\omega}_s + \boldsymbol{\omega}_d,\end{aligned} \tag{32}$$

where $\boldsymbol{\omega}_s$ and $\boldsymbol{\omega}_d$ are the arbitrage portfolios defined as $\boldsymbol{\omega}_s \equiv \mathbf{w}_m - \mathbf{w}_g$ and $\boldsymbol{\omega}_d \equiv \mathbf{w}_p - \mathbf{w}_m$. Note that the covariances between these parts are all zero:

$$\sigma_{gs} \equiv \mathbf{w}_g'\boldsymbol{\Sigma}\boldsymbol{\omega}_s = \mathbf{w}_g'\boldsymbol{\Sigma}(\mathbf{w}_m - \mathbf{w}_g) = 0, \tag{33a}$$

$$\sigma_{gd} \equiv \mathbf{w}_g'\boldsymbol{\Sigma}\boldsymbol{\omega}_d = \mathbf{w}_g'\boldsymbol{\Sigma}(\mathbf{w}_p - \mathbf{w}_m) = 0, \tag{33b}$$

$$\sigma_{sd} \equiv \boldsymbol{\omega}_s'\boldsymbol{\Sigma}\boldsymbol{\omega}_d = \mathbf{w}_m'\boldsymbol{\Sigma}(\mathbf{w}_p - \mathbf{w}_m) - \mathbf{w}_g\boldsymbol{\Sigma}(\mathbf{w}_p - \mathbf{w}_m) = 0. \tag{33c}$$

Equations (33a) and (33b) are zero since they are each the difference of the covariances of two portfolios with the global minimum-variance portfolio, and by (14) the covariance of every portfolio with $\mathbf{w}_g$ is equal to $1/A$. Equation (33c) is also zero. The second term is zero by (33b). The first term is zero by (29). It is the difference of the covariance of portfolios $\mathbf{w}_p$ and $\mathbf{w}_m$ with portfolio $\mathbf{w}_m$. Since $\mathbf{w}_p$ and $\mathbf{w}_m$ have the same expected returns, their covariances with $\mathbf{w}_m$, a minimum-variance portfolio, must be the same.

Thus, the variance of portfolio $\mathbf{w}_p$ can be separated into three parts:

$$\sigma_p^2 = \sigma_g^2 + \sigma_s^2 + \sigma_d^2. \tag{34}$$

σ_g^2 measures unavoidable risk, σ_s^2 measures the systematic risk associated with a level of expected return of $\bar{Z}_p$, and σ_d^2 measures diversifiable risk. Only the first two portions of the variance contribute to expected return.

EQUILIBRIUM: THE CAPITAL ASSET PRICING MODEL

The pricing results just given cannot be used to explain the expected returns observed in the market in equilibrium. The minimum-variance portfolios (with the exception of the global minimum-variance portfolio) cannot be identified until the vector of expected returns is known. Furthermore, even if investors do not choose portfolios through mean-variance analysis (so that there need be no optimal properties of the minimum-variance portfolios), the minimum-variance portfolios exist provided only that there are no riskless arbitrage opportunities (and means and variances are defined), and the pricing results of the previous section obtain. Thus, these results have no equilibrium content until some minimum-variance portfolio can be identified by another route. This identification is precisely what the capital asset pricing model accomplishes.

To derive the CAPM we make the following assumptions: (i) Each investor chooses a portfolio with the objective of maximizing a derived utility function of the form $V(\bar{Z}, \sigma^2)$ with $V_2 < 0$, $V_1 > 0$, and V concave. (ii) All investors have a common time horizon and homogenous beliefs about $\bar{\mathbf{z}}$ and $\mathbf{\Sigma}$. (iii) Each asset is infinitely divisible (iv) The riskless asset can be bought or *sold* in unlimited amounts.

These conditions are sufficient to show that each investor holds a minimum-variance portfolio. Intuitively, no other portfolio could be optimal, because the minimum-variance portfolio with the same expected return would be preferred since $V_2 < 0$. Furthermore, since all minimum-variance portfolios are combinations of any two minimum-variance portfolios, a separation or mutual fund theorem obtains, as previously explained.

Formally, the problem is

$$\text{Max } V(R + \mathbf{w}'(\bar{\mathbf{z}} - R\mathbf{1}), \mathbf{w}'\boldsymbol{\Sigma}\mathbf{w}), \tag{35}$$

where we have substituted for w_0 using the budget constraint. Solving (35) gives

$$\begin{aligned} 0 &= \frac{\partial V}{\partial \mathbf{w}} = V_1(\cdot)(\bar{\mathbf{z}} - R\mathbf{1}) + 2V_2(\cdot)\boldsymbol{\Sigma}\mathbf{w}, \\ \mathbf{w}^* &= \frac{-V_1(\cdot)}{2V_2(\cdot)}\boldsymbol{\Sigma}^{-1}(\bar{\mathbf{z}} - R\mathbf{1}). \end{aligned} \tag{36}$$

The second-order condition is met since

$$\begin{aligned} \frac{\partial^2 V}{\partial \mathbf{w}\, \partial \mathbf{w}'} &= 2V_2\boldsymbol{\Sigma} + V_{11}(\bar{\mathbf{z}} - R\mathbf{1})(\bar{\mathbf{z}} - R\mathbf{1})' \\ &\quad + 2V_{12}[\boldsymbol{\Sigma}\mathbf{w}(\bar{\mathbf{z}} - R\mathbf{1})' + (\bar{\mathbf{z}} - R\mathbf{1})\mathbf{w}'\boldsymbol{\Sigma}] + 4V_{22}\boldsymbol{\Sigma}\mathbf{w}\mathbf{w}'\boldsymbol{\Sigma} \end{aligned} \tag{37}$$

is negative definite. ($V_2(\cdot) < 0$, and $\boldsymbol{\Sigma}$ is positive definite. $V_{11} < 0$, $V_{22} < 0$, and $V_{11} + 4V_{12} + 4V_{22} < 0$ by concavity, and the other matrices are positive semidefinite with that multiplying V_{12} positively dominated.)

Comparing (36) to (19), we see that the optimal investment in the risky assets is proportional to the tangency portfolio. The remainder of wealth is invested in the riskless asset. Since all investors hold combinations of the tangency portfolio and the riskless asset, the aggregate demand for each risky asset must be in proportion to its representation in the tangency portfolio. In equilibrium, demand and supply are equal; therefore, the supply of each risky asset in the market portfolio must also be in proportion to the tangency portfolio: $\mathbf{w}_M \propto \mathbf{w}_t$. If the riskless asset is a financial security in zero net supply, then $\mathbf{w}_t$ is the market portfolio $\mathbf{w}_M$. In other cases the market portfolio will be somewhere to the left on the tangency line. Using (24) we can therefore write the Sharpe–Lintner CAPM pricing equation:

$$\bar{\mathbf{z}} - R\mathbf{1} = \boldsymbol{\beta}_M(\bar{Z}_M - R). \tag{38}$$

In the absence of a riskless asset, or if there are limits on its sale or purchase, a similar result can still be derived provided that (iv′) there are no restrictions on the sale of risky assets. (The assumption that $V_1 > 0$ is not required.) The same intuition is valid. The formal problem is

$$\text{Max } V(\mathbf{w}'\bar{\mathbf{z}}, \mathbf{w}'\boldsymbol{\Sigma}\mathbf{w}) + \lambda(1 - \mathbf{1}'\mathbf{w}). \tag{39}$$

The solution to (39) satisfies

$$\begin{aligned} 0 &= \frac{\partial V}{\partial \mathbf{w}} = V_1(\cdot)\bar{\mathbf{z}} + 2V_2(\cdot)\boldsymbol{\Sigma}\mathbf{w} - \lambda\mathbf{1}, \\ 0 &= 1 - \mathbf{1}'\mathbf{w}. \end{aligned} \tag{40}$$

The optimal portfolio is

$$\mathbf{w} = \frac{-V_1(\cdot)}{2V_2(\cdot)}\boldsymbol{\Sigma}^{-1}\bar{\mathbf{z}} + \frac{\lambda}{2V_2(\cdot)}\boldsymbol{\Sigma}^{-1}\mathbf{1}$$
$$= -\frac{BV_1}{2V_2}\mathbf{w}_d + \left(1 + \frac{BV_1}{2V_2}\right)\mathbf{w}_g \tag{41}$$

when λ is substituted out by using the budget constraint. Optimal portfolios are combinations of $\mathbf{w}_d$ and $\mathbf{w}_g$. Thus, aggregate demand is a combination of $\mathbf{w}_d$ and $\mathbf{w}_g$. In equilibrium, supply equals demand; therefore, the market portfolio must be a minimum-variance portfolio, and (29) describes expected returns:

$$\bar{\mathbf{z}} = \bar{Z}_z\mathbf{1} + (\bar{Z}_M - \bar{Z}_z)\boldsymbol{\beta}_M, \tag{42}$$

where z denotes a zero beta portfolio uncorrelated with the market. This is the Black CAPM or the "two-factor" model.

In the standard case when the expected return on the global minimum-variance portfolio is positive ($B > 0$), the expected return (and variance) on portfolio d exceeds that on portfolio g. Investors who are more "risk averse" ($-V_1/V_2$ is smaller) hold less of portfolio d, as expected.

The primary difference in the assumptions leading to these results is that short sales need not be permitted for the risky assets when unlimited riskless borrowing and lending is available, provided that $V_1 > 0$. In this case all investors will want to hold portfolios on the upper portion of the frontier. If an upper (lower) tangency exists, all investors will have a positive (negative) demand for the tangency portfolio. Since this is the market portfolio in equilibrium, the net demand for it must be positive. The first conclusion therefore is that an upper tangency must exist and $\bar{Z}_M > R$. Second, since each investor's demand for the market portfolio is positive and it is long in each asset, every investor's desired holding of every risky asset is positive and a no-short-sales constraint would not be binding. Without a riskless asset some short sales must be allowed in order to fashion every portfolio on the upper limb of the minimum variance hyperbola. Since the portfolios on the lower limb can then also be formed, restricting our attention to utilities with $V_1 > 0$ is not necessary. We demonstrate in Appendix B that $V_1 < 0$ is not consistent with expected utility maximization when a riskless asset is available, but it can be in the absence of one.

When there are restrictions on the riskless asset, such as only lending permitted or there is a higher borrowing than lending rate, but no restrictions on the other assets, then the zero beta version of the CAPM is still valid. These two cases are illustrated in Figure 4.5. The most risk-averse investors will hold tangency portfolio L combined with lending. Less risk-averse investors will hold long positions in both L and B. The

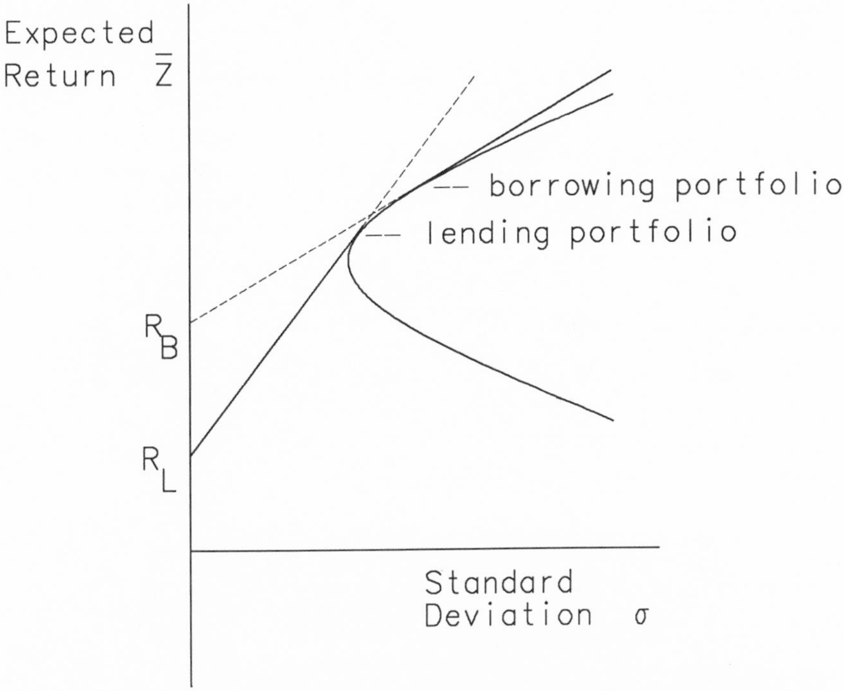

Figure 4.5 M-V Problem with Restricted Borrowing and Lending

least risk-averse investors will be overly long in *B* financed by borrowing or a short position in *L* if borrowing is not allowed. In any case each investor's demand for the risky assets will be some combination of portfolios *L* and *B*. Since these are both minimum-variance portfolios, aggregate demand will be minimum variance as well. In equilibrium, therefore, the market portfolio will be in the minimum-variance class.

To summarize, it is the mean-variance analysis that generates the separation theorem and the pricing result that relates expected returns to covariances with minimum-variance portfolios. The equilibrium analysis simply leads to the identification of the market portfolio as being minimum variance.

CONSISTENCY OF MEAN-VARIANCE ANALYSIS AND EXPECTED UTILITY MAXIMIZATION

Thus far we have simply assumed that investors' optimal policies consist of selecting among mean-variance efficient portfolios. In this section we explore the conditions under which this behavior maximizes expected utility.

The first case examined is quadratic utility. Suppose that an investor has a quadratic utility function defined over end-of-period wealth. We can choose the units of wealth so that the investor's initial endowment is unity, so the argument of the utility function is return. Also since utility is defined only up to an increasing linear transformation, we may write

$$u(Z) = Z - \frac{bZ^2}{2} \tag{43}$$

with complete generality.

For the utility function in (43), expected utility is

$$V(\bar{Z}, \sigma^2) \equiv Eu(\tilde{Z}) = \bar{Z} - \frac{b}{2}(\bar{Z}^2 + \sigma^2). \tag{44}$$

Thus, for quadratic utility of wealth functions, expected utility depends solely on the mean and variance of return. Furthermore, for risk-averse utility functions ($b > 0$), $V_2 < 0$, so only minimum-variance portfolios are held. If outcomes are confined to the range of increasing utility ($Z < 1/b$), then $V_1 > 0$, and only mean-variance efficient portfolios can be optimal.

From (44) we can see that the indifference curves in mean-standard deviation space are semicircles centered at $\bar{Z} = 1/b$, $\sigma = 0$. For the relevant portion ($\bar{Z} < 1/b$), they are convex so a tangency with the minimum-variance frontier exists.

Assuming quadratic utility has two drawbacks. First, all concave quadratic functions are decreasing after a certain point, so some care must be employed to assure that the outcomes remain in the lower, relevant range of utility. Second, quadratic utility functions display increasing absolute risk aversion

$$\begin{aligned} A(Z) &\equiv -\frac{u''(Z)}{u'(Z)} = \frac{b}{1 - bZ}, \\ A'(Z) &= \left(\frac{b}{1 - bZ}\right)^2 > 0. \end{aligned} \tag{45}$$

The more commonly adopted justification for mean-variance analysis is multivariate normally distributed returns. Since all weighted sums of multivariate normal random variables are normally distributed, and since a normal distribution is completely characterized by its mean and variance, all portfolios formed from such assets are completely described by their means and variances.

We can also demonstrate that only mean-variance efficient portfolios are optimal. Let $f(Z; \bar{Z}, \sigma^2)$ denote the normal denstiy function for the return on a portfolio. Then

$$V(\bar{Z}, \sigma^2) \equiv \int_{-\infty}^{\infty} u(Z)f(Z; \bar{Z}, \sigma^2)\,dZ$$
$$= \int_{-\infty}^{\infty} u(\bar{Z} + \sigma\varepsilon)n(\varepsilon)\,d\varepsilon, \tag{46}$$

where $\varepsilon \equiv (Z - \bar{Z})/\sigma$ is a standard normal deviate and $n(\cdot)$ is its density function. The partial derivative with respect to mean return is

$$V_1 = \int_{-\infty}^{\infty} u'(\bar{Z} + \sigma\varepsilon)n(\varepsilon)\,d\varepsilon > 0 \tag{47}$$

since $u'(\cdot)$ is uniformly positive. The partial derivative with respect to variance is

$$V_2 = \frac{1}{2\sigma}\frac{\partial V}{\partial \sigma} = \frac{1}{2\sigma}\int_{-\infty}^{\infty} u'(\bar{Z} + \sigma\varepsilon)\varepsilon n(\varepsilon)\,d\varepsilon. \tag{48}$$

The negativity of V_2 can now be deduced from the symmetry of $n(\cdot)$ and the positivity of u'. Alternatively, integrating by parts by using the property $\int \varepsilon n(\varepsilon)\,d\varepsilon = -n(\varepsilon)$ gives

$$V_2 = \frac{1}{2\sigma}\int_{-\infty}^{\infty} u''(\bar{Z} + \sigma\varepsilon)\sigma n(\varepsilon)\,d\varepsilon < 0 \tag{49}$$

since $u''(\cdot)$ is uniformly negative.

The indifference curves in mean-standard deviation space are again convex since

$$\frac{\partial^2 V}{\partial \bar{Z}^2} = \int u''(\cdot)n(\varepsilon)\,d\varepsilon < 0, \tag{50a}$$

$$\frac{\partial^2 V}{\partial \sigma^2} = \int u''(\cdot)\varepsilon^2 n(\varepsilon)\,d\varepsilon < 0, \tag{50b}$$

$$\frac{\partial^2 V}{\partial \bar{Z}^2}\frac{\partial^2 V}{\partial \sigma^2} - \left(\frac{\partial^2 V}{\partial \bar{Z}\,\partial \sigma}\right)^2 = \int u''(\cdot)n(\varepsilon)\,d\varepsilon \int \varepsilon^2 u''(\cdot)n(\varepsilon)\,d\varepsilon$$
$$-\left[\int \varepsilon u''(\cdot)n(\varepsilon)\,d\varepsilon\right]^2 \tag{50c}$$
$$= (-1)^2\left[\int g(\varepsilon)\,d\varepsilon \int \varepsilon^2 g(\varepsilon)\,d\varepsilon - \left(\int \varepsilon g(\varepsilon)\,d\varepsilon\right)^2\right].$$

The first two inequalities follow from the negativity of u''. The last expression is positive by the Cauchy–Schwarz inequality since $g(\varepsilon) = -u''(\cdot)n(\varepsilon)$ is a positive measure.

SOLVING A SPECIFIC PROBLEM

Consider an investor with utility function $U(W) = -e^{-a'W}$ facing an investment environment with a riskless asset and n risky assets distributed multivariate normally $N(\bar{\mathbf{z}}, \boldsymbol{\Sigma})$. Without loss of generality we can assume $u(Z) = -e^{-aZ}$, where $a = a'W_0$. Substituting for the budget constraint, we see that the investor's problem is

$$\text{Max } E\{-e^{-a[\mathbf{w}'(\tilde{\mathbf{z}} - R\mathbf{1}) + R]}\}. \tag{51}$$

Since $\mathbf{w}'\tilde{\mathbf{z}}$ is normally distributed with mean $\mathbf{w}'\bar{\mathbf{z}}$ and variance $\mathbf{w}'\boldsymbol{\Sigma}\mathbf{w}$, we can write the expectation in (51) as $-\phi(ia)$, where ϕ is the characteristic function of a normal distribution with mean and variance equal to that of the portfolio. Thus, the problem can be restated as

$$\text{Max}\left\{-\exp\left(-a[\mathbf{w}'(\bar{\mathbf{z}} - R\mathbf{1}) + R] + \frac{a^2\mathbf{w}'\boldsymbol{\Sigma}\mathbf{w}}{2}\right)\right\}. \tag{52}$$

The utility fucntion to be maximized in (52) is an ordinal function of mean and variance. Since it is ordinal, we can operate on it with the increasing function $\theta(x) = -(1/a)[\log(-x) - R]$ to give the problem

$$\text{Max}\,\mathbf{w}'(\bar{\mathbf{z}} - R\mathbf{1}) - \frac{a\mathbf{w}'\boldsymbol{\Sigma}\mathbf{w}}{2}. \tag{52'}$$

The solution to (52′) satisfies

$$\begin{aligned} \mathbf{0} = \bar{\mathbf{z}} - R\mathbf{1} - a\boldsymbol{\Sigma}\mathbf{w} \quad &\text{or} \quad \mathbf{w}^* = a^{-1}\boldsymbol{\Sigma}^{-1}(\bar{\mathbf{z}} - R\mathbf{1}). \\ w_0^* = 1 - \mathbf{1}'\mathbf{w}^* = 1 - a^{-1}(B - AR).& \end{aligned} \tag{53}$$

Comparing this to (19), we see that the risky assets are held in the same proportions as in the tangency portfolio in (19). The more risk averse is the investor (the higher is a), the fewer risky assets will be held.

THE STATE PRICES UNDER MEAN-VARIANCE ANALYSIS

Starting with the expected returns relation (38), we can compute state prices consistent with the CAPM as follows:

$$\begin{aligned} \bar{z}_i = R + \text{Cov}(\tilde{z}_i, \tilde{Z}_M)\frac{\bar{Z}_M - R}{\sigma_M^2} &\equiv R + \lambda\text{Cov}(\tilde{z}_i, \tilde{Z}_M), \\ \int \pi(s)z_i(s)\,ds = R + \lambda\int \pi(s)z_i(s)[Z_M(s) - \bar{Z}_M]\,ds&, \\ 1 = R^{-1}\int \pi(s)[1 - \lambda(Z_M(s) - \bar{Z}_M)]z_i(s)\,ds&, \end{aligned} \tag{54}$$

$$p(s) = R^{-1}\pi(s)[1 - \lambda(Z_M(s) - \bar{Z}_M)].$$

Although this pricing "vector" is clearly a set of supporting prices, it need not be the positive state pricing vector we seek. In particular, if the market portfolio is normally distributed, then $\tilde{Z}_M$ can be arbitrarily larger than its mean. For those states in which $\lambda(Z_M(s) - \bar{Z}_M) > 1$, the state pricing function given in (54) will be negative.

Since the CAPM equation above is an equilibrium relation, there must be an alternative way to describe state prices in which they are all positive, for a market in equilibrium cannot contain any arbitrage opportunities.

If the CAPM equilibrium arises because all investors have quadratic utility, then potential arbitrage opportunities are not a concern. Investors with quadratic utility will not take unlimited arbitrage positions, for this would increase their wealth past the point where marginal utility becomes negative, and the guaranteed profit of an arbitrage would only hurt.

With multivariate normal returns supporting the CAPM, however, there can be no arbitrage opportunities. This is ture for the equilibrium reason stated earlier. In addition, there can be no possible arbitrage opportunities among assets with normally distributed returns simply because no portfolio that has a completely nonnegative return can be constructed from the risky assets.

Valid positive state prices for the case of normally distributed asset returns can be constructed as follows. Consider the problem stated in Equation (51) of the previous section. The first-order conditions for this (unmodified) problem are

$$E[e^{-a\tilde{Z}^*}(\tilde{z}_i - R)] = 0. \tag{55}$$

From (53) an investor with risk aversion $a \equiv a_M \equiv B - AR > 0$ will hold just the tangency (market) portfolio. For this investor the first-order condition can be written as

$$\int \pi(s)\exp[-a_M Z_M(s)]z_i(s)ds = R\int \pi(s)\exp[-a_M Z_M(s)]\,ds \equiv K^{-1}. \tag{56}$$

Thus

$$p(s) = K\pi(s)\exp[-a_M Z_M(s)] > 0. \tag{57}$$

PORTFOLIO ANALYSIS USING HIGHER MOMENTS

Apart from tractability and tradition there are no reasons not to consider third and higher central moments in portfolio problems. Indeed, a close examination of these problems can provide understanding even for the mean-variance problem, which is sometimes otherwise missed through too much familiarity. We outline the equilibrium by using mean-variance-skewness analysis. (*Note*: Skewness usually means the third central moment divided by the cube of the standard deviation; here skewness is the unnormalized third central moment.)

To compute the skewness of a portfolio, $m^3 \equiv E[(\tilde{Z} - \bar{Z})^3]$, we need to know not only the assets' skewnesses but also the coskewnesses

$$m_{ijk} \equiv E[(\tilde{z}_i - \bar{z}_i)(\tilde{z}_j - \bar{z}_j)(\tilde{z}_k - \bar{z}_k)]. \tag{58}$$

Then

$$m_p^3 = \sum_1^N \sum_1^N \sum_1^N w_i w_j w_k m_{ijk}. \tag{59}$$

Now consider an investor with the derived utility function $V(\bar{Z}, \sigma^2, m^3)$ with optimal portfolio characterized by the moments $\bar{Z}_o$, σ_o^2, m_o^3. The portfolio combination of asset i and the optimal portfolio is characterized by the moments

$$\begin{aligned}
\bar{Z} &= (1 - w)\bar{Z}_o + w\bar{z}_i,\\
\sigma^2 &= (1 - w)^2\sigma_o^2 + 2w(1 - w)\sigma_{io} + w^2\sigma_i^2,\\
m^3 &= (1 - w)^3 m_o^3 + 3(1 - w)^2 w m_{ooi} + 3(1 - w)w^2 m_{oii} + w^3 m_i^3.
\end{aligned} \tag{60}$$

Since at the optimum, differential changes in the optimal portfolio leave utility unaffected,

$$\begin{aligned}
0 &= V_1 \frac{d\bar{Z}}{dw} + V_2 \frac{d\sigma^2}{dw} + V_3 \frac{dm^3}{dw}\bigg|_{w=0}\\
&= V_1(\bar{z}_i - \bar{Z}_o) + 2V_2(\sigma_{io} - \sigma_o^2) + 3V_3(m_{ioo} - m_o^3).
\end{aligned} \tag{61}$$

Rearranging (61) gives the expected return on asset i as a function of its covariance and coskewness with portfolio o and two utility measures

$$\bar{z}_i = \bar{Z}_o - \frac{2V_2}{V_1}(\sigma_{io} - \sigma_o^2) - \frac{3V_3}{V_1}(m_{ioo} - m_o^3). \tag{62}$$

Equation (62) also holds for the riskless asset if one is available, and since $\sigma_{0o} = m_{0oo} = 0$,

$$R = \bar{Z}_o + \frac{2V_2}{V_1}\sigma_o^2 + \frac{3V_3}{V_1}m_o^3. \tag{63}$$

Solving (63) for $2V_2/V_1$ and substituting into (62) yield

$$\bar{z}_i = R + \beta_i^o(\bar{Z}_o - R) + \frac{3V_3 m_o^3}{V_1}(\beta_i^o - \gamma_i^o), \tag{64}$$

$$\beta_i^o \equiv \frac{\sigma_{io}}{\sigma_o^2}, \qquad \gamma_i^o \equiv \frac{m_{ioo}}{m_o^3}.$$

Now if some investor's optimal portfolio is the market (see Chapter 5 and 6), then the first two terms in (64) duplicate the Sharpe–Lintner CAPM.

The deviations from that model can be either positive or negative; however, the contribution of the skewness term

$$\frac{\partial \bar{z}_i}{\partial m_{ioo}} = -\frac{3V_3}{V_1} \tag{65}$$

is easily signed. Assuming higher skewness is preferred, we see that a comparative static decrease in coskewness requires an increase in expected return to induce the same holding of the asset at the margin. The intuition is the same as in the mean-variance model. If both mean and skewness are desirable, then the investor can remain at the margin after the comparative static change only if m_o decreases when $\bar{Z}_o$ increases, and vice versa. Again, as in the mean-variance model, it is only the co-moment that matters. Skewness and m_{iio} are irrelevant at the margin, just as individual asset variances are. The intuition is that they provided no marginal tradeoff opportunities, since, as seen in (60), $\partial m^3/\partial w = m_{ioo} - m_o^3$ at $w = 0$. The co-moment m_{ioo}, however, contributes fully since skewness is the weighted average of this coskewnesses measure

$$m_o^3 = \sum w_i^* m_{ioo} \tag{66}$$

just as $\sigma_o^2 = \Sigma w_i^* \sigma_{io}$. A second explanation of m_{ioo}'s contribution to m_o^3 comes from its definition: $m_{ioo} \equiv E[(\tilde{z}_i - \bar{z}_i)(\tilde{Z}_o - \bar{Z}_o)^2]$. If this is positive, then $\tilde{z}_i$ tends to be above (below) its mean when the return on the remainder of $\tilde{Z}_o$ is very far from (close to) its mean. This tends to shift the density function of $\tilde{Z}_o$ to the right (left) for very high or low (intermediate) values. That is, it imparts a positive skewness.

The second utility term in the pricing relation can be eliminated by introducing a second portfolio. For example, let the subscript z denote the minimum variance portfolio uncorrelated with $\tilde{Z}_o$. Then, since (62) holds for $\bar{Z}_z$ and $\beta_z^o = 0$,

$$\bar{z}_i = R + \beta_i^o(\bar{Z}_o - R) + \frac{\gamma_i^o - \beta_i^o}{\gamma_z^o}(\bar{Z}_z - R). \tag{67}$$

Any uncorrelated portfolio could be used in place of $\tilde{Z}_z$; however, unlike in the mean-variance model each may have a different expected return. Different values of the parameter γ_z^o will correct for this.

Appendix A: The Budget Constraint

Throughout this chapter a strict budget constraint $\mathbf{1}'\mathbf{w} = 1$ was imposed, indicating that all wealth must be invested. In some cases the appropriate budget constraint should actually be $\mathbf{1}'\mathbf{w} \leqslant 1$; that is, no more than the investor's entire wealth can be invested. It might appear that the more stringent requirement is perfectly general since it would seem foolish ever to throw away wealth. Actually, in the standard mean-variance problem this can be done as a part of an optimal portfolio.

Consider the problem posed earlier with multivariate normally distributed asset returns and an investor with exponential utility but without a riskless asset. As in (52) the strictly constrained problem can be stated now as a Lagrangian:

$$L(\mathbf{w}, \lambda) \equiv \mathbf{w}'\bar{\mathbf{z}} - \frac{a\mathbf{w}'\mathbf{\Sigma}w}{2} - \lambda(\mathbf{1}'\mathbf{w} - 1). \tag{A1}$$

The first-order conditions are

$$\bar{\mathbf{z}} - a\mathbf{\Sigma}\mathbf{w} - \lambda\mathbf{1} = \mathbf{0}, \tag{A2a}$$

$$\mathbf{1}'\mathbf{w} - 1 = 0. \tag{A2b}$$

Solving (A2a) gives

$$\mathbf{w}^* = \frac{1}{a}[\lambda\mathbf{\Sigma}^{-1}\mathbf{1} + \mathbf{\Sigma}^{-1}\bar{\mathbf{z}}]. \tag{A3}$$

Premultiplying (A3) by $\mathbf{1}'$ and imposing the budget constraint (A2b) yield an equation in λ which can be solved, giving

$$\lambda = \frac{a - \mathbf{1}'\mathbf{\Sigma}^{-1}\bar{\mathbf{z}}}{\mathbf{1}'\mathbf{\Sigma}^{-1}\mathbf{1}} = \frac{a - B}{C}. \tag{A4}$$

Thus, the final solution for the optimal portfolio is

$$\mathbf{w}^* = \mathbf{\Sigma}^{-1}\mathbf{1}\frac{1 - B/a}{C} + \mathbf{\Sigma}^{-1}\bar{\mathbf{z}}\frac{1}{a}. \tag{A5}$$

The investor holds a combination of portfolios $\mathbf{w}_g$ and $\mathbf{w}_d$. The greater is the risk aversion, a, the more the investor holds of the former.

For the second problem the weak budget constraint can be restated as $\mathbf{1}'\mathbf{w} = b \leqslant 1$, where b is a control variable. For this problem the Lagrangian is

$$L(\mathbf{w}, \lambda, b) \equiv \mathbf{w}'\bar{\mathbf{z}} - \frac{a\mathbf{w}'\mathbf{\Sigma}\mathbf{w}}{2} - \lambda(\mathbf{1}'\mathbf{w} - 1) \tag{A6}$$

with the constraint $b \le 1$. Using the Kuhn–Tucker methodology, we obtain that the first-order conditions are (A2a) and

$$\frac{\partial L}{\partial \lambda} = -\mathbf{1}'\mathbf{w} + b = 0, \tag{A7a}$$

$$\frac{\partial L}{\partial b} = \lambda \ge 0, \tag{A7b}$$

$$(1 - b)\lambda = 0. \tag{A7c}$$

If $a < B$, then the same solution applies. This is true, because from (A4) λ is positive, so from (A7c) $b = 1$ and (A7a) is identical to (A2b). For larger values of a, λ must be set to zero to satisfy both (A7b) and (A7c). In this case the solution to (A2a) is $\mathbf{w}^* = \mathbf{\Sigma}^{-1}\bar{\mathbf{z}}/a$. The entire solution can be written as

$$\mathbf{w}^* = \mathbf{\Sigma}^{-1}\mathbf{1}\,\text{Min}\left[0, \frac{1 - B/a}{C}\right] + \mathbf{\Sigma}^{-1}\bar{\mathbf{z}}\frac{1}{a}. \tag{A8}$$

As before, the investor holds some combination of portfolios $\mathbf{w}_g$ and $\mathbf{w}_d$. If $B > 0$, investors who are sufficiently close to risk neutral are short in the first portfolio and long in the second. At higher levels of risk aversion, wealth is shifted from $\mathbf{w}_d$ into $\mathbf{w}_g$. For $a = \mathbf{1}'\mathbf{\Sigma}^{-1}\bar{\mathbf{z}}$ just $\mathbf{w}_d$ is held, but at this point the shifting into $\mathbf{w}_g$ stops. For even higher risk-aversion levels, wealth is discarded rather than being invested in $\mathbf{w}_g$.

The opportunity to freely discard wealth can be viewed as a riskless asset with a zero gross return to those investors who are sufficiently risk averse to desire this opportunity. Less risk-averse investors cannot, however, borrow at this rate, −100%. This solution is illustrated in Figure 4.3. The lower portion of the dashed line, which was used to locate portfolio d, can now be interpreted as the borrowing–lending line.

If $B < 0$ so that portfolio $\mathbf{w}_d$ is on the lower limb of the hyperbola, the solution appears even stranger. Now for risk-averse investors a must exceed B, so the solution for every investor is to short portfolio $\mathbf{w}_d$ and discard all wealth, including the proceeds from this short sale.

The explanation for these counterintuitive results lies in the unlimited liability embodied in the normal distribution and the interpretation of negative wealth implicit in exponential utility. Since the exponential function is decreasing over the entire real line, negative exponential utility views negative wealth as a defined concept and attributes less utility to larger bankruptcies. Were this not the case—that is, were, for example, $W = -100$ and $W = -1000$ to be considered equally undesirable—then the optimal solution would not have this characteristic. Wealth would not be discarded. Alternatively, if some asset had limited liability, its return was bounded below by −1, then it would always be preferable to invest in this asset rather than to discard wealth, or if consumption in the first period were modeled explicitly, the investor would just consume more and invest all remaining wealth.

Appendix B: The Elliptical Distributions

Multivariate normality is the usual, but not the only, distribution of returns for which mean-variance (or generally median-dispersion) analysis is fully consistent with expected utility maximization. Clearly, if there are only two assets and they have different expected returns, each possible portfolio is completely characterized by its mean return. A fortiori, mean-variance analysis is valid. For $n > 2$, Tobin originally conjectured that any family of two-parameter distributions would be consistent with mean-variance analysis, but this class is too broad. The important missing requirement was that any portfolio (i.e., linear combination) of the random returns also had to have a distribution in the same family.

The distributions which permit mean-variance analysis are the elliptical distributions, so called because the isoprobability contours are ellipsoidal. A vector $\tilde{\mathbf{x}}$ of n random variables is said to be elliptically distributed if its density function can be expressed as

$$f(\mathbf{x}) = |\boldsymbol{\Omega}|^{-1/2} g[(\mathbf{x} - \boldsymbol{\mu})'\boldsymbol{\Omega}^{-1}(\mathbf{x} - \boldsymbol{\mu}); n]. \tag{B1}$$

$\boldsymbol{\Omega}$ is the positive definite dispersion matrix, and $\boldsymbol{\mu}$ is the vector of medians. If variances exist, then the covariances matrix is proportional to $\boldsymbol{\Omega}$. If means exist, $\boldsymbol{\mu}$ is also the vector of means. Note that $g(\cdot)$ is a univariate function with parameter n. The functions $g(\cdot; n)$ in the same class but with different parameter values can be quite different in appearance. Membership in a particular class can be verified through the characteristic function, which does not depend on n.

The characteristic function of elliptical random variables has the form

$$\phi_n(\mathbf{t}) \equiv E[e^{i\mathbf{t}'\tilde{\mathbf{x}}}] = e^{i\mathbf{t}'\boldsymbol{\mu}}\Psi(\mathbf{t}'\boldsymbol{\Omega}\mathbf{t}) \tag{B2}$$

for some function Ψ which does not depend on n.

Multivariate normal random variables are the most well-known ellipticals. For these, $g(s; n) \propto \exp(-s/2)$ and $\Psi(T) = \exp(-T/2)$. Many other types are also possible. For example, the multivariate student t distribution with ν degrees of freedom is characterized by

$$g(s; n) \propto (\nu + s)^{-(n+\nu)/2}. \tag{B3}$$

(The multivariate Cauchy distribution, $\nu = 1$, is a special case of an elliptical distribution in which neither the means nor variances are defined.) In fact, any nonnegative function, when properly normalized, can be used as the basis of an elliptical distribution. Note that the $g(s)$ can be identically zero for sufficiently large s, so that the distribution of asset returns could be bounded above and below. Thus, the criticism of the CAPM—that it requires assets to have unlimited liability—although true for the normal case, is not generally valid.

The marginal distribution of any component of $\mathbf{x}$ is also elliptical of the same class. If $\mathbf{x}_1$ is a subvector of $\mathbf{x}$ of length ν, then its density function is

$$f(\mathbf{x}_1) = |\boldsymbol{\Omega}_{11}|^{-1/2} g[(\mathbf{x}_1 - \boldsymbol{\mu}_1)'\boldsymbol{\Omega}_{11}^{-1}(\mathbf{x}_1 - \boldsymbol{\mu}_1); \nu]. \tag{B4}$$

This can be easily demonstrated by evaluating $\phi_\nu(\mathbf{t}) = \phi_n(\mathbf{t}, \mathbf{0})$ by using (B2). More generally, weighted sums of any elliptical random variables have an identical joint elliptical form that depends only on their mean vector and dispersion matrix.

Let $\mathbf{v} \equiv \mathbf{Tx}$ be a set of weighted sums for any matrix $\mathbf{T}$. Then the mean (median) vector for $\mathbf{v}$ is $\mathbf{m} = \mathbf{T}\boldsymbol{\mu}$, and the dispersion matrix is proportional to the covariance matrix

$$\boldsymbol{\Delta} \equiv kE[(\mathbf{v} - \mathbf{m})(\mathbf{v} - \mathbf{m})'] = k\mathbf{T}E[(\mathbf{x} - \boldsymbol{\mu})(\mathbf{x} - \boldsymbol{\mu})']\mathbf{T}' = \mathbf{T}\boldsymbol{\Omega}\mathbf{T}'.$$

The characteristic function of $\mathbf{v}$ is

$$\begin{aligned}\phi_\mathbf{v}(\mathbf{t}) &\equiv E[e^{i\mathbf{t}'\mathbf{v}}] = E[e^{i\mathbf{t}'\mathbf{Tx}}] = \phi_\mathbf{x}(\mathbf{T}'\mathbf{t}) \\ &= e^{i\mathbf{t}'\mathbf{T}\boldsymbol{\mu}}\Psi(\mathbf{t}'\mathbf{T}\boldsymbol{\Omega}\mathbf{T}'\mathbf{t}) = e^{i\mathbf{t}'\mathbf{m}}\Psi(\mathbf{t}'\boldsymbol{\Delta}\mathbf{t}).\end{aligned} \tag{B5}$$

Since the characteristic function of $\mathbf{v}$ has the same form as the characteristic function of any subvector of $\mathbf{x}$ with the same number of elements, this proves the point.

To prove that "mean-variance" analysis is valid for any elliptical distribution for returns, we need only show that the distribution of any portfolio is completely specified by its mean and dispersion and that the latter is disliked, so that investors hold minimum dispersion portfolios. Of course when variances exist, any portfolio's variance is proportional to its dispersion, so optimal portfolios are minimum variance as well. The intuition behind these steps is identical to that for the multivariate normal case.

Any portfolio of risky assets $\tilde{Z}_p = \mathbf{w}'\tilde{\mathbf{z}}$ is a weighted sum, so if the assets have an elliptical distribution, the distribution of the portfolio is the appropriate marginal with characteristic function

$$\phi_p(t) = \phi_\mathbf{z}(t\mathbf{w}) = e^{it\mu}\Psi(t^2\omega^2), \tag{B6}$$

where $\mu = \mathbf{w}'\bar{\mathbf{z}}$ and $\omega^2 \equiv \mathbf{w}'\boldsymbol{\Omega}\mathbf{w}$ are the portfolio's mean (or median) return and dispersion. Now the mth central moment of $\tilde{Z}_p$ will be

$$i^{-m}\frac{d^m}{dt^m}\Psi(t^2\omega^2)\bigg|_{t=0}. \tag{B7}$$

It is clear that all odd moments will be zero, and even moments will be proportional to ω^m. Therefore, the distribution of any portfolio of risky assets is characterized completely by μ and ω.

If the riskless asset is included, then $\tilde{Z}_p - R = \mathbf{w}'(\tilde{\mathbf{Z}} - R\mathbf{1})$, which is a weighted sum of ellipticals. The latter is characterized by $\omega^2 \equiv \mathbf{w}'\boldsymbol{\Omega}\mathbf{w}$ and $\mu - R \equiv \mathbf{w}'(\bar{\mathbf{Z}} - R\mathbf{1})$ as just shown, but ω^2 is the portfolio's variance, which, as before, determines all the higher moments.

We now show that dispersion is disliked. For the density function of the portfolio's return $f(\tilde{Z}_p)$, expected utility is

$$\begin{aligned}\hat{V}(\mu, \omega) \equiv Eu(\tilde{Z}_p) &= \int_{-\infty}^{\infty} u(Z_p) f(Z_p)\, dZ_p \\ &= \int_{-\infty}^{\infty} u(\mu + \omega\xi) g(\xi^2; 1)\, d\xi.\end{aligned} \tag{B8}$$

The second line follows from the substitutions $\xi = (Z_p - \mu)/\omega$, $dZ_p = \omega\, d\xi$ Then

$$\begin{aligned}\hat{V}_2 &= \int_{-\infty}^{\infty} u'(\mu + \omega\xi)\xi g(\xi^2; 1)\, d\xi \\ &= \int_{0}^{\infty} \xi g(\xi^2; 1)[u'(\mu + \omega\xi) - u'(\mu - \omega\xi)]\, d\xi < 0.\end{aligned} \tag{B9}$$

The inequality follows from the concavity of u, which guarantees that the term in brackets is negative. Since variance is proportional to dispersion, ω, it is likeise disliked.

These two steps complete the proof that mean-variance analysis is valid for elliptical distributions, and the CAPM continues to obtain. Note that the CAPM would even be valid if investors disagreed about the distribution of returns, that is, about $g(\cdot)$, provided they had idential assessments about $\boldsymbol{\mu}$ and $\boldsymbol{\Omega}$. Although we shall not prove so here, for more than two assets this condition is also necessary for the validity of mean-variance analysis (but *not* for the CAPM; see Chapters 6 and 9) when a riskless asset is available.

When there is no riskless asset, the class of distributions permitting mean-variance analysis to be consistent with expected utility maximization is enlarged somewhat to

$$\tilde{\mathbf{z}} = \tilde{\varepsilon}_1\mathbf{1} + \tilde{\varepsilon}_2\mathbf{a} + \tilde{\mathbf{x}}, \tag{B10}$$

where the vector $\tilde{\mathbf{x}}$ is elliptically istributed around zero conditional on $\tilde{\boldsymbol{\varepsilon}}$. That is, the form of g may depend upon their realizations, but the dispersion matrix $\boldsymbol{\Omega}$ remains the same.

We shall not analyze this case in detail, but the intuition is straightforward. Since $\mathbf{w}'\mathbf{1} = \mathbf{1}$, any portfolio formed from these assets includes all the risk associated with $\tilde{\varepsilon}_1$. Consequently, investors "ignore" it and minimize the remaining risk. ($\tilde{\varepsilon}_1$ may affect the choice of which minimum-variance portfolio is chosen.) Also, for any portfolio,

$$\bar{Z}_p = \bar{\varepsilon}_1 + \bar{\varepsilon}_2 \mathbf{w}'\mathbf{a}, \tag{B11}$$

so the mean return (together with the exogenous quantities $\bar{\varepsilon}_1$ and $\bar{\varepsilon}_2$, which are the same for all portfolios) is a sufficient statistic for $\mathbf{w}'\mathbf{a}$, which is the amount of $\tilde{\varepsilon}_2$ risk included in the portfolio. Finally, since $\tilde{\mathbf{x}}$ is conditionally elliptical around zero given $\tilde{\boldsymbol{\varepsilon}}$, $E(\tilde{\mathbf{x}}|\boldsymbol{\varepsilon}) = \mathbf{0}$, implying $\text{Cov}(\tilde{\mathbf{x}}, \varepsilon_1) = \text{Cov}(\tilde{\mathbf{x}}, \tilde{\varepsilon}_2) = \mathbf{0}$. Thus

$$\text{Var}(\tilde{Z}_p) = \text{Var}(\tilde{\varepsilon}_1) + 2\mathbf{w}'\mathbf{a}\text{Cov}(\tilde{\varepsilon}_1, \tilde{\varepsilon}_2) + (\mathbf{w}'\mathbf{a})^2\text{Var}(\tilde{\varepsilon}_2) + \text{Var}(\mathbf{w}'\tilde{\mathbf{x}}). \tag{B12}$$

From (B12) it is clear that the portfolio's mean (which determines $\mathbf{w}'\mathbf{a}$) and variance (again together with the three exogenous variance numbers) are sufficient statistics for variance of the elliptical random variable affecting the portfolio's return. But we already know that the variance of a particular zero mean elliptical random variable is a sufficient statistic for its entire distribution. Thus, the portfolio mean and variance completely determine the distribution of the portfolio's return.

Again with more than two assets this condition is also necessary for the validity of mean-variance analysis in the absence of a riskless asset. We shall refer to this class of distributions as the augmented elliptical class.

Some Examples of Elliptical Variables

As stated previously, the number of different types of elliptical distributions is literally uncountable. To illustrate the properties of elliptical variables, we use the following simple example.

Let (x_1, x_2) be uniformly distributed on the unit circle. That is, the density function is

$$f(\mathbf{x}) = \begin{cases} \pi^{-1}, & \text{for } x_1^2 + x_2^2 \leq 1, \\ 0\ \ , & \text{elsewhere.} \end{cases} \tag{B13}$$

The marginal density of x_i can be obtained by integrating out x_j. Since $|x_j| \leq \sqrt{1 - x_i^2} \equiv L$,

$$f(x_i) = \int_{-L}^{L} \pi^{-1}\,dx_j = \frac{2}{\pi}(1 - x_i^2)^{1/2} \tag{B14}$$

for $x_i^2 \leq 1$ and zero elsewhere.

Note that as suggested earlier the marginal distribution can be quite different in appearance from the joint distribution. Also, the conditional distribution is obviously uniform; specifically

$$f(x_i|x_j) = \frac{f(\mathbf{x})}{f(x_j)} = \frac{(1 - x_j^2)^{-1/2}}{2} \quad \text{for } x_i^2 \le 1 - x_j^2.$$

Thus, we see that the marginal and conditional densities can be different in appearance as well. This latter fact indicates that the random variables are not independent even though each is conditionally independent of the other.

Now let $v \equiv ax_1 + bx_2$. The density function for this sum is

$$f(v) = \int f\left(x_1, \frac{v - ax_1}{b}\right) dx_1, \tag{B15}$$

where the integral is over the region where $x_i^2 + b^{-2}(v - ax_1)^2 \le 1$, giving

$$f(v) = \frac{2}{\pi}\left[1 - \frac{v^2}{a^2 + b^2}\right]^{1/2} \tag{B16}$$

for $v^2 \le a^2 + b^2$, and zero elsewhere. Comparing (B16) to (B12), we see that all linear combinations of x_1 and x_2 have the same distributional form as either x_i—namely,

$$f(v) = \frac{2}{\pi}\left(1 - \frac{v^2}{\omega^2}\right)^{1/2}, \tag{B17}$$

where ω is the semirange, a measure of dispersion.

This example demonstrates the properties of elliptical distributions and illustrates that mean-variance analysis (and hence the CAPM) can be valid even with substantially nonnormal returns. It is not, however, a particularly apt description of asset returns. One general and useful category of augmented elliptical random variables is the subordinated normal class.

A random vector of returns on the risky assets is said to be jointly subordinated normal if its distribution is conditionally normal. That is, it is distributed as $N(\tilde{p}\boldsymbol{\theta}, \tilde{q}\boldsymbol{\Upsilon})$, where $\tilde{p}$ and $\tilde{q}$ are scalar random variables independent of the normal deviates. q must be nonnegative with probability 1. $\tilde{p}$ and $\tilde{q}$ are called the *directing* variables. We will show that this class of distributions is augmented elliptical by demonstrating that all portfolios can be described by their means and variances alone.

Assume that the directing variables have the bivariate density $h(p, q)$ and characteristic function $\phi^h(t_1, t_2) \equiv E[\exp(it_1\tilde{p} + it_2\tilde{q})]$. Then the characteristic function of the unconditional distribution can also be derived. For a given portfolio of risky assets, $\mathbf{w}$, the conditional distribution is normal with *conditional* mean and *conditional* variance of

$$p\theta = p\mathbf{w}'\boldsymbol{\theta}, \qquad q\upsilon^2 = q\mathbf{w}'\boldsymbol{\Upsilon}\mathbf{w}, \tag{B18}$$

respectively. The characteristic function of the unconditional portfolio distribution is

$$\begin{aligned}\phi(t) &\equiv \int_{-\infty}^{\infty} e^{itZ}\left[\iint n\left(\frac{Z - p\theta}{\upsilon\sqrt{q}}\right)h(p, q)\,dp\,dg\right]dZ \\ &= \iint\left[\int_{-\infty}^{\infty} \mathrm{e}^{\mathrm{it}\mathrm{Z}}\,\mathrm{n}\left(\frac{\mathrm{Z} - \mathrm{p}\theta}{\upsilon\sqrt{q}}\right)dZ\right]h(p, q)\,dp\,dq \\ &= \iint \exp\left(it\theta p - \frac{t^2\upsilon^2 g}{2}\right)h(p, q)\,dp\,dq \qquad \text{(B19)} \\ &= \phi^h\left(\theta t, \frac{it^2\upsilon^2}{2}\right).\end{aligned}$$

In the second line we have assumed that it is permissible to change the order of the integration. In that case the innermost integral is the characteristic function of the normal distribution. The fourth line follows from the definition of ϕ^h. It is clear from (B19) that the distribution of returns on any portfolio is completely characterized by θ and υ since these two variables completely determine its characteristic function (together with the distribution of $\tilde{p}$ and $\tilde{q}$, which is, of course, the same for all portfolios). We next show tha the portfolio's mean and variance are sufficient statistics.

Evaluating the derivatives

$$\begin{aligned}\phi'(t) &= \theta\phi_1^h + it\upsilon^2\phi_2^h, \\ \phi(t) &= \theta^2\phi_{11}^h + 2i\theta\upsilon^2 t\phi_{22}^h - \upsilon^4 t^2\phi_{22}^h + i\upsilon^2\phi_2^h\end{aligned} \qquad \text{(B20)}$$

gives the moment as

$$E[\tilde{Z}] = \frac{1}{i}\phi'(0) = \frac{1}{i}\theta\phi_1^h(0, 0) = \theta E[\tilde{p}], \qquad \text{(B21a)}$$

$$\begin{aligned}E[\tilde{Z}^2] = -\phi''(0) &= -\theta^2\phi_{11}^h(0, 0) - i\upsilon^2\phi_2^h(0, 0) \\ &= \theta^2 E[\tilde{p}^2] + \upsilon^2 E[\tilde{q}],\end{aligned} \qquad \text{(B21b)}$$

$$\mathrm{Var}[\tilde{Z}] = \theta^2\mathrm{Var}[\tilde{p}] + \upsilon^2 E[\tilde{q}]. \qquad \text{(B21c)}$$

Thus, $\bar{Z}$ is a sufficient statistic for the conditional mean $p\theta$, and $\bar{Z}$ and $\mathrm{Var}(\tilde{Z})$ jointly determine the conditional variance $q\upsilon^2$. This concludes the proof; however, since (B19) holds for all portfolios, we can additionally use it and (B6) to write the multivariate characteristic function as

$$\begin{aligned}\phi(t) &\equiv E[e^{it\mathbf{w}'\tilde{\mathbf{z}}}] = \phi^h\left(t\mathbf{w}'\boldsymbol{\theta}, \frac{it^2\mathbf{w}'\boldsymbol{\Upsilon}\mathbf{w}}{2}\right), \\ \phi_{\mathbf{z}}(\mathbf{t}) &= \phi^h\left(\mathbf{t}'\boldsymbol{\theta}, \frac{i\mathbf{t}'\boldsymbol{\Upsilon}\mathbf{t}}{2}\right),\end{aligned} \qquad \text{(B22)}$$

where $\mathbf{t} = t\mathbf{w}$.

Whenever $\tilde{p}$, the random variable affecting the means, is a constant, the subordinated normals are elliptical, and a riskless asset can also be added to the opportunity set. In some cases when $\tilde{p}$ is not degenerate, there is an alternative choice of directing variables $\tilde{p}$ and $\tilde{q}$ with the former constant which yields the same distribution of returns. This will be true, for example, whenever $\tilde{p}$ and $\tilde{q}$ are independent and $\tilde{p}$ has a symmetric distribution. Again a riskless asset can be added. In other cases the unconditional distribution for the assets' returns are only in the augmented elliptical class, and no riskless asset is permitted.

Solving a Specific Problem

As a specific example take $\tilde{p}$ to be degenerate, that is $\tilde{p} \equiv 1$, and $\tilde{q}$ to have an exponential distribution

$$h(p, q) = \delta(p - 1)\, \lambda e^{-\lambda q}, \tag{B23a}$$

$$\phi^h(s, t) = e^{is}\left(1 - \frac{it}{\lambda}\right)^{-1}. \tag{B23b}$$

From (B22) and (B23b) the characteristic function of the risky assets is $e^{it'\boldsymbol{\theta}}(1 + \mathbf{t}'\boldsymbol{\Upsilon}\mathbf{t}/2\lambda)^{-1}$. the corresponding distribution

$$f(\mathbf{z}) = \left(\frac{\lambda}{2|\boldsymbol{\Upsilon}|}\right)^{1/2} \exp(-[2\lambda(\mathbf{z} - \boldsymbol{\theta})'\boldsymbol{\Upsilon}^{-1}(\mathbf{z} - \boldsymbol{\theta})]^{1/2} \tag{B24}$$

is known as the Laplace or double exponential distribution. Its mean vector is $\bar{\mathbf{z}} = \theta$, and its covariance matrix is $\boldsymbol{\Sigma} = \boldsymbol{\Upsilon}/\lambda$. The marginal distributions are symmetric, but the kurtosis is 6 ("excess" is 3), so they are "fat tailed."

An exponential utility investor, $u(Z) = -e^{-aZ}$, facing this opportunity set would solve the problem stated in (50). Using the characteristic function, we get that this is $\text{Max}[-e^{-aWR}\phi_{\mathbf{z}}(ia\mathbf{w})]$ or

$$\text{Min}\, e^{-a(R+\mathbf{w}'(\boldsymbol{\theta}-R\mathbf{1}))}\left(1 - \frac{\mathbf{w}'\boldsymbol{\Upsilon}\mathbf{w}}{2\lambda}\right)^{-1}. \tag{B25}$$

The first-order condition is

$$\begin{aligned} 0 &= \boldsymbol{\theta} - R\mathbf{1} - \frac{a\boldsymbol{\Upsilon}\mathbf{w}}{(1 - a^2\mathbf{w}'\boldsymbol{\Upsilon}\mathbf{w}/2\lambda)\lambda}, \\ w^* &= \frac{1 - a^2\mathbf{w}'\boldsymbol{\Sigma}\mathbf{w}/2}{a}\boldsymbol{\Sigma}^{-1}(\bar{\mathbf{z}} - R\mathbf{1}). \end{aligned} \tag{B26}$$

Recall that $\bar{\mathbf{z}} = \boldsymbol{\theta}$ and $\boldsymbol{\Upsilon} = \lambda\boldsymbol{\Sigma}$. Comparing (B26) to (53) we see that the investor's holdings in the risky assets are proportional in these two cases. We know this must be true because in each case the same two-fund separation obtains. He will, however, change the leverage of his portfolio.

Under the first investment environment the investor holds the fraction $\mathbf{1}'\mathbf{w}^* = (B - AR)/a$ in the risky assets. In the present economy the fraction $[1 - a^2\mathbf{w}'\boldsymbol{\Sigma}\mathbf{w}/2](B - AR)/a$ is placed at risk. To compute the expression in brackets in terms of exogenous quantities alone, define

$$\begin{aligned} v &\equiv a^2\mathbf{w}'\boldsymbol{\Sigma}\mathbf{w}, \\ v &= \left(1 - \frac{v}{2}\right)^2 (\bar{\mathbf{z}} - R\mathbf{1})'\boldsymbol{\Sigma}^{-1}\boldsymbol{\Sigma}\boldsymbol{\Sigma}^{-1}(\bar{\mathbf{z}} - R\mathbf{1}) \\ &= \left(1 - \frac{v}{2}\right)^2 (C - 2RB + R^2A) \equiv \left(1 - \frac{v}{2}\right)^2 b^2. \end{aligned} \tag{B27}$$

The second line follows from (B26). From (18) or Figure 4.4, b is the slope of the efficient frontier. (B27) is a quadratic equation in v.

Solving for v and substituting into (B27) give a total risky holding of

$$\mathbf{1}'\mathbf{w}^* = \frac{\sqrt{1 + 2b^2} - 1}{b^2}\frac{B - AR}{a}. \tag{B28}$$

Since $\sqrt{1 + 2b^2} - 1 < b^2$, the investor places fewer funds at risk in this economy. This is just the result expected because portfolio returns are now leptokurtotic, and the investor dislikes kurtosis. ($u^{(4)}(Z) < 0$.)

Preference Over Mean Return

We stated previously that whenever return distributions are such that mean-variance analysis is consistent with expected utility maximization and a riskless asset is available, then investors who prefer more to less will always prefer the portfolio with the highest mean among portfolios with the same variance. That is $V_1 > 0$, and investors' optimal portfolios are on the upper limb of the locus of minimum variance portfolios. On the other hand, the preference of higher mean is not true for some of the additional distributions permitted when no riskless asset is available.

To prove the first part of this statement, recall that mean-variance analysis is valid with a riskless asset only if all risky assets have an elliptical distribution. In this case the expected utility of any portfolio can be expressed via the derived utility function defined over mean and variance given in (B8). Evaluating the derivative gives

$$V_1 = \hat{V}_1 = \int_{-\infty}^{\infty} u'(\mu + \omega\xi)g(\xi^2; 1)\,d\xi > 0. \tag{B29}$$

The inequality follows from the assumption of positive marginal utility.

In the absence of a riskless asset the returns must only be elliptical conditional upon an arbitrary random vector $\tilde{\boldsymbol{\varepsilon}}$. The expected utility of a portfolio can still be written in terms of the mean and variance of the elliptical distribution

$$\hat{V}(\mu, \omega) \equiv Eu(Z_p) = \int u(\mu + \omega\xi) \int g(\xi^2, \boldsymbol{\varepsilon}; 1) f(\boldsymbol{\varepsilon})\, d\boldsymbol{\varepsilon}\, d\xi. \quad \text{(B30)}$$

As before,

$$\hat{V}_1 = \int u'(\cdot) \int g(\cdot) f(\cdot)\, d\boldsymbol{\varepsilon}\, d\xi > 0; \quad \text{(B31)}$$

however, now an increase in μ, holding ω constant, is not the same as an increase in $\bar{Z}_p$, holding σ_p constant, because σ_p may depend on μ through interactions via the distribution of $\boldsymbol{\varepsilon}$. If increasing $\bar{Z}_p$ increases both μ and ω, then a higher mean may not be preferred.

A specific illustration of a situation in which some investor, with positive marginal utility, holds a minimum-variance portfolio which mean return less than that on the global minimum-variance portfolio is the following simple example. Assume that there are two assets with returns $z_1 = \{1, 3\}$ and $z_2 = \{0, 6\}$. The two outcomes are each equally likely, and the returns are independent. Then $\bar{z}_1 = 2$, $\bar{z}_2 = 3$, $\sigma_1^2 = 1$, $\sigma_2^2 = 9$, and $\sigma_{12} = 0$. Because there are only two assets, all portfolios are minimum variance, and mean-variance analysis is obviously valid.

The global minimum-variance portfolio is $\mathbf{w}_g' = (0.9, 0.1)$, with $\bar{Z}_g = 2.1$ and $\sigma_g^2 = 0.9$. Since $\bar{Z}_g > \bar{z}_1$, asset 1 is on the lower, "inefficient" portion of the minimum-variance frontier. Nevertheless, asset 1 and the portfolios between asset 1 and the global minimum-variance portfolio are each preferred to the corresponding portfolio with the same variance on the upper limb by some investors. (They are each even the optimal portfolio for some investor.)

For example, the portfolio with the same variance as asset 1 is $\mathbf{w}' = (0.8, 0.2)$, with $\bar{Z}_p = 2.2$ and the four equally likely returns $\{0.8, 2.0, 2.4, 3.6\}$. For the utility function $-e^{-4Z}$, the expected utility of this portfolio is approximately $-.010$, whereas for aset 1 expected utility is about $-.009$. Thus, asset 1 is preferred to the portfolio even though the former is mean-variance dominated.

The reason asset 1 is preferred to the portfolio despite being mean-variance dominated is that its remaining moments are "better." Both distributions are symmetric, but all the even central moments for asset one are less than those for the portfolio. Since all even moments are "disliked" by exponential utility functions, there is a tradeoff between mean and these higher moments when comparing asset 1 and the portfolio. For exponential utility $-\exp(-aZ)$, the larger a is, the more important are the higher moments.

If all assets are joint elliptically distributed, then such tradeoffs cannot exist because all portfolios with the same variance have identical central moments of all orders. In the augmented elliptical class, however, these tradeoffs do arise through the variable $\tilde{\varepsilon}_2$, which links mean returns with the other moments.

5

Generalized Risk, Portfolio Selection, and Asset Pricing

In the CAPM, risk is measured by standard deviation or variance. As we saw in Chapter 4 this notion of risk is consistent with choice by expected utility maximization only under special conditions. In this chapter we examine a general definition of risk which is fully consistent with expected utility maximization.

THE BACKGROUND

In keeping with our previous practice we consider only single-argument, monotone increasing, concave utility functions. In most contexts the argument will be final wealth or return on initial wealth. We do not impose a boundedness condition, so that utility functions such as $u(Z) = \log Z$, which are not strictly von Neumann–Morgenstern utility functions, are allowed. Instead we consider only outcomes with bounded range. Under suitable regularity conditions all the results developed hold for unbounded outcomes whenever expected utility is defined.

It is natural to consider "risk" to be a property of the set of random outcomes which is disliked by risk averters. Whether or not something is disliked, however, depends upon the utility function used in the evaluation. That is, risk is a property defined for a class of utility functions. Naturally we would like a definition which is as broadly applicable as possible.

Risk generally conveys only the notion of uncertainty or dispersion of outcomes. That is, it is natural to think of the two normal distributions $N(0, 1)$ and $N(1, 1)$ as being equally risky, although the latter would be preferred under all increasing utility functions. Thus, in talking of risk we must correct preferences for location. We shall adopt the common practice and use the mean or expectation to measure location.

RISK: A DEFINITION

If uncertain outcomes $\tilde{X}$ and $\tilde{Y}$ have the same expectation, then $\tilde{X}$ is said to be *weakly less risky* than $\tilde{Y}$ for the class of utility functions, $\mathcal{U}$, if no individual with a utility function in $\mathcal{U}$ prefers $\tilde{Y}$ to $\tilde{X}$; that is,

$$E[u(\tilde{X})] \geqslant E[u(\tilde{Y})] \qquad \text{for all } u \text{ in } \mathcal{U}. \tag{1}$$

$\tilde{X}$ is said to be *less risky* than $\tilde{Y}$ without qualification if some individual prefers $\tilde{X}$; that is, the inequality in (1) is strict for some $u(\cdot)$.

For some restricted classes, this ordering is complete. For all pairs of random variables $\tilde{X}$ and $\tilde{Y}$ with the same mean but different distributions, either $\tilde{X}$ or $\tilde{Y}$ is less risky (or they have equal risk). The quadratic utility functions compose such a class, and $\tilde{X}$ is less risky than $\tilde{Y}$ if and only if $\text{Var}(\tilde{X}) < \text{Var}(\tilde{Y})$.

Even among complete orderings, however, variance is not the universal measure of riskiness. Consider the class of cubic utility functions $u(Z) = Z - cZ^3$ with $c > 0$ and outcomes bounded between 0 and $(3c)^{-1/2}$. For this class, expected utility can be written by using Equation (49) of the Mathematical Introduction in terms of distribution moments as

$$Eu(\tilde{Z}) = \bar{Z} - cE(Z^3) = \bar{Z} - c(m^3 + \bar{Z}^3 + 3\sigma^2\bar{Z}), \tag{2}$$

where m^3 is the third central moment of $\tilde{Z}$. Outcome 1 is preferred to outcome 2 with the same expectation if

$$c[3\bar{Z}(\sigma_2^2 - \sigma_1^2) + m_2^3 - m_1^3] > 0. \tag{3}$$

Thus, $m^3 + 3\bar{Z}\sigma^2$ is the proper measure of risk for all utility functions in this class.

Not only do different classes of utility functions have different risk measures, but, in general, no simple statistical risk measures can be defined because the ordering in (1) is only a partial one. That is, it is possible to find outcomes $\tilde{X}$ and $\tilde{Y}$ and utility functions u_1 and u_2 such that $Eu_1(\tilde{X}) > Eu_2(\tilde{Y})$ and $Eu_2(\tilde{X}) < Eu_2(\tilde{Y})$. For example, consider

$$X = \begin{cases} 0 \\ 4 \end{cases} \text{with probability} \begin{matrix} \frac{1}{2}, \\ \frac{1}{2}, \end{matrix} \qquad Y = \begin{cases} 1 \\ 9 \end{cases} \text{with probability} \begin{matrix} \frac{7}{8}, \\ \frac{1}{8}. \end{matrix} \tag{4}$$

then $\bar{X} = \bar{Y} = 2$, $\text{Var}(\tilde{X}) = 4$, and $\text{Var}(\tilde{Y}) = 7$. Any quadratic utility function will give a higher expected utility to $\tilde{X}$, but the utility function $u(X) = \sqrt{X}$ assigns a higher expected utility to $\tilde{Y}$.

$$Eu(\tilde{X}) = 1 < Eu(\tilde{Y}) = \tfrac{10}{8}. \tag{5}$$

In the class consisting of the square root utility function and all quadratic utilities, neither $\tilde{X}$ nor $\tilde{Y}$ can be said to be riskier.

Rothschild and Stiglitz proposed this notion of risk and developed its propterties in the most general case when the class $\mathcal{U}$ included all risk-averse utility functions. Henceforth, whenever it is stated that $\tilde{X}$ is less risky than $\tilde{Y}$ with no qualification about the relevant class of utility functions, it should be understood that this Rothschild–Stiglitz convention is adopted. In general, we only consider the subset of these which are strictly concave and at least twice differentiable.

While no single parameter like variance is sufficient to determine the risk of a random outcome in this general discussion, it is still true that increased riskiness implies a distribution which is more spread out.

MEAN PRESERVING SPREADS

We shall see that a random variable is less risky than a second if the density function of the latter can be obtained from that of the former by applying a series of mean preserving spreads.

A *mean preserving spread* (MPS) is defined as any function satisfying

$$s(x) = \begin{cases} \alpha & \text{for } c < x < c + t, \\ -\alpha & \text{for } c' < x < c' + t, \\ -\beta & \text{for } d < x < d + t, \\ \beta & \text{for } d' < x < d' + t, \\ 0 & \text{elsewhere,} \end{cases} \tag{6}$$

where $\alpha(c' - c) = \beta(d' - d)$, $\alpha > 0$, $\beta > 0$, $t > 0$, $c + t < c' < d - t$, and $d + t < d'$. Briefly, these conditions guarantee that $s(\cdot)$ has four distinct intervals of nonzero value with the middle two negative and the outside two positive. An example of an MPS is illustrated in Figure 5.1.

Two important properties of a mean preserving spread are, for $a < c$, $d' + t < b$,

$$\int_a^b s(x)\,dx = 0,$$

$$\begin{aligned} \int_a^b xs(x)\,dx &= \tfrac{1}{2}\alpha[(c + t)^2 - c^2 + c'^2 - (c' + t)^2] \\ &\quad + \tfrac{1}{2}\beta[d^2 - (d + t)^2 + (d' + t)^2 - d'^2] \\ &= t[\alpha c - \alpha c' + \beta d' - \beta d] = 0. \end{aligned} \tag{7}$$

Thus, if $f(x)$ is a density function defined over (a, b), and if $g(x) \equiv f(x) +$

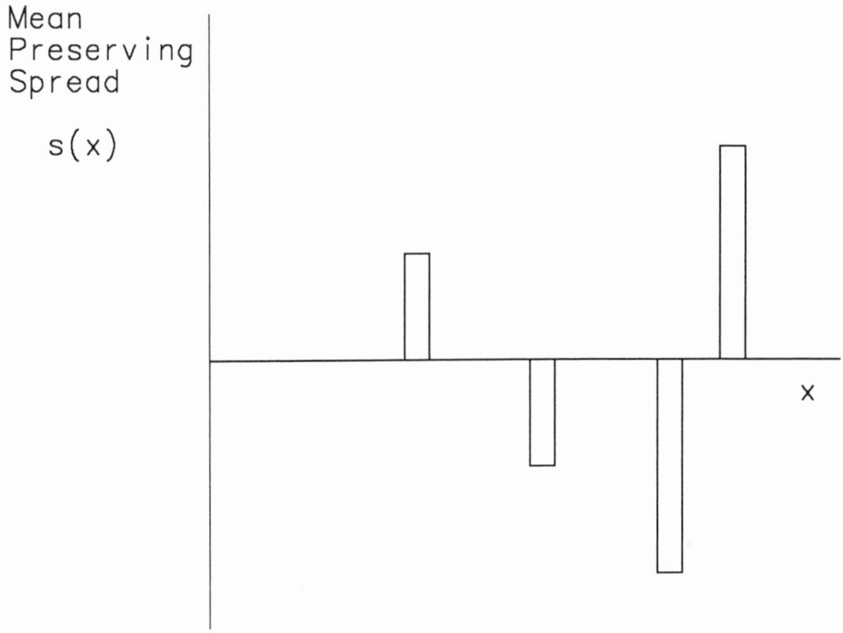

Figure 5.1 Mean-Preserving Spread

$s(x) > 0$, then $g(x)$ is also a density function defined over the same interval and having the same expectation.

$$\int_a^b g(x)\,dx = \int_a^b [f(x) + s(x)]\,dx = \int_a^b f(x) = 1,$$
$$\int_a^b xg(x)\,dx = \int_a^b xf(x)\,dx + \int_a^b xs(x)\,dx = \int_a^b xf(x)\,dx. \tag{8}$$

Figures 5.2 and 5.3 illustrate the density functions $f(x)$ and $g(x)$. Note that density mass of g is further away from all interior points between $c' + t$ and d. This interval need not include the mean of the distribution for $s(x)$ to constitute a mean preserving spread.

We now demonstrate that an outcome Y with density $g(\cdot)$ is riskier than an outcome X with density $f(\cdot)$. To do this we compare expected utilities

$$Eu(\tilde{X}) - Eu(\tilde{Y}) = \int_a^b u(z)[f(z) - g(z)]\,dz = -\int_a^b u(z)s(z)\,dz$$
$$= -\alpha\int_c^{c+t} u(z)\,dz + \alpha\int_c^{c'+t} u(z)\,dz + \beta\int_d^{d+t} u(z)\,dz - \beta\int_{d'}^{d'+t} u(z)\,dz \tag{9}$$

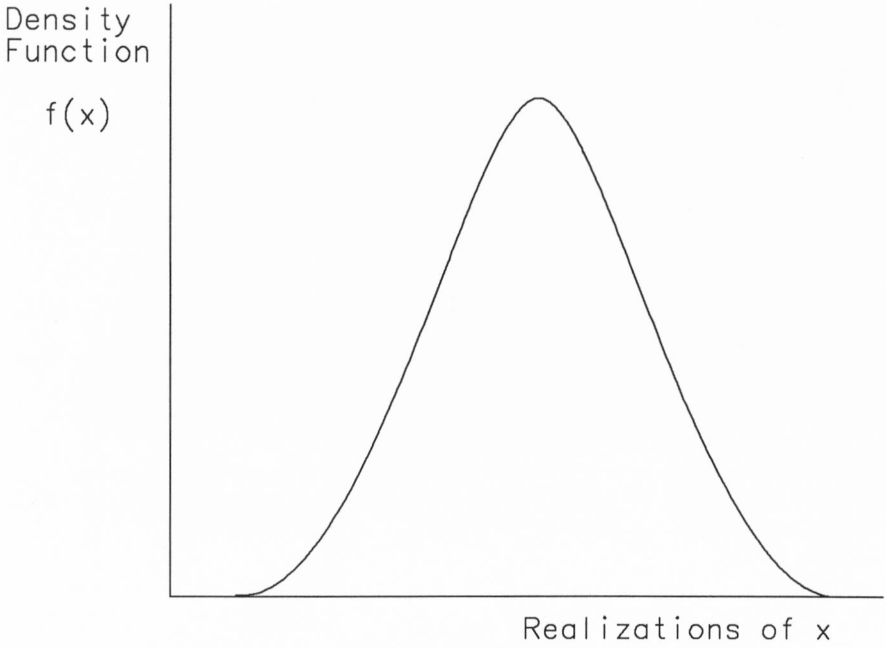

Figure 5.2 Original Density Function

$$= -\alpha \int_{c}^{c+t} [u(z) - u(z + c' - c)]\, dz + \beta \int_{d}^{d+t} [u(z) - u(z + d' - d)]\, dz$$

$$= -\alpha \int_{c}^{c+t} [u(z) - u(z + c' - c) - \frac{\beta}{\alpha}[u(z + d - c)$$

$$- u(z + d - c + d' - d)]]\, dz.$$

From the definition of an MPS $\beta/\alpha = (c' - c)/(d' - d)$, and from the mean value theorem $u(z + h) - u(z) = u'(z^*)h$ for some z^* in $[z, z + h]$; therefore, for some z_1^* in $[z, z + c' - c)$ and z_2^* in $[z + d - c, z + d' - c]$,

$$Eu(\tilde{X}) - Eu(\tilde{Y}) = \alpha(c' - c) \int_{c}^{c+t} [u'(z_1^*) - u'(z_2^*)]\, dz. \tag{10}$$

z_1^* and z_2^* depend upon z, but for each z, $z_2^* > z_1^*$ since their possible ranges do not overlap. Thus, since $u''(\cdot) \leqslant 0$, $u'(z_1^*) \geqslant u'(z_2^*)$, and the integrand is uniformly nonnegative, we have

$$Eu(\tilde{X}) - Eu(\tilde{Y}) \geqslant 0. \tag{11}$$

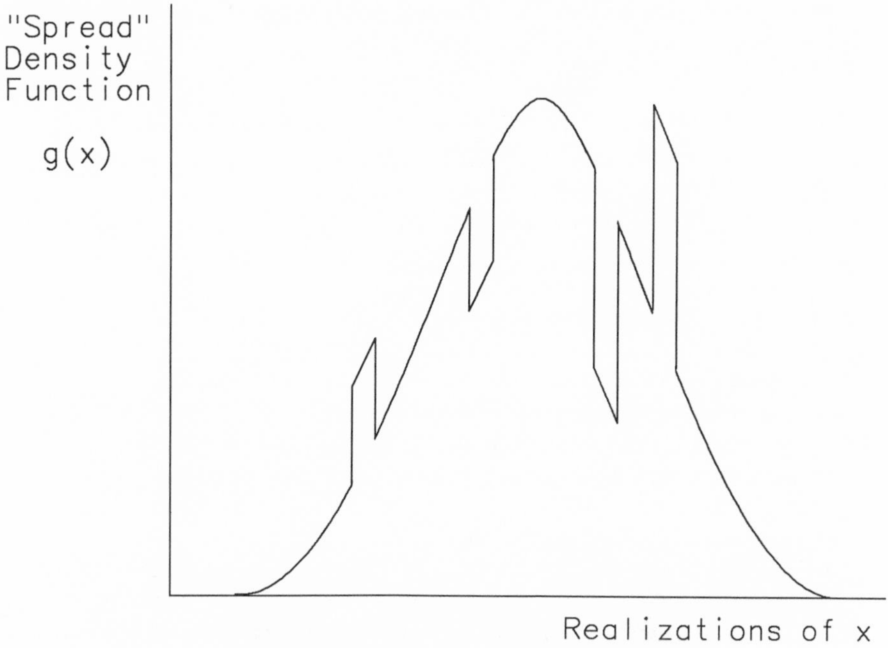

Figure 5.3 "Spread" Density Function

If we consider only strictly concave utilities, then the preference ordering in (11) is also a strict one.

By transitivity it is clear that a density function which can be obtained from another by a series of MPSs is riskier than the original as well. Examining density functions to see if they have this characterization, however, can be a tedious exercise. Fortunately, Rothschild and Stiglitz have developed precise relations for testing the relative riskiness of two outcomes.

ROTHSCHILD AND STIGLITZ THEOREMS ON RISK

If $\tilde{Y}$ differs from $\tilde{X}$ by the addition of mean preserving spreads, then $\tilde{Y}$ has a noiser distribution, as defined in the Mathematical Introduction. This notion is made precise next.

THEOREM 1 *Outcome $\tilde{X}$ is weakly less risky than outcome $\tilde{Y}$ if and only if $\tilde{Y}$ is distributed like $\tilde{X} + \tilde{\varepsilon}$ and $\tilde{\varepsilon}$ is a fair game with respect to $\tilde{X}$. That is,*

$$\tilde{Y} \overset{d}{=} \tilde{X} + \tilde{\varepsilon}, \qquad E(\tilde{\varepsilon}|X) = 0 \qquad \text{all } X. \tag{12}$$

Proof. We provide only the proof of sufficiency because that is all we require here. Taking conditional expectations and using Jensen's inequality give

$$E[u(\tilde{X} + \tilde{\varepsilon})|X] \leq u(E[\tilde{X} + \tilde{\varepsilon}|X]) = u(E[\tilde{X}|X] + E[\tilde{\varepsilon}|X]) = u(X). \quad (13)$$

Now taking expectations over all $\tilde{X}$ values gives

$$E[E[u(\tilde{X} + \tilde{\varepsilon})|X]] \equiv Eu(\tilde{X} + \tilde{\varepsilon}) \leq Eu(\tilde{X}). \quad (14)$$

Since $\tilde{X} + \tilde{\varepsilon}$ and $\tilde{Y}$ have the same distribution,

$$Eu(\tilde{Y}) = Eu(\tilde{X} + \tilde{\varepsilon}) \leq Eu(\tilde{X}). \qquad \text{Q.E.D.} \quad (15)$$

Note that for this theorem it is only required that $\tilde{Y}$ be distributed like $\tilde{X} + \tilde{\varepsilon}$; it need not be equal to the sum of those two random variables. Also, as stated in the Mathematical Introduction, the second condition in (12) is stronger than a lack of correlation but weaker than independence. Finally, the theorem does not preclude other relations between $\tilde{X}$ and $\tilde{Y}$ which are not expressed as $\tilde{Y} \overset{d}{=} \tilde{X} + \tilde{\varepsilon}$.

To illustrate this last point, consider the random variable $\tilde{X}$, which takes on the values +1 and −1 with equal probability. The random variable $\tilde{Y} \equiv 2\tilde{X}$ is clearly riskier. The most obvious way to indicate the distribution of $\tilde{Y}$ is by $\tilde{Y} \overset{d}{=} \tilde{X} + \tilde{X}$; however, $E(\tilde{X}|X) \neq 0$. The distribution of Y can also be described as $\tilde{Y} \overset{d}{=} \tilde{X} + \tilde{\varepsilon}$, where

$$\tilde{\varepsilon} = \begin{cases} 3 & \text{with probability } \frac{1}{4} \\ -1 & \text{with probability } \frac{3}{4} \end{cases} \text{when } X = -1, \quad \begin{cases} -3 & \text{with probability } \frac{1}{4} \\ +1 & \text{with probability } \frac{3}{4} \end{cases} \text{when } X = 1. \quad (16)$$

In this case $E(\tilde{\varepsilon}|X) = 0$.

With Theorem 1 it is easy to explain why variance is a valid measure of risk for normally distributed outcomes. If $\tilde{X}$ is normally distributed $N(\mu, a)$ and $\tilde{\varepsilon}$ is an independent normal $N(0, b)$, then $\tilde{X} + \tilde{\varepsilon}$ is also normal $N(\mu, a + b)$ and $E(\tilde{\varepsilon}|X) = 0$. Since b can be any nonnegative number, any normally distributed outcome Y with a variance $c > a$ is distributed like $\tilde{X} + \tilde{\varepsilon}$, where $\tilde{\varepsilon}$ is $N(0, c - a)$ and independent of X. If $c < a$ then $\tilde{X}$ is distributed like $\tilde{Y} + \tilde{\varepsilon}$, where $\tilde{\varepsilon}$ is $N(0, a - c)$ and independent of Y. Thus, the normal outcome with the large variance is the riskier one.

Although variance is not typically a complete measure of risk in this general sense with nonnormal outcomes, it should be noted that if $\tilde{Y}$ is riskier than $\tilde{X}$, then it must have at least as great a variance. We know this must be true because variance is a sufficient measure of risk under quadratic utility, which is in the class of concave utilities. To demonstrate this result, we first recall that if $E(\tilde{\varepsilon}|X) = 0$, then $\text{Cov}(X, \varepsilon) = 0$. If $\tilde{Y} \overset{d}{=} \tilde{X} + \tilde{\varepsilon}$, then

$$\begin{aligned} \text{Var}(\tilde{Y}) &= \text{Var}(\tilde{X} + \tilde{\varepsilon}) = \text{Var}(\tilde{X}) + \text{Var}(\tilde{\varepsilon}) + 2\text{Cov}(\tilde{X}, \tilde{\varepsilon}) \\ &= \text{Var}(\tilde{X}) + \text{Var}(\tilde{\varepsilon}) \geqslant \text{Var}(\tilde{X}). \end{aligned} \tag{17}$$

THE RELATIVE RISKINESS OF OPPORTUNITIES WITH DIFFERENT EXPECTATIONS

Thus far we have compared in riskiness only opportunities with the same expectation. If possible we would like to extend this notion in a compatible fashion to opportunities with different expectations. We can no longer say that $\tilde{X}$ is less risky than $\tilde{Y}$ if $Eu(\tilde{X}) \geqslant Eu(\tilde{Y})$ for all increasing, concave utility functions. Utility functions "sufficiently close" to risk neutral would always prefer the outcome with the higher mean, so, by this definition, $\tilde{X}$ could be less risky than $\tilde{Y}$ only if $\bar{X} \geqslant \bar{Y}$. This is clearly not in keeping with our intuition on riskiness.

If a riskless opportunity is available with outcome X_0, then Levy's extension to the Rothschild–Stiglitz definition could be used. He shows that if $\gamma\tilde{X} + (1 - \gamma)X_0$ has the same expectation as $\tilde{Y}$ and is less risky than $\tilde{Y}$ by Rothschild and Stiglitz's definition, then for any portfolio combination of $\tilde{Y}$ and the riskless opportunity, the combination of $\tilde{X}$ and the riskless opportunity which has the same mean will be weakly preferred by all risk-averse individuals. In this case it is meaningful to say that $\tilde{X}$ is less risky than $\tilde{Y}$.

There are two problems with Levy's definition. First, a riskless asset may not always be available, or it may not be meaningful to speak of portfolio combinations of the opportunities. Second, this definition is not compatible with the notion of riskiness used previously in the mean-variance problem. There we said asset 1 was riskier than asset 2 if $\sigma_1 > \sigma_2$. Under Levy's definition asset 1 is riskier than asset 2 if $\sigma_1/(\bar{z}_1 - R) > \sigma_2/(\bar{z}_2 - R)$.

To avoid these problems, we use the alternative definition that $\tilde{X}$ is (weakly) less risky than $\tilde{Y}$ if there exist constants a and b such that $E(\tilde{X} - a) = E(\tilde{Y} - b)$ and $\tilde{X} - a$ is (weakly) less risky than $\tilde{Y} - b$ in the sense of Rothschild and Stiglitz. That is, in place of using a proportional adjustment in the distribution, we use an additive adjustment to equate the means.

If we define $u_2(X) \equiv u_1(X - a)$, then the former is increasing and concave if and only if the latter is. Therefore, the definition in the preceding paragraph has the consistency property that relative riskiness is invariant to the choice of constants a and b, which equate the means of $\tilde{X}$

and $\tilde{Y}$. It is often convenient therefore to extend the definition as follows: $\tilde{X}$ is (weakly) less risky than $\tilde{Y}$ if $\tilde{X} - \bar{X}$ is (weakly) less risky than $\tilde{Y} - \bar{Y}$ in the sense of Rothschild and Stiglitz.

SECOND-ORDER STOCHASTIC DOMINANCE

The notion of riskiness developed here is closely related to that of second-order stochastic dominance. The distinction between the two ideas is that the latter also incorporates the correction for location. A random return $\tilde{X}$ displays weak second-order stochastic dominance over $\tilde{Y}$ if

$$\tilde{Y} \stackrel{d}{=} \tilde{X} + \tilde{\xi} + \tilde{\varepsilon}, \qquad E[\tilde{\varepsilon}|X + \xi] = 0, \tag{18}$$

where $\tilde{\xi}$ is a nonpositive random variable. Thus, second-order stochastic dominance results if there is some random variable $\tilde{\xi}$ such that $\tilde{X}$ first-order stochastically dominates $\tilde{X} + \tilde{\xi}$ (as described in Chapter 3) and $\tilde{Y}$ is weakly riskier than this latter quantity. The stochastic dominance is strict if either the probability that $\tilde{\xi}$ is negative is nonzero or $\tilde{\varepsilon}$ has positive dispersion so that $\tilde{Y}$ is strictly riskier than $\tilde{X} + \tilde{\xi}$.

THEOREM 2 *A necessary and sufficient condition that outcome $\tilde{Y}$ be preferred to outcome $\tilde{X}$ by no increasing concave utility function is that $\tilde{X}$ weakly stochastically dominates $\tilde{Y}$.*

Proof. Again, only a proof of sufficiency is provided. Since $\tilde{\varepsilon}$ is noise by Theorem 1,

$$Eu(\tilde{X} + \tilde{\xi}) \geq Eu(\tilde{X} + \tilde{\xi} + \tilde{\varepsilon}) \tag{19}$$

for all concave utilities. Since $\tilde{\xi}$ is nonpositive,

$$Eu(\tilde{X}) \geq Eu(\tilde{X} + \tilde{\xi}) \tag{20}$$

by first-order stochastic dominance. Finally, since $\tilde{Y}$ has the same distribution as $\tilde{X} + \tilde{\xi} + \tilde{\varepsilon}$, it follows that they have the same expected utility. Q.E.D.

As stated previously, the relation between riskiness and second-order stochastic dominance is strong, but the two concepts are not identical. If $\bar{X} \geq \bar{Y}$ and $\tilde{Y}$ is weakly riskier than $\tilde{X}$, then $\tilde{X}$ stochastically dominates $\tilde{Y}$. This is easily demonstrated since

$$\tilde{Y} \stackrel{d}{=} \tilde{X} + (\bar{Y} - \bar{X}) + \tilde{\varepsilon} \tag{21}$$

with $E[\tilde{\varepsilon}|X] = 0$. In (21) $\bar{Y} - \bar{X}$ is a degenerate nonpositive random variable.

Table 5.1 Summary of Preference Ordering Conditions

	Utility condition	Random Variable Condition	Distributional Condition[a]
Dominance	$EU(\tilde{X}+\tilde{W}) \geqslant EU(\tilde{Y}+\tilde{W})$ for any r.v. $\tilde{W}$ for all increasing utility functions	$\tilde{Y}=\tilde{X}+\xi$ $\xi \leqslant 0$	$\tilde{X} \geqslant \tilde{Y}$
1st-order Stochastic Dominance	$EU(\tilde{X}) \geqslant EU(\tilde{Y})$ for all increasing utility functions	$\tilde{Y} \overset{d}{=} \tilde{X}+\xi$ $\xi \leqslant 0$	$G(t) \geqslant F(t)$ for all t
2nd-order Stochastic Dominance	$EU(\tilde{X}) \geqslant EU(\tilde{Y})$ for all increasing, concave utility functions	$\tilde{Y} \overset{d}{=} \tilde{X}+\xi+\tilde{\varepsilon}$ $\xi \leqslant 0$ $E[\tilde{\varepsilon} \mid X+\xi]=0$	$\int_a^t [G(s)-F(s)]\,ds \equiv \Delta(t) \geqslant 0$ for all t
Increasing Risk	$EU(\tilde{X}) \geqslant EU(\tilde{Y})$ for all concave utility functions	$\tilde{Y} \overset{d}{=} \tilde{X}+\tilde{\varepsilon}$ $E[\tilde{\varepsilon} \mid X]=0$	$\Delta(t) \geqslant 0$ for all t $\Delta(b)=0$

[a] $\tilde{X}$ and $\tilde{Y}$ are random variables defined over the range $[a, b]$. The distribution functions are $F(X)$ and $G(Y)$, respectively.

On the other hand, if $\tilde{X}$ weakly stochastically dominates $\tilde{Y}$, then we can conclude that $\bar{X} \geq \bar{Y}$, but we cannot conclude that $\tilde{Y}$ is riskier than $\tilde{X}$ (in fact the opposite is possible). The former must be true since $Eu(\tilde{X}) \geq Eu(\tilde{Y})$ for linear utility only if $\bar{X} \geq \bar{Y}$. (If we wish to restrict our attention to strictly concave utility functions, then appropriate limiting arguments give us the same conclusion.) That the latter need not be true can be easily demonstrated. Let $\tilde{Y}$ be a uniform random variable on [0, 1] and $\tilde{X}$ a uniform random variable on [2, 4]. Clearly, $\tilde{X}$ is riskier than $\tilde{Y}$ (when de-meaned), but $\tilde{X}$ also dominates (and a fortiori first- and second-order stochastically dominates) $\tilde{Y}$.

It is also possible to construct examples in which $\tilde{X}$ does not first-order stochastically dominate $\tilde{Y}$ but does second-order stochastically dominate $\tilde{Y}$ without being less risky. Consider the following variables, each with four equally likely outcomes:

$$\begin{array}{ccccc} \tilde{X} & 30 & -10 & -10 & -10 \\ \tilde{\eta} & -30 & -1 & -1 & 0 \\ \tilde{\varepsilon} & 0 & 2 & -2 & 0 \\ \tilde{Y} & 0 & -9 & -13 & -10 \end{array} \tag{22}$$

Clearly, η is nonpositive, and

$$E(\tilde{\varepsilon}|x + \eta = 0) = E(\tilde{\varepsilon}|X + \eta = -11) = E(\tilde{\varepsilon}|X + \eta = -10) = 0.$$

Thus $\tilde{Y} = \tilde{X} + \tilde{\eta} + \tilde{\varepsilon}$ is second-order stochastically dominated by $\tilde{X}$. Note that $\bar{X} = 0 > \bar{Y} = -8$. Also $\tilde{X}$ does not first-order stochastically dominate $\tilde{Y}$ since $\text{Prob}[\tilde{X} \le -10] = .75 > \text{Prob}[\tilde{Y} \le -10] = .5$. The easiest way to prove that $\tilde{X} - \bar{X}$ is not less risky than $\tilde{Y} - \bar{Y}$ is to compute variances. $\text{Var}(\tilde{X}) = 300 > \text{Var}(\tilde{Y}) = 87.5$. Since a smaller variance is a necessary condition for being less risky, $\tilde{Y}$ cannot be riskier than $\tilde{X}$.

A summary of stochastic dominance and riskiness is provided in Table 5.1.

THE PORTFOLIO PROBLEM

As in Chapter 3 we denote the random variable return on asset i by $\tilde{z}_i$. We shall often wish to refer to a particular realization as z_{si}, which is the realized return on asset i given that the economy ends in state s. We denote the probability of state s by π_s.

Consider an investor who is faced with maximizing expected utility from his or her portfolio's return. The problem can be stated as follows: Choose the portfolio weights w_i to

$$\text{Max } Eu(\textstyle\sum w_i \tilde{z}_i) \tag{23}$$

subject to $\Sigma w_i = 1$. Forming the Lagrangian, $L \equiv Eu + \lambda(1 - \Sigma w_i)$, and differentiating give the first-order conditions

$$\frac{\partial L}{\partial w_i} = E[u(\cdot)\tilde{z}_i] - \lambda = 0 \qquad \text{all } i, \tag{24a}$$

$$\frac{\partial L}{\partial \lambda} = 1 - \textstyle\sum w_i = 0. \tag{24b}$$

If there is a riskless asset, it is convenient to use (24b) to rewrite (24a) as

$$E[u'(\textstyle\sum w_i \tilde{z}_i)(\tilde{z}_i - R)] = 0 \qquad \text{all } i. \tag{25}$$

THEOREM 3 *If a solution exists for the optimal portfolio for a strictly concave utility function and for a given set of assets, then the probability* *distribution of its return is unique. If there are no redundant assets, then the portfolio (i.e., w_i^*) is unique as well.*

Proof. We provide a proof only in the case when the outcome state is discrete. For each feasible portfolio $\mathbf{w}$ define a new set of control variables θ_s and the associated derived utility function V by

$$\theta_s \equiv \sum w_i Z_{si}, \qquad s = 1, \ldots, S, \tag{26a}$$

$$V(\theta_1, \ldots, \theta_S) \equiv \Sigma \pi_s u(\theta_s). \tag{26b}$$

Now the problem of choosing the set θ_s to maximize $V(\cdot)$ subject to feasibility [there exists a portfolio $\mathbf{w}$ satisfying (26a)] is the same as the standard portfolio problem. It is also a standard convex optimization problem with concave objective, so the optimum is unique.

To see that the portfolio $\mathbf{w}$ is also unique, write

$$\boldsymbol{\theta}^* = \mathbf{Z}\mathbf{w}^*, \tag{27}$$

where $\boldsymbol{\theta}^*$ is the vector of θ_s. If there are no redundant assets, then $\mathbf{Z}$ has full column rank and a unique left inverse $\mathbf{Z}^- = (\mathbf{Z}'\mathbf{Z})^{-1}\mathbf{Z}'$, so

$$\mathbf{w}^* = \mathbf{Z}^-\boldsymbol{\theta}^* \tag{28}$$

is also unique. Q.E.D.

SOLVING A SPECIFIC PROBLEM

One sample portfolio problem was provided in Chapter 4 for the case of normally distributed returns and exponential utility. Here we give another sample problem which does not depend upon mean-variance analysis.

Suppose there is a riskless asset with return R and a single risky asset whose return is h with probability π and k with probability $1 - \pi$. (To avoid arbitrage, $k < R < h$.) The investor has a power utility function $u(Z) = Z^\gamma/\gamma$ with relative risk tolerance $b = 1/(1 - \gamma)$. From (25) the optimal investment in the risky asset is the solution to

$$\pi[w(h - R) + R]^{\gamma-1}(h - R) + (1 - \pi)[w(k - R) + R]^{\gamma-1}(k - R) = 0. \tag{29}$$

Solving (29) for w gives

$$w = R\frac{(1 - \pi)^{-b}(R - k)^{-b} - \pi^{-b}(h - R)^{-b}}{(1 - \pi)^{-b}(R - k)^{1-b} + \pi^{-b}(h - R)^{1-b}}. \tag{30}$$

OPTIMAL AND EFFICIENT PORTFOLIOS

For a given set of asset returns, the portfolios which satisfy (24a) or (25) make up the set of optimal portfolios for the class of utility functions for u under consideration. If we speak of "optimal portfolios" with no specification of any class, the class of all increasing concave functions should be assumed.

Under mean-variance analysis and in the absence of short sale restrictions, possible optimal portfolios are those that have the highest mean return for a given variance. These portfolios are usually called mean-variance efficient. A similar but partial relation holds here, so that optimal portfolios are very often referred to as efficient without the mean-variance qualification. Efficient portfolios are those for which there are no other portfolios with the same or greater expected return and less risk.

We can also give the set of efficient portfolios the following heuristic characterization. If a utility function is analytic, it can be expressed as the Taylor expansion $u(Z) = u(\bar{Z}) + \cdots + u^{(n)}(\bar{Z})(Z - \bar{Z})^n/n! + \cdots$. Then if the sum $E[(Z - \bar{Z})^2]/2 + \cdots + E[(Z - \bar{Z})^n]/n!$ converges, expected utility can be stated in terms of the mean return and all the higher central moments. For quadratic utility $u^{(n)}(\cdot) = 0$ for $n > 2$, so only mean and variance matter. For cubic utility mean, variance, and skewness matter, and so on. In general, considering one more term, the nth, will expand the set of previously efficient portfolios by permitting new tradeoffs between the nth moment and the lower-order moments. The efficient set is the limit of these sets.

Two cautions are in order. First, this characterization is not exact unless proper account is taken of the constraints which must be imposed to ensure the utility function is uniformly increasing and concave. (See Chapter 4 for a discussion of this limitation in the context of the mean-variance model.) Second, just because a selection can be made by examining only a few moments of a portfolio's distribution does not mean that the efficient set must include only those portfolios with extremal values of a single moment when other moments are held fixed. This was true under mean-variance efficiency because $u'' < 0$ guaranteed that variance was disliked. Similarly, for extremal values of the kth moment to be optimal $u^{(k)}$ must be of uniform sign. As we saw in Chapter 1 this can be true over an unbounded range only if the derivatives alternate in sign. In this case odd moments are liked, and even moments are disliked.

THEOREM 4 *Let $\tilde{Z}_e$ denote the return on an efficient portfolio, optimal for some strictly increasing concave utility function, and $\tilde{Z}$ the return on any other distinct portfolio (one whose return is not identical). If $\tilde{Z}_e$ (i.e., $\tilde{Z}_e - \bar{Z}_e$) is weakly more risky than $\tilde{Z}$ (i.e., $\tilde{Z} - \bar{Z}$), then $\bar{Z}_e > \bar{Z}$.*

Proof. From the Rothschild–Stiglitz definition of risk,

$$Eu(\tilde{Z}_e) \leqslant Eu(\tilde{Z} - \bar{Z} + \bar{Z}_e) \qquad \text{for all } u. \tag{31}$$

Suppose $\bar{Z} > \bar{Z}_e$. Then

$$Eu(\tilde{Z}_e) < Eu(\tilde{Z}) \qquad \text{for all } u. \tag{32}$$

But this violates the assumption that $\tilde{Z}_e$ is the return on the (unique) utility maximizing portfolio for some utility function for which $Eu(\tilde{Z}_e) > Eu(\tilde{Z})$. Q.E.D.

In Theorem 4 if $\tilde{Z}_e$ is the return on an optimal portfolio for some quasi-increasing concave utility function, then we can only conclude that $\bar{Z}_e \geq \bar{Z}$, because the optimal portfolio for this utility function need not be unique. If there are no redundant assets, then the qualification that $Z \not\equiv Z_e$ is not required since no two portfolios could always have identical returns.

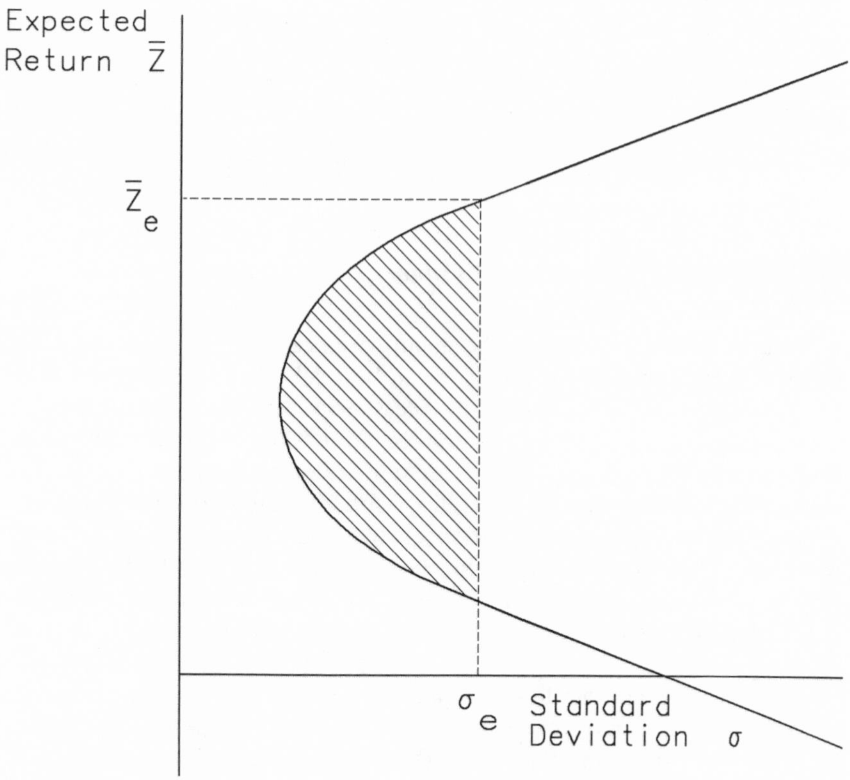

Figure 5.4 Portfolios with Less Risk than $\tilde{Z}_e$

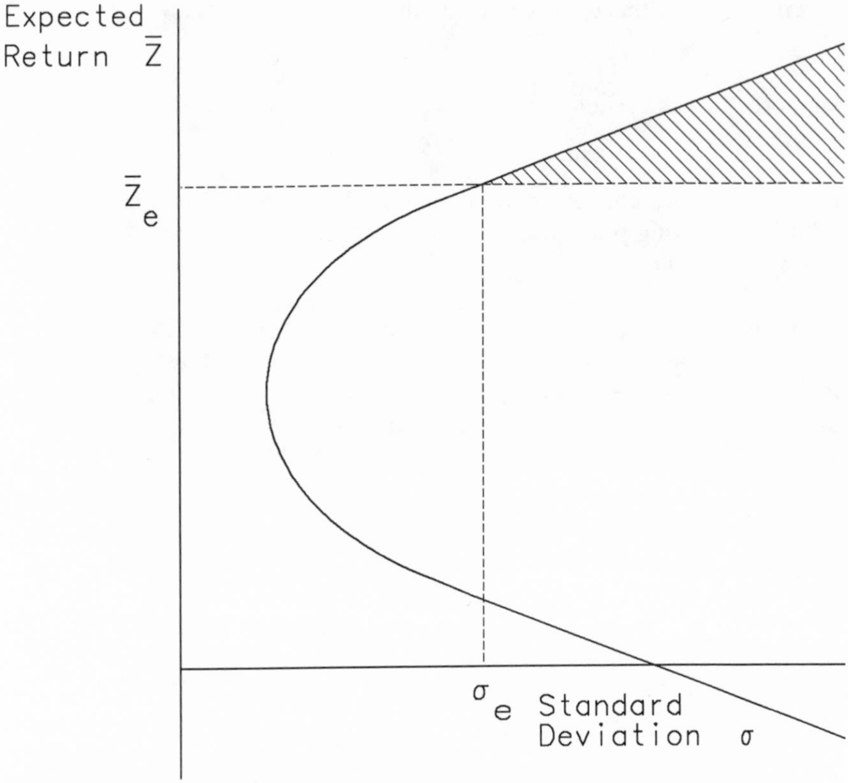

Figure 5.5 Portfolios with Higher Expected Returns than $\tilde{Z}_e$

Theorem 4 is equivalent to the mean-variance efficiency condition that $\bar{Z}_e > \bar{Z}$ if $\sigma_e^2 > \sigma^2$. That this is true can be easily seen in Figure 5.4. The shaded region includes all portfolios less risky than Z_e. Clearly, they all have smaller means. In a mean-variance context the converse is also true. If $\bar{Z} > \bar{Z}_e$, then $\sigma^2 > \sigma_e^2$. This is demonstrated in Figure 5.5. Now the shaded region includes all portfolios with expected returns above $\bar{Z}_e$. Clearly, they all have larger variances. We cannot make a similar statement about the converse here, however. It is possible to find portfolios with higher mean returns than $\bar{Z}_e$ but which are neither more nor less risky. Recall that the Rothschild–Stiglitz risk ordering is only a partial one.

With this theorem we have the natural CAPM-like corollaries that all efficient portfolios have expected returns in excess of the riskless return, and that the riskier an efficient portfolio, the higher its expected return. Just as in the mean-variance world, these results apply only to efficient portfolios. The proper measure of risk for individual securities equivalent to beta in the CAPM is developed later.

One further clarification about efficient portfolios is important. The set of efficient portfolios does not include every portfolio for which there is not another less risky portfolio with the same mean return. The latter set is similar to the set of minimum-variance portfolios in the mean-variance problem, which includes both the mean-variance efficient portfolios and the lower limb of the hyperbola (or lower projection of the capital market line with a riskless asset). These excluded portfolios correspond to solutions to (24a) where marginal utility is not uniformly positive, and investors trade off variance to get lower expected return.

VERIFYING THE EFFICIENCY OF A GIVEN PORTFOLIO

In some contexts it is important to verify whether or not a given portfolio is efficient. In the mean-variance problem this is a simple matter. In all mean-variance efficient portfolios, the mean and variance must satisfy the quadratic relation of Chapter 4, Equation (6), and the portfolio weights must satisfy the linear relations of Chapter 4, Equation (10). In general, we must either describe a utility function satisfying (24a) or (25) for the portfolio in question or prove that one does not exist.

We examine this problem for the case of discrete outcomes for the returns on the assets. We denote as separate events or, in the terminology to be adopted later, separate states those realizations which have distinct patterns of returns on the assets. The return on the ith asset in the sth state is Z_{si}. The portfolio in question will have a pattern of returns of

$$Z_s^* = \sum_i w_i^* Z_{si}. \tag{33}$$

We order states such that $Z_1^* \leqslant Z_2^* \leqslant \cdots \leqslant Z_S^*$. For a given utility function we also denote $v_s \equiv u'(Z_s^*)$. Then (24a) can be stated as

$$\sum \pi_s Z_{si} v_s = \lambda \qquad \text{all } i. \tag{34}$$

If u is a valid utility function, it must have positive marginal utility $v_s \geqslant 0$ and decreasing marginal utility $v_1 \geqslant v_2 \geqslant \cdots \geqslant v_S$. Since utility is defined only up to a linear transformation, the scale of the v's is arbitrary. To answer our question, therefore, we may set $\lambda = 1$ without loss of generality. Note that the only way in which the portfolio in question can affect the requirements above is through the ordering it imposes on the states. Thus, all portfolios which impose the same ordering on the v's are efficient if and only if there is a feasible solution to the problem

$$\sum \pi_s Z_{si} v_s = 1, \qquad i = 1, \ldots, N, \tag{35a}$$

$$v_s \geqslant v_{s+1}, \qquad s = 1, \ldots, S-1. \tag{35b}$$

$$\nu_S \geqslant 0. \tag{35c}$$

If there are no redundant securities, then the rank of the matrix (Z_{si}), and, therefore, of $(\pi_s Z_{si})$, is $N \leqslant S$, and (35a) imposes N constraints on the S unknowns. If $N = S$, then there is a unique solution to (35a), so only one ordering of the states represents efficient portfolios, and all efficient portfolios can be immediately identified as soon as one is found. This case is the "complete markets" problem discussed in Chapter 8.

If $N < S$, then all efficient portfolios need not have the same state ordering of their returns. As an example of this latter case consider a three-state two-asset economy. The matrix $(Z_{si})'$ is

state:	a	b	c
asset:			
1	0.6	1.2	3.0
2	2.4	1.5	0.6

(36)

With three states there is a potential for $3! = 6$ orderings; however, portfolios of only two assets can achieve at most only four of these. In this case portfolios holding more than $\frac{3}{5}$ in asset 1 will have returns ordered from low to high as (a, b, c). Those with $\frac{3}{7} < w_1 < \frac{3}{5}$ will be ordered (b, a, c). Those with $\frac{1}{3} < w_1 < \frac{3}{7}$ will be ordered (b, c, a). Finally, those with $w_1 < \frac{1}{3}$ will be ordered (c, b, a).

Which of these orderings represent efficient portfolios depends upon the probabilities of the states. With only two assets one of the extreme cases $w_1 = \pm\infty$ will correspond to the portfolio with the highest expected return, depending on which mean is higher. Investors with utility "close" to risk neutral will choose such portfolios, so in our example one of the orderings (a, b, c) or (c, b, a) will always indicate efficient portfolios. Suppose that the state probabilities are all $\frac{1}{3}$. Then $\bar{z}_1 = 1.6 > \bar{z}_2 = 1.5$, so $w_1 = \infty$ is the risk-neutral investors' choice, and the ordering (a, b, c) represents efficient portfolios. This means, as discussed before, that *all* portfolios with this ordering (i.e., all portfolios with $w_1 > \frac{3}{5}$) are efficient.

Other orderings also come from efficient portfolios. For example, the exponential class of utility functions $u(Z) = -e^{-aZ}$ has the following optimal portfolios:

a	0	.001	.01	.1	1	10	100	∞
w_1^*	∞	33.88	3.77	.75	.45	.40	.34	$\frac{1}{3}$

(37)

Plainly, each of the three regions with $w_1 > \frac{1}{3}$ is represented, whereas the last is not. Therefore, portfolios with $w_1 < \frac{1}{3}$ are probably not efficient. For now this is only a conjecture. As we shall see later, there is no guarantee that a single class of utility functions will generate all efficient portfolios even when there are only two assets. When there are more than

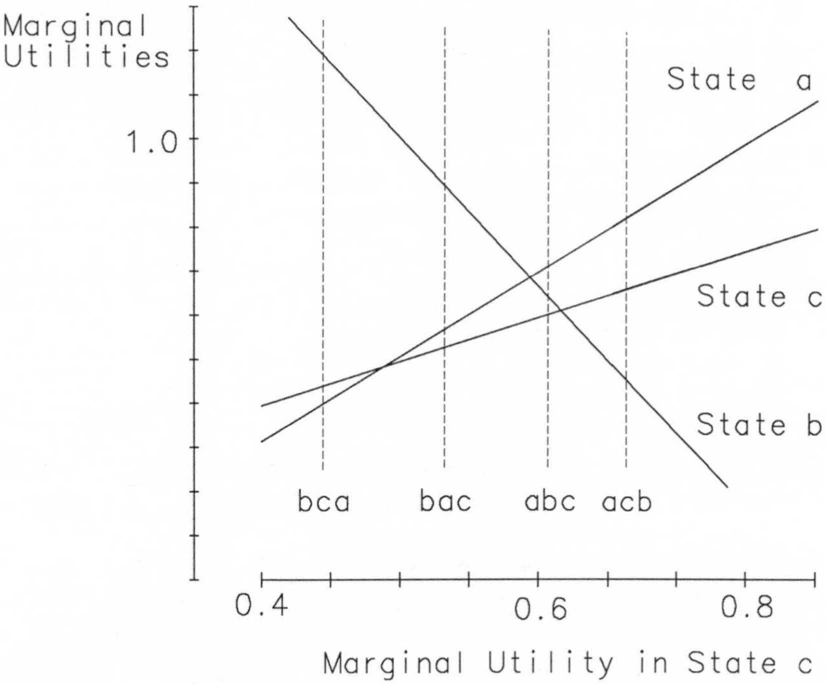

Figure 5.6 Marginal Utilities in Each State

two assets, a single class of utility functions almost certainly will not do so.

In general, we require a constructive method of demonstrating efficiency, that is, a method of finding all efficient orderings. The method following is one such.

To find all orderings representing efficient portfolios, we set up the system represented by (35a):

$$\begin{aligned} 0.2v_a + 0.4v_b + 1.0v_c &= 1.0, \\ 0.8v_a + 0.5v_b + 0.2v_c &= 1.0. \end{aligned} \tag{38}$$

The solution set to (38) is

$$v_a = \tfrac{21}{11} v_c - \tfrac{5}{11}, \qquad v_b = -\tfrac{38}{11} v_c + \tfrac{30}{11}, \tag{39}$$

which is graphed in Figure 5.6. From the figure it is clear that four orderings of utility represent efficient portfolios, namely,

$$v_b > v_c > v_a, \quad v_b > v_a > v_c, \quad v_a > v_b > v_c \quad v_a > v_c > v_b. \tag{40}$$

Recalling that marginal utility is inversely related to return, we see that the first three orderings in (40) correspond, in reverse order, to the first three orderings under Equation (36). This confirms our finding that all portfolios investing more than $\frac{1}{3}$ in asset 1 are efficient. It also confirms our guess that portfolios with $w_1 < \frac{1}{3}$ are not efficient. A portfolio with $Z_a < Z_c < Z_b$ would be efficient if it were feasible (without changing the economy). A portfolio with $Z_c < Z_a < Z_b$ would be inefficient even if available.

It is interesting to compare these results to those obtained by using mean-variance analysis. The variances are $\sigma_1^2 = 1.04$, $\sigma_2^2 = 0.54$, and $\sigma_{12} = -0.72$. The global minimum-variance portfolio holds

$$w_{g1} = \frac{\sigma_2^2 - \sigma_{12}}{\sigma_1^2 + \sigma_2^2 - 2\sigma_{12}} \approx 0.417. \tag{41}$$

Since there are only two assets, the mean-variance efficient frontier includes all portfolios with $w_1 \geqslant w_{g1}$. As we just saw, however, the efficient set includes those down to $w_1 = \frac{1}{3}$.

If the state probabilities are changed, then different orderings become efficient. For example, if the probabilities are $(\frac{1}{2}, \frac{1}{3}, \frac{1}{6})$, then the exponential class of utility functions has the following optimal portfolios:

$$\begin{array}{ccccccccc} a & 0 & .001 & .01 & .1 & 1 & 10 & 100 & \infty \\ w_1^* & -\infty & -227.24 & -22.35 & -1.86 & .19 & .37 & .34 & \frac{1}{3} \end{array} \tag{42}$$

Note that now $\bar{z}_2 > \bar{z}_1$ so a risk-neutral investor would select $w_1 = -\infty$. In this case two orderings are represented: (c, b, a) when $w_1^* < \frac{1}{3}$ and (b, c, a) when $\frac{1}{3} < w_1^* < \frac{3}{7}$. Note that not all portfolios in the second region are represented. w_1^* peaks at a value less than 0.38 between values of 8 and 9 for a, but $\frac{3}{7} > 0.42$. Nevertheless, we know that these other portfolios must also be efficient since they have the same state orderings as those for $a = 10$ or 100.

Using the constructive method for this case, we obtain that (35a) is

$$\begin{aligned} 0.3v_a + 0.4v_b + 0.5v_c &= 1.0, \\ 1.2v_a + 0.5v_b + 0.1v_c &= 1.0. \end{aligned} \tag{43}$$

The solution set is now

$$v_a = \tfrac{7}{11} v_c - \tfrac{10}{33}, \qquad v_b = \tfrac{30}{11} - \tfrac{19}{11} v_c, \tag{44}$$

which is plotted in Figure 5.7. Now only three orderings represent efficient portfolios

$$v_b > v_c > v_a, \quad v_c > v_b > v_a, \quad v_c > v_a > v_b. \tag{45}$$

Of these only the first two are feasible. Together they correspond to all portfolios with $w_1 < \frac{3}{7}$.

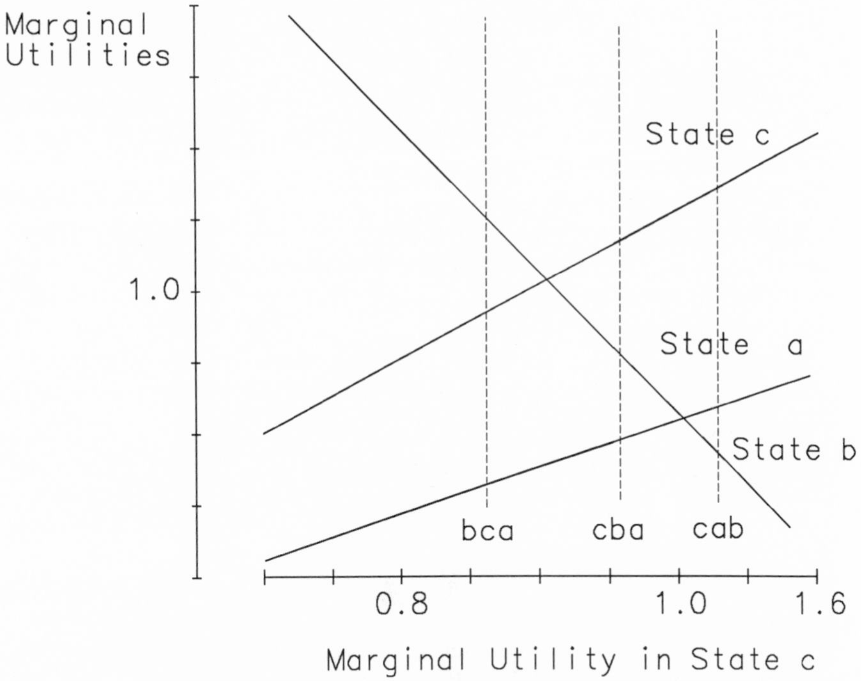

Figure 5.7 Marginal Utilities in Each State

Characterizing utility functions for which given portfolios are optimal is now a simple matter (although finding "nice" functions is not). For example, under the first set of probabilities, the efficient portfolio holding $w_1 = .4$ is optimal for $v_c = \frac{22}{55}$ (among other values), and from (39) $v_a = \frac{17}{55}$, $v_b = \frac{74}{55}$. This portfolio has returns $Z_a = 1.68$, $Z_b = 1.38$, $Z_c = 1.56$, so any utility function possessing $u'(1.68) = \frac{17}{55} < u'(1.56) = \frac{2}{5} < u'(1.38) = \frac{74}{55}$ will find it optimal.

A RISK MEASURE FOR INDIVIDUAL SECURITIES

In mean-variance analysis there are two risk measures: variance, determining the efficiency of portfolios, and beta, measuring the market risk of individual securities. The Rothschild–Stiglitz concept of risk is equivalent to the former. We now introduce a generalized measure of "systematic" risk.

Let $\tilde{Z}_e^k$ denote the return on efficient portfolio k, and let u be its associated utility function defined in (24a). Then the systematic risk of security i relative to portfolio k is defined by

$$b_i^k \equiv \frac{\mathrm{Cov}[u'(\tilde{Z}_e^k), \tilde{z}_i]}{\mathrm{Cov}[u'(\tilde{Z}_e^k), \tilde{Z}_e^k]}. \tag{46}$$

For now the name systematic risk for the measure b_i^k should be accepted through its role in (46) by analogy with the CAPM. The answer to why it is a measure of systematic risk is given in Chapter 9.

This measure has many properties similar to beta which are desirable properties of any systematic risk measure. First, it possesses the portfolio property that the b of a portfolio is the weighted average of the b's of the securities. Second, the ordering "security i is riskier by this measure than security j" is complete.

More importantly, if there is a riskless asset, excess expected returns are proportional to b. A proof follows immediately from (25). Since $E[u'(\tilde{Z}_e^k)\tilde{z}_i] = RE[u'(\tilde{Z}_e^k)]$,

$$\mathrm{Cov}[u'(\tilde{Z}_e^k), \tilde{z}_i] = RE[u'(\tilde{Z}_e^k)] - E[u'(\tilde{Z}_e^k)]\bar{z}_i = -E[u'(\tilde{Z}_e^k)](\bar{z}_i - R). \tag{47}$$

Now (47) holds for all assets including $\tilde{Z}_e^k$, so

$$b_i^k \equiv \frac{\mathrm{Cov}[u'(\tilde{Z}_e^k), \tilde{z}_i]}{\mathrm{Cov}[u'(\tilde{Z}_e^k), \tilde{Z}_e^k]} = \frac{\bar{z}_i - R}{\bar{Z}_e^k - R} \tag{48}$$

or $\bar{z}_i - R = b_i^k(\bar{Z}_e^k - R)$. By Theorem 3, $\bar{Z}_e^k > R$, so excess returns are positively proportional to this risk measure.

This result leads immediately to a second important result of order preservation. Asset i is riskier than (equally risky as) asset j with respect to an efficient portfolio if and only if it is riskier than (equally risky as) asset j with respect to any other efficient portfolio.

THEOREM 5 *(a)* $b_i^k > b_j^k$ *iff* $b_i^\ell > b_j^\ell$. *(b)* $b_i^k = b_j^k$ *iff* $b_i^\ell = b_j^\ell$.

Proof. From (48)

$$\frac{\bar{z}_i - R}{\bar{Z}_e^k - R} > \frac{\bar{z}_j - R}{\bar{Z}_e^k - R}, \tag{49}$$

and from Theorem 3 $\bar{Z}_e^k - R > 0$, so $\bar{z}_i > \bar{z}_j$. Now assume $b_i^\ell \leqslant b_j^\ell$. Then as before $\bar{z}_i \leqslant \bar{z}_j$. Together these imply that $\bar{z}_i > \bar{z}_j$, so this last assumption must be wrong and $b_i^\ell > b_j^\ell$. The proof of proposition (b) is similar. Q.E.D.

Theorem 5 guarantees that given the available set of assets the statement "security i has more systematic risk than security j" is unambiguous even if no efficient portfolio is specified. As a corollary to Theorem 5 all assets with expected returns equal to the riskless return have zero systematic risk with respect to all efficient portfolios.

THEOREM 6 *If assets i and j are efficient portfolios, then* $b_i^j > 0$. *That is, all efficient portfolios have positive systematic risk.*

Proof. From (48) $b_i^j = (\bar{z}_i - R)/(\bar{z}_j - R)$, and by Theorem 4 both numerator and denominator are positive. Q.E.D.

The results in Theorems 5 and 6 are similar to those obtained in the mean-variance problem with a riskless asset. There, however, the results were trivially true since all efficient portfolios were perfectly correlated. Here no such triviality exists.

If a riskless asset is not available, then we can use (24a) to obtain the pricing relation

$$\bar{z}_i - \bar{Z}_z^k = b_i^k(\bar{Z}_e^k - \bar{Z}_z^k). \tag{50}$$

$\bar{Z}_z^k$ denotes the expected return on a security with zero systematic risk with respect to the efficient portfolio k; that is, $b_z^k = 0$. (All such assets have the same expected return.) Just as in the mean-variance problem with no riskless asset, different efficient portfolios can have zero b portfolios with different expected returns.

SOME EXAMPLES

In two well-known and previously examined cases, the equilibrium condition in (48) simplifies to a CAPM-like relations. For quadratic utility $u'(\cdot)$ is linear in Z_e; hence, $b_i^k = \text{Cov}(\tilde{Z}_e^k, \tilde{z}_i)/\text{Var}(\tilde{Z}_e^k)$ is security i's beta with respect to efficient portfolio k. The other case is when all assets' returns are jointly normal. In this case $\tilde{Z}_e^k$ and $\tilde{z}_i$ are bivariate normal, so using Equation (62) of the Mathematical Introduction we see that b_i^k is again just the beta of security i with respect to portfolio k. In either case the CAPM results once it is established that the market portfolio is efficient.

For other distributional assumptions, except those examined in Chapter 4, it is generally difficult to simplify (46); however, simplification which leads to a testable relation is possible for some alternative utility assumption. For example, for isoelastic utility $u(Z) = Z^\gamma/\gamma$, so

$$b_i^k = \frac{\text{Cov}[\tilde{Z}_e^{\gamma-1}, \tilde{z}_i]}{\text{Cov}[\tilde{Z}_e^{\gamma-1}, \tilde{Z}_e]}, \tag{51}$$

and *if* the market portfolio is optimal for this utility function (see Chapter 6), we may be able to obtain an improved "CAPM" by estimating γ in a nonlinear regression. We would require isoelastic utility for a time series test because only then can utility of wealth always be renormalized to utility of return without changing its form.

As a final example consider the three-moment utility function example in Chapter 4. We had established the general first-order condition as

$$V_1(\bar{z}_i - \bar{Z}_e) + 2V_2(\sigma_{ie} - \sigma_e^2) + 3V_3(m_{iee} - m_e^3) = 0. \tag{52}$$

For the riskless asset $\bar{z}_0 = R$ and $\sigma_{0e} = m_{0ee} = 0$. Solving (52) gives

$$\frac{V_1}{V_3} = -\frac{2\sigma_e^2 V_2/V_3 + 3m_e^3}{\bar{Z}_e - R}. \tag{53}$$

Substituting this back into (52) gives

$$\begin{aligned} \bar{z}_i - \bar{Z}_e &= (\bar{Z}_e - R)\frac{2(V_2/V_3)(\sigma_{ie} - \sigma_e^2) + 3(m_{iee} - m_e^3)}{2(V_2/V_3)\sigma_e^2 + 3m_e^3}, \\ \bar{z}_i &= R + (\bar{Z}_e - R)\frac{2(V_2/V_3)\sigma_{ie} + 3m_{iee}}{2(V_2/V_3)\sigma_e^2 + 3m_e^3}. \end{aligned} \tag{54}$$

The final ratio in (54) must be interpreted as the general measure risk b_i.

To demonstrate this we use the only utility function for which analysis by the three moments is always valid—cubic utility,

$$u(Z) = aZ + bZ^2 + cZ^3. \tag{55}$$

Expanding expected utility in a Taylor's series gives

$$\begin{aligned} Eu(Z) &= u(\bar{Z}) + u'(\bar{Z})E(Z - \bar{Z}) + \tfrac{1}{2}u''(\bar{Z})E[(Z - \bar{Z})^2] \\ &\quad + \tfrac{1}{6}u'''(\bar{Z})E[(Z - \bar{Z})^3], \\ V(\bar{Z}, \sigma^2, m^3) &= a\bar{Z} + b(\sigma^2 + \bar{Z}^2) + c(m^3 + \bar{Z}^3 + 3\sigma^2\bar{Z}). \end{aligned} \tag{56}$$

Hence

$$V_1 = a + 2b\bar{Z} + 3c(\bar{Z}^2 + \sigma^2), \quad V_2 = b + 3c\bar{Z}, \quad V_3 = c. \tag{57}$$

The relative risk measure in (54) is then

$$\frac{(2b + 6c\bar{Z}_e)\sigma_{ie} + 3cm_{iee}}{(2b + 6c\bar{Z}_e)\sigma_e^2 + 3cm_e^3}. \tag{58}$$

For the general case in (48) we require

$$\begin{aligned} \mathrm{Cov}[u'(\tilde{Z}_e), \tilde{z}_i] &= \mathrm{Cov}[a + 2b\tilde{Z}_e + 3c\tilde{Z}_e^2, \tilde{z}_i] \\ &= 2b\sigma_{ie} + 3c\,\mathrm{Cov}(\tilde{Z}_e^2, \tilde{z}_i) \\ &= 2b\sigma_{ie} + 3c(m_{iee} + 2\bar{Z}_e\sigma_{ie}). \end{aligned} \tag{59}$$

Using (59) in the definition of b_i^k in (46), we derive

$$b_i^k = \frac{(2b + 6c\bar{Z}_e)\sigma_{ie} + 3cm_{iee}}{(2b + 6c\bar{Z}_e)\sigma_e^2 + 3cm_e^3}, \tag{60}$$

which is identical to (58).

Appendix: Stochastic Dominance

The concepts of first-order and second-order stochastic dominances were introduced in Chapter 3 and this chapter. In this appendix the properties of second-order strochastic dominance are explored further.

In Chapter 3 it was demonstrated that $\tilde{X}$ first-order stochastically dominated $\tilde{Y}$ if the cumulative distribution function of $\tilde{X}$ always lay below $\tilde{Y}$; that is,

$$F_X(t) \le G_Y(t) \tag{A1}$$

for all t in the domain $[a, b]$ of $\tilde{X}$ and $\tilde{Y}$. Similarly, second-order stochastic dominance obtains if and only if the cumulation of the cumulative distribution of $\tilde{X}$ always lies below that of $\tilde{Y}$; that is,

$$\int_a^t F(v)\,dv \le \int_a^t G(v)\,\mathrm{dv} \qquad \text{for all } t. \tag{A2}$$

To prove the sufficiency of this condition, define $\Delta(t) \equiv \int_a^t [G(v) - F(v)]\,dv$. Note from (A2) that $\Delta(t) \ge 0$ for all t in $[a, b]$ and $\Delta(a) = 0$. Now for any concave utility function, $u''(t)\Delta(t) < 0$, so

$$\begin{aligned} 0 &\ge \int_a^b u''(t)\Delta(t)\,\mathrm{dt} = \mathrm{u}'(t)\Delta(t)\Big|_a^b - \int_a^b u'(t)\Delta'(t)\,dt \\ &= [u'(t)\Delta(t) - u(t)\Delta'(t)]\Big|_a^b + \int_a^b u(t)\Delta''(t)\,dt \qquad \text{(A3)} \\ &= \{u'(t)\Delta(t) - u(t)[G(t) - F(t)]\}\Big|_a^b + \int_a^b u(t)[g(t) - f(t)]\,dt. \end{aligned}$$

Now $\Delta(a) = G(a) = F(a) = 0$ and $G(b) = F(b) = 1$, so

$$0 \ge u'(b)\Delta(b) + Eu(\tilde{Y}) - Eu(\tilde{X}). \tag{A4}$$

Because the first term is positive, the inequality can hold only if the expected utility of X exceeds that of Y. Note that this proof is valid only for twice differentiable utility functions. Proper limiting arguments can extend it for nondifferential but concave utilities.

To prove necessity, start with

$$0 \le \int_a^b u(t)[f(t) - g(t)]\,dt \tag{A5}$$

for all increasing concave u. Define the increasing concave function $m(t; s) \equiv \mathrm{Min}(t - s, 0)$. Also define

$$\begin{aligned} M(s) &\equiv \int_a^b m(t; s)[f(t) - g(t)]\,dt \\ &= \int_a^s (t - s)[f(t) - g(t)]\,dt \\ &= s[G(s) - F(s)] + \int_a^s t[f(t) - g(t)]\,dt. \end{aligned} \tag{A6}$$

From (A5), $M(s) \geq 0$ for all s. Integrating by parts gives

$$0 \leq s[G(s) - F(s)] + t[F(t) - G(t)]\Big|_a^s - \int_a^s [F(t) - G(t)]\,dt. \tag{A7}$$

The first term cancels the upper value of the second term. The lower value of the second term is zero because $F(a) = G(a) = 0$. Therefore,

$$0 \geq \int_a^s [F(t) - G(t)]\,dt, \tag{A8}$$

which is the same as (A2).

Nth-Order Stochastic Dominance

Nth-order order stochastic dominance is a further generalization which is applicable to all utility functions whose derivatives up through the Nth alternate in sign. (For example, third-order stochastic dominance covers the ranking of portfolios by risk-averse investors whose utility functions have a positive third derivative. This set includes only those with decreasing absolute risk aversion, the claimed relevant case.)

To discuss the higher-order stochastic dominance rules, we must define the repeated integrals of a probability distribution. (If the distribution is defined on an infinite or semi-infinite range, then the same analysis would hold, provided that the integrals in (A9) were defined. $F_n(Z)$, defined next, will exist for a distribution if and only if the first n moments of $\tilde{Z}$ exists.)

$$F(Z) \equiv F_0(Z) \equiv \int_a^Z f(t)\,dt, \qquad F_{n+1}(Z) \equiv \int_a^Z F_n(t)\,dt. \tag{A9}$$

Distribution F weakly stochastically dominates distribution G to the nth order if and only if

$$F_{n-1}(Z) \leqslant G_{n-1}(Z) \qquad \text{for all } a \leqslant Z \leqslant b, \tag{A10a}$$

$$F_k(b) \leqslant G_k(b) \qquad \text{for } k = 1, 2, \ldots, n - 2. \tag{A10b}$$

Furthermore, stochastic dominance rules of order n generate the complete set of efficient or optimal portfolios for all utility functions satisfying

$$(-1)^k u^{(k)}(Z) \leqslant 0 \qquad \text{for all } Z,\ k = 1, 2, \ldots, n. \tag{A11}$$

The stochastic dominance criteria above can also be expressed in terms of the lower partial moments of Z denoted by μ_n. Integrating by parts, we can rewrite the lower partial moment as

$$\begin{aligned}\mu_n(Z; F) \equiv \int_a^Z (Z-t)^n f(t)\,dt &= F(t)(Z-t)^n \Big|_a^Z \\ &\quad + n\int_a^Z (Z-t)^{n-1}F(t)\,dt \\ &= nF_1(t)(Z-t)^{n-1}\Big|_a^Z + n(n-1)\int_a^Z (Z-t)^{n-2}F_1(t)\,dt \\ &\ \ \vdots \\ &= n!\int_a^Z F_{n-1}(t)\,dt = n!F_n(Z).\end{aligned} \tag{A12}$$

In each step, the lead term is zero sinze $F_i(a) = 0$ and $(Z - Z)^i = 0$. Therefore (A7a), (A7b) can also be stated as

$$\mu_{n-1}(Z; F) \leqslant \mu_{n-1}(Z; G), \qquad a \leqslant Z \leqslant b, \tag{A13a}$$

$$\mu_k(b; F) \leqslant \mu_k(b; G), \qquad k = 1, 2, \ldots, n-2. \tag{A13b}$$

6

Portfolio Separation Theorems

In Chapter 5 we saw that the expected return on any asset could be written in terms of the interest rate, any investor's marginal utility function, and the joint probability distribution of the returns on the asset and this investor's optimal portfolio. Therefore, the pricing problem reduces to finding some efficient portfolio and the utility function associated with it. In particular, we will be interested in those cases when the market portfolio is efficient. One such case is already known to us from Chapter 4. Whenever mean-variance analysis is appropriate, the market portfolio is efficient, and the resulting equilibrium pricing can be expressed through the CAPM relation.

INEFFICIENCY OF THE MARKET PORTFOLIO: AN EXAMPLE

It might seem reasonable to expect that the market portfolio would always be an efficient combination. After all, in equilibrium, the market portfolio is just the wealth-weighted average of each investor's optimal portfolio, and all of these are efficient. Such reasoning would be correct if it were known that the set of efficient portfolios were convex. Unfortunately, such is not the case. The efficient set is not necessarily convex, as the following example proves. Suppose that three assets are available to investors and that they have the following pattern of returns:

Asset:		1	2	3	Portfolio: $(\frac{1}{2}, 0, \frac{1}{2})$	$(\frac{1}{4}, \frac{1}{2}, \frac{1}{4})$	$(-.5, -.4, 1.9)$	
State:	a	1.50	2.05	1.80	1.65	1.85	1.85	
	b	1.00	1.30	1.20	1.10	1.20	1.26	(1)
	c	1.40	0.95	1.20	1.30	1.125	1.20	
	d	1.30	1.25	1.20	1.25	1.25	1.13	

Any portfolio of these three assets may be held. The patterns of returns on three portfolios which we shall need are also given. The probability of each of the outcome states is $\frac{1}{4}$.

Consider two different investors possessing utility functions with the following properties:

$$u_1'(1.65) = 1 < u_1'(1.30) = 40 < u_1'(1.25) = 59 < u_1'(1.10) = 68, \tag{2a}$$

$$u_2'(2.05) = 21 < u_2'(1.30) = 28 < u_2'(1.25) = 39 < u_2'(0.95) = 40. \tag{2b}$$

Many utility functions satisfying (2a) or (2b) are possible because in both cases marginal utility meets the only two requirements—that it be positive and decreasing.

In the absence of a riskless asset, the criterion for an optimal portfolio for investor k, from Equation (26a) in Chapter 5

$$E[u_k'(Z^k)\tilde{z}_i] \equiv \sum_s \pi_s u_k'(Z_s^k)Z_{si} = \lambda_k \qquad \text{for } i = 1, 2, 3. \tag{3}$$

The first investor will optimally choose to hold the portfolio (.5, 0, .5) since

$$\begin{aligned} \tfrac{1}{4}(1.50 \times 1 + 1.00 \times 68 + 1.40 \times 40 + 1.30 \times 59) &= 50.55, \\ \tfrac{1}{4}(2.05 \times 1 + 1.30 \times 68 + 0.95 \times 40 + 1.25 \times 59) &= 50.55, \\ \tfrac{1}{4}(1.80 \times 1 + 1.20 \times 68 + 1.20 \times 40 + 1.20 \times 59) &= 50.55. \end{aligned} \tag{4}$$

Similarly, the second investor will choose the portfolio (0, 1, 0) since

$$\begin{aligned} \tfrac{1}{4}(1.50 \times 21 + 1.00 \times 28 + 1.40 \times 40 + 1.30 \times 39) &= 41.55, \\ \tfrac{1}{4}(2.05 \times 21 + 1.30 \times 28 + 0.95 \times 40 + 1.25 \times 39) &= 41.55, \\ \tfrac{1}{4}(1.80 \times 21 + 1.20 \times 28 + 1.20 \times 40 + 1.20 \times 39) &= 41.55. \end{aligned} \tag{5}$$

We now pose the question: Is the portfolio (.25, .5, .25), which is an equal mixture of these two investors' efficient portfolios, efficient as well? If it is not, then we have demonstrated that the efficient set is not convex. Furthermore, since these two investors could be alone in the market, we would have also proved that the market portfolio is not necessarily efficient.

The answer to the question posed is no. We could prove this by examining permitted orderings as in Chapter 5; however, we first choose the simpler and more direct method of finding a better portfolio. The portfolio (.25, .5, .25) is not efficient because it has a lower expected utility than the portfolio (−.5, −.4, 1.9) to any investor who prefers more to less. This is easily demonstrated by comparing the expected utility of these two portfolios:

$$\tfrac{1}{4}[u(1.85) + u(1.20) + u(1.125) + u(1.25)], \tag{6a}$$

$$\tfrac{1}{4}[u(1.85) + u(1.26) + u(1.20) + u(1.13)]. \tag{6b}$$

For any increasing u, the quantity in (6a) is smaller because its first two terms are equal to the first and third terms of (6b) and its third and fourth terms are smaller than the fourth and second terms in (6b).

Figure 6.1 demonstrates explicitly the nonconvexity of the efficient set.

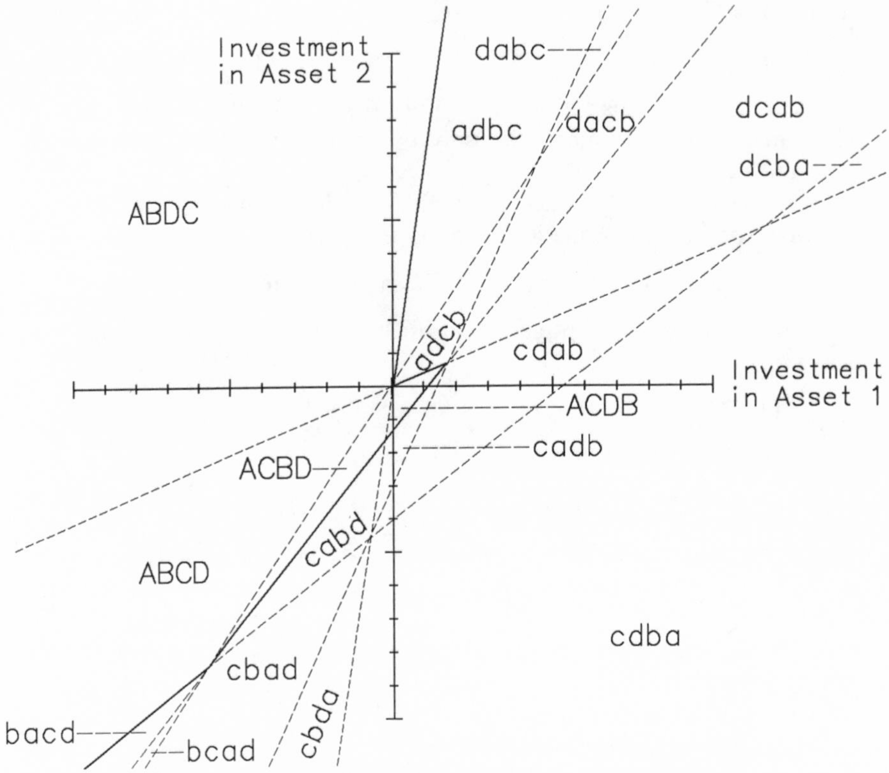

Figure 6.1 Example of Non-Convexity of Efficient Set

Each point (w_1, w_2) represents a feasible portfolio. Furthermore, since w_3 is pegged by the budget constraint, all portfolios are represented. Shown in the figure are the 18 possible portfolio types, as indicated by their ordered (from high to low) state returns. (The six unlisted permutations are not possible to achieve with feasible portfolios.)

The regions indicated by capital letters correspond to efficient portfolios. As already stated, the portfolio (0, 1, 0) is optimal for the utility function with the properties in (6b). Its returns are ordered *ABDC* from high to low. The portfolio (.5, 0, .5) is also efficient, and it lies in *ACDB*.

The portfolio (−.5, −.4, 1.9) is in the region *ABCD* and therefore must be efficient if the figure is correct. We do know that it dominates the portfolio (.25, .5, .25), but this is insufficient to prove that it is efficient. To do this, we must find an appropriate utility function. One such would be that characterized by

$$\begin{aligned} u'(1.85) &= .107 < u'(1.26) = .195 \\ &< u'(1.20) = .234 < u'(1.13) = .244. \end{aligned} \tag{7}$$

Marginal utility is positive and decreasing, and the first-order condition of optimality (Equation (26a) of Chapter 5) is satisfied for each asset:

$$\tfrac{1}{4}(1.50 \times .107 + 1.00 \times .195 + 1.4 \times .234 + 1.3 \times .244) = .250,$$
$$\tfrac{1}{4}(2.05 \times .107 + 1.30 \times .195 + 0.95 \times .234 + 1.25 \times .244) = .250, \quad (8)$$
$$\tfrac{1}{4}(1.80 \times .107 + 1.20 \times .195 + 1.20 \times .234 + 1.20 \times .244) = .250.$$

Similarly, the region *ACDB* is supported by the marginal utilities .079, .234, .224, .257 (among other values).

Many portfolios in the regions *adbc* and *adcb* are convex portfolio combinations of efficient portfolios lying in the regions *ABDC* and *ACDB*. All of them are inefficient, however, just as (.25, .5, .25) in the region *adbc* is.

This example shows that nonconvexity of the efficient set does not depend on risk aversion, since nowhere was it assumed that u was concave. Nonconvexity does, however, require strict monotonicity, a strict preference of more to less. Without strict monotonicity a constant utility function would be permitted and would be indifferent among all portfolios, so the efficient set would be the entire space of portfolios.

Although we worked in the context of a perfect market and with an unrestricted state space tableau, these assumptions were not crucial. The specific counterexample does satisfy the two often-imposed conditions of limited liability, $Z_{si} \geq 0$, and no bankruptcy, $\Sigma Z_{si} w_i^* > 0$. It does not meet the no-short-sales constraint; however, it could be suitably modified to do so.

The foregoing example is of minimal complexity. With just two assets the feasible set can be described by a single parameter (for example, w_1 or, if $\bar{z}_1 \neq \bar{z}_2$, $\bar{Z}_p$). Using mean-variance analysis, which is always valid for the case of two assets with different means, we have seen in Chapter 4 that the efficient set includes all portfolios satisfying $\bar{Z}_p \geq \bar{Z}_p^*$ for some $\bar{Z}_p^*$. These portfolios are those with $w_1 \geq w_1^*$ (if $\bar{z}_1 > \bar{z}_2$) or $w_1 \leq w_1^*$ (if $\bar{z}_1 < \bar{z}_2$). A set of this type is obviously convex. Therefore, at least three assets are required for the efficient set not to be convex. Furthermore, as we shall see in Chapter 8, there must be fewer assets than states for the market portfolio to be inefficient.

MUTUAL FUND THEOREMS

One way to limit the search for efficient portfolios is to prove that each investor's optimal portfolio is a combination of a few distinct "service" portfolios which are common to all investors. Such results are known as portfolio separation or mutual fund theorems. If N assets are available, then, with no short sales restriction, the set of feasible portfolio weights is the N-dimensional Euclidean space R^N. Each feasible portfolio is a vector in this space. A "k-fund" portfolio separation theorem indicates that the set of optimal portfolio weight vectors lies completely within a k-dimensional subspace of R^N. It should be obvious that k unique mutual funds cannot be specified, but that any k portfolios which span this subspace are acceptable. This was demonstrated in the mean-variance problem in which any two efficient portfolios traced out the entire efficient set.

If a riskless asset is available, it is often convenient to take it as one of the k mutual funds. This is always permissible whenever the problem includes investors with unboundedly large risk aversion because the riskless asset being optimal for such investors must then be in the efficient set. It can then be specified as one of the k mutual funds, and the other $k - 1$ can be made from the risky assets only. One economy in which this is not possible but separation does obtain is described in the last section of this chapter.

In an economy with K investors and N assets it is obvious that no more than $\min(K, N)$ mutual funds are required to form each (existing) investor's optimal portfolio. Such a theorem, however, is of no importance. To get nontrivial results, we must restrict the problem under consideration. There are three approaches which could be used: (1) restrict attention to some class of utility functions smaller than the increasing concave class; (2) restrict the class of returns distributions; (3) make restrictions of both types simultaneously.

Strictly speaking, only the third case could be fruitful since we always must impose some restrictions on both tastes and distributions to ensure against generalized paradoxes of the St. Petersburg type. However, if the only restrictions on tastes or returns required are those which ensure that expected utility is finite, we shall refer to these as cases 2 and 1, respectively. With this redefinition case 2 is closed. Both the necessary and sufficient conditions for distributional-based separation theorems are known. The necessary and sufficient conditions are also known for one- and two-fund taste-based separation theorems, and some necessary conditions are known for greater fund theorems. In the mixed case some results are known when a riskless asset is available and is one of the mutual funds or when the states of outcomes are completely spanned by asset returns. Each of these cases is discussed here.

It should be noted that, for $k > 2$, portfolio separation theorems, although limiting the efficient set, do not necessarily guarantee its convexity or, therefore, the efficiency of the market portfolio. This should be obvious from the previous example if we interpret the three securities there as the three mutual funds used by all investors.

As we shall see, the classes of utility functions which admit to mutual fund theorems are the same classes which permit individual utility functions to be combined into a meaningful aggregate utility function. We discuss the requirements for one-, two-, and k-fund separation both with and without a riskless asset. Throughout this chapter we are concerned only with the single-period portfolio problem, so we use only the utility function defined over returns, which was introduced in Chapter 3.

ONE-FUND SEPARATION UNDER RESTRICTIONS ON UTILITY

The necessary and sufficient condition for one-fund separation is that all investors have the same utility of return function up to a positive linear transformation. The sufficiency of this condition is obvious. That it is also necessary can be seen from the first-order condition of Equation (1) in Chapter 3. We require that $E[u_k'(\cdot)\tilde{Z}_i] = \lambda_k$ for all possible asset descriptions. If we consider the cases when the various assets have payoffs which are Dirac delta function, it is clear that for any two investors there must exist a constant γ_{kj} such that $u_k'(\cdot) = \gamma_{kj}u_j'(\cdot)$. Integrating once now gives the necessary condition.

In equilibrium this single mutual fund must be the market portfolio. Thus, the market portfolio is efficient, and the equilibrium pricing of the assets is given by Equations (50) and (52) of Chapter 5, where Z_e is the return on the market portfolio and $u(\cdot)$ is the common utility function.

TWO-FUND SEPARATION UNDER RESTRICTIONS ON UTILITY

As before, it is obvious that a sufficient condition for two-fund separation is that all investors have one of two utility functions up to positive linear transformations. In this case each investor will hold the portfolio optimal for either one or the other of the utility functions. No investor will hold a portfolio mix of these two.

The only known class of utility functions that permits two-fund separation for general markets of assets and which is not degenerate as previously described, but admits to mixtures of the two funds, is the quadratic class. This case was examined in Chapter 4 by mean-variance analysis. Other classes of utility functions do admit separation, however, if we assume the existence of a riskless asset that is used as one of the two separating mutual funds. This type of separation is often called "money separation." As we indicated earlier, this restriction can be imposed with no loss of generality so long as the classes of utility functions under consideration include those with infinite risk aversion.

From Equation (27) of Chapter 5 the optimal portfolio weights of the kth investor satisfy

$$E\left[u_k'\left(\sum_0^N w_{ik}\tilde{z}_i\right)(\tilde{z}_i - R)\right] = 0, \qquad i = 1, \ldots, n. \tag{9}$$

Since the riskless asset is one of the two mutual funds, the other need only include risky assets. Therefore, we wish to determine the classes of utility functions for which w_{ik}/w_{jk} $(i, j \neq 0)$ is the same for all investors. We will demonstrate that a sufficient condition for this result is that each investor's utility function satisfies

$$u_k'(Z) = (A_k + B_k Z)^{-c}. \tag{10}$$

The parameter c must be the same for all investors; A and B may vary. For concave utility c and B must have the same sign. Equation (10) includes $\exp(-\delta_k Z)$ as the limiting case when $A_k = 1$, $B_k = \delta_k/c$, as $c \to -\infty$.

To demonstrate this separation proposition, substitute (10) into (9) to obtain

$$E\left[\left(A_k + B_k \sum_{i=0}^n w_{ik}\tilde{z}_i\right)^{-c}(\tilde{z}_i - R)\right] = 0, \qquad i = 1, \ldots, N. \tag{11}$$

Now let us first examine the case when $A_k \equiv 0$. The first-order condition in (11) reduces to

$$B_k^{-c}E\left[\left(\sum_{i=0}^n w_{ik}\tilde{z}_i\right)^{-c}(\tilde{z}_i - R)\right] = 0, \qquad i = 1, \ldots, N. \tag{12}$$

It is obvious that the solution w_i^* to (12) is independent of B_k; that is, the same portfolio is chosen by each investor.

In the general case suppose that the investor first places an arbitrarily chosen fraction $1 - a_k$ of wealth in the riskless asset and then optimally invests the remaining fraction a_k of wealth in a portfolio of the risky and the riskless assets. Denote this last portfolio by α_0 and $\boldsymbol{\alpha}$, with $\Sigma_{i=0}^n \alpha_i = 1$. There is no loss of generality in this arbitrary division of the portfolio selection task since the riskless asset is included in the second, optimally selected, portfolio. The final portfolio weights are

$$w_{0k} = 1 - a_k + a_k\alpha_{0k}, \qquad w_{ik} = a_k\alpha_{ik}. \tag{13}$$

Now set the arbitrary constant $a_k = 1 + A_k/RB_k$. Substituting these portfolio weights into (11) gives

$$(B_k a_k)^{-c}E[(\Sigma\alpha_{ik}\tilde{z}_i)^{-c}(\tilde{z}_i - R)] = 0, \qquad i > 0. \tag{12'}$$

Equation (12′) is identical in form to (12), so the same result obtains and $\alpha_{ik} = \alpha_i$. The same constant for all investors with the same utility parameter c will satisfy (12′) and the portfolio summation constraint (both in terms of the α's and w's). Furthermore, for the risky assets $w_{ik} = \alpha_i a_k$, so

$$\frac{w_{ik}}{w_{jk}} = \frac{\alpha_i}{\alpha_j} \tag{14}$$

for all investors, and the desired result obtains.

The single-period marginal utility of wealth function associated with $u'(Z)$ is $U'(W) = (A_k + B_k W/W_0)^{-c}$. Integrating once and expressing the result in simplest form gives

$$\frac{(W - \hat{W}_k)^\gamma}{\gamma}, \qquad \gamma < 1, \tag{15a}$$

$$\frac{-(\hat{W}_k - W)^\gamma}{\gamma}, \qquad \gamma > 1, \tag{15b}$$

$$\ln(W - \hat{W}_k), \tag{15c}$$

$$-\exp(-\delta_k W). \tag{15d}$$

In (15a) and (15b) $\gamma = 1 - c$ and $\hat{W}_k = -W_{0k}A_k/B_k$. Log utility (15c) corresponds to $c = 1\,(\gamma = 0)$ and exponential utility (15d) to $c = -\infty$. (These functions are, of course, just the HARA or linear risk-tolerance utility functions of Chapter 1.) For $\gamma < 1$, $\hat{W}_k$ can be interpreted as the subsistence level of wealth minus any exogenous riskless income available to investor k at the end of the period from sources other than these assets. In these cases, if $W = \hat{W}_k$, marginal utility is infinite. Obviously, expected utility maximimization will require a portfolio which avoids $W \leqslant \hat{W}_k$ with certainty. For $\gamma > 1$, $\hat{W}_k$ is the satiation level of wealth, at which point marginal utility is zero. Beyond this point utility is either decreasing or convex, so we must confine our attention to the region $W \leqslant \hat{W}_k$.

Combining (12), (15a), (15c), and the definitions of $\hat{W}_k$ and a_k, we can write the dollar demand for the risky assets as

$$w_{ik}W_{0k} = \alpha_i\left(W_{0k} - \frac{\hat{W}_k}{R}\right), \qquad w_{0k}W_{0k} = \frac{\hat{W}_k}{R} + \alpha_0\left(W_{0k} - \hat{W}_k R\right). \tag{16}$$

Investors first place the present value of their subsistence level of wealth in the riskless asset and then divide their remaining wealth among all the assets, including the riskless one, in the proportions α_i. The portfolio represented by the vector of weights α_i is the optimal one for an investor with power utility $u(Z) = Z^\gamma/\gamma$.

For utility functions with $\gamma > 1$ demand for the assets is also linear in wealth as given in (16). In this case however the portfolio α_i represents the utility *minimizing* portfolio for the convex utility function Z^γ/γ. The investor's wealth must be bounded below the level of satiation, so the term in parenthesis must be negative. Therefore the investor takes a short position in this utility minimizing portfolio.

For exponential utility (15d) the demand functions are

$$w_{ik}W_{0k} = \frac{\alpha_i}{\delta_k}, \qquad w_{0k}W_{0k} = \frac{\alpha_0}{\delta_k} + \frac{\delta_k W_{0k} - 1}{\delta_k}, \tag{17}$$

so investors have a constant demand for the risky assets. The portfolio weights α_i represent the portfolio chosen by investors with absolute risk aversion equal to the reciprocal of their wealth, $U(W) = -\exp(-W/W_0)$, that is, an investor with unitary risk aversion over returns, $u(Z) = -\exp(-Z)$.

MARKET EQUILIBRIUM UNDER TWO-FUND, MONEY SEPARATION

For simplicity we assume that the rickless asset is in zero net supply throughout this section; that is, the riskless asset is borrowing or lending between investors. For the generalized power utility case we call the ratio $\hat{W}_k/W_{0k} \equiv d_k$ investor k's defensive ratio. It is clear from (16) that as this ratio is varied from $-\infty$ to ∞ all possible levels of lending from $w_0 = -\infty$ to ∞ (∞ to $-\infty$ if $\alpha_0 > 1$) will be possible. Thus, there is some value d_m for which $w_0 = 0$. We deem this value the "market's defensive ratio", since an investor with $d_k = d_m$ neither borrows nor lends but holds only the optimal portfolio of risky assets. Furthermore, since all investors have the same cautiousness, γ, and beliefs, in equilibrium all have the same optimal portfolio of risky assets, so this "average investor" must hold the market portfolio. We have now identified the efficient portfolio of one investor, so from Equation (52) in Chapter 5 we can write the equilibrium condition

$$\bar{z}_i - R = (\bar{Z}_m - R)\frac{\operatorname{Cov}[(\tilde{Z}_m - d_m)^{\gamma-1}, \tilde{z}_i]}{\operatorname{Cov}[(\tilde{Z}_m - d_m)^{\gamma-1}, \tilde{Z}_m]}. \tag{18}$$

The parameter d_m could be determined from a knowledge of d_k for all investors and the investment opportunities. (See Chapter 9 for details.) However, since the former are unobservable, we can, if we choose, simply view it as a parameter of the equilibrium relation which is to be determined empirically.

For exponential utility the quantity $\delta_k W_{0k}$ is crucial. It is obvious from (17) that two investors with different wealth and risk aversion, but with the product of the two and the same, will borrow or lend the same fraction of their wealth. We call this product d_k. As d_k varies from zero to ∞, all levels of lending will be possible. The value of d_k for which $w_{0k} = 0$ will define "the average investor," who, as before, holds the market portfolio in equilibrium. If we denote this value by d_m, then market equilibrium is given by

$$\bar{z}_i - R = (\bar{Z}_m - R)\frac{\text{Cov}[\exp(-d_m\tilde{Z}_m),\ \tilde{z}_i]}{\text{Cov}[\exp(-d_m\tilde{Z}_m),\ \tilde{Z}_m]}. \tag{19}$$

SOLVING A SPECIFIC PROBLEM

Suppose there are three equally likely outcome states and three assets with returns

asset:		0	1	2
	a	1	4	0
outcome:	b	1	0	5
	c	1	0	0

(20)

The first-order conditions (Equation (25) in Chapter 5) are

$$\begin{aligned} 3u'(w_0 + 4w_1) - u'(w_0 + 5w_2) - u'(w_0) &= 0, \\ -u'(w_0 + 4w_1) + 4u'(w_0 + 5w_2) - u'(w_0) &= 0. \end{aligned} \tag{21}$$

Solving (21) for the first two marginal utilities gives

$$u'(w_0 + 4w_1) = \frac{5u'(w_0)}{11}, \qquad u'(w_0 + 5w_2) = \frac{4u'(w_0)}{11}. \tag{22}$$

For generalized power utility $u'(Z) = (A + Z)^b$ the risky asset holdings are

$$\begin{aligned} w_1 &= (A + w_0)\frac{(5/11)^{1/b} - 1}{4}, \\ w_2 &= (A + w_0)\frac{(4/11)^{1/b} - 1}{5}, \end{aligned} \tag{23}$$

For generalized logarithmic utility, $b = -1$, $w_1 = 0.3(A + w_0)$, and $w_2 = 0.35(A + w_0)$, so $w_1/w_2 = \frac{6}{7}$ regardless of the value of A. For generalized square root utility, $b = -\frac{1}{2}$, $w_1 = 0.96(A + w_0)$ and $w_2 = 1.3125(A + w_0)$, so $w_1/w_2 \approx 1.37$.

DISTRIBUTIONAL ASSUMPTIONS PERMITTING ONE-FUND SEPARATION

One obvious case in which one-fund separation occurs is when all asset returns are independent and identically distributed. In this case, the optimal portfolio will be an equal investment in each asset. This is not the only distribution permitting separation, however. The necessary and sufficient conditions for one-fund separation among risk-averse investors are that asset returns are described by

$$\tilde{z}_i = \tilde{Y} + \tilde{\varepsilon}_i, \tag{24a}$$

$$E[\tilde{\varepsilon}_i | Y] = 0 \qquad \text{all } i, \tag{24b}$$

$$\sum w_i^m \tilde{\varepsilon}_i \equiv 0 \tag{24c}$$

for some set of w_i^m with $\Sigma w_i^m = 1$. The optimal portfolio for all investors holds the fraction w_i^m in asset i. Note that from (24b) all assets and portfolio have the same expected return.

We can verify the sufficiency of (24) by showing that this portfolio weakly (second-degree) stochastically dominates any other. From (24c) it has a return

$$\tilde{Z}_m = \sum w_i^m \tilde{Y} + \sum w_i^m \tilde{\varepsilon}_{\text{i}} = \tilde{\text{Y}}. \tag{25}$$

Any other portfolio has a return $\tilde{Z} = \tilde{Y} + \tilde{\varepsilon}$, where $\tilde{\varepsilon}$ is a weighted average of the individual risks. Using (24b) gives

$$E[\tilde{\varepsilon} | Z_m] = \sum w_i E[\tilde{\varepsilon}_i | Y] = 0, \tag{26}$$

so this portfolio is riskier than portfolio m and has the same mean return. Therefore it is stochastically dominated.

The necessity of (24) follows from the property of fair games established in the Mathematical Introduction. Let $\tilde{Z}$ denote the return on the assumed unique optimal portfolio. Without loss of generality we can write the return on any asset as

$$\tilde{z}_i = \tilde{Z} + \tilde{e}_i, \tag{27}$$

where $\tilde{e}_i$ is unspecified. The first property to be verified is that $E(\tilde{e}_j) = 0$. This must be true, because if it were not, some assets would have different expected returns and some, indeed "most," investors would hold different portfolios trading off risk and mean return. (We have verified this for investors with quadratic utility in Chapter 4, and one example is all we require here.)

From Equation in Chapter 5 $E[u'(\tilde{Z})\tilde{z}_i] = \lambda$ for all assets, including the optimal portfolio, so

$$\begin{aligned} 0 &= E[u'(\tilde{Z})(\tilde{z}_i - \tilde{Z})] = E[u'(\tilde{Z})\tilde{e}_i] \\ &= \text{Cov}[u'(\tilde{Z}), \tilde{e}_i]. \end{aligned} \tag{28}$$

The final equality follows from the definition of covariance and $\tilde{e}_i$'s zero mean. Since $\tilde{Z}$ was assumed universally optimal, (28) holds for all positive, decreasing functions $u'(\cdot)$. As shown in the Mathematical Introduction this requires that $E[\tilde{e}_i | \tilde{Z}] = 0$, verifying (24a) and (24b). Finally, the portfolio $\tilde{Z}$ has no residual risk, so (24c) is needed as well.

Once (27) and $E(\tilde{e}_i) = 0$ have been established, there might appear to be a simpler proof of (24b) than that just given. One might like to argue that $\tilde{Z}$ and $\tilde{z}_i$ have the same mean, but the former is universally preferred, that is, less risky, so from Theorem 2 in Chapter 5 we must have $E(\tilde{e}_i|Z) = 0$. The fault with this proof is that Theorem 2 would only require $\tilde{z}_i$ to be distributed like $\tilde{Z}$ plus noise, whereas here we wish to show that it is equal to $\tilde{Z}$ plus noise. So this "proof" using Theorem 2 would not preclude an asset with $\tilde{e}_i = \tilde{Z} - \bar{Z}$. Clearly, $E[\tilde{e}_i|Z] \neq 0$, even though $\tilde{z}_i$ is riskier than $\tilde{Z}$.

Equilibrium under this type of separation is a relatively simple matter. The universally optimal portfolio must be the market. Because all assets have the same expected return, $\bar{z}_i = \bar{Z}_m$.

At the beginning of this section it was stated that a set of N assets whose returns were independent and identically distributed would display one-fund separation with optimal portfolio $w_i^m = 1/N$. Since it is not obvious that i.i.d. random returns can be written as in (24), this is now demonstrated as a part of an example of one-fund separation.

Assume that the returns $\tilde{z}_i$ are i.i.d. Define $\tilde{Y} \equiv \Sigma \tilde{z}_i/N$ and $\tilde{\varepsilon}_i \equiv \tilde{z}_i - \tilde{Y}$. Properties (24a) and (24c) are satisfied by construction, so only (24b) remains to be proved. Since returns are identically distributed, $E(\tilde{\varepsilon}_i|Y) = k(Y)$ independent of i.

Thus,

$$k(Y) = \frac{1}{N}\Sigma E(\tilde{\varepsilon}_i|Y) = \frac{1}{N}\Sigma E(\tilde{z}_i - \tilde{Y}|Y)$$
$$= E\left[\frac{1}{N}\Sigma \tilde{z}_i - \tilde{Y}|Y\right] = E(\check{Y} - \tilde{Y}|Y) = 0. \quad (29)$$

DISTRIBUTIONAL ASSUMPTION PERMITTING TWO-FUND, MONEY SEPARATION

It is well known that all investors will hold the same portfolio of risky assets, levered up or down, when faced with a multivariate normal investment opportunity set. Tobin conjectured that "any 'two parameter' family" of distribution would also possess this property. This, however, was easily proved false by counterexample. On the other hand, the elliptical distributions of Chapter 4 also permit separation, so normality is not required, as claimed by Cass and Stiglitz. Even this extended characterization is incomplete, however.

A complete description of all possible distributions permitting two-fund, money separation is that there exist b_i, w_i^m, $\tilde{Y}$, and $\tilde{\varepsilon}_i$ such that returns satisfy

$$\tilde{z}_i = R + b_i\tilde{Y} + \tilde{\varepsilon}_i, \quad (30a)$$

$$E(\tilde{\varepsilon}_i | Y) = 0 \qquad \text{all } i, \tag{30b}$$

$$\sum w_i^m \tilde{\varepsilon}_i \equiv 0, \tag{30c}$$

$$\sum w_i^m = 1. \tag{30d}$$

w_i^m are the weights of the universally optimal risky-asset-only portfolio that all investors combine with the riskless asset. Until we verify this, however, we shall call it the residual risk-free portfolio to avoid confusion. For the riskless asset, of course, $b_0 = 0$, $\tilde{\varepsilon}_0 \equiv 0$.

The proof that (30) is sufficient for separation is straightforward. Let $\boldsymbol{\mu}' \equiv (0, w_1^m, \ldots, w_N^m)$ be the augmented row vector of the residual risk-free portfolio's weights, $\mathbf{b}' \equiv (0, b_1, \ldots, b_N)$ be the row vector of b coefficients, $\mathbf{w}$ be the vector of optimal weights for utility function u, and λ be the ratio of the systematic risks of the portfolios $\mathbf{w}$ and $\boldsymbol{\mu}$; that is, $\lambda \equiv \mathbf{w}'b/\boldsymbol{\mu}'\mathbf{b}$.

The portfolio $\mathbf{w}$ can be broken into three parts: investment in the residual-risk-free portfolio, borrowing or lending to achieve the desired leverage, and a residual arbitrage or zero-investment portfolio $\boldsymbol{\omega}$:

$$\mathbf{w} = \lambda\boldsymbol{\mu} + (1 - \lambda, 0, 0, \ldots, 0)' + \boldsymbol{\omega}. \tag{31}$$

$\boldsymbol{\omega}$ is an arbitrage portfolio since $\mathbf{1}'\boldsymbol{\omega} = \mathbf{1}'\mathbf{w} - \lambda\mathbf{1}'\boldsymbol{\mu} - (1 - \lambda) = 1 - \lambda - (1 - \lambda) = 0$, and it has no systematic risk because $\boldsymbol{\omega}'\mathbf{b} = \mathbf{w}'\mathbf{b} - \lambda\boldsymbol{\mu}'\mathbf{b} = 0$.

Now

$$\begin{aligned} E[\boldsymbol{\omega}'\tilde{\mathbf{z}} | \lambda\boldsymbol{\mu}'\tilde{\mathbf{z}} + (1 - \lambda)R] &= E[\boldsymbol{\omega}'\mathbf{b}\tilde{Y} + \boldsymbol{\omega}'\tilde{\boldsymbol{\varepsilon}} | \lambda\boldsymbol{\mu}'\mathbf{b}Y + \lambda\boldsymbol{\mu}'\boldsymbol{\varepsilon} + R] \\ &= E[\boldsymbol{\omega}'\tilde{\boldsymbol{\varepsilon}} | \lambda b_m Y + R] = 0. \end{aligned} \tag{32}$$

The first equality in (32) follows by the substitution of (30a) and $\boldsymbol{\omega}'\mathbf{1} = 0$. The second equality follows by (30c), the definition $b_m \equiv \boldsymbol{\mu}'\mathbf{b}$, and $\boldsymbol{\omega}'\mathbf{b} = 0$ from (31). The final equality follows from (30b).

Now the return on the presumed optimal portfolio is

$$\mathbf{w}'\tilde{\mathbf{z}} = [\lambda\boldsymbol{\mu}'\tilde{\mathbf{z}} + (1 - \lambda)R] + \boldsymbol{\omega}'\tilde{\mathbf{z}}. \tag{33}$$

But from (32) and Theorem 2 in Chapter 5, this "optimal" portfolio has the same mean and is weakly riskier in a Rothschild–Stiglitz sense than the portfolio $\lambda\boldsymbol{\mu}'\tilde{\mathbf{z}} + (1 - \lambda)R$. Unless $\boldsymbol{\omega} = \mathbf{0}$ the first portfolio is strictly riskier, so all risk averters prefer the latter. This contradicts the assumption that $\mathbf{w}$ is an optimal portfolio. But if $\boldsymbol{\omega} = \mathbf{0}$, then $\mathbf{w}$ is a combination of the residual risk-free portfolio and the riskless asset. Thus, separation has been proved.

The proof that the conditions in (30) are also necessary for separation goes as follows. If all possible investors display separation in their portfolio decisions holding combinations of the portfolio $\mathbf{w}$ and the riskless asset, then for each utility function u and portfolio $\mathbf{w}$ there must exist a λ such that

$$E[u(\lambda\boldsymbol{\mu}'\tilde{\mathbf{z}} + (1 - \lambda)R)] \geqslant E[u(\mathbf{w}'\tilde{\mathbf{z}})]. \tag{34}$$

Define $\tilde{q} \equiv \lambda\boldsymbol{\mu}'\tilde{\mathbf{z}} + (1 - \lambda)R \equiv \lambda\tilde{Z}_m + (1 - \lambda)R$. Then the value of λ which maximizes expected utility [and a fortiori satisfies (34)] is given by the first-order condition

$$E[u'(\tilde{q})(\tilde{Z}_m - R)] = 0. \tag{35}$$

The general first-order condition, given that $\tilde{q}$ is the optimal return, is, from Chapter 5,

$$E[u'(\tilde{q})(\tilde{z}_i - R)] = 0 \qquad \text{all } i. \tag{36}$$

For separation to the universally optimal as assumed, (35) must imply (36). Now without loss of generality we can write

$$\tilde{z}_i = R + \delta_i(\tilde{Z}_m - R) + \tilde{\varepsilon}_i, \tag{37}$$

with $E(\tilde{\varepsilon}_i) = 0$, by setting $\delta_i = (\bar{z}_i - R)/(\bar{Z}_m - R)$, provided we place no other restrictions on the $\tilde{\varepsilon}_i$. Clearly, $\tilde{\varepsilon}_m \equiv 0$, so (30c) is satisfied. Define $\tilde{Y} \equiv (\tilde{Z}_m - R)/b_m$ and $b_i \equiv b_m\delta_i$; then (37) is identical to (30a). To see that (30b) is also required, substitute (37) into (36) and use (35) to derive

$$\begin{aligned} 0 &= E[u'(\tilde{q})[\delta_i(\tilde{Z}_m - R) + \tilde{\varepsilon}_i]] \\ &= E[u'(\tilde{q})\delta_i(\tilde{Z}_m - R)] + E[u'(\tilde{q})\tilde{\varepsilon}_i] = E[u'(\tilde{q})\tilde{\varepsilon}_i], \\ 0 &= E[f(\tilde{Y})\tilde{\varepsilon}_i] \qquad \text{for all } f(\cdot), \text{ with } f' < 0 \text{ and } f > 0. \end{aligned} \tag{38}$$

The second line in (38) follows from (35). The third line follows from the definitions of $\tilde{q} \equiv R + \lambda b_m\tilde{Y}$ and $f(\tilde{Y}) \equiv u'(\tilde{q})$. The last line in (38) guarantees that $E(\tilde{\varepsilon}_i|Y) = 0$, as was demonstrated in the Mathematical Introduction. This completes the proof.

EQUILIBRIUM UNDER TWO-FUND, MONEY SEPARATION

We assume that $\bar{Y} \neq 0$. If it did, then $\bar{z}_i = R$ for all assets, and there is nothing to explain. Also, in this case two-fund separation is degenerate with all investors holding just the riskless asset.

If the riskless asset is in zero net supply, then just as in the mean-variance problem the optimal combination of risky assets must be the market portfolio in equilibrium. The equilibrium condition for the individual assets is also the same as in the CAPM.

From (29), $\overline{z}_i = R + b_i\overline{Y}$ and $\overline{Z}_m = R + b_m\overline{Y}$. Combining these results to eliminate $\overline{Y}$ gives

$$\overline{z}_i = R\frac{b_i}{b_m}(\overline{Z}_m - R). \tag{39}$$

If the variance of $\tilde{Y}$ exists, then the ratio of b's in (39) is the standard beta coefficient. From (30a) and (30b) $\tilde{Z}_m = R + b_m\tilde{Y}$ (i.e., the market has no $\tilde{\varepsilon}$ risk), so

$$\begin{aligned} \mathrm{Cov}(\tilde{z}_i, \tilde{Z}_m) &= \mathrm{Cov}(b_m\tilde{Y}, b_i\tilde{Y}) = b_m b_i \mathrm{Var}(\tilde{Y}), \\ \mathrm{Var}(\tilde{Z}_m) &= b_m^2 \mathrm{Var}(\tilde{Y}), \\ \beta_i &\equiv \frac{\mathrm{Cov}(\tilde{z}_i, \tilde{Z}_m)}{\mathrm{Var}(\tilde{Z}_m)} = \frac{b_i}{b_m}. \end{aligned} \tag{40}$$

If the variance of $\tilde{Y}$ is infinite as in a Pareto–Levy distribution, the ratio of b's in (39) is interpreted as a measure of codispersion divided by the market's dispersion.

CHARACTERIZATION OF SOME SEPARATING DISTRIBUTION

Now that we have established a complete description of all return structures permitting two-fund, money separation, it will be informative to show how these separating distributions compare to the elliptical distributions of Chapter 4. We know that the multivariate normal distribution, for example, exhibits two-fund separation; therefore, it must be possible to write any multivariate normal random variables as in (30). It is useful to demonstrate this directly, however, since (30) appears somewhat restrictive in form. Some generality results from using $N + 1$ random variables to describe N returns, and this is sufficient for all normal (or elliptical) distributions.

To demonstrate this let $\tilde{Y}$ be the excess return on the mean-variance tangency portfolio (the market portfolio under the CAPM). $\tilde{Y} = \tilde{Z}_m - R$. Then we can write the regression model

$$\tilde{z}_i = \alpha_i + \beta_i(\tilde{Z}_m - R) + \tilde{\varepsilon}_i. \tag{41}$$

The residuals are normally distributed and $\mathrm{Cov}(\tilde{\varepsilon}_i, \tilde{Z}_m) = 0$, so they are independent and, a fortiori, $E(\tilde{\varepsilon}_i | Z_m) = 0$. Therefore, $\alpha_i = R$ in equilibrium, and for the market portfolio $\Sigma\, w_i^m \tilde{\varepsilon}_i = 0$. With these conditions (41) has the same form as (30).

We would also like to answer the question, is (30) just another way to describe elliptical distributions or do we now have a large class?

The following example shows that we do, indeed, have a larger class. Suppose there are two risky assets with returns which satisfy (30a) with $b_1 = b_2 = 1$, and further suppose there are only four equally probable outcome states described by

State:	a	b	c	d
$\tilde{Y}$	1	1	2	2
$\tilde{\varepsilon}_1$	0.1	−0.1	0.2	−0.2
$\tilde{\varepsilon}_2$	−0.2	0.2	−0.4	0.4

Examination of the table shows that for $w_1 = \frac{2}{3}$, $w_2 = \frac{1}{3}$ the residual risk is always zero. Also (30b) holds. This distribution, however, is clearly not elliptical since it has discrete outcomes.

The separating distributions are a larger class than the distributions permitting mean-variance analysis because, in addition to the latter, the former also includes other distributions for which the efficient set happens to coincide with the mean-variance efficient set. In fact, it is clear from the equilibrium condition (39) and our discussion in Chapter 4 that the separating distributions are exactly those distributions for which the efficient and mean-variance efficient sets are identical.

To illustrate this point, consider a set of $N - 1$ joint normal random variables $\tilde{X}_i$ and an independent nonnormal random variable $\tilde{e}$ with a zero mean. Suppose there is an economy with assets whose returns are given by $\tilde{z}_i = \tilde{X}_i$ for $i < N - 1$, $\tilde{z}_{N-1} = \tilde{X}_{N-1} + \tilde{e}$, and $\tilde{z}_N = \tilde{X}_{N-1} - \tilde{e}$. Knowing the mean and variance of a portfolio formed from these assets will not completely describe the distribution of the portfolio's return. To determine that, we would also need to know how much $\tilde{e}$ risk was included. In all portfolios of potential interest to investors, however, assets $N - 1$ and N will be held in equal proportions and there will be no $\tilde{e}$ risk, so their returns will be normally distributed and completely described by their mean and variance.

To prove this statement, consider any portfolio $\mathbf{w}$ with $\tilde{e}$ risk (i.e., $w_{N-1} \neq w_N$) and a second portfolio $\boldsymbol{\omega}$ with the same weights, except $\omega_{N-1} = \omega_N = (w_{N-1} + w_N)/2$. The returns on these two portfolios are

$$\tilde{Z}_{\mathbf{w}} = \sum_1^N w_i\tilde{z}_i = \sum_1^{N-2} w_i\tilde{X}_i + (w_{N-1} + w_N)\tilde{X}_{N-1} + (w_{N-1} - w_N)\tilde{e},$$
$$\tilde{Z}_{\boldsymbol{\omega}} = \sum_1^N \omega_i\tilde{z}_i = \sum_1^{N-2} w_i\tilde{X}_i + (\omega_{N-1} + \omega_N)\tilde{X}_{N-1}. \tag{42}$$

But $\omega_{N-1} + \omega_N = w_{N-1} + w_N$, so $\tilde{Z}_{\mathbf{w}} = \tilde{Z}_{\boldsymbol{\omega}} + \delta\tilde{e}$. Since $\tilde{e}$ is independent of the $\tilde{X}_i$, it is independent of $\tilde{Z}_{\boldsymbol{\omega}}$; thus, $\tilde{Z}_{\mathbf{w}}$ is riskier than $\tilde{Z}_{\boldsymbol{\omega}}$, and has the same mean, so no one will hold it.

TWO-FUND SEPARATION WITH NO RISKLESS ASSET

Two- (risky) fund separation with no riskless asset will obtain if and only if all returns can be characterized as

$$\tilde{z}_i = \tilde{X} + b_i\tilde{Y} + \tilde{\varepsilon}_i, \tag{43a}$$

$$E[\tilde{\varepsilon}_i | X + \gamma Y] = 0 \qquad \text{all } i, \tag{43b}$$

$$\sum w_i^1 \tilde{\varepsilon}_i \equiv 0, \qquad \sum w_i^1 = 1, \tag{43c}$$

$$\sum w_i^2 \tilde{\varepsilon}_i \equiv 0, \qquad \sum w_i^2 = 1, \tag{43d}$$

$$\sum w_i^1 b_i \neq \sum w_i^2 b_i. \tag{43e}$$

The conditional expectation in (43b) must be zero for all values of γ between and including the minimum and maximum "b" value of all investors' portfolios. (*Note*: Ross gives the additional condition $\bar{z} = \bar{X} + b_i\bar{Y}$; however, this is redundant since it can be deduced from (43a) and (43b), which requires that $E(\tilde{\varepsilon}_i) = 0$.) The requirement (43e) guarantees that the two portfolios have distinct returns. A necessary condition for (43e) is that the vector of b's not be constant. If (43e) does not hold, separation still obtains, but it degenerates to one-fund separation.

The proof of this proposition is omitted because it is virtually identical to that for two-fund separation with a riskless asset. The basis of the proof involves showing that any portfolio which is not a combination of $\mathbf{w}^1$ and $\mathbf{w}^2$ is riskier than that combination of these two portfolios with the same expected return.

In this case all investors hold combinations of the two mutual funds and incur no residual risk. Because in equilibrium the market portfolio is one such combination, we may assume it to be the first portfolio with no loss of generality. By rescaling $\tilde{Y}$ if necessary, we set $b_m = 1$. We call the other portfolio number 0 for convenience of notation. (Recall that $b_0 \neq b_m = 1$.)

Solving for $\bar{X}$ and $\bar{Y}$ in terms of $\bar{Z}_0$ and $\bar{Z}_m$ and substituting back into (43a) give the equilibrium expression for expected returns:

$$\bar{z}_i = (1 - b_0)^{-1}(\bar{Z}_0 - b_0\bar{Z}_m + b_i(\bar{Z}_m - \bar{Z}_0)]. \tag{44}$$

For the choice of the second portfolio with $b_0' = 0$, (44) apparently reduces to the standard two-factor pricing model

$$\bar{z}_i = \bar{Z}_0 + b_i(\bar{Z}_m - \bar{Z}_0'). \tag{45}$$

b_i is not the beta of asset i, however, unless $\tilde{X}$ is a constant.

Nevertheless, the two-factor model does obtain. Rewrite (44) as

$$\bar{z}_i = \bar{Z}_0\left(1 - \frac{b_i - b_0}{1 - b_0}\right) + \bar{Z}_m\frac{b_i - b_0}{1 - b_0}. \tag{46}$$

Thus, the fraction $(b_i - b_0)/(1 - b_0)$ should be the beta of asset i if $\tilde{Z}_0$ is a true zero beta portfolio. From (43)

$$\text{Cov}[\tilde{z}_j, \tilde{Z}_m] = \text{Var}(\tilde{X}) + b_j\text{Var}(\tilde{Y}) + (1 + b_j)\text{Cov}(\tilde{X}, \tilde{Y}), \tag{47}$$

so a zero beta portfolio has

$$b_0 = -\frac{\mathrm{Var}(\tilde{X}) + \mathrm{Cov}(\tilde{X}, \tilde{Y})}{\mathrm{Var}(\tilde{Y}) + \mathrm{Cov}(\tilde{X}, \tilde{Y})}, \tag{48}$$

not $b_0 = 0$. Substituting (48) into the fraction in (46) gives

$$\frac{b_i - b_0}{1 - b_0} = \frac{b_i \mathrm{Var}(\tilde{Y}) + (1 + b_i)\mathrm{Cov}(\tilde{X}, \tilde{Y}) + \mathrm{Var}(\tilde{X})}{\mathrm{Var}(\tilde{Y}) + 2\mathrm{Cov}(\tilde{X}, \tilde{Y}) + \mathrm{Var}(\tilde{X})} = \frac{\sigma_{im}}{\sigma_m^2}, \tag{49}$$

as desired.

K-FUND SEPARATION

Investors will all hold combinations of no more than K risky mutual funds and the riskless asset if asset returns are given by

$$\tilde{z}_i = R + \sum_{k=1}^{K} b_i^k \tilde{Y}_k + \tilde{\varepsilon}_i, \tag{50a}$$

$$E(\tilde{\varepsilon}_i | Y_1, \ldots, Y_K) \qquad \text{all } i, \tag{50b}$$

$$\sum_{i=1}^{N} w_i^k \tilde{\varepsilon}_i \equiv 0 \qquad \text{all } k, \tag{50c}$$

$$\sum_{i=1}^{N} w_i^k = 1 \qquad \text{all } k, \tag{50d}$$

$$\mathrm{rank}(\mathbf{A}) = K, \tag{50e}$$

where w_i^k is the weight of security i in the kth common mutual fund and $a_{mk} \equiv \Sigma b_i^k w_i^m$. The conditions given here are stronger than needed. Conditions (50a)–(50d) are analogous to conditions (30a)–(30d) for two-fund separation. Equation (50e) guarantees that an investor can achieve any combination of factor loadings by using just the K common mutual funds. $\mathbf{A}$ is the $K \times K$ matrix of the mutual funds' b's on the factors. The proof of this assertion is almost identical to that of two-fund separation and is left to the reader.

As an example of three-fund separation with two risky funds, consider the structure

$$\tilde{z}_i = R + a_i + b_i \tilde{Y} + \tilde{u}_i. \tag{51}$$

The $\tilde{u}_i$ are multivariate normal random variables with zero mean and variance-covariance matrix $\mathbf{\Sigma}$ (typical element σ_{ij}). $\tilde{Y}$ is a nonnormal random variable independent of the u_i with zero mean, unit variance, and finite higher moments. For the riskless asset $a_0 = b_0 = \tilde{u}_0 = 0$.

Since multivariate normals fall within the two-fund separating class, $a_i + \tilde{u}_i$ could be decomposed into a common factor and independent residuals

$$a_i + \tilde{u}_i = c_i\tilde{X} + \tilde{\varepsilon}_i, \tag{52}$$

as demonstrated earlier. Then (51) could be rewritten in a form similar to (50:)

$$\tilde{z}_i = R + b_i\tilde{Y} + c_i\tilde{X} + \tilde{\varepsilon}_i. \tag{53}$$

From (53) and (50) it is immediate that three-fund separation obtains. It is more instructive, however, to demonstrate the separation directly as was done in the mean-variance problem. We first show that the distribution of any portfolio is completely distinguished by three parameters, a, b, and $\text{Var}(\tilde{u})$. The return on any portfolio is

$$\tilde{Z} = R + a + b\tilde{Y} + \tilde{u},$$

where

$$\begin{aligned} a &\equiv \sum_1^N w_i a_i, & b &\equiv \sum_1^N w_i b_i, \\ \tilde{u} &\text{ is } N(0, \sigma^2), & \sigma^2 &\equiv \sum_1^N \sum_1^N w_i w_j \sigma_{ij}. \end{aligned} \tag{54}$$

The riskless asset (number 0) contributes nothing to excess return, index risk, or residual variance, so the sums are only over assets 1 through N.

The mean return on the portfolio is $\bar{Z} = R + a$. Using the independence of $\tilde{Y}$ and $\tilde{u}$ we obtain the higher-order central moments

$$m_n \equiv E[(\tilde{Z} - R - a)^n] = E[(b\tilde{Y} + \tilde{u})^n] = \sum_{i=0}^{n} \binom{n}{i} E(\tilde{u}^i) b^{n-i} E(Y^{n-i}). \tag{55}$$

But $E(\tilde{u}^i) = 0$ for i odd and $E(\tilde{u}^i) = (i-1)(i-3) \cdots 3 \cdot 1 \cdot \sigma^i$ for i even, or, in general, $E(\tilde{u}^i) = C_i\sigma^i$. Therefore each higher moment

$$m_n = \sum_{i=0}^{n} \binom{n}{i} C_i \sigma^i b^{n-i} E(\tilde{Y}^{n-i}) \tag{56}$$

is exactly determined by σ^2 and b (and the exogenous moments of $\tilde{Y}$). Since knowing the mean of a distribution and all its integer moments completely characterizes it, any portfolio return distribution is uniquely determined by a, b, and σ^2.

Now consider the general "portfolio" problem of minimizing residual variance while holding mean and b fixed. (Since variance is $b^2 + \sigma^2$, minimizing residual risk minimizes variance for a fixed b; however, as we will show, it is the former interpretation that is important in this case.) To fix mean, we can fix the excess expected return a.

$$\text{Min } \frac{1}{2}\sum_1^N\sum_1^N w_i w_j \sigma_{ij} \tag{57}$$

$$\text{Subject to} \quad a = \sum_1^N w_i a_i, \qquad b = \sum_1^N w_i b_i.$$

Because the riskless asset does not contribute to a, b, or σ^2, we may exclude it from the minimization and need not impose the budget constraint. Forming the Lagrangian

$$\mathrm{L} \equiv \frac{1}{2}\sum_1^N\sum_1^N w_i w_j \sigma_{ij} - \lambda_1\left(\sum_1^N w_i a_i - a\right) - \lambda_2\left(\sum_1^N w_i b_i - b\right) \tag{58}$$

and minimizing give

$$0 = \frac{\partial L}{\partial w_i} = \sum_1^N w_j \sigma_{ij} - \lambda_1 a_i - \lambda_2 b_i, \tag{59a}$$

$$0 = \frac{\partial L}{\partial \lambda_1} = a - \sum w_i a_i, \tag{59b}$$

$$0 = \frac{\partial L}{\partial \lambda_2} = b - \sum w_i b_i. \tag{59c}$$

Solving (59a) and expressing the result in vector notation, we get

$$\mathbf{w}^* = \lambda_1 \mathbf{\Sigma}^{-1}\mathbf{a} + \lambda_2 \mathbf{\Sigma}^{-1}\mathbf{b}. \tag{60}$$

If we now define two portfolios as

$$\mathbf{w}_1 = \frac{\mathbf{\Sigma}^{-1}\mathbf{a}}{\mathbf{1}'\mathbf{\Sigma}^{-1}\mathbf{a}}, \qquad \mathbf{w}_2 = \frac{\mathbf{\Sigma}^{-1}\mathbf{b}}{\mathbf{1}'\mathbf{\Sigma}^{-1}\mathbf{b}}, \tag{61}$$

then (60) can be written as

$$\mathbf{w}^* = \hat{\lambda}_1 \mathbf{w}_1 + \hat{\lambda}_2 \mathbf{w}_2, \tag{62}$$

which shows that all optimal portfolios are linear combinations of only two distinct risky portfolios. The third mutual fund is the riskless asset. Different investors will hold different portfolios as determined by the individual "costs" of the various constraints reflected in their own multipliers.

The only remaining task is to show that optimal portfolios are actually characterized by minimum residual risk. That is, given two portfolios with returns $\tilde{Z}_i = R + a + b\tilde{Y} + \tilde{u}_i$, do all investors prefer i to j if $\sigma_i^2 < \sigma_j^2$? Since $\tilde{u}_i$ and $\tilde{u}_j$ are normally distributed, the answer is yes, as we saw in Chapter 5. The presence of $\tilde{Y}$ does not affect the relative riskiness of $\tilde{Z}_i$ and $\tilde{Z}_j$ since it is independent of both $\tilde{u}$'s.

The variance of the return on any portfolio is, from (55), $b^2 + \sigma^2$. If the distribution of $\tilde{Y}$ is not symmetric, then the third moment of the return on any portfolio is $b^3E(\tilde{Y}^3)$. Thus the portfolio analysis described here in terms of a, b, and σ^2 is equivalent to portfolio analysis by the first three moments. Joint distributions of the type in (51) are therefore one justification for three-moment portfolio analysis, as described in Chapter 4.

PRICING UNDER K-FUND SEPARATION

From (46a) it is clear that

$$\bar{z}_i = R + \sum_{k=1}^{K} b_i^k \bar{Y}_k, \tag{63}$$

since $E(\tilde{\varepsilon}_i) = 0$. This also holds for the K funds free from residual risk. With no loss of generality we can assume that each common mutual fund has a nonzero factor loading on only one factor. (Since $\mathbf{A}$ has full rank, we can always find some K combinations of mutual funds satisfying $\boldsymbol{\alpha}_k'\mathbf{1} = 1$ and $\mathbf{A}'\boldsymbol{\alpha}_k = \boldsymbol{\iota}_k$.) Let $\bar{Z}^k$ be the expected return on the mutual fund with a nonzero loading on the kth factor, and let $b^k = \sum w_i^k b_i^k$ be this factor loading. Then

$$\bar{Z}^k = R + b^k \bar{Y}_k. \tag{64}$$

Now (63) can be written as

$$\bar{z}_i = R + \sum_{i=1}^{K} \frac{b_i^k(\bar{Z}^k - R)}{b^k}. \tag{65}$$

Furthermore $\text{Cov}(\tilde{Z}_i, \tilde{Z}^k) = b_i^k b^k \,\text{Var}(\tilde{Y}^k)$ and $\text{Var}(\tilde{Z}^k) = (b^k)^2 \,\text{Var}(\tilde{Y}^k)$, so

$$\bar{z}_i = R + \sum_{i=1}^{K} \beta_i^k(\bar{Z}^k - R), \tag{66}$$

where β_i^k is a ratio of covariance to variance as in the CAPM.

THE DISTINCTION BETWEEN FACTOR PRICING AND SEPARATION

The pricing result in the previous section is not dependent on separation. The expected returns on a set of assets whose common variation depends on K factors must be linearly related to the assets' responses on these factors if just *one* risk-averse investor holds a portfolio which is free from residual risk.

Specifically assume a linear returns generating model

$$\tilde{z}_i = a_i + \sum_{k=1}^{K} b_i^k \tilde{f}_k + \tilde{\varepsilon}_i, \tag{67}$$

where $E(\tilde{f}_k) = 0$. If some investor holds a portfolio with no $\varepsilon -$ risk, then expected returns must be linear in the factor responses

$$a_i = R + \lambda_1 b_i^1 + \cdots + \lambda_K b_i^K, \tag{68}$$

so that the risk premium can be combined into the common factors. That is, Equation (67) may be written as

$$\tilde{z}_i = R + \sum b_i^k(\tilde{f}_k + \lambda_k) + \tilde{\varepsilon}_i, \tag{69}$$

which is (50a) for $\tilde{Y}_k \equiv \tilde{f}_k + \lambda_k$. We do not assume that K portfolios free of residual risk exist, however, so separation need not obtain (except when $K = 1$).

To demonstrate this result, regress the a_i on the b_i^k (in the population)

$$a_i = \lambda_0 + \lambda_1 b_i^1 + \cdots + \lambda_K b_i^K + v_i, \tag{70a}$$

$$\sum v_i = 0, \tag{70b}$$

$$\sum v_i b_i^k = 0 \qquad \text{for all } k. \tag{70c}$$

Now consider our risk-averse investor who has optimally chosen to hold a portfolio with no residual risk. Denote the return on the optimal portfolio by

$$\tilde{Z}^* = a^* + \sum_1^N \sum_1^K b_i^k w_i^* \tilde{f}_k. \tag{71}$$

He or she could change the holdings to $w_i^* + \gamma v_i$ since this addition is self-financing by (70b). From the assumed optimality of the original portfolio,

$$\begin{aligned} 0 &= \frac{\partial}{\partial\gamma}\left[Eu\left(\tilde{Z}^* + \gamma\sum_1^N v_i\tilde{z}_i\right)\right]\Bigg|_{\gamma=0} = E\left[u'(\tilde{Z}^*)\sum_1^N v_i\tilde{z}_i\right] \\ &= \mathrm{E}\left[u'(\tilde{Z}^*)\right]\sum_1^N v_i a_i + E\left[u'(\tilde{Z}^*)\sum_1^N\sum_1^K v_i b_i^k \tilde{f}_k\right] \\ &\quad + E\left[u'(\tilde{Z}^*)\sum_1^N v_i\tilde{\varepsilon}_i\right] \\ &= E[u'(\tilde{Z}^*)]\sum_1^n v_i a_i. \end{aligned} \tag{72}$$

The second term on the second line is zero from (70c). The third term is zero from the fair game property of the residuals, as proved in the Mathematical Introduction.

Since marginal utility is positive, $\sum v_i a_i = 0$. But a_i and v_i are the dependent variable and residual of a regression, so they cannot be orthogonal unless the fit is perfect—$v_i \equiv 0$. Furthermore, since this must hold for the riskless asset ($v_0 = 0$), $\lambda_0 = R$, and (68) obtains.

If the investor holding the portfolio which is free from residual risk has a quadratic utility function, then the residuals need only be uncorrelated with the factors for this property to hold.

General conditions under which at least one investor holds a portfolio completely free of residual risk are elusive. One set of conditions for which this will be true is the following: (1) One factor (or some linear combination of factors) is equal to the realized return on the market portfolio in excess of its mean ($\tilde{f}_k = \tilde{Z}_m - \bar{Z}_m$); and (2) there are as many linearly independent assets as outcome states (markets are complete, as in Chapter 8). The second condition guarantees that the market portfolio is efficient. The first condition specifies that it has no residual risk.

SEPARATION UNDER RESTRICTIONS ON BOTH TASTES AND DISTRIBUTIONS

The existence of mutual fund theorems which obtain under simultaneous restrictions on both tastes and distributions is a largely unexplored area. We did see previously that the existence of a riskless asset extended the allowable utility functions, permitting separation, but this is a relatively weak distributional restriction. Here we shall consider a simple example which is not of this type to show that extensions of the theory to this area are possible.

We assume that the random return on each asset i can take on only two distinct values z_i, not a random variable, or 0. The probability that $\tilde{z}_i = z_i$ is denoted by π_i. Furthermore, exactly $N - 1$ securities always have a return of zero; that is, $\text{Prob}[\tilde{z}_i = z_i, \tilde{z}_j = z_j] = 0$ for $i \neq j$ and $\Sigma\pi_i = 1$. This structure of returns is highly specialized; however, many general structures can be reduced to this case. In fact, the securities considered here are the Arrow–Debreu securities inherent in any complete market (see Chapter 8).

With this restriction on returns Cass and Stiglitz prove that the necessary and sufficient condition for two-fund separation is that each investor's utility function satisfy

$$A_k[u_k'(Z)]^\alpha + B_k[u_k'(Z)]^\beta = Z$$
$$\text{or} \tag{73}$$
$$[u_k'(Z)]^\alpha[A_k + B_k \log u_k'(Z)] = Z.$$

Here we only demonstrate separation for the utility function

$$u'(Z) = [-a_k Z + (a_k^2 Z^2 + 1)^{1/2}]^\gamma, \tag{74}$$

which is a special case of (73) for $\alpha = -\beta = 1/\gamma$ and $-A = B = \frac{1}{2}a$. For this function, marginal utility is positive for all $Z > 0$ and decreasing if $a\gamma$

> 0 since the Arrow–Pratt absolute risk-aversion measure is

$$-\frac{u''(Z)}{u'(Z)} = a\gamma(a^2Z^2 + 1)^{-1/2}. \tag{75}$$

Changing the signs of both a and γ leaves the Arrow–Pratt measure unchanged, so we may assume both parameters are positive.

Using the first-order condition (Equation (26a) in Chapter 5), we get

$$\lambda = E[u'(\tilde{Z}^*)\tilde{z}_i] = \sum_j \pi_j u'(\tilde{Z}_j^*)Z_{ji} = \pi_i u'(w_i z_i)z_i \qquad \text{for all } i. \tag{76}$$

The last line follows since $Z_{ji} = 0$—unless $j = i$, when $Z_{ii} = z_i$. For the utility function in (74) this can be expressed as

$$\left[\frac{\lambda}{\pi_i z_i}\right]^{1/\gamma} = -aw_i z_i + [a^2 w_i^2 z_i^2 + 1]^{1/2} \qquad \text{for all } i. \tag{77}$$

Adding $aw_i z_i$ and squaring both sides of (77) leave a linear equation to be solved for the optimal weights

$$w_i^* = \frac{[\pi_i z_i/\lambda]^{1/\gamma}}{2az_i} - \frac{[\lambda/(\pi_i z_i)]^{1/\gamma}}{2az_i}. \tag{78}$$

If we reintroduce the subscript k to denote different investors, (78) becomes

$$w_{ik}^* = \left(\frac{\lambda_k^{-1/\gamma}}{2a_k}\right)\left[\frac{(\pi_i z_i)^{1/\gamma}}{z_i}\right] - \left(\frac{\lambda_k^{1/\gamma}}{2a_k}\right)\left[\frac{(\pi_i z_i)^{-1/\gamma}}{z_i}\right]. \tag{79}$$

Notice that the terms in parentheses do not depend upon i, the asset, and the terms in brackets do not depend upon k, the investor. Also the Lagrange multipliers λ_k must be determined so that the portfolio constraint is satisfied. Thus (79) displays portfolio separation which can be expressed as

$$\begin{aligned} w_{ik}^* &= c_k w_i^1 + (1 - c_k)w_i^2, \\ w_i^1 &\equiv \frac{(\pi_i z_i)^{1/\gamma}}{z_i}\Bigg/\sum\frac{(\pi_j z_j)^{1/\gamma}}{z_j}, \\ w_i^2 &\equiv \frac{(\pi_i z_i)^{-1/\gamma}}{z_i}\Bigg/\sum\frac{(\pi_j z_j)^{-1/\gamma}}{z_j}. \end{aligned} \tag{80}$$

The Lagrange multiplier λ is positive from (76), and a, π_i, and z_i are likewise positive, so by comparing (80) to (79) we can see that $1 - c_k < 0$. That is, all investors short the second portfolio. This does not preclude an equilibrium, however, even though each asset is held long in the second portfolio. The net demand for each asset can still be positive.

As mentioned earlier, the set of portfolios spanned by two separating mutual funds need not include the riskless asset if the class of utility functions does not include any which are infinitely risk averse. We now demonstrate this for the economy just considered.

From (75) relative risk aversion is

$$a\gamma Z(a^2 Z^2 + 1)^{-1/2} \tag{81}$$

which is increasing in the parameter a. The maximum relative risk aversion is therefore γ at $a = \infty$. Suppose the economy is structured as

		π_s	asset: 1	2	3
outcome:	a	$\frac{1}{3}$	1	0	0
	b	$\frac{1}{3}$	0	$\sqrt{2}$	0
	c	$\frac{1}{3}$	0	0	2

and $\gamma = 1$. Then from (80) the first portfolio is equally weighted, and the second is divided in proportion to $(1, \frac{1}{2}, \frac{1}{4})$; that is, $\mathbf{w}^2 = (\frac{4}{7}, \frac{2}{7}, \frac{1}{7})$. The

Table 6.1 Summary of Conditions for Mutual Fund Theorems

	Restrictions on	
	Tastes	*Distributions*
One-fund separation	Equivalent Utility Functions $u_k(Z) = a + bu_j(Z)$	$\tilde{\mathbf{z}} = \tilde{Y}\mathbf{1} + \tilde{\boldsymbol{\varepsilon}}$ $E[\tilde{\boldsymbol{\varepsilon}} \mid Y] = \mathbf{0}$ $\exists \mathbf{w}$ such that $\mathbf{1}'\mathbf{w} = 1$, $\mathbf{w}'\tilde{\boldsymbol{\varepsilon}} = 0$
Two-fund separation	Quadratic Utility Functions $u_k'(Z) = A_k + B_k Z$	$\tilde{\mathbf{z}} = \tilde{X}\mathbf{1} + \tilde{Y}\mathbf{b} + \tilde{\boldsymbol{\varepsilon}}$ $E[\tilde{\boldsymbol{\varepsilon}} \mid X + \gamma Y] = \mathbf{0}$ $\exists \mathbf{w}_1$ and $\mathbf{w}_2$ such that $\mathbf{1}'\mathbf{w}_i = 1$, $\mathbf{w}_i'\tilde{\boldsymbol{\varepsilon}} = 0$ $\mathbf{w}_1'\mathbf{b} > \mathbf{w}_2'\mathbf{b}$
Two-fund separation with a riskless asset	HARA Utility Functions $u_k'(Z) = (A_k + B_k Z)^{-c}$	$\tilde{\mathbf{z}} = R\mathbf{1} + \tilde{Y}\mathbf{b} + \tilde{\boldsymbol{\varepsilon}}$ $E[\tilde{\boldsymbol{\varepsilon}} \mid Y] = \mathbf{0}$ $\exists \mathbf{w}$ such that $\mathbf{1}'\mathbf{w} = 1$, $\mathbf{w}'\tilde{\boldsymbol{\varepsilon}} = 0$ $\mathbf{w}'\mathbf{b} \neq 0$
Two-fund separation with joint restrictions	Every state insurable and utility function satisfying $A_k[u_k'(Z)]^\alpha + B_k[u_k'(Z)]^\beta = Z$ or $[u_k'(Z)]^\alpha\{A_k + B_k \log[u_k'(Z)]\} = Z$	

returns on the two portfolios are $(1/3, \sqrt{2}/3, 2/3)$ and $(4/7, 2\sqrt{2}/7, 2/7)$.

It is impossible to construct a riskless asset from these two portfolios. Equal returns can be achieved in states *a* and *c* by holding them in the proportion of 6 to 7. This gives a return pattern of $(6/13, 4\sqrt{2}/13, 6/13)$, which is not riskless. Any other relative holding will not give equal returns in states *a* and *c*.

If the state probabilities are changed to (.5, .25, .25), then the two portfolios are $\mathbf{w}^1 = (.5, .25, .25)$ and $\mathbf{w}^2 = (.4, .4, .2)$ with returns of $(.5, .25\sqrt{2}, .5)$ and $(.4, .4\sqrt{2}, .4)$. Since both portfolios have equal returns in states *a* and *c*, so will all combination. Now a riskless portfolio can be achieved by trading off this return and that in state *b*. The riskless portfolio is approximately .531 in $\mathbf{w}^1$ and .469 in $\mathbf{w}^2$, and the riskless return is 0.453. The reason the riskless asset can be constructed in this case is that $\pi_a z_a = \pi_c z_c$, so these two states are equivalent from the viewpoint of investor utility and may together be considered a single metastate. This issue is discussed in greater detail in Chapter 8.

7

The Linear Factor Model: Arbitrage Pricing Theory

LINEAR FACTOR MODELS

Throughout this chapter we assume that asset returns are described by the linear factor model

$$\tilde{z}_i = a_i + \sum_{k=1}^{K} b_{ik}\tilde{f}_k + \tilde{\varepsilon}_i,$$

$$E(\tilde{\varepsilon}_i) = E(\tilde{f}_k) = E(\tilde{\varepsilon}_i\tilde{\varepsilon}_j) = E(\tilde{\varepsilon}_i\tilde{f}_k) = E(\tilde{f}_k\tilde{f}_m) = 0, \tag{1}$$

$$E(\tilde{\varepsilon}_i^2) \equiv s_i^2 < S^2,$$

$$E(\tilde{f}_k^2) = 1,$$

unless otherwise noted. The $\tilde{f}_k$ are the *factors*, the b_{ik} are the *factor loadings*, and the $\tilde{\varepsilon}_i$ represent the *residual* or *idiosyncratic risks*. The factor loadings are bounded: $|b_{ij}| < b$.

This model can also be written conveniently in vector notation as

$$\tilde{\mathbf{z}} = \mathbf{a} + \mathbf{B}\tilde{\mathbf{f}} + \boldsymbol{\varepsilon}, \tag{2a}$$

$$E(\tilde{\boldsymbol{\varepsilon}}) = \mathbf{0}, \tag{2b}$$

$$E(\tilde{\mathbf{f}}) = \mathbf{0}, \tag{2c}$$

$$E(\tilde{\mathbf{f}}\tilde{\mathbf{f}}') = \mathbf{I}, \tag{2d}$$

$$E(\tilde{\boldsymbol{\varepsilon}}\tilde{\mathbf{f}}') = \mathbf{0}, \tag{2e}$$

$$E(\tilde{\boldsymbol{\varepsilon}}\tilde{\boldsymbol{\varepsilon}}') = \mathbf{D}, \quad \text{a diagnonal matrix.} \tag{2f}$$

Assumptions (2b)–(2e) are innocuous; (2c), (2d) can be met simply by subtracting any factor means and then orthogonalizing and rescaling the parameters. This does not change any of the stochastic properties of the set of factors. Conditions (2b), (2e) are always possible through the appropriate choices for **a** and **B**. Only the assumptions of uncorrelated residuals cannot be guaranteed. Relaxation of (2f) will be considered later.

SINGLE-FACTOR, RESIDUAL-RISK-FREE MODELS

Before studying the model in (2) in detail, it is useful to examine economies with no idiosyncratic (asset-specific) risk. Although these are very special cases, much of the intuition developed is useful in general.

Suppose that asset returns are related by a single-factor, residual-riskfree linear model

$$\tilde{z}_i = a_i + b_i\tilde{f}, \qquad i = 1, \ldots, n. \tag{3}$$

From the basic theorem of arbitrage pricing, any two assets with the same value of b must have the same expected return a. To price assets with different values of b, consider a portfolio of two assets, with $b_i \neq b_j$, $b_i \neq 0$, $b_j \neq 0$, formed by investing a fraction w in asset i and $1 - w$ in asset j. The return on this portfolio is

$$\tilde{Z} = w(a_i - a_j) + a_j + [w(b_i - b_j) + b_j]\tilde{f}. \tag{4}$$

If we choose $w^* = b_j/(b_j - b_i)$, then $\tilde{Z}^* = b_j(a_i - a_j)/(b_j - b_i) + a_j$, which is certain. Therefore, to avoid arbitrage, we must have $Z^* = R$. This condition can also be expressed as

$$\frac{a_j - R}{b_j} = \frac{a_i - R}{b_i} \tag{5}$$

or, since $\bar{z}_i = a_i$,

$$\bar{z}_i = R + b_i\lambda, \tag{6}$$

where λ is some constant known as the *factor risk premium*. From (6) it is clear that λ is equal to the excess expected return on any asset with $b = 1$. Even if no riskless asset naturally exists, a similar relation must still obtain since a riskless asset can be constructed from any two risky assets. All such constructed riskless assets must have the same return. Thus, when no explicit riskless asset exists,

$$\bar{z}_i = \lambda_0 + b_i\lambda_1 \tag{7}$$

for all assets described by (3).

MULTIFACTOR MODELS

For multifactor models a similar analysis can also be performed, provided that the factor loadings are "sufficiently different." The case of two factors is outlined next.

Suppose that asset returns are generated by the two-factor linear model

$$\tilde{z}_i = a_i + b_i\tilde{f}_1 + c_i\tilde{f}_2 \tag{8}$$

with the vectors **b**, **c**, and **1** not collinear. Choose a portfolio of three securities. The return on this portfolio is

$$\tilde{Z} = \sum w_i a_i + \tilde{f}_1 \sum w_i b_i + \tilde{f}_2 \sum w_i c_i. \tag{9}$$

If we select $\sum w_i b_i = \sum w_i c_i = 0$, then the portfolio is riskless; so if arbitrage opportunities are absent, $\Sigma w_i a_i = R$ or $\Sigma w_i(a_i - R) = 0$. These three conditions can be written as

$$\begin{pmatrix} a_1 - R & a_2 - R & a_3 - R \\ b_1 & b_2 & b_3 \\ c_1 & c_2 & c_3 \end{pmatrix} \begin{pmatrix} w_1 \\ w_2 \\ w_3 \end{pmatrix} = \begin{pmatrix} 0 \\ 0 \\ 0 \end{pmatrix}. \tag{10}$$

The matrix in (10) must be singular. Because the last two rows are not collinear we have

$$\bar{z}_i - R \equiv a_i - R = \lambda_1 b_i + \lambda_2 c_i \qquad \text{for all } i. \tag{11}$$

Again, if the riskless asset does not exist, we replace R by λ_0.

INTERPRETATION OF THE FACTOR RISK PREMIUMS

The only remaining issue is to identify λ_1 and λ_2. If we choose a portfolio with $\Sigma w_i b_i = 1$ and $\Sigma w_i c_i = 0$, then we see that its excess expected return $Z^1 - R$ is λ_1. Similarly, λ_2 is the excess expected return on a portfolio with $b = 0$ and $c = 1$. So λ_1 and λ_2 can be thought of as the excess return per unit risk associated with the f_1 and f_2 factors, and (11) may be written

$$\bar{z}_i = R + b_i(\bar{Z}^1 - R) + c_i(\bar{Z}^2 - R). \tag{12}$$

The relation in (11) or (12) can also be rewritten in terms of the expected excess return on any portfolios whose two risk components are in different proportions. For example, choose the market portfolio and any other for which $b_P/c_P \neq b_M/c_M$. Solve (11) for λ_1 and λ_2 in terms of the expected returns on these two portfolios. Then for any security i,

$$\bar{z}_i = R + b_i'(\bar{Z}_M - R) + c_1'(\bar{Z}_P - R),$$

where

$$b' \equiv \frac{b_i c_P - c_i b_P}{b_M c_P - c_M b_P}, \qquad c_i' \equiv \frac{c_i b_M - b_i c_M}{b_M c_P - c_M b_P}. \tag{13}$$

FACTOR MODELS WITH "UNAVOIDABLE" RISK

Up to now we have been assuming implicitly that the factor loadings are "sufficiently different." We outline now a case in which this is not true.

Consider the two-factor model just discussed and assume that $c_i = c - b_i$ (except $b_0 = c_0 = 0$). The previous derivation fails because we cannot form a portfolio of risky assets with $b = c = 0$, as we assumed.

This point is emphasized if we rewrite the factor model (8) as

$$\tilde{z}_i = a_i + b_i(\tilde{f}_1 - \tilde{f}_2) + c\tilde{f}_2 = a_i = b_i\tilde{f}_1' + \tilde{f}_2'. \tag{14}$$

(Note that the factors are no longer orthogonal or normalized, but this need not concern us.) Under this restructuring the loadings on $\tilde{f}_2'$ are obviously not "sufficiently different," and we will be unable to form a portfolio which has no $\tilde{f}_2'$ risk. Any portfolio formed will have the return

$$\tilde{Z} = a + b\tilde{f}_1' + \tilde{f}_2'. \tag{15}$$

The thing to note from (15) is that any two portfolios with the same value of b are perfectly correlated; therefore, by the basic theorem of arbitrage pricing, they must have the same expected return.

To price securities with different b's we introduce a^o, which is defined to be the expected return for a portfolio or security with $b = 0$. From the paragraph above, all such securities will have the same expected return, so a^o is well defined. Now consider forming two portfolios from assets i, j, and o (with $b_o = 0$) as follows:

$$w_i^+ = w_i^* + \delta_1, \quad w_j^+ = w_j^* + \delta_2, \quad w_o^+ = w_o^* - \delta_1 - \delta_2. \tag{16}$$

The two portfolios have the properties that

$$\begin{aligned} a^+ &= a^* + \delta_1(a_i - a^o) + \delta_2(a_j - a^o), \\ b^+ &= b^* + \delta_1 b_i + \delta_2 b_j. \end{aligned} \tag{17}$$

Suppose we choose $\delta_i b_i + \delta_2 b_j = 0$. Then $b^+ = b^*$, and, as above, $a^+ = a^*$. Therefore

$$0 = \delta_1(a_i - a^o) + \delta_2(a_j - a^o) = \delta_1\left[a_i - a^o - \frac{b_i}{b_j}(a_j - a^o)\right]. \tag{18}$$

Equation (18) must be true for any choice of δ_1. Thus,

$$\frac{a_i - a^o}{b_i} = \frac{a_j - a^o}{b_j} = \lambda. \tag{19}$$

The linear pricing relation is $a_i = a^o + \lambda b_i$ or

$$\bar{z}_i \equiv a_i = \bar{Z}^0 + b_i(\bar{Z}^1 - \bar{Z}^0), \tag{20}$$

where $\bar{Z}^0 = a^o$ is the expected return on any portfolio with $b = 0$, and $\bar{Z}^1$ is the expected return on a portfolio with $b = 1$. Note that the riskless return does not appear in this formula at all, unlike Equation (12). In that case riskless portfolios could be constructed by using only the risky assets. Such is not true here, so the absence of arbitrage opportunities alone cannot reveal any relation between the riskless rate and the expected returns on the risky assets. In particular, $\bar{Z}^0$ need not be equal to R. In general, $\bar{Z}^0 > R$ to compensate investors for bearing $\tilde{f}_2'$-type risk. $\bar{Z}^1$ can be greater than or less than $\bar{Z}^0$.

Using the same steps as Equations (44)–(49) in Chapter 6, Equation (20) can be reinterpreted as the "two-factor" form of the CAPM. Note, however, that here a riskless asset may be available and there need be no restrictions on borrowing.

We can reintroduce both factor loadings into the noarbitrage condition by selecting λ_0, λ_1, and λ_2 such that

$$a_i = a^o + \lambda b_i = \lambda_0 + \lambda_1 b_i + \lambda_2 c_i. \tag{21}$$

This relation remains valid for all assets if and only if the choices of factor risk premiums satisfy

$$a^o = \lambda_0 + c\lambda_2, \qquad \lambda = \lambda_1 - \lambda_2. \tag{22}$$

Since there are three variables and only two constraints in (22), this second relation is not unique, and any one of the three factor risk premiums may be arbitrarily specified. For example, if we take $\lambda_0 = R$, then the resulting no arbitrage expression is Equation (11). Thus, the previous "invalid" analysis does come to a valid conclusion, but only one of the many possible.

ASYMPTOTIC ARBITRAGE

We now examine the general linear factor model described in (1) or (2). Note the similarity in form between this model and the separating distribution model of Chapter 6. One important distinction is that in the latter we assumed a CAPM-like equilibrium or derived it directly from the fair-game assumption on the residuals. Here we are interested in proving this equilibrium, and we have introduced varying intercepts and weakened the fair-game assumption to a lack of correlation with the indices.

We no longer assume that zero residual-risk portfolios are available. Instead we assume that the residuals are mutually uncorrelated and that an infinite number of assets are available. These two assumptions guarantee that investors can form diversified portfolios with near zero residual risks. These portfolios play the role of the idiosyncratic risk-free portfolios of Chapter 6 and are discussed at length later. The assumed existence of an infinite number of assets is not, of course, true to life and means that the APT is only an asymptotic result for large economies.

One final item which should be noted is that the definition of arbitrage to be used here is also a limiting one. An asymptotic arbitrage opportunity is said to exist if there exists a sequence of arbitrage portfolios $\boldsymbol{\omega}^n$, $n = 1, \ldots,$ satisfying

$$\sum_1^n \omega_i^n = 0, \tag{23a}$$

$$\sum_1^n \omega_i^n \bar{z}_i \geq \delta > 0, \tag{23b}$$

$$\sum_1^n \sum_1^n \omega_i^n \omega_j^n \sigma_{ij} \to 0. \tag{23c}$$

(The notation here is deliberately vague. It is not required that the limit of the variance be zero. What is required is that for some infinite subsequence the limit be zero. However, if the $n + 1$ asset economy has the same parameters for the first n assets, $\bar{z}_i^n$ and σ_{ij}^n, as the n asset economy, then the existence of a subsequence arbitrage opportunity will imply the existence of a sequence arbitrage opportunity where the limit of the variance is zero.)

This notion of arbitrage is an obvious extension to the definition of a riskless arbitrage opportunity in Chapter 3. As seen there, the scale of an abitrage opportunity is arbitrary, so that an infinite profit can be earned by holding an unbounded position in the arbitrage portfolio. With an asymptotic arbitrage opportunity the question of scaling becomes a little trickier because the risk only vanishes in the limit. If $\boldsymbol{\omega}^n$ is a sequence defining an asymptotic arbitrage opportunity, then $\gamma\boldsymbol{\omega}^n$ is as well for any $\gamma > 0$. However, γ cannot become unbounded in an arbitrary fashion if (23c) is to remain valid. Clearly, it must depend on n. One construction that will work is to set $\gamma_n = (\boldsymbol{\omega}'\boldsymbol{\Sigma}\boldsymbol{\omega})^{-1/4}$. Then $\hat{\boldsymbol{\omega}}^n \equiv \gamma_n \boldsymbol{\omega}^n$ is an asymptotic arbitrage opportunity with a limiting infinite profit

$$\sum \hat{\omega}_i^n = \gamma_n \sum \omega_i^n = 0, \qquad \text{all } n, \tag{24a}$$

$$\sum \hat{\omega}_i^n \bar{z}_i = \gamma_n \sum \omega_i^n \bar{z}_i \geq \delta\gamma_n \to \infty, \tag{24b}$$

$$\sum\sum \hat{\omega}_i^n \hat{\omega}_j^n \sigma_{ij} = \gamma_n^2 \sum\sum \omega_i^n \omega_j^n \sigma_{ij} = [\sum\sum \omega_i^n \omega_j^n \sigma_{ij}]^{1/2} \to 0. \tag{24c}$$

A natural question to ask at this point is, What does an asymptotic arbitrage opportunity achieve for an investor? An ordinary arbitrage opportunity when practiced on unlimited scale guarantees infinite wealth and infinite certainty equivalent of return; that is, $u(\tilde{Z}_n) \to u(\infty)$. Chebyshev's inequality when applied to (24) shows that an asymptotic arbitrage opportunity guarantees an infinite wealth with probability 1. An infinite certainty equivalent wealth is not guaranteed, however.

As a counterexample, consider a sequence of random portfolio returns $\tilde{Z}_n$ with realizations $\{1 - n, 1 + n, 1\}$ with probabilities $\{n^{-3}, n^{-3}, 1 - 2n^{-3}\}$. Then for $u(Z) = -e^{-z}$,

$$\bar{Z}_n = 1 + n^{-3}[1 - n + 1 + n - 2] = 1, \tag{25a}$$

$$\sigma_n^2 = n^{-3}[(-n)^2 + n^2] = \frac{2}{n} \to 0, \tag{25b}$$

$$Eu(\tilde{Z}_n) = -\frac{1}{n^3}(e^{n-1} + e^{-n-1} - 2e^{-1}) - e^{-1} \sim -\frac{1}{n^3}e^{n-1}, \tag{25c}$$

which implies that in the limit the certainty equivalent wealth is $-\infty$. Although it would be difficult to construct an economy in which a sequence of arbitrage portfolios yielded this sequence of returns, the point is made that the opportunity to increase wealth without any investment commitment, even with vanishingly small risk, does not guarantee an increase in expected utility. Certain investors may refrain from taking advantage of some asymptotic arbitrage opporunities.

General conditions sufficient to guarantee that any asymptotic arbitrage opportunity will lead to bliss, $u(\infty)$, are not known. Concave utility functions which are bounded below will possess this property. Restrictions such as bounds on the assets' returns will be insufficient because portfolios could still have unbounded returns.

ARBITRAGE PRICING OF ASSETS WITH IDIOSYNCRATIC RISK

Given that there are no asymptotic arbitrage opportunities of the type described in (23), we can prove the following result.

THEOREM 1 *If the returns on the risky assets are given by a K factor linear model with bounded residual risk and there are no asymptotic arbitrage opportunities, then there exists a linear pricing model which gives expected returns with a mean square error of zero. That is, there are factors* $\lambda_0, \lambda_1, \ldots, \lambda_K$ *dependent on n such that*

$$\begin{gathered} v_i \equiv a_i - \lambda_0 - \sum_{k=1}^{K} b_{ik}\lambda_k, \\ \lim_{n\to\infty} \frac{1}{n}\sum_{i=1}^{n} v_i^2 \equiv \lim_{n\to\infty}\frac{1}{n}\|\mathbf{v}_n\|^2 = 0. \end{gathered} \tag{26}$$

Proof. Arbitrarily select n of the assets and number them 1 to n. "Regress" their expected returns a_i on the b_{ik} and a constant. Call the regression coefficients λ_k. (This "regression" is a thought experiment performed not on observations of the returns but on the true expectations. Mathematically, it is a projection of the vector **a** into the space spanned by **B** and the vector **1**. If the regression cannot be performed because of multicollinearity, arbitrarily prespecify a sufficient number of the λ_k to remove the collinearity.) The "residuals," v_i, of this regression are given by

$$a_i = \lambda_0 + \sum_{k=1}^{K} b_{ik}\lambda_k + v_i. \tag{27}$$

The v_i will be the same vector elements defined in (26). From the orthogonality property of regressions,

$$\sum_{i=1}^{n} v_i = 0, \tag{28a}$$

$$\sum_{i=1}^{n} v_i b_{ik} = 0, \qquad \text{all } k. \tag{28b}$$

Consider the arbitrage portfolio $\omega_i = v_i/\|\mathbf{v}_n\|\sqrt{n}$. The profit on it is

$$\begin{aligned}(\sqrt{n}\|\mathbf{v}_n\|)^{-1}\sum_1^n v_i\tilde{Z}_i &= (\sqrt{n}\|\mathbf{v}_n\|)^{-1}\sum_1^n v_i\left(a_i + \sum_1^k b_{ik}\tilde{f}_k + \tilde{\varepsilon}_i\right) \\ &= (\sqrt{n}\|\mathbf{v}_n\|)^{-1}\sum_1^n v_i(a_i + \tilde{\varepsilon}_i).\end{aligned} \tag{29}$$

The last line follows from (28b). The expected profit is

$$\begin{aligned}&(\sqrt{n}\|\mathbf{v}_n\|)^{-1}\sum_1^n v_i a_i \\ &= (\sqrt{n}\|\mathbf{v}_n\|)^{-1}\left[\lambda_0\sum_1^n v_i + \sum_1^K \lambda_k \sum_1^n v_i b_{ik} + \sum_1^n v_i^2\right] \\ &= \frac{\|\mathbf{v}_n\|}{\sqrt{n}}.\end{aligned} \tag{30}$$

The first two sums in the second line of (30) are zero from (28a), (28b). The variance of the profit is

$$(n\|\mathbf{v}_n\|)^2)^{-1}\sum_1^n v_i^2 s_i^2 \leq \frac{S^2}{n}. \tag{31}$$

Now suppose that the stated theorem is false; then the expected profit remains nonzero while its variance goes to zero as n is increased. But this would represent an arbitrage opportunity of the type defined in (23). Hence, $\|\mathbf{v}_n\|^2/n$ must vanish, and (26) obtains. Q.E.D.

The derived no arbitrage condition is

$$\frac{1}{n}\sum_{i=1}^{n}\left(a_i - \lambda_0 - \sum_{k=1}^{k} b_{ij}\lambda_k\right)^2 \to 0. \tag{32}$$

Each term in this infinite sum is nonnegative. The average term is zero;

therefore most of the terms (i.e., all but a finite numbr of them) must be negligible. To be precise, if the assets are ordered by their absolute pricing errors so that $|\nu_1| \geq |\nu_2| \geq \cdots \geq |\nu_i| \geq \cdots$, then for any δ no matter how small, there exists an N such that fewer than N of the assets are mispriced by more than δ:

$$|\nu_1| \cdots \geq |\nu_{N-1}| \geq \delta > |\nu_N| \geq |\nu_{N+1}| \geq \cdots. \tag{33}$$

This means that the linear pricing model

$$\bar{Z}_i = \lambda_0 + \sum_1^K b_{ik}\lambda_k \tag{34}$$

prices "most" of the assets "correctly," and all of the assets together with a negligible mean square error. However, it can be arbitrarily bad at pricing a finite number of the assets.

It may seem somewhat strange that the magnitudes of the residual variances do not enter the pricing bound in (26). Intuitively, we would expect that assets with little residual variation should be priced quite closely whereas those with high residual variances could deviate by more. In particular, we know that among assets with zero residual risk the pricing must be exact. This intuition is correct.

THEOREM 2 *Under the same conditions as in Theorem 1 the pricing errors must satisfy*

$$\lim_{n\to\infty} \frac{1}{n} \sum_{i=1}^{n} \frac{\nu_i^2}{s_i^2} = 0. \tag{35}$$

Proof. The proof is left to the reader. [*Hint*: Consider a weighted least squares "regression."]

As promised, this theorem provides the intuition, lacking in the previous theorem, that the pricing deviation permitted each asset depends critically on its residual variation. It does more than simply clarify this issue, however. It provides a stronger condition which must be met in economies with no arbitrage, as the following example demonstrates.

Consider an economy with no common factors; $a_i = i^{-1}$, $s_i^2 = i^{-2}$ for i even; and $a_i = -(i+1)^{-1}$, $s_i^2 = (i+1)^{-2}$ for i odd. Clearly, for all even n, $\lambda_n = 0$ is the best fit, and

$$\Sigma \nu_i^2 = 2^{-2} + 2^{-2} + 4^{-2} + 4^{-2} + \cdots = \frac{1}{2}\sum_1^{n/2} i^{-2} \tag{36}$$

converges to $\pi^2/6$, so $\Sigma \nu_i^2/n$ goes to zero, and Theorem 1 is satisfied. Equation (35) is violated, however, since

$$\sum_1^n \frac{\nu_i^2}{s_i^2} = \sum_1^n 1 = n, \tag{37}$$

so the limit in (35) is 1. Thus, the arbitrage portfolio $\omega_i = -\omega_{i-1} = i/n$ for i even presents an arbitrage opportunity with an expected profit and variance of

$$\sum_1^n \omega_i a_i = \frac{1}{n}\sum_1^n 1 = 1, \qquad \sum_1^n \omega_i^2 s_i^2 = \frac{1}{n^2}\left(\sum_1^n 1\right) = \frac{1}{n} \to 0. \tag{38}$$

If there is an upper bound S^2 on the residual variances as we have assumed, then Theorem 1 is a special case of Theorem 2 since $\Sigma v_i^2 \leqslant S^2 \Sigma v_i^2/s_i^2$.

The earlier theorem is still useful, of course, because the residual variances need not be known for its application. If residual variances are not bounded, then (35) does not imply (26); however, the proof of Theorem 1 is no longer valid either. If residual variances are bounded away from zero as well, then Theorems 1 and 2 are equivalent.

In these two theorems the factor premiums may change at each step along the way. It is also possible to prove that the mean square error goes to zero even for a fixed vector of factor premiums.

RISK AND RISK PREMIUMS

Unless something further about the nature of the factors in the linear generating model can be specified, no economic significance can be attached to the signs or magnitudes of the λ_k. In fact for any arbitrage-pricing-model economy, it is possible to create a different set of K uncorrelated factors with only one receiving a positive factor risk premium. The arbitrage model can be written as

$$\tilde{\mathbf{z}} = \mathbf{a} + \mathbf{B}\tilde{\mathbf{f}} + \tilde{\boldsymbol{\varepsilon}}, \tag{39a}$$

$$\mathbf{a} \approx \lambda_0 \mathbf{1} + \mathbf{B}\boldsymbol{\lambda}. \tag{39b}$$

Now consider a new set of factors created by an orthogonal transformation of the original set:

$$\hat{\mathbf{f}} \equiv \mathbf{T}'\mathbf{f}. \tag{40}$$

$\mathbf{T}$ is an orthogonal matrix with $\mathbf{TT}' = \mathbf{T}'\mathbf{T} = \mathbf{I}$, so $\mathbf{f} = \mathbf{T}\hat{\mathbf{f}}$. Then

$$\tilde{\mathbf{z}} = \mathbf{a} + \mathbf{BT}\hat{\mathbf{f}} + \tilde{\boldsymbol{\varepsilon}} \equiv \mathbf{a} + \hat{\mathbf{B}}\hat{\mathbf{f}} + \tilde{\boldsymbol{\varepsilon}}; \tag{41}$$

that is, $\mathbf{B} \equiv \hat{\mathbf{B}}\mathbf{T}'$. Substituting for $\mathbf{B}$ in (39b) gives

$$\mathbf{a} = \lambda_0 \mathbf{1} + \hat{\mathbf{B}}\mathbf{T}'\boldsymbol{\lambda}. \tag{42}$$

To substantiate our claim, we now need only show that $\mathbf{T}'\boldsymbol{\lambda}$ is a vector with only one nonzero element and that (41) is a proper linear generating model for the factors $\hat{\mathbf{f}}$. The latter is easily accomplished, since for any orrhogonal matrix $\mathbf{T}$,

$$E(\boldsymbol{\varepsilon}\hat{\mathbf{f}}') = E(\boldsymbol{\varepsilon}\mathbf{f}'\mathbf{T}) = E(\boldsymbol{\varepsilon}\mathbf{f}')\mathbf{T} = \mathbf{0}, \tag{43}$$

and

$$E(\hat{\mathbf{f}}\hat{\mathbf{f}}') = E(\mathbf{T}'\mathbf{f}\mathbf{f}'\mathbf{T}) = \mathbf{T}'E(\mathbf{f}\mathbf{f}')\mathbf{T} = \mathbf{T}'\mathbf{I}\mathbf{T}' = \mathbf{T}'\mathbf{T} = \mathbf{I}. \tag{44}$$

To establish the former, choose the heretofore arbitrary transformation matrix

$$\mathbf{T} = (\boldsymbol{\lambda}(\boldsymbol{\lambda}'\boldsymbol{\lambda})^{-1/2}, \mathbf{X}), \tag{45}$$

where X is any K by $K - 1$ matrix of mutually orthogonal unitary columns all orthogonal to $\boldsymbol{\lambda}$. By construction $\mathbf{T}$ is an orthogonal matrix; therefore

$$\mathbf{I} = \mathbf{T}'\mathbf{T} = (\mathbf{T}'\boldsymbol{\lambda}(\boldsymbol{\lambda}'\boldsymbol{\lambda})^{-1/2}, \mathbf{T}'\mathbf{X})$$

and

$$(1, 0, \ldots, 0)' = \frac{\mathbf{T}'\boldsymbol{\lambda}}{(\boldsymbol{\lambda}'\boldsymbol{\lambda})^{1/2}}, \qquad ((\boldsymbol{\lambda}'\boldsymbol{\lambda})^{1/2}, 0, \ldots, 0)' = \mathbf{T}'\boldsymbol{\lambda}. \tag{46}$$

The fact that a K factor model can be "reduced" to a different model with only one priced factor must not be construed as a criticism of the original model. This "simplification" cannot be performed until all the original factor risk premium are known. (*Aside*: We have already seen something similar in a different context. In Chapter 4 we saw that assets could be priced in terms of two mean-variance efficient portfolios; however, these portfolios could not be identified unless all expected rates of return were known.)

The principal lesson to be learned is that in virtually any equilibrium only a portion of the uncertainty brings compensation. This can be true even when an unpriced risk is common to many or all assets. No meaningful economic statement has been made, however, until the priced and unpriced sources of risk are identified. The CAPM is one case in which this identification is made. We will encounter others in Chapters 13 and 15.

Even if certain factors are unpriced, it is useful to know the asset loadings on that factor despite the fact that they do not affect expected returns. For example, in an event study it would be useful to remove the common unpriced component as well as the common priced component of an asset's return to reduce the variation in the residual.

FULLY DIVERSIFIED PORTFOLIOS

Even though the factors may not be identified with any specific macroeconomic variables, the factor premiums may be given portfolio interpretations under certain conditions. Before doing so, however, we must introduce a new concept.

A *fully diversified portfolio* is the limit of a sequence of positive net investment portfolios whose weights satisfy

$$\lim_{n\to\infty} n\sum_{1}^{n} w_i^2(n) \leq C < \infty. \tag{47}$$

It is obvious that w_i must vanish for each asset in a fully diversified portfolio. In particular, w_i must be $O(n^{-1})$ for "most" assets. Fully diversified portfolios have no residual risk in the limit since

$$\lim_{n\to\infty} \sum w_i^2 s_i^2 \leq \lim_{n\to\infty} (n\sum w_i^2)\left(\frac{S^2}{n}\right) = 0. \tag{48}$$

There are also less than fully diversified portfolios with no residual risk. One example is the limit of the sequence in which $w_i(n) = n^{-3/4}$ for the first $n/2$ assets and $2/n - n^{-3/4}$ for the second half. In this case

$$\sum w_i^2(n) = \frac{n}{2}n^{-3/2} + \frac{n}{2}\left(\frac{2}{n} - n^{-3/4}\right)^2 = \frac{2}{n} + \frac{1}{\sqrt{n}} - \frac{2}{n^{3/4}}. \tag{49}$$

For large n then the residual risk is less than $S/\sqrt{n}$, so it vanishes in the limit. Nevertheless, the limit in (47) is $\sqrt{n}$, which is not bounded.

THEOREM 3 *The expected returns on all fully diversified portfolios are given correctly with zero error by any linear pricing model satisfying Theorem 1.*

Proof. From Equation (30) the expeted return on the portfolio in the nth step of the sequence is

$$\lambda_0 + \sum w_i b_{ik}\lambda_k + \sum w_i v_i, \tag{50}$$

so the theorem is proved if the third term vanishes. By the Cauchy–Schwarz inequality

$$(\sum w_i v_i)^2 \leq \sum w_i^2 \sum v_i^2 = (n\sum w_i a^2)\left(\sum \frac{v_i^2}{n}\right). \tag{51}$$

But the first term on the right hand side is bounded, and the second vanishes in the limit. Q.E.D.

If we can create a fully diversified portfolio with $b_{pk} = 1$ and $b_{pj} = 0$ for all other factors, then $\lambda_0 + \lambda_k$ is the expected return on this portfolio. Similarly, λ_0 is the expected return on a fully diversified portfolio with no factor risk (if such is feasible), but since it has no residual risk either, $\lambda_0 = R$.

If there is only one factor and if the market portfolio is fully diversified, then $b_M\lambda = \bar{Z}_M - R$, and the no arbitrage condition may be written as

$$\bar{z}_i - R \approx \frac{b_i}{b_M}(\bar{Z}_M - R) \approx \frac{\sigma_{iM}}{\sigma_M^2}(\bar{Z}_M - R) \equiv \beta_i(\bar{Z}_M - R). \quad (52)$$

The second approximation follows since

$$\beta_i = \frac{b_i b_M + w_{iM}s_i^2}{b_M^2 + s_M^2} = \left[\frac{b_i}{b_M} + \frac{w_{iM}s_i^2}{b_M^2}\right]\left[1 + \frac{s_M^2}{b_M^2}\right]^{-1}, \quad (53)$$

and w_{iM} and s_M^2 are zero in the limit for fully diversified portfolios.

Despite the formal identity between the relation in (52) and the equilibrium in Equation (39) of Chapter 6 for a market whose securities' returns are members of a "separating distribution," there is a fundamental difference in the underlying economics of these two models. The separating distribution (CAPM) relation is a market equilibrium, whereas the linear model relation is a "no arbitrage" condition. Now although there obviously can be no arbitrage possibilities in a market at equilibrium, the converse is not true. The absence of arbitrage opportunities does not necessarily imply that the market is in equilibrium.

There are two consequences of this distinction which are important for empirical work. The first is that the APT relation (52) will hold for a subset of asset returns which meets its assumptions even if all asset returns do not. (This is not true, in general, for the separating distribution equilibrium.) We are justified in ignoring some assets in empirical tests so long as the number of assets actually considered is "sufficiently great" to permit diversification. In addition, finding the true market portfolio is not crucial. Any fully diversified index may be used as a proxy for the market. Thus, the linear model can furnish at least a partial answer to the objection that the true market has never been identified.

Using mean-variance analysis, we can base the equilibrium on any mean-variance efficient portfolio and its zero beta portfolio; however, the intercept term of the relation is equal to the risk-free rate only if the tangency (market) portfolio is used. For any other mean-variance efficient portfolio the intercept term is the expected return on a risky portfolio which is uncorrelated with it. In the APT, on the other hand, the relation will always include the riskless return as the intercept term for any choice of fully diversified index. The reason for this difference is simple to explain. A riskless asset can be constructed from the risky assets by forming a well-diversified portfolio with $b = 0$. So under the linear factor model, the efficient frontier hyperbola is degenerate, consisting of two rays from the point R. (*Note*: When there is more than one factor, it may not be always be possible to construct a portfolio which is complete free from risk.)

Since both the CAPM and the single-factor linear model have conclusion (52), all tests verify (or reject) either theory if they look only at this pricing relation. To the extent that an improper market portfolio has been used in tests, what has actually been tested is actually closer to the single-factor linear model. Furthermore, most tests use diversified portfolios which are highly mutually correlated (e.g., in Black, Jensen, and Scholes all forty portfolios for the subperiods had correlations with the market in excess of .87). Thus, these tests come close to testing only Equation (6) as applied to well-diversified portfolios and not the individual asset pricing Equation (52).

In a multifactor model at most one of them can be identified with the market portfolio. Nevertheless, the interpretation that λ_k is proportional to the expected excess return on a fully diversified portfolio with a single source of factor risk is still valid, provided that both such a portfolio and a fully diversified zero factor risk portfolio are feasible. We now examine conditions under which we can create these portfolios.

INTERPRETATION OF THE FACTOR PREMIUMS

To simplify the notation of this section, we define the augmented factor loading matrix to be the partitioned matrix $\hat{\mathbf{B}}_n = (\mathbf{1}, \mathbf{B}_n)$. Its dimensions are n by $K + 1$. We assume for now that for large n it has rank $K + 1$. Obviously, $\mathbf{B}_n$ must have rank K for sufficiently large n or the factor loadings are collinear, so there is an unavoidable risk as before. This is also clearly the case if any columns are collinear with a constant vector. In either case it will be impossible to form a portfolio with only a single source of factor risk.

We also define $\mathbf{Q}_n \equiv \hat{\mathbf{B}}_n'\hat{\mathbf{B}}_n/n$ and assume that the sequence $\mathbf{Q}_n$ has a limit. This assumption is not crucial, but it greatly simplifies the exposition. $\mathbf{Q}_n$ has the same size, $K + 1$ square, independent of n, so it has a limit if each element does. Furthermore, these are all bounded:

$$q_{11} = 1; \qquad |q_{1i}| = |q_{i1}| = \left|\sum_1^n b_{ki}\right| \Big/ n \leqslant b;$$

and for $i, j > 1$,

$$|q_{ij}| = \left|\sum_1^n b_{ki} b_{kj}\right| \Big/ n \leqslant b^2.$$

Now consider the sequence of portfolio formation problems using $n = K + 1, K + 2, \ldots$ assets:

$$\text{Min } \tfrac{1}{2}\sum w_i^2,$$

$$\text{Subject to } \sum w_i = 1,$$

$$\sum w_i b_{ik} = 1, \tag{54}$$
$$\sum w_i b_{ij} = 0, \qquad j \neq k.$$

Form the Lagrangian $L = \frac{1}{2}\mathbf{w}'\mathbf{w} + \boldsymbol{\gamma}'(\mathbf{c} - \hat{\mathbf{B}}'\mathbf{w})$, where $\boldsymbol{\gamma}$ is a vector of Lagrange multipliers and $\mathbf{c}$ is a vector with 1 in the first and kth spots and 0's elsewhere. Minimizing gives

$$\mathbf{0} = \mathbf{w} - \hat{\mathbf{B}}\boldsymbol{\gamma}, \tag{55a}$$
$$\mathbf{0} = \mathbf{c} - \hat{\mathbf{B}}'\mathbf{w}. \tag{55b}$$

Multiplying (55a) by $\hat{\mathbf{B}}'$ gives $\mathbf{0} = \hat{\mathbf{B}}'\mathbf{w} - \hat{\mathbf{B}}'\hat{\mathbf{B}}\boldsymbol{\gamma} = \mathbf{c} - \hat{\mathbf{B}}'\hat{\mathbf{B}}\boldsymbol{\gamma}$ or $\boldsymbol{\gamma} = (\hat{\mathbf{B}}'\hat{\mathbf{B}})^{-1}\mathbf{c}$. (*Note*: This inverse exists because $\hat{\mathbf{B}}$ has full column rank.) Substituting back into (55a) gives

$$\mathbf{w} = \hat{\mathbf{B}}(\hat{\mathbf{B}}'\hat{\mathbf{B}})^{-1}\mathbf{c}. \tag{56}$$

This portfolio has a single source of factor risk, as desired. It is fully diversified if

$$n\mathbf{w}'\mathbf{w} = n\mathbf{c}'(\hat{\mathbf{B}}'\hat{\mathbf{B}})^{-1}\hat{\mathbf{B}}'\hat{\mathbf{B}}(\hat{\mathbf{B}}'\hat{\mathbf{B}})^{-1}\mathbf{c} = \mathbf{c}'\mathbf{Q}^{-1}\mathbf{c} \tag{57}$$

is bounded. Since $\mathbf{c}$ and $\mathbf{Q}$ are finite in size, the quantity in (57) can be unbounded only if $\mathbf{Q}_n$ becomes "singular in the limit." [*Note*: $\mathbf{Q}_n$ must be nonsingular for all finite n because $\mathbf{B}_n$ is of full column rank.) Similarly, if $\mathbf{c}$ is a vector with a 1 for the first element and 0's elsewhere, the created portfolio has no factor risk and is fully diversified. Its expected return, therefore, must be $\lambda_0 = R$. Thus, the portfolio interpretation

$$a_i \approx R + \sum b_{ik}(a^k - R), \tag{58}$$

where a^k is the expected return on a fully diversified portfolio with one unit of k risk and no other risk, is valid provided $\mathbf{Q}$ is nonsingular.

This condition is the limiting equivalent of the requirement that the factor loadings not be collinear in the idiosyncratic risk-free economy. It is most easily understood by considering examples in which it is not true.

Example 1 Suppose there is a single factor and all but m assets have the same $b_i = b$. Without loss of generality take these to be the first m and set $\bar{b} \equiv \Sigma_1^m b_i/m$ and $\bar{d} \equiv \Sigma_1^m b_i^2/m$. The for $n > m$,

$$\mathbf{Q}_n = n^{-1}\begin{pmatrix} n & m\bar{b} + (n-m)b \\ m\bar{b} + (n-m)b & m\bar{d} + (n-m)b^2 \end{pmatrix}. \tag{59}$$

In the limit

$$\mathbf{Q}_\infty = \begin{pmatrix} 1 & b \\ b & b^2 \end{pmatrix}. \tag{60}$$

Example 2 Suppose there is a single factor, and all assets have different factor loadings $b_i = b - 2^{-i}$. In this case

$$\mathbf{Q}_n = n^{-1}\begin{pmatrix} n & nb + 1 - 2^{-n} \\ nb + 1 - 2^{-n} & nb^2 + (1 - 4^{-n})/3 \end{pmatrix}. \tag{61}$$

Again $\mathbf{Q}_\infty$ is given by (60).

Example 3 Suppose there are two factors with loadings b_i and $c_i = 1 - b_i + 2^{-i}$. Then

$$\mathbf{Q}_n = \begin{pmatrix} 1 & \bar{b} & 1 - \bar{b} \\ \bar{b} & \bar{d} & \bar{b} - \bar{d} \\ 1 - \bar{b} & \bar{b} - \bar{d} & 1 - 2\bar{b} + \bar{d} \end{pmatrix} + n^{-1}\sum_{1}^{n} 2^{-i}\begin{pmatrix} 0 & 0 & 1 \\ 0 & 0 & b_i \\ 1 & b_i & 2(1 - b_i) + 2^{-i} \end{pmatrix} \tag{62}$$

If the b_i are bounded, then the second matrix vanishes in the limit and the first is singular.

In each of these examples the factor loadings, including a vector of 1's, are close enough to collinear so that fully diversified portfolios cannot be formed with arbitrary factor responses. Specifically, in Example 1, to form a portfolio with b_p substantially different from b requires nonnegligible investment in some of the first m assets, so any such portfolio cannot be fully diversified.

Exercises for the Reader

1. If $\mathbf{Q}_\infty$ is singular but $\mathbf{B}_n'\mathbf{B}_n/n$ has a nonsingular limit, show that

$$a_i \approx a^o + \sum_{1}^{K-1} b_{ik}(a^k - a^o), \tag{63}$$

where a^k is as defined before and a^o is the expected return on a portfolio with a zero factor loading on the first $K - 1$ factors. (*Note*: The omitted factor is not completely arbitrary and might not be the last.)

2. If $\mathbf{Q}_\infty$ has rank r and $\mathbf{B}_n'\mathbf{B}_n/n$ has a limiting rank of $r - 1$, show that

$$a_i \approx R + \sum b_{ik}(a^k - R), \tag{64}$$

where the sum is taken over $r - 1$ values of k.

3. If both $\mathbf{Q}_\infty$ and $\mathbf{B}_n'\mathbf{B}_n/n$ have rank r in the limit, show that

$$a_i \approx a^o + \sum b_{ik}(a^k - a^o), \tag{65}$$

where the sum is taken over $r - 1$ values of k. The portfolio associated with a^o has $b_{ik} = 0$ for these values of k.

These exercises show two things. First, as seen in Exercise 2, a complete lack of correlation among the residuals is not necessary for the APT to hold. Essentially what is required is a sufficient lack of correlation for the law of large numbers to apply. Second, the pricing model can appear in a "Sharpe–Lintner" or "Black" form.

PRICING BOUNDS IN A FINITE ECONOMY

It has been claimed that the APT is not testable because its pricing is meaningful only in an economy with infinite assets. One response to this criticism is to ignore it and test for an exact linear relation among expected returns. In certain respects this is justified. The CAPM, for example, is based on strong assumptions and yields (objectionably) strong conclusions. The APT, on the other hand, is based on relatively weak assumptions, and it only suggests a "conclusion." A strong assumption can be made at this point to claim that the conclusion is exact.

A second response is to strengthen the original assumptions, so that the pricing equation becomes exact. We consider this in the next section.

A final response is to derive pricing bounds for each asset. These can then be checked for violations. To show how this can be done, we consider as an example a combination of the CAPM and linear factor models.

Assume that all asset returns are described by the generating model in (1) and that the CAPM pricing result holds. Since $\sigma_{im} = \Sigma b_{ik} b_{mk} + w_{im} s_i^2$, expected returns can be written as

$$\begin{aligned} a_i &= \frac{1}{\sigma_m^2}(\Sigma b_{ik} b_{mk} + w_{im} s_i^2)(a_m - R) \\ &= \sum b_{ik}\left(b_{mk}\frac{a_m - R}{\sigma_m^2}\right) + w_{im} s_i^2 \frac{a_m - R}{\sigma_m^2}. \end{aligned} \tag{66}$$

The terms in parentheses can be interpreted as factor premiums λ_k, so the pricing error is

$$v_i = w_{im} s_i^2 \frac{a_m - R}{\sigma_m^2}. \tag{67}$$

The size of this error is unknown unless the market portfolio is identified; however, it can be bounded. For any value-weighted market proxy $0 \leqslant w_{im} \leqslant w_{ip}$. Thus, if relative risk aversion is assumed to be less than some bound, the pricing errors are also bounded. For example, if relative risk aversion is less than 20, then a typical stock whose value is about 1/2000 of the NYSE will have a pricing bound of $0 < v_i < s_i^2/100$.

Note that this result answers both the objection that the APT is not testable and that the CAPM is not testable, since the market is not observable. On the other hand, it also assumes *both* mean-variance maximization and a factor structure.

If we are unwilling to assume the CAPM, the residuals from the APT can still be bounded if other strong assumptions are made. The following theorem of Dybvig is stated without proof.

THEOREM 4 *Assume that the returns on all assets are given by the linear factor model (1) with $\tilde{f}_1, \ldots, \tilde{f}_k, \tilde{\varepsilon}_1, \ldots, \tilde{\varepsilon}_n$ all mutually independent. The residuals are bounded below by −100%. The portfolio* $\mathbf{w}$ *is the optimal holding of some investor with a von Neumann–Morgenstern utility function which is strictly increasing, concave, has bounded absolute risk aversion $-u''(Z)/u'(Z) < A$, and has $u'''(Z) \geq 0$. Then for each asset*

$$a_i = R + \sum b_{ik}\lambda_k + v_i, \qquad |v_i| \leq w_i s_i^2 A e^{w_i A}. \tag{68}$$

The assumptions on the utility function and the assumption that the $\tilde{\varepsilon}_i$ are bounded assure that small contributions to returns by the $\tilde{\varepsilon}_i$ cannot have large utility effects. The assumption that the residuals and factors are independent guarantees that the residual risk is uncorrelated with the utility of returns on the factors. It has the same role here as in Equation (72) of Chapter 6.

EXACT PRICING IN THE LINEAR MODEL

Thus far we have shown that the APT holds with a zero mean square error. That is, "most" assets are priced with negligible error. Under what conditions can we assert that *all* assets are priced with negligible error, or, equivalently, that the total error converges to zero? Sufficient conditions for this stronger result are that at least one investor chooses to hold a fully diversified portfolio, and that each asset's idiosyncratic risk be a fair game with respect to all the factors

$$E(\tilde{\varepsilon}_i | f_1, f_2, \ldots, f_K) = 0. \tag{69}$$

In the limit a fully diversified portfolio has no idiosyncratic risk, so exact pricing follows, as shown for a finite number of assets in Chapter 6.

The question remaining is, What requirements are needed to assure that some investor holds a fully diversified portfolio? It seems natural to view idiosyncratic risk as nonmarket risk which is not priced and conclude that all investors would hold fully diversified portfolios. However, this parallel is deceptive, and the reasoning is circular. In some cases a significant portion of the total risk of the economy comes from the idiosyncratic risk of a few assets. In these circumstances it is priced, and the APT fails—at least for these assets.

As a simple example of a linear factor economy in which not all assets are priced exactly by the arbitrage relation, consider the set of assets with returns

$$\tilde{z}_1 = a_1 + \tilde{\varepsilon}_1, \qquad \tilde{z}_i = a + \tilde{\varepsilon}_i, \quad i = 2, \ldots, \infty. \tag{70}$$

The ε_i, $i > 1$, are independent and identically distributed. This is a zero factor economy. If $a = R$, assets 2, 3, ... are priced exactly right. However, if $a_1 \neq R$, then asset 1 is not priced correctly. Can such an economy exist in equilibrium? The answer is yes.

Suppose that the assets are scale-free investment opportunities. By symmetry, investors will purchase assets 2, 3, ... equally. In the limit this portfolio must duplicate the riskless asset.

Assume that $\tilde{\varepsilon}_1$ is normally distributed with mean zero and variance s^2, and that all investors have exponential utility $u(Z) = e^{-\delta Z}$. From Equation (53) in Chapter 4, the optimal portfolio is the fraction w in asset 1 and $1 - w$ in the riskless asset (the equally weighted portfolio of 2, 3, ...), where w is

$$w = \frac{a_1 - R}{\delta s^2}. \tag{71}$$

Thus it is perfectly consistent to find $a_1 \neq R$, and in this case investors do not hold fully diversified portfolios. (It would be possible to construct a one-factor model fitting a and a_1 exactly by having the factor affect only asset 1. However, in this case the factor loadings on the factor are not sufficiently different. That is, $\mathbf{Q}_\infty$ is singular.)

The following theorem, which is stated without proof, gives sufficient conditions under which the arbitrage model holds exactly in the limit.

THEOREM 5 *If (i) the returns on the risky assets are given by the K factor linear generating model in (36) with* $E(\tilde{\varepsilon}_i | f_1, \ldots, f_K) = 0$, *(ii) the market proportion supply of each asset is negligible, (iii) the loadings on each factor are spread "evenly" among many securities (i.e.,* $\mathbf{Q}_n$ *is nonsingular in the limit), (iv) no investor takes an unboundedly large position in any security, and (v) marginal utility is bounded above zero, then the linear pricing relation in (26) holds, and the pricing errors converge to zero in the sense that*

$$\lim_{n\to\infty} \sum_1^n v_i^2 = 0. \tag{72}$$

Assumptions (ii) and (iii) together describe a "fully diversified economy." Condition (ii) assures that no asset is a significant proportion of the market portfolio. Condition (iii) serves two purposes. First, many of the coefficients b_{ik} ($i = 1, 2, \ldots$) must be nonzero for each k. That is, each $\tilde{f}_k$ affects a nonnegligible proportion of the asset returns. (Note that this does not say that only a finite number are unaffected. For example, $\tilde{f}_1$ could influence only the odd-numbered assets.) Second, there can be no severe multicollinearity in the columns of the factor loading matrix. That is, each factor must make an identifiable independent contribution to the risk of the economy. In a fully diversified economy, all investors can simultaneously hold fully diversified portfolios with the factor effects distributed among them in any fashion.

Assumptions (iv) and (v) guarantee that each investor's portfolio is an "interior" optimum; (iv) assures that risk aversion does not vanish so that variance is always disliked; (v) assures that expected return is always valued.

In this theorem $\lambda_0 = R$, provided that the riskless asset exists. Each λ_k is (asymptotically) exactly equal to the expected return on an asset with $b_{ik} = 1$ and $b_{ij} = 0$ for $j \neq k$.

8

Equilibrium Models with Complete Markets

In this chapter we examine the equilibrium that results in a market in which each state is insurable. Recall from the definition in Chapter 2 that a state is insurable if it is possible to construct a portfolio of assets that has a nonzero return in that state alone.

The definition of complete markets given here is a relatively simple one. There are many other definitions that have been used as well. The distinction among the definitions depends on exactly what criteria are used to differentiate states from one another. For our purposes states are distinguished only by the returns on marketed assets. Thus, there can be no possibility for disagreement or confusion on the part of the investors as to which state has been realized. We are not faced with the problems that sometimes arise if a state's definition depends on some individual's private information. That is, there are no moral hazard or adverse selection problems which arise, for example, in realistic insurance problems.

NOTATION

The insured portfolio that can be constructed which pays one dollar if a particular state occurs is called an *Arrow–Debreu* security in honor of the two economists who developed the idea of complete markets. Other names that are also used are *state security*, *pure security*, and *state contingent claim*.

Since the payoff to the state s Arrow–Debreu security is one dollar if and only if state s occurs, its price at the beginning of the period must be p_s, that is, the sth component of the economy's supporting price vector. Because every state is insurable, the supporting price vector is completely determined with unique state prices (unless arbitrage opportunities are available).

To demonstrate this construction, let the N vector $\mathbf{n}$ represent a portfolio of traded assets; n_i is the number of shares of asset i held in the portfolio. To construct the Arrow–Debreu securities for a complete market, we require S portfolios $\mathbf{n}_s$ such that

$$\mathbf{Y}\mathbf{n}_s = \boldsymbol{\iota}_s, \qquad s = 1, \ldots, S, \tag{1}$$

where $\boldsymbol{\iota}_s$ is an N vector with a 1 in the sth spot and 0's elsewhere (i.e., it is the sth column of the $N \times N$ identity matrix).

Equation (1) can also be written as

$$\mathbf{YN} = \mathbf{I}, \tag{2}$$

where $\mathbf{N} = (\mathbf{n}_1, \mathbf{n}_2, \ldots, \mathbf{n}_S)$. If there are fewer than S securities, then it is clear that no solution to (2) exists, and the market cannot be complete. If there are exactly S securities and their payoffs are linearly independent (there are no redundant securities), then $\mathbf{N} = \mathbf{Y}^{-1}$ satisfies (2). For $N > S$, $\mathbf{Y}$ will still have full row rank S if there are S linearly independent assets. Therefore, $\mathbf{Y}$ has a left inverse $\mathbf{Y}^{-} \equiv (\mathbf{Y}'\mathbf{Y})^{-1}\mathbf{Y}'$ and $\mathbf{N} = \mathbf{Y}^{-}$ is a possible (but not the only) collection of state securities.

VALUATION IN COMPLETE MARKETS

This method can also be used to determine the state prices in terms of the values of the primitive assets. Since $\mathbf{p}'\mathbf{Y} = \mathbf{v}'$, we have from (2) that

$$\mathbf{v}'\mathbf{N} = \mathbf{p}'\mathbf{YN} = \mathbf{p}'\mathbf{I} = \mathbf{p}'. \tag{3}$$

More often we will wish to express the value of the primitive assets in terms of the state prices. This is just the usual valuation given in Chapter 2:

$$\mathbf{v} = \mathbf{Y}'\mathbf{p}. \tag{4}$$

Since markets are complete, there is an Arrow–Debreu security for each state. A portfolio holding one of each of these is a riskless asset. Thus, a riskless asset always exists in a complete market, and the relation given in Chapter 2, $R = (\mathbf{1}'\mathbf{p})^{-1}$, gives the riskless rate.

PORTFOLIO SEPARATION IN COMPLETE MARKETS

In a complete market, investors will be indifferent between choosing portfolios made up of only the S state securities and having complete freedom to choose from these plus all N primary assets. Consider an investor who selects a portfolio of firms and state securities with n_i shares of each of the former and ν_s' shares of each of the latter. The budget constraint is

$$W_0 = \sum_{i=1}^{N} n_i V_i + \sum_{s=1}^{S} \nu_s' p_s, \tag{5}$$

and the final wealth in state s is

$$W(s) = \sum_{i=1}^{N} n_i Y_{si} + \nu'_s. \tag{6}$$

Now consider the alternative portfolio strategy, investing in only the state securities, which holds $\nu_s = \Sigma n_i Y_{si} + \nu'_s$ shares of state security s. Clearly, the end-of-period wealth will be identical. Furthermore, if the investor is a price taker, the budget constraint is also satisfied since

$$\begin{aligned} \sum_{s=1}^{S} p_s \nu_s &= \sum_{s=1}^{S} p_s \nu'_s + \sum_{i=1}^{N} n_i \sum_{s=1}^{S} p_s Y_{si} \\ &= \sum_{s=1}^{S} p_s \nu'_s + \sum_{i=1}^{N} \mathrm{n_i V_i} = \mathrm{W_0}. \end{aligned} \tag{7}$$

The second line follows from Equation (5).

Of course, in equilibrium the primary assets must actually be held. However, this can be done through financial intermediaries. Suppose that mutual funds buy all the primary assets and finance this by issuing

$$\sum N_i Y_{si} \equiv \dot{N}_s \tag{8}$$

shares of state security s for each state. (N_i is the number of shares of primary asset i.) The intermediaries are exactly hedged.

This portfolio separation theorem is not as strong a result as those in Chapter 4 and 6. Here only redundant assets are eliminated from consideration, but the remaining state securities can generate a portfolio with any pattern of returns that the complete set can. In the previous theorems some portfolio return patterns which are feasible with the set of individual assets are not possible with the "separating" portfolios.

For example, consider an economy whose assets conform to a separating distribution as described in Chapter 6 with $R = 2$, $b_1 = 1$, $b_2 = 2$, and

state	index, Y	ε_1	ε_2	z_1	z_2
1	1	0.6	−0.6	1.6	1.4
2	1	−0.6	0.6	0.4	2.6
3	2	0.1	−0.1	2.1	3.9
4	2	−0.1	0.1	1.9	4.1

(9)

To eliminate residual risk, in this economy *all* investors will hold the two risky assets in equal proportion, thus creating a risky portfolio with return pattern (1.5, 1.5, 3.0, 3.0) which has equal returns in states 1 and 2 and in states 3 and 4. Even after combining this portfolio with the riskless asset, these same equalities hold. Thus, the mutual fund theorem "precludes" the return pattern (1.6, 0.4, 2.1, 1.9), for example, but this is clearly feasible by holding just asset 1.

THE INVESTOR'S PORTFOLIO PROBLEM

Suppose the investor has a utility function of the form $U(W_1, s)$. Strictly speaking, we need not include future wealth as an argument of next period's utility since the state outcome uniquely determines W_1. However, at times it will be useful to assume that utility is *state independent* so that only wealth directly affects the level of utility $U(W_1, s) = U(W_1)$. This is the case we have examined in previous chapters. Furthermore, even in the general case, the two-argument formulation is convenient notation because we wish to think of W_1 as something under the investor's partial control while the state realized cannot be controlled at all.

The investor's problem can now be stated as

$$\text{Max} \sum_{s=1}^{S} \pi_s U(\nu_s, s) \tag{10}$$

$$\text{Subject to} \quad \sum \nu_s p_s = W_0,$$

where π_s denotes the subjective probabilities that the different states will occur, and ν_s, the decision variable, denote the numbers of shares of the state securities the investor puchases. (From the previous section only the state securities need be considered, and $W_1(s) = \nu_s$.)

Form the Lagrangian

$$L = \sum \pi_s U_1(\nu_s, s) + \lambda[W_0 - \sum \nu_s p_s]. \tag{11}$$

Then

$$0 = \frac{\partial L}{\partial \lambda} = W_0 - \sum \nu_s p_s,$$

$$0 = \frac{\partial L}{\nu_s} = \pi_s U_1(\nu_s, s) - \lambda p_s. \tag{12}$$

Thus, in choosing a portfolio, an investor equates expected marginal utility per dollar spent in each state:

$$\pi_s \frac{U_1(\nu_s, s)}{p_s} = \lambda > 0 \quad \text{for all } s. \tag{13}$$

As in the portfolio problems in Chapter 3, if consumption occurs at time zero, then λ is the marginal utility of first-period consumption.

Since all state security prices are positive, an "interior" solution to Equation (12) is guaranteed so long as $U_1(0, s) = \infty$, $U_1(\infty, s) = 0$, and $\pi_s > 0$, for all s. (The first requirement is not necessary if there are no short sale constraints, and negative wealth has a meaningful interpretation.) The requirement of positive subjective state probabilities is crucial. Unless $\pi_s > 0$, the investor will short the state s security to whatever extent is possible, and no unconstrained equilibrium will result.

PARETO OPTIMALITY OF COMPLETE MARKETS

It is a well-known result that the competitive equilibrium in a complete market is Pareto optimal. That is, there is no feasible reallocation of state claims that leaves all investors at least as well off in terms of expected utility and makes one investor better off. Note that the only feasibility criterion to be applied is that of aggregate supplies of the various assets; individual budget constraints need not be considered. This result can be easily demonstrated for local changes in the allocations as follows.

Suppose individual k's portfolio of state securities is changed by the vector $d\nu_s^k$. Then

$$\begin{aligned} dE[U^k(W_k, s)] &= \sum_s \pi_s^k U_1^k(\nu_s^k, s)\, d\nu_s^k \\ &= \lambda_k \sum_s p_s\, d\nu_s^k. \end{aligned} \tag{14}$$

The second line follows from Equation (13). Since $\lambda > 0$,

$$\lambda_k^{-1}\, dEU^k = \sum_s p_s\, d\nu_s^k. \tag{15}$$

Summing over all investors gives

$$\sum_k \lambda_k^{-1}\, dEU^k = \sum_s p_s \sum_k d\nu_s^k = 0 \tag{16}$$

since $\Sigma_k d\nu_s^k \equiv 0$ to maintain allocations equal to aggregate supplies. But if the gross change in the left-hand side is zero and the summand is positive for one investor, it must be negative for at least one other investor. Thus, since $\lambda_k > 0$ for all investors, $dEU^k > 0$ implies $dEU^j < 0$ for some j.

This result also holds for noninfinitesimal changes in portfolios and for nondifferentiable utility functions.

COMPLETE AND INCOMPLETE MARKETS: A COMPARISON

The equilibrium condition in Equation (13) is similar to that derived for general markets in Chapter 3. There [Equation (6b)] it was given that

$$E[U'(W\tilde{Z}^*)\tilde{z}_i]W = \lambda' \qquad \text{for all } i. \tag{17}$$

This result is a weaker form of the one given in (13).

The return $\tilde{z}_s$ on each Arrow–Debreu security is p_s^{-1} if state s occurs, and zero if any other state occurs. Therefore, for utility functions which depend only on wealth,

$$E[U'(W\tilde{Z}^*)\tilde{z}_s] = \frac{\pi_s U'(\nu_s)}{p_s} = \lambda. \tag{18}$$

For any other asset $Z_{si} = Y_{si}/v_i$ and

$$E[U'(W\tilde{Z}^*)\tilde{z}_i] = \sum_s \frac{\pi_s U'(\nu_s) Y_{si}}{v_i}$$

$$= \sum_s \frac{\lambda p_s Y_{si}}{v_i} = \lambda. \tag{19}$$

The second equality follows from Equation (13). Equation (19) verifies (17).

PARETO OPTIMALITY IN INCOMPLETE MARKETS: EFFECTIVELY COMPLETE MARKETS

The Pareto optimality result above does not generally obtain in incomplete markets. It is true that a competitive incomplete market will achieve a constrained Pareto optimal allocation of securities; however, there generally will be a Pareto improvement if new financial securities are introduced to complete the market.

To demonstrate this result, consider a very simple market with one asset and two equally probable states. The outcome space is $\mathbf{y} = (1, a)'$ per share with $a > 1$. Each share currently sells for v = one dollar. The portfolio problem can be considered a constrained complete market problem. The constraint is $\nu_2 = a\nu_1$. Thus, it may be stated as

$$\text{Max} \sum .5U(\nu_s)$$

$$\text{Subject to} \quad \nu_2 = a\nu_1, \qquad v\nu_1 = 1. \tag{20}$$

The second constraint is the budget constraint. The only feasible solution to Equation (20) is $\nu_1 = 1$, $\nu_2 = a$.

What set of Arrow–Debreu prices would support this alkocation for a given investor in a complete market? From Equation (12) $\hat{p}_s = .5\lambda^{-1}U'(\nu_s)$ so for this example $\hat{p}_1/\hat{p}_2 = U'(1)/U'(a)$. Also from (5) $v = 1 = \hat{p}_1 + a\hat{p}_2$. Solving this system for the required allocation gives

$$\hat{p}_1 = \frac{U'(1)}{U'(1) + aU'(a)}, \qquad \hat{p}_2 = \frac{U'(a)}{U'(1) + aU'(a)}. \tag{21}$$

Were this investor in a complete market and facing the prices given in (21), he or she would not care if they were now forced to hold only the single asset described previously. Thus, we may consider the prices in (21) to be the subjective complete market state prices that this investor perceives.

In general, two different investors will perceive different subjective prices, and both would profit from the creation of Arrow–Debreu financial securities. For example, with power utility $\hat{p}_1/\hat{p}_2 = a^{1-\gamma}$. With two such investors there are feasible state prices p_1 and p_2 satisfying

$$a^{1-\gamma_1} > \frac{p_1}{p_2} > a^{1-\gamma_2}, \tag{22}$$

at which the more risk-averse investor (smaller γ) would be willing to purchase some of the state 1 security from the less risk-averse investor in exchange for state security 2.

Incomplete markets are not necessarily Pareto inefficient. For example, in the simple economy just described, an investor with utility function $U(W) = -\exp[-\delta W]$, with $\delta = (a - 1)^{-1}\ln a$, would perceive subjective relative prices of

$$\frac{p_1}{p_2} = \exp([-(a - 1)^{-1}\ln a](1 - a)) = a. \tag{23}$$

But a log utility investor ($\gamma = 0$ earlier) would perceive the same subjective prices. Therefore, no gains would accrue from completing the market since trades could only occur at the relative prices $a{:}1$, and both investors are indifferent toward marginal trades at this price. In cases like this when incomplete markets are Pareto efficient, the market is said to be *effectively complete.*

Effective completeness can arise through "happenstance" as in the foregoing example. It also obtains whenever all investors are identical in tastes and endowments (and beliefs), since such investors would behave identically and could not perceive different subjective state prices. If all investors have HARA utility with the same cautiousness and a riskless asset is available, then portfolio separation into the riskless asset and the market occurs, and effective completeness again arises.

Note, however, that all asset returns belonging to some separating distribution, as described in Chapter 6, does not guarantee effective completeness even though the same market separation occurs. Investors generally perceive different subjective state prices and would profit from the completion of the market. (An example is given in Chapter 9.)

Other general categories of effectively complete markets could also be outlined. One important case is discussed in the next section. Here we shall simply argue that in the frictionless economies generally studied, it will always be in the interests of investors to create new financial securities until markets are effectively complete. Once this is accomplished, all complete market properties obtain. This is a general justification for analyzing the economic properties of complete markets even though actual markets are obviously far from complete.

PORTFOLIO SEPARATION AND EFFECTIVE COMPLETENESS

We saw in the previous section that some investors might want to hold two (or more) state securities in the same proportions. This result was utility specific, however. We now explore general conditions under which this result obtains. That is, we derive partial separation results with no restrictions on utility.

Suppose that there are two or more states in which $p_s = b\pi_s$. Then for state-independent utility of wealth the first-order condition (13) or (18) for each of these states is

$$U'(\nu_s) = \frac{\lambda p_s}{\pi_s} = b\lambda. \tag{24}$$

If U' is strictly decreasing, it is invertible; thus,

$$\nu_s = g(b\lambda), \tag{25}$$

where g is the inverse function for U'. That is, the investor has the same wealth in each of these states.

If all investors have state-independent utility of wealth and share homogeneous beliefs, then this is true for all investors and $\nu_s^k/\nu_\sigma^k = 1$ for each investor. Furthermore, since

$$\frac{W_s^k}{W_\sigma^k} = \frac{\nu_s^k p_s / W_0^k}{\nu_\sigma^k p_\sigma / W_0^k} = \frac{p_s}{p_\sigma} = \frac{\pi_s}{\pi_\sigma}, \tag{26}$$

investors' portfolios always contain these state securities in the same proportions. The last step in (26) follows from the assumption $p_s = b\pi_s$.

The condition in (26) is the standard one for a separation theorem. Investors are indifferent between being able to invest in the original state securities or having only a mutual fund of the state securities, associated with the states for which $p_s = b\pi_s$, which holds them in proportion to their state prices p_s.

The intuition behind this result is straightforward. Investors' utilities depend only upon wealth, and in each of these states all investors have the same terminal wealth. Therefore they need not distinguish between the states but maximize expected utility by buying state claims to wealth in proportion to the states' probabilities.

Rather than speaking of separation theorems, we can adopt the alternative course of making the state partititoning coarser. For homogeneous beliefs and state-independent utility of wealth the only states which need to be distinguished are those in which aggregate wealth (or the return on the market portfolio) differs. If there are state securities for each of these metastates, then the market is effectively complete and our previous results, except one, hold.

The one result we must change is the pricing equation (5). Knowledge of the metastate which obtains may be insufficient to determine the terminal value of the asset. Let us index the Ω different metastates by ω and denote the set of states composing metastate ω by S_ω. Then the pricing equation is

$$v_i = \sum_{\omega=1}^{\Omega} P_\omega E(Y_{si}|\omega), \tag{27}$$

where $P_\omega \equiv \Sigma p_s$ for all states in the set S_ω, (i.e., states in which $p_s = b_\omega \pi_s$). The proof of (27) consists of reducing it to (5). Since

$$E(Y_{si}|\omega) = \sum_{S_\omega} \pi_s Y_{si} \Big/ \sum_{S_\omega} \pi_s \tag{28}$$

and

$$P_\omega = \sum_{S_\omega} p_s = b_\omega \sum_{S_\omega} \pi_s, \tag{29}$$

we have

$$\begin{aligned} v_i &= \sum_{\omega=1}^{\Omega} \Big(b_\omega \sum_{S_\omega} \pi_s\Big) \sum_{S_\omega} \pi_s Y_{si} \Big/ \sum_{S_\omega} \pi_s \\ &= \sum_{\omega=1}^{\Omega} b_\omega \sum_{S_\omega} \pi_s Y_{si} = \sum_{\omega=1}^{\Omega} \sum_{S_\omega} p_s Y_{si} \\ &= \sum_{s=1}^{S} p_s Y_{si}, \end{aligned} \tag{30}$$

which is (5).

EFFICIENT SET CONVEXITY WITH COMPLETE MARKETS

We saw in Chapter 6 that the efficient set (the set composed of the optimal portfolio for each increasing concave utility function) need not be convex. One important conclusion of this finding is that the market portfolio may not be efficient, so that the generalized pricing equation of Chapter 5 might not be applicable. If markets are complete, however, the efficient set must be convex and therefore include the market portfolio. In the following discussion we consider only state-independent utility functions $U(W, s) = U(W)$ and homogeous beliefs. This is in keeping with the previous analysis of this question. Furthermore, if we permitted arbitrary state dependencies in utility, then we could not preclude any portfolio as inefficient. The efficient set would be the universe of portfolios and necessarily convex.

To demonstrate this convexity we start by rewriting (13):

$$U'(v_s) = \frac{\lambda p_s}{\pi_s}. \tag{31}$$

Since $\lambda > 0$, $u'' < 0$, and $u' > 0$, v_s is a monotone decreasing function of p_s/π_s. Furthermore, as this quantity is the same for all investors, the across state ranking of wealth is the same for all investors—the across state ranking of aggregate wealth. Without loss of generality we number the states in increasing order of aggregate wealth available. Then efficient portfolios include only those in which

$$v_1 \leq v_2 \leq \cdots \leq v_S. \tag{32}$$

As we now show, *all* feasible portfolios with this ordering are efficient. To accomplish this, we must demonstrate that there exists an increasing concave utility function satisfying (31) for each pattern satisfying the ordering (32). For a given pattern define a function which passes through the points $f(v_s) = p_s/\pi_s$. Since $p_s > 0$, $\pi_s > 0$, this function is positive. From our previous discussion

$$\frac{p_1}{\pi_1} \geq \frac{p_2}{\pi_2} \geq \cdots \geq \frac{p_S}{\pi_S}. \tag{33}$$

Thus, $f(\cdot)$ is decreasing. The integral of f is therefore increasing and concave, so it can be considered a utility function. Utility functions are defined only up to a positive linear transformation, so this procedure will work with any positive value of λ.

We have just proved the following result.

LEMMA *Assume that markets are complete, investors have homogeneous expectations and select their portfolio by maximizing the expectation of an increasing concave utility function, and markets are frictionless. Number the states in order of increasing aggregate wealth. A necessary and sufficient condition for a portfolio to be efficient is that it will result in state contingent wealth, v_s, satisfying $v_1 \leq v_2 \leq \cdots \leq v_S$.*

We can now prove the central result.

THEOREM *Assume that the conditions of the lemma are met. Then the efficient set is convex, and the market portfolio is efficient.*

Proof. The proof is by contradiction. Let $\mathbf{v}^1$ and $\mathbf{v}^2$ be efficient portfolios, and let $\mathbf{v} = \gamma\mathbf{v}^1 + (1 - \gamma)\mathbf{v}^2$ be inefficient for some γ in (0, 1). Since $\mathbf{v}$ is inefficient, by the lemma,

$$v_s > v_{s+1} \qquad \text{for some } s. \tag{34}$$

Since $\mathbf{v}$ is a convex combination of $\mathbf{v}^1$ and $\mathbf{v}^2$, this implies that

$$\gamma v_s^1 + (1-\gamma)v_s^2 > \gamma v_{s+1}^1 + (1-\gamma)v_{s+1}^2,$$
$$\gamma(v_s^1 - v_{s+1}^1) + (1-\gamma)(v_s^2 - v_{s+1}^2) > 0. \tag{35}$$

But portfolios 1 and 2 are efficient, so $v_s^i < v_{s+1}^i$ and γ and $1-\gamma$ are both positive. This represents a contradiction, so $\mathbf{v}$ cannot be inefficient. Q.E.D.

The key to the convexity of the efficient set is the monotonic relation between the state results (returns) on all efficient portfolios. Without complete markets this result is not guaranteed. In fact, if we check the counterexample to convexity given in Chapter 6, we see that the two cited efficient portfolios have returns which are not monotonically related.

CREATING AND PRICING STATE SECURITIES WITH OPTIONS

State securities for each of the metastates defined before can be created as portfolios of the primary assets, provided the number of linearly independent primary assets is equal to the number of metastates. If there are fewer, the introduction of a single type of financial security is sufficient to complete the market. What is required are call options on the market portfolio. Denote the value per share of the market portfolio in state s by M_s. Number the states in increasing order of M_s, and by suitably redefining the size of one share if necessary, ensure that $M_{s+1} > M_s + 1$ and $M_1 > 1$.

To create a state security for state σ, consider a call option on M with exercise price M_σ. Its terminal value in state s is

$$C_\sigma(s) = \begin{cases} 0, & s \leqslant \sigma, \\ M_s - M_\sigma, & s > \sigma. \end{cases} \tag{36}$$

Consider a second call option on M with exercise price $M_\sigma + 1$. Its terminal value in state s is

$$\hat{C}_\sigma(s) = \begin{cases} 0, & s \leqslant \sigma, \\ M_s - M_\sigma - 1, & s > \sigma. \end{cases} \tag{37}$$

Note that $M_{\sigma+1} - M_\sigma - 1 > 0$ by our scaling assumption.

A portfolio long one C_σ and short one $\hat{C}_\sigma$ will be worth

$$C_\sigma(s) - \hat{C}_\sigma(s) = \begin{cases} 0, & s \leqslant \sigma, \\ 1, & s > \sigma. \end{cases} \tag{38}$$

A portfolio short one C_σ and one $\hat{C}_{\sigma-1}$ and long one $\hat{C}_\sigma$ and one $C_{\sigma-1}$ will be worth

$$-C_\sigma(s) + \hat{C}_\sigma(s) - \hat{C}_{\sigma-1}(s) + C_{\sigma-1}(s) = \begin{cases} 1, & s = \sigma, \\ 0, & s \neq \sigma. \end{cases} \quad (39)$$

Note that the expression in Equation (39) is similar to a second partial derivative.

Suppose that the market portfolio has a continuum of possible outcomes for a continuum of states $M = M(s)$. Since $M(s)$ is different in each metastate, we can henceforth denote the state by M. Let $p(M)\,dM$ denote the current price of one dollar to be paid if the terminal metastate is in the interval $(M, M + dM)$. Then the current value of any asset with final conditional expected value $\bar{Y}(M)$ in metastate M is, by analogy with Equation (27),

$$v = \int \bar{Y}(M)p(M)\,dM. \quad (40)$$

Consider a call option with exercise price X on the market portfolio. From Equation (40) its current price is

$$C(M, X) = \int_X^\infty (M - X)p(M)\,dM. \quad (41)$$

Then by Leibniz's rule (Equation (15) of the Mathematical Introduction)

$$\frac{\partial C(M, X)}{\partial X} = \int_X^\infty - p(M)\,dM - (X - X)p(X) = -\int_X^\infty p(M)\,dM,$$
$$\frac{\partial^2 C(M, X)}{\partial X^2} = p(X). \quad (42)$$

If the Black–Scholes (or Rubinstein) option model holds for M (see Chapter 14) and its log has a normal distribution with variance σ^2, then the price "per unit state" conditional on a current state of M_0 is

$$p(M) = \frac{1}{M\sigma R} n\left(\frac{\ln(M_0 R/M) - \frac{1}{2}\sigma^2}{\sigma}\right) \equiv R^{-1}\hat{\pi}(M|M_0), \quad (43)$$

where $n(\cdot)$ is the standard normal density function.

To interpret these state prices note that, under the option model's lognormality assumption, the probability of state M occurring is

$$\pi(M|M_0) = (M\sigma)^{-1} n\left(\frac{ln(M_0\bar{Z}/M) - \frac{1}{2}\sigma^2}{\sigma}\right), \quad (44)$$

There $\bar{Z}$ is the expected return on the market portfolio. Then if β is the appropriate discount factor for the asset v, that is, its expected return, we may write its current value as

$$v = \beta^{-1} \int \bar{Y}(M)\pi(M \mid M_0)\, dM. \tag{45}$$

Under state pricing v is

$$v = R^{-1} \int \bar{Y}(M)\hat{\pi}(M \mid M_0)\, dM. \tag{46}$$

Here we have used a "risk-adjusted" probability density and discounted at the riskless rate. Consequently, state pricing is more in keeping with the certainty equivalent approach to valuation than with the discounted expected value methodology in Equation (45). This is the basis for risk-neutral pricing that is discussed in Chapters 14–19.

Of course, in a single-period world there will always be a (unique) discount factor β which gives the proper valuation. In fact, Equation (45) and (46) can be used to determine this discount factor (under the option model's conditions):

$$\beta = R\left[\int \bar{Y}(M)\pi(M \mid M_0)\, dM \Big/ \int \bar{Y}(M)\hat{\pi}(M \mid M_0)\, dM\right]. \tag{47}$$

If we could view this single-period world "between" the periods, however, the discounting method in Equation (45) would not be generally valid because the discount factor β depends on the interim states.

If we wish to construct state securities for all the substates of the metastates so that we have a state security for each pattern of payoffs on the primary assets, we will have to use more than options on the market portfolio. If there is any asset or financial security whose value is different in each state, then we can use the foregoing method to construct state securities by using this asset in place of the market portfolio. If no such asset exists, we can construct the state securities by using the following method. To create a state security for state σ, we determine the value of each of the N primary assets in that state, $Y_{\sigma i}$. Then treating each asset as if it were the market portfolio, we form a portfolio of call options written on it which pays one dollar if $Y_{si} = Y_{\sigma i}$, and zero dollars otherwise. Note that for each asset there may be many $s \neq \sigma$ for which this one-dollar payoff occurs. However, only in state σ will the payoff be one dollar on each portfolio of calls, because by assumption there are no two states in which the value of all assets are the same.

Now form a superportfolio holding one portfolio of call options on each assets. In state σ its value will be N, and in all other states its value will be less than N. Consequently, a call option with exercise price $N - 1$ on this superportfolio will be worth one dollar in state σ and zero dollars in all other states.

9

General Equilibrium Considerations in Asset Pricing

Up to now we have been using partial equilibrium analysis to study portfolio selection problems. In particular, we have assumed that the assets' price dynamics or probability distributions and investors' individual assessments about them were given exogenously. In this chapter we examine the consequence of relaxing this assumption.

We will also use this opportunity to explore each of the models in more detail by using the insights developed from the study of the other models.

RETURNS DISTRIBUTIONS AND FINANCIAL CONTRACTS

In a single-period model it is certainly permissible to specify exogenously the joint probability distribution of the end-of-period values of the assets if we think of these assets as previously committed fixed investments which cannot be reversed—for example, fields of already planted seeds. If trading takes place only at equilibrium prices, then this is equivalent to specifying the form of the joint probability distribution of returns as well. If we think instead of a "seed" economy with assets representing various fields of differing fertility, it is perfectly all right to specify the returns distributions directly, provided that they have stochastic constant returns to scale. In either case the equilibrium solution will not be materially affected. The only remaining issue is whether the equilibrium can be affected by investors making financial contracts (side bets) among themselves.

We have studied four single-period models of asset pricing: the CAPM relation and the related distributional based separation model (Chapters 4 and 6), the general utility relation and the associated utility-based separation model (Chapters 5 and 6), the arbitrage pricing theory (Chapter 7), and the complete markets model (Chapter 8).

The creation of new financial securities clearly cannot affect the equilibrium reached in a complete market because the "new" assets must be already spanned by the original marketed assets which already provided insurance against each state. Similarly, the equilibrium under taste aggregation cannot be affected by the creation of financial securities because the equilibrium description is completely independent of any assumptions about returns distributions (provided only that they are sufficiently well behaved so that expected utility is defined).

The reason is basically the same as for complete markets. If all investors have utility functions which are sufficiently similar (e.g., exponential) to permit aggregation, then the market must be effectively complete (Pareto optimal) even prior to the creation of the financial assets. In this case all investors agree on the "shadow" prices for the states not insurable with the original assets and therefore must assess the same (utility) value for any possible financial asset. That is, no investor will have any motive to trade the new assets or hold any amount of them in his portfolio except zero.

With complete markets any possible financial asset is already in existence. With utility aggregation any possible financial asset (in zero net supply) is irrelevant.

The arbitrage relation of the linear factor model cannot be upset by the creation of financial assets because the introduction of new assets *in equilibrium* certainly can introduce no arbitrage opportunities. In any case the arbitrage pricing theory's linear relation holds for any subset of (an infinite number of) assets regardless of what other investments may be available.

The separating distribution model (CAPM), however, might be affected by the introduction of financial assets if they do not have returns which are related in the proper linear fashion with conditionally mean zero residuals.

As an example of this point consider an economy with the following three assets: riskless storage $R = 1$ and two investments whose returns are independent normal random variables $\tilde{z}_1 \sim N(2, 4)$ and $\tilde{z}_2 \sim N(3, 8)$. Since these returns are drawn from a separating distribution, we can use mean-variance analysis to compute the weights in the tangency portfolio. From Equation (16) of Chapter 4 they are

$$w_{it}^* = K\frac{\bar{z}_i - R}{\sigma_i^2}, \tag{1}$$

with K chosen so that the weights sum to 1. In this case $w_1^* = w_2^* = \frac{1}{2}$. The tangency portfolio has an expected return of 2.5 and a variance of 3.

Assuming that each investor is sufficiently risk averse to invest some wealth in riskless storage, then the tangency portfolio is the market portfolio of risky assets. (Since the riskless asset need not be in zero net supply in this economy, the market portfolio may actually be on the line connecting the tangency portfolio with the riskless asset. Nevertheless, the form of the CAPM pricing model will be unchanged.) The betas of the two assets are given by the formula $\beta_i = w_{im}\sigma_i^2/\sigma_m^2$. These values are $\frac{2}{3}$ and $\frac{4}{3}$, respectively.

How is the equilibrium affected when markets for financial contracts are opened? Consider a call option with an exercise price of two dollars written on a one-dollar investment in asset number 1. Call this asset 3. Its return is

$$\tilde{z}_3 = \frac{\text{Max}(\$1 \cdot \tilde{z}_1 - \$2, 0)}{C}, \tag{2}$$

where C is its current price.

Since $\bar{z}_1 = 2$, the nonzero portion of this return is the right half of a normal distribution. Thus, the expected return on asset 3 can be computed as

$$\begin{aligned} C \cdot \bar{z}_3 &= \int_2^\infty (z_1 - 2) n\left(\frac{z_1 - \bar{z}_1}{\sigma_1}\right) dz_1, \\ \bar{z}_3 &= \frac{\sigma_1}{C\sqrt{2\pi}} \approx \frac{0.798}{C}. \end{aligned} \tag{3}$$

It covariances are $\sigma_{23} = 0$ by independence and

$$\begin{aligned} \sigma_{13} &= E[\tilde{z}_3(\tilde{z}_1 - \bar{z}_1)] \\ &= \frac{E[\text{Max}(\tilde{z}_1 - 2, 0)(\tilde{z}_1 - 2)]}{C} = \frac{\sigma_1^2}{2C} = \frac{2}{C}. \end{aligned} \tag{4}$$

The next to last equality follows from the symmetry of $\tilde{z}_1$ about its mean of 2. Finally, its own variance is

$$\begin{aligned} \sigma_3^2 &= \frac{E[(\text{Max}(\tilde{z}_1 - 2, 0))^2]}{C^2} - \bar{z}_3^2, \\ &\frac{1}{C^2}\left(\frac{1}{2}\sigma^2 - \frac{1}{2\pi}\sigma_1^2\right) \approx \frac{1.36338}{C^2}. \end{aligned} \tag{5}$$

With these preliminaries out of the way we can now examine the pricing of this call option by various types of investors. We will look at four distinct economies. In the first three all investors have identical utility functions, and in the last their utilities differ.

When all investors are identical, the equilibrium price of the option must be such that every investor holds exactly zero of it since it is in zero net supply. In this case, its price would not actually be observable. However, it is possible to compute the shadow price at which demand is exactly zero. This is easily done because the option, which is not held by any investor, does not affect the equilibrium of the other assets.

Scenario 1. Homogeneous Quadratic Utility: Suppose that all investors have the utility function $u(Z) = Z - bZ^2/2$ and assume that $b > [\bar{Z}_t + \sigma_t^2/(\bar{Z}_t - R]^{-1} = \frac{2}{9}$, so that they have positive demand for the riskless asset.

All investors have quadratic utility, so the CAPM holds even though the option's return is not normally distributed. The market portfolio (of risky assets) is equally weighted with an expected return of 2.5 and a variance of 3. The option's beta is $\beta_3 = .5(\sigma_{13} + \sigma_{23})/\sigma_m^2 = 1/3C$. Using (3) and the CAPM pricing relation gives

$$\frac{0.798}{C} \approx \bar{z}_3 = R + \beta_3(\bar{Z}_m - R) = 1 + \frac{1}{3C}1.5, \tag{6}$$

or $C \approx 0.298$, $\bar{z}_3 \approx 2.679$, and $\beta_3 \approx 0.843$.

Scenario 2. Homogeneous Exponential Utility: If all investors have the utility function $u(Z) = -\exp(-aZ)/a$, then each will have a positive demand for the riskless asset as long as $a > (\bar{Z}_t - R)/\sigma_t^2 = \frac{1}{2}$. (See the sample problem in Chapter 4 for details.) As before, no investor will hold the option, and the previous equilibrium is not affected. Each investor holds the equally weighted market portfolio. The shadow price for the option can be determined from the equilibrium condition of Chapter 5.

$$\bar{z}_3 = R + b_3(\bar{Z}_m - R) = 1 + 1.5b_3,$$

where

$$b_3 \equiv \frac{\text{Cov}[\exp(-a\tilde{Z}_m), \tilde{z}_3]}{\text{Cov}[\exp(-a\tilde{Z}_m), \tilde{Z}_m]}, \tag{7}$$

which, in general, is not equal to β_3.

To calculate b_3, we compute the denominator by using the property of bivariate normals, $\text{Cov}[f(\tilde{x}), \tilde{y}] = E[f'(\tilde{x})]\text{Cov}(\tilde{x}, \tilde{y})$ (see Equation (62) of the Mathematical Introduction):

$$\begin{aligned} \text{Cov}[\exp(-a\tilde{Z}_m), \tilde{Z}_m] &= E[-a\exp(-a\tilde{Z}_m)]\sigma_m^2 \\ &= -a\exp\left[-a\bar{Z}_m + \frac{a^2\sigma_m^2}{2}\right]\sigma_m^2. \end{aligned} \tag{8}$$

For the numerator, from the independence of $\tilde{z}_2$ and $\tilde{z}_1$,

$$\begin{aligned} \text{Cov}[\exp(-a\tilde{Z}_m), \tilde{z}_3] &= E[\tilde{z}_3\exp(-a\tilde{Z}_m)] - \bar{z}_3 E[\exp(-a\tilde{Z}_m)] \\ &= E\left[\exp\left(\frac{-a\tilde{z}_2}{2}\right)\right]E\left[\tilde{z}_3\exp\left(\frac{-a\tilde{z}_1}{2}\right)\right] \\ &\quad - \bar{z}_3 E[\exp(-a\tilde{Z}_m)]. \end{aligned} \tag{9}$$

Evaluating these two expressions gives $b_3 \approx 0.678$, independent of the parameter a. From (7) $\bar{z}_3 \approx 2.017$. Finally, from (3) $C \approx 0;.798/\bar{z}_3 \approx 0.396$.

In this case the CAPM describes the returns on assets 1 and 2, but *not* on asset 3. The call option price is substantially higher because its systematic risk and, therefore, its expected return are significantly lower.

Aside: The price of the call option and, hence, b_3 can also be calculated by the method to be introduced in Chapter 14:

$$\begin{aligned} C &= \left(1 - \frac{X}{R}\right) N\left(\frac{R - X}{\sigma}\right) + \frac{\sigma}{R} n\left(\frac{R - X}{\sigma}\right) \\ &= -N\left(\frac{1}{2}\right) + 2n\left(\frac{1}{2}\right) \approx 0.396, \end{aligned} \tag{10}$$

verifying the results above.

Scenario 3. Homogeneous Power Utility: If the utility function for all investors is $u(Z) = Z^{\gamma}/\gamma$ with $\gamma \leqslant 0$, then $u(0) = -\infty$ and no investor will accept any possibility of ending with zero or negative wealth. Therefore, only the riskless asset will be held in the original economy.

When the option is introduced, the demand for the original two assets will remain zero, but each investor might want to take a long position in the call because an option has limited liability. No investor would be willing to sell options, however, since their unlimited potential for upside gains means that short positions do not have limited liability. Since the options are in zero net supply, there can be no purchases by investors without matching sales. Thus, the price must be such that no one will want to buy. As shown in Chapter 3, an investor forming a portfolio from a riskless asset and a single risky asset will have a nonzero demand for the latter only if the expected return on the risky asset is equal to the riskless return (provided also, of course, that expected utility is defined). Thus,

$$C \approx \frac{0.798}{R} = 0.798. \tag{11}$$

A comparison of the three scenarios is shown in the table:

	Quadratic Utility	Exponential Utility	Power Utility
Call Price C	0.298	0.396	0.798
Expected Return $\bar{z}_3$	2.679	2.017	1.000
Systematic Risk β_3, b_3	0.843	0.678	not defined

Note that in each case the value of the option is independent of the parameter of the common utility function. (In fact, as we shall see later in this chapter different investors could have different parameter values so long as they all had quadratic or exponential utility and this result would still be valid.) Only in the first case does the CAPM relation describe the expected returns on all assets. In the second scenario the CAPM relation is valid only among the original assets. This latter result would also be true for any common utility function.

We are now ready to examine the case of heterogeneous utilities. We will look at an economy composed of some investors with quadratic utility and others with power utility; however, the qualitative results that we get are quite general.

Scenario 4. Heterogeneous Utilities: Suppose that some investors have quadratic utility and some investors have power utility. In the original economy the power utility investors will choose to invest their entire wealth in the riskless asset as described under the previous scenario. The quadratic utility investors will diversify. Since the returns distributions are given exogenously, they are unaffected by the presence of the power utility investors, and the quadratic utility investors will hold the same portfolio as outlined under scenario 1.

The risky-asset-only market portfolio will still be mean-variance efficient since it is the optimal portfolio of a quadratic utility investor. (The power utility investors do not hold any of the risky assets.) Therefore, the CAPM equation will describe the relation among the expected returns.

When the option is introduced, the power utility investors may wish to buy. As shown in Chapter 3 and discussed earlier in this Chapter, they will have a positive demand for the option if and only if its expected return is greater than the riskless return of 1; that is, if and only if its price is less than 0.798. They will never want to sell the option. Quadratic utility investors, on the other hand, will wish to buy (sell) the option if its price is less (more) than 0.298, as shown in scenario 1. Thus, there will be an equality of supply and demand for some price in the range (0.298, 0.798).

Exactly what price prevails will depend on the relative wealths of the two classes of investors and on the parameters, b and γ, of their utility functions. There are two considerations. The higher the relative wealth of the quadratic utility investors, the smaller (i.e., the closer to 0.298) will be the price. The more risk averse are the power (quadratic) utility investors, the less will be their demand to buy (sell) and the lower (higher) will be the resulting price. Calculation of the price in terms of these quantities is a tedious exercise. However, any value in the given range is the equilibrium price for some value of the ratio of the relative wealths of the two classes of investors. To avoid this calculation, we finish the example in general in terms of the price of the call option C.

At a given option price, a quadratic utility investor faces an opportunity set characterized by $R = 1$, $\bar{\mathbf{z}} = (2, 3, 0.798/C)'$ and covariance matrix

$$\boldsymbol{\Sigma} = \begin{pmatrix} 4 & 0 & 2/C \\ 0 & 8 & 0 \\ 2/C & 0 & 1.36/C^2 \end{pmatrix} \tag{12}$$

The tangency portfolio (the optimal risky-asset-only portfolio, assuming that the investor is sufficiently risk averse to hold the riskless asset) is given by Equation (16) of Chapter 4.

$$\mathbf{w}_t = \frac{\boldsymbol{\Sigma}^{-1}(\bar{\mathbf{z}} - R\mathbf{1})}{\mathbf{1}'\boldsymbol{\Sigma}^{-1}(\bar{\mathbf{z}} - R\mathbf{1})} \tag{13}$$

with expected return $\bar{Z}_t = \mathbf{w}_t'\bar{\mathbf{z}}$ and variance $\sigma_t^2 = \mathbf{w}_t'\boldsymbol{\Sigma}\mathbf{w}_t$.

For example, if $C = \frac{1}{3}$ the mean-variance tangency portfolio is $\mathbf{w}_t \approx (.579, .484, -.063)'$ with an expected return and variance of approximately 2.459 and 3.802 respectively. The options shorted by the quadratic utility investors are held by the power utility investors. Therefore, the (risky-asset) market portfolio is in proportion .579 to .484 to 0 or $\mathbf{w}_m \approx (.545, .455, 0)'$ with an expected return and variance of $\bar{Z}_m \approx 2.455$ and $\sigma_m^2 \approx 2.844$. The assets' betas are

$$\boldsymbol{\beta} = \frac{\boldsymbol{\Sigma}\mathbf{w}_m}{\sigma_m^2} \approx (0.767,\ 1.280,\ 1.150)'. \tag{14}$$

The predicted (by the CAPM) expected returns would be (2.116, 2.862, 2.673), whereas the true expected returns are (2, 3, 2.393). Thus, in this case, even the original assets are "mispriced" after the option is introduced.

At this point our tentative conclusion must be that the introduction of financial assets may cause a complete breakdown of the distributional-based asset-pricing models. Not only is the model incorrect for the financial assets, but it also fails to describe the relation among the returns on the original assets. Since financial assets with highly nonnormal returns are fairly common, this breakdown could be a fatal blow to models like the CAPM.

The described breakdown of the CAPM pricing relation for the original assets does not occur if the *original* market is effectively complete (or Pareto optimal) since there will be no desire to trade the newly created assets on the part of any investor. However, this is of little comfort since strong assumptions about utility must be met for the original very limited market to be effectively complete. Scenarios 1, 2, and 3 are specific examples of effectively complete markets.

Fortunately, the breakdown also may be avoided even when the original market is not effectively complete. Two sufficient conditions that guarantee the CAPM relation among the original assets after the introduction of financial assets are that a sufficient number of new assets are introduced to make the market effectively complete and that the *form* of the distribution of returns on the original assets is not disturbed (e.g., the distribution of returns remains multivariate normal). The exact result is stated next.

THEOREM 1 *Assume that each primary asset is either a previously fixed (and nonreversible) investment or a discretionary investment with stochastic constant returns to scale. In the absence of financial assets, the returns on the primary assets have a multivariate normal distribution (or more generally any of the elliptical distributions). Then a CAPM pricing (but not separation) equilibrium obtains for the primary assets in both the original market with no financial assets and in a market effectively completed by the introduction of financial assets in zero net supply.*

Proof. That the CAPM obtains in the original market is immediate since all the assets are jointly normally distributed. The proof that the CAPM pricing relation is valid in the completed market has two steps.

First, all of the primary assets have a multivariate normal (or elliptical) distribution in the completed market. This is obvious for the discretionary investments whose returns distributions are given exogenously. If we use a * to denote quantities in the completed market, then for the discretionary investments $\tilde{z}_i^* = \tilde{z}_i$ and $v_i^* = v_i$. For the fixed investment assets the new returns in the completed market, $\tilde{z}_i^*$, are

$$\tilde{z}_i^* = \frac{\tilde{y}_i}{v_i^*} = \frac{\tilde{z}_i v_i}{v_i^*}. \tag{15}$$

Obviously $\tilde{\mathbf{z}}^*$ is multivariate normal (or elliptical) because $\tilde{\mathbf{z}}$ is.

The remainder of the proof relies on the efficiency of the market portfolio in an effectively complete market (which was proved in the previous chapter). Since the market portfolio is efficient, then, by definition, there is some utility function for which it is the optimal portfolio. Now consider the portfolio problem for this utility function when the returns are those in the completed market but there is a constraint that no investment be made in the financial assets. Since all "available" assets are now multivariate normal (elliptical), the optimal portfolio is mean-variance efficient. But this artificial constraint is obviously not binding, so the optimal portfolio is still the (completed market) market portfolio. Therefore, the market portfolio is mean-variance efficient within the subset of primary assets, and the CAPM pricing relation holds. Q.E.D.

It should be noted that the market portfolio may differ in the pre- and postcompleted economies, as may the covariance structure. Thus, the equilibrium pricing relation need not be exactly the same. Nevertheless, they both have the same form with expected excess returns proportional to betas. The constant of proportionality is the expected excess return on the market portfolio.

In addition, portfolio separation (i.e., the CAPM "mutual fund" theorem) need no longer obtain. Investors may optimally hold substantially different portfolios even though they all agree that only the market is mean variance efficient. The pricing and separation results of the CAPM can now be viewed as distinct rather than causally linked as they were in Chapter 4. This decoupling is similar to that in Chapter 6, where it was shown that the pricing results for linear factor models required only that at least one investor hold a portfolio with no idiosyncratic risk.

As we saw in Chapter 8 if markets are not effectively complete, then there are always two or more investors whose expected utility would be increased by the introduction of some financial asset(s). If investors are not constrained from creating new trading opportunities and it is not costly to do so, then the market should always be effectively complete. This may justify the assumption of a CAPM *pricing* equation even in an economy with options or other financial assets with highly nonnormal returns distributions.

SYSTEMATIC AND NONSYSTEMATIC RISK

In each of the models that we studied, some risks were compensated and others were not. This distinction was clearest in the arbitrage pricing theory. Factor risk was pervasive in the economy, whereas idiosyncratic risk could be eliminated from every investors' portfolio by diversification. Consequently, idiosyncratic risk was not systematic, and investors who chose to bear it received no compensation in the form of higher expected returns for doing so.

In the CAPM nonsystematic risk was that portion of returns uncorrelated with the return on the market portfolio. In this case the concept of systematic versus nonsystematic risk is a little more precise but less intuitive.

In Chapter 5 the mean-variance notion of systematic risk was generalized for any distribution of returns and any utility function. The systematic risk measure of security i relative to efficient portfolio k was defined as

$$b_i^k \equiv \frac{\mathrm{Cov}[u_k'(\tilde{Z}_e^k),\ \tilde{z}_i]}{\mathrm{Cov}[u'(\tilde{Z}_e^k),\ \tilde{Z}_e^k]}, \qquad (16)$$

where $u_k(\cdot)$ denotes the utility function for which efficient portfolio k is optimal.

If the random-variable marginal utility $u'(\tilde{Z}_e^k)$ is denoted by $\tilde{v}_k$, then the standard regression

$$\tilde{z}_i = \gamma_{ik} + \delta_{ik}\tilde{v}_k + \tilde{\varepsilon}_{ik} \tag{17}$$

defines the nonsystematic risk of asset i with respect to portfolio k as $\tilde{\varepsilon}_{ik}$—that portion of the return which is uncorrelated with the marginal utility provided by portfolio k. Note that $b_{ik} = \delta_{ik}/\delta_{kk}$, so δ_{ik} measures systematic risk.

In general, exactly what is considered nonsystematic risk by this definition will depend on the choices of benchmark portfolio and utility function. In an effectively complete market, however, the marginal utilities of all investors are exactly proportional (see Chapter 8). Thus, for all k, the $\tilde{v}_k$ are perfectly correlated and $\tilde{\varepsilon}_{ik} \equiv \tilde{\varepsilon}_{ij}$, so there is an unequivocal measure of nonsystematic risk agreed upon by all investors. This is even true if some or all investors have state-dependent utility functions.

It is not necessarily true in this general context that any risk that is uncorrelated with returns on the market portfolio is nonsystematic in nature. A sufficient condition for a risk to be nonsystematic in an effectively complete market is that it be a fair game with respect to the market. That is, if the return on an asset is decomposed as

$$\tilde{z}_i = \tilde{\zeta}_i + \tilde{\xi}_i \qquad \text{with } E[\tilde{\xi}_i | Z_m] = 0 \tag{18}$$

and the market is effectively complete, then $\tilde{\xi}_i$ is nonsystematic risk. $\tilde{\zeta}_i$ may be systematic risk, nonsystematic risk, or partially each. It was demonstrated in the previous chapter that when markets are effectively complete, the efficient set is convex, so that the market portfolio is itself efficient. That is, there is a utility function $u_m(\cdot)$ for which the market portfolio is the optimal holding. But since the marginal utilities of all investors are proportional $\tilde{v}_k = a\tilde{v}_m \equiv au'(\tilde{Z}_m)$, and anything uncorrelated with the marginal utility of the market portfolio is uncorrelated with the marginal utility of any investor. Since $\tilde{\xi}_i$ is a fair game with respect to the return on the market portfolio, it must be uncorrelated with the marginal utility of it (see the Mathematical Introduction). Thus, it is unequivocally nonsystematic risk.

MARKET EFFICIENCY WITH NONSPECULATIVE ASSETS

In Chapter 3 the important concept of market efficiency was introduced. The theorem that was proved was a "no trade" theorem. If investors had common prior beliefs, then even if they had different information, they would all refrain from trading purely speculative claims, and each asset would be priced so that its expected return was equal to the riskless return.

The basic intuition for this result was that in a purely speculative market the risk of the assets was not inherent to the economy and could be avoided by every investor. Investors would trade therefore only when they believed they were receiving a favorable "bet." Each investor realized that all of the other investors also thought this way, so whenever some other investor was willing to take the opposite side of a transaction, this had to be understood as being based on some information that the first investor did not know. Realizing this, both investors would revise their beliefs until they came into concordance.

If markets are not purely speculative, then this result no longer holds. Investors may be willing to take unfavorable "bets" if they offset some of the risk of their other holdings. That is, an investor may trade to get a favorable return *or* to reduce risk. It is, however, possible to separate these two motives for trade and derive a "no trade" theorem in other than purely speculative markets. Like the previous theorem in this chapter, this result also depends on the market being effectively complete.

The basic structure of the economy is as follows. There is an initial round of trading in which a Pareto optimal allocation of period-0 consumption and period-1 wealth is achieved. That is, the initial round of trading takes place in an effectively complete market. After this equilibrium is reached, investors consume. Then they receive private information, and the market reopens for trading. In this second round, investors may also learn from the equilibrium price or other public information. Each investor knows that this is the structure of the economy and knows before the first round of trading all the possible states (i.e., the private information does not cause any investor to believe that the structure of the economy is changed or that any new states are possible).

For simiplicity of notation we will assume that investors have common prior beliefs and that each has a strictly concave, time-additive and state-independent utility function for period-0 consumption and period-1 wealth. These assumptions can be weakened. State independence and time additivity are not required at all. Pareto optimality of a complete market allocation is all that is required, and this holds for state-dependent utility as well. The weakening of common priors is dicussed later.

As in Chapter 3, the kth investor's private information and the public information are denoted by ϕ_k and Φ, respectively. $\mathbf{v}_k$ is the optimal portfolio of investor k after the first round of trading; ν_{sk} is the number of pure state s claims that investor k holds (his wealth if state s occurs). Therefore, the random variable $\tilde{\nu}_k$ with realizations ν_{sk} will denote investor k's wealth in period 1.

q will denote various prior probabilities. For example, $q(s, \phi_k, \Phi)$ is the probability that investor k with receive signal ϕ_k, the public signal will be Φ, and state s will occur. Similarly, $q(s|\phi_k, \Phi)$ is the conditional probability that state s will occur if investor k receives signal ϕ_k and the public receives information Φ. Since investors have common priors, they would make the same assessments given the same information, and these probabilities are the same for all investors. (Of course, investors do not need to agree on the probabilities of the various states after receiving their private signals because, in general, they receive different signals.)

We can now prove a "no trade" theorem for the second round similar to that in Chapter 3. The intuition for no second round trading is that all of the risk sharing and diversification was accomplished in the first round so all investors recognize any attempts to trade in the second round as speculation on information.

THEOREM 2 *In the market environment just described with a Pareto optimal allocation achieved in a first round of trading and homogeneous priors, investors refrain from trading in the second round.*

Proof. Assume that second round trading does occur, then there is a set of reallocations of the state securities $\boldsymbol{\delta}_k(\phi_k, \Phi)$ (a random-variable addition to period-1 wealth $\tilde{\delta}$ with realization δ_{ks}) which is feasible (19a) and weakly preferred by each investor (19b)

$$\sum_{k=1}^{K} \tilde{\delta}_k \equiv 0, \tag{19a}$$

$$E[U_k(\tilde{v}_k + \tilde{\delta}_k) | \phi_k, \Phi] \geqslant E[U_k(\tilde{v}_k) | \phi_k, \Phi]. \tag{19b}$$

(The condition in (19a) considers only global feasibility and not individual wealth constraints; however, since the original assumption is concerned only about Pareto optimality, this is not a concern.)

Now consider the reallocation of state securities

$$\boldsymbol{\Delta}_k \equiv \sum_{\phi_k, \Phi} q(\phi_k, \Phi)\, \boldsymbol{\delta}_k(\phi_k, \Phi) \tag{20}$$

and the associated random additions to wealths $\tilde{\Delta}_k$. Note that this allocation is the ex ante expectation (based on the prior probabilities) of the assumed superior allocation $\boldsymbol{\delta}_k(\phi_k, \Phi)$. Since all investors agree on the prior probabilities, this reallocation is also (globally) feasible.

$$\sum_{k=1}^{K} \boldsymbol{\Delta}_k \equiv \sum_{\phi_k, \Phi} q(\phi_k, \Phi) \sum_{k=1}^{K} \boldsymbol{\delta}_k(\phi_k, \Phi) = 0, \tag{21}$$

the inner sum being zero for all ϕ_k and Φ. In addition, unlike $\boldsymbol{\delta}_k(\phi_k, \Phi)$, the reallocation $\boldsymbol{\Delta}_k$ does not depend on any private information or public information learned in the second round of trading, so it could be incorporated into the first round of trading.

For a given outcome state

$$\begin{aligned} U_k(v_{ks} + \Delta_{ks}) &\equiv U_k[v_{ks} + \sum_{\phi_k, \Phi} q(\phi_k, \Phi)\delta_{ks}(\phi_k, \Phi)] \\ &\geqslant \sum_{\phi_k, \Phi} q(\phi_k, \Phi)\, U_k[v_{ks} + \delta_{ks}(\phi_k, \Phi)], \end{aligned} \tag{22}$$

where the last step follows from Jensen's inequality. Taking the unconditional expectation of both sides of (22) and reordering the conditional expectations yield

$$\begin{aligned} E[U_k(\tilde{v}_k + \tilde{\Delta}_k)] &\geq E\Big[\sum_{\phi_k, \Phi} q(\tilde{\phi}_k, \tilde{\Phi})\, U_k[\tilde{v}_k + \delta_k(\tilde{\phi}_k, \tilde{\Phi})]\Big] \\ &= E[E\{U_k[\tilde{v}_k + \delta_k(\tilde{\phi}_k, \tilde{\Phi})] | \tilde{\phi}_k, \tilde{\Phi}\}]. \end{aligned} \tag{23}$$

But by (19b) the inner expectation is at least as large as that of the utility of the original portfolio, so

$$E[U_k(\tilde{v}_k + \tilde{\Delta}_k)] \geq E[U_k(\tilde{v}_k)]. \tag{24}$$

That is, based on the information available at the time of the first round of trading, the set of portfolios $\mathbf{v}_k + \mathbf{\Delta}_k$ is at least as good as the set of portfolios $\mathbf{v}_k$. Furthermore, since utility is strictly concave, the set of portfolios $\mathbf{v}_k + \mathbf{\Delta}_k/2$ is strictly better than the set of portfolios $\mathbf{v}_k$, violating the assumption that the latter were ex ante Pareto optimal. Q.E.D.

The three important requirements in this theorem are that the original market be Pareto optimal, that investors have common interpretations of the same information, and that investors not be able to change their consumption plans at time zero after learning their private information. If the second condition were not true, then the reallocation described in (20) would not necessarily have been feasible. The sum over investors in the right-hand side of Equation (21) could not be taken inside the probability $q(\phi_k, \Phi)$ because it would differ for different investors. The assumption of a common interpretation of information is somewhat weaker than common priors, but the latter is a familiar assumption that suits our purposes well.

If period-0 consumption plans could be changed, then (19b) would not be the most general way to state that an individual's lot had improved. Expected utility of end-of-period wealth could decrease, provided that period-0 consumption were increased sufficiently to offset this. In this case we could no longer draw (24) as a conclusion of (23).

If the original market were not Pareto optimal, then finding a new allocating (at possibly changed prices) which was preferred by all investors would not be a contradiction. The proposed reallcoation might simply be infeasible in the original (obviously incomplete) market. An example is given after the next theorem.

Note that we do not require in this theorem or the next that any investor know what trades others might wish to make. That is, the potential trade of any investor $\boldsymbol{\delta}_k$ may depend on private information. Of course, each investor must know that the set of trades is feasible. Similarly, no investor needs to know any other investor's utility function. He or she need only know that every other investor is risk averse.

Although no trades will occur in the second round, it does not follow that the prices will not change. In fact, we should expect them to change, so that the original allocation is still an equilibrium with respect to each investor's new information.

Each investor's information set includes both private and public information; however, as we will show the public information dominates in importance, and investors' beliefs must become homogeneous. This result is reminiscent of one in Chapter 3. There we saw that investors had to agree that the expected return on each speculative asset was equal to 1 plus the interest rate.

THEOREM 3 *Assume that each agent is strictly risk averse with a continuously differentiable utility function. Assume also that a first round of trading takes place which results in a Pareto optimal equilibrium with supporting state prices* **p**. *If private information is received by each investor and the market reopens after period-0 consumption has taken place, then the resulting new supporting price vector* $\hat{\mathbf{p}}$ *will reveal sufficient information to make each investor's assessment of the new state probabilities equal to what they could learn from prices alone:*

$$q(s|\phi_k, \Phi) = q(s|\hat{\mathbf{p}}). \tag{25}$$

Proof. Since the original allocation is Pareto optimal, the expected marginal utility of each investor in a given state is proportional to the supporting state price

$$q(s)U_k'(\nu_{ks}) = \lambda_k p_s \tag{26}$$

for all k and s. Furthermore, since this same allocation remains Pareto optimal after the second round of trading, as proved in Theorem 2, then

$$q(s|\phi_k, \Phi)U_k'(\nu_{ks}) = \hat{\lambda}_k \hat{p}_s \tag{27}$$

for the same allcoation $\mathbf{v}_k$ for all k and s. Together these conditions imply tht

$$\begin{gathered} q(s|\phi_k, \Phi) = (\hat{\lambda}_k \hat{p}_s)(\lambda_k p_s)^{-1} q(s) \\ \text{or} \\ \frac{q(s|\phi_k, \Phi)}{q(\sigma|\phi_k, \Phi)} = \frac{\hat{p}_s/\hat{p}_\sigma}{p_s/p_\sigma} \frac{q(s)}{q(\sigma)}. \end{gathered} \tag{28}$$

Since the right-hand side of (28) does not depend on any information other than the original (common) probabilities and the new and old prices, then neither does the left-hand side. Furthermore, since the probabilities of a set of mutually exclusive and collectively exhaustive events are completely determined by their ratios (and that their sum is 1), none of the individually assessed probabilities can differ. Q.E.D.

In the absence of an effectively complete market, resulting in a Pareto optimal allocation in the first round of trading, neither Theorem 2 nor 3 necessarily holds. There can be additional trading after new information arrives in the market, and the equilibrium in the second round need not completely reveal this new information.

To illustrate this, consider the following ecoomy. There is a riskless asset and a single risky asset with possible returns 0, 2, 4, and 6. There is one investor with quadratic utility and other investors with other types of utility functions. All investors start with homogeneous priors. After a first round of trading, the quadratic utility investor receives a private signal, either α or β. The probability of each signal is $\frac{1}{2}$, and they indicate that the state probabilities are either $\boldsymbol{\pi}'_\alpha = (.2, .4, .1, .3)$ or $\boldsymbol{\pi}'_\beta = (.3, .1, .4, .2)$. The prior beliefs are $\boldsymbol{\pi} = .5(\boldsymbol{\pi}_\alpha + \boldsymbol{\pi}_\beta) = (.25, .25, .25, .25)'$.

No matter which signal the quadratic utility investor receives, he or she will compute that the mean return and variance on the risky asset are 3 and 5, respectively. The quadratic utility investor will also come to the same conclusion based solely on the prior information. Since mean and variance are all that is important to an investor with quadratic utility, the new information will not create any incentive to alter the portfolio chosen previously.

Obviously the new information will not affect the equilibrium price, and it cannot be revealed to the other investors thereby even though it would be valuable to them. For example, since the third moment of the return on the risky asset is 2.4 based on the probabilities $\boldsymbol{\pi}_\alpha$ and -2.4 based on the probabilities $\boldsymbol{\pi}_\beta$, an investor with an exponential utility function who likes skewness would wish to purchase more (less) of the risky asset if he or she knew that the signal α (β) had been received.

Somewhat more complicated examples could be constructed in which the price changes with the release of the new information, but it is still not fully revealed by the new price. Other examples can be constructed to show that trades can occur, and none, some, or all of the information is revealed.

PRICE EFFECTS OF DIVERGENT OPINIONS

In the previous section we examined conditions under which investors' private heterogeneous beliefs would become homogeneous. In this section we consider the price effects of any remaining divergence in investors' opinions.

To simplify the structure as much as possible, we will confine our attention to assets which have a value of zero in all but one state. If the market is complete, then as discussed in Chapters 2 and 8 it is always possible to create an Arrow–Debreu security (or insurance portfolio) for each state. In this case the imposed restriction entails no loss of generality. More typically, only some of the states are insurable. In this latter case the results here will hold only for the state securities of these states, and a modified method of analysis would have to be used for the states that are not insurable.

Consider the Arrow–Debreu security for insurable state s. The first-order condition for optimality of investor k's portfolio is, from Equation (7) of Chapter 3,

$$ {}_k\pi_s u_k'(w_s^k z_s) z_s = 1, \tag{29} $$

where we have assumed without loss of generality that the remaining assets have been formed into portfolios, creating new assets all of which have a return of zero in state s. Expressing this in terms of the direct utility function for weatlh, we have

$$ {}_k\pi_s U_k'(\nu_s^k) = \lambda_k p_s, \tag{30} $$

where ν_s^k is the number of unit payoff state securities held (i.e., it is investor k's wealth in state s), and λ_k is a positive Lagrange multiplier. Note that (30) is just the first-order condition (Equation (13) of Chapter 8) for asset selection in a complete market.

Since $U'' < 0$, U' has an inverse function $f(\cdot)$ which is monotone decreasing:

$$ \nu_s^k = f_k\left(\frac{\lambda_k p_s}{{}_k\pi_s}\right). \tag{31} $$

Equation (31) can now be summed across investors. The left-hand side of the sum is aggregate wealth in state s. For fixed values of λ_k and ${}_k\pi_s$, the right-hand side of the sum is a monotone decreasing function of p_s. Therefore, it too has an inverse and

$$ p_s = F_s(W_s, {}_1\pi_s, {}_2\pi_s, \ldots, {}_k\pi_s), \tag{32} $$

where W_s is aggregate wealth in state s. Thus, *in a given economy* the Arrow–Debreu price for an insurable state depends only on aggregate wealth in that state and the pattern of beliefs about that state.

The phrase "in a given economy" in the sentence above is quite important. We wish to discuss the comparative statics of the function in (32), but in doing so we must keep the economy the same. For example, a single probability cannot be changed by itself since each investor's subjective probabilities must sum to one. Therefore, in the discussion to follow each comparative static must be interpreted as a cros-sectional comparison between two otherwise identical states within a given economy.

It is clear from the preceding analysis that the state price is a decreasing function of the aggregate wealth available in that state, but our main concern is how the beliefs affect the price. It would seem obvious that that the state price of an insurable state should be an increasing function of each investor's subjective probability of that state. It is straightforward to show that this is the case. Consider Equation (31). In a state where ${}_k\pi_s$ is higher, to maintain the equality for the same wealth, p_s must be higher as well. Thus, as conjectured, the state price is an increasing function of each investor's subjective probability that the state will occur.

In examining the effects of heterogeneity in beliefs, the relevant measure for each investor is the marginal utility weighted probability, ${}_k\xi_s \equiv {}_k\pi_s/\lambda_k$. In general, wealthier or more risk-tolerant investors will have lower marginal utilities (smaller λ_k), and, therefore, their beliefs will have a greater impact on prices. We shall refer to ${}_k\xi_s$ as a util-probability.

To isolate the effects of heterogeneity of beliefs, we examine an economy of investors with identical utility functions. In this case the functions $f_k(\cdot)$ in (31) are all identical, and this equation can then be expressed as

$$W_s = \sum_{k=1}^{K} f\left(\frac{p_s}{{}_k\xi_s}\right). \tag{33}$$

We know already that the state price is a decreasing function of aggregate wealth; therefore; we can determine the effect of the change in beliefs by analyzing (33) directly. For some simple cases we should be able to determine the function $f(\cdot)$ from the common utility function of the investors, but we have a more general tool already in our arsenal.

The sum in (33) can be considered to be K times the equally weighted average of some function $f(\cdot)$ of $p_s/{}_k\xi_s$. By analogy with the Rothschild–Stiglitz analysis of riskiness, W_s will be less (more) than W_σ if $f(\cdot)$ is a concave (convex) function of the utility weighted probabilities and the state σ util-probabilities are equal to the state s util-probabilities plus a mean-preserving spread.

The only remaining problem is to determine the shape of the function $f(\cdot)$. Since it is the inverse of the marginal utility function, $f(U'(W)) \equiv W$, and

$$1 = \frac{\partial f}{\partial W} = f'(\cdot)U''(W), \tag{34a}$$

$$0 = \frac{\partial^2 f}{\partial W^2} = f''(\cdot)[U''(W)]^2 + f'(\cdot)U'''(W). \tag{34b}$$

Solving for the derivatives of $f(\cdot)$, we get

$$f'(\cdot) = \frac{1}{U''(W)}, \tag{35a}$$

$$f''(\cdot) = \frac{-U'''(w)}{[U''(W)]^3}. \tag{35b}$$

Finally, we can determine the shape of $f(\cdot)$ with respect to ${}_k\xi_s$:

$$\frac{\partial f}{\partial({}_k\xi_s)} = \frac{-f'(\cdot)p_s}{{}_k\xi_s^2}, \tag{36a}$$

$$\begin{aligned}\frac{\partial^2 f}{\partial({}_k\xi_s)^2} &= \frac{p_s}{U'(W)_k\xi_s^3}\left(2 - \frac{p_s U'''(W)}{{}_k\xi_s[U''(W)]^2}\right)\\ &= \frac{p_s}{U''(W)_k\xi_s^3}\left(2 - \frac{U'(W)U'''(W)}{[U''(W)]^2}\right).\end{aligned} \tag{36b}$$

The last equality follows from $U'(W) = p_s/{}_k\xi_s$. Since $U''(W)$ is negative, the function $f(\cdot)$ is concave or convex as the term in brackets is positive or negative.

With the above facts we can state the effects of an increased dispersion in beliefs in the following theorem.

THEOREM 4 *In the market environment just described, a mean-preserving spread in the utility weighted beliefs across the population of investors will decrease (increase) the state price for an insurable state if the elasticity of relative risk aversion is greater (less) than 1 minus the relative risk aversion.*

Proof. Given our preceding analysis, the only thing remaining to be demonstrated is the relation between the elasticity of relative risk aversion and the concavity of $f(\cdot)$. Since relative risk aversion is $R(W) \equiv -WU''(W)/U'(W)$, we have

$$\frac{dR(W)}{dW} = -\frac{U''(W) + WU'''(W)}{U'(W)} + \frac{W[U''(W)]^2}{[U'(W)]^2},$$

$$\begin{aligned}\frac{WR'(W)}{R(W)} - 1 + R(W) &= 1 + \frac{WU'''(W)}{U''(W)} - \frac{WU''(W)}{U'(W)} - 1 + R(W)\\ &= R(W)\left(2 - \frac{U'''(W)U'(W)}{[U''(W)]^2}\right).\end{aligned} \tag{37}$$

The final term in brackets is also what appears in (36b). Therefore, since relative risk aversion is positive, the function $f(\cdot)$ is concave if and only if the elasticity of relative risk aversion exceeds relative risk aversion less 1. Q.E.D.

For example, if the common utility function is in the power family, $U(W) = W^\gamma/\gamma$, then relative risk aversion is $1 - \gamma$, and the elasticity of relative risk aversion is zero. Thus, $f(\cdot)$ is concave (convex) for power utility functions with negative (positive) exponents. In other words, among investors who are more (less) risk averse than log utility investors, a mean-preserving spread in beliefs across the population of investors will decrease (increase) the price of insurance for a particular state.

Estimates of relative risk aversion vary, but all that I have seen exceed unity. Thus, the typical case is that more dispersion in beliefs should lower prices of state securities.

UTILITY AGGREGATION AND THE "REPRESENTATIVE" INVESTOR

The three important results of this chapter all depended on the market's being effectively complete. When this is the case, then (i) the CAPM (or distributional-based) pricing relation holds for the primary assets even in the presence of financial assets and the absence of portfolio separation; (ii) all investors agree on what risks are systematic (and compensated) and nonsystematic; and (iii) the market is informationally efficient with respect to all private information revealed in the publicly observable price.

The proof of each of these results depended either explicitly or implicitly on the existence of a representative investor—one whose optimal portfolio was the market portfolio. The assumption of a representative investor is a common one in economic models. Even in cases when no explicit assumption of the existence of a representative investor must be made in a proof, the intuition behind many results is sharpened by examining the actions of such an individual.

Although a complete or effectively complete market guarantees that a representative investor does exist, it is not necessarily the case that it is easy to describe him. The utility function of the representative investor can be determined only in special cases.

The representative investor's utility function is completely determined by the separate investors' utility functions and their wealths and is independent of the assets available only when all investors have HARA utility functions with the same cautiousness.

For example, suppose that all investors have exponential utility $U_k(W) = -\exp(-\delta_k W)$ or $u_k(Z) = -\exp(-a_k Z)$, where $a_k = \delta_k W_{0k}$. In this case the representative investor also has an exponential utility function with a risk tolerance equal to the average risk tolerance across all investors (i.e., the risk aversion of the representative investor is equal to the harmonic mean of the investors' risk aversions).

Recall from Chapter 6 [Equation (17)] that the dollar demand for the ith risky asset by the kth investor is

$$w_{ik}W_{0k} = \frac{\alpha_i}{\delta_k}, \tag{38}$$

where α_i is the portfolio demand for asset i by an investor with unit wealth and unit risk aversion. Aggregating (38) over all investors gives

$$\alpha_i \sum \delta_k^{-1} = \sum w_{ik}W_{0k} = w_{im}W_{0m} \equiv \frac{\alpha_i}{\delta_m}, \tag{39}$$

or $\delta_m^{-1} \equiv \Sigma\delta_k^{-1}$, the harmonic mean of the individual risk aversions. The second equality in (39) follows from the equality of supply and demand in equilibrium. The final line serves as a definition of the aggregate or representative investor. A single investor who owned all of the economy's wealth and who had an exponential utility function with risk aversion δ_m would have the same demand for each of the assets as in the original economy. Thus, the same equilibrium would be valid. In terms of the utility of returns function, the absolute risk aversion is a wealth-weighted harmonic mean

$$a_m^{-1} = W_m\left(\sum \frac{W_{0k}}{a_k}\right). \tag{40}$$

From the results in Chapters 5 and 6, we could use this representative utility function together with the market portfolio to price all assets.

Harmonic means are never large than arithmetic means and are lower unless every component in the average is the same. Therefore, the risk aversion over returns of the representative investor (or the "market") is less than the wealth-weighted average of the risk aversions, and, othr things being equal, investors with a lower risk aversion have a greater influence on the risk aversion of the representative investor. This last result follows intuitively because more risk-tolerant investors will be willing to purchase (or sell short) more shares of stock even with the same wealth. At the extreme, one risk-neutral investor, $a_k = 0$ (with positive wealth), will make the market risk neutral. Also, as we would expect, investors with a larger wealth have a greater impact on the risk aversion of the market and therefore on returns and prices.

Similar aggregation results hold for each of the generalized power families of utilities. Suppose all investors have utility functions of the form $U(W) = (W - \hat{W})^\gamma$. From Eqution (16) of Chapter 6 the dollar demand for the ith risky asset by the kth investor is

$$w_{ik}W_{0k} = \alpha_i\left(W_{0k} - \frac{\hat{W}_k}{R}\right), \tag{41}$$

where α_i is the portfolio demand for asset i of an investor with $\hat{W}_k = 0$. Aggregating (41) over all investors gives

$$\sum w_{ik} W_{0k} = \alpha_i \sum \left(W_{0k} - \frac{\hat{W}_k}{R} \right) \equiv \alpha_i \left(W_{0m} - \frac{\hat{W}_m}{R} \right). \tag{42}$$

This is obviously the same demand that would arise from a single investor with all the economy's wealth and a subsistence wealth level of $\hat{W}_m = \sum \hat{W}_k$. The appropriate utility of return function is therefore $u_m(Z) = (Z - \hat{Z})^\gamma/\gamma$, where $\hat{Z} \equiv \sum \hat{W}_k / \sum W_{0k}$.

10

Intertemporal Models in Finance

All of the models examined to this point have been single-period models. In this chapter we begin our examination of intertemporal models. Intertemporal models share many of the characteristics of single-period models; however, there are certain important differences as well.

PRESENT VALUES

It is assumed that the reader of this text is familiar with the arithmetic for computing present values as taught in any introductory text in finance. This section gives merely the briefest review of these mechanics.

Let $\tilde{d}_1$, $\tilde{d}_2$, ... be a series of cash dividends on an asset at times 1, 2, ..., and let v_0 and $\tilde{v}_1$, $\tilde{v}_2$ ... be the series of exdividend prices for the asset at times 0, 1, ... If k is the appropriate *discount rate* or *required rate of return* for this asset, then

$$v_t = \sum_{\tau=t+1}^{T} \frac{E[\tilde{d}_\tau]}{(1 + k)^{\tau-t}} + \frac{E[\tilde{v}_T]}{(1 + k)^{T-t}}. \tag{1}$$

If the discount rate is changing over time (but is known ex ante), then the denominators are replaced by the appropriate products. If the applicable discount rate is also stochastic, then the expectation must be taken of the entire sum at once.

The formula given in (1) is the natural analog of the single-period relation $v = E[\tilde{y}]/\bar{z}$ given in Chapter 2, where $k \equiv \bar{z} - 1$ is the expected rate of return and $\tilde{y}$ is the payoff, dividend plus terminal value. Equation (1) follows from this relation by induction and must hold for any choice of T.

STATE DESCRIPTION OF A MULTIPERIOD ECONOMY

Suppose that at time t there are a number of different states that can occur. Over time a particular evolution or history of the economy, $\tilde{s}_{t+1}$, $\tilde{s}_{t+2}$, ..., $\tilde{s}_T$ will occur. We shall denote a generic history of this type lasting from time $t + 1$ through time T by h_{tT}. That is, h_{tT} is a random vector of length $T - t$ with realizations $(\tilde{s}_{t+1}, \tilde{s}_{t+2}, \ldots, \tilde{s}_T)'$.

Consider two specific histories commencing at the same time t and lasting through T and $T + \tau$ $(\tau > 0)$, h_{tT} and $h_{t,T+\tau}$. If the elements of the former match the first $T - t$ elements of the latter vector, then $h_{t,T+\tau}$ is a possible future of $h_{t,T}$.

As in previous chapters, a state (at a point in time) is completely characterized by the payoffs on the available assets; however, we may now need to distinguish between cash disbursements and "value payoffs." For example, asset 1 paying a one dollar per share dividend and being worth ten dollars per share is a different state than when it is worth eleven dollars and pays no dividend even if all other things are the same. Obviously, particular evolutions are completely characterized by the unfolding histories of asset prices and cash payments.

In the intertemporal model each history has an associated "state" price which we denote by $p(h_{tT}|h_{0\tau})$. This state price is the value at time τ and after history $h_{0\tau}$ of one dollar at time T if and only if the economy evolution matches the prescribed history h_{tT} during the period t to T of the future. Note that we have assumed that the dollar is paid as soon as the history is confirmed even if the economy continues past the date T. (For $\tau > t$ the state price is interpreted as $p(h_{tT}|h_{0\tau}) = p(h_{\tau T}|h_{0\tau})$ if the history h_{tT} has not yet been contradicted by $h_{t\tau}$, and as zero otherwise.)

As in the single-period model, the state prices support the observed asset values. Let $d_i(h_{0t})$ be the cash disbursement (dividend) on asset i at time t if history h_{0t} has occurred. Similarly, let $v_i(h_{0t})$ be the asset's exdividend value at time t after the history h_{0t}. The states prices support the values at time t if

$$v_i(h_{0t}) = \sum_{\tau=t+1}^{T} \sum_{h_{t\tau}} d_i(h_{0\tau}) p(h_{0\tau}|h_{0t}) + \sum_{h_{tT}} v_i(h_{0T})\, p(h_{0T}|h_{0t}). \qquad (2)$$

The terms in the inner sum are the current, that is, time t, values of each of the stochastic dividend payments at a particular point in time τ. They are analogous to the terms $E[\tilde{d}_\tau]/(1 + k)^{\tau-t}$ in (1). Similarly, the final sum is the current value of the terminal payoff or value (ex dividend) of the asset at time T. The outer sum is the sum of each of these contributions. It is analogous to the summation in (1). As in the simple present-value framework, the dividend at each point in time has an independent and additive contribution to value.

Again, the equation in (2) must be valid for every choice of T. That is, the value of an asset today must be the present value of its next T dividends plus the present value of its exdividend price at that time. However, this last price is the present value (at that time) of the next dividend plus the price at this second date, and so on.

In the absence of all arbitrage opportunities, the state price for each possible history must be positive. A complete set of positive state prices is also a sufficient condition for the absence of arbitrage. The proof of this statement is omitted since it is identical to that in Chapter 2 for a single-period economy. In the intertemporal economy there is also another reltion that will hold among the state prices, namely, at time τ

$$p(h_{tT}|h_{0\tau}) = \sum_{h_{\tau u}} p(h_{tu}|h_{0\tau})p(h_{uT}|h_{0u}) \tag{3}$$

for all u. The sum in (3) is over all still possible histories $h_{\tau u}$, noting that this history also affects the second state price. Typically, $0 < \tau < t < u < T$ for this equation, but with state prices of impossible histories taken to be zero as above, this restriction is not required.

The proof of the necessity of this condition in a complete market (one in which claims against all possible evolutions are available at every time) is straightforward. Consider a portfolio formed at time τ consisting of $p(h_{uT}|h_{0u})$ state claims against each possible evolution $h_{\tau u}$ which is consistent with h_{tT}, the evolution for which the state price is desired. Whatever history is realized by time u, the value of this portfolio will be equal to $p(h_{uT}|h_{0u})$ (including 0 if h_{tT} is no longer possible). This is just sufficient to purchase a further claim for one dollar for the rest of the history h_{uT}. In addition, since the cost of each of these particualr state claims at time u is $p(h_{tu}|h_{0\tau})$, the total cost of the portfolio is

$$\sum_{h_{\tau u}} p(h_{tu}|h_{0\tau})p(h_{uT}|h_{0u}), \tag{4}$$

which is just the claimed value for $p(h_{tT}|h_{0\tau})$.

The convolution relation in Equation (3) is the same as the Kolmogorov relation among probabilities in a Markov Chain. The reason for this similarity should be obvious. In both cases a particular state (or history) at time T can only be reached by means of some intervening state (or history) at time u. The total probability of achieving a particular state is equal to the sum of the probabilitis of all possible paths. Similarly, the cost of insuring against any possible evolution must be equal to the cost of insuring separately against its mutually exclusive and collectively exhaustive components. If it were not, then an arbitrage opportunity would be available.

As with the positivty of state prices in a single-period model, this "requirement" is one that *can* always be met if there are no arbitrage opportunities. If the intertemporal market is complete, then the state prices are unique, and it must be met. If the market is incomplete, however, there may be other supporting state price vectors which violate this condition because an incomplete market puts fewer constraints on possible supporting pricing vectors than a complete market.

It is clear from Equation (3) that all of the evolutionary path prices are completely determined by the one-period ahead state prices $p(s_{t+1}|h_{0t})$.

We shall see that this has implications for the mechancis of trading as well. It need not be the case that state contingent claims against all possible evolutions are necessary for the market to be complete if investors can trade every period.

Since the evolution or history state prices are completely determined by the single-period state prices, all of the single period results of Chapter 2 remain valid. In particular, there is for each period a set of risk-neutral "probabilities" under which the expected rate of return on each asset is equal to the interest rate. A common way to make use of this result is through a *martingale pricing process*. This measure is related to the single-period state price per unit probability.

In an intertemporal content, we can define a stochastic process, $\tilde{\Lambda}_t$, which prices all assets according to the rule

$$v_t = \frac{1}{\Lambda_t}\left(\sum_{\tau=t+1}^{T} E_t[\tilde{\Lambda}_\tau \tilde{d}_\tau] + E_t[\tilde{\Lambda}_T \tilde{v}_T]\right). \tag{5}$$

For $T = t + 1$ (5) becomes

$$\tilde{\Lambda}_t v_t = E_t[\tilde{\Lambda}_{t+1}(\tilde{v}_{t+1} + \tilde{d}_{t+1})], \tag{6}$$

which is exactly Equation (59a) of Chapter 2 for the normalization $\Lambda_t = 1$.

Until some equilibrium is specified, the exact stochastic process for $\tilde{\Lambda}_t$ cannot be determined. However, since (6) applies to all assets including the riskless asset, it is clear that $\tilde{\Lambda}_t$ is expected to decrease in proportion to the riskless discount factor; that is, $E_t[\tilde{\Lambda}_{t+1}] = \Lambda_t/R$.

The related stochastic process $\tilde{\Theta}_t \equiv \tilde{\Lambda}_t R$ can be used in place of $\tilde{\Lambda}_t$. This process prices according to the rule

$$v_t = \frac{1}{\Theta_t}\left(\sum_{\tau=t+1}^{T} \frac{E_t[\tilde{\Theta}_\tau \tilde{d}_\tau]}{R^{\tau-t}} + \frac{E_t[\tilde{\Theta}_T \tilde{v}_T]}{R^{T-t}}\right) \tag{7a}$$

or

$$\Theta_t v_t = E_t\left[\frac{\tilde{\Theta}_{t+1}(\tilde{v}_{t+1} + \tilde{d}_{t+1})}{R}\right]. \tag{7b}$$

If the sure rate of interest is changing deterministically, then the denominators in (7a) are replaced with the appropriate products as in (1). If the interest rate is itself stochastic, then this product is inside the expectation. This topic is covered in more detail in Chapter 18 on the term structure of interest rates.

The process $\tilde{\Theta}_t$ is a martingale since $E_t[\tilde{\Theta}_{t+1}] = \Theta_t$, and it is referred to as a martingale pricing process. This name is also often applied to $\tilde{\Lambda}_t$ as well. Although this process is not itself a martingale, $\tilde{\Lambda}_t \tilde{P}_t$ is a martingale if $\tilde{P}_t$ is the value of any asset or portfolio of assets with all dividends reinvested.

THE INTERTEMPORAL CONSUMPTION INVESTMENT PROBLEM

In many respects the intertemporal consumption-investment problem is similar to the single-period problem. One major difference is that the utility of return function is not as easily derived from the direct utility function. We shall return to the problem of the derived utility function in the next chapter.

Consider an investor who is concerned about his current consumption and his consumption in the next T periods. (The last period's consumption is often assumed to be a bequest.) This investor faces the portfolio problem

$$\text{Max } E[\hat{U}(C_0, \tilde{C}_1, \ldots, \tilde{C}_T; \tilde{h}_{0T})] \tag{8}$$

subject to a budget constraint and certain feasibility constraints. The presence of h_{0T} in the utility function allows for any state dependencies in utility of consumption. Recall that h_{0T} records the entire history, so that the utility realized from a particular stream of consumption may depend on all of the past (and future) states.

The formal statement of the problem in (8) looks exactly like a single-period portfolio problem with T consumption goods in the first period. In this case the different consumption goods are consumption in the different periods. In fact, this appearance is not accidental; the intertemporal consumption portfolio problem can be treated in exactly this fashion. Indeed, if there are no further assumptions made about the structure of the economy or preferences, there is no other way to handle the problem.

One advantage of this correspondence is that many of the single-period multiple good results are immediately applicable in a multiperiod context. We have not previously dealt with multiple-good models explicitly; however, many of the single-good results remain true. In particular, if markets are complete (each history is insurable), then the achieved allocation is Pareto optimal. Furthermore, as shown in the previous chapter, once the first round of trading is finished, there will be no subsequent trading based on private information. That is, the markets can close at time zero and need never reopen.

A sufficient condition on preferences for this multiple-good interpretation to be reducible to a single-good interpretation is that the utility function display temporal independence. In this case as shown in Chapter 1, the utility function can be represented in either a multiplicative or additive form. Although either will do, we will concentrate on the more commonly assumed additive form. (An example of the consumption investment problem with a multiplicative utility function is provided in the appendix to the next chapter.)

Specifically, we assume that the utility function can be written as

$$\hat{U}(C_0, \ldots, C_T; h_{0T}) = \sum_{t=0}^{T} U(C_t, h_{0t}). \tag{9}$$

The assumed utility independence guarantees that the contribution to utility at any point in time depends only on the past and current states of the world.

Under the assumption of time additive utility, the function to be maximized in Equation (8) can be restated as

$$\begin{aligned} E[\hat{U}(C_0, C_1, \ldots, C_T; h_{0T})] &\equiv \sum_{h_{0T}} \pi(h_{0T}) \sum_{t=0}^{T} U(C_t, h_{0t}) \\ &= \sum_{t=0}^{T} \sum_{h_{0T}} \pi(h_{0t})\, U(C_t, h_{0t}) \sum_{h_{tT}} \pi(h_{tT}|h_{0t}) \\ &= \sum_{t=0}^{T} \sum_{h_{0t}} \pi(h_{0t})\, U(C_t, h_{0t}). \end{aligned} \tag{10}$$

The second equality follows by reversing the order of the summations and splitting the history into two parts. The final equality follows since the inner sum of the previous expression is of the probabilities of all possible futures, so it is unity. In addition, this means that the outer sum need only consider all histories h_{0t}.

Comparing this final maximand with that for a single-period model, $\Sigma \pi_s U(C, s)$, we see that they are obviously of the same form with states replaced by evolutions of states. (The probabilities of all the evolutions add not to 1 but to T, but this is a normalization only and has no effect on the problem.) It is clear now that for the market to be effectively complete, it is not necessary that there be "state" claims for all possible evolutions. At most all that is required is state claims for all possible histories commencing at the present. If these state claims all exist, we say the economy has a complete static market. This is distinguished later from a complete dynamic market.

If markets are complete in this static sense, then the solution in Chapter 8 can be applied immediately. The first order conditions are, from Equation (12) of Chapter 8,

$$0 = \frac{\partial L}{\partial \lambda} = W - C_0 - \Sigma p(h_{0t})\nu_{0t}, \tag{11a}$$

$$0 = \frac{\partial L}{\partial C_0} = U'(C, h_{00}) - \lambda, \tag{11b}$$

$$0 = \frac{\partial L}{\partial \nu_{0t}} = \pi(h_{0t})U'(\nu_{0t}, h_{0t}) - \lambda p(h_{0t}) \qquad \text{for all } t, \tag{11c}$$

where ν_{0t} is the number of pure state claims held for evolution h_{0t}, and L and λ are the Lagranian and Lagrange multiplier.

With complete static markets $p(h_{0t})$ will be proportional to the probability of the history $\pi(h_{0t})$ and to the marginal utility of the investor in that case. As in the single-period model, these marginal utilities are perfectly correlated across investors, so a representative investor can be defined who holds the market portfolio. The achieved allocation is Pareto optimal, and new information can only affect all investors' beliefs in comparable ways. Consequently, no trading takes place after time zero.

As argued before, there will always be incentives for some investors to introduce new assets or new kinds of assets until the market has become complete or effectively so. The number of securities required for the intertemporal static market to be complete, however, would typical be enormous, even relative to the usually large number of securities required for a complete single-period market. As we shall see, another mode for the completion of a multiperiod market is through explicit intertemporal trading. This trading occurs not only because of changes in private information but as the result of shifts in the investment opportunities available—shifts that are observable to all.

Of course, even with dynamic trading of the primitive assets, it may not be possible to create a market that is complete or effectively complete. Nevertheless, in the absence of a complete static market, investors would typically rebalance their portfolios in an attempt to maximize their expected utility.

COMPLETION OF THE MARKET THROUGH DYNAMIC TRADING

To illustrate dynamic completion of a market, consider the following economy with three assets. Each asset is originally worth one dollar per share. There are six states with realized returns

$$\mathbf{Z} = \begin{pmatrix} 0 & 1 & 2 \\ 2 & 0 & 1 \\ 1 & 2 & 0 \\ 1 & 1 & 0 \\ 1 & 0 & 2 \\ 2 & 2 & 1 \end{pmatrix} \qquad \boldsymbol{\pi} = \begin{pmatrix} 1/4 \\ 1/8 \\ 1/8 \\ 1/4 \\ 1/8 \\ 1/8 \end{pmatrix}. \tag{12}$$

The expected return on each asset is 1, and the covariance matrix is

$$\boldsymbol{\Sigma} = \frac{1}{4}\begin{pmatrix} 2 & 0 & -1 \\ 0 & 2 & -1 \\ -1 & -1 & 3 \end{pmatrix}. \tag{13}$$

Since all assets have the same expected rate of return, any investor with quadratic utility will hold the global minimum variance portfolio. This is

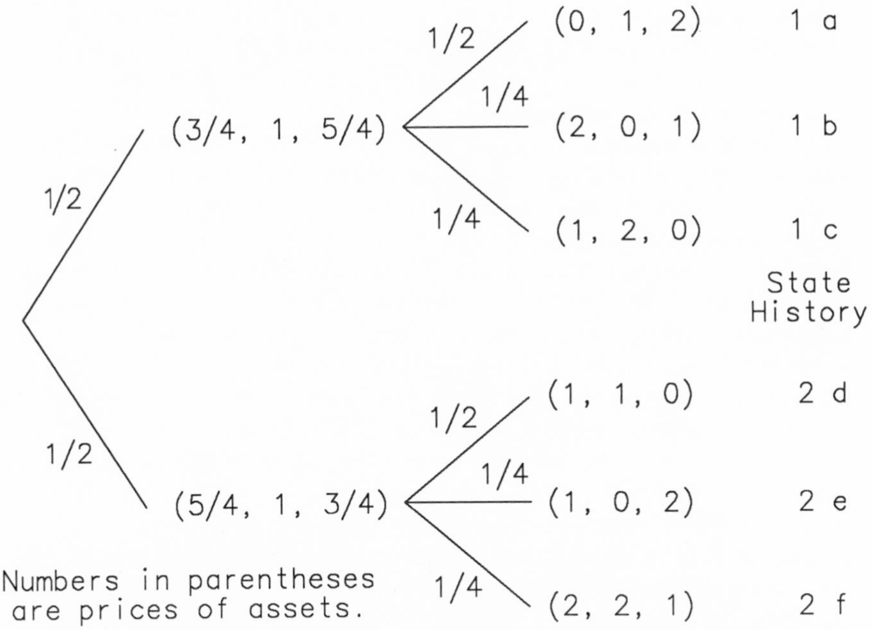

Figure 10.1 History of Dynamically Complete Market

$$\mathbf{w}_g' = \frac{\mathbf{1}'\mathbf{\Sigma}^{-1}}{\mathbf{1}'\mathbf{\Sigma}^{-1}\mathbf{1}} = (\tfrac{1}{3}, \tfrac{1}{3}, \tfrac{1}{3})'. \tag{14}$$

The global minimum variance portfolio has a pattern of returns of $\{1\ 1\ 1\ \frac{2}{3}\ 1\ 1\frac{2}{3}\}$. The first and fourth outcomes have probabilities of $\frac{1}{4}$, whereas the others have probabilities of $\frac{1}{8}$. Its expected return is 1 and its variance is $\frac{1}{12}$. For a utility function of $u(Z) = Z - (b/2)Z^2$, the investor's expected utility is $1 - 13b/24$.

Now suppose that trading is allowed between time periods 0 and 1 after some new information has arrived which lets investors conclude that certain states are no longer possible. The possible evolutions of the economy are illustrated in Figure 10.1. The lines in the figure indicate possible histories, and the numbers give their probabilities. Two outcomes are possible at time $\frac{1}{2}$. In the first only states a, b, and c remain possible, and the assets are worth $\frac{3}{4}$, 1, and $\frac{5}{4}$, respectively. In the second outcome only states d, e, and f are still possible, and the assets are worth $\frac{5}{4}$, 1, and $\frac{3}{4}$. (*Note*: The interim prices have been set at the conditional expected values of the final prices. Since the original expected returns were all unity, this is a consistent equilibrium.)

Before solving for the quadratic utility investor's optimal portfolio policy when rebalancing is allowed at time $\frac{1}{2}$, let us see how the market can be completed by using dynamic portfolio strategies. The first step in doing this is to construct the single-period insurance portfolios. The portfolio $\mathbf{n}_1$ which is long $\frac{5}{4}$ of a share of asset 3 and short $\frac{3}{4}$ of a share of asset 1 provides at time 0 insurance against outcome 1 at time $\frac{1}{2}$. It costs $\frac{1}{2}$ and is worth 0 in outcome 1 and 1 in outcome 2. The portfolio $\mathbf{n}_2$ which is long $\frac{5}{4}$ of a share of asset 1 and short $\frac{1}{4}$ of a share of asset 3 provides insurance against outcome 2.

The reader can also check that the portfolios of $\mathbf{n}'_a = \frac{1}{9}(-2, 1, 4)$, $\mathbf{n}'_b = \frac{1}{9}(4, -2, 1)$, and $\mathbf{n}'_c = \frac{1}{9}(1, 4, -2)$ formed after outcome 1 provide insurance against states a, b, and c, respectively. The first costs $\frac{1}{2}$, and the other two cost $\frac{1}{4}$ each per dollar insurance at time 1. Similarly, the portfolios of $\mathbf{n}'_d = (4, -3, -2)$, $\mathbf{n}'_e = (1, -1, 0)$, and $\mathbf{n}'_f = (-2, 2, 1)$ formed after outcome 2 provide insurance against states d, e, and f, respectively. Again, the first costs $\frac{1}{2}$, and the other two cost $\frac{1}{4}$ each.

It is possible to construct insurance against each evolution, and hence every final state, with a dynamic portfolio which trades these single-period insurance portfolios. To insure against evolution $1b$, for example, an investor would spend $\frac{1}{8}$ dollar on portfolio $\mathbf{n}_1$. This would provide him with $\frac{1}{4}$ dollar if state 1 occurred. He could then use this to buy portfolio $\mathbf{n}_b$. Thus, he would end up with one dollar if the evolution was state 1 followed by state b, and nothing if any other sequence occurred. Any other evolution could similarly be insured.

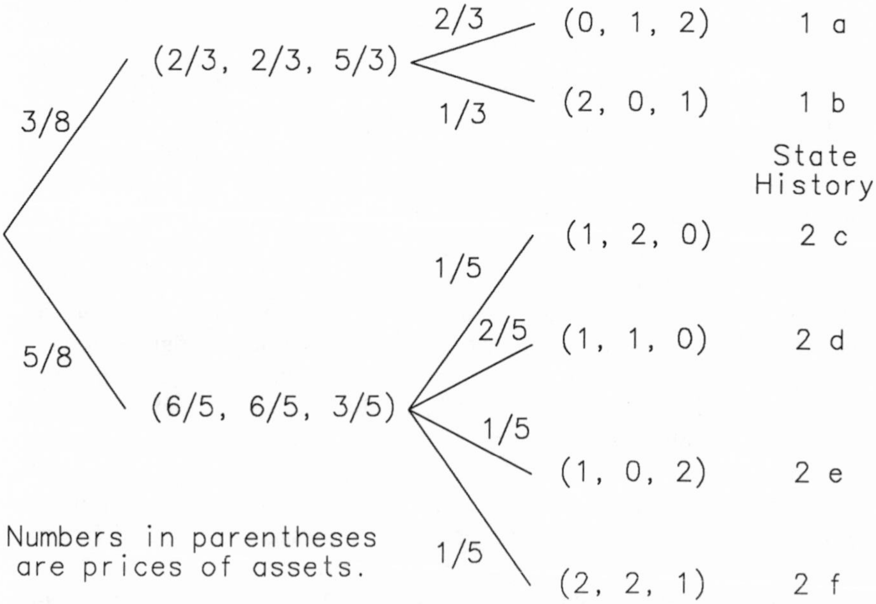

Figure 10.2 History of Incomplete Market

Since every final state is insurable, a riskless asset can be constructed. This obviously is the global minimum-variance portfolio, and it is the policy that our quadratic utility investor will follow. In this case the investor's expected utility is $1 - b/2$, which exceeds the expected utility previously achievable by $b/24$.

This economy can be made complete with dynamic trading because each of the separate one-period markets is complete. At time 0 there are two linearly independent assets, and there are two possible states at time $\frac{1}{2}$. (Note that one-half share each of assets 1 and 3 duplicates asset 2.) In each state at time $\frac{1}{2}$ there are three linearly independent assets equal in number to the three remaining possible states at time 1.

Notice how the situation is changed if state c follows outcome 2 rather than 1. This economy is illustrated in Figure 10.2. The prices at time $\frac{1}{2}$ are now different because different possibilities have been eliminated. The original prices are the same, however, since the total probabilities of states a–f remain the same. Now the market is incomplete after outcome 2, so the intertemporal market cannot be completed by dynamic trading. We do not yet have the tools for solving an intertemporal problem of this type. They will be developed in the next chapter.

INTERTEMPORALLY EFFICIENT MARKETS

In Chapters 3 and 9 the concept of an efficient market was introduced and expanded upon. There the primary concern was on the aggregation of diverse information into a market price which revealed some or all of the relevant information to all investors. In this section we address another aspect of efficient markets, the behavior over time of asset prices. This aspect of efficient markets is much closer in spirit to the idea of a "random walk" in prices than to rational expectations. To emphasize this difference, we assume that all investors have the same beliefs.

All of the efficient markets results depend on the following lemma, which was proved in the Mathematical Introduction:

LEMMA *Let $\tilde{x}$ be any random variable with $E[|\tilde{x}|] < \infty$, and let $\{\tilde{z}_t\}_0^T$ be the related stochastic process $\tilde{z}_t \equiv E_t[\tilde{x}]$. Then $\tilde{z}_t$ is a martingale.*

THEOREM 1 *If an asset with a single payoff $\tilde{d}_T$ at time T is priced according to (1), then the stochastic process $\tilde{x}_t \equiv (1 + k)^{T-t}\tilde{v}_t$ is a martingale with respect to any subset of the information used in forming the expectations in (1), and the expected compound rate of return on the asset is equal to the discount rate, k, per period over any interval.*

Proof. For this asset the relevant stochastic process is $\tilde{x}_t = E_t[\tilde{d}_T]$. But this is a martingale by the lemma. Clearly, $E_t[\tilde{v}_{t+\tau}]/v_t = (1 + k)^\tau$, and since there are no dividends, this is the total expected rate of return. Q.E.D.

Although all theorems are tautologies, this theorem appears so little removed from the obvious that it has often caused confusion. The important assumption is that the information set used in verifying that $\tilde{x}_t$ is a martingale is no more precise than that used in computing the price originally by the formula in (1). That is, if the "market" sets the price v_t using (1), then $(1 + k)^{T-t}\,\tilde{v}_t$ is a martingale with respect to any subset of the market's information. The practical statement in the theorem is that the returns realized on average must be equal to the "fair" rate of return used in determining values in the market place.

Unlike the theorems in Chapters 3 and 9, this theorem does *not* say that an investor who possesses superior information (has information not included in the expectation in (1) that sets the market price) cannot earn a return above the fair return on average. Whether or not he will do so depends upon whether or not his information is revealed or reflected in the market price or other publicly observed information. In other words, this theorem is *not* one about fully revealing prices.

If the relevant information set used in computing the expectations consists of the current and past prices, then this form of efficient market theory is often called a random walk theory. Note, however, that, strictly speaking, $\tilde{x}_t$ need not be a random walk. The distribution of changes in $\tilde{x}_t$ can vary over time. For example, its variance can change. Only its expectation must remain the same.

If the asset's discount rate is changing deterministically over time, then an obvious adjustment is made in the definition of the martingale $\tilde{x}_t$. If the asset's discount rate is varying randomly over, then the following related theorem is valid.

THEOREM 2 *Let $\tilde{v}_t$ be the time series of values of an asset with a single payoff $\tilde{d}_T$ at time T, and, let $\tilde{\Lambda}_t$ be the martingale pricing process introduced in (5). If there are no arbitrage opportunities, then the stochastic process $\tilde{x}_t \equiv \tilde{\Lambda}_t\tilde{v}_t$ is a martingale with respect to any subset of the information used in forming the expectations in (5).*

Proof. The proof follows immediately from Equation (6). Q.E.D.

Again, the important assumption is that the expectation used in verifying that $\tilde{\Lambda}_t\tilde{v}_t$ is a martingale can be no more precise than that used in computing the "present value" in (5). In each period investors will expect to earn at the appropriate discount rate or required rate of return. This statement follows from the isomorphism of Equation (6) and Equation

(59a) in Chapter 2, which gives the single-period rate of return.

In addition, since we have seen that multiperiod state prices for histories are determined by the single-period state prices, the expected rate of return over any interval will be the required rate of return as well. Since $\tilde{\Lambda}_t \tilde{v}_t$ is a martingale, $E_t[\tilde{\Lambda}_\tau \tilde{v}_\tau] = \Lambda_t v_t$ and

$$\Lambda_t v_t = \operatorname{Cov}(\tilde{\Lambda}_T, \tilde{v}_T) + E[\tilde{\Lambda}_T]E[\tilde{v}_T],$$

$$\frac{E_t[\tilde{v}_T]}{v_t} = \frac{\Lambda_t}{E_t[\tilde{\Lambda}_T]}\left(1 - \frac{\operatorname{Cov}(\tilde{\Lambda}_T, \tilde{v}_T)}{\Lambda_t v_t}\right) \tag{15}$$

$$= R^{T-t}\left[1 - \operatorname{Cov}\left(\frac{\tilde{\Lambda}_T}{\Lambda_t}, \frac{\tilde{v}_T}{v_t}\right)\right].$$

This result is the obvious intertemporal analog of Equation (60b) of Chapter 2 and gives the required $T - t$ period rate of return.

For assets with multiple payoffs, similar results hold as well. The stochastic process that is a martingale is $\tilde{\Lambda}_t$ multiplied by the accumulated value obtained by reinvesting all dividends in the same asset (the product of all the single-period returns and the original value); that is

$$\tilde{x}_\tau \equiv \tilde{\Lambda}_\tau v_t \left(\frac{\tilde{v}_{t+1} + \tilde{d}_{t+1}}{\tilde{v}_t}\right) \cdots \left(\frac{\tilde{v}_\tau + \tilde{d}_\tau}{\tilde{v}_{\tau-1}}\right).$$

INFINITE HORIZON MODELS

All of the intertemporal results above hold in infinite horizon models as well. The only caution concerns the behavior of asset values at infinity. Consider pricing an infinitely lived asset with Equation (1). Normally we would write

$$v_t = \sum_{\tau=t+1}^{\infty} \frac{E[\tilde{d}_\tau]}{(1 + k)^{\tau-t}}. \tag{16}$$

However, to be precise we should express this as the limit

$$v_t = \sum_{\tau=t+1}^{\infty} \frac{E[\tilde{d}_\tau]}{(1 + k)^{\tau-t}} + \lim_{T\to\infty}\left(\frac{E[\tilde{v}_T]}{(1 + k)^{T-t}}\right). \tag{17}$$

The first term in (17) is sometimes called the *fundamental value* or *market fundamental*. The second term is know as a *price bubble*. In order for (17) and (16) to be the same, the price bubble must vanish. This condition is the *transversality condition*.

In most contexts the transversality condition must hold or "infinite horizon" arbitrage opportunities will be present. This has nothing to do with possible undefined or infinite expectations in (16) or (17). They can even appear in certainly models. To demonstrate that it is not uncertainty that causes the problems, the ensuing discussion is mostly in terms of certainty models with a constant interest rate $r \equiv R - 1$.

For example, consider a consol bond which pays a one-dollar coupon per year. The value at time t, B_t, computed by Equation (16) is

$$B_t = \sum_{\tau=t+1}^{\infty} \frac{1}{(1 + r)^{\tau-t}} = \frac{1}{r}. \tag{18}$$

This price, which is the present value of the cash payments, is the *market fundamental.*

This familiar result is commonly assumed to be the only "correct" price series. However, consider the price series $b_t = [1 + (rb - 1)(1 + r)^t]/r$, where b is the price at time 0. Note that for $b = 1/r$ this series is a constant: $b_t = 1/r$, the market fundamental. However, for $b \neq 1/r$, the price is always greater or less than this correct value. Nevertheless, even for other values of b this price series induces a realized rate of return over the period t to $t + 1$ of

$$\frac{b_{t+1} - b_t + 1}{b_t} = \frac{(1/r)(rb - 1)(1 + r)^t[(1 + r) - 1] + 1}{(1/r)[1 + (rb - 1)(1 + r)^t]}, \tag{19}$$

which is equal to r, the required rate of rturn on a riskless asset.

In addition, the present value formula (1) when applied for any finite interval gives

$$\begin{aligned} &\sum_{\tau=t+1}^{T} \frac{1}{(1 + r)^{\tau-t}} + \frac{[1 + (rb - 1)(1 + r)^T]/r}{(1 + r)^{T-t}} \\ &= \frac{1}{r}[1 - (1 + r)^{t-T}] \\ &\quad + \frac{1}{r}[(1 + r)^{t-T} + (rb - 1)(1 + r)^t] \\ &= b_t, \end{aligned} \tag{20}$$

confirming again that this is a "valid" price series. Furthermore, if investors believe that the price will follow this time path, there will be no reason for deviation from it since the rate of return is always equal to the riskless rate, justifying the assumption that the asset is riskless. Thus, the price series fulfills the rational expectations requiement as well.

The difference between the market fundamental and the actual price, $(rb - 1)(1 + r)^t/r$, is the price bubble. Note that the present value of the price bubble is a constant, $b - 1/r$. This is a general result for all price bubbles in a certainty model. (With uncertainty, the present expected value of a price bubble is a martingale.) Price bubbles are therefore self-supporting. That is, they are similar to pyramid or Ponzi schemes in which growth is justified only by the assumption of further growth.

It would appear that the price series for any value of b is valid, but $b_t = 1/r$ is the generally accepted correct answer. In what sense is the market fundamental more valid than these other price series? The problem with the other price series is that there are arbitrage opportunities. If the original value b is less than $1/r$, then the price will become negative at some time. But the bond has only positive payoffs, so there is an obvious arbitrage opportunity in buying the bond (for a negative amount) and receiving positive payments. The fact that the price becomes increasingly negative does not negate the arbitrage because the investor is never forced to sell and suffer this loss. The price at $t = \infty$ is not a terminal value in the sense that any final reckoning is required; it is merely the limit of the series.

If, on the other hand, $b > 1/r$, then there is an arbitrage associated with selling the claim and financing the position by investing $1/r$ dollars in a series of one-period riskless assets paying interest at the rate r. The interest is always sufficient to pay the coupons on the short sale, so there is no remaining liability. The fact that the price is growing without limit is no problem. If the short position gets called, a new one can be established at the same price (assuming as always a competitive market with price-taking behavior).

Thus, only the price series $b_t = 1/r$ has no arbitrage opportunities. Another argument establishing that this is the only reasonable price is through the stationarity of the economy. Since the interest rate, the coupon payments, and the remaining time on the contract are all constant, the only reasonable price series is a constant as well.

Mathematically these other price series are usually discarded by positing the transversality condition $(1 + r)^T v_T \to 0$ as $T \to \infty$. Any price series established when $b \neq 1/r$ violates this condition. From (20) it is clear that this limit is not zero but $b(1 + r)^t$ at time t. If we impose the transversality condition, only $b_t = 1/r$ remains as a valid price series.

For assets with uncertain payments the transversality condition is lim $E_t[\tilde{v}_T]/(1 + k)^T = 0$ as $T \to \infty$. To illustrate this, consider a mutual fund which buys one of the consols described before. Rather than distributing income, it reinvests all coupons received in more consols.

If $1/r$ dollars are invested originally in the mutual fund, one consol can be purchased. The one-dollar coupon at the end of the first year will purchase r additional consols. At the end of the next year $1 + r$ in coupons will be received, enabling the purchase of $r + r^2$ in additional consols. The number of consols held at time t (after the latest purchase) will be $(1 + r)^t$ for a portfolio value of $(1 + r)^t/r$.

Suppose that the fund has no set termination date. Conditional on its still being in operation at time t, it will terminate and distribute its assets with probability π (a constant). Then the unconditional probability of distribution at time t is $(1 - \pi)^{t-1}\pi$. The expected value of the payoff at time t is $(1 - \pi)^{t-1}\pi(1 + r)^t/r$, and the present value of the original investment is

$$\sum_{t=1}^{\infty} \frac{(1 - \pi)^{t-1}\pi(1 + r)^t}{r(1 + r)^t} = \frac{\pi}{r}\sum_{t=1}^{\infty}(1 - \pi)^{t-1} = \frac{1}{r}, \tag{21}$$

as it should be. The tth term is $(1 - \pi)^{t-1}\pi/r$, which vanishes as $t \to \infty$, as required by the transversality condition.

Under some conditions, the transversality condition will not hold. In Chapters 14 and 17, for example, we will see that the value of a European call option of infinite maturity is typically positive even though its only "distribution" is at $t = \infty$.

11

Discrete-time Intertemporal Portfolio Selection

An investor is assumed to choose a consumption stream and portfolio to Max $E[\hat{U}(C_0, C_1, \ldots, C_{T-1}, W_T)]$, where, for simplicity, the date of death T is assumed known and the utility function is assumed additively separable:

$$\hat{U}(C_0, C_1, \ldots, W_T) = \sum_{t=0}^{T-1} U(C, t) + B(W_T, T), \tag{1}$$

where $U(\cdot)$ is the concave utility of consumption, and $B(\cdot)$ is the concave utility of bequest.

At time t an investor knows the prices $P_i(t)$ of the securities, wealth $W(t)$, and current noncapital income $Y(t)$. He or she then chooses to consume $C(t)$ and buy $N_i(t)$ shares of each asset subject to the constraint

$$W(t) + Y(t) - C(t) \equiv I(t) = \sum_0^N N_i(t)P_i(t). \tag{2}$$

Define $w_i(t) \equiv N_i(t)P_i(t)/I(t)$ and $\tilde{z}_i(t) = \tilde{P}_i(t+1)/P_i(t)$. The $t + 1$ price is cum dividend. Then

$$\begin{aligned} W(t+1) &= I(t)\sum_{i=0}^{N} w_i(t)z_i(t) \\ &= [W(t) - C(t) + Y(t)]\left[\sum_{i=1}^{N} w_i(t)[z_i(t) - R] + R\right], \end{aligned} \tag{3}$$

where the constraint $\Sigma w_i = 1$ has been substituted out.

Also define the derived utility of wealth function

$$\begin{aligned} J[W(t), t] &\equiv \text{Max } E_t\left[\sum_{s=t}^{T-1} U(C, s) + B(W_T, T)\right], \\ J[W(T), T] &\equiv B[W(T), T]. \end{aligned} \tag{4}$$

In writing J as a function of time, we are recognizing both its explicit effect through age and time preference and its implicit effect through changes in the opportunities and the information available to the investor.

With one year to go in his or her life the investor solves the problem

$$\begin{aligned} J[W(T-1), T-1] &= \underset{C,\mathbf{w}}{\text{Max}}\ E_{T-1}[U(C, T-1) + B[\tilde{W}(T), T)]] \\ &= \underset{C,\mathbf{w}}{\text{Max}}[U(C, T-1) + E_{T-1}B[\tilde{W}(T), T)]]. \end{aligned} \tag{5}$$

Then using (5) and (3), we derive the first-order conditions

$$0 = U_C(C, T-1) - E_{T-1}\left[B_{W_T}(\cdot)\left(\sum_1^N w_i[\tilde{z}_i - R] + R\right)\right], \tag{6a}$$

$$0 = E_{T-1}[B_{W_T}(\cdot)(\tilde{z}_i - R)]. \tag{6b}$$

Since $U(\cdot)$ and $B(\cdot)$ are concave, the second-order coditions will be satisfied. It is possible, however, that the optimal solution C^* will be negative. We assume for the moment that this is not the case. This issue as well as short sale constraints will be examined later.

Equation (6a) can be rewritten as $U_C = E[\tilde{Z}^* B_W]$, which demonstrates that the current marginal utility of consumption is equal to expected future marginal utility of wealth. Using (6b) we can also express this as

$$U_C = E_{T-1}[B_W\tilde{Z}^*] = RE_{T-1}[B_W]. \tag{7}$$

Notice that (7) says that current marginal utility of consumption is equal to accumulated (not discounted) expected future marginal utility. This seeming paradox is cleared up when we realize that the utility functions include an implicit discounting term. If we separate the personal discounting factor from utility $U(C, t) = \delta^t u(C)$ and $B(W, T) = \delta^T b(W)$, then (7) becomes

$$u_C = \delta R E_{T-1}(b_W), \tag{8}$$

and expected future marginal utility *is* discounted, but only to the extent that the personal rate of time preference exceeds the riskless rate.

This relation can be expressed in a third fashion as follows. "Substitute" the formal solutions C^* and w_i^* into (5) and, assuming these policies are differentiable with respect to W, differentiate using (3) and the chain rule:

$$J_W = U_C\frac{\partial C^*}{\partial W} + E_{T-1}\left[B_W(\cdot)\left[\tilde{Z}^*\left(1 - \frac{\partial C^*}{\partial W}\right) + \sum_{i=1}^N(\tilde{z}_i - R)I^*\frac{\partial w_i^*}{\partial W}\right]\right], \tag{9}$$

where $I^* = W - C^* + Y$ and $\tilde{Z}^* = \Sigma_0^n w_i\tilde{z}_i$. Rearranging terms gives

$$\begin{aligned} J_W = [U_C - E_{T-1}[\tilde{Z}^* B_W(\cdot)]]\frac{\partial C^*}{\partial W} + I^*\sum_1^N\frac{\partial w_i^*}{\partial W}E_{T-1}[B_W(\cdot)(\tilde{z}_i - R)] \\ + E_{T-1}[B_W(\cdot)\tilde{Z}^*]. \end{aligned} \tag{10}$$

The first term is zero from (7), the second term is zero from (6b). Thus

$$J_W = E_{T-1}[B_W(\cdot)\tilde{Z}^*] = RE_{T-1}[B_W(\cdot)] = U_C. \tag{11}$$

The last two equalities follow from (7). Equation (11) is known as the "envelope condition." It will appear again later.

Moving back to the previous period we solve

$$\begin{aligned} J[W(T-2), T-2] &= \text{Max}(U(C, T-2) + \text{E}_{T-2}[U(\tilde{C}, T-1) \\ &\quad + B(\tilde{W}, T)]) \\ &= \underset{T-2}{\text{Max}}(U(C, T-2) \\ &\quad + E_{T-2}\underset{T-1}{\text{Max}}\, E_{T-1}[U(\tilde{C}, T-1) + B(\tilde{W}, T)]) \\ &= \underset{T-2}{\text{Max}}(U(C, T-2) + E_{T-2}J[\tilde{W}(T-1), T-1]). \end{aligned} \tag{12}$$

But this problem is of the same form as (5) with J replacing B. Similarly, for any previous period we have

$$\begin{aligned} J[W(t), t] &= \text{Max}\left(U(C, t) + E_t\left[\sum_{s=t+1}^{T-1} U(\tilde{C}, s) + B(\tilde{W}, T)\right]\right) \\ &= \text{Max}[U(C, t) + E_t(J[\tilde{W}(t+1), t+1])]. \end{aligned} \tag{13}$$

Again the problem is identical to (5) in form. Solutions are given by equations similar to (6), and by identical manipualtions we can show that Equation (11) is valid at each point of time. The characterization of the optimal decisions is thus

$$U_C(C, t) = E_t[J_W((W - C)\tilde{Z}^*, t+1)\tilde{Z}^*], \tag{14a}$$

$$E_t[J_W((W - C)\tilde{Z}^*, t+1)(\tilde{z}_i - R)] = 0, \qquad i = 1, \ldots, n. \tag{14b}$$

If the optimal policies are differentiable, then, as before, (14a) can be reexpressed as $U_C(C, t) = J_W(W, t)$, which is the envelope condition. It indicates that an investor first consumes until marginal utility of consumption equals marginal utility of wealth (discounted expected marginal utility of future consumption and bequest). The optimal portfolio is then determined for the single-period problem in (14b).

Caution: This interpretation of (14) is an intuitive one and should not be accepted literally. The consumption choice in (14a) cannot be made "first" because $J(W, t)$ generally depends upon the optimal portfolio. Furthermore, the portfolio choice problem in (14b) is not identical to a single-period problem, since, in general, next period's derived utility function depends implicitly on future optimal portfolios which depend on future investment opportunities. These distinctions will be made clear in the following examples.

Example 1. Logarithmic utility, $Y \equiv 0$.

Let $U(C, t) = \delta^t \ln(C)$, $B(W, T) = \delta^T \ln(W)$. Then from (6a)

$$U_C = E_{T-1}[B_{W_T}[(W_{T-1} - C^*)\tilde{Z}^*, T]\tilde{Z}^*]$$

$$\frac{\delta^{T-1}}{C^*} = E_{T-1}\left[\frac{\tilde{Z}^*\delta^T}{(W_{T-1} - C^*)Z^*}\right] = \frac{\delta^T}{W_{T-1} - C^*}, \tag{15}$$

or $C^*_{T-1} = W_{T-1}/(1 + \delta)$. In this case the optimal level of consumption is independent of the rates of return available, and the Caution can safely be ignored. Consumption is proportional to wealth and decreasing in δ. For a zero rate of time preference ($\delta = 1$) one-half of the remaining wealth is consumed. The other half is saved. With positive time preference $\delta < 1$, more than one-half of the remaining wealth is consumed.

To determine the optimal portfolio we use (6b)

$$E_{T-1}[B_W(\cdot)\tilde{z}_i] = RE_{T-1}[\mathrm{B_W}(\cdot)]$$

$$\delta^T E_{T-1}\left[\frac{\tilde{z}_i}{\tilde{Z}^*(W_{T-1} - C)}\right] = \delta^T R E_{T-1}\left[\frac{1}{Z^*(W_{T-1} - C)}\right] \tag{16}$$

$$E_{T-1}\left[\frac{\tilde{z}_i}{\tilde{Z}^*}\right] = RE_{T-1}\left[\frac{1}{\tilde{Z}^*}\right], \qquad i = 1, \ldots, n.$$

If we multiply both sides of the last line of (16) by w_i^* and sum over all assets, we get $E(1) = RE[1/\tilde{Z}^*]$, so we can also express the optimal portfolio as

$$E_{T-1}\left[\frac{\tilde{z}_i}{\tilde{Z}^*}\right] = 1, \qquad i = 0, 1, \ldots, n. \tag{17}$$

The solution to the implicit problem in (16) or (17) is exactly the same portfolio formed by a log utility investor in a single-period world.

To determine the optimal policies in the previous period, we must first obtain $J(W, T - 1)$. Using the envelope condition and (15) and integrating once give

$$\begin{aligned} J_W(W, T-1) &= U_C = \frac{\delta^{T-1}}{C^*} = \frac{\delta^{T-1}(1+\delta)}{W_{T-1}}, \\ J(W, T-1) &= \delta^{T-1}(1+\delta)\ln W + k, \end{aligned} \tag{18}$$

where k is a constant of integration. Alternatively, from (5),

$$\begin{aligned} J[W, T-1] &= \delta^{T-1}\ln C^* + E_{T-1}B[\tilde{W}_T^*, T] \\ &= \delta^{T-1}\ln\left(\frac{W}{1+\delta}\right) + \delta^T E_{T-1}\ln[\tilde{Z}^*(W - C^*)] \end{aligned}$$

$$= \delta^{T-1}\ln\left(\frac{W}{1+\delta}\right) + \delta^T E_{T-1}\ln\tilde{Z}^* \tag{19}$$

$$+ \delta^T \ln\left[W\left(1 - \frac{1}{1+\delta}\right)\right]$$

$$= \delta^{T-1}(1+\delta)\ln W + \delta^{T-1}\left[\delta\ln\left(\frac{\delta}{1+\delta}\right)\right.$$

$$\left. - \ln(1+\delta) + \delta E_{T-1}\ln\tilde{Z}^*\right]$$

$$= \delta^{T-1}(1+\delta)\ln W + \Phi(T-1).$$

When the problem (12) for the second to last period is solved, similar manipulations show that $J(W, T-2)$ is also logarithmic. In fact we can show in general that the derived utility function is always logarithmic. We establish this proposition by induction as follows. Assume that $J(W, t+1) = \delta^{t+1}f(t+1)\ln W + \Phi(t+1)$. The using (14a) we get

$$U_C = \frac{\delta^t}{C^*} = E_t[J_W(\cdot)\tilde{Z}^*] = \delta^{t+1}f(t+1)E_t\left[\frac{\tilde{Z}^*}{(W_t - C^*)\tilde{Z}^*}\right]. \tag{20}$$

Solving for optimal consumption gives

$$C_t^* = [1 + \delta f(t+1)]^{-1}W_t \equiv h(t)W_t. \tag{21}$$

Substituting for C^* in (13) gives

$$J(W, t) = \delta^t\ln[h(t)W]$$

$$+ E_t\{\delta^{t+1}f(t+1)\ln[\tilde{Z}^*W(1-h(t))] + \Phi(t+1)\} \tag{22}$$

$$= \delta^t[1 + \delta f(t+1)]\ln W + \Phi(t).$$

Thus the proposition is established for $f(t) = 1 + \delta f(t+1)$ and $\Phi(t)$ defined in (25). Evaluating the former recursively and setting $f(T) = 1$ give

$$f(t) = 1 + \delta + \cdots + \delta^{T-t} = \frac{1 - \delta^{T-t+1}}{1-\delta}. \tag{23}$$

From (21) and (23) optimal consumption is thus

$$C(t) = \frac{1-\delta}{1-\delta^{T-t+1}}W(t), \tag{24}$$

a deterministic fraction of wealth. This is an important property which is unique to log utility among all additively separable types of utility functions. (Appendix A gives an example of a non-time-additive utility function for which this property also holds.)

The recursion relation for $\Phi(t)$,

$$\Phi(t) = \delta^{t+1} f(t+1)\left[\ln\left(\frac{f(t)-1}{f(t)}\right) - \frac{\ln f(t)}{\delta f(t+1)} + E_t \ln \tilde{Z}^*\right], \tag{25}$$
$$+ E_t[\Phi(t+1)],$$

shows that $\Phi(t)$ does depend upon future opportunities through $\Phi(t+1)$. Nevertheless, this does not affect the optimal portfolio, which depends only on the partial derivative J_W, which is unaffected by Φ. From (14b) the optimal portfolio is given by

$$\delta^t f(t) E_t\left[\left[\left(\frac{f(t)-1}{f(t)}\right) W \sum_0^n w_i \tilde{z}_i\right]^{-1} (\tilde{z}_i - R)\right] = 0. \tag{26}$$

But this problem is exactly the one solved by a single-period log utility investor.

Therefore, in the case of log utility both cautions given earlier can be ignored. Consumption does not depend upon the current or future available returns, and the portfolio choice problem is a strict single-period problem unaffected by future investment opportunities.

Example 2. Power utility, $U(C, t) = \delta^t C^\gamma/\gamma$, $B(W, T) = \delta^T W^\gamma/\gamma$.

From (6a) the final consumption decision is given by

$$\begin{aligned} U_C &= E_{T-1}[B_W(\cdot)\tilde{Z}^*] \\ \delta^{T-1}(C^*)^{\gamma-1} &= \delta^T E_{T-1}[(W_{T-1} - C^*)^{\gamma-1}(\tilde{Z}^*)^\gamma] \\ \frac{1}{\delta}\left(\frac{C^*}{W_{T-1} - C^*}\right)^{\gamma-1} &= E_{T-1}[(\tilde{Z}^*)^\gamma]. \end{aligned} \tag{27}$$

Solving the last line in (27) for optimal consumption gives

$$\begin{aligned} C^*_{T-1} &= a_{T-1} W_{T-1}, \\ a_{T-1} &\equiv [1 + (E_{T-1}[(\tilde{Z}^*)^\gamma]\delta)^{1/(1-\gamma)}]^{-1}. \end{aligned} \tag{28}$$

Unlike the logarithmic utility case above, optimal consumption in this example does depend upon the investment opportunities available. The final optimal portfolio can be obtained from (6b). It is described by

$$\begin{aligned} E_{T-1}[B_W(\cdot)\tilde{z}_i] &= R E_{T-1}[B_W(\cdot)] \\ \delta^T E_{T-1}[(W_{T-1} - C^*)^{\gamma-1}(\tilde{Z}^*)^{\gamma-1}\tilde{z}_i] &= R\delta^T E_{T-1}[(W_{T-1} - C^*)^{\gamma-1}(\tilde{Z}^*)^{\gamma-1}] \\ E_{T-1}[(\tilde{Z}^*)^{\gamma-1}\tilde{z}_i] &= R E_{T-1}[(\tilde{Z}^*)^{\gamma-1}], \qquad i = 1, 2, \ldots, n. \end{aligned} \tag{29}$$

Thus, the final optimal portfolio problem can still be solved independently from the consumption–savings decision, as in Example 1.

Evaluating the derived utility of wealth function using (28) and the envelope condition gives

$$J_W(W, T-1) = U_C(C^*, T-1) = \delta^{T-1}(a_{T-1}W)^{\gamma-1},$$
$$J(W, T-1) = \frac{\delta^{T-1}a_{T-1}^{\gamma-1}W^\gamma}{\gamma} + k \tag{30}$$

where k is a constant of integration. Alternatively, using (5) gives

$$\begin{aligned} J(W, T-1) &= \frac{\delta^{T-1}(C^*)^\gamma}{\gamma} + E_{T-1}(B[(W - C^*)\tilde{Z}^*, T]) \\ &= \delta^{T-1}\frac{(aW)^\gamma}{\gamma} + \delta^T\frac{((1-a)W)^\gamma}{\gamma}E_{T-1}[(\tilde{Z}^*)^\gamma] \\ &= \delta^{T-1}\frac{W^\gamma}{\gamma}a^{\gamma-1}\left[a + \frac{\delta(1-a)^\gamma}{a^{\gamma-1}}E[(\tilde{Z}^*)^\gamma]\right] \\ &= \frac{(\delta^{T-1}a_{T-1}^{\gamma-1})W^\gamma}{\gamma}, \end{aligned} \tag{31}$$

since, from (27) and (28), the term in brackers is unity. Thus, $k = 0$.

When the portfolio–consumption problem for $T - 2$ is solved as in (12), we must evaluate the expectation

$$E_{T-2}[J(W_{T-1}, T-1)] = \frac{\delta^{T-1}}{\gamma}E_{T-2}[\tilde{W}_{T-1}^\gamma \tilde{a}_{T-1}^{\gamma-1}]. \tag{32}$$

As before, optimal consumption is the solution to $U_C = E[\tilde{Z}^*J_W]$:

$$\delta^{T-2}C^{\gamma-1} = \delta^{T-1}E_{T-2}[\tilde{Z}^\gamma \tilde{a}_{T-1}^{\gamma-1}](W_{T-2} - C)^{\gamma-1},$$
$$\text{or} \tag{33}$$
$$C_{T-2}^* = W_{T-2}[1 + (\delta E_{T-2}(\tilde{a}_{T-1}^{\gamma-1}\tilde{Z}^\gamma))^{1/(1-\gamma)}]^{-1}.$$

So consumption depends upon both the current and future investment opportunities through Z and a_{T-1}, respectively.

The optimal portfolio is given by

$$\delta^{T-1}E_{T-2}[(W_{T-2} - C_{T-2})^{\gamma-1}(\tilde{Z}^*)^{\gamma-1}\tilde{a}_{T-1}^{\gamma-1}(\tilde{z}_i - R)] = 0$$
$$E_{T-2}[\tilde{a}_{T-1}^{\gamma-1}(\tilde{Z}^*)^{\gamma-1}(\tilde{z}_i - R)] = 0, \tag{34}$$

so this choice also depends upon future opportunities. The portfolio problem in (34) can be thought of as a single-period problem, but here, unlike Example 1, utility of end-of-period wealth is state dependent. Marginal utility is proportional to $a_{T-1}^{\gamma-1}$, which depends on rates of return available at $T - 1$.

Similar results obtain for all previous periods. Assume that $J(W, t+1)$

$= \delta^{t+1} a_{t+1}^{\gamma-1} W^\gamma/\gamma$. Then from (14a),

$$\begin{aligned} U_C &= E_t[J_W(\tilde{W}, t+1)\tilde{Z}_t^*] \\ \delta^t C^{\gamma-1} &= \delta^{t+1}(W_t - C)^{\gamma-1} E_t[(\tilde{Z}^*)^\gamma \tilde{a}_{t+1}^{\gamma-1}]. \end{aligned} \tag{35}$$

We can solve as in (28) to obtain

$$C_t^* = a_t W_t, \qquad a_t \equiv [1 + (\delta E_t[(\tilde{Z}_t^*)^\gamma \tilde{a}_{t+1}^{\gamma-1}])^{1/(1-\gamma)}]^{-1}. \tag{36}$$

From (14b) the optimal portfolio is characterized by

$$\begin{aligned} E_t[\delta^{t+1} \tilde{a}_{t+1}^{\gamma-1}(W_t - C_t)^{\gamma-1}(\tilde{Z}_t^*)^{\gamma-1}(\tilde{z}_i - R)] &= 0 \\ E_t[(\tilde{a}_{t+1}\tilde{Z}_t^*)^{\gamma-1}(\tilde{z}_i - R)] &= 0. \end{aligned} \tag{37}$$

As before, optimal consumption depends upon current and future investment opportunitis through $\tilde{Z}_t^*$ and $\tilde{a}_{t+1}$, and the utility function associated with the implicit single-period problem is state dependent.

Finally, substituting into (13) gives

$$\begin{aligned} J(W, t) &= (\delta^t (a_t W)^\gamma + \delta^{t+1} E_t[W^\gamma (1 - a_t)^\gamma (\tilde{Z}^*)^\gamma \tilde{a}_{t+1}^{\gamma-1}])\frac{1}{\gamma} \\ &= \delta^t \left(\frac{W^\gamma}{\gamma}\right) a_t^\gamma [1 + \delta E_t[(a_t^{-1} - 1)^\gamma (\tilde{Z}^*)^\gamma \tilde{a}_{t+1}^{\gamma-1}]] \\ &= \frac{\delta^t a_t^\gamma}{\gamma}[1 + (\delta E_t[(\tilde{Z}_t^*)^\gamma \tilde{a}_{t+1}^{\gamma-1}])^{1/(1-\gamma)}] W^\gamma \\ &= \frac{\delta^t a_t^{\gamma-1} W^\gamma}{\gamma}. \end{aligned} \tag{38}$$

The last step follows from the definition of a_t in (36). Thus, the derived utility of wealth function maintains its state-dependent power form as assumed.

If $(\tilde{Z}_t^*)^\gamma$ and $\tilde{a}_{t+1}^{\gamma-1}$ are uncorrelated, then the single-period problem embodied in (34) and (37) has state-independent utility of end-of-period wealth. Typically this will be true only if $\tilde{a}_{t+1}$ and the returns $\tilde{z}_{it}$ are statistically independent. In this case the investor behaves (optimally) in a myopic fashion. In the general case when the investment opportunity set is changing stochastically over time, the portfolio held by a multiperiod investor takes into account the future beyond the next period as well. We will return to this general case after examining investing with a constant oportunity set in more detail.

Example 3. Power utility with a constant opportunity set.

If the opportunities available at time $T - 1$ are known at time $T - 2$, then, from (28), a_{T-1} will be known at $T - 2$. In that case this variable will not affect the portfolio problem embodied in (34). By induction then, if the investment opportunities available at time $t + 1, \ldots, T - 1$ are known at time t, then a_{t+1} will be known at time t. Again the portfolio problem embodied in (37) will be unaffected. Furthermore, if the opportunity sets are known to be the same each period, then the same portfolio will be chosen each time. This portfolio solves the single-period problem

$$\text{Max } E[(\Sigma w_i \tilde{z}_i)^{\gamma-1}(\tilde{z}_i - R)]. \tag{39}$$

Define $\alpha \equiv E[(\Sigma w_i^* z_i)^\gamma]$. As just indicated, this is a constant. Evaluating (36) recursively, we get

$$\begin{aligned} a_t^{-1} &= 1 + (\delta\alpha)^{1/(1-\gamma)} + \cdots + (\delta\alpha)^{(T-t)/(1-\gamma)} \\ a_t &= \frac{1 - \delta\alpha}{1 - (\delta\alpha)^{(T-t+1)/(1-\gamma)}}. \end{aligned} \tag{40}$$

Recalling that a_t is the fraction of wealth consumed at time t, we see that (40) is a generalization of (24) for log utility ($\gamma = 0$ implying $\alpha = 1$).

Now consider the specific portfolio problem in Chapter 6. There is a single risky asset with two possible payoffs $h > R$ and $k < R$. If these two outcomes are equally likely, the optimal portfolio is

$$w^* = R\frac{(R - k)^{-b} - (h - R)^{-b}}{(R - k)^{1-b} + (h - R)^{1-b}}, \tag{41}$$

where $b = 1/(1 - \gamma)$. Optimal consumption is given by (40), where

$$\alpha = \tfrac{1}{2}R^\gamma(h - k)^\gamma[(h - R)^{1-b} + (R - k)^{1-b}]^{1-\gamma}. \tag{42}$$

Example 4. Power utility with a changing opportunity set.

As we observed in Example 2, the *future* investment opportunity sets affect the current portfolio decision for any power utility investor, except in the special case $\gamma = 0$ (log utility). This effect is indirect through the influence of future optimal consumption choices. As in standard price theory, we can decompose this effect into "income" and "substitution" effects.

A beneficial change in investment opportunities (e.g., an increase in any expected rate of return) makes future consumption cheaper to acquire relative to current consumption, so investors consume less currently (substitution effect). But this change also increases overall welfare which induces greater current consumption (income effect). For the log utility case, these two effects exactly cancel.

To understand these two effects we examine a simple two-period, three-date economy with consumption and portfolio decisions at $t = 0, 1$ and bequest at $t = 2$. Over the final interval only a riskless asset is available. In the first interval there is also a risky asset.

The standard two-good cross-substitution Slutsky equation, which measures the change in the quantity of the ith good, Q_i, with respect to a change in the price of the jth good, P_j, is

$$\frac{dQ_i}{dP_j} = \left.\frac{\partial Q_i}{\partial P_j}\right|_U - Q_j \left.\frac{\partial Q_i}{\partial W}\right|_{P_i, P_j}. \tag{43}$$

The first term is the substitution effect, and the second is the income effect. At $t = 1$, $Q_1 = C_1$, $Q_2 = W_2$, $P_1 = 1$, and $P_2 = R^{-1}$. Substituting into (43) and using $dP_2/dR = -R^{-2}$ give

$$\begin{aligned} \frac{dC_1}{dR} = \frac{dP_2}{dR}\frac{dC_1}{dP_2} &= \frac{dP_2}{dR}\left[\left.\frac{\partial C_1}{\partial R}\right|_J \frac{dR}{dP_2} - W_2 \left.\frac{\partial C_1}{\partial W}\right|_R\right] \\ &= -R^{-2}\left[-R^2 \left.\frac{\partial C_1}{\partial R}\right|_J - W_2 \left.\frac{\partial C_1}{\partial W_1}\right|_R\right] \\ &= \left.\frac{\partial C_1}{\partial R}\right|_J + (W_1 - C_1)R^{-1} \left.\frac{\partial C_1}{\partial W_1}\right|_R, \end{aligned} \tag{44}$$

since $W_2 = (W_1 - C_1)R$.

Now consider an investor with power utility and a zero rate of time preference, $\delta = 1$. From (31) and (28), $J(W, 1) = a^{\gamma-1}(C/a)^{\gamma}/\gamma = C^{\gamma}/a\gamma$. Using the implicit function theorem, we obtain the substitution effect

$$\begin{aligned} \left.\frac{\partial C}{\partial R}\right|_J = -\frac{\partial J/\partial R}{\partial J/\partial C} &= -\frac{(C^{\gamma}/\gamma)(\gamma/(1-\gamma))R^{\gamma/(1-\gamma)-1}}{C^{\gamma-1}/a} \\ &= -a^2 W \frac{1}{1-\gamma} R^{\gamma/(1-\gamma)-1}, \end{aligned} \tag{45}$$

which is uniformly negative. From (28) the income effect is

$$(W - C)R^{-1}\frac{\partial C}{\partial W} = W(1 - a)R^{-1}a, \tag{46}$$

which is uniformly positive. The net effect is

$$\begin{aligned} \frac{dC}{dR} &= a^2 W R^{-1}\left[-\frac{1}{1-\gamma}R^{\gamma/(1-\gamma)} + a^{-1} - 1\right] \\ &= -a^2 W R^{-1} R^{\gamma/(1-\gamma)}\left(\frac{\gamma}{1-\gamma}\right). \end{aligned} \tag{47}$$

Note that $a^{-1} = 1 + R^{\gamma/(1-\gamma)}$ from (28). The only term of ambiguous sign is γ. Thus, if $\gamma < 0$, $dC/dR > 0$, so the income effect dominates. For $\gamma > 0$ the substitution effect dominates. For log utility the two effects net out.

At time 1 the investor's derived utility function is

$$J(W, 1) = \frac{(1 + R^{\gamma/(1-\gamma)})^{1-\gamma} W^{\gamma}}{\gamma}. \tag{48}$$

Now suppose that at time 0 the interest rate which will be prevaling at $t = 1$ is not known. Investors only know that there are two equally likely realizations, R_1 and R_2, with $R_1 < R_2$. At time 0 there is a riskless asset with a return of R and a risky asset on which a return of $2R$ is realized if R_1 prevails at time 1, and a return of 0 is realized otherwise.

The expected return on this risky asset is just R, so no single-period risk-averse investor would hold any of it long or short. (From (41), $h - R = R - k = R$, so $w^* = 0$.) Multiperiod investors might want some, however. Let a_i denote the utility parameter in state i: $a_i = 1/(1 + R_i^{\gamma/(1-\gamma)})$. From (34) the first-order condition is

$$\begin{aligned} 0 &= .5(a_1[w2R + (1 - w)R])^{\gamma-1}(2R - R) + .5(a_2(1 - w)R)^{\gamma-1}(-R) \\ &= .5R^{\gamma}([a_1(1 + w)]^{\gamma-1} - [a_2(1 - w)]^{\gamma-1}). \end{aligned} \tag{49}$$

The demand for the risky asset is

$$w = \frac{a_2 - a_1}{a_2 + a_1} = \frac{R_1^{\gamma/(1-\gamma)} - R_2^{\gamma/(1-\gamma)}}{R_1^{\gamma/(1-\gamma)} + R_2^{\gamma/(1-\gamma)}}. \tag{50}$$

Log utility inverstors ($\gamma = 0$) have a zero demand for this asset. It does not have a favorable risk return tradeoff because $\bar{z} = R$, and they have no desire to hedge against changes in the interest rate.

For more risk tolerant ($\gamma > 0$) investors the demand is negative. These investors take short positions in this risky asset to increase wealth in state 2 where the high interest rate prevails. Previously we saw that the substitution effect dominated for these investors. That is, they consumed less when the interest rate was high. Thus, their portfolio selected at time 0 serves to smooth their consumption at time 1 by yielding more wealth, and hence consumption, in states when the interest rate is high, and they would tend to consume less. In fact, in this simple world the income is smoothed completely. The relative consumption in the two states is

$$\frac{C_1}{C_2} = \frac{a_1 W_1}{a_2 W_2} = \frac{a_1(W_0 - C_0)(2Rw + R(1 - w))}{a_2(W_0 - C_0)R(1 - w)} = \frac{a_1(1 + w)}{a_2(1 - w)} = 1. \tag{51}$$

For more risk-averse investors ($\gamma < 0$) the opposite is true. They hold the risky asset in long positions to create more wealth in the low interest rate state. This negates the net income effect on these investors.

This "hedging" behavior is not merely to smooth consumption over time. It characterizes portfolio formation even in the absence of intermediate consumption. Investors who save and reinvest all their wealth each period and do not consume until the final period would not choose the same portfolio as investors with a single-period horizon. Nor would they choose the same portfolio as other investors who consume only at the same time as they, but who were constrained not to adjust their portfolios each period.

The unconstrained investor with a horizon of more than one period will readjust his portfolio each period, so that he will have relatively more wealth in those states when his marginal utility of wealth is the highest. His utility is obviously affected by the investment oportunity set even when he has no desire to consume, so his marginal utility is as well.

In the example just considered, any investor is obviously better off when the interest rate is higher because the same portfolio policy will lead to higher terminal wealth and therefore higher terminal utility. The same policy does not generally remain optimal, of course. Some investors view this improvement in welfare as an opportunity to seek higher returns and invest more heavily in the risky asset. Other investors see the improvement as an opportunity to achieve improved safety and concentrate more on the safe asset. We will examine this issue in more detail in Chapter 13.

Example 5. HARA utility.

For simplicity of notation we write $B(W, T) = \delta^T(W - \hat{C})^\gamma/\gamma$ and $U(C, t) = \delta^t(C - \hat{C})^\gamma/\gamma$, $\gamma < 1$, but all the results obtain for exponential utility and utility of the form $(\hat{C} - C)^\gamma/\gamma$, $\gamma > 1$. $\hat{C}$ can also be different in each period with $\hat{W}_t$ as defined in (52) suitably adjusted. Finally, we assume that the investment opportunity set is constant. Without this last assumption the results are modified to account for state-dependent utility of wealth for each period prior to the last. This issue is discussed further later.

The basic result to be shown in this example is that this investor behaves in a very similar fashion to an investor with power utility ($\hat{C} = 0$) as in the single-period model, and that HARA properties of the direct utility function are replicated in the indirect utility function. This result is equivalent to the single-period result obtained in Chapter 6. Specifically, if we define

$$\hat{W}_t \equiv \hat{C} \sum_{s=t}^{T} R^{t-s}, \tag{52}$$

then the optimal consumption and portfolio choices as a function of wealth are

$$C_t^*(W) = \hat{C} + \frac{W - \hat{W}_t}{W} C_t^P, \tag{53a}$$

$$w_{0t}^*(W) = \frac{\hat{W}_{t+1}}{(W - C_t^*)R} + \frac{\hat{W} - C_t^* - \hat{W}_{t+1}/R}{W - C_t^*} w_0^P, \tag{53b}$$

$$w_{it}^*(W) = \frac{W - C_t^* - \hat{W}_{t+1}/R}{W - C_t^*} w_i^P, \qquad i = 1, \ldots, n, \tag{53c}$$

where C^p and w_i^p are the optimal choices of a power utility investor with the same exponent. Note that different investors with the same γ hold the risky assets in the same relative proportions. The derived utility of wealth function is

$$J(W, t) = J^p(W - \hat{W}_t, t) = \frac{\delta^t f(t)(W - \hat{W}_t)^\gamma}{\gamma}. \tag{54}$$

To verify all these results, we first assume (54) and use the envelope condition (14a) $U_C = J_W$ to obtain optimal consumtpion:

$$\begin{aligned} f(t)(W - \hat{W}_t)^{\gamma-1} &= (C^* - \hat{C})^{\gamma-1} \\ C^* &= \hat{C} + [f(t)]^{1/(\gamma-1)}(W - \hat{W}_t). \end{aligned} \tag{55}$$

Since the power utility investor consumes the fraction $f(t)^{1/(\gamma-1)}$ of his wealth, (55) confirms (53a).

To verify that (53b), (53c) give the optimal portfolio, first note that

$$\sum_0^n w_i^* = (W - C)^{-1}\left[\frac{\hat{W}}{R} + \left(W - C - \frac{\hat{W}}{R}\right)\sum w_i^p\right] = 1, \tag{56}$$

so the budget constraint is satisfied. Also from (53b), (53c),

$$\tilde{Z}^* = \sum w_{it}^* \tilde{z}_i = (W - C)^{-1}\left[\hat{W}_{t+1} + \left(W - C - \frac{\hat{W}_{t+1}}{R}\right)\sum w_i^p \tilde{z}_i\right], \tag{57}$$

or

$$\begin{aligned} (W_t - C_t)\tilde{Z}^* - \hat{W}_{t+1} &= \left(W_t - C_t - \frac{\hat{W}_{t+1}}{R}\right)\tilde{Z}^p \\ &= (W_t - C_t + \hat{C} - \hat{W}_t)\tilde{Z}^p, \end{aligned} \tag{58}$$

where the last equality follows from the definition in (52). Substituting (58) into (14b) gives

$$\begin{aligned} &\delta^t f(t) E_t[((W - C)\tilde{Z}^* - \hat{W}_{t+1})^{\gamma-1}(\tilde{z}_i - R)] \\ &= \delta^t f(t)(W_t - C_t + \hat{C} - \hat{W}_t)^{\gamma-1} E_t[(\tilde{Z}^p)^{\gamma-1}(\tilde{z}_i - R)]. \end{aligned} \tag{59}$$

Since the portfolio $\tilde{Z}^p$ is optimal for power utility investors, the expression in (59) is zero, verifying that (14b) holds for the portfolio $\tilde{Z}^*$; that is (53b), (53c) do describe the optimal portfolio.

Our final task is to verify that the derived utility function is given correctly by (54). We proceed by backward inductioin. From (13), the optimum in (55), and (58),

$$J(W, t) = U(C^*, t) + E_t[J(\tilde{W}, t + 1)]$$

$$
\begin{aligned}
&= \frac{\delta^t(C^* - \hat{C})^\gamma}{\gamma} + \delta^{t+1} f(t+1) E_t\left(\frac{(\tilde{W}_{t+1} - \hat{W}_{t+1})^\gamma}{\gamma}\right) \\
&= \delta^t [f(t)]^{\gamma-1} \frac{(W - \hat{W}_t)^\gamma}{\gamma} + \delta^{t+1} f(t+1) E_t\left[\frac{(W - \hat{W}_t)^\gamma}{\gamma(\tilde{Z}^P)^\gamma}\right] \\
&\equiv \frac{\delta^t f(t)(W - \hat{W}_t)^\gamma}{\gamma},
\end{aligned}
\tag{60}
$$

for $f(t)$ the solution to

$$
f(t) = [f(t)]^{\gamma/(\gamma-1)} + \delta f(t+1) E[(\tilde{Z}^P)^\gamma]. \tag{61}
$$

If the investment opportunity set is changing deterministically, then similar reasoning with subitable changes gives virtually identical results. If the investment opportunity is stochastic, but the interest rate is constant (or deterministically changing), then $\hat{W}_t$ is defined in (52), and the optimal choices given in (53) are still valid. The derived utility of wealth function in (54), however, must be modified as in (38). If the riskless rate changes stochastically, then, in general, derived utility is no longer of the HARA form.

These three examples can be summarized with the following observations:

1. For investors with time-additive log utility, optimal consumption is a deterministic fraction of wealth which depends solely on the investor's remaining lifetime and rate of time preference. The optimal portfolio selected each period is identical to that chosen by a single-period log utility investor.

2. For investors with power utility other than log facing a constant or deterministically changing investment opportunity set, similar results obtain; however, the savings rate is a deterministic function of the opportunity set. If the opportunity set is constant over time, then the investor chooses identical portfolios each period.

3. For investors with nonpower HARA utility facing a constant or deterministically changing opportunity set, the savings rate and portfolio are stochastic because they depend upon wealth. However, for a constant opportunity set the risky assets are always held in the same proportions (over time and by investors with different $\hat{C}$).

4. In general, non-log-utility investors facing a stochastic investment opportunity set will alter their portfolios from that chosen by an otherwise identical single-period investor if it is possible to "hedge" against unfavorable changes in opportunities. Hedging of this type is usually possible unless the opportunity shifts are statistically independent of contemporaneous and earlier returns.

5. Investors with time-additive power utility of consumption and bequest also have state-dependent power derived utility of wealth functions.

If utility is logarithmic or the opportunity set is nonstochastic, then derived utility is state independent. Similar results are obtained for other HARA utility functions if the riskless rate is nonstochastic.

SOME TECHNICAL CONSIDERATIONS

Throughout the analysis in this Chapter we have assumed that the formal solutions were in fact the true optimal solutions to our problem. This need not be the case if there are unrecognized constraints or the function which we are maximizing is not concave. We address the last issue first.

Since $U(C, t)$ and $B(W, T)$ are concave in C and W, the second-order necessary conditions for a maximum at $T - 1$ are met in the problem stated in (6a) and (6b). Similarly, if $J(W, t)$ is concave in W, then the second-order conditions for a maximum for the choice at time $t - 1$ are met. Differentiating the envelope condition in (14a) with respect to W gives

$$U_{CC}C_W^* = J_{WW}. \tag{62}$$

$U(\cdot)$ is concave in C, and consumption is a normal good, so $C_W^* \geqslant 0$; therefore, $J_{WW} \leqslant 0$ and the second-order necessary conditions are met. (Typically, $C_W^* > 0$, so J is strictly concave, but see the following.) In the first appendix to this Chapter we see that for utility of consumption which is not additive over time this condition is not met. It is possible for an investor to be risk preferring, $J_{WW} > 0$, even though utility is concave in *each* period's consumption.

If there are short sale constraints, then the implied portfolio problem in (14b) is explicitly modified to include the Kuhn–Tucker conditions; that is, for short sale constraints (14b) becomes

$$\frac{\partial EJ}{\partial w_i} = E_t[J_{W_{t+1}}(\cdot)(\tilde{z}_i - R)] \leqslant 0, \tag{63a}$$

$$w_i\frac{\partial EJ}{\partial w_i} = 0. \tag{63b}$$

Equation (63a) indicates that we are either at the optimum or utility could be increased by decreasing our holding of asset i. However, from (63b) the latter is true only if $w_i = 0$, and we are therefore constrained from doing so.

The analysis for deriving the envelope condition in (11) (or the case for $t < T - 1$) is still valid. Equation (6a) can be rewritten as (7) because the only assets for which (6b) does not hold are those with $w_i = 0$. Equation (10) remains valid. Furthermore, from (7) its first term is still zero. From (63b) each summand in the second term for which $w_i^* > 0$ is also zero.

Those assets for which the optimal solution would otherwise be negative (in the absence of the short sales constraint) do not satisfy (6b); however, by continuity of the optimal solutions a small change in wealth will keep these weights at zero (i.e., $\partial w_i/\partial W = 0$), so they also contribute nothing to the sum in the second term. Therefore, the envelope condition (11) still holds.

The envelope condition does collapse when there are explicit constraints on consumption. The most obvious example is if consumption must be nonnegative, as is usually the case. Replacing (6a) we then have

$$U_C \leqslant E[B_W(\cdot)\tilde{Z}^*], \tag{64a}$$

$$C(U_C - E[B_W(\cdot)\tilde{Z}^*]) = 0. \tag{64b}$$

Workig through the steps in (7)–(11) then gives the envelope inequality

$$U_C \leqslant J_W, \tag{65}$$

with equality holding whenever $C > 0$.

Appendix A: Consumption Portfolio Problem when Utility Is Not Additively Separable

Previously we were concerned only with additively separable utility. We now outline one case for which the utility function is not additively separable. We assume instead that utility has the multiplicative form

$$\hat{U}(C_0, \ldots, C_{T-1}) = \frac{1}{\gamma} B[W_T, T] \prod_{t=0}^{T-1} U(C(t), t). \tag{A1}$$

As discussed in Chapter 1 this is the other general class of utility function displaying independence. In particular, we examine a family of utility functions similar to the power family characterized by $U(C, t) = C^{\gamma(t)}$. Note that this family has isoelastic margial utility since

$$\frac{d \ln U_C}{d \ln C} = \frac{d[\ln \gamma(t) + (\gamma(t) - 1)\ln C]}{d \ln C} = \gamma(t) - 1. \tag{A2}$$

If we let $\gamma(t) = \gamma\delta^t$ (with $\delta > 0$), then (A1) can be written as in Equation (71) of Chapter 1:

$$\hat{U}(C, W) = \frac{1}{\gamma}(\exp\{\gamma[\Sigma\delta^t \ln C_t + \delta^T \ln W_T]\}), \tag{A3}$$

with $\gamma \neq 0$ and δ measuring temporal risk aversion and time preference, respectively.

To solve the consumption–portfolio problem, we introduce the derived utility of wealth function

$$\begin{aligned} J(W, t) &= \text{Max } E_t[\hat{U}(C_0, C_1, \ldots, W_T)] \\ &= \frac{1}{\gamma}\left(\prod_{s=0}^{t-1} C_s^{\gamma(s)}\right) \text{Max } E_t\left[\left(\prod_{s=t}^{T-1} C_s^{\gamma(s)}\right) W_T^{\gamma(T)}\right]. \end{aligned} \tag{A4}$$

We denote the quantity outside the Max(·) in the second line of (A4) by $f(t)$.

At the next to last period we must solve

$$J(W, T-1) = f(T-1)\,\text{Max}\, C_{T-1}^{\gamma(T-1)} E(W_T^{\gamma(T)}). \tag{A5}$$

Since $W_T = (W_{T-1} - C_{T-1})[\Sigma w_i(z_i - R) + R]$, we get the necessary first-order conditions

$$\begin{aligned} 0 &= \frac{\partial J}{\partial C} \\ &= f(T-1)E[\gamma(T-1)C^{\gamma(T-1)-1}\tilde{W}_T^{\gamma(T)} - \gamma(T)C^{\gamma(T-1)}\tilde{W}_T^{\gamma(T)-1}\tilde{Z}^*], \end{aligned} \tag{A6a}$$

$$\begin{aligned} 0 &= \frac{\partial J}{\partial w_i} \\ &= f(T-1)E[C^{\gamma(T-1)}\gamma(T)\tilde{W}_T^{\gamma(T)-1}(W_{T-1} - C)(\tilde{z}_i - R)]. \end{aligned} \tag{A6b}$$

Substituting $\tilde{W}_T = (W_{T-1} - C_{T-1})\tilde{Z}^*$ and collecting common factors in (A6a) give

$$\begin{aligned} 0 = {} & f(T-1)C_{T-1}^{\gamma(T-1)-1}(W_{T-1} - C_{T-1})^{\gamma(T)-1}E[\tilde{Z}^{\gamma(T)}] \\ & \times [\gamma(T-1)(W_{T-1} - C_{T-1}) - \gamma(T)C], \end{aligned} \tag{A7}$$

or

$$C_{T-1}^* = \frac{\gamma(T-1)}{\gamma(T) + \gamma(T-1)} W_{T-1} = \frac{1}{1+\delta} W_{T-1}, \tag{A8}$$

independent of the investment opportunity set and identical to the result for time-additive logarithmic utility in (12).

From (A6b) the optimal portfolio is characterized by

$$E\left[\gamma(T)(W_{T-1} - C_{T-1})^{\gamma(T)}\left(\sum_0^N w_i^* \tilde{z}_i\right)^{\gamma(T)-1}(\tilde{z}_i - R)\right] = 0. \tag{A9}$$

So the optimal portfolio is identical to that which would be chosen by a single-period investor with power utility $W^{\gamma(T)}/\gamma(T)$.

If we now substitute the optimal portfolio and consumption choices into (A5), we get the derived utility of wealth

$$J(W, T-1) = f(T-1)\delta^{\gamma(T)} E[(\tilde{Z}^*)^{\gamma(T)}]\left(\frac{W}{1+\delta}\right)^{\gamma(T)+\gamma(T-1)}. \tag{A10}$$

Since the optimal portfolio choice is independent of wealth, from (A9), this may be written as

$$J(W, T-1) = f(T-1) g(\tilde{\mathbf{z}}, \delta, \gamma, T-1) W^{\alpha(T-1)}. \tag{A11}$$

Thus we see that the solution technique will remain the same. If we continue with the dynamic programming, we find that derived utility of wealth function is again of the power utility form, so (if the investment opportunity set is nonstochastic) the optimal portfolio will be independent of wealth. We show by induction that the derived utility function is always of this power form $f(t)g(t)W^{\alpha(t)}$. We are particularly interested in the function α because this measures relative risk aversion. From (A4)

$$\begin{aligned} J(W, t) &= f(t) \operatorname{Max} E_t\left[\left(\prod_{s=t}^{T-1} C_s^{\gamma(s)}\right) W_T^{\gamma(T)}\right] \\ &= f(t) \operatorname*{Max}_t C_t^{\gamma(t)} E_t \operatorname*{Max}_{t+1} E_{t+1}\left[\left(\prod_{s=t+1}^{T-1} C_s^{\gamma(s)}\right) \tilde{W}_T^{\gamma(T)}\right] \\ &= f(t) \operatorname{Max}\left[\frac{C_t^{\gamma(t)} E_t J(\tilde{W}_{t+1}, t+1)}{f(t+1)}\right], \end{aligned} \tag{A12}$$

which is similar to the Bellman result for time-additive utility. Substituting the assumed form for $J(W, t+1)$ gives

$$J(W, t) = f(t) \operatorname{Max}[C_t^{\gamma(t)} E_t(g(t+1) W_{t+1}^{\alpha(t+1)})]. \tag{A13}$$

The first-order condition for consumption is

$$\begin{aligned} 0 &= \frac{\partial J}{\partial C} \\ &= f(t) E_t[g(t+1)[\gamma(t) C_t^{\gamma(t)} \tilde{W}_{t+1}^{\alpha(t+1)} - \alpha(t+1) C_t^{\gamma(t)} \tilde{W}_{t+1}^{\alpha(t+1)-1} Z^*)] \\ &= f(t) C_t^{\gamma(t)-1}(W_t - C_t)^{\alpha(t+1)-1} \\ &\quad \times [\gamma(t)(W_t - C_t) - \alpha(t+1) C_t] E(g(t+1) Z^{\alpha(t+1)}). \end{aligned} \tag{A14}$$

This gives

$$C_t^* = \frac{\gamma(t)}{\gamma(t) + \alpha(t+1)} W_t. \tag{A15}$$

As with time-additive logarithmic utility, optimal consumption is proportional to wealth and independent of current and future investment opportunities.

The first-order condition for the portfolio weights is for $i = 1, \ldots, n$,

$$\begin{aligned} 0 &= \frac{\partial J}{\partial w_i} \\ &= f(t)\alpha(t+1)C_t^{\gamma(t)}(W_t - C_t)^{\alpha(t+1)-1} \\ &\quad \times E_t\left[g(t+1)\left(\sum_0^N w_i \tilde{z}_i\right)^{\alpha(t+1)-1}(\tilde{z}_i - R)\right]. \end{aligned} \tag{A16}$$

The optimal portfolio is again independent of wealth. It is identical to that chosen by a single-period, isoelastic utility investor with state-dependent utility, this time with power $\alpha(t+1)$. Now the utility function is state dependent through $g(t+1)$.

To determine the derived utility of wealth function, we substitute (A15) and $\tilde{W}_{t+1} = (W_t - C_t)\tilde{Z}^*$ into (A13) and obtain

$$\begin{aligned} J(W, t) &= f(t)\left(\frac{\gamma(t)}{\gamma(t) + \alpha(t+1)}\right)^{\gamma(t)}\left(\frac{\alpha(t+1)}{\gamma(t) + \alpha(t+1)}\right)^{\alpha(t+1)} \\ &\quad \times E[g(t+1)(\tilde{Z}^*)^{\alpha(t+1)}]W^{\gamma(t)+a(t+1)} \\ &\equiv f(t)g(t)W^{\alpha(t)}. \end{aligned} \tag{A17}$$

From (A17) the new exponent of wealth is $\alpha(t) \equiv \alpha(t+1) + \gamma(t)$. By induction

$$\alpha(t) = \sum_{s=t}^{T} \gamma(s) = \gamma \sum_{s=t}^{T} \delta^s = \frac{\gamma\delta^t(1 - \delta^{T-t+1})}{1 - \delta}. \tag{A18}$$

Note that $\alpha(t)$ is of uniform sign. The expression $1 - \alpha(t)$ is the measure of relative risk aversion for portfolio decisions at time $t - 1$, so, for all t, investors with positive (negative) γ are always more (less) risk tolerant than an investor with log utility, $\alpha(t) \equiv 0$. Furthermore,

$$\Delta\alpha(t) \equiv \alpha(t+1) - \alpha(t) = -\gamma\delta^t, \tag{A19}$$

so as an investor ages portfolio choice reflects relative risk aversion which approaches unity (but never gets closer to it than $1 - \gamma\delta^T$).

One curiosity is that $\alpha(t+1) < 1$ need not imply that $\alpha(t) < 1$. Thus, an investor can be risk preferring when young and risk averse at an older age. (This is true even though utility of consumption is concave *for each period.*) A sufficient condition for risk aversion at every age is that the investor be sufficiently risk averse over consumption ($\gamma \leqslant 0$). For more risk-tolerant investors, $\gamma > 0$, the condition $1 - \delta \geqslant \gamma$ guarantees risk aversion at all ages.

A word of explanation: Even though the utility function employed here is concave in *each* of its arguments, it is not a concave function of all of its arguments. The distinction can be clarified by the folowing simple example. Suppose the investor must make two portfolio decisions (at $t = 0$, $t = 1$) and one consumption decision at $t = 1$. Whatever wealth is left at $t = 2$ is consumed. The utility function, defined over first-period consumption and second-period wealth, is

$$\hat{U}(C, W) = \frac{1}{\gamma} C^{\gamma\delta} W^{\gamma\delta^2} \tag{A20}$$

with $\delta < 1$ and $\gamma < 1$. Now sine

$$\begin{aligned} \frac{\partial^2 \hat{U}}{\partial C^2} &= \delta(\gamma\delta - 1)C^{\gamma\delta-2}W^{\gamma\delta^2} < 0, \\ \frac{\partial^2 \hat{U}}{\partial W^2} &= \delta^2(\gamma\delta^2 - 1)C^{\gamma\delta}W^{\gamma\delta^2-2} < 0, \\ \frac{\partial^2 \hat{U}}{\partial C \partial W} &= \gamma\delta^3 C^{\gamma\delta-1}W^{\gamma\delta^2-1} \gtreqless 0, \end{aligned} \tag{A21}$$

utility is concave in each argument. However, to be a concave function of all its arguments, we require as well that the determinant of the Hessian matrix be negative; that is

$$\begin{aligned} 0 &< \frac{\partial^2 \hat{U}}{\partial W^2}\frac{\partial^2 \hat{U}}{\partial C^2} - \left(\frac{\partial^2 \hat{U}}{\partial C \partial W}\right)^2 \\ &= \delta^3 C^{2\gamma\delta-2}W^{2\gamma\delta^2-2}[(\gamma\delta - 1)(\gamma\delta^2 - 1) - \gamma^2\delta^3] \\ &= \delta^3 C^{2\gamma\delta-2}W^{2\gamma\delta^2-2}[1 - \gamma\delta - \gamma\delta^2], \end{aligned} \tag{A22}$$

or

$$\gamma\delta + \gamma\delta^2 \equiv \alpha(0) < 1.$$

Therefore, if the utility function is concave (in *both* its arguments simultaneously) the investor will have a derived utility function which is also concave. The same rule holds true for longer time periods as well. Utility is concave (in *all* its arguments) only if

$$\sum_{s=0}^{T} \gamma(s) < 1, \tag{A23}$$

which is sufficient for a risk-averse derived utility of wealth function as shown in (A18).

Returning to the derivation of the derived utility function in (A17), we see that the multiplier $g(t)$ is defined as

$$g(t) \equiv \left(\frac{\gamma(t)}{\gamma(t) + \alpha(t+1)}\right)^{\gamma(t)}\left(\frac{\alpha(t+1)}{\gamma(t) + \alpha(t+1)}\right)^{\alpha(t+1)} \tag{A24}$$

$$\times\ E[g(t+1)(\tilde{Z}^*)^{\alpha(t+1)}].$$

From our discussion $\gamma(\cdot)$ and $\alpha(\cdot)$ have the same sign, so both terms in parentheses are positive. Using the definition of $\alpha(\cdot)$ in (A18), we can write

$$\begin{aligned} g(t) &= |\alpha(t)|^{-\alpha(t)}|\alpha(t+1)|^{\alpha(t+1)}|\gamma(t)|^{\gamma(t)}E[g(t+1)(\tilde{Z}^*)^{\alpha(t+1)})] \\ &= |\alpha(t)|^{-\alpha(t)}\left[\prod_{s=t}^{T}|\gamma(s)|^{\gamma(s)}\tilde{Z}_s^{\alpha(s+1)}\right]. \end{aligned} \tag{A25}$$

The last step follows by induction.

Appendix B: Myopic and Turnpike Portfolio Policies

One major difficulty with the programming problems in this chapter is that they are hard to implement. In Chapter 13 we shall see that the problems are simplified to a great extent when we examine them in a continuous-time framework. Other procedures for simplifying them have also been suggested. In this appendix we outline a few of these other approaches.

The growth optimal policy is concerned with choosing the best portfolio for investors who neither make additions to nor withdrawals from their invested wealth and are concerned with investing for the "long run." That is, they are to maximize their expected utility of wealth at some point in the distant future.

For our purposes we will assume a constant investment opportunity set and search for the best fixed portfolio policy. For investors with power utility functions, a fixed policy will be globaly optimal. In other cases, outlined here, fixed policies are "asymptotically optimal." We also limit our consideration to portfolios with limited liability.

Growth Optimal Portfolios

Let $\tilde{Z}(t)$ represent 1 plus the rate of return on a portfolio with limited liability in period t. Then the T-period return is

$$\frac{\tilde{W}(T)}{W(0)} = \prod_{t=1}^{T}\tilde{Z}(t) = \exp\left[\sum_{T=1}^{T}\ln\tilde{Z}(t)\right] \equiv e^{\Sigma y(t)}, \tag{B1}$$

where $\tilde{y}(t)$ is the continuously compounded rate of return over the period

$t - 1$ to t. Let $\bar{y} \equiv E[\tilde{y}]$ denote the geometric mean return over the period. Since the opportunity set is constant and the portfolio policy fixed, $\bar{y}$ is an intertemporal constant. Now if $\tilde{y}$ also has a finite variance, then by the strong law of large numbers

$$\lim_{T\to\infty} \frac{1}{T}\left[\ln\left(\frac{\tilde{W}(T)}{W(0)}\right)\right] = \lim\left[\frac{1}{T}\sum_{t=1}^{T} \tilde{y}(t)\right] = \bar{y},$$
$$\lim\left[\frac{W(T)}{W(0)}\right] = \begin{cases} \infty, & \bar{y} > 0, \\ 1, & \bar{y} = 0, \\ 0, & \bar{y} < 0. \end{cases} \tag{B2}$$

Therefore, persistent portfolio choices with a positive (negative) compound rate of return lead ultimately to bliss (ruin) with probability 1.

Clearly then, it would appear that all "long-term" investors who make no additions to or withdrawals from their portfolios should select portfolios with a positive geometric mean. Furthermore, intuitively we might suspect that "the higher $\bar{y}$ the better." This is true in the following sense. Let $\tilde{y}^*$ represent the continuously compounded return on the portfolio chosen to have the maximum geometric mean return. Then for any other portfolio policy with continuously compounded returns $\tilde{y}(t)$, the set of random variables $\tilde{\rho}(t) = \tilde{y}^*(t) - \tilde{y}(t)$ has the property

$$E(\tilde{\rho}(t)) > 0 \qquad \text{for all } t. \tag{B3}$$

By the law of large numbers then as T approaches ∞,

$$\lim \frac{1}{T}\left[\ln\left(\frac{W^*(T)}{W(T)}\right)\right] = \lim\left[\frac{1}{T}\sum_{t=1}^{T} (\tilde{y}^*(t) - \tilde{y}(t))\right]$$
$$= \lim\left[\frac{1}{T}\sum_{t=1}^{T} \tilde{\rho}(t)\right] > 0, \tag{B4}$$

and if $\tilde{y}^*(t)$ is a strict maximum, then $\lim(1/T)[\ln(W^*/W)] = \infty$.

The growth optimal policy is then to select each period the portfolio which maximizes

$$\text{Max}\, E_t[\ln \tilde{Z}(t)] = \text{Max}\, E_t\left[\ln\left(\sum_{i=0}^{N} w_i \tilde{z}_i\right)\right]. \tag{B5}$$

That is, we solve the one-period problem *as if* utility were logarithmic. For this reason the growth optimal policy is also sometimes called the MEL (maximum expected logarithm) policy.

A Caveat

It is true that if an investor chooses at each point of time the portfolio with the highest compound rate of return, then over a "sufficiently long" period he or she will "almost certainly" have higher terminal wealth and higher utility. However, he or she need not, and in general will not, have selected a portfolio which maximizes *expected* utility.

Consider the portfolio problem of an investor with a T-period horizon and a power utility function W_T^γ/γ. As shown in Example 3 such an investor will optimally choose a fixed portfolio when faced with a constant opportunity set. Let $\tilde{Z}_t(\gamma)$ denote the one-period return on the portfolio optimal for this investor. (Note that $\tilde{Z}_t(0)$ is the return on the growth optimal portfolio.) $\tilde{Z}_t(\gamma)$ will be independently and identically distributed over time.

For a particular investor the certainty equivalent (initial) wealth for the growth optimal policy is the solution W_c to

$$\frac{E\{[W_0 \Pi \tilde{Z}_t(0)]^\gamma\}}{\gamma} = \frac{E\{[W_c \Pi \tilde{Z}_t(\gamma)]^\gamma\}}{\gamma}. \tag{B6}$$

That is, the certainty equivalent wealth is that amount an investor could start with and achieve the same expected utility as by starting with actual wealth and following the growth optimal policy.

Solving (B6) gives

$$\frac{W_c}{W_0} = \left\{\frac{E[(\tilde{Z}(0))^\gamma]}{E[(\tilde{Z}(\gamma))^\gamma]}\right\}^{T/\gamma} \equiv \omega^T. \tag{B7}$$

Since $\tilde{Z}(\gamma)$ is the optimal policy, the fraction inside the braces is less (greater) than 1 for positive (negative) γ. In either case $\omega < 1$. Thus, for any horizon the certaity equivalent wealth of the growth optimal policy is less than the investor's initial wealth. In fact, for far distant horizons, the certainty equivalent wealth of the growth optimal policy becomes negligible.

One other caution is also in order. It is not true that among investors who consume optimally from their wealth that those with logarithimic utility will have the highest geometric mean growth rate and therefore come to dominate in the market.

Myopic Portfolio Policies

If an investor's optimal portfolio depends only upon current wealth and the distribution of returns currently available, the portfolio choice is said to be *myopic*. In Example 1 we found that investors with logarithmic utility display complete myopia. (In fact, they follow the myopic growth optimal policy described previously.) Investors with power utility also behave myopically *if* security returns are statistically independent of changes in the investment opportunities available, as we saw in Examples 2 and 3.

A related concept is "partial myopia." A portfolio policy is said to be *partially myopic* if the risky assets are always held in the same proportions while the degree of leverage varies. We saw in Chapter 7 and Example 5 of this Chapter that only the power γ of the HARA utility functions affected the distribution of wealth among the risky assets. Consequently, investors with HARA utility behave in a partially myopic fashion when facing constant investment opportunities. Partial myopia also obtains if the investment opportunity set is stochastic but statistically independent of the prior period's returns.

Turnpike Portfolio Policies

When a myopic portfolio choice policy results in a portfolio with constant weights, a "turnpike portfolio" is said to result. The power utility functions are the only additive ones for which turnpikes exist for the joint consumption–investment decision. However, when only terminal wealth is consumed and the horizon is distant, many (investment only) problems for other utility functions have solutions whose limiting behavior defines a turnpike.

For example, suppose that investment opportunities are constant and that utility of terminal wealth is of the HARA form $B(W) = (W - \hat{W})^\gamma/\gamma$. Then from (32) derived utility is always of the form

$$J(W, t) = f(t)\frac{(W - \hat{W}_t)^\gamma}{\gamma}, \tag{B8}$$

where $\hat{W}_t \equiv \hat{W}R^{t-T}$ from (30). It is clear that for a distant horizon, $T - t \gg 0$, and $R > 1$, $\hat{W}_t$ becomes negligible. Thus all HARA utility of terminal wealth investors with the same cautiousness hold the same turnpike portfolio when the horizon is distant.

This result can be extended to all utility of terminal wealth functions for which the Arrow–Pratt measure of relative risk aversion converges uniformly to $1 - \gamma$ as $W \to \infty$; that is, if the interest rate is positive and

$$\lim_{W\to\infty} R(W) = 1 - \gamma, \tag{B9}$$

where $R(W) \equiv -B''(W)W/B'(W)$, then all investors with the same limiting relative risk aversion follow the same turnpike.

12

An Introduction to the Distributions of Continuous-Time Finance

We saw in Chapter 11 that in many cases the intertemporal consumption–portfolio problem could be restated as a single-period problem by introducing a derived utility of wealth function in place of the utility fucntion defined over lifetime consumption. Although the consumption–portfolio problem can then be solved in principle, the actual solution is by no means easy to determine, and the resulting equilibrium is often difficult to analyze. In a single-period framework this same problem is solved by resorting to mean-variance analysis, which simplifies the problem because the portfolio demands are then the solutions to a set of simultaneous linear equations.

As we saw in Chapter 4, the only class of utility functions for which mean-variance analysis and expected utility maximization are always consistent is the quadratic class. The only probability distributions for which they are always consistent are the elliptical ones with finite means and variances. (For the elliptical distributions with infinite variances, other measures of dispersion may be used in a general mean-dispersion analysis.) However, for certain other types of distributions, mean-variance analysis may be approximately correct (at least for most utility functions). The types of distributions for which this is true are known as *compact distributions*. As we shall see, these distributions are intimately connected with the distributions usually used in continuous-time finance problems.

COMPACT DISTRIBUTIONS

Let $\tilde{x}$ be a random variable with $E[\tilde{x}] = 0$, $\text{Var}[\tilde{x}] = 1$, and finite central moments of all orders $E[\tilde{x}^k] \equiv m_k$. Define a new random variable

$$\tilde{\xi} \equiv \mu t + f(t)\tilde{x} \equiv \mu t + t^{\delta}g(t)\tilde{x}, \tag{1}$$

where $\delta > 0$ is the lowest power of t in the expansion of $f(\cdot)$ around zero so that the limit of $g(t)$ as t goes to zero is σ, a constant. (*Note*: This is not the only fashion in which compact random variables can be characterized,

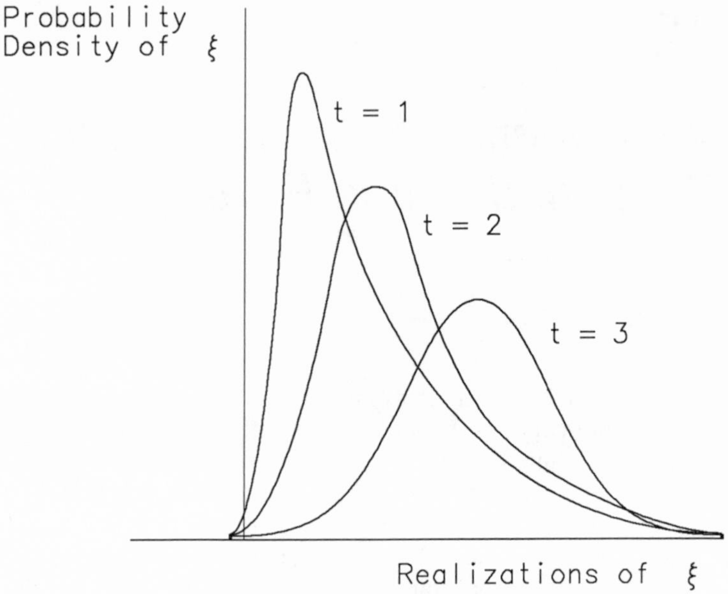

Figure 12.1 Example of a Compact Distribution

but it will suit our purposes. In some cases we might also wish the distribution of $\tilde{x}$ to be indexed by t. The important distinguishing property of compact random variables is given in Equation (5).)

One important property of variables like $\tilde{\xi}$ is that there is a negligible probability that they can take on any value very different from their means. By Chebyshev's inequality

$$\text{Prob}\{|\tilde{x}| > \varepsilon\} < \frac{1}{\varepsilon^2}. \tag{2}$$

Therefore

$$\text{Prob}\{|\tilde{\xi} - \mu t| > \varepsilon\} < \frac{t^{2\delta} g^2(t)}{\varepsilon^2}. \tag{3}$$

As $t \to 0$, the numerator of the right-hand side of (3) goes to zero while the denominator remains fixed. Thus, for any $\varepsilon > 0$ there is some T such that $T^{2\delta} g^2(T) < \varepsilon^3$ for all $t < T$; therefore, the probability that $\tilde{\xi}$ deviates from its mean by more than ε can be made less than ε for any positive ε no matter how small. Figure 12.1 illustrates this property, showing how the probability distribution collapses to a spike as t goes to zero.

This property is shared by all random variables with vanishingly small variances and is not the reason they are called compact. Their compactness has to do with the relative importance of their variances compared to their higher central moments.

The mean and central moments of $\tilde{\xi}$ are

$$\begin{aligned} \bar{\xi} &\equiv E[\tilde{\xi}] = \mu t, \\ M_k &\equiv E[(\tilde{\xi} - \bar{\xi})^k] = E[t^{k\delta} g^k(t) x^k] = t^{k\delta} g^k(t) m_k. \end{aligned} \tag{4}$$

For compact random variables like $\tilde{\xi}$ the higher-order moments are negligible relative to the variance for sufficiently small t.

$$\begin{aligned} L_k &\equiv \lim_{t \to 0} \frac{M_k}{M_2} = \lim_{t \to 0} t^{(k-2)\delta} g^{k-2}(t) m_k \\ &= \sigma^{k-2} m_k \lim_{t \to 0} t^{(k-2)\delta} = 0. \end{aligned} \tag{5}$$

In comparing the mean and variance, we find

$$\begin{aligned} L &\equiv \lim_{t \to 0} \frac{M_2}{\bar{\xi}} = \lim_{t \to 0} \frac{g^2(t) t^{2\delta - 1}}{\mu} \\ &= \frac{\sigma^2}{\mu} \lim_{t \to 0} t^{2\delta - 1}. \end{aligned} \tag{6}$$

Thus, for $\frac{1}{2} < \delta$, $L = 0$, For $\delta = \frac{1}{2}$, $L = \sigma^2/\mu$. For $0 < \delta < \frac{1}{2}$, the ratio becomes unbounded. Therefore, in general, for small t if $\delta > \frac{1}{2}$, only the expectation "matters"; that is, $\tilde{\xi}$ is essentially a constant. For $\delta < \frac{1}{2}$ only the variance "matters"; and for $\delta = \frac{1}{2}$ expectations and variances have equal importance. The higher-order moments never "matter." From Equation (47) in the Mathematical Introduction it is clear that this is also true for noncentral moments. For convenience in what follows, we shall often express compactness, using noncentral moments.

COMBINATIONS OF COMPACT RANDOM VARIABLES

We now consider combinations of compact random variables. Let $\tilde{\xi} \equiv a_1\tilde{\xi}_1 + a_2\tilde{\xi}_2$. With no loss of generality assume $\delta_1 \leqslant \delta_2$ and, to avoid trivial cases, $a_i \neq 0$. The central moments of the sum are

$$\bar{\xi} = (a_1\mu_1 + a_2\mu_2)t, \tag{7a}$$

$$\begin{aligned} M_k &\equiv E[(\tilde{\xi} - \bar{\xi})^k] \\ &= \sum \binom{k}{i} (a_1 g_1 t^{\delta_1})^i (a_2 g_2 t^{\delta_2})^{k-i} E[x_1^i x_2^{k-i}] \\ &= A t^{k\delta_1} + o(t^{k\delta_1}). \end{aligned} \tag{7b}$$

For sufficiently small t all higher-order central moments are small compared to the variance, so $\tilde{\xi}$ is also compact.

As in the univariate case, if $\frac{1}{2} < \delta_1$ (the smaller value), the variance is negligible relative to the mean, and each variable as well as the sum is a "constant"; for $\delta_1 < \frac{1}{2}$ the mean is negligible compared to the variance. The mean and variance are of equal importance if $\delta_2 \geqslant \delta_1 = \frac{1}{2}$. In the last case if $\delta_2 = \delta_1 = \frac{1}{2}$, then both $\tilde{\xi}_1$ and $\tilde{\xi}_2$ contriute to the variance:

$$\mathrm{Var}(\tilde{\xi}) = (a_1^2\sigma_1^2 + 2a_1a_2\sigma_{12} + a_2^2\sigma_2^2)t. \tag{8}$$

If $\delta_2 > \delta_1 = \frac{1}{2}$, then only $\tilde{\xi}_1$ contributes to the variance

$$\mathrm{Var}(\tilde{\xi}) = a_1^2\sigma_1^2 t + o(t). \tag{9}$$

To summarize, a combination of compact random variables is also compact with characteristic parameter $\delta = \mathrm{Min}(\delta_i)$. Both the mean and variance of the combination are important only if $\delta = \frac{1}{2}$, and only the random variables with δ_i also equal to $\frac{1}{2}$ contribute to the variance in the limit.

IMPLICATIONS FOR PORTFOLIO SELECTION

Consider the general single-period portfolio problem of Chapters 2 or 5 or the single-period problem embedded in the multiperiod problem of the previous chapter. Let $\tilde{\zeta}_p \equiv \tilde{Z}_p - 1$ denote the rate of return on a generic portfolio. By Taylor's theorem the objective to be maximized is

$$\begin{aligned} Eu(\tilde{Z}_p) &= Eu(1 + \tilde{\zeta}_p) \\ &= E[u(1) + u'(1)\tilde{\zeta}_p + \tfrac{1}{2}u''(1)\tilde{\zeta}_p^2 + u'''(1 + k\tilde{\zeta})O(\tilde{\zeta}_p^3)] \qquad (10) \\ &= a + b\mu t - c[\mathrm{Var}(\tilde{\zeta}_p) + \bar{\zeta}_p^2] + E[u'''(1 + k\tilde{\zeta}_p)O(\tilde{\zeta}_p^3)], \end{aligned}$$

where $a \equiv Eu(1)$, $b \equiv Eu'(1) > 0$, $c \equiv -Eu''(1)/2 < 0$, and $0 \leqslant k \leqslant 1$. Now if u''' is defined in a neighborhood of 1, $\tilde{\zeta}_p$ has a compact distribution, and the investor does not consider unboundedly large positions in any assets, then the fourth term is $O(M_3)$. Furthermore, the scalar a has no effect on decisions, so defining $u(1) = a = 0$, we have

$$\frac{Eu(\tilde{Z}_p)}{t} \sim b\mu_p - c\sigma_p^2 t^{2\delta - 1} \qquad \text{as } t \downarrow 0. \tag{11}$$

For sufficiently small t, investors will avoid all portfolios with $\delta < \frac{1}{2}$. If only these are available, all investors will act in the limit in a "super-risk-averse" fashion and select the global minimum-variance portfolio (that with the largest δ). If there are some portfolios with $\delta \geqslant \frac{1}{2}$, then investors will select among them by using mean-variance analysis. Portfolios with $\delta > \frac{1}{2}$ will be considered to be riskless assets.

We will be concerned primarily with the latter case under which mean-variance analysis is approximately correct. The following example demonstrates the sense in which and the limit to which the mean-variance solution is approximately correct.

Assume there is one safe asset with return $R = 1 + rt$ and one risky asset with return $\tilde{z} = h$ with probability π and $\tilde{z} = k$ with probability $1 - \pi$; $k < R < h$; h and k are given by

$$\begin{aligned} h &\equiv 1 + \mu t + \sigma\sqrt{\frac{(1-\pi)t}{\pi}}, \\ k &\equiv 1 + \mu t - \sigma\sqrt{\frac{\pi t}{1-\pi}}. \end{aligned} \tag{12}$$

The properties of the asset's rate of return $\tilde{\xi} \equiv \tilde{z} - 1$ are

$$\begin{aligned} E[\tilde{\xi}] &= \mu t, \\ \mathrm{Var}[\tilde{\xi}] &= \sigma^2 t, \\ E[(\tilde{\xi} - \bar{\xi})^3] &= \sigma^3 \frac{1 - 2\pi}{\sqrt{\pi(1-\pi)}} t^{3/2} \equiv \gamma\sigma^3 t^{3/2}, \\ E[(\tilde{\xi} - \bar{\xi})^k] &= O(t^{k/2}), \end{aligned} \tag{13}$$

so it is compact, as defined earlier.

For a logarithmic utility investor, the optimal holding of the risky asset is given by Equation (30) of Chapter 5 as

$$\begin{aligned} w^*(t) &= R\frac{\pi(h-R) + (1-\pi)(k-R)}{(h-R)(R-k)} \\ &= (1+rt)\frac{\mu - r}{\sigma^2}\left[1 - \gamma\frac{\mu - r}{\sigma}t^{1/2} - \left(\frac{\mu - r}{\sigma}\right)^2 t\right]^{-1}. \end{aligned} \tag{14}$$

To obtain the approximate mean-variance solution, we first calculate

$$a \equiv u(1) = 0, \quad b \equiv u'(1) = 1, \quad c \equiv -u''(1) = \tfrac{1}{2}. \tag{15}$$

Then the approximating maximization problem in (11) is

$$\mathrm{Max} \quad (1 - w)r + w\mu - \frac{w^2\sigma^2}{2} \tag{16}$$

with solution

$$w_2^* = \frac{\mu - r}{\sigma^2}. \tag{17}$$

This solution matches the true solution in the limit since $w_2^* = w^*(0)$. The match is exact, however, *only* in the limit. The two solutions will typically differ for $t \neq 0$. If we carry the Taylor expansion further, it is possible to get an even better approximation to the correct solution. Since $u'''(1) = 2$, we can express expected utility as

$$Eu(\tilde{Z}_p) = \bar{\zeta}_p - \tfrac{1}{2}[\mathrm{Var}(\tilde{\zeta}_p) + \bar{\zeta}_p^2] + \tfrac{1}{3}[E(\tilde{\zeta}_p - \bar{\zeta}_p)^3 + 3\mathrm{Var}(\tilde{\zeta}_p)\bar{\zeta}_p + \bar{\zeta}_p^3]. \tag{18}$$

Substituting from (13) and keeping only the low-order terms give

$$Eu(\tilde{Z}_p) = [r + w(\mu - r)]t - \frac{w^2\sigma^2 t}{2} + \frac{\gamma w^2 \sigma^2 t^{3/2}}{3} + O(t^2). \tag{19}$$

The optimal approximate portfolio weight is

$$w_3^*(t) = \frac{1}{2\gamma\sigma\sqrt{t}}\left[1 - \left[1 - \frac{4(\mu - r)\gamma\sqrt{t}}{\sigma}\right]^{1/2}\right]. \tag{20}$$

We can compare the true and the two approximating solutions by using their expansions in powers of $\sqrt{t}$:

$$\begin{aligned} w_2^*(t) &= \frac{\mu - r}{\sigma^2}, \\ w_3^*(t) &= \frac{\mu - r}{\sigma^2} + \gamma\frac{(\mu - r)^2}{\sigma^3}\sqrt{t} + \gamma^2\frac{2(\mu - r)^3}{\sigma^4}t + o(t), \\ w^*(t) &= \frac{\mu - r}{\sigma^2} + \gamma\frac{(\mu - r)^2}{\sigma^3}\sqrt{t} \\ &\quad + \frac{\mu - r}{\sigma^2}\left[r + \frac{(\mu - r)^2}{\sigma^2}(1 + \gamma^2)\right]t + o(t). \end{aligned} \tag{21}$$

It can be seen that the mean-variance-skewness approximation provides a better fit than the mean-variance approximation since it matches in its first two terms. If we continued this exercise by finding the n moment solution, we would find that it provided an even better approximation, matching the true solution up to the $(n - 2)$th power of $\sqrt{t}$.

"INFINITELY DIVISIBLE" DISTRIBUTIONS

One reasonable condition for this probability convergence model would be as the limit of portfolio decisions over shorter and shorter time intervals. The approximation would be good if prices could not change drastically in a short period of time with rates of return having compact distributions. In this case, portfolio analysis using only a few moments might be salvageable for general utility functions over short time periods. The mean-variance solution would be exact in the limit.

To examine problems in this limit economy, we must be able to model prices and other variables of interest as stochastic processes, or time series, in continuous time. The class of processes we will use are those called *infinitely divisible*.

Let $\tilde{X}$ be a random variable. It is said to be infinitely divisible if for all n,

$$\tilde{X} = \tilde{x}_1 + \tilde{x}_2 + \cdots + \tilde{x}_n, \tag{22}$$

where $\tilde{x}_1, \ldots, \tilde{x}_n$ are independent and identically distributed random variables. It is not required that the n variables $\tilde{x}_1, \ldots, \tilde{x}_n$ have the same distribution as the m variables $\tilde{x}_1, \ldots, \tilde{x}_m$ for $m \neq n$. In fact, this will be the case only for normal (or other stable) random variables.

If $\tilde{Y}(t)$ is a stochastic process where $\tilde{Y}(t + 1) - \tilde{Y}(t)$ has independent increments distributed like $\tilde{X}_t$, then

$$\begin{aligned} \tilde{Y}(T) - Y(0) &= \sum \tilde{X}_t \\ &= \tilde{x}_{11} + \cdots + \tilde{x}_{1n} + \tilde{x}_{21} + \cdots + \tilde{x}_{2n} + \cdots \\ &\quad + \tilde{x}_{t1} + \cdots + \tilde{x}_{tn}, \end{aligned} \tag{23}$$

and $\tilde{Y}(t)$ is called an infinitely divisible stochastic process.

Infinitely divisible stochastic variables or processes are easily distinguished by means of their characteristic functions. The characteristic function of the sum of two independent random variables is equal to the product of the two variables' characteristic functions. Therefore, if $\tilde{X}$ is infinitely divisible, then there must exist a series of characteristic functions $\phi_n(s)$ such that

$$\phi_X(s) = [\phi_n(s)]^n \qquad \text{for all } n. \tag{24}$$

Infinitely divisible stochastic processes may be compact, but they need not be. For all infinitely divisible variables, compact or not, the inverse of the number of independent summands takes the role of t in Equation (1). That is, we can think of time as broken into equal parts during each of which an independent increment to the price occurs. Since an infinitely divisible random variable is composed of independent increments, both its mean change and variance (if finite) must be proportional to the number of incremental parts; that is, they must be of equal importance. This can also be demonstrated with the characteristic function:

$$\begin{aligned} \phi'_X(s) &= n[\phi_n(s)]^{n-1}\phi'_n(s), \\ \phi''_X(s) &= n(n - 1)[\phi_n(s)]^{n-2}[\phi'_n(s)]^2 + n[\phi_n(s)]^{n-1}\phi''_n(s). \end{aligned} \tag{25}$$

Therefore, recalling that $\phi(0) = 1$, we get

$$\begin{aligned} E[\tilde{X}] &= -i\phi'_X(0) = -in\phi'_n(0) = nE[\tilde{x}_n], \\ \text{Var}[\tilde{X}] &= -\phi''_X(0) - \bar{X}^2 = -n(n - 1)[\phi'_n(0)]^2 - n\phi''_n(0) - \bar{X}^2 \end{aligned}$$

$$= n(n-1)\bar{x}_n^2 + n[\text{Var}(\tilde{x}_n) + \bar{x}_n^2] - n^2\bar{x}_n^2 \tag{26}$$
$$= n\ \text{Var}[\tilde{x}_n].$$

One example of an infinitely divisible and compact stochastic process is one in which changes over a unit interval of time have a normal distribution with mean μ and variance σ^2. This process is infinitely divisible because the change can be expressed as the sum of n independent normal variables with means μ/n and variances σ^2/n for any value of n. In addition, the characteristic function of a normal variable $\tilde{X}$ can be written in product form as in (24):

$$\phi_X(s) = \exp\left(i\mu s - \frac{s^2\sigma^2}{2}\right) = \left[\exp\left(\frac{i\mu s}{n} - \frac{s^2\sigma^2}{2n}\right)\right]^n. \tag{27}$$

The component parts are also compact since $\tilde{x}_n = \mu t + \sqrt{t}\tilde{e}$, where $\tilde{e}$ is a standard normal variate, and $t = 1/n$. Both the mean and variance of $\tilde{x}_n$ are proportional to $1/n$, and its even kth central moments are proportional to $n^{-k/2}$. (Its odd moments are, of course, zero.) Normal random processes are the only kind that are both compact and infinitely divisible.

The sum of two or more independent chi-squared random variables also has a chi-squared distribution. Therefore, a stochastic process whose increments have a chi-squared distribution is also infinitely divisible, but it is not compact. The characteristic function for a chi-squared variable with ν degrees of freedom is

$$\phi_X(s) = (1 - 2is)^{-\nu/2} = [(1 - 2is)^{-(\nu/n)/2}]^n, \tag{28}$$

so it can be expressed as the sum of n independent chi-squared random variables each with ν/n degrees of freedom. The means and variances are ν/n and $2\nu/n$, respectively. Again, they are of equal importance; however, in this case the third central moment is $8\nu/n$, so the ratio of it to variance is 4 for all n. Higher central moments are also proportional to $1/n$, so the chi-squared process is not compact.

WIENER AND POISSON PROCESSES

The limit of the infinitely divisible and compact normal stochastic process described above is known as *Brownian motion* or a *Wiener process*. Strictly speaking the latter name applies only to a process with a mean of 0 and a variance of 1 per unit time interval; nevertheless, both names are often used interchangeably. Wiener processes are very important tools in continuous-time financial models. The increments to Brownian motion can be modeled as the limit of

$$\Delta\tilde{\beta} = m\,\Delta t + \sigma\tilde{e}\sqrt{\Delta t} + o(\Delta t), \tag{29}$$

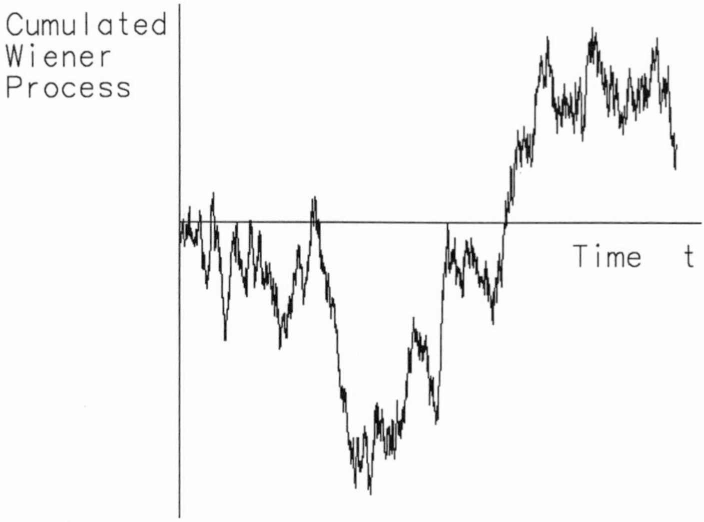

Figure 12.2 Example of a Wiener Process

where $\tilde{e}$ is a standard normal variate with zero mean and unit variance. The limit of $\tilde{e}\sqrt{\Delta t}$ is therefore the increment to a Wiener process. Wiener processes are examined in more detail in Chapter 16.

The property of a Wiener process which makes it compact is the continuity of its sample paths. That is, for any realization of a Wiener process there are no discontinuous changes. The chi-squared process, on the other hand, is not compact and has discontinuities. The prototypical discontinuous stochastic process is the Poisson process.

A mean zero Poisson process is one which drifts downward (upward) deterministically at the rate λ most of the time but with probability $\lambda \Delta t$ increases (decreases) discountinuously by one unit over an interval of length Δt. The times of these discontinuities are independent.

A Wiener process and a Poisson process are illustrated in Figures 12.2 and 12.3, respectively. Each has an expected change of 0 and a variance of 1 per unit time. The Wiener process has no discontinuities, being made up of many tiny random changes. This is illustrated by the apparent "fuzziness" of its sample path. A line with any breadth at all cannot show all the values achieved by a Wiener process without apparently retracing over itself. The Poisson process, on the other hand, with no obvious "fuzziness" in its sample path has only a few apparent random changes. Of course, this is really an illusion since the discontinuities can occur at any point in time, so the change over any interval is uncertain.

It is apparent from these figures that financial price series are more like Wiener processes, and this is how we shall choose to model them. The major drawback to this choice is that there is absolutely no possibility of

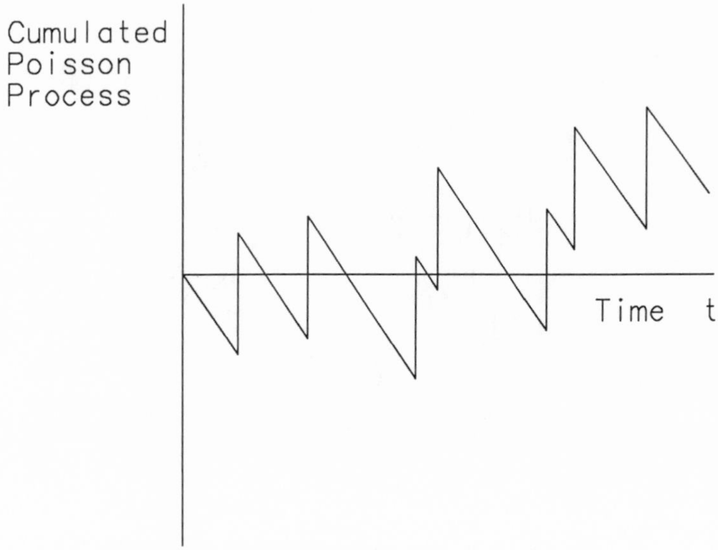

Figure 12.3 Example of a Poisson Process

abrupt changes (discontinuities) in the price. On the other hand, the substantial advantage is the validity of mean-variance analysis. On a more practical level, virtually any continuous-time stochastic process can be expressed as a sum of Brownian motion and Poisson processes, so studying the former will provide a basis for more general models.

Since a normally distributed stochastic process (Brownian motion) is the only kind that is both compact and infinitely divisible, it might seem that we would be severely restricted as to the kinds of returns distributions that we could model if we confine our attention to these types. Fortunately, many other distributions can be modeled by allowing the mean and/or variance of the normal distribution to change as a function of the price level or other variables.

As a typical example, stock prices will often be postulated to behave like

$$\tilde{S}(t + \Delta t) - S(t) \equiv \Delta\tilde{S}(t) = \alpha(S)S\,\Delta t + \sigma(S)S\tilde{e}\sqrt{\Delta t} + o(\Delta t), \quad (30)$$

where $\tilde{e}\sqrt{\Delta t}$ is the increment to a Wiener process as in (29), and α and σ^2 are the current mean rate of return and variance of return. For example, if they are constants, then, as we will show in the limit of continuous time ($\Delta t \to 0$) the process produces lognormally distributed prices.

DISCRETE-TIME APPROXIMATIONS FOR WIENER PROCESSES

In Chapter 16 we will learn how to utilize Wiener processes in financial models. Until then we will be content to use discrete-time approximations. There are two different convenient approximations to a Wiener process. The first is to represent the normal distribuiton over the period Δt by a two-point distribution. This is a binomial process and will be used primarily in Chapter 14 on option pricing.

Let $\Delta\tilde{\varepsilon}$ be a binomial random variable with two equally likely outcomes, $\Delta\varepsilon_{1,2} = \Delta t \pm \sqrt{\Delta t}$. Then

$$E[\tilde{\varepsilon}] = \Delta t, \qquad \mathrm{Var}[\tilde{\varepsilon}] = \Delta t. \tag{31}$$

If $1/\Delta t$ is an integer, then $\tilde{\varepsilon}(1) - \varepsilon(0)$ will have a binomial distribution of $1/\Delta t + 1$ points with a mean and variance of unity. In the limit as $\Delta t \to 0$ this will approach the standard normal distribution of $\tilde{e}$ over a period of one unit of time.

The second approximation is constructed by actually taking the limit of the discrete process in (29). The most important tool for working with Wiener processes is Ito's lemma. Ito's lemma describes the behavior of functions of Wiener processes. It will be introduced in a more formal fashion in Chapter 16. For the approximation approach we need merely use a Taylor expansion.

Let $\tilde{\beta}(t)$ be the Brownian motion process whose increments are described in (29), and let $f[\beta(t)]$ be some twice continuously differentiable function of the Brownian motion process. Expanding $f(\cdot)$ in a Taylor series gives

$$\begin{aligned} f[\tilde{\beta}(t + \Delta t)] = f[\beta(t)] + f'[\beta(t)]\Delta\tilde{\beta} + \tfrac{1}{2}f''[\beta(t)](\Delta\tilde{\beta})^2 \\ + \tfrac{1}{6}f'''[\beta(t + k\,\Delta t)](\Delta\tilde{\beta})^3, \end{aligned} \tag{32}$$

where $0 \leqslant k \leqslant 1$. Subtracting $f(\cdot)$ from both sides and substituting for $\Delta\tilde{\beta}$ from (29), we derive

$$\Delta\tilde{f} = f'(\cdot)(\mu\,dt + \sigma\tilde{e}\sqrt{\Delta t}) + \tfrac{1}{2}f''(\cdot)\sigma^2\tilde{e}^2\Delta t + o(\Delta t). \tag{33}$$

Therefore, the expected and uncertain components in the change in $f(\cdot)$ are

$$E[\Delta\tilde{f}] = [f'(\cdot)\mu + \tfrac{1}{2}f''(\cdot)\sigma^2]\Delta t + o(\Delta t), \tag{34a}$$

$$\Delta\tilde{f} - E[\Delta\tilde{f}] = \sigma\tilde{e}\sqrt{\Delta t} + o(\sqrt{\Delta t}). \tag{34b}$$

The second derivative term is relevant in (34a) since $E[\tilde{e}^2] = 1$. Its contribution to the uncertainty, however, is small relative to the term $\tilde{e}\sqrt{\Delta t}$.

To the smallest-order approximation these two quantities are all that is required. If $f(\cdot)$ is a function of both the Brownian process and time, then the ordinary derivatives are replaced with partial derivatives, and the partial derivative with respect to time is also included in the expected change in (34a).

As an example, let $\tilde{S}(t) = \exp[\tilde{\beta}(t)]$. Then $f' = f'' = S$ and

$$\Delta\tilde{S} = (\mu + \tfrac{1}{2}\sigma^2)S\,\Delta t + \sigma S\tilde{e}\sqrt{\Delta t} + o(\Delta t). \tag{35}$$

Comparing (35) with (30), we see that they are the same for $\alpha \equiv \mu + .5\sigma^2$. Since $\tilde{e}$ is normally distributed, $\tilde{S}$ is obviously lognormally distributed, verifying the statement made earlier.

13

Continuous-Time Portfolio Selection

Suppose that the realized rates of return on all securities are infinitely divisible and compact with means and variances of equal importance. Let $\tilde{\zeta}(t)$ denote the rate of return $\tilde{\zeta}(t) \equiv \Delta P/P = \alpha\,\Delta t + \sigma\tilde{e}\sqrt{\Delta t} + o(\Delta t)$, where ΔP denotes the cum dividend price change if a dividend is paid, and $\tilde{e}$ is a standard normal random variable. The moments of $\tilde{\zeta}$ are denoted by

$$
\begin{aligned}
E[\tilde{\zeta}] &\equiv E\left[\frac{\Delta P}{P}\right] \equiv \alpha\,\Delta t + o(\Delta t),\\
E[\tilde{\zeta}^2] &\equiv E\left[\frac{\Delta P^2}{P^2}\right] = \sigma^2\Delta t + o(\Delta t),\\
\mathrm{Var}[\tilde{\zeta}] &= \sigma^2\Delta t + o(\Delta t),\\
\mathrm{Cov}[\tilde{\zeta}_i, \tilde{\zeta}_j] &\equiv E\left[\frac{\Delta P_i \Delta P_j}{P_i P_j}\right] - E\left[\frac{\Delta P_i}{P_i}\right]E\left[\frac{\Delta P_j}{P_j}\right]\\
&= \sigma_i\sigma_j\Delta t\,\mathrm{Cov}(\tilde{e}_i, \tilde{e}_j) + o(\Delta t) \equiv \sigma_{ij}\Delta t + o(\Delta t),
\end{aligned}
\tag{1}
$$

and higher moments are $o(\Delta t)$. In the first four sections of this Chapter we assume that the parameters α_i and σ_{ij}, including the interest rate $\alpha_0 \equiv r$, are constant. For future reference note that to $o(\Delta t)$ variance and the second raw moment are equal.

The continuous-time version of the portfolio selection problem is given in (2), where we have again assumed time-additive and state-independent utility of consumption. Consumption is now measured as a flow or rate of consumption per unit time.

$$
\mathrm{Max}\, E_0\left[\int_0^T U[C(t), t]\,dt + B[W(T), T]\right]. \tag{2}
$$

To solve this problem we approximate it as the discrete-time problem of Chapter 11 as follows: At time t the lump sum $C(t)\,\Delta t$ is taken from wealth and used to finance consumption at a constant rate from t to t +

Δt. The remaining wealth $W(t) - C(t)\,\Delta t$ is invested in the portfolio characterized by weights $w_i(t)$. This portfolio is not rebalanced until $t + \Delta t$. Our approximate problem can now be stated as

$$\operatorname{Max} \sum_{t=0}^{T-\Delta t} \int_t^{t+\Delta t} U[C(s), s]\,ds + B[W(T), T] \tag{3a}$$

Subject to

$$W(t + \Delta t) = [W(t) - C(t)\,\Delta t] \sum_{i=0}^{N} w_i(t)(1 + \tilde{\zeta}_i(t)). \tag{3b}$$

For simplicity we have assumed that there is no wage income.

Using an exact two-term Taylor expansion for the integral in (3a), we have

$$\begin{aligned} \int_t^{t+\Delta t} U[C(s), s]\,ds &= U[C(t), t]\,\Delta t + U_t[C(t^*), t^*]\Delta t^2 \\ &= U[C(t), t]\,\Delta t + o(\Delta t) \end{aligned} \tag{4}$$

for some t^* in the interval $[t, t + \Delta t]$. note that $C(t^*) = C(t)$ by construction, so we are not required to take the partial derivative with respect to C in the expansion.

The wealth accumulation equation (3b) can be reexpressed in difference form as

$$\begin{aligned} W(t + \Delta t) &= [W(t) - C(t)\,\Delta t]\textstyle\sum w_i + [W(t) - C(t)\,\Delta t]\textstyle\sum w_i \zeta_i, \\ \Delta W(t) &= -C(t)\,\Delta t + [W(t) - C(t)\,\Delta t]\textstyle\sum w_i \tilde{\zeta}_i, \end{aligned} \tag{5a}$$

with properties

$$E_t[\Delta W(t)] = -C\,\Delta t + W\textstyle\sum w_i \alpha_i \Delta t + o(\Delta t), \tag{5b}$$

$$\begin{aligned} \operatorname{Var}_t[\Delta W(t)] &= (W - C\,\Delta t)^2 \operatorname{Var}[\textstyle\sum w_i \tilde{\zeta}_i] \\ &= (W - C\,\Delta t)^2 \sum_1^N \sum_1^N w_i w_j \sigma_{ii}\,\Delta t + o(\Delta t) \\ &= W^2 \sum_1^N \sum_1^N w_i w_j \sigma_{ij}\,\Delta t + o(\Delta t), \end{aligned} \tag{5c}$$

$$E_t[(\Delta W(t))^k] = o(\Delta t) \qquad \text{for } k > 2. \tag{5d}$$

As in Equations (4) of Chapter 11 define the derived utility of wealth function

$$J[W(t), t] \equiv \operatorname{Max} E_t\left[\int_t^T U(C, s)\,ds + B[W(T), T]\right]. \tag{6}$$

Using conditional expectations and maximizations, we derive the equivalent of Equation (13) of Chapter 11, namely,

$$J[W(t), t] \equiv \operatorname{Max} E_t\left[\int_t^{t+\Delta t} U(C, s)\, ds + J[W(t + \Delta t), t + \Delta t]\right]. \tag{7}$$

Expand $J(\cdot)$ by Taylor's theorem to get

$$\begin{aligned} J[W(t + \Delta t), t + \Delta t] = J(W, t) &+ \frac{\partial J}{\partial t}\Delta t + \frac{\partial J}{\partial W}\Delta W + \frac{1}{2}\frac{\partial^2 J}{\partial W^2}\Delta W^2 \\ &+ \frac{1}{2}\frac{\partial^2 J}{\partial t^2}\Delta t^2 + \frac{\partial^2 J}{\partial t \partial W}\Delta t \Delta W + \theta, \end{aligned} \tag{8}$$

where θ includes terms $\Delta W^k \Delta t^j$ with $k + j \geqslant 3$. Taking the expectation of (8) gives

$$\begin{aligned} E_t[J(W + \Delta W, t + \Delta t)] = J(W, t) &+ \frac{\partial J}{\partial t}\Delta t + \frac{\partial J}{\partial W}E_t[\Delta W] \\ &+ \frac{1}{2}\frac{\partial^2 J}{\partial W^2}\operatorname{Var}[\Delta W] + o(\Delta t). \end{aligned} \tag{9}$$

Substituting (9) and (5) into (7), subtracting J from both sides of the equation, and using our approximation $\int_t^{t+\Delta t} U(C, s)\, ds = U(C, t)\Delta t + o(\Delta t)$, we get

$$\begin{aligned} 0 = \operatorname{Max}\Bigg[U(C, t) &+ \frac{\partial J}{\partial t} + \frac{\partial J}{\partial W}\left[-C + W\sum_0^N w_i \alpha_i\right] \\ &+ \frac{W^2}{2}\frac{\partial^2 J}{\partial W^2}\sum_1^N\sum_1^N w_i w_j \sigma_{ij} + o(\Delta t^0)\Bigg]. \end{aligned} \tag{10}$$

The choice variables are consumption and the portfolio weights. These are determined using ordinary calculus. To maximize with respect to the w_i, substitute out the constraint $\Sigma_{i=0}^N w_i = 1$ to get

$$\sum_{i=0}^N w_i \alpha_i = \sum_{i=1}^N w_i(\alpha_i - r) + r,$$

where $r = \alpha_0$ is the interest rate. Then the first-order conditions are

$$\frac{\partial U}{\partial C} = \frac{\partial J}{\partial W}, \tag{11a}$$

$$0 = \frac{\partial J}{\partial W}W(\alpha_i - r) + \frac{\partial^2 J}{\partial W^2}W^2\sum_{j=1}^N w_j^* \sigma_{ij}. \tag{11b}$$

(11a) is the envelope condition again and (11b) is the standard set of *linear* equations we get in mean-variance analysis with solution

$$w_i^* = -\frac{\partial J/\partial W}{W\partial^2 J/\partial W^2}\sum_{j=1}^{N} v_{ij}(\alpha_j - r), \tag{12}$$

where v_{ij} are the elements of $(\sigma_{ij})^{-1}$. Since w_i^*/w_j^* is independent of utility, in equilibrium all investors must hold the market portfolio (levered) and, as in the single-period case, it is mean-variance efficient so

$$\alpha_i - r = \frac{\sigma_{im}}{\sigma_m^2}(\alpha_m - r) \equiv \beta_i(\alpha_m - r); \tag{13}$$

that is, the CAPM holds for the continuously compounded rates of return.

Investors' portfolios differ only in desired leverage. To find the optimal leverage, we must determine the derived utility of wealth function. An example of a completely solved problem is given next.

SOLVING A SPECIFIC PROBLEM

Consider an investor with isoelastic utility of consumption $U(C, t) = e^{-\rho t}C^\gamma/\gamma$ and no motive for bequest. Since he will always hold the market, we can assume that it is the only risky asset. In this case (10) becomes

$$0 = \text{Max}\left[\frac{e^{-\rho t}C^\gamma}{\gamma} + J_t + J_W[W(w(\alpha - r) + r) - C] \right. \tag{14}$$

$$\left. + \frac{1}{2}w^2W^2\sigma^2 J_{WW}\right]$$

where subscripts on J denote partial differentiation. Substituting the optimal solution $w^* = (-J_W/WJ_{WW})(\alpha - r)/\sigma^2$ from (12) gives

$$0 = e^{-\rho t}\frac{(C^*)^\gamma}{\gamma} + J_t + J_W(rW - C^*) - \frac{J_W^2(\alpha - r)^2}{J_{WW}\sigma^2} + \frac{1}{2}\frac{J_W^2(\alpha - r)^2}{J_{WW}\sigma^2}. \tag{15}$$

From (11a) $C^* = (e^{\rho t}J_W)^{1/(\gamma-1)}$; thus

$$0 = e^{-\rho t}\left(\frac{1}{\gamma} - 1\right)(e^{\rho t}J_W)^{\gamma/(\gamma-1)} + J_t + rWJ_W - \frac{1}{2}\frac{(\alpha - r)^2}{\sigma^2}\frac{J_W^2}{J_{WW}}. \tag{16}$$

As you can imagine, this iiis a difficult partial differential equation to solve unless you make a lucky guess.

A trick which often helps is to consider the infinite horizon problem first; that is, $J(W, t) = \text{Max}\,E[\int_t^\infty e^{-\rho s}\,U(C)\,ds]$. For this problem define $I(W) \equiv e^{\rho t}J(W, t)$. To see that it is independent of t, we have

$$I(W) = \text{Max}\,E\left[\int_t^\infty e^{\rho(t-s)}\,U(C)\,ds\right]$$

$$= \operatorname{Max} E\left[\int_0^\infty e^{-\rho v} U(C)\, dv\right] \tag{17}$$

for $v = s - t$. Then $J_t = -\rho I e^{-\rho t}$, $J_W = e^{-\rho t} I'$, $J_{WW} = e^{-\rho t} I''$. Substituting into (16) and dividing out $e^{-\rho t}$ leave

$$0 = \left(\frac{1}{\gamma} - 1\right)(I')^{\gamma/(\gamma-1)} - \rho I + rWI' - \frac{1}{2}\left(\frac{\alpha - r}{\sigma}\right)^2 \frac{(I')^2}{I''}. \tag{18}$$

For (18) we guess a solution of the form $I(W) = AW^\gamma/\gamma$. Substitution into (18) leaves

$$0 = AW^\gamma\left[\frac{1-\gamma}{\gamma}A^{1/(\gamma-1)} - \frac{\rho}{\gamma} + r - \frac{1}{2}\left(\frac{\alpha - r}{\sigma}\right)^2 \frac{1}{\gamma - 1}\right], \tag{19}$$

verifying this solution form for the constant

$$A = \left[\frac{\gamma}{1-\gamma}\left[\frac{\rho}{\gamma} - r - \frac{1}{2}\left(\frac{\alpha - r}{\sigma}\right)^2 \frac{1}{1-\gamma}\right]\right]^{\gamma - 1} \equiv a^{\gamma-1}, \tag{20}$$

provided that $a > 0$. If $a < 0$, then the solution method we have used is not valid. From (22) optimal consumption is formally negative if $a \leqslant 0$, but this obviously cannot be true. Even if negative consumption is meaningful, its utility is not defined for power utility functions. A second condition required for a valid solution is $\rho \geqslant 0$. Together the constraints on ρ and a imply

$$\rho > \operatorname{Max}\left\{0, \gamma\left[r + \frac{1}{2}\left(\frac{\alpha - r}{\sigma}\right)^2 \frac{1}{1-\gamma}\right]\right\}. \tag{21}$$

This requirement is known as the transversality condition. For those familiar with the optimal growth literature it will be recognized as the stochastic equivalent of $\rho > \operatorname{Max}(0, \gamma r)$, which is required there for a well-defined solution. An intuitive explanation for this requirement is that in its absence an investor could achieve infinite expected utility by one plan or another. For $\rho < 0$, $U(C, \infty) = \infty$ for any consumption plan with $C > 0$, so many plans could achieve infinite expected utility. For $\rho > 0$, $U(C, \infty)$ vanishes, but if $\gamma > 0$ and the transversality condition is violated the investor achieves infinite expected utility by saving his entire wealth. (From (22) the optimal rate of consumption is zero if $a \leqslant 0$.) For $\gamma \leqslant 0$ saving one's entire wealth and consuming nothing currently could never be optimal, since $U(0, t) = -\infty$.

Given that the transversality condition holds, the optimal portfolio choices are given by (12a) and (11a) as

$$w^* = \frac{\alpha - r}{(1-\gamma)\sigma^2}, \qquad C^* = aW. \tag{22}$$

We can now tackle the finite horizon case with the guessed solution

$J(W, t) = e^{-\rho t}A(t)W^\gamma/\gamma$. Substituting into (16) verifies this guess, leaving

$$0 = \left[(1-\gamma)A^{\gamma/(\gamma-1)} - \rho A + A' + \gamma r A - \frac{1}{2}A\left(\frac{\alpha-r}{\sigma}\right)^2 \frac{\gamma}{\gamma-1}\right]\frac{e^{-\rho t}W^\gamma}{\gamma}, \tag{23}$$
$$0 = A'(t) + (\gamma-1)[aA(t) - A^{\gamma/(\gamma-1)}(t)],$$

with boundary condition $A(T) = 0$. This first-order equation is of the Bernoulli type and can be solved by the change of variable $A(t) = [B(t)]^{1-\gamma}$. Making this substitution in (23) leaves $B'(t) = aB(t) - 1$. Thus, the function $A(t)$ has the solution

$$A(t) = \left[\frac{1 - e^{a(t-T)}}{a}\right]^{1-\gamma}. \tag{24}$$

The optimal portfolio and consumption choices are

$$w^*(t) = w^* = \frac{\alpha - r}{(1-\gamma)\sigma^2}, \qquad C^*(t) = \frac{a}{1 - e^{a(t-T)}}W(t). \tag{25}$$

These solutions are valid for any values of the parameters. The tranversality condition is not relevant since infinite wealth cannot be accumulated in a finite lifetime. The optimal portfolio is the same from one period to the next; however, the optimal rule for consumption changes over time. [For $a = 0$ the consumption rule is to plan on dividing consumption equally over the remaining time, $C^*(t) = W(t)/(T - t)$.]

Although we shall not analyze it here, the optimal plan in (25) can lead to many types of behavior. For example, if the value $t^* = T + \ln(1 - a/\alpha^*)/a$ is defined and in the range $(0, T)$, then the investor will plan on saving more than his income from 0 to t^* and then spend his savings during t^* to T. This is the usual "hump savings" phenomenon.

For both the finite and infinite horizon cases, the optimal portfolio is independent of wealth, consumption, and impatience, ρ. The greater is the risk aversion, the smaller the expected return, the higher the interest rate, or the higher the risk, the less will be held of the risky asset. Optimal consumption does depend upon the distribution or returns (except in the log utility case ($\gamma = 0$), for which $a = \rho$). The greater the impatience, ρ, the more will the investor consume. For $\gamma > 0$, the investor will consume more when the market price of risk $(\alpha - r)/\sigma$ is smaller. This is to be expected, since the greater is γ the less risk averse is the investor, and he will hold a larger fraction of his wealth in the market. If the premium is smaller, he is hurt more than those concentrating more in bonds. For $\gamma < 0$ the opposite is true.

TESTING THE MODEL

To test the model just developed, we require estimates of the various parameters. Since we have assumed that α_i, σ_i, and σ_{ij} are constants, we can use standard sampling methods to obtain their estimates. We shall also assume that the relative market weight of each asset is constant, so that α_m, σ_{im}, and σ_m will be stationary. P_m denotes the price of "one share" of the market portfolio.

With constant α_i and σ_i asset prices are, as we shall see momentarily, lognormally distributed. Since standard econometric methods are designed for normal random variables, it is useful to transform the data by defining $\tilde{y}(t; \Delta t) \equiv \ln[\tilde{P}(t + \Delta t)/P(t)]$. By Taylor expansion $\ln[1 + x] = -\Sigma_1^\infty(-1)^n x^n/n$; hence

$$\begin{aligned} \tilde{y}(t; \Delta t) &= \frac{\Delta \tilde{P}}{P} - \frac{1}{2}\frac{\Delta \tilde{P}^2}{P^2} + o(\Delta \tilde{P}^2) \\ &= (\alpha - \tfrac{1}{2}\sigma^2)\,\Delta t + \sigma\tilde{e}\sqrt{\Delta t} + o(\Delta t). \end{aligned} \tag{26}$$

From (26) it is clear that the $\tilde{y}(t; \Delta t)$ are in the limit independent and identically distributed normal random variables. (Returns are therefore i.i.d. lognormal variables.) This is an important feature, since with continuous lognormal prices the constructed $\tilde{y}$'s will be independent normals regardless of the frequency of data collection.

To estimate $\hat{\beta}_i$, consider the "market model" regression equation

$$\tilde{y}_i(t; \Delta t) = a_i + b_i \tilde{y}_m(t; \Delta t) + \tilde{\varepsilon}_i(t; \Delta t). \tag{27}$$

We will find

$$b_i = \frac{\mathrm{Cov}[\tilde{y}_i, \tilde{y}_m]}{\mathrm{Var}[\tilde{y}_m]} = \frac{\hat{\sigma}_{im}\,\Delta t}{\hat{\sigma}_m^2\,\Delta t} = \hat{\beta}_i,$$

as desired, independent of the observation interval.

One *apparent* way to test the model would be to use the cross-sectional regression

$$\bar{y}_i = \gamma_0 + \gamma_1 \hat{\beta}_i + \tilde{u}_i. \tag{28}$$

In (28) $\hat{\gamma}_1 = \hat{\mathrm{Cov}}[\bar{y}_i, \hat{\beta}_i]/\hat{\mathrm{Var}}(\hat{\beta}_i)$, where $\hat{\mathrm{Cov}}(\cdot)$ and $\hat{\mathrm{Var}}(\cdot)$ refer to the cross-sectional statistics of the sample. It is well known that plim $\hat{\beta}_i = \beta_i$ and plim $\bar{y}_i = E(y_i)$. From (26) and (13), the latter is

$$E(y_i) = (\alpha_i - \tfrac{1}{2}\sigma_i^2)\,\Delta t = (r + \beta_i(\alpha_m - r) - \tfrac{1}{2}\sigma_i^2)\,\Delta t.$$

Therefore even if we properly adjust for the measurement error bias in beta (for example, by using different periods to estimate $\hat{\gamma}_1$ and $\hat{\beta}_i$), the test $\hat{\gamma}_1 = (\bar{y}_m - r)\,\Delta t$ is biased and inconsistent:

$$
\begin{aligned}
E(\hat{\gamma}_1) = \operatorname{plim} \hat{\gamma}_1 &= \frac{\operatorname{Cov}[(r + \beta_i(\alpha_m - r) - \tfrac{1}{2}\sigma_i^2)\,\Delta t,\ \beta_i]}{\operatorname{Var}(\beta_i)} \\
&= \left[\alpha_m - r - \frac{1}{2}\frac{\operatorname{Cov}(\sigma_i^2, \beta_i)}{\operatorname{Var}(\beta_i)}\right]\Delta t,
\end{aligned}
\tag{29a}
$$

$$
E[\hat{\gamma}_1 - (\bar{y}_m - r)\,\Delta t] = \operatorname{plim}(\cdot) = \frac{1}{2}\left[\sigma_m^2 - \frac{\operatorname{Cov}(\sigma_i^2, \beta_i)}{\operatorname{Var}(\beta_i)}\right]\Delta t, \tag{29b}
$$

where Cov(·) and Var(·) now refer to cross-sectional statistics of the population. As is readily apparent, only by coincidence would the right-hand side of (29b) be zero, as we would "expect." It is easy to show that the estimate of γ_0 is similarly biased and inconsistent.

If we include $\hat{\beta}_i^2$ and/or residual variance $s_i^2 \equiv \sigma_i^2 - \beta_i^2\sigma_m^2$ as other explanatory variables in (28), then on average they will have nonzero regression coefficients. For example, for the regression

$$
\bar{y}_i = \gamma_0 + \gamma_1\hat{\beta}_i + \gamma_2\hat{\beta}_i^2 + \gamma_3\hat{s}_i^2 + \tilde{u}_i \tag{30}
$$

we have

$$
\begin{aligned}
&\operatorname{plim} \hat{\gamma}_0 = r, && \operatorname{plim} \hat{\gamma}_1 = \alpha_m - r, \\
&\operatorname{plim} \hat{\gamma}_2 = -\tfrac{1}{2}\sigma_m^2, && \operatorname{plim} \hat{\gamma}_3 = -\tfrac{1}{2},
\end{aligned}
\tag{31}
$$

since $E(\bar{y}_i) = r + \beta_i(\alpha_m - r) - \frac{1}{2}(\beta_i^2\sigma_m^2 + s_i^2)$. Again (31) does not give the results "expected."

We are even worse off if the average raw returns are used as the left-hand side variables because they are not linearly related to β:

$$
\begin{aligned}
1 + E\left[\frac{\Delta P_i}{P_i}\right] &= \exp(\alpha_i\,\Delta t + o(\Delta t)) \\
&= \exp[(r + \beta_i(\alpha_m - r)\,\Delta t + o(\Delta t)].
\end{aligned}
\tag{32}
$$

One way to verify the model which does not require nonlinear techniques or the estimation of extraneous numbers, such as s_i^2 in (30) or the population covariance of β_i and σ_i^2 in (29), is to use the following test. Equation (27) is used to obtain estimates $\hat{\beta}_i$ which are subjected to the cross-sectional regression

$$
\overline{\ln\left(1 + \frac{\Delta P_i}{P_i}\right)} = \gamma_0 + \gamma_1\hat{\beta}_i + \tilde{u}_i. \tag{33}
$$

In this case, $\hat{\gamma}_0$ and $\hat{\gamma}_1$ are unbiased and consistent estimators of $r\,\Delta t$ and $(\alpha_m - r)\,\Delta t$, respectively. The latter can also be stated in terms of the observed mean

$$E\left[\hat{\gamma}_1 - \ln\left(1 + \frac{\overline{\Delta P_m}}{P_m}\right) + r\,\Delta t\right] = \text{plim}(\cdot) = 0, \tag{34}$$

which does not require knowledge of the unobservable expected rate of return on the market portfolio. These limiting relations can be derived from (32) as follows:

$$\begin{aligned} \ln\left(1 + E\left[\frac{\Delta P_i}{P_i}\right]\right) &= [r + \beta_i(\alpha_m - r)]\,\Delta t + o(\Delta t) \\ &= r\,\Delta t + \beta_i\left[\ln\left(1 + E\left(\frac{\Delta P_m}{P_m}\right)\right) - r\,\Delta t\right] + o(\Delta t). \end{aligned} \tag{35}$$

The important distinction between these tests is in their left-hand-side variables. Neither of the two natural choices are correct for the simplest test of the continuous-time CAPM. Rather, the log of the average return is required.

EFFICIENCY TESTS USING THE CONTINUOUS-TIME CAPM

One standard test for efficiency is to look at the intercept of the market model regression. However, for the continuous-time market model regression in (27) the intercept term a_i has the properties

$$\begin{aligned} E(a_i) &= \text{plim } a_i = E(y_i) - \beta_i E(y_m) \\ &= [r(1 - \beta_i) + \tfrac{1}{2}(\beta_i \sigma_m^2 - \sigma_i^2)]\,\Delta t + o(\Delta t) \\ &= [r(1 - \beta_i) + \tfrac{1}{2}[\sigma_m^2 \beta_i(1 - \beta_i) - s_i^2]]\,\Delta t + o(\Delta t). \end{aligned} \tag{36}$$

Naively we would expect $r(1 - \beta_i)$, so standard efficiency tests could be misleading.

One way to counteract this problem is to use the continuous-time equivalent of the Treynor measure. To test efficiency, examine

$$\frac{\ln(1 + \overline{\Delta P_i/P_i}) - r\,\Delta t}{\beta_i} \gtrless ln\left(1 + \frac{\overline{\Delta P_m}}{P_m}\right) - r\,\Delta t. \tag{37}$$

If the greater than sign applies (and $\beta_i > 0$), the security in question outperformed the market on a risk-adjusted basis and vice versa. To see that the test in (37) is indeed an unbiased and consistent one for efficiency, we need only examine the formula in (35).

Another common type of market efficiency test is the event study. Typically, the CAPM is used to construct "residuals" which are then tracked over a period of time which includes the event of interest. The simplest residual construction procedure would be to estimate $\hat{a}_i$ and $\hat{b}_i$ in

(27) and then use as the residual for period $(t, t + \Delta t)$

$$v_i(t, \Delta t) \equiv y_i(t; \Delta t) - \hat{a}_i - \hat{b}_i v_m(t, \Delta t). \tag{38}$$

While this technique would be unbiased and consistent, it is not the most efficient because it fails to impose the equilibrium relation between a_i and b_i. Equation (36) could be used for this; however, that would require estimating σ_m^2 and σ_i^2.

One partial solution to this problem is to construct residuals as follows:

$$\begin{aligned} v_i = 1 &+ \frac{\Delta P_i}{P_i} \\ &- \exp\left\{\left[r(1 - \beta_i) + \frac{\beta_i(1 - \beta_i)\sigma_m^2}{2}\right]\Delta t\right\}\left(1 + \frac{\Delta P_m}{P_m}\right)^{\beta_i}. \end{aligned} \tag{39}$$

These residuals do have a zero mean since $\beta_i y_m \sim N[(\alpha_m - \frac{1}{2}\sigma_m^2)\beta_i, \beta_i^2\sigma_m^2]$, so

$$E\left[\left(1 + \frac{\Delta P_m}{P_m}\right)^{\beta_i}\right] = \exp\left[\left(\beta_i\alpha_m - \frac{1}{2}\beta_i\sigma_m^2 + \frac{1}{2}\beta_i^2\sigma_m^2\right)\Delta t\right]. \tag{40}$$

This technique avoids estimation of σ_i^2, although it does require an estimte of σ_m^2. Fortunately, it should be possible to estimate the latter more precisely. The disadvantage of this scheme is that the constructed residuals will not be normally distributed.

EXTENDING THE MODEL TO STOCHASTIC OPPORTUNITY SETS

We have apparently derived a very strong result. The CAPM holds for continuously compounded rates of return if prices have continuous sample paths. Unfortunately, we have made the subtle but crucial assumption that an investor can measure his well being at any point of time by knowing only his wealth; that is, in (6) we *assumed* that $J(\cdot)$ is independent of "the state of the world." Clearly, if, for example, relative commodity prices change, then utility of consumption will be state dependent and so will J. However, even if utility of consumption is state independent, there may be induced dependencies in the J function if α_i, σ_{ij}, or r vary randomly over time, as we saw in discrete time in Examples 2 and 3 of Chapter 11.

Suppose there is a single state variable which describes changes in these variables; that is, one or more of α_i, σ_{ij}, and r are functions of x. We assume x has a compact distribution $\Delta x = \mu\,\Delta t + s\tilde{e}_x\sqrt{\Delta t} + o(\Delta t)$ such that

$$E_t[\Delta x] = \mu\,\Delta t + o(\Delta t),$$

$$\text{Var}_t[\Delta x] = s^2\Delta t + o(\Delta t), \tag{41}$$

$$\text{Cov}_t\left[\Delta x, \frac{\Delta \text{P}_\text{i}}{\text{P}_\text{i}}\right] = \rho_{\text{ix}} \text{s}\sigma_\text{i}\,\Delta\text{t} + \text{o}(\Delta t) = \sigma_{ix}\Delta t + o(\Delta t).$$

We solve the problem as we did previously except now the Taylor expansion of $J(\cdot)$ replacing (8) is

$$\begin{aligned} J[W + \Delta W, x + \Delta x, t + \Delta t] &= J(W, x, t) + J_t\Delta t + J_W\Delta W + J_x\Delta x \\ &+ \tfrac{1}{2}J_{WW}\Delta W^2 + \tfrac{1}{2}J_{xx}\Delta x^2 + J_{xW}\Delta x\,\Delta W + \tfrac{1}{2}J_{tt}\Delta t^2 \\ &+ J_{tW}\Delta t\,\Delta W + J_{tx}\Delta t\,\Delta x + \theta, \end{aligned} \tag{42}$$

where θ contains terms $\Delta W^i\,\Delta t^j\,\Delta x^k$ with $i + j + k \geqslant 3$. Taking expectations

$$\begin{aligned} E_t[J(W + \Delta W, x + \Delta x, t + \Delta t)] &= J + J_t\Delta t + J_W E[\Delta W] + J_x E[\Delta x] \\ &+ \tfrac{1}{2}J_{WW}\text{Var}[\Delta W] + \tfrac{1}{2}J_{xx}\text{Var}[\Delta x] \\ &+ J_{xW}\text{Cov}[\Delta x, \Delta W] + o(\Delta t) \end{aligned} \tag{43}$$

and substituting (43), (41), and (5) into (7), we derive

$$\begin{aligned} 0 = \text{Max}\Bigg[& U(C, t) + J_t + J_W\left(-C + W\sum_0^N w_i\alpha_i\right) \\ & + \frac{W^2}{2}J_{WW}\sum_1^N\sum_1^N w_i w_j\sigma_{ij} + J_x\mu + \tfrac{1}{2}J_{xx}s^2 + J_{Wx}W\sum_1^N w_i\sigma_{ix}\Bigg] \\ & + o(\Delta t). \end{aligned} \tag{44}$$

As before, $\partial U/\partial C = \partial J/\partial W$. The portfolio constraint is substituted out, giving $\Sigma_0^N w_i\alpha_i = r + \Sigma_1^N w_i(\alpha_i - r)$, so now the optimal weights satisfy

$$0 = J_W W(\alpha_i - r) + J_{WW}W^2\sum_{j=1}^N \frac{w_j^*}{\sigma_{ij}} + J_{Wx}W\sigma_{ix}. \tag{45}$$

(45) may be written in matrix form after dividing by W:

$$\mathbf{0} = J_W(\boldsymbol{\alpha} - r\mathbf{1}) + J_{WW}W\boldsymbol{\Sigma}\mathbf{w}^* + J_{Wx}\boldsymbol{\sigma}, \tag{46}$$

where Σ is the covariance matrix of returns and $\boldsymbol{\sigma}' = (\sigma_{1x}, \ldots, \sigma_{nx})$ is a row vector of the covariances of each of the assets with changes in the state variable. The solution to (46) is

$$\mathbf{w}^* = -\frac{J_W}{WJ_{WW}}\boldsymbol{\Sigma}^{-1}(\boldsymbol{\alpha} - r\mathbf{1}) - \frac{J_{xW}}{WJ_{WW}}\boldsymbol{\Sigma}^{-1}\boldsymbol{\sigma},$$

$$\text{or} \tag{47}$$

$$w_i^* = -\frac{J_W}{WJ_{WW}}\sum_{j=1}^N v_{ij}(\alpha_j - r) - \frac{J_{xW}}{WJ_{WW}}\sum_{j=1}^N v_{ij}\sigma_{jx}.$$

In general, w_i^*/w_j^* is not independent of preferences; however, if we define $D \equiv (-J_W/WJ_{WW})\mathbf{1}'\boldsymbol{\Sigma}^{-1}(\boldsymbol{\alpha} - r\mathbf{1})$ and $H \equiv (-J_{xW}/WJ_{WW})\mathbf{1}'\boldsymbol{\Sigma}^{-1}\boldsymbol{\sigma}$, then we may write (47) as

$$\mathbf{w}^* = D\mathbf{t} + H\mathbf{h}, \quad \mathbf{t} \equiv \frac{\boldsymbol{\Sigma}^{-1}(\boldsymbol{\alpha} - r\mathbf{1})}{\mathbf{1}'\boldsymbol{\Sigma}^{-1}(\boldsymbol{\alpha} - r\mathbf{1})}, \quad \mathbf{h} \equiv \frac{\boldsymbol{\Sigma}^{-1}\boldsymbol{\sigma}}{\mathbf{1}'\boldsymbol{\Sigma}^{-1}\boldsymbol{\sigma}} \tag{48}$$

for $\mathbf{t}$ and $\mathbf{h}$ independent of individual preferences and $\mathbf{1}'\mathbf{d} = \mathbf{1}'\mathbf{h} = 1$. Thus, all investors form their own portfolios by buying "shares" in two risky "mutual funds" $\mathbf{t}$ and $\mathbf{h}$. Note that these two portfolios do not include the riskless asset, which is held separately by each investor for adjusting the risk of his portfolio.

From (48) portfolio $\mathbf{t}$ is identical to the single portfolio in the previous problem. It is the *t*angency portfolio of the frontier hyperbola and the borrowing lending line. As before, it is used to provide optimal diversification. The second portfolio $\mathbf{h}$ is a "*h*edge" portfolio. As shown below the correlation of portfolio $\mathbf{h}$ with the state variable x is the maximum absolute correlation possible for any portfolio formed from this set of risky assets. In this sense it provides the best hedge against changes in the state variable. (Note that the portfolio $\mathbf{t}$ may have any correlation with x.)

The squared correlation coefficient of any portfolio's return with changes in the state variable x is $\rho^2 = (\mathbf{w}'\boldsymbol{\sigma})^2/(\mathbf{w}'\boldsymbol{\Sigma}\mathbf{w})s^2$. The (unconstrained) extrema, $\hat{\mathbf{w}}$, of ρ^2 satisfy

$$\mathbf{0} = \frac{\partial \rho^2}{\partial \mathbf{w}} = 2(\mathbf{w}'\boldsymbol{\Sigma}\mathbf{w})^{-2}s^{-2}[(\mathbf{w}'\boldsymbol{\Sigma}\mathbf{w})(\mathbf{w}'\boldsymbol{\sigma})\boldsymbol{\sigma} - (\mathbf{w}'\boldsymbol{\sigma})^2\boldsymbol{\Sigma}\mathbf{w}]$$

or (49)

$$\hat{\mathbf{w}} = (\hat{\mathbf{w}}'\boldsymbol{\sigma})^{-1}(\hat{\mathbf{w}}'\boldsymbol{\Sigma}\hat{\mathbf{w}})\boldsymbol{\Sigma}^{-1}\boldsymbol{\sigma}.$$

Comparing (49) and (48), we see that $\mathbf{h}$ and $\hat{\mathbf{w}}$ are both proportional to $\boldsymbol{\Sigma}^{-1}\boldsymbol{\sigma}$, so they must represent the same portfolio. Substituting $\hat{\mathbf{w}} = \mathbf{h}$ into (49) confirms this equality despite the fact that we have imposed no constraint on the maximization just performed. Since $\mathbf{h}$ is an unconstrained extremum and $\mathbf{1}'\mathbf{h} = 1$, it follows that $\mathbf{h}$ is a constrained portfolio extremum as well. (The reason we could get away without imposing the constraint is that the correlation coefficient ρ is homogeneous of degree zero in $\mathbf{w}$, so that $\rho(a\mathbf{w}) = \rho(\mathbf{w})$. Thus we are free to normalize $\hat{\mathbf{w}}$ after finding the extremum.) A check of the second-order condition confirms that $\mathbf{h}$ does provide a maximum.

INTERPRETING THE PORTFOLIO HOLDINGS

Portfolios $\mathbf{t}$ and $\mathbf{h}$ are used to reduce fluctuations in consumption over time. To see this, we examine two related portfolio problems, minimizing the variance of the growth rates in wealth and consumption subject to consuming C^* and earning an expected rate of return on the portfolio equal to that on the portfolio optimally chosen, $r + (\boldsymbol{\alpha} - r\mathbf{1})'\mathbf{w}^*$. For the first problem we form the Lagrangian $L \equiv \sigma_W^2 + \lambda(\alpha^* - r - (\boldsymbol{\alpha} - r\mathbf{1})'\mathbf{w})$, where σ_W^2 is given in (5). Differentiating for the risky assets gives

$$\mathbf{0} = \frac{\partial L}{\partial \mathbf{w}} = 2W^2\boldsymbol{\Sigma}\mathbf{w} - \lambda(\boldsymbol{\alpha} - r\mathbf{1}) \tag{50}$$

with solution $\mathbf{w}^{**} = (\lambda/2W^2)\boldsymbol{\Sigma}^{-1}(\boldsymbol{\alpha} - r\mathbf{1})$. $\mathbf{w}^{**}$ is proportional to $\mathbf{t}$ as defined in (48). Thus some linear combination of $\mathbf{t}$ and the riskless asset would represent the best return-risk tradeoff if wealth were the proper criterion for judging. Portfolio $\mathbf{h}$ is not used. This portfolio obviously differs from the optimal portfolio described in (47), (48). The explanation for this difference is obvious. Utility comes only indirectly from wealth. Consumption is the underlying key, so we now consider minimizing its variance.

Optimal consumption depends upon wealth, age, and the state of the world, $C^*(W, x, t)$. Following the same steps as in (42) and (43), we find that

$$\begin{aligned}\Delta C^* &= C_t^*\,\Delta t + C_W^*\,\Delta W + C_x^*\,\Delta x + \tfrac{1}{2}C_{WW}^*\,\Delta W^2 + \tfrac{1}{2}C_{xx}^*\,\Delta x^2 \\ &\quad + C_{xW}^*\,\Delta W\,\Delta x + o(\Delta t^n\,\Delta x^m\,\Delta W^p), \qquad n + m + p \geqslant 3.\end{aligned} \tag{51}$$

From (51), the variance of growth in consumption is

$$\begin{aligned}\sigma_C^2 &= C_W^{*2}\sigma_W^2 + C_x^{*2}s^2 + 2C_W^*C_x^*\,\sigma_{xW} + o(\Delta t) \\ &= C_W^{*2}\,W^2\mathbf{w}'\boldsymbol{\Sigma}\mathbf{w} + C_x^{*2}s^2 + 2C_W^*C_x^*\,W\mathbf{w}'\boldsymbol{\sigma} + o(\Delta t).\end{aligned} \tag{52}$$

Forming the Lagrangian $L \equiv \sigma_C^2 + \lambda(\alpha^* - r - (\boldsymbol{\alpha} - r\mathbf{1})'\mathbf{w})$ and differentiating for the risky assets' portfolio weights give

$$\mathbf{0} = \frac{\partial L}{\partial \mathbf{w}} = 2C_W^{*2}\,W^2\boldsymbol{\Sigma}\mathbf{w} + 2C_W^*C_x^*\,W\boldsymbol{\sigma} - \lambda(\boldsymbol{\alpha} - r\mathbf{1}) \tag{53}$$

with an optimum at

$$\mathbf{w}^{**} = \frac{\lambda}{2W^2C_W^{*2}}\boldsymbol{\Sigma}^{-1}(\boldsymbol{\alpha} - r\mathbf{1}) - \frac{C_x^*}{WC_W^*}\boldsymbol{\Sigma}^{-1}\boldsymbol{\sigma}. \tag{54}$$

Therefore, the set of consumption variance-minimizing portfolios is a linear combination of $\mathbf{t}$, $\mathbf{h}$, and the riskless asset. Furthermore, if we differentiate the envelope condition (11a) (along the optimal consumption path) with respect to W and x, we get

$$U_{CC}\frac{\partial C^*}{\partial W} = J_{WW}, \qquad U_{CC}\frac{\partial C^*}{\partial x} = J_{Wx}. \tag{55}$$

Thus, we can interpret

$$-\frac{J_{Wx}}{J_{WW}W} = -\frac{\partial C^*/\partial x}{(\partial C^*/\partial W)W}$$

and the correspondence between the second terms in (54) and (47) is complete; that is, the consumption variance-minimizing portfolio holds exactly the same amount of **h** as does the investor's optimal portfolio. Furthermore, since the expected returns (and therefore excess returns) on the two portfolios are the same, the holdings of **t** and the riskless asset must also be the same (except in the case when $\mathbf{t}'\boldsymbol{\alpha} = r$; since **t** is the mean-variance tangency portfolio this can be true only in the singular case $\boldsymbol{\alpha} = r\mathbf{1}$).

We now explore what factors influence the hedging behavior of investors in an economy. Investor k's demands for the risky assets were given in (48) as

$$\mathbf{w}^k = D^k\mathbf{d} + H^k\mathbf{h}. \tag{56}$$

Taking a wealth-weighted average of (56) by multiplying by W^k, summing, and dividing by ΣW^k give (in equilibrium) the market portfolio weights as

$$\begin{aligned}\boldsymbol{\mu} &\equiv (\textstyle\sum W^k)^{-1}(\sum \mathbf{w}^k W^k) = (\sum W^k)^{-1}[\mathbf{d}\sum D^k W^k + \mathbf{h}\sum H^k W^k] \\ &\equiv \mathbf{t}D^m + \mathbf{h}H^m.\end{aligned} \tag{57}$$

Individual demand equations can then be rewritten as

$$\mathbf{w}^k = \left(\frac{D^k}{D^m}\right)\boldsymbol{\mu} + \left(H^k - \frac{H^m D^k}{D^m}\right)\mathbf{h}. \tag{58}$$

To simplify this exposition, let us assume that market participants have introduced a financial contract which provides a perfect hedge against changes in x. (With frictionless contracting some investors would always desire to do this except under singular conditions.) We refer to this asset as asset number h. Obviously, it will be the hedging portfolio, so **h** is a vector with a 1 in the hth position and 0's elsewhere. Furthermore, since financial assets are in zero net supply, they cannot be part of the market portfolio. Thus, $\mu_h = 0$ and, from (58),

$$w_h^k = H^k - \frac{H^m D^k}{D^m}. \tag{59}$$

(*Note*: Asset h can be in portfolio **t** even though it is absent from the market.)

The first term of the demand function, H^k, is a measure of individual aversion to changes in x, $-J_{xW}/WJ_{WW}$, multiplied by the technological constant $\mathbf{1}'\mathbf{\Sigma}^{-1}\boldsymbol{\sigma}$. Because asset h is perfectly (positively or negatively) correlated with changes in x, $\boldsymbol{\sigma}$ is the hth column of $\mathbf{\Sigma}$ multiplied by σ_{hx}/σ_h^2, as shown in (60):

$$\begin{aligned}\sigma_{ix} &= \rho_{ix}\sigma_i s = \pm\frac{\rho_{ih}\sigma_i s\sigma_h^2}{\sigma_h^2} \\ &= \sigma_{ih}\left(\pm\frac{s\sigma_h}{\sigma_h^2}\right) = \frac{\sigma_{ih}\sigma_{xh}}{\sigma_h^2}.\end{aligned} \tag{60}$$

The + or − sign in (60) applies as $\rho_{hx} = \pm 1$, respectively. The product of $\mathbf{\Sigma}^{-1}$ and the hth row of $\mathbf{\Sigma}$ is a vector of zeroes with a 1 in the hth position, so $\mathbf{1}'\mathbf{\Sigma}^{-1}\boldsymbol{\sigma} = \sigma_{hx}/\sigma_h^2$. Thus

$$H = \frac{-J_{xW}}{WJ_{WW}}\frac{\sigma_{hx}}{\sigma_h^2}, \qquad \text{sgn}(H) = \text{sgn}(\sigma_{hx}J_{xW}). \tag{61}$$

The "market" factor H^m is the wealth-weighted average of the individual factors H^k.

If the market as a whole is neutral about x ($H^m = 0$), then, for a positive correlation between asset h and x, investor k will have a long (short) demand for asset h if increases in x increase marginal utility of wealth. This hedging behavior increases wealth in states when x is high (low); that is, the portfolio is constructed in an attempt to increase wealth in those states where it has the highest marginal utility. In this way utility losses in one variable tend to be offset by utility gains in the other. For negative correlation between x and asset h, the reverse hedging will occur.

If the market is not neutral about x, then the average aversion to changes in x and individual risk aversion also affect an individual's hedging demands. The expression D^k/D^m is investor k's relative risk tolerance divided by the wealth-weighted average relative risk tolerance of all investors. If all investors are equally risk tolerant, then this ratio is unity, and any individual's hedging demand depends upon the differences between this investor's propensity to hedge and the average propensity. At the other extreme, if each investor has an equal (and positive) propensity to hedge, $H^k = H^m > 0$, then hedging demands depend only upon risk tolerance. Those investors who are more (less) risk tolerant than average will be short (long) the hedge portfolio. That is, it is the investors who are less risk averse than average who go against their natural propensity and supply the asset with which hedging is performed. This is exactly what our intuition about risk aversion would suggest.

EQUILIBRIUM IN THE EXTENDED MODEL

Rewrite (46) as

$$a^k(\boldsymbol{\alpha} - r\mathbf{1}) = \boldsymbol{\Sigma}\mathbf{w}^k W^k - b^k\boldsymbol{\sigma}, \tag{62}$$

where superscripts refer to investors, $a \equiv -J_W/J_{WW}$, and $b \equiv -J_{Wx}/J_{WW}$. Then sum across investors and divide by $\Sigma_k a^k$ to get

$$\boldsymbol{\alpha} - r\mathbf{1} = A\boldsymbol{\Sigma\mu} - B\boldsymbol{\sigma} \quad \text{or} \quad \alpha_i - r = A\sigma_{im} - B\sigma_{ix}, \tag{63}$$

where $A \equiv \Sigma W^k/\Sigma a^k$, $B \equiv \Sigma b^k/\Sigma a^k$, and $\boldsymbol{\mu} \equiv \Sigma \mathbf{w}^k W^k/\Sigma W^k$ is the average investment in each asset across investors. These must be the market weights in equilibrium. Premultiply (63) by $\boldsymbol{\mu}'$ and $\mathbf{h}'$ to get

$$\alpha_m - r = A\sigma_m^2 - B\sigma_{mx}, \qquad \alpha_h - r = A\sigma_{hm} - B\sigma_{hx}. \tag{64}$$

We can now solve (64) for A and B and introduce them back into (63) to derive

$$\begin{aligned} \alpha_i - r &= \frac{\sigma_{im}\sigma_{hx} - \sigma_{ix}\sigma_{mh}}{\sigma_m^2\sigma_{hx} - \sigma_{mx}\sigma_{mh}}(\alpha_m - r) + \frac{\sigma_{ix}\sigma_m^2 - \sigma_{im}\sigma_{mx}}{\sigma_{hx}\sigma_m^2 - \sigma_{mx}\sigma_{mh}}(\alpha_h - r) \\ &= \beta_i^m(x)(\alpha_m - r) + \beta_i^h(x)(\alpha_h - r). \end{aligned} \tag{65}$$

Here the β will be recognized as the multiple regression coefficients of security i's logged return on the logged returns of the market and portfolio h, using x as an instrumental variable for the latter.

Because of the unique construction of portfolio h to have maximum correlation, this expression can be simplified. We can evaluate the vector of covariances (σ_{ih}) by using the definition of $\mathbf{h}$:

$$(\sigma_{ih}) = \boldsymbol{\Sigma}\mathbf{h} = \frac{\boldsymbol{\Sigma\Sigma}^{-1}\boldsymbol{\sigma}}{\mathbf{1}'\boldsymbol{\Sigma}^{-1}\boldsymbol{\sigma}} = \frac{\boldsymbol{\sigma}}{\mathbf{1}'\boldsymbol{\Sigma}^{-1}\boldsymbol{\sigma}}. \tag{66}$$

Thus, $\sigma_{ix} = k\sigma_{ih}$ and

$$\begin{aligned} \beta_i^m(x) &= \frac{\sigma_{im}k\sigma_h^2 - k\sigma_{ih}\sigma_{mh}}{\sigma_m^2 k\sigma_h^2 - k\sigma_{mh}^2} = \beta_i^m, \\ \beta_i^h(x) &= \frac{k\sigma_{ih}\sigma_m^2 - \sigma_{im}k\sigma_{mh}}{k\sigma_h^2\sigma_m^2 - k\sigma_{mh}^2} = \beta_i^h, \end{aligned} \tag{67}$$

which are the ordinary multiple regression coefficients without the instrumental variable, just as if portfolio h provided a perfect hedge. Note in particular that $\sigma_{ih} = 0$ if and only if $\sigma_{ix} = 0$.

If the state variable is uncorrelated with the market, then by (66) $\sigma_{mh} = 0$ as well, and the equilibrium simplifies to

$$\alpha_i - r = \frac{\sigma_{im}}{\sigma_m^2}(\alpha_m - r) + \frac{\sigma_{ih}}{\sigma_h^2}(\alpha_h - r), \tag{68}$$

where the coefficients are now both OLS coefficients from separate regressions. This case is not as special as it may seem because we are free to choose as the state variable in place of x the residuals after "regressing" x on the market. (By regression here we refer to an operation on the population distribution and not a time series regression which would have to be performed on a sample distribution.) The hedge portfolio is, of course, different for this state variable.

In some cases the dual beta equilibrium (65), (68) reduces to the continuous-time equivalent of the single beta (Sharpe–Lintner) CAPM (13). This will be true if x changes deterministically over time, so there is no need to hedge. The single beta CAPM also holds if changes in x are uncorrelated with the return on every asset, so there is no possible hedge. In this latter case, however, we should expect investors to create a financial contract which provided a hedge against x, and the CAPM would not describe its expected return.

If all investors have log utility, then $J_{Wx} = 0$ and no investor desires to hedge so the hedge portfolio has no premium beyond that explained by the CAPM

$$\alpha_h - r = \beta_h(\alpha_m - r) \equiv \frac{\sigma_{hm}}{\sigma_m^2}(\alpha_m - r). \tag{69}$$

Substituting this and (67) into (65) gives

$$\begin{aligned}\alpha_i - r &= \left[(\sigma_{im}\sigma_h^2 - \sigma_{ih}\sigma_{mh}) + \frac{\sigma_{hm}}{\sigma_m^2}(\sigma_{ih}\sigma_m^2 - \sigma_{im}\sigma_{mh})\right]\frac{\alpha_m - r}{\sigma_h^2\sigma_m^2 - \sigma_{mh}^2} \\ &= \frac{\sigma_{im}}{\sigma_m^2}(\alpha_m - r),\end{aligned} \tag{70}$$

which is the single beta CAPM. This is also true if investors' utilities differ, but the net demand for the hedge portfolio is in equilibrium when (69) holds. (*Note*: In this case only the pricing result, not the separation result, of the CAPM obtains.)

Finally, if $\boldsymbol{\alpha} - r\mathbf{1} = b\boldsymbol{\sigma}$, then the portfolios $\mathbf{t}$ and $\mathbf{h}$ are identical, so both must correspond to the market. Separation and the single beta CAPM follow immediately.

CONTINUOUS-TIME MODELS WITH NO RISKLESS ASSET

When no riskless asset is available, most of the development of the problem remains identical. The maximimand in (10) or (44) becomes a

Lagrangian with the addition of the constraint $\lambda(\Sigma_1^n w_i - 1)$, and the sum in the J_W term is over the risky assets $1, \ldots, n$.

The envelope condition still holds and the first-order condition for the portfolio weights is

$$\mathbf{0} = WJ_W\boldsymbol{\alpha} + W^2J_{WW}\boldsymbol{\Sigma}\mathbf{w}^* + WJ_{Wx}\boldsymbol{\sigma} + \lambda\mathbf{1}. \tag{71}$$

The optimal solution is

$$\mathbf{w}^* = -\frac{J_W}{WJ_{WW}}\boldsymbol{\Sigma}^{-1}\boldsymbol{\alpha} - \frac{J_{xW}}{WJ_{WW}}\boldsymbol{\Sigma}^{-1}\boldsymbol{\sigma} - \frac{\lambda\boldsymbol{\Sigma}^{-1}\mathbf{1}}{WJ_W}. \tag{72}$$

The three vectors in (72) can be scaled to represent portfolios. The first resulting portfolio $\mathbf{d} \equiv \boldsymbol{\Sigma}^{-1}\boldsymbol{\alpha}(\mathbf{1}'\boldsymbol{\Sigma}^{-1}\boldsymbol{\alpha})^{-1}$ is the portfolio on the minimum-variance hyperbola which is at the tangency point of a line passing through the origin. This is demonstrated by setting $r = 0$ in the definition of $\mathbf{t}$ in (48). The second portfolio is the hedge portfolio $\mathbf{h}$ as before. The third portfolio $\mathbf{g} \equiv \boldsymbol{\Sigma}^{-1}\mathbf{1}/(\mathbf{1}'\boldsymbol{\Sigma}^{-1}\mathbf{1})$ is the global minimum-variance portfolio. Each investor's optimal portfolio can be constructed as a combination of these three portfolios so three-fund separation still obtains.

Both of the portfolios $\mathbf{d}$ and $\mathbf{g}$ are on the minimum-variance hyperbola, and they are used together by the investors to achieve maximum diversification. As in the single-period problem, any two minimum-variance portfolios can be chosen in place of $\mathbf{d}$ and $\mathbf{g}$ since they span the entire hyperbola. Unlike the single-period problem, however, the market portfolio need not be a combination of $\mathbf{d}$ and $\mathbf{g}$. (This will be true if the state variable x is irrelevant for all investors. In this case two-fund separation obtains. The usual choices for the two portfolios are the market and its associated zero beta portfolio, and the Black version of the CAPM, $\alpha_i = \alpha_z + \beta_i(\alpha_m - \alpha_z)$, describes expected returns.)

When the state variable x does matter, the equilibrium condition must be derived as in the previous section. From (71)

$$a^k\boldsymbol{\alpha} = \boldsymbol{\Sigma}\mathbf{w}^kW^k - b^k\boldsymbol{\sigma} - c^k\mathbf{1}, \tag{73}$$

where a and b are defined as in (62), and $c \equiv -\lambda/WJ_{WW}$. Aggregating across investors gives

$$\boldsymbol{\alpha} = A\boldsymbol{\Sigma}\boldsymbol{\mu} - B\boldsymbol{\sigma} - C\mathbf{1}, \tag{74}$$

where $A \equiv (\Sigma a^k)^{-1}$, $B \equiv A\Sigma b^k$, $C \equiv A\Sigma c^k$. Now we premultiply both sides of (74) by $(\boldsymbol{\mu} - \mathbf{z})'$, $(\mathbf{h} - \mathbf{z})'$, and $\mathbf{z}'$, where $\mathbf{z}$ is the vector of portfolio weights for a zero beta portfolio, giving

$$\begin{aligned} \alpha_m - \alpha_z &= A\sigma_m^2 - B(\sigma_{mx} - \sigma_{zx}), \\ \alpha_h - \alpha_z &= A\sigma_{hm} - B(\sigma_{hx} - \sigma_{zx}), \\ \alpha_z &= -B\sigma_{zx} - C. \end{aligned} \tag{75}$$

Solving (75) for A, B, and C permits us to write (74) as

$$\alpha_i - \alpha_z = \frac{\sigma_{im}(\sigma_{hx} - \sigma_{zx}) - \sigma_{hm}(\sigma_{ix} - \sigma_{zx})}{\sigma_m^2(\sigma_{hx} - \sigma_{zx}) - \sigma_{hm}(\sigma_{mx} - \sigma_{zx})}(\alpha_m - \sigma_z) + \frac{(\sigma_{ix} - \sigma_{zx})\sigma_m^2 - \sigma_{im}(\sigma_{mx} - \sigma_{zx})}{\sigma_m^2(\sigma_{hx} - \sigma_{zx}) - \sigma_{hm}(\sigma_{mx} - \sigma_{zx})}(\alpha_h - \alpha_z). \tag{76}$$

As before, $\sigma_{ix} = k\sigma_{ih}$ and after redefining the state variable it may be assumed that $\sigma_{xm} = \sigma_{hm} = 0$. Thus

$$\alpha_i - \alpha_z = \frac{\sigma_{im}}{\sigma_m^2}(\alpha_m - \alpha_z) + \frac{(\sigma_{ih} - \sigma_{zh})\sigma_m^2 + \sigma_{im}\sigma_{zh}}{\sigma_m^2(\sigma_h^2 - \sigma_{zh})}(\alpha_h - \alpha_z). \tag{77}$$

The first term in (77) is the standard Black CAPM relation. The coefficient of the second term is not an OLS coefficient as in (68), except when σ_{zh} equals zero. Note that different zero beta portfolios will have different expected rates of return if they have different correlations with the hedge portfolio.

STATE-DEPENDENT UTILITY OF CONSUMPTION

In the previous sections the derived utility function had an induced state dependency caused by stochastic shifts in the investment opportunity set. We now examine the portfolio–consumption problem when the direct utility function is state dependent.

If utility of consumption depends upon a single state variable x, which may, but need not, also measure changes in the opportunity set, then the previously derived solution (47) is still correct. Portfolio choices still satisfy the same three-fund separation theorem. The three mutual funds are also the same, but the allocations will typically change. The equilibrium relation in (65) or (76) is also still correct.

The one change that must be made is in the interpretation of the portfolio holdings. With state-dependent direct utility, we have in place of the second result of (55)

$$J_{Wx} = U_{CC}\frac{\partial C^*}{\partial x} + U_{Cx}. \tag{78}$$

Unless $U_{Cx} = 0$ the holdings of portfolio **h** in (54) and (47) are no longer the same; thus, in general, investors do *not* hold consumption variance minimizing portfolios. For state-dependent utility of consumption, optimal portfolios are marginal utility variance-minimizing portfolios.

To demonstrate this result, we must first determine how utility changes over time. Using a Taylor expansion for $\Delta U'$ (we use primes to denote partial derivatives with respect to C and subscripts for other partial derivatives) gives

$$\Delta U' = U'_t\,\Delta t + U''\,\Delta C^* + U'_x\,\Delta x + \tfrac{1}{2}U'''\,\Delta C^2 + \tfrac{1}{2}U'_{xx}\,\Delta x^2 + U''_x\,\Delta C\,\Delta x + o(\Delta t). \tag{79}$$

From (79) and (51)

$$\Delta U' - E[\Delta U'] = U''C^*_W(\Delta W - \Delta W) + (U''C^*_x + U'_x) \times (\Delta x - \Delta z) + o(\sqrt{\Delta t}). \tag{80}$$

The variance of marginal utility is therefore

$$\sigma^2_{U'} = (U''C^*_W)^2\sigma^2_W + 2U''C^*_W(U''C^*_x + U'_x)\sigma_{Wx} + (U''C_x + U'_x)^2\sigma^2_x + o(\Delta t), \tag{81}$$

where

$$\sigma^2_W = \mathbf{w}'\boldsymbol{\Sigma}\mathbf{w}W^2, \qquad \sigma_{Wx} = \mathbf{w}'\boldsymbol{\sigma}W.$$

Forming the Lagrangian $L \equiv \sigma^2_{U'} + \lambda[\alpha^* - (r + \mathbf{w}'(\boldsymbol{\alpha} - r\mathbf{1}))]$ and differentiating for the risky assets gives

$$\mathbf{0} = \frac{\partial L}{\partial \mathbf{w}} = 2(U''C^*_W W)^2\boldsymbol{\Sigma}\mathbf{w} + 2U''C^*_W(U''C^*_x + U'_x)W\boldsymbol{\sigma} - \lambda(\boldsymbol{\alpha} - r\mathbf{1}) \tag{82}$$

with an optimum at

$$\mathbf{w}^{**} = \frac{\lambda}{2(U''C^*_W W)^2}\boldsymbol{\Sigma}^{-1}(\boldsymbol{\alpha} - r\mathbf{1}) - \frac{U''C^*_x + U'_x}{U''C^*_W W}\boldsymbol{\Sigma}^{-1}\boldsymbol{\sigma}. \tag{83}$$

Again we find the variance-minimizing portfolio to be composed of **t**, **h**, and the riskless asset. Using (78) and the first result in (55), we confirm that the holdings of the hedge portfolio in (83) and (47) are the same. As before, the holdings of the other two components in $\mathbf{w}^{**}$ must be identical to those in the optimal portfolio $\mathbf{w}^*$ since expected returns were constrained to be equal.

SOLVING A SPECIFIC PROBLEM

For HARA utility of consumption $U(C, t) = e^{-\rho t}(C - \hat{C})^\gamma/\gamma$, with $\hat{C} \geqslant 0$, the derived utility of wealth function for a single exogenous state variable and (unless $\hat{C} = 0$) a constant interest rate is partially separable and can be written in the form

$$J(W, x, t) = e^{-\rho t} Q(x, t) \frac{[W - \hat{C}(1 - e^{-r(T-t)})/r]^{\gamma}}{\gamma}. \tag{84}$$

Notice that the negative term in brackets is the riskless present value of the investor's future subsistence consumption flow $\hat{C}$. Thus, HARA utility maximizers acts *as if* they first escrowed that amount in the riskless asset and had power utility defined over the remainder of their wealth. The same general result goes through if $\hat{C}$, r, or ρ are deterministic functions of time.

For an investor with power utility, $\hat{C} = 0$, the problem in the previous section reduces to determining $Q(\cdot)$. Substituting (84) into (44) and using $C^* = WQ^{1/(\gamma-1)}$ from the envelope condition, we get

$$\begin{aligned}(1 - \gamma)Q^{\gamma/(\gamma-1)} + Q_t + \left[\gamma \sum_{0}^{N} w_i \alpha_i + \frac{1}{2}\gamma(\gamma - 1)\sum\sum w_i w_j \sigma_{ij} - \rho\right] Q \\ + [\mu + \gamma \sum w_i \sigma_{ix}] Q_x + \frac{1}{2} s^2 Q_{xx} = 0.\end{aligned} \tag{85}$$

By substituting the optimal portfolio weights from (47), Equation (85) becomes

$$\begin{aligned}(1 - \gamma)Q^{\gamma/(\gamma-1)} + Q_t + \left[\gamma r - \rho + \frac{\gamma}{2(1-\gamma)} A_1\right] Q + \left[\mu + \frac{\gamma}{1-\gamma} A_2\right] Q_x \\ + \frac{1}{2}\frac{\gamma}{1-\gamma}\frac{A_3 (Q_x)^2}{Q} + \frac{1}{2} s^2 Q_{xx} = 0,\end{aligned} \tag{86}$$

where

$$\begin{aligned} A_1 &\equiv \sum\sum(\alpha_i - r)v_{ij}(\alpha_j - r) = (\boldsymbol{\alpha} - r\mathbf{1})'\boldsymbol{\Sigma}^{-1}(\boldsymbol{\alpha} - r\mathbf{1}), \\ A_2 &\equiv \sum\sum(\alpha_i - r)v_{ij}\sigma_{jx} = (\boldsymbol{\alpha} - r\mathbf{1})'\boldsymbol{\Sigma}^{-1}\boldsymbol{\sigma}, \\ A_3 &\equiv \sum\sum \sigma_{ix} v_{ij} \sigma_{jx} = \boldsymbol{\sigma}'\boldsymbol{\Sigma}^{-1}\boldsymbol{\sigma}. \end{aligned}$$

In general, (86) will not admit an analytical solution unless A_1, A_2, A_3, r, μ, and s^2 are particularly simple functions of x.

For generalized power utility functions ($\hat{C} \neq 0$) the same steps apply formally once we make the change of variables $c \equiv C - \hat{C}$ and $M \equiv W - \hat{C}(1 - e^{-r(T-t)})/r$. However, in general, any value $c^* > 0$ is a possible solution; hence, to meet the requirement that $C^* > 0$, we required $\hat{C} > 0$. Note, avoiding the mere possibility of the optimal (interior) solution becoming negative when $\hat{C} < 0$ affects the *form* of the solution (84) so that it is no longer of the HARA class.

As a specific example suppose that there is a single risky asset. Its expected rate of return, α, is equal to the interest rate, and its variance is σ^2. The interest rate r, which is changing over time, is the state variable. The parameters of its movement, μ and s, are constant with the former zero; that is, the interest rate is not expected to change. Changes in the interest rate are perfectly negatively correlated with returns on the risky asset. This example is the continuous-time equivalent of the one in Chapter 11.

Before solving this problem explicitly, note that the risky asset provides a perfect hedge against changes in the state variable. This, however, is *all* that it does. It has no risk premium while having risk. In a single-period model any risk-averse investor would avoid this asset entirely. As seen in a similar problem in Chapter 11, this is not the case here. There is a hedging demand for this asset.

To solve this problem, we first determine the constants in (86):

$$A_1 = \frac{(\alpha - r)^2}{\sigma^2} = 0, \quad A_2 = \frac{(\alpha - r)(-s\sigma)}{\sigma^2} = 0, \quad A_3 = \frac{(-s\sigma)^2}{\sigma^2} = s^2. \tag{87}$$

Assume that the investor consumes only at time T and has a power utility function $U(C) = C^\gamma/\gamma$. Since there is consumption only at time T, his rate of time preference, ρ, can be set to zero arbitrarily. Substituting (87) into (86) and noting that the lead term is also zero, since there is no consumption before time T, we get

$$Q_t + \gamma r Q + \frac{1}{2}\frac{\gamma}{1-\gamma}s^2\frac{Q_r^2}{Q} + \frac{1}{2}s^2 Q_{rr} = 0. \tag{88}$$

The boundary condition is $Q(r, T) = 1$.

A method for solving this equation is discussed in Chapter 18 where a very similar equation is handled. The solution is

$$Q(r, t) = \exp\left[\gamma r(T - t) + \frac{1}{6}s^2\gamma^2\left(\frac{1}{1-\gamma}\right)(T - t)^3\right]. \tag{89}$$

Relevant partial derivatives are $J_W = QW^{\gamma-1}$, $J_{WW} = (\gamma - 1)QW^{\gamma-2}$, $J_r = (T - t)QW^\gamma$, and $J_{Wr} = \gamma(T - t)QW^{\gamma-1}$. From (47) the optimal holding of the risky asset by this investor is therefore

$$w^* = \frac{-J_{rW}}{WJ_{WW}}\frac{-s\sigma}{\sigma^2} = -\frac{\gamma(T-t)}{1-\gamma}\frac{s}{\sigma}. \tag{90}$$

As in Chapter 11, we see that an investor whose utility function shows more risk tolerance than log utility will have a negative demand for the risky asset. Investors who are more risk averse will have a positive demand.

Regardless of sign, the investor's demand for the risky asset is proportional to s, the standard deviation of the state variable, and inversely proportional to σ, the standard deviation of the risky asset's return. These are expected results. The higher is s the more risk is there to hedge, and the higher is σ the more risk does any particular holding of the risky asset remove.

Note also that as time passes and the date for consumption approaches, the hedging demand grows smaller in absolute value. Again this behavior should be expected. The investor is not directly concerned about the interest rate. His worry is only about how much wealth he can accumulate. As time passes, he becomes less concerned about future levels of the interest rate because there is a shorter remaining time during which he will invest. In the limit as $t \to T$, the demand for the risky asset goes to zero, which is the demand of a single-period investor.

A partial understanding of these results comes from considering the type of risky asset that fits the description of this model. One such asset is a zero coupon bond maturing at time T. (When interest rates rise, the prices of long-term bonds fall or rise less than was expected. Furthermore, as shown in Chapter 18, when there is a single state variable governing interest rate changes, the correlation is -1.) Over the entire investment period this asset is riskless. It might seem natural that an investor who is more risk averse (higher γ) would wish to invest a higher percentage of his wealth in this "safe" asset. This explanation cannot be complete, however, because it is not clear why any risk-averse investor would wish to short such an asset.

The substitution and income effect explanation as given in Chapter 11 cannot be used here because there is no consumption until time T, but similar reasoning does apply. First note that $J_r = (T - t)QW^{\gamma} > 0$; that is, an increase in the interest rate is beneficial to any investor. This result should be obvious. If the interest rate increased and investors did not alter their portfolios they would reach time T with more wealth and higher utility. Therefore, the optimal response to an increase in the interest rate cannot make any investor worse off.

In the simple model here investors do not alter their portfolios when the interest rate changes, as can be seen in (90). Nevertheless, the level of the interest rate does affect their utility, and the fact that the interest rate *can* change causes investors to hold different portfolios than they otherwise would. This can be seen in the effect of an interest rate increase on marginal utility. The partial derivative $\partial J_W/\partial r = \gamma(T - t)QW^{\gamma-1}$ has the same sign as γ. Thus, in certain respects, for γ positive (negative), an increase (decrease) in the interest rate is like a decrease in wealth, which also increases marginal utility.

An explanation of this last statement requires the understanding that interest rate risk is not like the risk of assets in portfolios. Asset risk is due to the uncertainty about contemporaneous returns. It is measured by covariances, which add. Interest rate risk, on the other hand, is uncertainty over time. An unexpected change in the interest rate now affects all future returns, so interest rate risk "compounds" over time.

To illustrate this for the given model, note that with no consumption the derived utility function is just the expectation of $\tilde{W}_T^\gamma/\gamma$. The expected rate of return on the portfolio is always r_t since both assets have this expected return. Terminal wealth is therefore $\tilde{W}_T = W_t \exp[r_t(T - t) + \tilde{\varepsilon}_t]$. The random variable $\tilde{\varepsilon}_t$ captures effects of both future interest rate changes and the unanticipated portion of the return on the risky asset; however, (for this simple problem) its distribution is independent of the level of wealth and the interest rate. (Note also that $E[\tilde{\varepsilon}] \neq 0$.) This is what gives a derived utility function of the form verified in (89), namely,

$$J(W, r, t) = f(t)(W_t \exp[r_t(T - t)])^\gamma/\gamma.$$

At time t an investor is concerned about two outcomes at time $t + \Delta t$: the level of wealth and the interest rate. To study the latter risk, we shall consider a sequential resolution of the two components of uncertainty. Consider an investor who at time t is faced with a one-time risk about the interest rate. Currently, the investor does not know what the interest rate will be. In a moment this uncertainty will be resolved, resulting in an interest rate of $\tilde{r} \equiv r + \tilde{\eta}$, where $E[\tilde{\eta}] = 0$ (so that r is the expected level). This gamble about the current interest rate is to be resolved immediately (i.e., before the portfolio must be formed at time t.) We denote by $J(W, \tilde{r}, t)$ and $J(W, r, t)$, respectively, the utility before and after this static uncertainty is resolved. Then

$$\begin{aligned} J(W, \tilde{r}, t) &= f(t) E\left[\frac{(W \exp[(r + \tilde{\eta})(T - t)])^\gamma}{\gamma}\right] \\ &= f(t)\left(\frac{W^\gamma}{\gamma}\right) E(\exp[\gamma(r + \tilde{\eta})(T - t)]) \qquad (91) \\ &> f(t)\left(\frac{W^\gamma}{\gamma}\right) \exp(\gamma E[r + \tilde{\eta}](T - t)) = J(W, r, t). \end{aligned}$$

The inequality follows since $\exp(\gamma x)$ is a strictly convex function of x for $\gamma > 0$. The final equality follows since $E[\tilde{\eta}] = 0$. In this case interest rate is actually liked even though the investor is risk averse in the usual sense. For $\gamma < 0$ the inequality is reversed, and interest rate risk is disliked.

The same basic analysis remains valid even when the uncertainty about the interest rate and the portfolio's return are resolved simultaneously. For investors whose relative risk aversion is less than unity uncertainty about the interest rate is actually beneficial.

A NOMINAL EQUILIBRIUM

Strictly speaking, the analysis performed in this chapter should be done in real, rather than nominal, terms because it is the real level of consumption which enters an investor's utility function. However, most tests of the model have been conducted in nominal terms due to measurement problems. Unfortunately, the equilibrium given in (13) or (65) will not hold in general for nominal returns. A nonzero expected rate of inflation will impose no problems since it will increase all expected nominal returns equally, and the equilibrium is given in excess return form. The difficulty arises because real and nominal covariances may be differentially affected by *unanticipated* inflation.

Suppose real returns are as given in (1) and that the price level moves according to $\Delta\pi/\pi = \mu\,\Delta t + s\tilde{e}_\pi\sqrt{\Delta t} + o(\Delta t)$. Then the nominal price of any asset $\hat{P} \equiv P\pi$ will evolve according to

$$\Delta\hat{P} = \pi\,\Delta P + P\,\Delta\pi + \Delta P\,\Delta\pi + o(\Delta t). \tag{92}$$

The nominal return is then

$$\begin{aligned}\frac{\Delta\hat{P}}{\hat{P}} &= \frac{\Delta P}{P} + \frac{\Delta\pi}{\pi} + \frac{\Delta P}{P}\frac{\Delta\pi}{\pi} + o(\Delta t)\\ &= (\alpha + \mu + \rho\sigma s)\,\Delta t + (\sigma\tilde{e}_p + s\tilde{e}_\pi)\sqrt{\Delta t} + o(\Delta t)\\ &\equiv \hat{\alpha}\,\Delta t + \hat{\sigma}\hat{e}\sqrt{\Delta t} + o(\Delta t).\end{aligned} \tag{93}$$

From (93) the asset's nominal dynamics can be expressed in real quantities as

$$\hat{\alpha}_i = \alpha_i + \mu + \sigma_{i\pi} + \frac{o(\Delta t)}{\Delta t}, \tag{94a}$$

$$\hat{\sigma}_i^2 = \sigma_i^2 + 2\sigma_{i\pi} + s^2 + \frac{o(\Delta t)}{\Delta t}, \tag{94b}$$

$$\hat{\sigma}_{im} = \sigma_{im} + \sigma_{i\pi} + \sigma_{m\pi} + s^2 + \frac{o(\Delta t)}{\Delta t}, \tag{94c}$$

$$\hat{\sigma}_{i\pi} = \sigma_{i\pi} + s^2 + \frac{o(\Delta t)}{\Delta t}. \tag{94d}$$

Alternatively, solving (94d) for the real covariance, we can write the real return dynamics by using nominal quantities as

$$\alpha_i = \hat{\alpha}_i - \mu + s^2 - \hat{\sigma}_{i\pi} + \frac{o(\Delta t)}{\Delta t}, \tag{95a}$$

$$\sigma_i^2 = \hat{\sigma}_i^2 - 2\hat{\sigma}_{i\pi} + s^2 + \frac{o(\Delta t)}{\Delta t}, \tag{95b}$$

$$\sigma_{im} = \hat{\sigma}_{im} - \hat{\sigma}_{i\pi} - \hat{\sigma}_{m\pi} + s^2 + \frac{o(\Delta t)}{\Delta \mathrm{t}}. \tag{95c}$$

Notice the apparent asymmetry in these results, with s^2 appearing to increase both the nominal and real variances and covariances.

Since the real investment opportunities are stationary over time, equilibrium will be given by a modified form of (13), namely, $\alpha_i - \alpha_z = \beta_i(\alpha_m - \alpha_z)$, where z denotes a real zero beta portfolio. This relation holds for all securities, including the nominal riskless asset, so solving for α_z in terms of α_0 gives $\alpha_z = (1 - \beta_0)^{-1}(\alpha_0 - \beta_0\alpha_m)$, and equilibrium is then

$$\begin{aligned}\alpha_i &= \frac{\alpha_0 - \beta_0\alpha_m}{1 - \beta_0}(1 - \beta_i) + \beta_i\alpha_m \\ &= (\alpha_0 - \alpha_m)\frac{1 - \beta_i}{1 - \beta_0} + \alpha_m.\end{aligned} \tag{96}$$

Recall that the β's are measured in real terms. To introduce nominal betas, we use (95) to rewrite

$$\begin{aligned}\frac{1 - \beta_i}{1 - \beta_0} &= \frac{\sigma_m^2 - \sigma_{im}}{\sigma_m^2 - \sigma_{0m}} \\ &= \frac{\hat{\sigma}_m^2 - 2\hat{\sigma}_{m\pi} + s^2 - \hat{\sigma}_{im} + \hat{\sigma}_{i\pi} + \hat{\sigma}_{m\pi} - s^2}{\hat{\sigma}_m^2 - 2\hat{\sigma}_{m\pi} + s^2 + \hat{\sigma}_{m\pi} - s^2} \\ &= \frac{\hat{\sigma}_m^2 - \hat{\sigma}_{m\pi} - \hat{\sigma}_{im} + \hat{\sigma}_{i\pi}}{\hat{\sigma}_m^2 - \hat{\sigma}_{m\pi}} = 1 - \frac{\hat{\sigma}_{im} - \hat{\sigma}_{i\pi}}{\hat{\sigma}_m^2 - \hat{\sigma}_{m\pi}}.\end{aligned} \tag{97}$$

Combining (95a), (96) and (97) yields the nominal equilibrium

$$\hat{\alpha}_i = r + \hat{\sigma}_{i\pi} + \frac{\hat{\sigma}_{im} - \hat{\sigma}_{i\pi}}{\hat{\sigma}_m^2 - \hat{\sigma}_{m\pi}}(\hat{\alpha}_m - \hat{\sigma}_{m\pi} - r). \tag{98}$$

If stocks provide a negligible hedge against inflation. $\hat{\sigma}_{i\pi} = 0$, then (98) reduces to the desired nominal equilibrium

$$\hat{\alpha}_i = r + \hat{\beta}_i(\hat{\alpha}_m - r). \tag{99}$$

At the other extreme, if stocks are a perfect inflation hedge, $\sigma_{i\pi} = 0$, then from (94d) $\hat{\sigma}_{i\pi} = s^2$, and the nominal equilibrium is

$$\hat{\alpha}_i = r + \hat{\beta}_i(\hat{\alpha}_m - r) + \frac{s^2}{\hat{\sigma}_m^2 - s^2}(\hat{\beta}_i - 1)(\hat{\alpha}_m - r - \hat{\sigma}_m^2), \tag{100}$$

which differs from the "expected" result by the last premium term.

The expected real rate of return on the nominal risk-free asset is $\alpha_0 = \alpha_z + \beta_0(\alpha_m - \alpha_z)$. Using (95a), (95c), and (94d), we get

$$r - \mu + s^2 = \alpha_z + \frac{-\hat{\sigma}_{m\pi} + s^2}{\sigma_m^2}(\alpha_m - \alpha_z) = \alpha_z. \tag{101}$$

The last equality in (101) is obtained by noting that $\hat{\sigma}_{i\pi} = s^2$ for all assets, including, therefore, the market. Substituting for $\hat{\alpha}_m$ from (94a), $\hat{\sigma}_m^2$ from (94b), and r from (101) into the premium in (100) gives

$$\begin{aligned} \hat{\alpha}_i - r - \beta_i(\hat{\alpha}_m - r) &= \frac{s^2}{\hat{\sigma}_m^2 - s^2}(\beta_i - 1)(\alpha_m - \alpha_z - \hat{\sigma}_m^2 + s^2) \\ &= s^2(\beta_i - 1)\left(\frac{\alpha_m - \alpha_z}{\sigma_m^2} - 1\right) \\ &= s^2(1 - \beta_i)(1 - R_m), \end{aligned} \tag{102}$$

where R_m is the relative risk aversion of the "market."

Equation (102) implies that if the market is more (less) risk averse than logarithmic, then high (low) beta stocks have positive premiums (in nominal terms). Thus, this model is consistent with the Black–Jensen–Scholes "zero beta" effect if investors have risk aversion less than unity.

14

The Pricing of Options

Options are examples of derivative securities or contingent claims. The value of an option depends on the prices of one or more other assets and the contractual right of its owner to take certain actions under specified conditions. The two most common types of options are calls, which give the owner the right to purchase the underlying asset, and puts, which confer the right to sell. The basic ideas developed here, however, can also be used to value more complex option-like securities such as callable or convertible bonds. These extensions are covered in Chapters 17–19. Here we shall develop the basic results using only puts and calls.

In addition to the underlying asset, each put or call option must specify two other items to completely describe the contract: the expiration date and the exercise or striking price. With a call the underlying asset can be acquired upon the payment of the exercise price; with a put the asset can be sold for the exercise price.

Options come in two varieties. American options can be exercised at any time on or before the expiration date. The so-called European options can be exercised only on the expiration date. This terminology is not quite accurate. Although American options are traded in the United States and Canada (and now Europe), the standard (theoretical) European option is not actually traded in Europe, or anywhere else, although it is similar to the French prime contract in certain respects.

DISTRIBUTION AND PREFERENCE-FREE RESTRICTIONS ON OPTION PRICES

Let $F(S, t; T, X)$, $f(S, t; T, X)$, $G(S, t; T, X)$, and $g(S, t; T, X)$ denote the values at time t of American and European calls and American and European puts with expiration date T and exercise price $X \geqslant 0$ written on an asset (stock) with a current or spot price of S. As always, we assume that both the stock and the option trade in perfect markets with no taxes or transactions costs.

For any type of option its value derives solely from the net proceeds received upon exercise. For a European option, exercise can occur only at the maturity date T. At that time the owner of a call option has to decide between paying X and receiving one share of stock worth S_T or letting the call expire unexercised. Clearly, the call will be exercised if $S_T > X$. If $S_T < X$, the option will be allowed to expire. If $S_T = X$, then either action may be taken with each giving proceeds of exactly zero. Note that in a perfect market the price originally paid for the option is a sunk cost and does not affect the decision to exercise in any way. With capital gains taxes or other frictions, the optimal exercise policy might deviate from the simple rule give here.

For an American call option the problem is more difficult. The same decision will be made at maturity. In addition, exercise can also take place at any time prior to maturity. No exercise will occur when $S_t < X$. However, an investor will not necessarily exercise his American call as soon as $S_t > X$ because the value embodied in waiting may be worth more than the immediate profit.

For puts similar reasoning applies. At maturity puts will be exercised if $S_T < X$. American puts might be exercised prior to maturity, but only when $S_t < X$.

It is assumed throughout this chapter that the stock has limited liability. This implies (among other things) that $S_t = 0$ if and only if $\tilde{S}_T \equiv 0$ for all $T > t$. The options also have limited liability to the owner, but not the writer (short party), by construction since the owner can choose not to exercise and throw the option away.

Propositions 1–7 are very basic statements which depend only on the assumption that investors prefer more to less and therefore will permit the existence of no dominated securities. The proof, or intuition, of each proposition is also given.

PROPOSITION 1

$$F(\cdot) \geqslant 0,\ G(\cdot) \geqslant 0,\ f(\cdot) \geqslant 0,\ g(\cdot) \geqslant 0.$$

PROPOSITION 2

$$F(S, T; T, X) = f(S, T; T, X) = \text{Max}(S - X, 0),$$
$$G(S, T; T, X) = g(S, T; T, X) = \text{Max}(X - S, 0).$$

PROPOSITION 3

$$F(S, t; T, X) \geqslant S - X, \qquad G(S, t; T, X) \geqslant X - S.$$

PROPOSITION 4 *For* $T_2 > T_1$,

$$F(\cdot; T_2) \geqslant F(\cdot; T_1) \quad \textit{and} \quad G(\cdot; T_2) \geqslant G(\cdot; T_1).$$

PROPOSITION 5 $F(\cdot) \geqslant f(\cdot)$ *and* $G(\cdot) \geqslant g(\cdot)$.

PROPOSITION 6 *For* $X_1 > X_2$,

$$F(\cdot;\, X_1) \leqslant F(\cdot;\, X_2) \quad \textit{and} \quad f(\cdot;\, X_1) \leqslant f(\cdot;\, X_2),$$

$$G(\cdot;\, X_1) \geqslant G(\cdot;\, X_2) \quad \textit{and} \quad g(\cdot;\, X_1) \geqslant g(\cdot;\, X_2).$$

PROPOSITION 7 $S \equiv F(S, t; \infty, 0) \geqslant F(S, t; T, X) \geqslant f(S, t; T, X)$.

PROPOSITION 8 $f(0, \cdot) = F(0, \cdot) = 0$.

Proposition 1 merely restates the limited liability of option contracts. Since the owners of the options have a choice about exercising, they need never commit additional funds to their positions (beyond the initial payment).

Proposition 2 states that at maturity the option will be exercised if it has a positive *intrinsic value* (defined as $S - X$ for calls and $X - S$ for puts); otherwise it will be discarded unused. Proposition 3 gives the no arbitrage condition that American options must sell for at least their "intrinsic value," their value when exercised, or an immediate profit could be made by purchasing the option and exercising. This need not hold for European options since they cannot be exercised prior to maturity, making this arbitrage unavailable.

Propositions 4 and 5 follow from the dominance argument that additional rights cannot have negative value. In Proposition 4 the right to exercise during (T_1, T_2) is considered. In Proposition 5 it is the right to exercise strictly before the expiration date that is considered.

Proposition 6 states that calls (puts) are nonincreasing (nondecreasing) functions of the exercise price. When applied to European options this is a special case of Proposition 9. For both Amerian and European options it can be generally proved with a straightforward dominance argument. Whenever the first call is exercised for a profit of $\tilde{S} - X_1$, the second call could be exercised for a strictly greater profit of $\tilde{S} - X_2$.

Proposition 7 follows directly from Propositions 4 and 6 (first inequality) and Proposition 5 (second inequality). Proposition 8 follows from Proposition 7 and the limited liability of long positions in options. Propositions 7 and 8 are the only ones that have depended on the assumptions that $X \geqslant 0$ and the stock has limited liability.

Figure 14.1 illustrates these propositions. The numerical label in each region refers to the number of the proposition which precludes the call option price from being in that range.

The next set of propositions deals specifically with European options. Again the results depend only on the absence of arbitrage opportunities. In Chapter 2 it was demonstrated that the absence of arbitrage is equivalent to the existence of a set of positive state prices which support all assets' values. For our current purposes we need distinguish only among

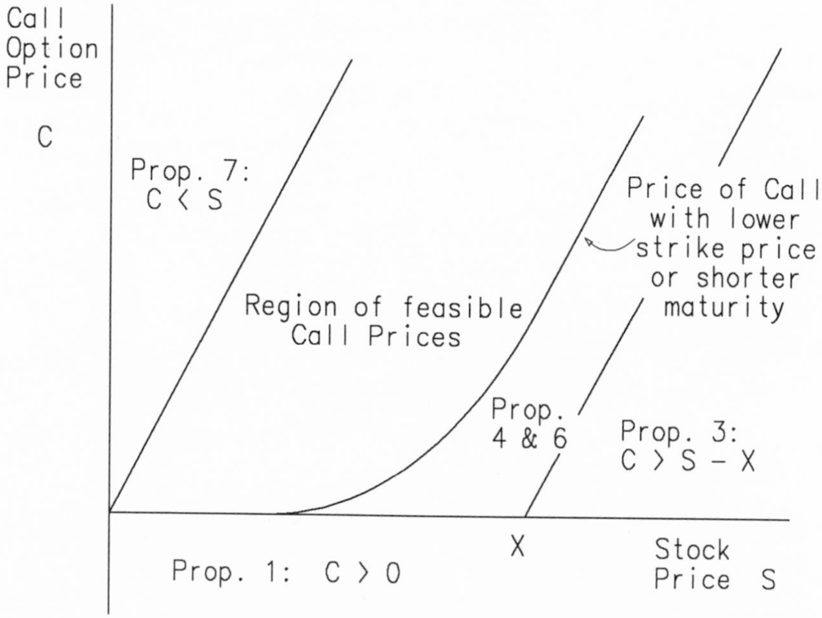

Figure 14.1 Restrictions on Option Values

metastates (unions of states) in which the asset underlying the option has distinct values. For simplicity we shall refer to these metastates simply as states for the remainder of the chapter.

We assume that these states are ordered in increasing value. Let p_s be the current value of a pure state security which pays one dollar in the state when $\tilde{S}_T = s$. Also define $P(t, T)$ as the present value of one dollar for sure at time T. We assume that the sure rate of interest is always positive, so that $P(t, T) < 1$ for $t < T$. Then

$$P(t, T) = \sum p_s, \tag{1a}$$

$$f(S_t, t; T, X) = \sum p_s \operatorname{Max}(s - X, 0) = \sum_{s \geq X} p_s(s - X). \tag{1b}$$

We give two proofs of each of the next three propositions and demonstrate this duality by using these state prices and actually constructing the arbitrage portfolios.

PROPOSITION 9 *If the stock has no distributions (dividends) between t and T, then $f(S, t; T, X) \geq S - XP(t, T)$.*

Proof.

$$f(\cdot) = \sum p_s \operatorname{Max}(s - X, 0) \geq \sum p_s(s - X) = \sum p_s s - X \sum p_s. \tag{2}$$

The inequality follows since the terms which are included in the second sum and excluded from the first are nonpositive. If the stock pays no dividends, then $S = \Sigma p_s s$, giving, along with (1a), the desired result. Q.E.D.

PROPOSTION 10 *For* $X_2 > X_1$,

$$f(\cdot, X_1) - f(\cdot, X_2) \leqslant P(t, T)(X_2 - X_1).$$

Proof.

$$\begin{aligned} f(\cdot, X_1) - f(\cdot, X_2) &= \sum p_s(\mathrm{Max}(s - X_1, 0) - \mathrm{Max}(x - X_2, 0)) \\ &= \sum_{x \geqslant X_1} p_s(X_2 - X_1) \leqslant P(t, T)(X_2 - X_1). \end{aligned} \tag{3}$$

Q.E.D.

PROPOSITION 11 *A call option price is a convex function of the exercise price; that is, for* $X_1 > X_2 > X_3$,

$$f(\cdot, X_2) \leqslant \lambda f(\cdot, X_1) + (1 - \lambda)f(\cdot, X_3),$$

where $\lambda \equiv (X_3 - X_2)/(X_3 - X_1)$.

Proof. Since $\mathrm{Max}(s - X, 0)$ is convex in X, so is the positive linear sum $\Sigma p_s \mathrm{Max}(s - X, 0)$. Specifically,

$$\begin{aligned} &\lambda f(\cdot, X_1) + (1 - \lambda)f(\cdot, X_3) - f(\cdot, X_2) \\ &\quad = \sum p_s(\lambda \mathrm{Max}(s - \mathrm{X}_1, 0) + (1 - \lambda)\mathrm{Max}(x - X_3, 0) - \mathrm{Max}(s - X_2, 0)) \\ &\quad = \sum_{X_1 \leqslant s \leqslant X_2} p_s \lambda(s - X_1) + \sum_{X_2 \leqslant s \leqslant X_3} p_s(\lambda s - \lambda X_1 - s + X_2) \geqslant 0. \end{aligned} \tag{4}$$

The first sum clearly has only positive terms. The second sum also has only positive terms; since $\lambda < 1$, the summand is decreasing in s, so the smallest term is zero when $s = X_3$. Q.E.D.

PROPOSITION 12 *A portfolio of long positions in simultaneously maturing options is worth at least as much as option on the portfolio of the same number of shares of each of the underlying stocks; that is, for* $n_i > 0$,

$$\sum n_i f_i(S_i, t; T, X_i) \geqslant f(\sum n_i S_i, t; T, \sum n_i X_i).$$

Proof. We show the proof for two assets. The proof for more follows by induction. Let n and m be the number of shares and options of the two stocks. Let the state (s, σ) denote the times when $S_{T1} = s$ and $S_{T2} = \sigma$, and let $p_{s\sigma}$ be the state price for this state. Then

$$nf_1 + mf_2 = n\sum_{\sigma} \sum_{s > X_1} p_{s\sigma}(s - X_1) + m\sum_{s} \sum_{\sigma > X_2} p_{s\sigma}(\sigma - X_2)$$

$$
\begin{aligned}
&= \sum_A p_{s\sigma}(ns - nX_1 + m\sigma - mX_2) + \sum_B p_{s\sigma} n(s - X_1) \\
&\quad + \sum_C p_{s\sigma} m(\sigma - X_2) \qquad (5) \\
&= f(nS_1 + mS_2, t; T, nX_1 + mX_2) + \text{nonnegative terms.}
\end{aligned}
$$

A denotes the set of states when $ns + m\sigma > nX_1 + mX_2$; B denotes the set of states excluding those in A when $s > X_1$; C denotes the set of states not in A when $\sigma > X_2$. Note that the intersection of sets B and C is empty. The sums over these sets include only nonnegative terms, so ignoring them gives the desired result. Q.E.D.

The intuition for the result in Proposition 12 again depends on the necessity that a free right cannot have negative value. An option on a portfolio is the same as a portfolio of options which all must be exercised simultaneously. With a portfolio of options the investor has the additional right of separate exercises.

The alternative proofs of these propositions consist of constructing one portfolio that would dominate another if the proposition were false. For Proposition 9 we compare owning the stock to owning the option plus a loan promising X dollars:

Final Outcomes	Initial investment S_t	$f + XP(t, T)$
$S_T < X$	S_T	X
$S_T \geq X$	S_T	S_T

The portfolio in the last column always has at least as great a final value, so it must have at least as large an initial value. If $S_T < X$ is possible, then $S_t < f(\cdot) + XP(t, T)$.

For Proposition 10 a vertical option spread is compared to a loan promising $X_2 - X_1$ dollars:

Final Outcomes	Initial investment $f(\cdot, X_1) - f(\cdot, X_2)$	$P(t, T)(X_2 - X_1)$
$S_T < X_1$	0	$X_2 - X_1$
$X_1 \leq S_T < X_2$	$S_T - X_1$	$X_2 - X_1$
$X_2 \leq S_T$	$X_2 - X_1$	$X_2 - X_1$

Again the second column of payoffs is never less than the first and is bigger, except when $X_2 \leq S_T$.

For Proposition 11 we compare the single option f_2 to the portfolio $\lambda f_1 + (1 - \lambda) f_3$:

Final Outcomes	Initial investment f_2	$\lambda f_1 + (1 - \lambda)f_3$
$S \leqslant X_1$	0	0
$X_1 < S_T \leqslant X_2$	0	$\lambda(S_T - X_1)$
$X_2 < S_T \leqslant X_3$	$S_T - X_2$	$\lambda(S_T - X_1)$
$X_3 < S_T$	$S_T - X_2$	$S_T - X_2$

Again the portfolio in the last column is never less valuable and is more valuable whenever $X_1 < S_T < X_3$, so it must have a higher initial value if this outcome is possible.

A similar construction applies to Proposition 12; however, the resulting table is cumbersome. The two portfolios to be compared are a portfolio of options and the corresponding option on the portfolio of stocks. The former is worth more in states within the sets B and C as described before.

The put–call parity theorem can also be proved in a similar fashion.

PROPOSITION 13 *(The Put–Call Parity Relation)*

$$g(S, t; T, X) = f(S, t; T, X) - S + XP(t, T).$$

Proof. The payoff on the portfolio which is long one call and the lending and short one share of the stock is $\text{Max}(S - X, 0) - S + X = \text{Max}(X - S, 0)$. This is also the payoff on a put, so the two must have the same current value. Q.E.D.

Proposition 13 can be used to prove propositions similar to 11 and 12 for European puts on stocks with no payouts (dividends). These propositions are stated without proof.

PROPOSITION 14 *A put option price is a convex function of X.*

PROPOSITION 15 *A long portfolio of put options is worth at least as much as a put option on the portfolio of underlying stocks.*

Similarly, applying the put–call parity theorem to Propositions 9 and 10, we derive the following: (i) $g(\cdot) \geqslant 0$, and (ii) put option prices are nondecreasing in the exercise price, respectively. These, of course, are just the limited liability of puts and Proposition 6. In other words, third proofs of Proposition 9 and 10 start with the limited liability of puts or Proposition 6, respectively, and apply the put–call parity theorem.

Propositions 9–15 apply to European options. For these options the time path of the stock's price is not a relevant consideration for the basic constraints just outlined. Neither does the time path of the stock price affect the value of these options. Only the terminal value of the stock is relevant. With American options this need not be the case. Interim values of the stock may be important because they can affect the decision to exercise prior to the option's expiration.

PROPOSITION 16 *For a stock paying no dividends* $F(S, t; T, x) \geqslant S - XP(t, T)$. *In this case exercise of the American call will never occur prior to maturity, and* $F(\cdot) \equiv f(\cdot)$.

Proof. From Propositions 5 and 9, $F \geqslant f \geqslant S - XP(t, T)$. Furthermore, since $P(\cdot) < 1$ for $t < T$, $F > S - X$, which is the option's value when exercised. Since the option is always worth more "alive" than when exercised, exercise will never occur prior to maturity. Finally, since the extra right of the American call is never used, the American call is worth no more than its European counterpart. Q.E.D.

If the stock pays dividends, then exercise of a call prior to maturity may be optimal, since otherwise any dividend will not be received. This problem is discussed in more detail in Chapter 17.

The corresponding theorem about American puts is not true. In general, the right to exercise early has positive value. To illustrate this, suppose that the stock price has dropped to a point where $S_t < X - XP(t, T)$. In this case the value of immediate exercise, $X - S$ is greater than the riskless present value of the maximum proceeds from exercise at maturity, $P(t, T)X$. Therefore, waiting until expiration cannot be optimal.

For European puts and calls with the same striking prices, the optimal exercise strategies are exact complements. At maturity one and only one of the two will be exercised. (If the options are just at-the-money, $S_T = X$, then both may be exercised at a zero value.) For American puts and calls the optimal exercise strategies are not exact complements. The difference in the exercise strategies for American options means that the put–call parity theorem is not valid. A related result does hold.

PROPOSITION 17 *(Put–Call Relation for American Options)*

$$G(T, t; T, X) \geqslant F(S, t; T, X) - S + XP(t, T).$$

Proof. If the stock pays no dividends, then $G(\cdot) \geqslant g(\cdot)$ and $F(\cdot) = f(\cdot)$ by Propositions 5 and 16. The relation given then follows from the put–call parity relation for European options. If the stock does pay dividends, it may pay to exercise the call option prior to its maturity. If it is exercised at time τ, the portfolio is worth $S - X - S + XP(\tau, T) < 0$, while the put must have a positive value. If the call is not exercised prior to its maturity, then the portfolio and the put will have the same values as in the proof of Proposition 13. Q.E.D.

One proposition which has not been derived here is that a call (put) option's value be an increasing (decreasing), convex function of the underlying stock price. These properties probably appear to be eminently reasonable, perhaps in the first case even "obvious." Nevertheless, these comparative statics results do not appy in all cases.

To illustrate this, consider the following economy. If the price of the asset on which the option is based is 50, then after one period the price will change to either 100 or 0. If the price is 60, then after one period the price will change to either 70 or 50. In both cases the supporting prices of the state with the increased and decreased values are each equal to $\frac{1}{2}$. This is a valid economy since $50 = .5 \times 100 + .5 \times 0$ and $60 = .5 \times 70 + .5 \times 50$.

Now consider a call option with an exercise price of 60. If the stock price is 50, then it is worth

$$f(50; 60) = .5 \times (100 - 60) + .5 \times 0 = 20. \tag{6}$$

If the stock price is 60, then the call is worth

$$f(60; 60) = .5 \times (70 - 60) + .5 \times 0 = 5. \tag{7}$$

Clearly, the call option's value is not an increasing function of the stock price for this stochastic process. In addition, since $f(0; 60) = 0$, the function is not convex either. Using the put–call parity theorem, Proposition 13, we can also see that the put with an exercise price of 60 would not be decreasing or convex in the stock price.

Even assuming a *proportional* stochastic process for the underlying asset is insufficient to guarantee this result, as has been claimed. A proportional stochastic process is one in which the distribution of percentage changes in the stock price does not depend on the level of the stock price. A lognormal distribution with constant mean and variance is the prototype of proportional stochastic processes.

As a counterexample to this second assertion, consider an asset with the following dynamics. If the stock price is 40, then four different realizations, {56, 44, 36, 24}, are possible, each equally likely. If the stock price is 50, then the four possibilities are {70, 55, 45, 30}. Again the probability of each otucome is $\frac{1}{4}$. In each case the stock price can increase or decrease by 40% or 10%, so the stochastic process is proportional.

Suppose in the first case that the supporting state prices are {.4, .1, .1, .4} and in the second case that they are {.02, .48, .48, .02}. Then the values of calls with an exercise price of 55 are, in the two cases,

$$f(40; 55) = .4 \times (56 - 55) = .4, \tag{8a}$$

$$f(50; 55) = .02 \times (70 - 55) = .3. \tag{8b}$$

Again we see that the call option-pricing function need not be increasing with an increase in the price of the underlying stock.

An assumption that is sufficient for these two propositions is that the supporting price for a state resulting from a particular percentage return be independent of the level of the current stock price. That is, if $p(S_T|S_t)$ is the state price for the metastate in which the outcome is $\tilde{S}_T$ conditional on the current state of S_t, then for all $\lambda > 0$,

$$p(\lambda S_T|\lambda S_t) = p(S_T|S_t) = P\left(\frac{S_T}{S_t}\right). \tag{9}$$

Since the risk-neutralized probabilities are proportional to the state prices $\hat{\Pi}(S_T/S_t) \equiv R \cdot P(S_T/S_t)$, this assumption is equivalent to saying that the risk-neutralized stochastic process for the stock is proportional, and the interest rate is the same for every initial state. This last assumption guarantees that the normalizing constant in the denominator $R = \Sigma P(S_T/S_t)$ is the same.

We can now demonstrate that put and call option prices are monotone, convex functions of the stock price. We do this as a part of the following more general proposition.

PROPOSITION 18 *If the risk-neutralized stochastic process for the stock price is proportional, then put and call option prices are homogeneous of degree one in the stock price and the exercise price, and they are monotone convex functions of the former.*

Proof. For a proportional risk-neutralized stochastic process, the supporting price for a particular level of return does not depend on the current stock price, so

$$\begin{aligned} f(\lambda S_t; \lambda X) &= \sum p(\lambda S_T|\lambda S_t)\,\text{Max}(\lambda S_T - \lambda X, 0) \\ &= \sum P\left(\frac{S_T}{S_t}\right)\text{Max}(\lambda S_T - \lambda X, 0) \\ &= \lambda \sum P\left(\frac{S_T}{S_t}\right)\text{Max}(S_T - X, 0) = \lambda f(S_t; X). \end{aligned} \tag{10}$$

The remainder of the proof follows immediately from the properties of homogeneous functions. For $S_2 > S_1$,

$$\begin{aligned} f(S_2; X) - f(S_1; X) &= f(S_2; X) - \left(\frac{S_1}{S_2}\right) f\left(S_2; \frac{S_2 X}{S_1}\right) \\ &= f(S_2; X) - f\left(S_2; \frac{S_2 X}{S_1}\right) + \left(1 - \frac{S_1}{S_2}\right) f\left(S_2; \frac{S_2 X}{S_1}\right). \end{aligned} \tag{11}$$

The last term is nonnegative because, by assumption, $S_1 < S_2$ and $f(\cdot) >$

0. The difference of the first two terms is nonnegative by Proposition 6.

To demonstrate convexity, start with the relation in Proposition 11. For $X_2 = \lambda X_1 + (1 - \lambda)X_3$ and $\lambda > 0$,

$$f(1; X_2) \leqslant \lambda f(1; X_1) + (1 - \lambda)f(1; X_3). \tag{12}$$

Now define $\gamma = \lambda X_2/X_1$ (note that $1 - \gamma = (1 - \lambda)X_2/X_3$) and $S_i = 1/X_i$. Using the homogeneity of the option function gives

$$\frac{1}{X_2}f(S_2; 1) \leqslant \frac{1}{X_1}f(S_1; 1) + \frac{1 - \lambda}{X_3}f(S_3; 1)$$

$$\text{or} \tag{13}$$

$$f(S_2; X) \leqslant \gamma f(S_1; X) + (1 - \gamma)f(S_3; X).$$

The proof for put options can be done in a similar manner, or it follows from the put–call parity theorem. Q.E.D.

If other assumptions are made concerning the risk-neutralized stochastic process for the stock price, then additional restrictions on option values can be derived. Some of these restrictions will be discussed later in the chapter after the development of the Black–Scholes model.

OPTION PRICING: THE RISKLESS HEDGE

To demonstrate the risk-neutral or preference-free pricing of options, which is the breakthrough of the Black–Scholes methodology, we first consider a simple case. Suppose that over each period of time the stock price can change in only one of two ways. It increases from S to hS or decreases to kS with (subjective) probabilities of π and $1 - \pi$, respectively; h or k is 1 plus the realized rate of return on the stock. To avoid arbitrage, $h > R > k$. We denote the price of a call option on this asset with exercise price X and n periods until maturity by $C(S, n; X)$ or $C(S, n)$ when there is no possibility of confusion.

Consider a portfolio short one call option and long m shares of stock. The value of this portfolio next period is $mkS - C(kS, n - 1)$ or $mhS - C(hS, n - 1)$ with probabilities $1 - \pi$ and π, respectively. The value of m can be chosen such that these two quantities are identical; that is, $mhS - C(hS, n - 1) = mkS - C(kS, n - 1)$. The value of m that sets the two portfolio outcomes equal is

$$m = \frac{C(hS, n - 1) - C(kS, n - 1)}{(h - k)S}. \tag{14}$$

After one period this portfolio will be worth

$$\frac{kC(hS, n-1) - hC(kS, n-1)}{h-k} \tag{15}$$

with certainty. To avoid arbitrage, this quantity must be equal to the current value of the portfolio multiplied by 1 plus the risk-free rate.

$$R[mS - C(S, n)] = \frac{kC(hS, n-1) - hC(kS, n-1)}{h-k},$$

$$\begin{aligned} RC(S, n) &= \frac{R-k}{h-k}C(hS, n-1) + \frac{h-R}{h-k}C(kS, n-1) \\ &\equiv \hat{\pi}C(hS, n-1) + (1-\hat{\pi})\,C(kS, n-1). \end{aligned} \tag{16}$$

Note that $\hat{\pi} \equiv (R-k)/(h-k)$, defined in the last line of (16), has certain probability-like properties. Namely, $0 < \hat{\pi} < 1$ and the "probabilities" of the two mutually exclusive and collectively exhaustive states sum to 1. Today's option price is therefore the "expected" value of its price next period discounted to the present at the riskless rate. Using these same '"probabilities," we obtain the expected return on the stock

$$\hat{E}(\tilde{z}) = \hat{\pi}h + (1-\hat{\pi})k = \frac{(R-k)h + (h-R)k}{h-k} = R. \tag{17}$$

This analysis demonstrates that the probabilities $\hat{\pi}$ and $1 - \hat{\pi}$ are the risk-neutralized probabilities as introduced in Chapters 2 and 10 for the outcome states distinguishable by observing only the stock's price. Furthermore, the risk-neutralized probabilities are unique and cannot be changed by the introduction of a derivative asset like the option because there are only two states, which are already spanned completely by the stock and the riskless asset. This, of course, provides an alternative way of deriving (16).

Let p_h and p_k be the state prices associated with the two metastates when the stock price increases and decreases, respectively. Then the supporting equations for the riskless asset and the stock are

$$p_hR + p_kR = 1, \tag{18a}$$

$$p_hh + p_kk = 1. \tag{18b}$$

The solutions to (18) are $p_h = (R-k)/R(h-k)$ and $p_k = (h-R)/R(h-k)$. If these two state prices are used to value the options, we get (16).

Since $C(S, 0)$ is a known function, namely, $\text{Max}(S - X, 0)$, we can use (16) to determine $C(S, 1)$ for all possible values of S. Continuing, we can determine $C(S, n)$ recursively from $C(S, n-1)$. An easier route to the price is to use the risk-neutralized probabilities in a risk-neutral pricing methodology. If the step sizes h and k are the same each period, then the probability distribution for $\tilde{S}_T$ after n periods is (under the risk-neutral probabilities)

$$\hat{\text{Prob}}[S_T = Sh^i k^{n-i}] = \frac{n!}{i!(n-i)!}\hat{\pi}^i(1-\hat{\pi})^{n-i}. \tag{19}$$

Hence,

$$\begin{aligned} C(S, n; X) &= R^{-n} \sum_{i=I}^{n} \frac{n!}{i!(n-i)!}\hat{\pi}^i(1-\hat{\pi})^{n-i}(Sh^i k^{n-i} - X) \\ &= SB\left(n - I, n; \frac{k(1-\hat{\pi})}{R}\right) - XR^{-n}B(n - I, n; 1 - \hat{\pi}). \end{aligned} \tag{20}$$

In the first line I is the smallest integer satisfying $h^i k^{n-i} S > X$. In the second line $B(j, \text{N}; \pi)$ is the cumulative binomial distribution function; that is, the probability of getting j or fewer successes out of N independent trials when the probability of each success is π.

Despite its apparent complexity, Equation (20) can be interpreted in a straightforward fashion. The expression $B(n - I, n; 1 - \hat{\pi})$ is the risk neutralized probability that the option will mature in-the-money. Thus, $XB(\cdot)$ is the expected value of the exercise payment, and $XR^{-n}B(\cdot)$ is its present value. The first term can be rewritten as

$$R^{-n}S\left[\frac{R^n B(n - I, n; k(1-\hat{\pi})/R)}{B(n - I, n; 1 - \hat{\pi})}\right]B(n - I, n; 1 - \hat{\pi}).$$

Here $S[R^n B(\cdot)/B(\cdot)]$ is the expected value of S_T conditional on $S_T \geqslant X$. This is multiplied by the probability of recceiving the stock (the probability that the option expires in-the-money) and then discounted by R^{-n} to give the present value.

OPTION PRICING BY THE BLACK–SCHOLES METHODOLOGY

The key assumption underlying the Black–Scholes option-pricing model is that the stock's price dynamics are compact as in the portfolio problem of Chapter 13; that is,

$$\frac{\Delta S}{S} = \alpha\,\Delta t + \sigma\tilde{e}\sqrt{\Delta t} + o(\Delta t), \tag{21}$$

where α is the instantaneous expected rate of return and σ^2 is the variance rate; α can be stochastic or depend aribtrarily on S and t or other state variables; σ is assumed to be a constant for simplicity. If σ is a function of only the prevailing stock price and time, then the analysis up to Equation (37) remains valid (with the exception of the digression); however, a different final solution results.

The solution to the option-pricing problem could be obtained as the appropriate limiting form of the given binomial model as outlined in

Chapter 12. It is more instructive, however, to give a separate development to this important model and compare the resulting answers.

We start by *assuming* that the return dynamics on the option are also compact. If $F(S, t)$ is the option's price, then

$$\frac{\Delta F}{F} = \alpha'(S, t; T)\,\Delta t + \sigma'(S, t; T)\tilde{e}'\sqrt{\Delta t} + o(\Delta t), \tag{22}$$

where α' and σ' are the instantaneous expected rate of return and standard deviation of return on the option, respectively. They may depend on the level of the stock price, time, and the option being priced.

Expanding the option-pricing function by using Taylor's theorem as in Chapter 12, we get

$$\begin{aligned} F(S + \Delta S, t + \Delta t) = F(S, t) &+ F_S\,\Delta S + F_t\,\Delta t + \tfrac{1}{2}F_{SS}\,\Delta S^2 \\ &+ \tfrac{1}{2}F_{tt}\,\Delta t^2 + F_{St}\,\Delta S\,\Delta t + \theta, \end{aligned} \tag{23}$$

where θ contains terms of $\Delta S^i\,\Delta t^j$ with $i + j > 2$ and is $o(\Delta t)$. We now separate the change in the option value into its expected and random components. The expected price change is

$$\begin{aligned} E[\Delta F] &= F_S E[\Delta S] + F_t\,\Delta t + \tfrac{1}{2}F_{SS}E[\Delta S^2] + F_{St}E[\Delta S]\,\Delta t + o(\Delta t) \\ &= F_S\alpha S\,\Delta t + F_t\,\Delta t + \tfrac{1}{2}F_{SS}\sigma^2 S^2\,\Delta t + o(\Delta t). \end{aligned} \tag{24}$$

Thus, the expected rate of return on the option is

$$\alpha' \equiv \frac{E[\Delta F]}{F\,\Delta t} = \frac{\alpha S F_S + F_t + \tfrac{1}{2}F_{SS}\sigma^2 S^2}{F} + \frac{o(\Delta t)}{\Delta t}. \tag{25}$$

The uncertain component of the price change is

$$\begin{aligned} \Delta F - E[\Delta F] = F_S(\Delta S - E[\Delta S]) &+ \tfrac{1}{2}F_{SS}(\Delta S^2 - E[\Delta S^2]) \\ &+ F_{St}\,\Delta t(\Delta S - E[\Delta S]) + o(\Delta t). \end{aligned} \tag{26}$$

Since $\Delta S - E[\Delta S] = \sigma S\tilde{e}\sqrt{\Delta t} + o(\Delta t)$ and $\Delta S^2 - E[\Delta S^2] = O(\Delta t)$, we have

$$\sigma'\tilde{e}' \equiv \frac{\Delta F - E(\Delta F)}{F\sqrt{\Delta t}} = \frac{SF_S\sigma\tilde{e}}{F} + \frac{O(\Delta t)}{\sqrt{\Delta t}}. \tag{27}$$

In the limit as $\Delta t \to 0$, α' is the first term in (25), $\sigma' = SF_S\sigma/F$, and $\tilde{e}' \equiv \tilde{e}$. This last equality implies that, in the limit, the return on the stock and option are perfectly correlated.

A BRIEF DIGRESSION

We now take a brief digression from the Black–Scholes derivation.

Suppose that the expected rate of return on the stock and the option were known. We could then rewrite (25) to $o(\Delta t)$ as

$$\tfrac{1}{2}\sigma^2 S^2 F_{SS} + \alpha S F_S - \alpha'(S, t; T)F + F_t = 0. \tag{28}$$

With α and α' known, Equation (28) is well specified, and its solution subject to $F(0, t) = 0$, $F(S, T) = \mathrm{Max}(S - X, 0)$, and $F(S, t) \leqslant S$ would give the option price.

Now suppose that α' were a constant. In this case the value of the option would be the discounted value of its expected payoff

$$\begin{aligned} F(S, t) &= e^{-\alpha'(T-t)} E[\mathrm{Max}(S_T - X, 0)|S_t] \\ &= e^{-\alpha'(T-t)} \int_X^\infty (S_T - X)\pi(S_T|S)\, dS_T, \end{aligned} \tag{29}$$

where $\pi(S_T|S)$ is the probability density function of the terminal stock price conditional on its current value S. That is, for α' constant, (29) is the formal integral solution to (28) subject to the boundary conditions $F(S, T) = \mathrm{Max}(S - X, 0)$, $F(0, t) = 0$, and $F(S, t) \leqslant S$.

For constant α and σ, the stock price at T will be lognormally distributed as shown in Chapter 12 with density function

$$\pi(S_T|S) = \frac{1}{S_T \sigma\sqrt{T-t}}\, n\!\left(\frac{\ln(S_T/S) - (\alpha - \frac{1}{2}\sigma^2)(T-t)}{\sigma\sqrt{T-t}}\right), \tag{30}$$

where $n(\cdot)$ is the unit normal density function. Substituting (30) into (29) and evaluating the integral by using Equation (69) of the Mathematical Introduction, we get

$$F(S, t) = e^{-\alpha'(T-t)}[e^{\alpha(T-t)} S N(x_1) - X N(x_2)],$$

where

$$\begin{aligned} x_1 &\equiv \frac{\ln(S/X) + (\alpha + \frac{1}{2}\sigma^2)(T-t)}{\sigma\sqrt{T-t}}, \\ x_2 &\equiv x_1 - \sigma\sqrt{T-t}. \end{aligned} \tag{31}$$

Note that as T gets large $x_1 \to \infty$ and $x_2 \to \pm\infty$; therefore, for large T the option price is asymptotically equal to

$$S e^{(\alpha-\alpha')(T-t)} - X e^{-\alpha'(T-t)} N(\pm\infty). \tag{32}$$

We know from Proposition 7 that a perpetual (nonexpiring) call option is equal in value to the stock, but this can be true in (32) only if $\alpha' = \alpha$. Thus, either the two expected rates of return are equal or α' is not constant. (We are free to assume that α and σ are constants since they are exogenous to the option-pricing problem.)

α' will not be equal to α, except under special conditions, because in percentage terms an option is riskier than its associated stock and, therefore, assuming that $\alpha > r$, it commands a higher expected rate of return. Thus, the expected rate of return on an option must not be constant in general. This is to be expected since the risk characteristics of an option obviously change over time as the stock price increases or decreases and the maturity shortens.

With α' an unknown function of the stock price and time, (28) is not a complete specification of the option-pricing problem. To solve the problem, we need to determine α' in some fashion or find a way to avoid the need to know it. As in the discrete-time binomial model the answer is in the formation of a riskless hedge.

THE CONTINUOUS-TIME RISKLESS HEDGE

In the discrete-time problem we avoided the need to know either the stock's or the option's expected rate of return by using the risk-neutralized probabilities which were completely specified by the stock's price dynamics but did not depend explicitly on the true probabilities (which determine the expected rate of return). A similar approach is also valid in continuous time.

Consider forming a portfolio by investing a fraction w in the option and $1 - w$ in the stock. The return on this portfolio is

$$\begin{aligned}\frac{\Delta P}{P} &= w\frac{\Delta F}{F} + (1 - w)\frac{\Delta S}{S} \\ &= [w\alpha' + (1 - w)\alpha]\,\Delta t + [w\sigma' + (1 - w)\sigma]\tilde{e}\sqrt{\Delta t} + o(\Delta t).\end{aligned} \tag{33}$$

For the choice $w = \sigma/(\sigma - \sigma')$ the term multiplying $\tilde{e}$ is zero, so the portfolio is riskless, and, to negate the possibility of arbitrage, we must have $\Delta P/P = r\,\Delta t + o(\Delta t)$. Then from (33)

$$w\alpha' + (1 - w)\alpha = r \quad \text{or} \quad w(\alpha' - r) + (1 - w)(\alpha - r) = 0.$$

Substituting for w and rearranging terms, we derive

$$\frac{\alpha - r}{\sigma} = \frac{\alpha' - r}{\sigma'}, \tag{34}$$

which is the continuous-time restatement of the no arbitrage condition (Equation (5) of Chapter 7).

These steps and results are analogous to those in (14) and (15) in the binomial model earlier. Thus the risk premium on the option is

$$\alpha' - r = \frac{\sigma'}{\sigma}(\alpha - r). \tag{35}$$

Substituting in (35) for α' and σ' from (25) and (27) gives

$$\frac{\alpha S F_S + F_t + \frac{1}{2}\sigma^2 S^2 F_{SS}}{F} - r = \frac{S F_S}{F}(\alpha - r). \tag{36}$$

Collecting terms yields the Black–Scholes partial differential equation for option pricing:

$$\tfrac{1}{2}\sigma^2 S^2 F_{SS} + rSF_S - rF + F_t = 0. \tag{37}$$

This equation is equivalent to the difference equation (16) for the binomial model. Note that it is identical to (28) with $\alpha' = \alpha = r$. Since r and σ were assumed to be constants, we know the solution by analogy with (28) and (31). We denote the solution in this special case by the Black–Scholes call option function, $W(\cdot)$:

$$\begin{aligned} F(S, t) &= W(S, \tau; X, r, \sigma) \equiv SN(d_1) - Xe^{-r\tau}N(d_2), \\ &\text{where } \tau \equiv T - t, \\ d_1 &\equiv \frac{\ln(S/X) + (r + \frac{1}{2}\sigma^2)\tau}{\sigma\sqrt{\tau}}, \\ d_2 &\equiv d_1 - \sigma\sqrt{\tau}. \end{aligned} \tag{38}$$

Table 14.1 Black–Scholes Option Prices (for $S = 100$, $r = 10\%$)

X	$\sigma = .2$			$\sigma = .3$		
		$\tau =$			$\tau =$	
	.25	.50	.75	.25	.50	.75
80	21.99	24.03	26.04	22.25	24.76	27.17
90	12.65	15.29	17.72	13.71	17.03	19.91
100	5.30	8.28	10.88	7.22	10.91	13.98
110	1.47	3.74	5.99	3.22	6.52	9.45
120	0.27	1.42	2.98	1.23	3.67	6.17

X	$\sigma = .4$			$\sigma = .5$		
		$\tau =$			$\tau =$	
	.25	.50	.75	.25	.50	.75
80	22.88	26.08	28.97	23.83	27.76	31.14
90	15.12	19.15	22.52	16.68	21.44	25.30
100	9.16	13.58	17.17	11.11	16.26	20.38
110	5.12	9.34	12.89	7.07	12.16	16.31
120	2.66	6.25	9.55	4.33	8.98	12.99

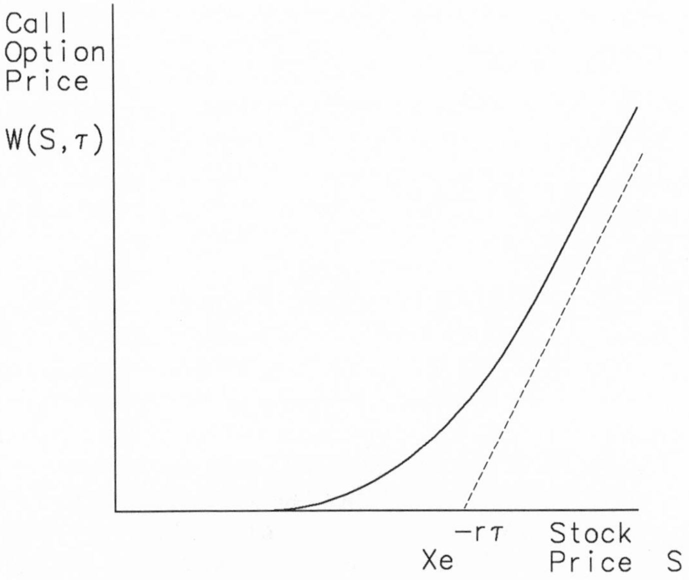

Figure 14.2 Black-Scholes Option Values

For future reference note that, despite the notation, it was not assumed that F represented a call option in deriving (37). This partial differential equation is the general pricing equation for all derivative assets. The soluttion given in (38) is of course that for a call option. For other derivative assets other formulae would result.

Call option values are given in Table 14.1 and plotted in Figure 14.2. We can see that the most actively traded call options (six months, at-the-money) are worth around 10% as much as their associated stock.

THE OPTION'S PRICE DYNAMICS

Equation (25) gives the relation between the option's and the stock's expected rates of return. Substituting from (36), we get for the call option

$$\alpha'(\cdot) = r + \frac{SW_S}{W}(\alpha - r). \tag{39}$$

Similarly, using (27), we get the option's standard deviation

$$\sigma'(\cdot) = \frac{SW_S}{W}\sigma. \tag{40}$$

The excess expected rate of return and standard deviation are proportional to these same two quantities for the stock. The constant of proportionality is in each case the call option's price elasticity

$$\eta_W \equiv \frac{SW_S}{W} = \frac{SN(d_1)}{SN(d_1) - Xe^{-r\tau}N(d_2)}. \tag{41}$$

It is clear from (41) that $\eta_W > 1$, so that the option is riskier in percentage terms than the stock and, therefore, from (39) has a higher risk premium (in absolute value) as well.

Despite the risk-neutral pricing fiction in the Black–Scholes option pricing model, it is clear from Equation (39) that the option's expected rate of return is not equal to the risk-free rate unless the stock's expected rate of return is as well. In general, the option can have a positive, negative, or zero risk premium, depending on the stock's risk premium.

This characterization applies in general whether or not the continuous-time version of the CAPM is valid. That is, the risk premium referred to is the total risk premium and not just that associated with the option's or stock's comovement with the market. For example, if the intertemporal CAPM with hedging portfolios describes returns, then any option will have all the same hedging characteristics as its associated stock because they are perfectly correlated. Thus from (40) all of its β's will be proportional to those of the stock.

Table 14.2 gives representative values for call option elasticities using the Black–Scholes formula. We can see that typical options are substantially riskier in percentage terms than their associated common stocks. Out-of-the-money options are riskier in percentage terms than in-the-money options because they have smaller values. While a given change in the stock price will cause a smaller change in an out-of-the-money option's price, this will be a larger percentage change. In the limit as S/X goes to zero, the elasticity becomes infinite.

Short maturity options are also riskier for the same reason. Perhaps suprising at first is the indication that riskier stocks have options with smaller elasticities. But again the basic reason is the same: More risk on the stock increases the value of the option, and the option's elasticity is a measure of percentage risk. In the limit as either σ or τ goes to infinity, the elasticity goes to unity, its lowest value.

THE HEDGING PORTFOLIO

The hedged portfolio constructed in (33) can also now be described. The fractional investment in the option is

$$w = \frac{\sigma}{\sigma - \sigma'} = \frac{1}{1 - \eta_W} < 0. \tag{42}$$

Table 14.2 Black–Scholes Option Elasticities (for $S = 100$, $r = 10\%$)

	$\sigma = .2$			$\sigma = .3$		
X	$\tau =$ .25	.50	.75	$\tau =$ .25	.50	.75
80	4.52	4.07	3.70	4.31	3.71	3.31
90	7.21	5.75	4.91	6.03	4.69	3.99
100	11.67	8.03	6.42	8.25	5.81	4.74
110	17.46	10.72	8.14	10.77	7.01	5.51
120	23.87	13.64	9.97	13.43	8.25	6.30

	$\sigma = .4$			$\sigma = .5$		
X	$\tau =$ .25	.50	.75	$\tau =$ .25	.50	.75
80	3.98	3.32	2.93	3.64	2.99	2.62
90	5.12	3.94	3.36	4.44	3.41	2.91
100	6.43	4.60	3.79	5.30	3.84	3.20
110	7.83	5.28	4.23	6.19	4.27	3.48
120	9.27	5.95	4.67	7.09	4.70	3.75

An equally, if not more, important portfolio is the *replicating* portfolio. This is the combination of stock with the riskless asset that duplicates the option. Solving (33) gives

$$\begin{aligned}\frac{\Delta F}{F} &= \frac{w-1}{w}\frac{\Delta S}{S} + \frac{1}{w}\frac{\Delta P}{P} = \frac{w-1}{w}\frac{\Delta S}{S} + \frac{1}{w} r\,\Delta t + o(\Delta t)\\ &= \eta_W \frac{\Delta S}{S} + (1-\eta_W) r\,\Delta t + o(\Delta t).\end{aligned} \tag{43}$$

Since $\eta_W > 1$, the call option is equivalent to a levered position in the stock financed by borrowing. In terms of absolute price variation,

$$\begin{aligned}\Delta F &= W_S\,\Delta S + (W - SW_S) r\,\Delta t + o(\Delta t)\\ &= N(d_1)\,\Delta S - Xe^{-r\tau} N(d_2) r\,\Delta t + o(\Delta t)\end{aligned} \tag{44}$$

so the call option's unexpected price change is as much as that on $N(d_1) < 1$ shares of stock.

Table 14.3 Black–Scholes Option Deltas (for $S = 100$, $r = 10\%$)

	$\sigma = .2$			$\sigma = .3$		
X	$\tau =$ .25	.50	.75	$\tau =$ .25	.50	.75
80	0.994	0.977	0.965	0.958	0.918	0.899
90	0.912	0.879	0.870	0.827	0.799	0.795
100	0.618	0.664	0.698	0.595	0.634	0.662
110	0.257	0.401	0.488	0.347	0.457	0.521
120	0.064	0.194	0.297	0.165	0.302	0.389

	$\sigma = .4$			$\sigma = .5$		
X	$\tau =$ .25	.50	.75	$\tau =$ .25	.50	.75
80	0.910	0.866	0.849	0.868	0.829	0.817
90	0.774	0.755	0.756	0.741	0.731	0.737
100	0.589	0.625	0.652	0.589	0.625	0.652
110	0.401	0.493	0.546	0.438	0.519	0.567
120	0.246	0.372	0.446	0.307	0.422	0.487

The number $N(d_1)$ is commonly called the option's *hedge ratio* and is usually denoted by the Greek letter Δ (although here Δ is always a symbol for a change or first difference in another variable). Table 14.3 gives values for option Δ's. Typically a change of one dollar in the price of a share of stock causes a 50 to 60 cent change in the price of an at-the-money option.

In-the-money options behave more like their associated common stock than do out-of-the-money options and, consequently, have higher Δ's. Any option is basically a combination of the stock and a loan fixed in size. For in-the-money options, the amount of stock in the replicating portfolio is higher. In the limit as S/X goes to zero, Δ goes to zero as well.

An increase in σ or τ can either increase or decrease Δ. If an option is currently out-of-the-money, then a higher variance or longer maturity makes it more likely that it may mature in-the-money. This tends to lead to a higher Δ. For an option currently in-the-money, the opposite is true. In the limit for large σ or τ, Δ goes to one.

COMPARATIVE STATICS

We know from Proposition 6 that $W_X < 0$. For the Black–Scholes function this is easily verified:

$$\frac{\partial W}{\partial X} = -e^{-r\tau}N(d_2) < 0. \tag{45}$$

From Proposition 4 and the equality of American and European calls (Proposition 16), we have $W_\tau > 0$. We have also already used the property $W_S = N(d_1) > 0$. We now derive the other comparative statics.

It is easy to verify by inspection that the Black–Scholes call option function is homogeneous of degree one in the stock price and the present value of the exercise price and depends on the stock's variance only through the term $\sigma^2\tau$. Consequently, it can be written as

$$W(S, \tau; X, r, \sigma) = Xe^{-r\tau}\hat{W}(\xi, v; 1, 0, 1),$$

$$\text{where } \xi \equiv \frac{S}{Xe^{-r\tau}}, \qquad v \equiv \sigma^2\tau, \tag{46}$$

and $\hat{W}$ is the normalized option price.

Thus, under the Black–Scholes conditions the price of a call option expressed in units of $Xe^{-r\tau}$ depends only on the two quantities: ξ, the normalized stock price, a measure of how far in- or out-of-the-money the option is, and v, a measure of the total uncertainty in the stock price over the remaining life of the option.

The two remaining comparative statics are

$$\frac{\partial W}{\partial \sigma^2} = Xe^{-r\tau}\tau\frac{\partial \hat{W}}{\partial v} > 0, \tag{47a}$$

$$\frac{\partial W}{\partial r} = -\tau Xe^{-r\tau}\left[\hat{W} - \xi\frac{\partial \hat{W}}{\partial \xi}\right] = \tau Xe^{-r\tau}N(d_2) > 0. \tag{47b}$$

The inequality in (47a) follows from Propositions 4 and 16 and the fact that v is the "maturity" of this modified option.

Both of these results can be supported intuitively. An increase in the interest rate ought to decrease the present value of the exercise payment. An increase in variance will make extreme outcomes more likely, but for the option the worsening of the out-of-the-money outcomes will not matter. More generally, since the payoff functions of both puts and calls are convex in the stock price, it would seem by Jensen's inequality that an increase in the dispersion of the outcomes would increase the expected payoff and therefore the value. These intuitions are fine in the case of a diffusion model but can be deceptive under more general conditions as outlined later. Note that as the variance goes to infinity, the option price approaches the stock price S. That is, the uncertainty effect alone is sufficient to guarantee the result in Proposition 7.

The second partial derivatives are mostly indeterminate. The Black–Scholes value is a convex function of the exercise price, as proved in general in Proposition 11. It is also a convex function of the stock price, as proved in Proposition 18, since the risk-neutralized stochastic process is lognormal.

$$\frac{\partial^2 W}{\partial X^2} = \frac{S}{X^2\sigma\sqrt{\tau}}n(d_1) > 0, \tag{48a}$$

$$\frac{\partial^2 W}{\partial S^2} = \frac{1}{S\sigma\sqrt{\tau}}n(d_1) > 0. \tag{48b}$$

THE BLACK–SCHOLES PUT PRICING FORMULA

Since Equation (37) is the general one for the pricing of derivative assets on stocks with no dividends, it can also be used to value European puts. In this case the boundary conditions to use are $g(S, T) = \text{Max}(X - S, 0)$, $g(0, t) = Xe^{-r(T-t)}$, and $g(\infty, t) = 0$. It can also be derived by applying the put–call parity theorem to (38). This latter method gives the Black–Scholes European put function

$$\begin{aligned} P(S, \tau; X, r, \sigma) &\equiv W(S, t) - S + Xe^{-r\tau} \\ &= S[N(d_1) - 1] + Xe^{-r\tau}[1 - N(d_2)] \\ &= -SN(-d_1) + Xe^{-r\tau}N(-d_2). \end{aligned} \tag{49}$$

The put option's elasticity is

$$\begin{aligned} \eta_P \equiv \frac{SP_S}{P} &= \frac{SW_S - S}{W - S + Xe^{-r\tau}} \\ &= \frac{-SN(-d_1)}{-SN(-d_1) + Xe^{-r\tau}N(-d_2)}, \end{aligned} \tag{50}$$

which is negative and greater than 1 in absolute value. Thus, puts are riskier than their associated stock and have risk premiums of the opposite sign but larger in absolute value. The Δ of a put option is opposite in sign to that of a call with the same striking price and maturity. Put elasticities and price sensitivities, Δ's, can be computed from Table 14.2 and 14.3 from the relations

$$W\eta_W - P\eta_P = S, \tag{51a}$$

$$\Delta_P \equiv P_S = W_S - 1 = \Delta_W - 1. \tag{51b}$$

Like the call option function, the Black–Scholes put option function is homogeneous of degree one in the stock price and the present value of the exercise price. Also like the call option, the European put depends on σ only through the term $\sigma^2\tau$:

$$\begin{aligned} P(S, \tau; X, r, \sigma) & Xe^{-r\tau}\hat{P}(\xi, v; 1, 0, 1) \\ &= Xe^{-r\tau}[\hat{W}(\xi, v; 1, 0, 1) - \xi - 1]. \end{aligned} \tag{52}$$

The comparative statics of the put function can also be determined from the put–call parity relation:

$$\frac{\partial P}{\partial S} = \frac{\partial W}{\partial S} - 1 = N(d_1) - 1 < 0, \tag{53a}$$

$$\frac{\partial P}{\partial X} = \frac{\partial W}{\partial X} + e^{-r\tau} = -N(d_2) + 1 > 0, \tag{53b}$$

$$\begin{aligned} \frac{\partial P}{\partial r} = \frac{\partial W}{\partial r} - \tau X e^{-r\tau} &= -\tau X e^{-r\tau}\left[\hat{W} - \xi\frac{\partial \hat{W}}{\partial \xi} + 1\right] \\ &= -\tau X e^{-r\tau}[1 - N(d_2)] < 0, \end{aligned} \tag{53c}$$

$$\frac{\partial P}{\partial \sigma^2} = \frac{\partial W}{\partial \sigma^2} > 0, \tag{53d}$$

$$\frac{\partial P}{\partial \tau} = \frac{\partial W}{\partial \tau} - rXe^{-r\tau} \gtrless 0, \tag{53e}$$

$$\frac{\partial^2 P}{\partial X^2} = \frac{\partial^2 W}{\partial X^2} > 0, \tag{53f}$$

$$\frac{\partial^2 P}{\partial S^2} = \frac{\partial^2 W}{\partial S^2} > 0. \tag{53g}$$

The only indeterminate comparative static is (53e). An increase in maturity lowers a European put's value by lowering the present value of the exercise price which is received if it is exercised; however, it also increases the put's value by increasing the total uncertainty about the terminal stock price. This dichotomy is clear when we employ the homogeneity restriction that the put depends on r, τ, and σ only through the products $r\tau$ and $\sigma^2\tau$, as introduced in Equation (52). Therefore,

$$\frac{\partial P}{\partial \tau} = \left[\frac{r}{\tau}\frac{\partial}{\partial r} + \frac{\sigma^2}{\tau}\frac{\partial}{\partial \sigma^2}\right]P = \frac{r}{\tau}\frac{\partial P}{\partial r} + \frac{\sigma^2}{\tau}\frac{\partial P}{\partial \sigma^2}. \tag{54}$$

The second term, which is the uncertainty effect, is positive from (53d). The first term is the present value effect and is negative from (53c).

THE BLACK–SCHOLES MODEL AS THE LIMIT OF THE BINOMIAL MODEL

In this section we demonstrate that the Black–Scholes model is the limit of the binomial model introduced in the beginning of the chapter. Recall that for the binomial model the stock's return could only take on one of two realizations, h or k. The resulting call option price is

$$C(S, n; X) = SB\left(n - I, n; \frac{k(1-\pi)}{R}\right) - XR^{-n}B(n - I, n; 1 - \hat{\pi}), \tag{20}$$

where $B(\cdot)$ is the cumulative binomial distribution function, and $\hat{\pi}$ is the risk-neutralized probability of an increase in price: $\hat{\pi} \equiv (R - k)/(h - k)$.

Now choose the step sizes, h and k, as

$$\begin{aligned} h &\equiv 1 + \alpha\,\Delta t + \sigma\sqrt{\frac{(1-\pi)\,\Delta t}{\pi}}, \\ k &\equiv 1 + \alpha\,\Delta t - \sigma\sqrt{\frac{\pi\Delta t}{1-\pi}}. \end{aligned} \tag{55}$$

where π is the true probability of an increase in price. As shown in Chapter 12, the properties of the asset's rate of return are

$$E[\tilde{z}] = 1 + \alpha\,\Delta t, \qquad \mathrm{Var}[\tilde{z}] = \sigma^2\,\Delta t. \tag{56}$$

The return will have a binomial distribution with characteristic probability π. It is well known that the limit of a binomial distribution is a normal distribution with the same mean and variance, so the true distribution will converge to the desired diffusion.

The only remaining issue is to show that the limiting form of (20) is the Black–Scholes function. Although this could be done directly by taking limits in (20), it is simpler and more informative to show that the limit of the risk-neutralized binomial distribution is the risk-neutralized diffusion.

The risk-neutralized process is also binomial, so its limiting form is also normal. To determine the parameters, let $R = 1 + r\,\Delta t$. Then since $h - k = \sigma\sqrt{\pi(1-\pi)\,\Delta t}$, the risk-neutralized probability $\hat{\pi}$ is

$$\begin{aligned} \hat{\pi} &\equiv \frac{R-k}{h-k} = \frac{(r-\alpha)\,\Delta t + \sigma\sqrt{\pi\,\Delta t/(1-\pi)}}{\sigma\sqrt{\pi(1-\pi)\,\Delta t}} \\ &= \pi + \frac{(r-\alpha)\sqrt{\Delta t}}{\sigma\sqrt{\pi(1-\pi)}} \equiv \pi + \theta\sqrt{\Delta t}. \end{aligned} \tag{57}$$

The first two moments of the risk-neutralized process are

$$\begin{aligned} \hat{E}[\tilde{z}] &\equiv \hat{\pi}h + (1-\hat{\pi})k = 1 + \alpha\,\Delta t + \theta(h-k)\sqrt{\Delta t} \\ &= 1 + \alpha\,\Delta t + (r-\alpha)\,\Delta t = 1 + r\,\Delta t, \end{aligned} \tag{58a}$$

$$
\begin{aligned}
\hat{\text{Var}}[\tilde{z}] &= \hat{\pi}h^2 + (1 - \hat{\pi})k^2 - (1 + r\,\Delta t)^2 \\
&= \pi h^2 + (1 - \pi)k^2 + \theta\sqrt{\Delta t}(h^2 - k^2) - (1 + r\,\Delta t)^2 \\
&= \sigma^2\,\Delta t + (1 + \alpha\,\Delta t)^2 - (1 + r\,\Delta t)^2 + \theta\sqrt{\Delta t}(h^2 - k^2) \qquad (58b) \\
&= \sigma^2\,\Delta t + (\alpha - r)\sigma(\Delta t)^{3/2}\frac{2\pi - 1}{\sqrt{\pi(1 - \pi)}} + r(\alpha - r)(\Delta t)^2.
\end{aligned}
$$

Thus, in the risk-neutralized economy, the mean rate of return is always the interest rate, and in the limit the risk-neutralized variance is the true variance. This completes the demonstration.

PREFERENCE-FREE PRICING: THE COX–ROSS–MERTON TECHNIQUE

Equation (37) is identical to (28) if the expected return on both the stock and the option are equal to the sure rate of interest. This isomorphic relation between the two equations permits the use of the so-called risk-neutral pricing method as in the binomial model. Expectations are formed with the risk-neutralized probabilities, and discounting is then done with the risk-free rate. It is important to remember, however, that this is just a fiction. The actual expected return on the option will not equal r unless α, the expected rate of return on the stock, is itself is equal to r.

It is perhaps less confusing to call this technique "preference-free" pricing because any self-consistent set of returns on the stock and option could be assumed and the same valuation would result. The hedging derivation assures us that this is true, for it is based only on the absence of arbitrage, and there can be no arbitrage opportunities in *any* potential equilibrium including the options. Therefore, since the option's value can and has been completely determined by the absence of arbitrage alone, this value must obtain in any equlibrium consistent with the assumptions made.

For example, we could assume that the investment opportunity set (apart from the option) was stationary over time. Then all investors would have identical demands for the risky assets (forcing a zero gross demand for the option), and the continuous-time version of the CAPM would hold. The option is not represented in the market portfolio, so the latter's return dynamics are also constant over time. The equilibrium expected return on any asset, including the option, would then be given by

$$\alpha_i = r + \beta_i(\alpha - r), \qquad (59)$$

where $\beta_i \equiv \sigma_{im}/\sigma_m^2$, as usual. For the stock

$$\sigma_{im} \equiv \text{Cov}(\sigma_i\tilde{e}_i,\ \sigma_m\tilde{e}_m). \qquad (60)$$

For the option

$$\sigma'_{im} = \text{Cov}(\sigma'_i \tilde{e}_i,\ \sigma_m \tilde{e}_m) = \frac{SF_S}{F}\text{Cov}(\sigma_i \tilde{e}_i,\ \sigma_m \tilde{e}_m). \tag{61}$$

From (60) and (61), $\beta' = \beta SF_S/F$. Thus, from (59),

$$\alpha' = r + \frac{SF_S}{F}\beta(\alpha_m - r) = r + \frac{SF_S}{F}(\alpha - r). \tag{62}$$

If this is substituted into (28), the Black–Scholes option differential equation is obtained without the assumption that a perfect hedge could be formed. Thus, the continuous-time version of the CAPM is a sufficient condition for obtaining the Black–Scholes formula for option pricing. Note, however, that the hedging argument is more general. For one thing it does not depend on any properties of the returns on other assets.

MORE ON GENERAL DISTRIBUTION-FREE PROPERTIES OF OPTIONS

Propositions 1, 7, and 9 permit a call option's price to be bracketed by $\text{Max}(0,\ S - XP(t,\ T)) \leqslant F(S,\ t) \leqslant S$. The range of option prices permitted by these bounds is quite wide, however. If additional assumptions are made about the nature of the risk-neutral stochastic process, these bounds can be narrowed.

One interesting and useful assumption is that the ratio of the risk-neutral probabilities to the true probabilities is a decreasing function of the stock price; that is, $\hat{\pi}_s/\pi_s \leqslant \hat{\pi}_\sigma/\pi_\sigma$ for $s < \sigma$. This assumption guarantees that the stock has a positive beta. This ratio is $\hat{\pi}_s/\pi_s = R\Lambda_s$, where Λ_s is the martingale pricing measure for the metastates distinguished by the stock's prices. Since the martingale measure is also proportional to each investor's average marginal utility in each of these metastates, the assumption that it is decreasing implies that on average every investor is better off in states when the stock's price is higher.

PROPOSITION 19 *If the state price per unit probability is a monotone decreasing function of the stock price, then a call option's value is bounded by*

$$P(t,\ T)\{E[\text{Max}(S_T - X,\ 0) - S_T]\} + S_t \leqslant F(S_t,\ t) \leqslant \frac{E[\text{Max}(S_T - X,\ 0)]}{E[S_T]/S_t}$$

Proof. Consider a portfolio with $S_t - F(S_t,\ t)$ dollars invested in bonds maturing at time T and one call option worth $F(S_t,\ t)$. The payoff on this portfolio at time T is $\text{Max}(S_T - X, 0) + (S_t - F)/P(t, T) \equiv h(S_T)$. This payoff function is a positive constant for $S_T < X$. Above this level it increases dollar for dollar with the terminal stock price; thus, there is either one or no values S_T^* for which $h(S_T^*) = S_T^*$. Since the portfolio is currently worth as much as one share of stock, its payoff cannot always exceed that on the stock or it would dominate the stock. Thus, there must be exactly one value S_T^* of equality.

Since the portfolio and the stock have the same current value,

$$0 = \sum p_s[h(s) - s] = \sum \pi_s \Lambda_s [h(s) - s]. \tag{63}$$

We can split this sum at s^* into two parts. The first sum has only positive terms, whereas the second is entirely negative. Since Λ_s is decreasing in s,

$$\begin{aligned} 0 &\geqslant \sum_{s<s^*} \pi_s \Lambda_{s^*}[h(s) - s] + \sum_{s \geqslant s^*} \pi_s \Lambda_{s^*}[h(s) - s] \\ &= \Lambda_{s^*} \sum \pi_s [h(s) - s] \\ &\qquad\qquad \text{or} \\ 0 &\geqslant E[h(\tilde{S}_T) - \tilde{S}_T] \\ &= E[\text{Max}(\tilde{S}_T - X, 0) - \tilde{S}_T] + \frac{S_t - F(\cdot)}{P(t, T)}. \end{aligned} \tag{64}$$

The last inequality follows since $\Lambda_s > 0$ for all s. Solving this last inequality for $F(\cdot)$ gives the lower bound.

To verify the upper bound, we compare a portfolio of $S_t/F(S_t, t)$ options to a share of stock. The payoff on this portfolio is $S_t \,\text{Max}(S_T - X, 0)/F(S_t, t) \equiv H(S_T)$. Again, this function has a single crossing point where $H(S_T^*) = S_T^*$. This time the portfolio's value exceeds the price of a share of stock when $S_T > S_T^*$.

Since the portfolio is currently worth the same as one share of stock, $E[\tilde{\Lambda}(H(\tilde{S}_T) - \tilde{S}_T)] = 0$. Separating the sum as before gives

$$0 \leqslant E[H(\tilde{S}_T) - \tilde{S}_T] = E\left[\frac{S_t \text{Max}(\tilde{S}_T - X, 0)}{F(S_t, t)} - \tilde{S}_T\right]. \tag{65}$$

Solving this last inequality for $F(\cdot)$ gives the upper bound. Q.E.D.

These bounds give a range for the option value which is substantially narrower than that provided by the earlier propositions. For example, if the distribution of the stock price is lognormal with an expected rate of return of α and a logarithmic variance of σ^2, then the lower and upper bounds in Proposition 19 are

$$\begin{aligned} F(S, t) &\geqslant e^{(\alpha - r)(T-t)} W(S, T - t; X, \alpha, \sigma) - S(e^{(\alpha - r)(T-t)} - 1), \\ F(S, t) &\leqslant W(S, T - t; X, \alpha, \sigma). \end{aligned} \tag{66}$$

Table 14.4 Proposition 19 Bounds on Option Prices (for $S = 100$, $r = 10\%$, $\alpha = 18\%$)

		$\sigma = .2$			$\sigma = .3$	
X	Black–Scholes	Lower Bound	Upper Bound	Black–Scholes	Lower Bound	Upper Bound
80	24.01	23.97	25.84	24.75	24.56	26.42
90	15.27	15.01	17.10	17.01	16.55	18.60
100	8.26	7.49	9.77	10.88	10.01	12.23
110	3.73	2.30	4.71	6.50	5.19	7.52
120	1.41	−0.56	1.91	3.65	1.94	4.35

		$\sigma = .4$			$\sigma = .5$	
X	Black–Scholes	Lower Bound	Upper Bound	Black–Scholes	Lower Bound	Upper Bound
80	26.06	25.75	27.57	27.73	27.32	29.11
90	19.13	18.55	20.55	21.41	20.76	22.71
100	13.55	12.65	14.80	16.23	15.32	17.40
110	9.31	8.07	10.33	12.12	10.95	13.14
120	6.23	4.68	7.03	8.95	7.52	9.80

Note that for $\alpha = r$, the upper and lower bounds are equal, so only the Black–Scholes price is possible for a "zero beta" stock. This result should come as no surprise, given the Cox–Ross–Merton technique of pricing. Also the lower bound can give a negative value for options that are substantially out-of-the-money.

Table 14.4 illustrates the bounds that are provided by Proposition 19.

The Black–Scholes put and call option functions depend on five variables: the price of the stock, the time until maturity, the exercise price, the stock's variance, and the interest rate. Of the seven comparative statics results given before for each type of option, two were not related to the general properties derived in the beginning of the chapter. In particular, we did not develop the distribution-free properties that a call (put) option's value would be higher if the interest rate were higher (lower), or the riskiness of the underlying asset were higher. In addition, we needed to assume that the risk-neutral stochastic process for the stock return was proportional in order to prove that the option price was a monotone, convex function of the stock price, and we demonstrated by counterexample that this was not true in general.

To show that monotonicity of the option function is not a general property of changes in riskiness or the interest rate, we use the economy outlined in the following table. There are two stocks both with a current price of 30. Stock 2 is obviously riskier than stock 1 even by the strong Rothschild–Stiglitz definition of risk since $\tilde{S}_2 = \tilde{S}_1 + \tilde{\varepsilon}$, where $\tilde{\varepsilon}$ is equal to +4 or −2 with probability $\frac{1}{3}$ and $\frac{2}{3}$ conditional on $S_1 = 20$, and is equal to +8 or −4 with probability $\frac{1}{3}$ and $\frac{2}{3}$ conditional on $S_1 = 40$.

Characteristic	State			
	a	*b*	*c*	*d*
State probability π_s	$\frac{1}{12}$	$\frac{1}{6}$	$\frac{1}{4}$	$\frac{1}{2}$
Supporting price p_s	.3	.2	.1	.4
Stock 1's value $\tilde{S}_1$	20	20	40	40
Stock 2's value $\tilde{S}_2$	24	18	48	36
Payoff on option on stock 1 with $X = 37$	0	0	3	3
Payoff on option on stock 2 with $X = 37$	0	0	11	0

Clearly, the option on stock 2 is worth only 1.1, which is less than the value of 1.5 for the option on the first stock. Note that the expected payoff on option 2 *is* greater than that on option 1 ($\frac{11}{4}$ as compared to $\frac{9}{4}$). This must be the case (at least weakly) since stock 2's payoff is more variable and the option *payoff* is a convex function of the stock price. However, the appropriate discount rate on option 2 is also much higher (150% versus 50%) because option two pays off only in a state *c* whose state price is low relative to its probability of occurrence. That is, state *c* corresponds to one in which wealth is high and, therefore, marginal utility is low. Failure to recognize that this latter effect can negate the former is the error in the intuition given before based on Jensen's inequality alone.

Why does this property hold for the Black–Scholes diffusion model? The answer is relatively straightforward. Consider first a discrete-time economy with risk-neutral investors. In this economy if the expected payoff on one asset is higher than on another, then its price must be higher as well. That is, the second effect cannot negate the first in a risk-neutral economy because all assets' discount rates are equal, so that each state price must be proportional to the state's probability of occurrence. (The proportionality constant is $P(t, T)$.)

Furthermore, in the Black–Scholes case the risk-neutral "adjustment" of the Cox–Ross–Merton type leaves the variance parameter unchanged. Therefore, the stock with the higher variance parameter also has more price dispersion in the risk-neutralized economy. This means that its (risk-neutralized) expected payoff is higher, and since discount rates are all equal, its options must be more valuable as well.

From this analogy we can derive a valid general proposition relating the riskiness of the stock to the option's price.

PROPOSITION 20 *If* $S_1 = S_2$ *at time t, but the latter is riskier at time T when measured using the risk-neutralized probabilities* $\hat{\pi}_s \equiv p_s/\Sigma p_s$ *(using information available at time t), the* $f_1(S_1, t; T, X) \leq f_2(S_2, t; T, X)$. *The same result is valid for European puts and, if there are no dividends, American calls.*

To illustrate the interest rate effect in discret time, consider the same economy. Since the sum of the state prices is 1, the interest rate is 0. If the interest rate is changed, then one or more of the state prices must change as well. Suppose that the interest rate changes to 25%. Then the sum of the state prices must now be 0.8.

If p_a drops by 0.2 to accomplish this, then both options will retain all their value. If p_d decreases by 0.2, then the price of the option on the second stock will not change, and the price of the option on the first stock will decrease. If p_d becomes 0.1 while p_c increases to 0.2, the price of the option on the second stock will actually increase.

For this Black–Scholes comparative static to be correct, obviously changes in the interest rate cannot affect state prices in this last way in diffusion models. For the lognormal model this is obviously the case. A change in the interest rate merely shifts the lognormal density to a new location. For more complicated models these types of changes are also disallowed.

15

Review of Multiperiod Models

This chapter ties together the various multiperiod models of the previous five chapters. In it we will discuss not only the similarities and linkages between the models, but we will also talk about the limitations of each. As in Chapter 9, various general equilibrium concerns will also be discussed.

Since all equilibrium models must be characterized by the absence of arbitrage opportunities, a martingale pricing process must exist for each model. Recall that apart from a normalization factor that changes over time, a martingale pricing process is just the state price per unit probability. One obvious way to compare models is therefore to compare their martingale pricing processes.

THE MARTINGALE PRICING PROCESS FOR A COMPLETE MARKET

From Equation (7b) of Chapter 10 the value v_t of an asset is given by

$$\Lambda_t v_t = E_t[\tilde{\Lambda}_{t+1}(\tilde{v}_{t+1} + \tilde{d}_{t+1})] \quad \text{or} \quad 1 = E\left[\left(\frac{\tilde{\Lambda}_{t+1}}{\Lambda_t}\right)\tilde{z}\right], \tag{1}$$

where Λ_t is the martingale pricing process. If markets are complete, then from Equations (11b), (11c) of Chapter 10 the state price per unit probability is $p_{s,t+1}/\pi_{s,t+1} = U'(C_{s,t+1})/U'(C_t)$ for any investor's utility function. Thus, it is also true that

$$1 = E\left[\left[\frac{U'(\tilde{C}_{t+1})}{U'(C_t)}\right]\tilde{z}\right]. \tag{2}$$

It is clear by comparing (1) and (2) that marginal utility is (at least) one valid martingale pricing process for a complete market.

This result can be expressed in a fashion more in keeping with our previous use as

$$\bar{z} = R + R\,\mathrm{Cov}\left[\left[\frac{U'(\tilde{C}_{t+1})}{U'(C_t)}\right], \tilde{z}\right]. \tag{3}$$

Equation (3) is derived from (2) by substituting the covariance for the expectation of the product and recalling that the expectation of the ratio of this "martingale" pricing process for any two consecutive periods is $1/R$. In this form it is clear that the risk premium on any asset is proportional to its covariance with each investor's marginal utility just as in the single-period complete-market model.

Although the equilibrium condition just developed appears to be investor specific, this is not the case. As we saw, the ratio of marginal utilities for each investor equals the ratio of the common stochastic process $\tilde{\Lambda}_t$. Thus, Equation (3) holds for per capita consumption as well when the utility function is that of the representative investor. Unfortuantely, this representative utility function will not be known generally, so this equilibrium relation will be of little use.

THE MARTINGALE PROCESS FOR THE CONTINUOUS-TIME CAPM

For continuous-time models we can do a little better. We know that the martingale process is a stochastic process with the properties

$$E[\Delta\tilde{\Lambda}] = -r\Lambda\,\Delta t + o(\Delta t), \tag{4a}$$

$$E[\Delta(\tilde{\Lambda}\tilde{P})] = 0 + o(\Delta t), \tag{4b}$$

where P is the value of any portfolio with all its dividends reinvested. These properties are the continuous-time equivalents of $E[\tilde{\Lambda}_{t+1}] = \Lambda_t/R$ and Equation (7b) of Chapter 10. The stochastic evolution for $\tilde{\Lambda}_t$ can therefore be written as

$$\Delta\tilde{\Lambda} = -r\Lambda\,\Delta t + s\Lambda\tilde{\varepsilon}_\Lambda\sqrt{\Delta t} + o(\Delta t), \tag{5}$$

where $\tilde{\varepsilon}_\Lambda$ and s are as yet unspecified. They are chosen to satisfy (4b). The standard deviation s may depend on Λ, t, or other variables of concern to investors.

These conditions are not sufficient to determine the martingale pricing process uniquely. In fact, there is generally no unique pricing process even in very simple economies. This can be illustrated for the continuous time CAPM with a static investment opportunity set. One stochastic process that satisfies the martingale pricing conditions is

$$\tilde{\Lambda}_t \equiv \exp\left[\left(\frac{\lambda}{2}(\alpha_m + r - \sigma_m^2) - r\right)t\right]\tilde{P}_{mt}^{-\lambda}, \tag{6}$$

where α_m and σ_m^2 are the instantaneous expected rate of return and variance of the market portfolio, $\lambda \equiv (\alpha_m - r)/\sigma_m^2$ is the market price of risk, and P_{mt} is the accumualted value (with all dividends reinvested) at time t of one dollar invested in the market portfolio at time zero.

Since the evolution of $\tilde{P}_m$ is

$$\Delta\tilde{P}_m = \alpha_m P_m \Delta t + \sigma_m P_m \tilde{\varepsilon}_m \sqrt{\Delta t} + o(\Delta t), \tag{7}$$

the stochastic evolution of $\tilde{\Lambda}_t$ is

$$\begin{aligned}\Delta\tilde{\Lambda}_t = &\left(\frac{\lambda}{2}(\alpha_m + r - \sigma_m^2) - r\right)\exp(\cdot)P_{mt}^{-\lambda}\Delta t - \lambda\exp(\cdot)P_{mt}^{-\lambda-1}\Delta\tilde{P}_m \\ &+ \frac{1}{2}\lambda(\lambda+1)\exp(\cdot)P_{mt}^{-\lambda-2}(\Delta\tilde{P}_m)^2 + o(\Delta t).\end{aligned} \tag{8}$$

Simplifying terms leaves

$$\begin{aligned}\frac{\Delta\tilde{\Lambda}_t}{\Lambda_t} &= -r\,\Delta t - \lambda\sigma_m\tilde{\varepsilon}_m\sqrt{\Delta t} + o(\Delta t) \\ &= -r\,\Delta t + \frac{r-\alpha_m}{\sigma_m}\tilde{\varepsilon}_m\sqrt{\Delta t} + o(\Delta t).\end{aligned} \tag{9}$$

Equation (9) verifies condition (4a). To verify (4b) we take any other portfolio with dynamics

$$\Delta\tilde{P}_i = \alpha_i P_i \Delta t + \sigma_i P_i \tilde{\varepsilon}_i \sqrt{\Delta t} + o(\Delta t). \tag{10}$$

Then the evolution of the product $\tilde{\Lambda}\tilde{P}_i$ is

$$\begin{aligned}\Delta(\tilde{\Lambda}\tilde{P}_i) &= P_i\,\Delta\tilde{\Lambda} + \Lambda\,\Delta\tilde{P}_i + \Delta\tilde{\Lambda}\,\Delta\tilde{P}_i + o(\Delta t) \\ &= \Lambda P_i[-r + \alpha_i - \lambda\sigma_m\sigma_i\mathrm{Cov}(\tilde{\varepsilon}_m, \tilde{\varepsilon}_i)]\,\Delta t \\ &\quad + \Lambda P_i[-\lambda\sigma_m\tilde{\varepsilon}_m + \sigma_i\tilde{\varepsilon}_i]\sqrt{\Delta t} + o(\Delta t),\end{aligned} \tag{11}$$

and

$$\frac{E[\Delta(\tilde{\Lambda}\tilde{P}_i)]}{\Lambda P_i} = \left[-r + \alpha_i + \frac{(\alpha_m - r)\sigma_{im}}{\sigma_m^2}\right]\Delta t = 0. \tag{12}$$

Since the term in brackets is zero from the continuous-time CAPM pricing relation, the product $\tilde{\Lambda}\tilde{P}_i$ is a martingale.

As stated previously, the martingale pricing process is not uniquely determined. The general form of valid martingale pricing processes is $\hat{\Lambda}_t = \tilde{\Lambda}_t\tilde{u}_t$, where $\tilde{\Lambda}_t$ is as defined in (6), and $\tilde{u}_t$ is any martingale diffusion process which is statistically independent of the returns on all of the assets.

This generalization is easily verified to be valid since $\Delta\hat{\Lambda} = u\,\Delta\tilde{\Lambda} + \Lambda\,\Delta\tilde{u} + \Delta\tilde{\Lambda}\,\Delta\tilde{u} + o(\Delta t)$, and

$$E\left[\frac{\Delta\hat{\Lambda}}{\hat{\Lambda}}\right] = E\left[\frac{\Delta\tilde{\Lambda}}{\Lambda}\right] + E\left[\frac{\Delta\tilde{u}}{u}\right] + \mathrm{Cov}\left(\frac{\Delta\tilde{\Lambda}}{\Lambda}, \frac{\Delta\tilde{u}}{u}\right) + o(\Delta t). \tag{13}$$

The first term is $-r\Delta t$, and the last two are zero since $\tilde{u}_t$ is itself a martingale and is independent of all asset returns and, hence, of $\tilde{\Lambda}_t$, which depends only on the market portfolio. Similarly,

$$\Delta(\hat{\Lambda}\tilde{P}_i) = \Lambda P_i \Delta\tilde{u} + u\,\Delta(\tilde{\Lambda}\tilde{P}_i) + \Delta\tilde{u}\,\Delta(\tilde{\Lambda}\tilde{P}_i) + o(\Delta t).$$

The expectation of this is also zero since both $\tilde{u}$ and $\tilde{\Lambda}\tilde{P}_i$ are martingales and they are independent.

A CONSUMPTION-BASED ASSET-PRICING MODEL

To determine a martingale pricing process for the intertemporal asset model when the investment opportunity set is stochastic, it is convenient to first express the equilibrium in terms of consumption. As we saw in Chapter 13, each investor with a state-independent (direct) utility of consumption function chooses that portfolio which minimizes the variance of his consumption for a given level of expected return. By analogy with the static CAPM, in which the variance of wealth is minimized subject to the same constraint, we might suspect that betas with consumption would be the appropriate sufficient statistic to measure the priced risk of a single security. This suspicion is correct as we will show.

Continuing the practice of Chapter 13, we assume that there is a single state variable which summarizes changes in the opportunity set. This assumption is one of convenience in notation only. The analysis is exactly the same if there are more state variables.

The equation for the demand for the risky assets is Equation (47) of Chapter 13:

$$\mathbf{w}^* W = -\frac{J_W}{J_{WW}}\boldsymbol{\Sigma}^{-1}(\boldsymbol{\alpha} - r\mathbf{1}) - \boldsymbol{\Sigma}^{-1}\boldsymbol{\sigma}\frac{J_{Wx}}{J_{WW}}. \tag{14}$$

Since $U_C = J_W$ at the optimum, we have $J_{WW} = U_{CC}C_W^*$ and $J_{Wx} = U_{CC}C_x^*$. Substituting these into (14) and rearranging terms give

$$\boldsymbol{\Sigma}\mathbf{w}^* W C_W^* + \boldsymbol{\sigma} C_x^* = -\frac{U_C}{U_{CC}}(\boldsymbol{\alpha} - r\mathbf{1}). \tag{15}$$

The first term on the left-hand side is the product of the covariance of each asset with the investor's wealth and the marginal change in consumption with a change in wealth. The second term is the product of the covariance of each asset with the state variable and the marginal change in consumption with a change in the state variable. That is, the left-hand side of (15) is the sum of two vectors of partial covariances of each of the assets with this investor's optimal consumption. In the first term W varies while x remains fixed, and in the second term x varies while W remains unchanged. Since these are the only two variables that affect consumption, the left-hand side of (15) is the vector of covariances of returns on each asset with this investor's optimal consumption.

Averaging (15) over investors, we get

$$\mathbf{g} = T^m(\boldsymbol{\alpha} - r\mathbf{1}), \tag{16}$$

where $\mathbf{g}$ is the vector of covariances of per capita consumption, G, with the assets, and T^m is the average of the investors' risk tolerances. If we premultiply (16) by the weights in any portfolio, $\mathbf{w}_p'$, then the covariance of returns on this portfolio with per capita consumption is

$$\sigma_{pG} = \mathbf{w}_p'\mathbf{g} = T^m\mathbf{w}_p'(\boldsymbol{\alpha} - r\mathbf{1}) = T^m(\alpha_p - r). \tag{17}$$

Solving for T^m and substituting into (16), we get

$$\alpha_i - r = \frac{\sigma_{iG}}{\sigma_{pG}}(\alpha_p - r). \tag{18}$$

The fraction σ_{iG}/σ_{pG} replaces the beta with respect to the market portfolio of the simple static CAPM. It is the ratio of the covariance of the return on asset i with per capita consumption to the covariance of the return on any portfolio p with per capita consumption. It can be measured as the instrumental variable regression coefficient from the regression of asset i's returns on the returns on portfolio p, using per capita consumption as an instrument for the latter. Note that it is not important that portfolio p be the market portfolio. It can be any portfolio with a nonzero covariance with per capita consumption.

If there is a portfolio whose returns are perfectly correlated with changes in per capita consumption, then this portfolio is the natural one to choose. In this case (18) can be simplified to

$$\alpha_i - r = \frac{\sigma_{ig}}{\sigma_g^2}(\alpha_g - r), \tag{19}$$

where the subscript g denotes the portfolio which is perfectly correlated with per capita consumption, and the beta is now an OLS regression coefficient just as in the simple static model.

If no riskless asset is available, then a "zero beta" version of this model holds. The expected rate of return on any asset is

$$\alpha_i - \alpha_z = \frac{\sigma_{iG}}{\sigma_{pG}}(\alpha_p - \alpha_z), \tag{18$'$}$$

where z denotes a portfolio whose return is uncorrelated with the changes in aggregate consumption. Equation (19) is similarly modified, as are the following results.

THE MARTINGALE MEASURE WHEN THE OPPORTUNITY SET IS STOCHASTIC

If there is a portfolio which is perfectly correlated with per capita consumption, then by analogy with the static CAPM it is clear that

$$\tilde{\Lambda}_t \equiv \exp\left[\left(\frac{\lambda}{2}(\alpha_g + r - \sigma_g^2) - r\right)t\right]\tilde{P}_{gt}^{-\lambda} \tag{20}$$

is a valid martingale pricing process, where now $\lambda \equiv (\alpha_g - r)/\sigma_g^2$ is the market price of risk in this economy. When no such portfolio exists (or even if it does), then per capita consumption itself can be used to create a pricing process.

Per capita consumption follows a diffusion process with

$$\frac{\Delta G}{G} = \mu_G \Delta t + \sigma_G \tilde{\varepsilon}_G \sqrt{\Delta t} + o(\Delta t). \tag{21}$$

A martingale pricing process is

$$\tilde{\Lambda}_t = \exp\left[\left(\frac{\lambda}{2}(\mu_G + r - \sigma_G^2) - r\right)t\right]\tilde{G}_t^{-\lambda}, \tag{22}$$

where $\lambda \equiv (\alpha_p - r)/\sigma_{pG}$ is the market price of risk in this model. The subscript p denotes any portfolio.

As in the static model, the evolution of $\tilde{\Lambda}_t$ is

$$\begin{aligned}\Delta\tilde{\Lambda}_t = {} & \left(\frac{\lambda}{2}(\mu_G + r - \sigma_G^2) - r\right)\exp(\cdot)\, G_t^{-\lambda}\,\Delta t \\ & - \lambda \exp(\cdot)\, G_t^{-\lambda-1}\,\Delta\tilde{G} \\ & + \tfrac{1}{2}\lambda(\lambda + 1)\exp(\cdot)\, G_t^{-\lambda-2}(\Delta\tilde{G})^2 + o(\Delta t).\end{aligned} \tag{23}$$

Simplifying terms leaves

$$\frac{\Delta\tilde{\Lambda}_t}{\Lambda_t} = -r\,\Delta t - \lambda\sigma_G\tilde{\varepsilon}_G\sqrt{\Delta t} + o(\Delta t). \tag{24}$$

Equation (24) verifies condition (4a). To verify (4b), we take any other portfolio with dynamics as given in (10). Then the evolution of the product $\tilde{\Lambda}\tilde{P}_i$ is

$$\begin{aligned}\Delta(\tilde{\Lambda}\tilde{P}_i) &= P_i\,\Delta\tilde{\Lambda} + \Lambda\,\Delta\tilde{P}_i + \Delta\tilde{\Lambda}\,\Delta\tilde{P}_i + o(\Delta t) \\ &= \Lambda P_i[-r + \alpha_i - \lambda\sigma_G\sigma_i \mathrm{Cov}(\tilde{\varepsilon}_G, \tilde{\varepsilon}_i)]\,\Delta t \\ &\quad + \Lambda P_i[-\lambda\sigma_G\tilde{\varepsilon}_G + \sigma_i\tilde{\varepsilon}_i]\sqrt{\Delta t} + o(\Delta t),\end{aligned} \tag{25}$$

and

$$E\frac{[\Delta(\tilde{\Lambda}\tilde{P}_i)]}{\Lambda P_i} = \left[-r + \alpha_i - \frac{\alpha_p - r)\sigma_{iG}}{\sigma_{pG}}\right]\Delta t. \tag{26}$$

Since the term in brackets is zero from the continuous-time CAPM pricing relation in (18), the product $\tilde{\Lambda}\tilde{P}_i$ is a martingale.

A COMPARISON OF THE CONTINUOUS-TIME AND COMPLETE MARKET MODELS

As we have just seen, per capita consumption is a valid martingale pricing process in the continuous-time model. This property is reminiscent of the complete market model where "aggregate" marginal utility was a martingale pricing process. This similarity might appear puzzling at first. We know from the first-order conditions of single-period models that every investor's marginal utility can serve as state prices (or a martingale process). However, this result can be aggregated only when the marginal utilities of all investors are perfectly related. Generally, this occurs only when markets are complete, but there is no obvious necessity that the continuous-time, diffusion market be complete, and since the "number of states" is infinite, this would seem highly unlikely. Thus, it is not obvious why the diffusion models should have this apparent "complete market's" property.

As shown in Chapter 10, under certain conditions an intertemporal market can be completed not only by the addition of more assets but also by dynamic trading strategies of long-lived assets. Dynamic trading can serve to complete the market, provided that the number of assets is as large as the multiplicity of the evolutionary path of the economy.

In this and the next section we shall examine this issue in some detail. We shall see that if all assets follows diffusions, then the set of states that are described just in terms of asset prices can always be insured against through dynamic portfolio strategies. Thus, the market is complete in the sense we have used for single-period models. However, the set of states defined more narrowly so as to distinguish among different values of the state variables that measure changes in the opportunity set as well as among different asset prices may not be insurable.

We demonstrate first how the market with states distinguished only by prices is complete. We have seen that any diffusion process is the limit of binomial processes in which over a single interval of time only two different outcomes are achievable. Therefore, a market with a riskless asset and a single risky asset following a diffusion process is the limit of markets with two assets and just two states. Since the assets' returns are not collinear, the market is obviously complete for each approximation. Completion of the limiting market also seems reasonable.

With a riskless asset and two risky assets, whose returns are each modeled by a binomial process, it would appear that there are four states and only three assets. This market is obviously not complete. In general, for N risky assets it would seem that there are 2^N states with only $N + 1$ assets. Fortunately, this rich a description is not required: N joint diffusion processes can be modeled as the limit of a single $(N + 1)$-nomial process, that is, a single process with $N + 1$ outcomes.

This proposition is illustrated for two risky assets. There are three outcome states characterized by

State	Probability	Return on Asset 1	Return on Asset 2
a	π_a	h_1	h_2
b	π_b	h_1	k_2
c	π_c	k_1	k_2

The individual outcomes are

$$h_i \equiv 1 + \alpha_i \Delta t + \sigma_i \sqrt{\frac{(1 - \pi_i)\Delta t}{\pi_i}}, \qquad k_i \equiv 1 + \alpha_i \Delta t - \sigma_i \sqrt{\frac{\pi_i \Delta t}{1 - \pi_i}}, \tag{27}$$

where π_i is the probability that the return on asset i is h_i; that is, $\pi_1 = \pi_a + \pi_b$ and $\pi_2 = \pi_a$.

Each asset price process has only two outcomes and is binomial of the same type as introduced in Chapters 10 and 14. As shown in the latter chapter, a single process like this has as a limit a diffusion process with expected rate of return α_i and a variance of σ_i^2. The only remaining issue is to show that the joint behavior does not degenerate in the limit; that is, that any correlation between the assets is possible. This can be proved as follows. The covariance of the returns on the two assets is

$$\begin{aligned}\sigma_{12} = {} & \pi_a \sigma_1 \sqrt{\frac{(1 - \pi_1)\Delta t}{\pi_1}} \sigma_2 \sqrt{\frac{(1 - \pi_2)\Delta t}{\pi_2}} \\ & - \pi_b \sigma_1 \sqrt{\frac{(1 - \pi_1)\Delta t}{\pi_1}} \sigma_2 \sqrt{\frac{\pi_2 \Delta t}{1 - \pi_2}} \\ & + \pi_c \sigma_1 \sqrt{\frac{\pi_1 \Delta t}{1 - \pi_1}} \sigma_2 \sqrt{\frac{\pi_2 \Delta t}{1 - \pi_2}}.\end{aligned} \tag{28}$$

Substituting for the probabilities π_1 and π_2 and collecting terms the correlation coefficient is

$$\rho_{12} = \frac{\sigma_{12}}{\sigma_1 \sigma_2} = \left(\frac{\pi_a \pi_c}{(\pi_a + \pi_b)(\pi_c + \pi_b)} \right)^{1/2} (1 - \pi_b). \tag{29}$$

For $\pi_b = 0$, the correlation is perfect. As π_b is increased to 1 (and therefore π_a and π_c are decreased to 0), the correlation coefficient decreases continuously to 0. All negative values for the correlation coefficient can be achieved by assigning the return h_2 to states b and c and k_2 to state a.

For three or more risky assets a similar proof applies. only $N + 1$ separate states are required to achieve any pattern of correlation coefficients among the assts. Unfortunately, the exact description of the states to select often proves tricky.

FURTHER COMPARISONS BETWEEN THE CONTINUOUS-TIME AND COMPLETE MARKET MODELS

We saw in the previous section that dynamic trading could render the diffusion market complete over states distinguished only by different asset prices. In this section we explore the implications of this result for consumption-based pricing. If the market is truly complete in the broader sense of providing insurance against change in the state variables as well, then (i) the allocation of consumption should be Pareto optimal; (ii) since twice differentiable utility functions are locally linear, changes in the consumption flows of all investors should be perfectly correlated; and (iii) we would have our justification for consumption-based pricing which we already know to be valid.

In the general model of Chapter 13, the covariance between the optimal amounts of consumption of any two investors is

$$\begin{aligned} \operatorname{Cov}(\Delta C^k, \Delta C^j) = {} & C_W^k C_W^j \operatorname{Cov}(\Delta W^k, \Delta W^j) + C_x^k C_W^j \operatorname{Cov}(\Delta x, \Delta W^j) \\ & + C_W^k C_x^j \operatorname{Cov}(\Delta x, \Delta W^k) + C_x^k C_x^j \operatorname{Var}(\Delta x) + o(\Delta t), \end{aligned} \tag{30}$$

where subscripts on C^k denote partial derivatives of investor k's optimal consumption. To evaluate this expression, we use the optimal demands in Equation (15):

$$\begin{aligned} \mathbf{w}^k W C_W^k &= \boldsymbol{\Sigma}^{-1}\left(-\frac{U_C}{U_{CC}}(\boldsymbol{\alpha} - r\mathbf{1}) - \boldsymbol{\sigma} C_x^k \right) \\ &= \boldsymbol{\Sigma}^{-1}\left(T^k(\boldsymbol{\alpha} - r\mathbf{1}) - \boldsymbol{\Sigma}\mathbf{h}\frac{\sigma_{xh}}{\sigma_h^2} C_x^k \right), \end{aligned} \tag{31}$$

where T^k is investor k's absolute risk tolerance and $\boldsymbol{\sigma}$, the vector of covariances between the assets and the state variable, has been repalced by $\boldsymbol{\Sigma}\mathbf{h}\sigma_{xh}/\sigma_h^2$ by using Equation (60) of Chapter 13; $\mathbf{h}$ is the vector of portfolio weights in the hedge portfolio. Thus, defining $\gamma \equiv \sigma_{xh}/\sigma_h^2$,

$$\begin{aligned} C_W^k \operatorname{Cov}(\Delta x, \Delta W^k) &= \boldsymbol{\sigma}'\mathbf{w}^k W^k C_W^k = \gamma \mathbf{h}'\boldsymbol{\Sigma}\mathbf{w}^k W^k C_W^k + o(\Delta t) \\ &= \gamma \mathbf{h}'[T^k(\boldsymbol{\alpha} - r\mathbf{1}) - \gamma \boldsymbol{\Sigma}\mathbf{h} C_x^k] \\ &= \gamma T^k(\alpha_h - r) - \gamma^2 \sigma_h^2 C_x^k + o(\Delta t) \end{aligned} \tag{32}$$

and

$$\begin{aligned} &C_W^k C_W^j \operatorname{Cov}(\Delta W^k, \Delta W^j) = C_W^k C_W^j W^k W^j (\mathbf{w}^k)'\boldsymbol{\Sigma}\mathbf{w}^j \\ &= [T^k(\boldsymbol{\alpha} - r\mathbf{1}) - \gamma \boldsymbol{\Sigma}\mathbf{h} C_x^k]'\boldsymbol{\Sigma}^{-1}[T^k(\boldsymbol{\alpha} - r\mathbf{1}) - \gamma \boldsymbol{\Sigma}\mathbf{h} C_x^k] \\ &= C_x^k C_x^j \gamma^2 \sigma_h^2 - \gamma(\alpha_h - r)(T^k C_x^j + T^j C_x^k) + T^k T^j A + o(\Delta t), \end{aligned} \tag{33}$$

where $A \equiv (\boldsymbol{\alpha} - r\mathbf{1})'\boldsymbol{\Sigma}^{-1}(\boldsymbol{\alpha} - r\mathbf{1})$. Substituting (32) and (33) into (30) and collecting terms give

$$\operatorname{Cov}(\Delta C^k, \Delta C^j) = C_x^k C_x^j \operatorname{Var}(\Delta x)(1 - \rho_{xh}^2) + T^k T^j A, \tag{34a}$$

$$\operatorname{Var}(\Delta C^k) = (C_x^k)^2 \operatorname{Var}(\Delta x)(1 - \rho_{xh}^2) + (T^k)^2 A, \tag{34b}$$

where ρ_{xh} is the correlation coefficient between returns on portfolio **h** and changes in the state variable x.

If this correlation is perfect (portfolio **h** provides a perfect hedge), then the correlation between any two investors' consumption flows is also unity:

$$\operatorname{Corr}(\Delta C^k, \Delta C^j) = \frac{A T^k T^j}{\sqrt{A}\, T^k \sqrt{A}\, T^j} = 1. \tag{35}$$

If portfolio **h** does not provide a perfect hedge, then the consumption flows of any two investors will typically be less than perfectly correlated.

Therefore, if a perfect hedge against changes in the state variable is available, then the allcoation of consumption is Pareto optimal; that is, the market is (effectively) complete. It should be clear why this one additional condition is all that is required. If there is a perfect hedge for the state variable among the existing assets, then the states jointly distinguished by different state variables and asset prices must also be distinguished by different asset prices alone. That is, no new states need to be added to the description of the economy, even if we wish to distinguish among outcomes of x. And since we already know that the market is complete with respect to states distinguished by different asset prices, it is also complete in this wider sense as well.

In the absence of a perfect hedge against changes in the state variable, typically investors' individual consumption flows will not be perfectly correlated. However, given their own tastes regarding changes in the state variable, investors will form those portfolios which induce the highest correlation between their own consumption and per capita consumption. This, of course, is not a conscious action on the part of any investor; it is a product of the equilibrium in which investors are trying to minimize the risk of their consumption flow streams and maximize the expected rate of return on their portfolios.

Consider investors who are following their optimal consumption portfolio plans over time. Now suppose that for a single period (one instant) they are going to deviate from their optimal portfolio plans and choose instead those portfolios which maximize the correlation between their consumption and per capital consumption. Since they will return to following their optimal plans immediately, the amount of consumption at the next instant (and all subsequent times) is determined exogenously to the problem now under consideration. Thus, this correlation coefficient is well defined.

The choice variables under their control are the portfolio weights of the individual assets; therefore, the portfolio chosen must have the property that the partial covariance between per capita consumption and the return on each asset, holding their (induced) personal consumption fixed, is zero. If this were not the case, the correlation between $\Delta\tilde{C}$ and $\Delta\tilde{G}$ could be increased by changing the weight of the corresponding asset. The partial correlation coefficient between two random variables $\tilde{x}$ and $\tilde{y}$, holding a third random variable $\tilde{z}$ fixed, is

$$\rho_{xy|z} = \frac{\rho_{xy} - \rho_{xz}\rho_{vz}}{\sqrt{1-\rho_{xz}^2}\sqrt{1-\rho_{yz}^2}}. \tag{36}$$

Therefore, for the maximum correlation between per capita and individual consumption, $\rho_{iG} = \rho_{iC}\rho_{CG}$ for each asset.

Now examine this artificial portfolio problem in detail. The correlation coefficient is the ratio of the covariance to the product of the standard deviations. Therefore,

$$\frac{\partial \operatorname{Corr}(\Delta\tilde{C}, \Delta\tilde{G})}{\partial \mathbf{w}} = (\sigma_C\sigma_G)^{-1}\frac{\partial\sigma_{CG}}{\partial\mathbf{w}} - \frac{1}{2}\sigma_{CG}\sigma_G^{-1}\sigma_C^{-3}\frac{\partial\sigma_C^2}{\partial\mathbf{w}}. \tag{37}$$

The covariance between $\Delta\tilde{C}$ and $\Delta\tilde{G}$ is $WC_W^*\mathbf{w}'\mathbf{g} + C_x^*\sigma_{xG}$, so the first partial derivative in (37) is

$$\frac{\partial\sigma_{CG}}{\partial\mathbf{w}} = WC_W^*\mathbf{g}. \tag{38}$$

The second partial derivative is given in Equation (53) of Chapter 13 as

$$\frac{\partial\sigma_C^2}{\partial\mathbf{w}} = 2C_W^{*2}W^2\boldsymbol{\Sigma}\mathbf{w} + 2C_W^*C_x^*W\boldsymbol{\sigma}. \tag{39}$$

Substituting (38) and (39) into (37) and solving for $\mathbf{w}$ give

$$\mathbf{w}^{**}W = \frac{\sigma_C^2}{\sigma_{CG} C_W^*}\boldsymbol{\Sigma}^{-1}\mathbf{g} - \frac{C_x^*}{C_W^*}\boldsymbol{\Sigma}^{-1}\boldsymbol{\sigma}. \tag{40}$$

As shown in Chapter 13, the fraction in the second term is equal to J_{Wx}/J_{WW}, so the second term matches the second term in (14). From (17) $\mathbf{g} = T^m(\boldsymbol{\alpha} - r\mathbf{1})$, and $T^m = \sigma_{pG}/(\alpha_p - r)$ for any portfolio p. In addition, from Equation (55) of Chapter 13, $C_W^* = (U_C/U_{CC}) = (J_{WW}/J_W)$, and, from (15), $-U_C/U_{CC} = \sigma_{pC}/(\alpha_p - r)$. Making these substitutions in (40) yields

$$\mathbf{w}^{**}W = -\frac{\sigma_C^2 \sigma_{pG}}{\sigma_{CG}\sigma_{Cp}}\frac{J_W}{J_{WW}}\boldsymbol{\Sigma}^{-1}(\boldsymbol{\alpha} - r\mathbf{1}) - \frac{J_{Wx}}{J_{WW}}\boldsymbol{\Sigma}^{-1}\boldsymbol{\sigma}. \tag{41}$$

Finally, the first fraction is just the ratio of correlation coefficients $\rho_{iG}/\rho_{iC}\rho_{CG}$, which was shown to be 1 just after Equation (36). Thus, the portfolio in (41) is the same as that in (14), the solution to the standard portfolio problem, and investors' portfolio choices *do* maximize the correlation between their consumption and per capita consumption.

This result provides the explanation why the consumption-based intertemporal asset-pricing model does not require the additional assumption that there be a perfect hedge for the state variable, which would complete the market and make it Pareto optimal. As shown before, since each investor's consumption has maximal correlation with per capita consumption, any portion of the unanticipated change in individual consumption which is uncorrelated with per capita consumption is uncorrelated with each of the assets' returns as well and vice versa.

In all of our models of equilibrium, each asset's risk premium is proportional to its covariance with every investor's marginal utility (and in the continuous-time models with consumption as well). But as we have just seen, in the continuous-time model per capita consumption provides a perfect instrumental variable for individual consumption in determining risk premiums, because although they are not perfectly correlated, they are both correlated with exactly the same "portions" of each asset's return. This assures that each investor makes the same assessment about what risks do not matter. This "portion" of the risk is nonsystematic risk, which receives no compensation in equilibrium.

The primary lesson of this comparison is that a continuous-time diffusion-model assumption is essentially the same as an assumption of complete markets in discrete-time models. New derivative assets, such as options, are spanned by already existing assets. If there is a perfect hedge for all state variables of interest, then the achieved allocation of consumption is Pareto optimal. If no perfect hedges exist, then a "second-best" solution obtains. Each investor's consumption is as highly correlated as possible, ensuring that all investors make exactly the same assessment of what is "unimportant" risk.

MORE ON THE CONSUMPTION-BASED ASSET-PRICING MODEL

The consumption-based asset-pricing model in continuous time is really more general than the foregoing derivation would indicate. If investors are free to choose the level of their consumption with no constraints other than their own budgets, and if each consumption flow rate follows a diffusion process, then the pricing relations in (18) and/or (19) will be valid for every asset whose price path is also a diffusion.

To demonstrate the generality of the consumption pricing result, consider an investor who is at an optimum. He or she is thinking about consuming c units more at the present and financing this by decreasing the investment in a particular asset. He or she will then move back to the optimal consumption path after the next instant by consuming less at $t + \Delta t$. This policy would change expected lifetime utility by

$$\begin{aligned}\Delta U(c) &= U(C_t + c, t) + E_t[U(\tilde{C}_{t+\Delta t} - c\tilde{z}_i, t + \Delta t)] \\ &\quad - U(C_t, t) - E_t[U(\tilde{C}_{t+\Delta t}, t + \Delta t)].\end{aligned} \tag{42}$$

Since the investor is already at his or her optimum, the choice of $c = 0$ must maximize (42). Assuming the investor's utility function is differentiable, we get

$$0 = \frac{\partial \Delta U(0)}{\partial c} = U_C(C_t, t) - E_t[U_C(\tilde{C}_{t+\Delta t}, t + \Delta t)\tilde{z}_i]. \tag{43}$$

This equation is, of course, just a reconfirmation that the ratio of future to current marginal utility is a martingale pricing process.

Equation (43) must hold for all assets, including the riskless asset, so we can simplify it to

$$0 = E_t[\tilde{U}_C(C_{t+\Delta t}, t + \Delta t)(\tilde{z}_i - R)]. \tag{44}$$

Now expand this expression in a Taylor series to get

$$\begin{aligned}0 &= E_t([U_C + U_{CC}\Delta\tilde{C} + \tfrac{1}{2}U_{CCC}(\Delta C)^2 + \theta] \\ &\quad \times [(\alpha_i - r)\Delta t + \sigma_i\tilde{e}_i\sqrt{\Delta t} + \theta_i] \\ &= E_t([U_C + U_{CC}\Delta\tilde{C}][(\alpha_i - r)\Delta t + \sigma_i\tilde{e}_i\sqrt{\Delta t}]) + o(\Delta t) \\ &= [(\alpha_i - r)U_C + U_{CC}\sigma_{iC}]\Delta t + o(\Delta t),\end{aligned} \tag{45}$$

where both partial derivatives are evaluated at C_t^*. This equation is equivalent to (15), and the consumption model relation in (18) or (19) follows immediately.

Note that in the derivation of this result is was not assumed that any asset prices except the ith followed diffusion processes nor that frictions, such as taxes or transactions costs, or explicit or implicit constraints were absent in the market for trading of these other assets. For example, this result is perfectly consistent with investors having human capital which is not tradable. The assumptions required are that *this* asset trades without frictions and that its price and consumption follow diffusion processes.

Even homogeneous expectations are not required in obtaining this result. If investors have different beliefs, then (45) can be expressed explicitly as

$$0 = E([U_C^k + U_{CC}^k \Delta\tilde{C}][(\alpha_i^k - r)\Delta t + \sigma_i^k \tilde{e}_i^k \sqrt{\Delta t}] | \phi_k, \Phi), \qquad (46)$$

where the index k refers to different investors. ϕ_k is investor k's private information, and Φ is publicly available information. α_i^k, σ_i^k, and $\tilde{e}_i^k$ represent investor k's beliefs about the diffusion process on asset i. We can now take the expectation of (46) conditional on just the public information. Public information is obviously (weakly) less informative than the union of public and any investor's private information, so

$$0 = E([U_C^k + U_{CC}^k \Delta\tilde{C}][(\alpha_i - r)\Delta t + \sigma_i \tilde{e}_i \sqrt{\Delta t}] | \Phi), \qquad (47)$$

where now α_i, σ_i, and $\tilde{e}_i$ represent beliefs based on just the public information. When (47) is aggregated, we get (18) or (19) for the relations among "public" beliefs.

It should be noted that the relation between aggregate consumption and asset returns in (18) or (19) need not hold for any single investor's beliefs since one investor need not conclude that another is at his own optimum; that is, it is possible that

$$0 \neq E([U_C^k + U_{CC}^k \Delta\tilde{C}][(\alpha_i^j - r)\Delta t + \sigma_i^j \tilde{e}_i^j \sqrt{\Delta t}] | \phi_j, \Phi). \qquad (48)$$

The consumption pricing result need be true only based on that portion of the information that is common knowledge.

MODELS WITH STATE-DEPENDENT UTILITY OF CONSUMPTION

The results in the previous sections no longer hold when the direct utility function of consumption is state dependent. As seen in Chapter 13 investors with state-dependent utility of consumption do not choose portfolios which minimize the variance of the flow of their consumption (subject to an expected rate of return constraint). Instead their portfolio choices can be characterized as those which minimize the variance of their marginal utilities.

All of the results of the previous sections can be easily and obviously extended. Marginal utility now takes the place of consumption. (Since the envelope condition still holds in this model, $J_W = U_C$, we can use either direct or indirect marginal utility.) If there are perfect hedges for each of the state variables, then investors will choose portfolios which assure that their marginal utilities are perfectly correlated. If perfect hedges are not available, then individual portfolios are constructed so that the correlations are as high as possible. In either case the appropriate martingale pricing process is marginal utility.

The CAPM form of the equilibrium can be expressed as

$$\alpha_i - r = \frac{\sigma_{iJ'}}{\sigma_{pJ'}}(\alpha_p - r), \tag{49}$$

where $\sigma_{iJ'}$ is the covariance of returns on asset i with changes in some investor's marginal utility, and p denotes any portfolio with a nonzero correlation with marginal utility. A martingale pricing process is

$$\tilde{\Lambda}_t = \exp\left[\left(\frac{\lambda}{2}(\mu_{J'} + r - \sigma_{J'}^2) - r\right)t\right](\tilde{J}'_t)^{-\lambda}. \tag{50}$$

As before λ is the model-specific price of risk. In this case $\lambda \equiv (\alpha_p - r)/\sigma_{pJ'}$.

DISCRETE-TIME UTILITY-BASED OPTION MODELS

To illustrate the use of a martingale pricing process, we will examine option pricing in a discrete-time context. The Black–Scholes option-pricing model and the related binomial model were derived by using the absence of riskless arbitrage and strong distributional assumptions. This permitted the formation of a perfect replica for the option through a dynamically controlled portfolio of the stock and borrowing that exactly hedged the option. In the absence of conditions which permit a perfect hedge, it is possible to derive an identical pricing model by making strong assumptions about utility.

Let $H(S_T)$ be a function which describes the payoff to an option or general derivative asset or contingent claim at time T, and let $f(S_t, t)$ be its value at time t. For example, for a call $H(S) = \text{Max}(S - X, 0)$. Based on the absence of arbitrage alone, we know that there is a martingale pricing process $\tilde{\Lambda}_t$ which values all assets through expectations alone. For the stock and the opiton this means that

$$S_0 = \frac{E[\tilde{S}_T\tilde{\Lambda}_T]}{\Lambda_0}, \tag{51a}$$

$$f(S_0, 0) = \frac{E[H(\tilde{S}_T)\tilde{\Lambda}_T]}{\tilde{\Lambda}_0}. \tag{51b}$$

Now suppose that $\tilde{S}_t$ and $\tilde{\Lambda}_t$ have a joint lognormal distribution. The mean and variance of $\log(\tilde{S}_T/S_t)$ per unit time are $(\alpha - .5\sigma^2)$ and σ^2. The mean and variance of $\log(\tilde{\Lambda}_T/\Lambda_t)$ per unit time are $-r - .5s^2$ and s^2. [Recall that if $\tilde{x}$ is normal with mean μ and variacne v, then $\exp(\tilde{x})$ is lognormal with an expected value of $\exp(\mu + .5v)$.] The correlation per unit time of the two logarithms is ρ.

The product $\tilde{S}_T\tilde{\Lambda}_T$ is also lognormal with

$$E[\tilde{S}_T\tilde{\Lambda}_T] = \mathrm{S}_t\Lambda_t \exp[(\alpha - r - \tfrac{1}{2}\sigma^2 - \tfrac{1}{2}s^2 + \tfrac{1}{2}(\sigma^2 + s^2 + 2\rho\sigma s))(T - t)]. \tag{52}$$

Comparing (52) and (51a), we see that

$$\alpha - r + \rho s\sigma = 0. \tag{53}$$

To value the option, note that $\ln \tilde{\Lambda}_t = b \ln \tilde{S}_t + \tilde{u}_t$, where $b \equiv \rho\sigma s/\sigma^2$ is the regression coefficient, and $\tilde{u}_t$ is a normal random variable independent of $\tilde{S}_t$. Since there is no intercept in the regression equation, $\tilde{u}_t$ is not a zero mean residual. Its mean and variance are $-r - b\alpha + .5(b\sigma^2 - s^2)$ and $s^2 - b^2\sigma^2$ per unit time. Thus, (51b) can be evaluated as follows:

$$\begin{aligned} E[H(\tilde{S}_T)\tilde{\Lambda}_T] &= E[H(\tilde{S}_T)E(\tilde{\Lambda}_T|S_T)] = E[H(\tilde{S}_T)\tilde{S}_T^b]E[e^{\tilde{u}}] \\ &= E[H(\tilde{S}_T)\tilde{S}_T^b]\Lambda_0 S_0^{-b} \exp[(b[.5\sigma^2(1 - b) - \alpha] - r)T]. \end{aligned} \tag{54}$$

The lognormal density function for the return on the stock is

$$\left(\frac{\sqrt{2\pi}\,\sigma S_T}{S_0}\right)^{-1} \exp\left(-\frac{\ln(S_T/S_0) - \alpha T + .5\sigma^2 T}{2\sigma^2 T}\right). \tag{55}$$

Substituting (53)–(55) into (51b) gives

$$f(S_0, 0) = \frac{e^{-rT} S_0}{\sqrt{2\pi}\,\sigma} \int \frac{H(s)}{s} \exp\left(-\frac{\ln(s/S_0) - rT + .5\sigma^2 T}{2\sigma^2 T}\right) ds. \tag{56}$$

In (56) the expected rate of return has been replaced with the interest rate, and discounting is also at the riskless rate. This is clearly a "risk-neutral" valuation with a lognormally distributed stock price, so the resulting option price must be given by the Black–Scholes option formula. Thus, we see that the Black–Scholes model can be derived without the assumption of a diffusion process.

The strong assumption of this model is that the martingale process has a lognormal distribution. Under what conditions will this be true? Apart from singular situations, the only cases in which the martingale pricing process is likely to have a lognormal distribution is if any investor's consumption has a lognormal distribution and his or her utility is isoelastic or if some investor's utility is exponential and his or her consumption has a normal distribution. Stated in this way the assumption that the martingale pricing process had a lognormal distribution, which was easy to state, becomes an assumption about endogenous variables which is difficult to interpret.

RETURNS DISTRIBUTIONS IN THE INTERTEMPORAL ASSET MODEL

We will close this chapter with a final look at the assumption of stationarity. This assumption is one that makes many of the models much simpler, for then each period is, in many respects, a repeat of previous periods. Since prices are endogenous in many models, however, this assumption may have unforeseen consequences.

In the simple form of the intertemporal CAPM of Chapter 13 it was assumed that the investment opportunity set was constant over time. In general, this assumption is questionable. Less obviously, it can lead to unexpected restrictions on prices and/or other undsirable side results.

One proposition of the intertemporal model is the mutual fund or separation theorem that all investors hold the market portfolio of risky assets. The only difference among investors' optimal portfolios is the degree of leverage they choose to use.

Any investor's demands for the risky assets are in proportion to $\mathbf{w} \propto \boldsymbol{\Sigma}^{-1}(\boldsymbol{\alpha} - r\mathbf{1})$. If the investment opportunity set is constant over time, then the right-hand side of this relation is constant, and the demand of any investor for each risky asset must be a constant proportion of that part of his wealth he invests in risky assets. Since this is true of all investors and they all hold the market portfolio, the market portfolio weights must be constant over time.

Let P_{it}, N_{it}, and w_i^m denote the price per share of asset i at time t, the number of shares of asset i held by an investor at time t, and the market proportion of asset i. Then

$$\frac{N_{it}P_{it}}{N_{jt}P_{jt}} = \frac{w_i^m}{w_j^m} \qquad \text{for all } t. \tag{57}$$

Since the right-hand side of (57) is constant, we can use this relation to establish the price relative (return excluding any dividend paid) for asset i over the (discrete or infinitesimal) period t to $t + 1$ as

$$\frac{P_{i,t+1}}{P_{it}} = \frac{(N_{j,t+1}/N_{i,t+1})P_{j,t+1}}{(N_{jt}/N_{it})P_{jt}}. \tag{58}$$

If firms i and j do no new equity financing over the period, then $N_{k,t+1} = N_{kt}$ and (58) reduces to

$$\frac{P_{i,t+1}}{P_{it}} = \frac{P_{j,t+1}}{P_{jt}}; \tag{59}$$

that is, the price relatives must be identical. Over any period during which any two firms issue no new shares and pay no dividends the returns on their shares must be the same. Note that this does not say that their prices are expected to be in the same proportion, but that they *must* remain in the same proportion.

If firms do refinance, but the number of shares to be issued is known at the beginning of the period, then their price relatives must be proportional. In either case the returns over periods of no dividend payments must be perfectly correlated. Certainly this is a testable implication of the intertemporal CAPM which is easily refutable. Even with uncertain financing, Equation (58) places severe restrictions on the independence of asset returns.

To allow asset returns to have completely arbitrary interrelations, we must assume that equilibrium is achieved each period *only through supply adjustments* and not by price adjustments. One economy of this type is a "seed-based" trade where fields with different return characteristics are available freely and in arbitrary scale. Equilibrium is achieved by allocation of the planting, a supply adjustment.

This criticism of the intertemporal CAPM has a kinship with the objection to the single-period CAPM, which argues that it cannot be valid because all investors obviously do *not* hold the market portfolio. These retorts are technically valid, but they miss the point of the exercise. The CAPM and similar models are not normative models of investor behavior; they are positive models about the relation between risk, both systematic and unsystematic, and expected returns. And they appear to do a reasonable job at this. In any case the theoretical purist can fall back on the consumption- or marginal-utility-based CAPM which do not rely on stationarity.

16

An Introduction to Stochastic Calculus

DIFFUSION PROCESSES

A diffusion process is a continuous-time stochastic process which is compact and infinitely divisible, as introduced in Chapter 12. All diffusion processes have sample paths through time which are continuous. Heuristically, this means that the path can be drawn without lifting your pen from the graph. Although continuous, diffusion processes are "infinitely" variable and are not differentiable. Diffusion processes and functions of diffusion processes are often used in dynamic models in finance.

A single-variance (i.e., Markov) diffusion process is written formally as

$$dx(t) = \mu(x, t)\,dt + \sigma(x, t)\,d\omega(t). \tag{1}$$

The first term in (1) is the expected change in x at time t, and the second term is the uncertain component of the change. $d\omega$ is a standard diffusion process (a Wiener process) which is the limit of a Gaussian random variable; that is,

$$d\omega(t) \equiv \lim_{\Delta t \to 0} \sqrt{\Delta t}\,\tilde{u}, \tag{2}$$

where $\tilde{u}$ is standard normal deviate with density

$$f(u) = (2\pi)^{-1/2} e^{-u^2/2}. \tag{3}$$

Shortly, we will need to know the moments of u. These are

$$\mu_k \equiv E(u^k) = \begin{cases} 0, & k \text{ odd}, \\ (k-1)(k-3)\cdots 3 \times 1, & k \text{ even}. \end{cases} \tag{4}$$

ITO'S LEMMA

Ito's lemma is used to determine the differential of a function of a diffusion process. It may be considered the stochastic calculus equivalent to the "chain rule." If $F(x, t)$ is a twice continuously differentiable function of x and a once continuously differentiable function of t, then Ito's lemma states that

$$\begin{aligned} dF(x, t) &= \frac{\partial F}{\partial x} dx + \frac{\partial F}{\partial t} dt + \frac{1}{2}\frac{\partial^2 F}{\partial x^2} \mathrm{dx}^2 \\ &= \frac{\partial F}{\partial x} dx + \left[\frac{\partial F}{\partial t} + \frac{1}{2}\sigma^2(x, t)\frac{\partial^2 F}{\partial x^2}\right] dt. \end{aligned} \tag{5}$$

The second line of (5) follows from the formal multiplication rules $dt^2 = dz\, dt = 0$, $d\omega^2 = dt$. If x were a certain process, $\sigma = 0$, then (5) would be a familiar result from calculus. We derive Ito's lemma after discussing the properties of Wiener processes.

PROPERTIES OF WIENER PROCESSES

$$E[d\omega] = 0, \tag{6a}$$

$$E[(d\omega)^2] = dt, \tag{6b}$$

$$E[(d\omega)^n] = \mu_n (dt)^{n/2}, \qquad n > 2. \tag{6c}$$

These properties follow immediately from the definition of $d\omega(t)$ in (2). In fact, the second and higher moments of $d\omega$ are not random in the sense defined later, and we have the stronger results

$$(d\omega)^2 = dt + O(dt^2), \tag{6b'}$$

$$(d\omega)^n = \mu_n (dt)^{n/2} + O(dt^n), \qquad n > 2. \tag{6c'}$$

Thse results can be demonstrated, by using Chebyshev's inequality

$$\begin{aligned} \text{Prob}[|(d\omega)^n - E[(d\omega)^n]| \geqslant \theta] &\leqslant \frac{E[[(d\omega)^n - E((d\omega)^n)]^2]}{\theta^2} \\ = \frac{E[(d\omega)^{2n}] - E^2[(d\omega)^n]}{\theta^2} &= \frac{(\mu_{2n} - \mu_n^2)(dt^n)}{\theta^2} = O(dt^n). \end{aligned} \tag{7}$$

Thus, the probability of a deviation of $(dz)^n$ from its mean is negligible compared to its mean in magnitude.

DERIVATION OF ITO'S LEMMA

If $x(t)$ were a certain process [i.e., $dx = \mu(x, t)\, dt$], we could use Taylor's expansion to write

$$\Delta F = \frac{\partial F}{\partial x}\Delta x + \frac{\partial F}{\partial t}\Delta t$$

$$+ \frac{1}{2}\left[\frac{\partial^2 F}{\partial x^2}(\Delta x)^2 + 2\frac{\partial^2 \mathrm{F}}{\partial x\,\partial t}\Delta \mathrm{x}\,\Delta t + \frac{\partial^2 F}{\partial t^2}\Delta t^2\right] + R, \tag{8}$$

where R is $O(\Delta t^n)O(\Delta x^m)$, $m + n \geqslant 3$. Since $\Delta x = \mu\,\Delta t + o(\Delta t)$, Equation (8) becomes

$$\Delta F = \frac{\partial F}{\partial x}\Delta x + \frac{\partial F}{\partial t}\Delta t + o(\Delta t), \tag{9}$$

which we write formally as

$$dF = \frac{\partial F}{\partial x}dx + \frac{\partial F}{\partial t}dt. \tag{10}$$

When $x(t)$ is an Ito process, we have

$$(\Delta x)^n = (\mu\,\Delta t + \sigma\,\Delta\omega)^n = \sum_{i=0}^{n}\binom{n}{i}\sigma^i(\Delta\omega)^i(\mu\,\Delta t)^{n-i}. \tag{11}$$

For $n = 2$ we have, from (6b′),

$$(\Delta x)^2 = (\mu\,\Delta t)^2 + 2\mu\,\Delta t\sigma\,\Delta\omega + \sigma^2(\Delta\omega)^2 = \sigma^2\,\Delta t + o(\Delta t). \tag{12}$$

For $n > 2$ we have, from (6b′), (6c′),

$$\begin{aligned}(\Delta x)^n &= (\mu\,\Delta t)^n + n(\mu\,\Delta t)^{n-1}\sigma\,\Delta\omega \\ &\quad + \sum_{i=2}^{n}\binom{n}{i}(\mu\,\Delta t)^{n-i}\sigma^i[\mu_i(\Delta t)^{i/2} + o(\Delta t^i)] \\ &= o(\Delta t^{n/2}).\end{aligned} \tag{13}$$

Thus, (8) becomes

$$\Delta F = \frac{\partial F}{\partial t}\Delta x + \frac{\partial F}{\partial t}\Delta t + \frac{1}{2}\frac{\partial^2 F}{\partial x^2}(\Delta x)^2 + o(\Delta t), \tag{14}$$

which we write formally as

$$dF = \frac{\partial F}{\partial x}dx + \frac{\partial F}{\partial t}dt + \frac{1}{2}\frac{\partial^2 F}{\partial x^2}\sigma^2\,dt. \tag{15}$$

MULTIDIMENSIONAL ITO'S LEMMA

For a function of several Ito processes there is a vector form of Ito's lemma. For

$$dx_i(t) = \mu_i(\mathbf{x}, t)\,dt + \sigma_i(\mathbf{x}, t)\,d\omega_i, \tag{16}$$

and $\mathrm{Cov}(d\omega_i, d\omega_j) \equiv \rho_{ij}$, $\sigma_{ij} \equiv \rho_{ij}\sigma_i\sigma_j$, we have

$$dF(\mathbf{x}, t) = \sum_i \frac{\partial F}{\partial x_i} dx_i + \frac{\partial F}{\partial t} dt + \frac{1}{2} \sum_i \sum_j \frac{\partial^2 F}{\partial x_i \partial x_j} \sigma_{ij}\, dt. \tag{17}$$

This is also written as follows:

$$\begin{aligned} d\mathbf{x}(t) &= \boldsymbol{\mu}(\mathbf{x}, t)\, dt + \mathbf{S}(\mathbf{x}, t)\, d\boldsymbol{\omega}. \\ dF(\mathbf{x}, t) &= \left[\boldsymbol{\mu}' \frac{\partial F}{\partial \mathbf{x}} + tr\left(\mathbf{SS}' \frac{\partial^2 F}{\partial \mathbf{x}'}\right)\right] dt = \left(\frac{\partial F}{\partial \mathbf{x}}\right)' \mathbf{S}\, d\boldsymbol{\omega}. \end{aligned} \tag{18}$$

In this case $\mathbf{x}$ is a vector of dimension n, $d\boldsymbol{\omega}$ is a vector of m ($\leq n$) independent Wiener processes, $\boldsymbol{\mu}$ is a vector function of dimension n, and $\mathbf{S}$ is an $n \times m$ matrix. Although the Wiener processes are independent, the x's need not be since two dx's may depend on the same $d\omega$'s through $\mathbf{S}$. The variance-covariance matrix of $d\mathbf{x}$ is $\mathbf{SS}'$. (It is of rank no more than m.)

FORWARD AND BACKWARD EQUATIONS OF MOTION

If x evolves according to the Markov diffusion process defined in (1) and $f(x, t; x_0, t_0)$ is the probability density function for x at time t conditional on $x(t_0) = x_0$, then f satisfies the partial differential equations of motion. They are the backward Kolmogorov equation

$$\frac{1}{2}\sigma^2(x_0, t_0)\frac{\partial^2 f}{\partial x_0^2} + \mu(x_0, t_0)\frac{\partial f}{\partial x_0} + \frac{\partial f}{\partial t_0} = 0, \tag{19}$$

and the forward Kolmogorov (or Fokker–Planck) equation

$$\frac{1}{2}\frac{\partial^2}{\partial x^2}[\sigma^2(x, t)f] - \frac{\partial}{\partial x}[\mu(x, t)f] - \frac{\partial f}{\partial t} = 0. \tag{20}$$

Each is to be solved subject to the condition $f(x, t_0; x_0, t_0) = \delta(x - x_0)$. That is, at time t_0, x can only be located at x_0, so the density at that time is represented by the Dirac delta function. Here we shall deal only with time homogeneous processes; that is, $\sigma = \sigma(x)$ and $\mu = \mu(x)$.

If $\sigma(x) > 0$ and $|\mu(x)| < \infty$, then, unless constrained, x can take on all real values and $f(\cdot) > 0$ everywhere. Two types of constraints are sometimes imposed. If $f(x_1^+, t)$ is constrained to be 0, then x_1 is said to be an *absorbing barrier* from above. The interpretation is that once $x = x_1$ at t_1, $x = x_1$ for all $t > t_1$. If $\frac{1}{2}\partial[\sigma^2(x)f(x, t)]/\partial x - \mu(x)f(x, t)$ is constrained to zero at $x = x_1$, then x_1 is said to be a *reflecting barrier*. The interpretation is that whenever x reaches the value x_1 it will immedately return in the direction from which it came.

If $\sigma(x_1) = 0$, then x_1 is said to be a *natural barrier*. When $\mu(s_1) = 0$, it is a natural absorbing barrier. When $\mu(x_1, t) < 0$ (> 0) then it is a natural reflecting barrier from below (above). In each case the heuristic interpretation is that at $x = x_1$, dx must have the same sign as $\mu(\cdot)$ with certainty since the variance terms is zero. With natural barriers the constraints mentioned before need not be imposed when solving Equations (19) and (20). Solutions will naturally satisfy them.

EXAMPLES

If $\mu(x) = \mu$ and $\sigma(x) = \sigma$ are constants, then x is said to be Brownian motion with drift. It can be verified in this case that the solution to (19) and (20) is

$$f(x, t; x_0, t_0) = n[(x - x_0 - \mu(t - t_0))(\sigma^2(t - t_0))^{-1/2}] \tag{21}$$

for $n(\cdot)$ the standard normal density function.

If $\mu(x) = \mu x$ and $\sigma(x) = \sigma x$, then x is said to be geometric Brownian motion. Defining $w = \ln x$ and using Ito's lemma, we get

$$dw = \frac{1}{x}dx + \frac{1}{2}\left(-\frac{1}{x^2}\right)dx^2 = \left(\mu - \frac{1}{2}\sigma^2\right)dt + \sigma\, d\omega. \tag{22}$$

Thus w is normally distributed with mean $w_0 + (\mu - \sigma^2/2)(t - t_0)$, and x is lognormally distributed. For geometric Brownian motion, 0 is an absorbing barrier since $\mu(0) = \sigma(0) = 0$. This makes geometric Brownian motion a good choice for modeling asset prices. Once the asset's value falls to zero, it can never again become positive. If it could, this would be an arbitrage opportunity.

If $\mu(x) = k(\overline{x} - x)$ and $\sigma(x) = \sigma$, then x is said to be an Ornstein–Unlenbeck process. Defining $w = (x - \overline{x})\exp(k(t - t_0))$ and using Ito's lemma, we get

$$\begin{aligned} dw &= e^{k(t-t_0)}\,dx + \tfrac{1}{2}\cdot 0 \cdot dx^2 + k(x - \overline{x})e^{k(t-t_0)}\,dt \\ &= e^{k(t-t_0)}[k(\overline{x} - x)\,dt + \sigma\, d\omega + k(x - \overline{x})\,\mathrm{dt}] \\ &= e^{k(t-t_0)}\sigma\, d\omega. \end{aligned} \tag{23}$$

In this case it is straightforward to identify that

$$\begin{aligned} f(w, t; w_0, t_0) &= n\left(\frac{w - w_0}{s(t)}\right), \\ s^2(t) &\equiv \sigma^2\int_{t_0}^{t} e^{2k(t-t_0)}\,dt = \frac{\sigma^2}{2k}[1 - e^{-2k(t-t_0)}]. \end{aligned} \tag{24}$$

Substituting for x, its density function is

$$f(x, t; x_0, t_0) = n\left(\frac{x - \overline{x} - (x_0 - \overline{x})e^{-k(t-t_0)}}{s(t)}\right). \tag{25}$$

As a final example, we shall solve for Brownian motion with an absorbing barrier at zero. For convenience we examine only the case $\mu = 0$. We could determine this density by solving (19) or (20) subject to the appropriate absorbing barrier boundary condition; however, it is more instructive to solve this problem as follows.

Let $x(t)$ be a Brownian motion with an absorbing barrier at zero starting from a point $x_0 > 0$. Let $\hat{x}(t)$ be the same Brownian motion with no absorbing barrier. Then for any $X > 0$,

$$\text{Prob}[x(T) \geqslant X] = \text{Prob}[\hat{x}(T) \geqslant X, \inf \hat{x}(t) > 0] \equiv P, \tag{26}$$

since if $\hat{x}(t)$ goes below zero, $x(t)$ will be absorbed and could never later end above zero.

Clearly, by the law of total probability,

$$\text{Prob}[\hat{x}(T) \geqslant X] = P + \text{Prob}[\hat{x}(T) \geqslant X, \inf \hat{x}(t) \leqslant 0]. \tag{27}$$

Any path $\hat{x}(t)$ contributing to the second term in (27) must pass through the origin. But since $\hat{x}(t)$ follows a symmetric random walk, it is equally likely to rise or fall afterwards, so

$$\begin{aligned}\text{Prob}[\hat{x}(T) \geqslant X, \inf \hat{x}(t) \leqslant 0] &= \text{Prob}[\hat{x}(T) \leqslant -X, \inf \hat{x}(t) \leqslant 0] \\ &= \text{Prob}[\hat{x}(T) \leqslant -X]\end{aligned} \tag{28}$$

because the second condition is redundant. Note that Prob $[\inf \hat{x}(t) = 0] = 0$, so it does not matter into which of the two sets this case is put.

Solving (27) for P and using (28), we have

$$\begin{aligned}P &= \text{Prob}[\hat{x}(T) \geqslant X] - \text{Prob}[\hat{x}(T) \leqslant -X] \\ &= 1 - N\left(\frac{X - x_0}{\sigma\sqrt{T - t_0}}\right) - N\left(\frac{-X - x_0}{\sigma\sqrt{T - t_0}}\right) \\ &= -N\left(\frac{X - x_0}{\sigma\sqrt{T - t_0}}\right) + N\left(\frac{X + x_0}{\sigma\sqrt{T - t_0}}\right),\end{aligned} \tag{29}$$

and the density function for $X > 0$ is

$$f(X, T; x_0, t_0) = \frac{-\partial P}{\partial X} = n\left(\frac{X - x_0}{\sigma\sqrt{T - t_0}}\right) - n\left(\frac{X + x_0}{\sigma\sqrt{T - t_0}}\right). \tag{30}$$

It is a simple matter to verify that (30) satisfies (19) and (20) since it is a linear combination of two solutions. Furthermore, $f(0, T; x_0, t_0) = 0$, as required. Note that the total probability mass above zero is less than unity; that is, $1 - F(0^+, T) < 1$. This shortfall is the probability that absorption has occurred.

For the case of an absorbing barrier when $x(t)$ is Brownian motion with drift the density function is

$$n\left[\frac{X - x_0 - \mu(T - t_0)}{\sigma\sqrt{T - t_0}}\right] - \exp\left(\frac{-2\mu x_0}{\sigma^2}\right) n\left[\frac{X + x_0 - \mu(T - t_0)}{\sigma\sqrt{T - t_0}}\right]. \tag{31}$$

This density function will be useful in future problems. We note here that its characteristic function can be easily determined from that of the normal density (Equation (55), Mathematical Introduction):

$$\phi(q) = \exp\left[iq(x_0 + \mu(T - t_0)) - \frac{q^2\sigma^2(T - t_0)}{2}\right] \times\left[1 - \exp\left(-2x_0\left(iq + \frac{\mu}{\sigma^2}\right)\right)\right]. \tag{32}$$

FIRST PASSAGE TIME

Often the probability density of the first time that $x(t)$ achieves some value is required. These problems can be solved in a similar fashion. Suppose we need to know the distribution of the first time that the origin is crossed or reached. If $G(t; x_0, t_0)$ is this distribution function and $F(x, t; x_0, t_0)$ is the distribution function for the same diffusion process with an absorbing barrier at the origin, then for $x_0 > 0$,

$$1 - G(t; x_0, t_0) = 1 - F(0^+, t; x_0, t_0); \tag{33}$$

that is, the probability that the origin has not yet been reached is the probability that absorption has not occurred. For Brownian motion with drift the first passage time density and distribution can be determined from (31) and (33).

$$g(t; x_0, t_0) = x_0[\sigma^2(t - t_0)^3]^{-1/2} n\left[\frac{x_0 + \mu(t - t_0)}{\sigma\sqrt{t - t_0}}\right], \tag{34a}$$

$$G(t; x_0, t_0) = N\left(\frac{-x_0 - \mu(t - t_0)}{\sigma(t - t_0)^{1/2}}\right) + \exp\left(\frac{-2\mu x_0}{\sigma^2}\right) N\left(\frac{-x_0 + \mu(t - t_0)}{\sigma(t - t_0)^{1/2}}\right). \tag{34b}$$

The first passage time distribution can also be determined without first obtaining the distribution of x. From (33) it is clear that the first passage time distribution (and density) satisfies the Kolmogorov backward equation but not the forward equation. The appropriate boundary conditions are $G(t; x_0, t_0) = 0$ for $x_0 > 0$ and $G(t; 0, t_0) = 1$.

One way to proceed is by defining the Laplace transform (or characteristic function) of g

$$L(q; x_0) = \int_0^\infty e^{-qt} g(t; x_0)\, dt. \tag{35}$$

Taking Laplace transforms of the backward equation (19) term by term gives

$$\frac{1}{2}\sigma^2\frac{\partial^2 L}{\partial x_0^2} + \mu\frac{\partial L}{\partial x_0} + \int_0^\infty e^{-qt}\frac{\partial g}{\partial t_0} = 0. \tag{36}$$

By time homogeneity $\partial g/\partial t_0 = -\partial g/\partial t$, so integrating by parts in the last term of (36) leaves an ordinary differential equation in x_0:

$$\tfrac{1}{2}\sigma^2 L'' + \mu L' - qL = 0. \tag{37}$$

The solutions to linear differential equations with constant coefficients are sums of exponentials—in this case

$$\begin{aligned} L(x_0) &= A\exp[x_0\theta_1(q)] + B\exp[x_0\theta_2(q)], \\ \theta_{1,2} &\equiv \frac{-\mu \pm \sqrt{\mu^2 + 2q\sigma^2}}{\sigma^2}. \end{aligned} \tag{38}$$

From (38) $\theta_2 < 0 < \theta_1$; also

$$L(q;\, x_0) \leqslant L(0;\, x_0) \equiv \int_0^\infty g(t)\, dt \leqslant 1$$

for all positive x_0. But $L(q;\, \infty)$ is unbounded unless $A = 0$. For $x_0 = 0$ absorption occurs immediately, so $g(t) = \delta(t)$, and, from (7) in the Mathematical Introduction, $L(q) = e^{-q0} = 1$. Thus, $B = 1$ and

$$L(q) = \exp[x_0\theta_2(q)]. \tag{39}$$

Inversion of (39) yields (34).

From (35) and (39) the probability of eventual absorption is

$$\pi = L(0) = \exp\left[\frac{-x_0(\mu + |\mu|)}{\sigma^2}\right] = \begin{cases} \exp\left(\dfrac{-2x_0\mu}{\sigma^2}\right), & \mu > 0, \\ 1, & \mu \leqslant 0. \end{cases} \tag{40}$$

The mean time to absorption is

$$-L'(0) = x_0\theta_2'(0)L(0) = \begin{cases} \dfrac{x_0}{|\mu|}, & \mu > 0, \\ \infty, & \mu \geqslant 0. \end{cases} \tag{41}$$

MAXIMUM AND MINIMUM OF DIFFUSION PROCESSES

The probability density of the minimum (or maximum) value reached by a diffusion process can also be determined by using the absorbing barrier problem. Equation (29) gives

$$P \equiv \text{Prob}[\hat{x}(T) \leqslant X, \inf\hat{x}(t) > 0]. \tag{42}$$

Since $\inf(\hat{x}(t)) \leqslant \hat{x}(T)$ by definition, evaluating for $X = 0$ gives $\text{Prob}[\inf\hat{x}(t) > 0]$ as

$$-N\left(\frac{-x_0}{\sigma\sqrt{T - t_0}}\right) + N\left(\frac{x_0}{\sigma\sqrt{T - t_0}}\right) = 2N\left(\frac{x_0}{\sigma\sqrt{T - t_0}}\right) - 1. \quad (43)$$

Because of the uniformity of this diffusion process, we can interpret (43) as

$$\text{Prob}[x_0 - \inf(x(t)) < X] = 2N\left(\frac{X}{\sigma\sqrt{T - t_0}}\right) - 1, \qquad X \geqslant 0. \quad (44)$$

For a diffusion process with drift we can use the density function in (31) to determine the distribution of the minimum.

DIFFUSION PROCESSES AS SUBORDINATED WIENER PROCESSES

Let $\omega(t)$ be a Wiener process (a diffusion process with $\mu = 0$, $\sigma = 1$). Let $b(t)$ be a strictly monotonic differentiable, positive and deterministic function, and let $a(t)$ and $c(t)$ be differentiable and deterministic functions. Then the process

$$x(t) = a(t)\omega[b(t)] + c(t) \quad (45)$$

is a diffusion process. Using Ito's lemma gives

$$\begin{aligned} dx(t) &= a'(t)\omega[b(t)]\,dt + c'(t)\,dt + a(t)\,d\omega[b(t)] \\ &= \left[c'(t) + \left(\frac{a'}{a}\right)[x(t) - c(t)]\right]dt + a(t)\,d\omega[b(t)] \end{aligned} \quad (46)$$

with properties

$$\begin{aligned} E[dx] &= \left[c'(t) + \frac{a'(t)}{a(t)}[x(t) - c(t)]\right]dt, \\ \text{Var}[dx] &= E[dx^2] + o(dt) = a^2(t)E[d\omega^2(b(t))] + o(dt) \\ &= a^2(t)|b'(t)|\,dt + o(dt). \end{aligned} \quad (47)$$

Thus, we may write

$$dx(t) = \left[c'(t) + \frac{a'(t)}{a(t)}[x(t) - c(t)]\right]dt + a(t)\sqrt{|b'(t)|}\,d\hat{\omega}(t), \quad (48)$$

where $\hat{\omega}(t)$ is a second standard Wiener process.

For example the Ornstein–Uhlenbeck process with $\bar{x} = 0$ in (23)–(25) can be represented by the choices $a(t) = \exp(-kt)$ and $b(t) = (\sigma^2/2k)\exp(2kt)$.

EXTREME VARIATION OF DIFFUSION PROCESSES

Diffusion processes are compact in the sense defined in Chapter 12 and have continuous sample paths. However, despite this continuity, their paths are nowhere differentiable. The simplest way to illustrate the non-differentiability of diffusion processes is as follows. Consider

$$\lim_{s \to t} E_t\left[\left[\frac{\omega(s) - \omega(t)}{s - t}\right]^2\right] = \lim_{s \to t} \frac{\text{Var}[\omega(s) - \omega(t)]}{(s - t)^2}$$
$$= \lim_{s \to t} \frac{1}{s - t} = \infty. \tag{49}$$

On the other hand, if a Wiener process has a finite derivative $\omega'(t)$, then

$$|\omega'(t)| \equiv \left|\lim_{s \to t} \frac{\omega(s) - \omega(t)}{s - t}\right| < \infty. \tag{50}$$

Clearly these two conditions are incompatible.

We can see that diffusion processes' paths, although continuous, must have "kinks" everywhere. Technically it is said that a diffusion process has "unbounded variation." This means that the path has infinite length and is not rectifiable; that is, for any set of $n + 1$ time points $t_i = t_0 + i(T - t_0)/n$,

$$\lim_{n \to \infty} \sum_{i=1}^{n} |\omega(t_i) - \omega(t_{i-1})| = \infty. \tag{51}$$

In fact, whenever $x(\tau) = X$, then $x(t) = X$ "infinitely often" in the range $[\tau, \tau + \varepsilon]$ no matter how small ε is (provided only that its drift is bounded and its variance is bounded away from zero). Because this is an important property of diffusion processes, we give two proofs: a short and heuristic mathematical proof followed by an economic proof.

We know that a Wiener process returns to the value $\omega(t)$ infinitely often over $[t, \infty)$. Now consider the transformed process

$$x(t) = t\left[\omega\left(\frac{1}{t}\right) - c\right]; \tag{52}$$

that is, $a(t) = t$, $b(t) = 1/t$, and $c(t) = -ct$. This process has an Ito representation, which can derived from (48),

$$dx = \frac{x}{t}dt + d\hat{\omega}. \tag{53}$$

As t gets large, $x(t)$ becomes indistinguishable from Wiener process since $\mu \to 0$. Now choose c so that $x(T) = 0$. Then x must take on the value zero "infinitely often" in $[T, \infty)$ for all T sufficiently large. But from (52) then ω must take on the value c infinitely often in $(0, 1/T]$ no matter how small $1/T$ is.

An economic proof that a Wiener process undergoes extreme variation relies on the option model, which was developed in a previous chapter. Consider the branching process model of stock prices used in Equations (14)–(20) of Chapter 14. From S the stock price can only change to hS or kS in a single period.

Instead of the hedge employed there, consider the hedge which is always short one option and has borrowed the present value of X dollars. (To simplify the exposition, assume that the riskless rate is zero.) Also it holds one share of stock whenever $S > X$ and X dollars in cash whever $S < X$. This portfolio is worth zero at maturity and with one exception is self-financing. The exception occurs when the stock price jumps from a level at or above X to a level below X or vice versa. In the former case X dollars in cash are required by the strategy, but the stock sale does not raise this. In the latter case $S > X$, and one share of stock could not be purchased with the cash on hand. The most cash that could be required as an input is either when the stock price falls from X to kX, necessitating $(1 - k)X$ dollars, or when the stock price rise from X^- to hX, requiring $(h - 1)X$ dollars. We shall assume that the former is larger in magnitude.

Therefore over the life of this option hedge the expected required input is less than $X(1 - k)$ multiplied by $\bar{N}$, the expected number of times that the option goes in or out of the money.

Now consider the diffusion limit of the example above. To achieve a compact distribution, $1 - k$ and $h - 1$ must approach unity like $(\Delta t)^{1/2}$. Thus, the total expected required input is less than

$$\bar{N}(\Delta t)X(1 - k)(\Delta t)^{1/2}, \tag{54}$$

which goes to zero unless $1/\bar{N}(\Delta t^{1/2}) = O(\Delta t^{1/2})$. Suppose this quantity does go to zero; then the hedge described has a vanishingly small expectation of required new financing, Furthermore, it is worth zero at maturity. Thus, its value must currently be vanishingly small; that is,

$$\text{Max}(S, X) - C - X = 0. \tag{55}$$

In truth $C > \text{Max}(S - X, 0)$ so (55) cannot be even approximately true. We must therefore conclude that $\bar{N} \to \infty$, or that the diffusion limit of the binomial process is "infinitely variable."

STATISTICAL ESTIMATION OF DIFFUSION PROCESSES

Suppose that we have monitored the diffusion process $dx = \mu\, dt + \sigma\, d\omega$ over the interval $(0, T)$, in the process taking N equally spaced observations (separated by $\Delta t = T/N$ units of time). The standard unbiased estimates of μ and σ^2 are

$$\hat{\mu}\,\Delta t = \frac{1}{N}\sum_1^N \Delta x_t, \tag{56a}$$

$$\hat{\sigma}^2\,\Delta t = \frac{1}{N-1}\sum_1^N (\Delta x_t)^2 - \hat{\mu}(\Delta t)^2. \tag{56b}$$

It is easy to see that this estimate of the mean can also be expressed as

$$\hat{\mu} = \frac{1}{T}(x_T - x_0). \tag{57}$$

Thus, its variance is

$$\operatorname{Var}(\hat{\mu}) = T^{-2}\operatorname{Var}(\tilde{x}_T) = \frac{\sigma^2}{T}. \tag{58}$$

Similarly, the variance of $\hat{\sigma}^2$ is

$$\operatorname{Var}(\hat{\sigma}^2) = \frac{2\sigma^4}{N-1} = \frac{2\sigma^4\,\Delta t}{T - \Delta t}. \tag{59}$$

Comparing (58) and (59), we see that the precision of the mean estimate can be increased only by lengthening the period over which the sampling is conducted. The precision of the variance estimate is also increased in this way. In addition, it can be increased by sampling more often during $(0, T)$. For a diffusion process, where, in principle, we can sample infinitely often, the precision can be made arbitrarily high over any nonzero interval with sufficiently frequent sampling.

The same result is also true for a diffusion process with a level or time-dependent variance. For example, consider the diffusion $dx = \mu f(x, t)\,dt + \sigma g(x, t)\,d\omega$. Now let $z \equiv G(x)$, where $G(x) \equiv \int (1/g(s))\,ds$. Then the diffusion process for G is $dG = \mu_G\,dt + \sigma\,dw$, and σ can be estimated as above. Note that the nonconstancy of the mean change in G is not a problem. In fact, it is clear from (56b) that the instantaneous variance of a diffusion can be accurately estimated by using just the mean squared change in the process if the period between observations is sufficiently small. The square of the mean change need not be subtracted since it is of order Δt^2, whereas the variance is of order Δt.

The theoretical implication of this is that all investors must agree about the variance of any continuously observable diffusion process. This conclusion is based on only the weakest supposition about rational expectations or market efficiency. No investor need learn any other investor's private information from the current price before trading. He need only look at past prices.

We can see, for example, that under the Black–Scholes assumptions all investors must agree about the model price of an option since of all the variables that affect the option price, the only possible source of disagreement, the stock's variance, has just been eliminated. In certain respects this finding is comforting. The Black–Scholes option-pricing model is based on the absence of arbitrage. It would be disconcerting to find that two investors could disagree on the price and have each believe that if the other's price prevailed in the market, there would be an arbitrage opportunity.

As a practical matter, sampling cannot be done continuously. So estimates of the variance will not have infinite precision. In addition, when trying to estimate the variance of a price series, it is not necessarily better to sample as often as possible. Fluctuations of the "price" between the bid and ask will cause the sample variance to appear too high. In fact, the tendency for daily returns to display negative first-order serial correlation is evidence that the bid–ask spread has some effect even on daily data.

There is another way to improve the estimate of the variance without looking at each transaction. One way to accomplish this is to use the quoted high and low prices as well as the closing price. For example, assume that the logarithm of a stock's price is Brownian motion without drift. As we saw previously, a nonzero drift will have a minimal affect. The distribution of the range r of values observed over an interval of length t is

$$\text{Prob}(r < R, t) = \sum_{n=1}^{n} (-1)^n 2n\left[N\left(\frac{(n+1)R}{\sigma\sqrt{t}}\right) + N\left(\frac{(n-1)R}{\sigma\sqrt{t}}\right) - 2N\left(\frac{nR}{\sigma\sqrt{t}}\right)\right] \tag{60}$$

for $R \geqslant 0$. The moments of this distribution are

$$E(r) \approx 1.596\,\sigma\sqrt{t}, \tag{61a}$$

$$E(r^2) \approx 2.773\,\sigma^2 t, \tag{61b}$$

$$E(r^4) \approx 10.819\,\sigma^4 t^2. \tag{61c}$$

From (61b), $(.361/t)r^2$ is an an unbiased estimate of the sample variance per unit time; thus

$$\hat{\sigma}_r^2 = \frac{.361}{Nt}\sum_{n=1}^{N} r_n^2 \tag{62}$$

is also an unbiased estimator of the variance per unit time calculated from N observations of the range over periods of length t.

Using (61c), we obtain the variance of this estimator as

$$\text{Var}(\hat{\sigma}_r^2) = N\left(\frac{.361}{Nt}\right)^2 \text{Var}(r^2) = \frac{.130}{Nt^2}[E(r^4) - E^2(r^2)] = \frac{.407}{N}\sigma^4. \tag{63}$$

The variance of the standard estimator (the averaged squared log price changes) is $2\sigma^4/N$, so the efficiency of the former is about five times as great for an equal number of observation days.

Some cautions must be observed when employing this estimator. Equation (60) gives the distribution function of the range for a Wiener process with no drift. For Brownian motion with drift this estimate will be biased high. (To see that the bias is upwards, consider the case when the variance is very small. The range will then primarily reflect the expected change.) Nevertheless, for typical daily stock price data, the square of the expected change is less than 1% of the variance, so, at least in this case, the bias should be small.

Also contributing to an upward bias in this estimator is the bid–ask spread. The daily high is most likely to occur as a market purchase at the specialist's asking price. The low will usually be at the bid. If the "true" price is assumed to be the average of these two, then the observed range will typically exceed the "true" range by the bid–ask spread, and the range estimator will be biased high by approximately $1.152s\sigma/\sqrt{t} + .361s^2/t$. Of course, the standard variance estimator is also subject to a bid–ask spread bias. If we assume that daily closing prices represent bids and asks independently and with equal probability, then, on average, one-half of the observed daily returns will be incorrect by plus or minus the spread. Thus, the standard estimator will be biased high by one-half the square of the bid–ask spread.

There is also an offsetting tendency for a negative bias in this estimator. Since prices are not observed continuously, the quoted high and low need not be the true high and low. In fact, if there is any degree of independence between the stochastic price path and executed trades, then, due to the extreme variation of Ito processes, the quote range will be less than the true range with probability 1. The smaller the trading volume, the more severe will this problem be.

One final problem is causd by the overnight closing of markets. The daily range estimator measures the variance only while the market is open. Multiplying it by the number of trading days in a year will cause an understimate of the annual variance because this ignores the risk of holding stock overnight. Were the variance rate the same overnight and during the day, this could be corrected by dividing the annualized number by the fraction of the time that the market is open. It is likely, however, that the overnight variance rate is smaller. In this case it must be separately estimated. The standard method applied by using close to open prices would work, for example.

17

Advanced Topics in Option Pricing

AN ALTERNATIVE DERIVATION

In Chapter 14 we saw that the Black–Scholes option function was the solution to a particular partial differential equation. In deriving this equation we had to assume that the option function was twice differentiable to obtain expressions for the option's expected rate of return and variance. Simple economic intuition assures that an option price should be a continuous function of the underlying stock price. However, we have no economic rationale for asserting that it be differentiable. In fact the function

$$F(S, \tau) = \gamma W(S, \tau) + (1 - \gamma)\text{Max}[S - Xe^{-r\tau}, 0], \tag{1}$$

where $W(\cdot)$ is the Black–Scholes formula (Equation (38) in Chapter 14), and $0 < \gamma < 1$ satisfies all of the "rationality" constraints for call options given in Chapter 14 and yet is not everywhere differentiable. Other examples of this type can also be constructed. Similarly, there is no obvious reason why the option price could not be a function of other stochastic variables in addition to the stock price. Again the derivation in Chapter 14 would not be valid. We now prove that this form of solution is not tenable.

Assume that the stock price dynamics are of the Ito type,

$$\frac{dS}{S} = \alpha(\cdot)\,dt + \sigma(S, t)\,d\omega, \tag{2}$$

and σ is a deterministic function of S and t. The expected rate of return, α, may be a function of other, possibly stochastic, variables. Assume also that the interest rate is constant.

We construct a portfolio worth P dollars by buying $n(S, t)$ shares of stock and borrowing $nS - P$ dollars. The dynamics of this portfolio's value are

$$dP = n\,dS - (nS - P)r\,dt = n(\alpha - r)S\,dt + rP\,dt + nS\sigma\,d\omega. \tag{3}$$

We now specify the number of shares of stock to be held at any point of time as $n(S, t) \equiv \partial Q(S, t)/\partial S$, where Q is a twice differentiable function to be defined shortly. By Ito's lemma Q evolves according to

$$dQ = [\alpha S Q_S + \tfrac{1}{2}\sigma^2(\cdot)S^2 Q_{SS} + Q_t]\,dt + \sigma(\cdot)SQ_S\,d\omega. \tag{4}$$

Consider the quantity $dP - dQ$. From (3) and (4) this is

$$dP - dQ = [-rSQ_S + rP - \tfrac{1}{2}\sigma^2(\cdot)S^2 Q_{SS} - Q_t]\,dt. \tag{5}$$

Define the yet unspecified function Q as the solution to the differential equation

$$\tfrac{1}{2}\sigma^2(\cdot)S^2 Q_{SS} + rSQ_S + Q_t = rQ \tag{6}$$

subject to $Q(0, t) = 0$, $Q(S, t) \leq S$, $Q(S, T) = \text{Max}(S - X, 0)$. [*Aside*: We know, at least for σ a constant, that such a function exists. In fact, it is obvious from (6) that Q would be the Black–Scholes option function ($Q_t = -Q_\tau$). For nonconstant σ, Q is a generalized "Black–Scholes" type solution. However, we are *not* asserting here that it is the true option price. We use it solely as a mathematical construct formally defined by (6).]

From (5) and (6)

$$dP - dQ = r(P - Q)\,dt. \tag{7}$$

If we select the original amount to invest to be $P(0) = Q(S, 0)$, then from (7) $P(t) \equiv Q(S(t), t)$. So the portfolio is worth $\text{Max}(S(T) - X, 0)$ at $t = T$. This is the same value a call option has at maturity. Consequently, if the option sold at $t = 0$ for C which was more (less) than $P(0)$, an investor could write (purchase) the option and buy (sell) the portfolio described. This strategy would generate a current inflow of $|P(0) - C|$ with no future liability. Thus it presents an arbitrage opportunity.

It is important to recall that we have not assumed that the option function was differentiable, that the option had to sell at an equilibrium price at all points in the future, or even that continuous trading in the option was possible. Rather we have demonstrated that if a solution to a particular equation exists, then it is possible to construct a self-financing portfolio of stock and bonds whose value is always numerically equal to the function. Since the constructed function takes on the value $\text{Max}(S_T - X, 0)$ at T, the portfolio is worth as much as the the call option at that time. By arbitrage the call must always be worth as much as the portfolio. And since the portfolio's value is numerically equal to the function, the constructed function gives the only no arbitrage value for the option.

Furthermore, the only properties intrinsic to call options that were used were the boundary conditions for (6); therefore, a similar proof applies to any contingent claim whose value depends solely on the contemporaneous stock price and time. This should be kept in mind throughout the remainder of this Chapter, even though we use the term "option" generically. As a reminder of this generality, we will denote "options" by the function $H(S, t)$.

A REEXAMINATION OF THE HEDGING DERIVATION

In the original derivation of the Black–Scholes option equation a riskless hedge portfolio was formed by using the stock and option. There it was assumed (Equation (33) of Chapter 14) that the portfolio's return was

$$\frac{dP}{P} = w\frac{dH}{H} + (1 - w)\frac{dS}{S}. \tag{8}$$

The choice $w = \sigma/(\sigma - \sigma')$, where σ' is the standard deviation of the option's return, was claimed to eliminate all risk from the portfolio. From Equation (40) of Chapter 14 $\sigma' = (SH_S/H)\sigma$, so the proper hedge ratio is a function of the stock price and is stochastic.

Once we recognize this, it is clear that the proper expansion of the dynamics of the portfolio's path should, by Ito's lemma, include terms in the changes in the portfolio weighting, but these do not appear in (8). Suppose the portfolio holds N shares of stock and n options. Then $P = NS + nH$, and using Ito's lemma gives

$$\begin{aligned} dP &= N\,dS + S\,dN + dS\,dN + n\,dH + H\,dn + dH\,dn, \\ \frac{dP}{P} &= \frac{nH}{NS + nH}\frac{dH}{H} + \frac{NS}{NS + nH}\frac{dS}{S} + \frac{S\,dN + dS\,dN + H\,dn + dH\,dn}{P}. \end{aligned} \tag{9}$$

The first two terms of the second line of (9) are $w\,dH/H + (1 - w)\,dS/S$, as in (8). If the original derivation is correct, the remaining fraction must be zero. Its numerator can be rewritten as $(S + dS)\,dN + (H + dH)\,dn$. This is just the change in the portfolio shares at the new prices. Since the portfolio is "self-financing," this expression is zero, and the derivation is valid. In a similar fashion the dynamic budget constraint imposed in the continous-time consumption portfolio problem negates the need for considering differentials in the portfolio weights.

THE OPTION EQUATION: A PROBABILISTIC INTERPRETATION

In Chapter 14 we said that the option price could be interpreted as the discounted "expected" value of the terminal payoff, where the expectation and discounting are taken by assuming the stock's and option's expected rates of return were both r. We now provide a basis for that statement.

The option equation is

$$\tfrac{1}{2}\sigma^2 S^2 H_{SS} + rSH_S - rH + H_t = 0. \tag{10}$$

We wish to verify the solution

$$H(S, t) = e^{-r(T-t)}\int_0^\infty \text{Max}(S_T - X, 0) f(S_T, T; S, t)\, dS_T, \tag{11}$$

where f is the risk-neutralized density function of S_T, the stock price at time T conditional on the current stock price $S_t = S$. Defining $\text{Max}(S_T - X, 0) = M(S_T)$ and using Leibniz's rule to differentiate (11) give

$$\begin{aligned} H_t &= rH + e^{-r(T-t)}\int_0^\infty M(S_T) f_t\, dS_T, \\ H_S &= e^{-r(T-t)}\int_0^\infty M(S_T) f_S\, dS_T, \\ H_{SS} &= e^{-r(T-t)}\int_0^\infty M(S_T) f_{SS}\, dS_T. \end{aligned} \tag{12}$$

Substituting into (10) gives

$$e^{-r(T-t)}\int_0^\infty M(S_T)[\tfrac{1}{2}\sigma^2 S^2 f_{SS} + rSf_S + f_t]\, dS_T = 0. \tag{13}$$

But the term inside the square brackets is the backward equation [(19) of Chapter 16] for a lognormal diffusion. Since f is the density function of this diffusion, the term is identically zero, which verifies (11). Since $S = 0$ is an absorbing barrier for the lognormal process, $f(S_T, T; 0) = \delta(S_T)$. Thus,

$$H(0, t) = e^{-r(T-t)}\int_0^\infty M(S_T)\delta(S_T)\, dS_T = 0,$$

as required. Finally, $f(S_T, T; S, T) = \delta(S_T - S)$, and from Equation (7) of the Mathematical Introduction

$$H(S, T) = \int_0^\infty M(S_T)\delta(S_T - S)\, dS_T = M(S).$$

The valuation equation in (11) can also be given a state space interpretation. The expression $e^{-r(T-t)}f(\cdot)$ can be interpreted as the price of a pure state contingent claim paying one dollar at time T if and only if the stock price is S_T at that time. To obtain the option's value, we sum the values of all state-contingent payoffs. For a further discussion of this topic see Chapter 8.

OPTIONS WITH ARBITRARY PAYOFFS

As mentioned previously, the derivations provided in this chapter and Chapter 14 apply to any option-like contingent claim. The preference-free or state space valuations also obtain in general. The value of any asset, whose fundamental valuation equation is given by (6), which satisfies $H(0, t) = 0$ and $H(S, t) < S$, and whose terminal value is $H(S, T) = h(S)$, is

$$H(S, t) = e^{-r(T-t)} \int_0^\infty h(S_T) f(S_T, T; S, t)\, dS_T$$
$$= e^{-r(T-t)} \hat{E}_t[h(S_T)]. \tag{14}$$

OPTION PRICING WITH DIVIDENDS

When the underlying common stock pays dividends, the option pricing problem is considerably complicated. First the "rationality" condition prohibiting early exercise may no longer be valid. Second, the (possibly) stochastic state variables determining the size of the dividends affect the option's value and must be included in the Ito expansion leading to the partial differential equation of option pricing.

The first problem will be dealt with later in this chapter; the second is postponed to Chapter 19. To avoid them for the moment, we consider only European options, so that premature exercise is precluded, and we assume that the dividends to be paid are a known function of the contemporaneous stock price and time. In this case no additional source of uncertainty affecting the option's price has been added, so it remains a function of only the stock price and time.

With these two assumptions the derivation of the option equation is changed but little. Let $D(S, t)$ denote the dividends paid per unit time on the stock. Although standard call options do not receive dividends, it will be convenient for other problems to examine the general case now. $\hat{D}(S, t)$ is the "dividend" paid to the option owner by the option writer.

The stock price dynamics are as assumed in (2); however, α is no longer the expected rate of return. It now represents the expected rate of price appreciation; that is, the expected rate of return is $\alpha + D(S, t)/S$. The dynamics of H are as given in (4). H itself is now defined as the solution to

$$0 = \tfrac{1}{2}\sigma^2(\cdot)S^2 H_{SS} + [rS - D(S, t)]H_S + H_t - rH + \hat{D}(S, t) \tag{15}$$

subject to the same boundary conditions as before. Thus, the general rule is that the term multiplying H_S is the expected risk-neutral price change on the stock, and the term with no derivatives, $-rH + \hat{D}$, is the negative of the expected risk-neutral price change on the option.

Consider the portfolio described previously but with the net dividends from the stock over those paid on one option reinvested in the portfolio. The value of this portfolio evolves according to

$$\begin{aligned} dP &= n\,dS - (nS - P)r\,dt + [nD(\cdot) - \hat{D}(\cdot)]\,dt \\ &= [n(\alpha - r)S + nD - \hat{D} + rP]\,dt + nS\sigma\,d\omega. \end{aligned} \tag{16}$$

From (4), (16), (15), and $n \equiv H_S$, the quantity $dP - dH$ is

$$\begin{aligned} dP - dH &= [-(rS - D)H_S - \tfrac{1}{2}\sigma^2 S^2 H_{SS} - H_t - \hat{D} + rP]\,dt \\ &= r(P - H)\,dt. \end{aligned} \tag{17}$$

Thus, the portfolio which starts with $P = H(S, 0)$ dollars pays dividends at the rate $\hat{D}(\cdot)$ and at the maturity of the option has the same value as one option. As before, $H(\cdot)$ the solution to (15) must be the price of the option.

Dividends are paid at distinct points in time, t_i, which are, at least to a first approximation, reliably forecastable. So

$$D(S, t) = \sum_i D_i(S)\delta(t - t_i), \tag{18}$$

where $\delta(\cdot)$ is the Dirac delta function. In some cases formal manipulations can handle a dividend stream of this type in the option equation (15). However, the delta function is not "well behaved," and it is often easier to use a multistep procedure. Another solution method involves approximating the dividend function by a similar continuous stream or flow of (infinitesimal) dividends. A third method is to price all options in terms of the value of the stock ex all dividends. These three methods are outlined in examples.

Example 1. Suppose that the stock pays a dividend at time t_1 which is proportional to the contemporaneous stock price, $D(S, t) = \gamma S^- \delta(t - t_1)$. S^- denotes the stock price at t_1 just prior to the dividend payment, and S^+ denotes the exdividend price. Assuming that the Miller–Modigliani proposition obtains, $S^+ = (1 - \gamma)S^-$. After t_1 no further dividends are paid, so the Black–Scholes assumptions hold; thus $H(S^+, t_1^+) = W(S^+, T - t_1)$. By continuity of H and the M–M proposition, $H(S^-, t_1^-) = H(S^+, t_1^+) = W[S^-(1 - \gamma), T - t_1]$. The option price for points of times before t_1 can now be determined as the solution to (15) subject to the boundary condition at t_1 just given. Using the risk-neutral or state space pricing method gives

$$H(S, t) = \exp[-r(t_1 - t)]\int_0^\infty f(S^-, t_1; S, t)W[S^-(1 - \gamma), T - t_1]\,dS^-$$

$$= W[S(1 - \gamma), T - t]. \tag{19}$$

If n dividends are to be paid prior to the expiration of the option, we can determine the option price by induction:

$$H(S, t) = W[S(1 - \gamma)^n, T - t]. \tag{20}$$

Example 2. The proportional dividends in Example 1 can be approximated by the continuous dividend flow $D(S, t) = \gamma' S$. The pricing equation (15) becomes

$$0 = \tfrac{1}{2}\sigma^2 S^2 H_{SS} + (r - \gamma')SH_S + H_t - rH. \tag{21}$$

A solution to (21) can be obtained from Equations (16) and (19) of Chapter 14 with $\alpha' = r$ and $\alpha = r - \gamma'$. Alternatively, we can make the substitutions $\tau \equiv T - t$, $Y \equiv Se^{-\gamma'\tau}$, $G(Y, \tau) \equiv H(S, \tau)$. Then

$$\begin{aligned} H_S &= G_Y \frac{\partial Y}{\partial S} = e^{-\gamma'\tau} G_Y, \\ H_{SS} &= e^{-2\gamma'\tau} G_{YY}, \\ H_t &= -G_\tau - G_Y \frac{\partial Y}{\partial \tau} = -G_\tau + \gamma' S e^{-\gamma\tau} G_Y. \end{aligned} \tag{22}$$

Substituting these partial derivatives into (21) yields

$$0 = \tfrac{1}{2}\sigma^2 Y^2 G_{YY} + rYG_Y - G_\tau - rG \tag{23}$$

with solution $G(Y, t) = W(Y, T - t)$. Thus

$$H(S, t) = W(Se^{-\gamma'(T-t)}, T - t). \tag{24}$$

The validity of this dividend approximation is apparent from (20) and (24). If there are m (possibly a fraction) dividend payments per unit time, then the flow rate is $\gamma' = m\gamma$, and the number of payments prior to the expiration of the option is $n = m(T - t)$. The adjustment factor is therefore $(1 - \gamma)^n = (1 - \gamma'/m)^{m(T-t)}$. In the continuous limit

$$\lim_{m\to\infty} \left[\left(1 - \frac{\gamma'}{m}\right)^m\right]^{(T-t)} = [e^{-\gamma'}]^{(T-t)}, \tag{25}$$

which is identical to the factor in (24). (*Aside*: For large S, $H \sim Se^{-\gamma\tau} - Xe^{-r\tau} < S - X$, so premature exercise will be optimal. This verifies the caution given earlier.)

In the formulas in (20) and (24) the expressions $S(1 - \gamma)^n$ and $Se^{-\gamma'(T-t)}$ are the values of owning the stock at time t *without* the right to the dividends between t and T. This methodology can be extended to any dividend payout function $D(S, t)$ as follows.

Let $Z(S, t; T)$ denote the value of a European option expiring at time

T with an exercise price of zero. Since the exercise price is zero and the stock price cannot go negative, this option will always be exercised. Its current value is therefore equal to the stock's current price less the value of the intervening dividends. Z is the solution to (15) with the boundary condition $Z(S, T) = S$. By Ito's lemma the dynamics for Z are

$$\begin{aligned} dZ &= [Z_S(\alpha S - D) + \tfrac{1}{2}Z_{SS}\sigma^2 S^2 + Z_t]\,dt + \sigma S Z_S\,d\omega \\ &\equiv \alpha_Z Z\,dt + \sigma_Z Z\,d\omega. \end{aligned} \tag{26}$$

Note that there are no dividends on the zero-exercise price option, so α_Z is its expected rate of return.

For any other option let $H(S, t) \equiv G(Z, t)$. Then $H_S = G_Z Z_S$, $H_{SS} = G_{ZZ}Z_S^2 + G_Z Z_{SS}$, $H_t = G_Z Z_t + G_t$, and substituting into (15) gives

$$\begin{aligned} 0 &= [\tfrac{1}{2}\sigma^2 S^2 Z_{SS} + (rS - D)Z_S + Z_t]G_Z + \tfrac{1}{2}\sigma^2 S^2 Z_S^2 G_{ZZ} - rG + G_t \\ &= \tfrac{1}{2}\sigma_Z^2 Z^2 G_{ZZ} + rZG_Z - rG + G_t. \end{aligned} \tag{27}$$

The term in brackets in the first line of (27) is equal to rZ from (15) and σ_Z is defined in (26). This last line is the standard no dividend Black–Scholes equation. If σ_Z is a constant, then

$$G(Z, t; T) = W(Z, T - t). \tag{28}$$

Thus Equations (20) and (24) are special cases of (28).

Z is a current and therefore certain payment for receiving the stock at time T. In a forward contract one party, the long, agrees at time t to pay a fixed price, the forward price $F(S, t; T)$ at the maturity of the contract for delivery of the stock. This is also a certain payment resulting in the same delivery. Thus, $F(S, t; T) = Z(S, t; T)e^{r(T-t)}$, and option values can also be expressed in terms of a forward price for the stock $W(Fe^{-r(T-t)}, T - t)$.

If the "option" or contingent claim receives dividends, similar methodology applies. The general solution to (15) subject to the limited liability constraints, and the terminal valuation $H(S, T) = h(S)$ is

$$H(S, t) = \hat{E}_t\left[e^{-r(T-t)}h(S_T) + \int_t^T e^{-r(u-t)}\hat{D}(S_u, u)\,du\right], \tag{29}$$

where the expectation is taken with respect to the diffusion process $dS = (rS - D)\,dt + \sigma\,d\omega$. Because the expectations operator is linear, we can value the terminal receipt and the flow of dividends separately. Valuing the latter part then is only a matter of computing the expectation of functions of a random variable.

OPTIONS WITH PAYOFFS AT RANDOM TIMES

The previous problems have all involved the valuation of uncertain payments which occurred at known points of time. We now examine problems in which the payment is known but its timing is uncertain.

As an example of this kind of problem, we price a "down-and-out" call option. This option contract becomes null, unexercisable, if the stock price declines to the "knockout" price prior to maturity. When this occurs, a rebate is given. The two potential payments to this option are related because once the rebate is received, the option is worthless at maturity.

Let $K(t)$ denote the knockout price and $R(t)$ the rebate at time t. The price of down-and-out option maturing at T is the solution to

$$\tfrac{1}{2}\sigma^2 S^2 D_{SS} + rSD_S - rD + D_t = 0, \qquad S > K(t), \tag{30a}$$

Subject to

$$D[K(t), t] = R(t), \qquad S(u) > K(u), \quad u < t, \tag{30b}$$

$$D(S, T) = \text{Max}(S - X, 0) \qquad \text{for } S > K(T). \tag{30c}$$

For simplicity we have assumed that the option is European and that $X > K(T)$.

The solution to (30) by using the risk-neutral pricing technique is

$$\begin{aligned} D(S, t) &= e^{-r(T-t)}\int_X^\infty (S_T - X) f(S_T, T; S, t)\, dS_T \\ &\quad + \int_t^T e^{-r(u-t)} R(u) g[u; K(\cdot), S, t]\, du. \end{aligned} \tag{31}$$

The function $f(\cdot)$ is the (defective) density for the stock price at time T with an absorbing barrier $K(t)$ imposed and conditional on the current stock price S, and $g(\cdot)$ is the first passage time density of S through the absorbing barrier $K(t)$.

Although this problem may appear to be quite different conceptually from previous examples, they can be interpreted very similarly. The first term in (31) gives that portion of the option's value due to exercising the option as in previous examples. The second term gives the portion of the option's value arising from the rebate. This term is very similar to a stream of dividends: $R(u)g(u; \cdot)$ is the "expected" value of the rebate payment at time u, and $e^{-r(u-t)}$ is the risk-neutral discount factor.

To verify this solution, we differentiate (31) by using Leibniz's rule:

$$D_S = e^{-r(T-t)}\int_X^\infty (S_T - X) f_S\, dS_T + \int_t^T e^{-r(u-t)} R(u) g_S\, du,$$

$$D_{SS} = e^{-r(T-t)}\int_X^\infty (S_T - X) f_{SS}\, dS_T + \int_t^T e^{-r(u-t)} R(u) g_{SS}\, du, \quad (32)$$

$$D_t = e^{-r(T-t)}\int_X^\infty (S_T - X)(rf + f_t)\, dS_T + R(t)g(t)$$
$$+ \int_t^T e^{-r(u-t)} R(u)(rg + g_t)\, du.$$

If $S > K(t)$, then $g(t) = 0$, and substituting (32) into (30a) gives

$$\begin{aligned} &e^{-r(T-t)}\int_X^\infty (S_T - X)[\tfrac{1}{2}\sigma^2 S^2 f_{SS} + rSf_S + rf - rf + f_t]\, dS_T \\ &+ \int_t^T e^{-r(u-t)} R(u)[\tfrac{1}{2}\sigma^2 S^2 g_{SS} + rSg_S + rg - rg + g_t]\, du = 0. \end{aligned} \quad (33)$$

The terms inside the brackets are the backward equation of a lognormal diffusion [(19) of Chapter 16]. The function f and the first passage time density g are known solutons, so [30a] is verified.

At $t = T$, $f(\cdot) = \delta(S_T - S)$, so from (7) in the Mathematical Introduction the first integral in (33) is $\text{Max}(S - X, 0)$. The second integral vanishes becaue its upper and lower limits are the same. This verifies (30c). Once the absorbing barrier is reached, $f(S_T) \equiv 0$ for all $S_T > X > K(t)$, so the first integral is zero. On the other hand, $g[u; K(t), K(t), t] = \delta(u - t)$, so the second integral is $R(t)$. This verifies (30b).

For a constant knockout price and a rebate of zero the solution to (30) or (31) is, for $S > K$,

$$D(S, t; T, X, K, 0) = W(S, T - t; X) - \left(\frac{S}{K}\right)^{-\gamma} W\left(K, T - t; \frac{SX}{K}\right). \quad (34)$$

When the rebate is a positive constant R, the second integral in (31) must be evaluated. The first passage time density was given in Equation (34a) of Chapter 16. Let $z \equiv \log(S/K)$, $\mu \equiv r - \sigma^2/2$, $\hat{\mu} \equiv r + \sigma^2/2$. Then this second integral is

$$\begin{aligned} &R\int_t^T e^{-r(u-t)} g(u; z; \mu)\, du \\ &= R\int_t^T z[2\pi\sigma^2(u - t)^3]^{-1/2} \exp\left[-r(u - t) - \frac{[z + \mu(u - t)]^2}{2\sigma^2(u - t)}\right] du \\ &= Re^z \int_t^T g(u; z; \hat{\mu})\, du = R\frac{S}{K} G(T; z, t; \hat{\mu}) \\ &= R\frac{S}{K}\left[N\left(\frac{-z - \hat{\mu}(T - t)}{\sigma(T - t)^{1/2}}\right) + \exp\left(-\frac{2\hat{\mu}z}{\sigma^2}\right) N\left(\frac{-z + \hat{\mu}(T - t)}{\sigma(T - t)^{1/2}}\right)\right]. \end{aligned} \quad (35)$$

OPTION PRICING SUMMARY

The general contingent claims equation can now be written as

$$0 = \tfrac{1}{2}\sigma^2 S^2 H_{SS} + (rS - D)H_S - rH + H_t + \hat{D}, \quad \underline{S}(t) < S < \overline{S}(t), \tag{36a}$$

$$H(S, T) = h(S), \tag{36b}$$

$$H(\overline{S}(t), t) = \overline{h}(t), \tag{36c}$$

$$H(\underline{S}(t), t) = \underline{h}(t), \tag{36d}$$

where $h(S)$ is the contractually specified value of the option at termination of the contract, $\overline{h}(t)$ and $\underline{h}(t)$ are also contractually specified payments received if and when the stock price first reaches $\overline{S}(t)$ or $\underline{S}(t)$. The value of the "option," the solution to (36), is

$$\begin{aligned} H(S, t) = {} & e^{-r(T-t)} \int h(S_T) f(S_T, T)\, dS_T \\ & + \int_t^T e^{-r(u-t)} \int \hat{D}(S_u, u) f(S_u, u)\, dS_u\, du \\ & + \int_t^T e^{-r(u-t)} [\overline{h}(u)\overline{g}(u) + \underline{h}(u)\underline{g}(u)]\, du, \end{aligned} \tag{37}$$

where f is the defective density and $\overline{g}$ and $\underline{g}$ are first passage time densities to the upper and lower barriers, respectively.

PERPETUAL OPTIONS

In certain applications, the option, like the underlying stock, has an indefinite life. If the stock's dynamics, the dividend streams, and the boundary conditions (36c), (36d) are time independent, then the option's value will not depend upon time either, and (36a) reduces to an ordinary differential equation. Since ordinary differential equations are substantially easier to handle than partial differential equations, perpetuities are often used as approximations for long-lived contingent claims as well.

When valuing perpetual claims, however, certain precautions must be taken to handle infinities. The next example illustrates the type of problem which can arise.

Consider the perpetual down-and-out option with a constant knockout price K and constant rebate R. Equation (27) modified for a perpetuity is

$$\tfrac{1}{2}\sigma^2 S^2 D'' + rSD' - rD = 0, \qquad S > K, \tag{38a}$$

subject to

$$D(K) = R. \tag{38b}$$

The solution to (38) can be obtained by evaluating the limits of (34) and (35):

$$\begin{aligned} D(S, t; \infty, X, K, R) &= S - \left(\frac{S}{K}\right)^{-\gamma} K + R\left(\frac{S}{K}\right)^{-\gamma} \\ &= S + (R - K)\left(\frac{S}{K}\right)^{-\gamma} \end{aligned} \tag{39}$$

In general, the finite maturity solution would not be known, so the perpetual solution could not be obtained as a limit. The solution method is illustrated here.

Equation (38a) is a homogeneous, linear, second-order differential equation, so all solutions are linear combinations of two distinct fundamental solutions. It is easy to verify that these solution are S and $S^{-\gamma}$, for $\gamma \equiv 2r/\sigma^2$. Thus

$$D(S) = AS + BS^{-\gamma}. \tag{40}$$

(38b) serves to establish one link between the two constants A and B, namely, $B = (R - AK)K^{\gamma}$. From (39) it is clear that the proper choice is $A = 1$; however, to establish this, a second boundary condition is required. Since an ordinary option can be no more valuable than the stock, the most that a down-and-out option can exceed the stock price by is the rebate. Thus $0 \le D(S) \le S + R$. These conditions are insufficient to establish the constants. In fact any value of A between 0 and 1 inclusive will satisfy them. To verify this assertion, note that

$$\begin{aligned} D(S) &= A\left(S - K\left(\frac{S}{K}\right)^{-\gamma}\right) + R\left(\frac{S}{K}\right)^{-\gamma}, \\ D(S) - S - R &= (A - 1)S + R\left[\left(\frac{S}{K}\right)^{-\gamma} - 1\right] - AK\left(\frac{S}{K}\right)^{-\gamma}. \end{aligned} \tag{41}$$

For $S > K$ (the relevant range), the first line of (41) is uniformly positive and the second line negative, term-by-term, for $0 \leqslant A \leqslant 1$.

If the option were American, the no arbitrage condition $D \geqslant S - X$ would determine the constant A. Arbitrage by exercise always exists for some sufficiently large S whenever $A < 1$ because $D(S) \sim AS$. For a European option, arbitrage by exercise is not possible, so this condition cannot be imposed; however, it does provide the same answer. The American option's value is strictly greater than $S - X$, so it will never be exercised. The American feature is therefore of no additional value, so $A = 1$ for the European option as well, and (39) is verified.

It is interesting to decompose the down-and-out value. The portion due to receipt of the rebate is, from (37),

$$D^R = R\int_0^\infty e^{-rt} g(t;\, K,\, S,\, t)\, dt = R\left(\frac{S}{K}\right)^{-\gamma}, \tag{42}$$

where $g(\cdot)$ is the first passage time density. The Laplace transform of this density for absolute Brownian motion was given in the last chapter. The solution given comes from a comparison of the integral in (42) with Equation (35) of Chapter 16 and the definitions $x_0 = \ln(S/K)$ and $\mu = r - \sigma^2/2$. The remainder of the option's value $S - K(S/K)^{-\gamma}$ comes from the right to exercise the option. Note that the value of this right is independent of the exercise price and is positive even though exercise never literally will occur in finite time. Even more paradoxically this right has value even if the probability of ultimately receiving the rebate, which nullifies the right to exercise, is unity. (This is the case for $\sigma^2 > 2r$; see Equation (40) in Chapter 16 and recall that $\mu = r - \sigma^2/2$.)

This is where the problem of "infinities" arises. Even though the probability of exercise is vanishingly small, the future expected benefit when doing so is unbounded. Together these give a finite present value, as we now show. Define $z \equiv \ln(S/K)$ and $t_0 = 0$; then z follows an absolute diffusion with risk-neutralized drift of $\mu = r - \sigma^2/2$ and an absorbing barrier at zero. The density function for z is given in Equation (31) of Chapter 16. The expected value of the stock price if no knockout (no absorption) has occurred is

$$E^+(S) \equiv E[S(T);\, S(t) > K) = K\int_K^\infty e^z f(z)\, dz. \tag{43}$$

But the integral in (43) is a special case of the characteristic function $\phi(-i)$. Using Equation (32) in Chapter 16, we get

$$\begin{aligned} E^+(S) &= K\exp\left[z + \mu T + \frac{\sigma^2 T}{2}\right]\left[1 - \exp\left(-2z\left(1 + \frac{\mu}{\sigma^2}\right)\right)\right] \\ &= Se^{rT}\left[1 - \left(\frac{S}{K}\right)^{-(\gamma+1)}\right] = e^{rT}\left[S - K\left(\frac{S}{K}\right)^{-\gamma}\right]. \end{aligned} \tag{44}$$

The risk-neutral present value of receiving the stock conditional upon no previous rebate is $S - K(S/K)^{-\gamma}$ *regardless* of when receipt actualy occurs. The present value of the exercise payment after an infinite time is zero so the option portion of the down-and-out is also $S - K(S/K)^{-\gamma}$.

OPTIONS WITH OPTIMAL EARLY EXERCISE

Up to this point we have concentrated on European options and have considered their American counterparts only in situations when exercise would never occur prior to maturity. We now turn out attention to options for which the American feature has strictly positive value.

The simplest problem of this type is the call option written on the dividend paying stock examined in Example 1. Premature exercise will occur only just before the stock goes exdividend. If the option remains unexercised at the exdividend moment, $H(S^+, t_1^+) = W(S^+, T - t_1)$. If the option is exercised, then $H(S^-, t_1^-) = S^- - X$. Since the owner of the option chooses whether to exercise, he or she will do so only if $S^- - X > W(S^+, T - t_1)$; therefore

$$H(S^-, t_1^-) = \text{Max}[S^- - X, W(S^-(1 - \gamma), T - t_1)]. \tag{45}$$

In analogy with (19),

$$H(S, t) = \exp[-r(t_1 - t)]\int_0^\infty H(S^-, t_1^-)f(S^-, t_1; S, t)\,dS^-. \tag{46}$$

If more than one dividend remains, then the option can be priced by induction. If dividends are approximated as a continuous flow, or if for other reasons exercise can occur at any time, then an alternative method must be employed.

We denote the as yet unknown optimal exercise strategy by $\bar{S}(t)$. If $S = \bar{S}(t)$ at time t, then whatever rights are embodied in the (still alive) option are to be used. The option is then worth $H(\bar{S}(t), t) = \bar{S}(t) - X$, an amount which is determinable at $t = 0$. If the optimal exercise strategy were known, then the problem would be identical to the one with payoffs at random times as stated in (36) and solved formally in (37).

Usually the optimal strategy is not known but must be determined simultaneously with the actual valution. In principle we could solve (36) for arbitrary strategies $\hat{S}(t)$. Call these solution functionals $f(S, t; \hat{S}(t))$. Then the option value is

$$\begin{aligned} H(S, t) &= \text{Max}[f(S, t; \hat{S}(t))], \\ \bar{S}(t) &= \arg\max[f(S, t; \hat{S}(t)], \end{aligned} \tag{47}$$

where the maximization has been taken over the class of all feasible functions $\hat{S}(\cdot)$. H is the maximum since the holders of the option will choose the strategy $\bar{S}$ which is best, that is, the one producing the greatest option value. In a competitive market the option will sell for no less (and no more) than this maximized value.

To value options with this method requires solving a difficult calculus of variations problem. An equivalent attack on this problem imposes the "high-contract" or "smooth pasting" condition

$$\frac{\partial H(\bar{S}(t), t)}{\partial S} = \frac{\partial \bar{H}(\bar{S}, t)}{\partial \bar{S}}, \tag{48}$$

provided $\bar{H}$ is differentiable. To see the equivalence, note that $f(\hat{S}, t; \hat{S})$

$= \bar{H}(\hat{S}, t)$. Consider the total derivative of f along the path $S = \hat{S}$:

$$\left.\frac{\partial \bar{H}(\bar{S}, t)}{\partial \bar{S}}\right|_{\bar{S}=\hat{S}} = \left.\left[\frac{\partial f(S, t; \hat{S})}{\partial S} + \frac{\partial f(S, t; \hat{S})}{\partial \hat{S}}\right]\right|_{S=\hat{S}}. \tag{49}$$

By definition, at the optimum $\hat{S} = \bar{S}$, $\partial f/\partial \hat{S} = 0$. Thus $\partial f(\bar{S}, t)/\partial S \equiv \partial H(\bar{S}, t)/\partial S = \partial \bar{H}/\partial \bar{S}$.

As an example of a problem of this type, we choose the perpetual American put option. Proceeding as in (47), we select $\hat{S}$ as the exercise strategy and denote the (conditional) option price by f. Then

$$\tfrac{1}{2}\sigma^2 S^2 f'' + rSf' - rf = 0, \tag{50a}$$

$$f(\hat{S}) = X - \hat{S}, \tag{50b}$$

$$f(\infty) = 0. \tag{50c}$$

The general solution to (50a) is

$$f(S) = AS + BS^{-\gamma}. \tag{51}$$

Satisfaction of (50c) requires that $A = 0$. From (50b) then, $B = \hat{S}^{\gamma}(X - \hat{S})$, so

$$f(S, \hat{S}) = (S - \hat{S})\left(\frac{S}{\hat{S}}\right)^{-\gamma}. \tag{52}$$

Maximizing over $\hat{S}$ gives $-(S/\hat{S})^{-\gamma} + \gamma(X - \hat{S})(S/\hat{S})^{-\gamma}/\hat{S} = 0$, or

$$\bar{S} = \frac{\gamma}{1 + \gamma}X \tag{53}$$

and $H(S) = f(S, \bar{S})$. The high-contact condition is verified since

$$H'(\bar{S}) = -\gamma\frac{(X - \bar{S})}{\bar{S}} = -1 = \frac{\partial(X - \bar{S})}{\partial \bar{S}}.$$

(*Note*: The payoff function Max$(X - S, 0)$ is not everywhere differentiable. Nevertheless, it is differentiable over the relevant range since $\bar{S} < X$ on an an priori basis.)

The callable call option is an example of a problem in which the high-contact condition does not obtain. A callable call option is an option on which the writer retains the right to either repurchase it for the call price K or force the holder to exercise. Under an arbitrary call policy $\hat{S}$, a perpetual callable call is the solution to (50a) subject to

$$f(\hat{S}) = \text{Max}(K, \hat{S} - X), \tag{54a}$$

$$f(0) = 0. \tag{54b}$$

The general solution is given in (51). (54b) places the requirement that

$B = 0$. From (54a) $A = K/\hat{S}$ if $\hat{S} < K + X$ and $A = (\hat{S} - X)/\hat{S}$ if $\hat{S} > K + X$. Thus

$$f(S) = \frac{\text{Max}(K, \hat{S} - X)S}{\hat{S}}. \tag{55}$$

The value of $\hat{S}$ is selected by the writer of the option, so it will be chosen to minimize the value of f.

$$\frac{\partial f(S)}{\partial \hat{S}} = \begin{cases} -\dfrac{SK}{\hat{S}^2}, & \hat{S} < K + X, \\ \dfrac{SX}{\hat{S}^2}, & \hat{S} > K + X. \end{cases} \tag{56}$$

Since f is decreasing for $\hat{S} < K + X$ and increasing for $\hat{S} > K + X$, $\hat{S} = K + X$ must be the minimizing value. Therefore, the callable call is worth

$$H(S) = \frac{K}{K + X}S. \tag{57}$$

The derivative of H is $K/(K + X)$, and the derivative of the payoff function $\text{Max}(K, \hat{S} - X)$ is 0 or 1 in the two relevant regions. At the boundary $\hat{S} = K + X$ the right derivative is 1, and the left derivative is 0. We might conclude therefore that the high-contact condition implies $0 \leqslant H' \leqslant 1$. Although this is true, it is insufficient to specify the solution completely.

OPTIONS WITH PATH-DEPENDENT VALUES

Previously we have considered the pricing of three types of options: those whose "payments" accrued at fixed times and were functions of only the contemporaneous stock price and time, those whose payments were deterministic but occurred at unknown times, and those whose payments were discrete mixtures of these two types. We now examine options whose payments are fixed in time but depend in amount upon the past history of the stock price.

Before learning to price such options, we must first determine if they are hedgable as are ordinary puts and calls. If a riskless hedge can be created for them by using only the stock and default-free bonds, then the Cox–Ross–Merton preference-free pricing technique can be employed. If no hedge is possible, then some equilibrium model must be used.

As a simple example of this type of option, consider a call with a stochastic (at issuance) exercise price equal to the average stock price during its life $(0, T)$; that is, $X = A(T)/T$, where

$$A(T) = \int_0^T S(t)\,dt. \tag{58}$$

The price of this option is a function of time and the two state variables $S(t)$ and $A(t)$. The evolution of the latter is, by the mean value theorem,

$$dA(t) = \lim_{\Delta t \to 0} \int_t^{t+\Delta t} S(u)\,du = \lim_{\Delta t \to 0} S(t^*)\,\Delta t = S(t)\,dt. \tag{59}$$

Since dA is deterministic, a riskless hedge for this option requires only eliminating the stock-induced risk. This is accomplished by holding F_S shares of stock short for each option.

The appropriate pricing equation for this asset is therefore

$$\tfrac{1}{2}\sigma^2 S^2 F_{SS} + rSF_S + SF_A + F_t = 0, \tag{60a}$$

$$F(0, A, t) = 0, \tag{60b}$$

$$F_1(\infty, A, t) = 1, \tag{60c}$$

$$F(S, \infty, t) = 0, \tag{60d}$$

$$F(S, A, T) = \operatorname{Max}\left(S - \frac{A}{T}, 0\right). \tag{60e}$$

Note that since A is locally deterministic, only a first derivative term appears, and the drift term for A is unadjusted. Furthermore, since only a first partial derivative term for A appears, only one A boundary condition is needed.

A solution to (60) in a closed form is possible, but since the option in question is an artificial example it would have little use. However, we can use this problem to illustrate one additional property which is often helpful in pricing problems. All parts of Equation (60) are linearly homogeneous in S and A; therefore, the option price should be as well. (The deduction that $F(\cdot)$ is linearly homogeneous in S and A can also be made just from the terms of the contract and the homogeneity of the stock's price dynamics.)

Because of the linear homogeneity, we can write $F(S, A, t) \equiv AG(x, t)$, where $x \equiv S/A$. Since $F_S = G_x$, $F_{SS} = G_{xx}/A$, $F_A = G - xG_x$, and $F_t = AG_t$, Equation (60) becomes

$$\tfrac{1}{2}\sigma^2 x^2 G_{xx} + (rx - x^2)G_x + (x - r)G + G_t = 0, \tag{61a}$$

$$G(0, t) = 0, \tag{61b, d}$$

$$G_x(\infty, t) = 1, \tag{61c}$$

$$G(x, T) = \operatorname{Max}\left(x - \frac{1}{T}, 0\right). \tag{61e}$$

The fact that (60) can be rewritten as (61) in terms of x alone confirms our intuition.

As a more difficult example we now examine an option which permits its owner to purchase at the maturity date T one share of a nondividend paying stock upon a payment equal to the minimum stock price reached during its life; that is, $X = m(0, T)$, where

$$m(0, T) = \min[S(t): 0 \leqslant t \leqslant T]. \tag{62}$$

This option's price is a function of the time and two state variables $S(t)$ and $m(0, t)$ with evolutions

$$\begin{aligned} dS &= \alpha S\,dt + \sigma(S, t)S\,d\omega, \\ dm &= \begin{cases} 0, & S > m, \\ 0, & S = m,\ dS \geqslant 0, \\ -dS, & S = m,\ dS < 0. \end{cases} \end{aligned} \tag{63}$$

The option's price dynamics are

$$\begin{aligned} dH = {} & H_t\,dt + H_S\,dS + \tfrac{1}{2}H_{SS}\,dS^2 + H_m\,dm + \tfrac{1}{2}H_{mm}\,dm^2 \\ & + H_{mS}\,dm\,dS + o(dt). \end{aligned} \tag{64}$$

Only the terms $H_S\,dS$ and $H_m\,dm$ contribute [to $O(\sqrt{dt})$] to the uncertain portion of the option's price change, and the latter does so only when $S = m$. Whenever $S > m$, $dm = 0$ and this option is perfectly hedged with H_S shares of stock. When $S = m$, however, it would appear that two hedge ratios are relevant: H_S if the stock price should rise, and $H_S - H_m$ should it fall. As we cannot know in advance which will happen, a perfect hedge can be constructed from the stock alone only if these two ratios are equal; that is, $H_m = 0$. Fortunately, this is true when $S = m$. (*Note*: It is not true when $S > m$.)

Before proving the preceding statement, the following intuition is offered. Because Ito processes are "infinitely" variable, the probability that the stock price will never fall below its current value even in a very short interval of time is vanishingly small. Therefore, when $S = m$ the probability that the minimum price reached in the future will still be only m is correspondingly negligible. Thus, small changes in m leave the option's value unaffected.

To prove that $H_m = 0$ when $S = m$, we first write the general valuation equation

$$\begin{aligned} H(S(t), m(0, t), t; T) &= PV[S(T) - m(0, T)] \\ &= PV[S(T)] - PV[m(0, T)], \end{aligned} \tag{65}$$

where $PV(\cdot)$ is the appropriately risk-adjusted discounted expected value operator. As this option will always be exercised, the present value of the payoff can be decomposed into its two parts as in (65). Furthermore, since no dividends are paid on the stock, $PV[S(T)] = S(t)$. Thus, the value of the option is determined only by the probability distribution of the minimum. We do not require knowledge of the joint distribution of $S(T)$ and $m(0, T)$.

To show that $H_m = 0$ when $S = m$, we need now only show that the distribution of $M \equiv m(0, T)$ is independent of $m \equiv m(0, t)$ when $S = m$, and to prove the latter it is sufficient to prove that all the moments of M are independent of m. Let $m' \equiv m(t, T)$ denote the minimum reached after the current time, and let $dF(m')$ be its density function. The nth moment of M is

$$\mu_n = \int_0^S [\text{Min}(m, m')]^n \, dF(m') = \int_0^m (m')^n \, dF + m^n \int_m^S dF. \tag{66}$$

Using Leibniz's rule and noting that the density function $dF(m')$ is independent of the past maximum m, we get

$$\frac{\partial \mu_n}{\partial m} = m^n \, dF(m) - m^n \, dF(m) + nm^{n-1} \int_m^S dF. \tag{67}$$

The first two terms cancel, and evaluating this integral at $S = m$ gives

$$\left.\frac{\partial \mu_n}{\partial m}\right|_{m=S} = nS^{n-1} \int_S^S dF. \tag{68}$$

Since an Ito process does not permit any discrete probability mass at any point, this integral is zero, and the result is proved.

We have now proved that this option can be hedged, so the preference-free pricing methodology is applicable, and

$$H(S, m, t; T) = S - e^{-r(T-t)} \int_0^S \text{Min}(m, m') \, d\hat{F}(m'), \tag{69}$$

where $d\hat{F}$ is the risk-neutral density function for the minimum of a diffusion process. If the stock price follows geometric Brownian motion, σ a constant, then the density function in Chapter 16 can be used to determine an explicit solution for H.

In this section we have examined two simple path-dependent options. We demonstrated that they were both hedgable and, consequently, that the preference-free pricing methodology was applicable. These two results carry over to all options with payoffs determined by arbitrary functions of their primitive asset's past history. The only requirements are that the primitive asset's price follow an Ito process and that the expected value of the payoff be defined.

OPTION CLAIMS ON MORE THAN ONE ASSET

The same methods can be applied if the value of the contingent claim depends on more than one other asset. In this case the portfolio that replicates the option requires investment in all of the underlying assets that give it value. After going through the Black–Scholes hedging argument, we will have risk-neutralized the resulting partial differential equation by replacing the expected rates of return on the option and all of the assets by the riskless interest rate.

For an option whose value depends on the prices of two other assets, both of which are following lognormal diffusions, the partial differential equation is

$$\begin{aligned}\tfrac{1}{2}\sigma_1^2 S_1^2 F_{11} + \tfrac{1}{2}\sigma_2^2 S_2^2 F_{22} + \rho\sigma_1\sigma_2 S_1 S_2 F_{12} \\ + rS_1E_1 + rS_2E_2 - rF + F_t = 0.\end{aligned} \tag{70}$$

As an example of a problem of this type, consider an option to exchange one asset for another. The value of an option to exchange asset 1 for asset 2 on or before a maturity date T will be the solution to (70) with the terminal condition $F(S_1, S_2, T) = \text{Max}(S_2 - S_1, 0)$.

To solve this problem, we can use the same homogeneity transformation that we used in Equation (61). Namely, let $F(S_1, S_2, t) \equiv S_1G(x, t)$, where $x \equiv S_2/S_1$. Then $F_2 = G_x$, $F_{22} = G_{xx}/S_1$, $F_1 = G - xG_x$, $F_{11} = x^2G_{xx}/S_1$, $F_{12} = -xG_{xx}/S_1$, $F_t = S_1G_t$. Substituting these expressions into (70) gives

$$\tfrac{1}{2}[\sigma_1^2 + \sigma_2^2 - 2\rho\sigma_1\sigma_2]x^2G_{xx} + G_t = 0 \tag{71}$$

$$\text{Subject to} \quad G(x, T) = \text{Max}(x - 1, 0),$$

$$G(0, t) = 0.$$

Equation (71) will be recognized as the standard Black–Scholes pricing equation and boundary conditions for a call on an asset whose proportional variance is $\nu^2 \equiv \sigma_1^2 + \sigma_2^2 - 2\rho\sigma_1\sigma_2$ and whose exercise price is 1 and when the interest rate is zero. (ν^2 is the proportional instantaneous variance of the ratio S_2/S_1.) Therefore, the solution is $G(x, t; T) = W(x, \tau; 1, 0, \nu^2)$, and

$$F(S_1, S_2, t; T) = S_1W\left(\frac{S_2}{S_1}, \tau; 1, 0, \nu^2\right) = W(S_2, \tau; S_1, 0, \nu^2). \tag{72}$$

Comparing this solution to that for a standard option, we can see that S_1 replaces every occurrence of $Xe^{-r\tau}$. This is a natural result. The latter expression is the present value of the exercise payment (conditional upon its being made). The riskless discount rate is used because the amount of the payment is known. In the present case the value of the payment is unknown (even conditional upon its being made). Nevertheless, S_1 is clearly the present value of the exercise payment (conditional upon its occurrence).

OPTION CLAIMS ON NONPRICE VARIABLES

The option pricing methodology can also be applied to claims whose payoffs depend upon variables other than the values of marketed assets. As examples, an executive's compensation may depend on the firm's earnings and the coupon on a floating rate bond depends upon some interest rate or index.

If the underlying state variable follows a diffusion

$$dx = \mu(x, t)\,dt + \sigma(x, t)\,d\omega, \tag{73}$$

then the claim has a value written as $F(x, t)$ which is the solution to the partial differential equation

$$\tfrac{1}{2}\sigma^2 F_{xx} + \mu F_x + F_t - \alpha F = 0 \tag{74}$$

subject to the boundary conditions appropriate for the contract; for example, $F(x, T) = V(x)$. Here α is the expected rate of return on the "option." (We assume no payouts on the claim prior to expiration.)

The problem inherent in Equation (74) is that α must be determined exogenously, for example, by some equilibrium pricing model. In this respect it resembles the option pricing equation (Equation (28) in Chapter 14) before the hedging argument was applied to set both expected returns to the risk-free rate. In general, α may depend upon both x and t. It cannot depend upon other variables because we have assumed that F does not. It may, of course, depend on parameters of the contract, such as its expiration date.

If F is one of a class of claims depending on x, then we can partially determine α. The uncertain component of the rate of return on F is

$$\frac{dF}{F} - \alpha\,dt = \left(\frac{F_x}{F}\right)\sigma\,d\omega. \tag{75}$$

If there is another claim, G, whose value also depends upon x, then (74) and (75) also hold for it. Furthermore, since their returns are perfectly correlated, to prevent arbitrage we must have

$$\frac{\alpha_F - r}{F_x/F} = \frac{\alpha_G - r}{G_x/G} = \lambda(x, t). \tag{76}$$

Here λ cannot depend upon any specific features of either claim in question. For example, it cannot depend upon the expiration date of either claim. In fact, if the problem is stationary (μ and σ^2 do not depend upon t), then α can depend only on x and the time to maturity $\tau \equiv T - t$. In this case λ cannot depend upon time.

Substituting (76) into (74) gives the modified equation

$$\tfrac{1}{2}\sigma^2 F_{xx} + (\mu - \lambda)F_x + F_t - rF = 0. \tag{77}$$

Equation (77) represents a "half-step" towards the option equation. α has been risk neutralized to r. Also the problem of identifying or estimating $\alpha(x, t; T)$ $[\alpha(x, \tau)]$ has been dimensionally reduced to finding $\lambda(x, t)$ $[\lambda(x)]$.

We can complete the second half-step if x is the value of a traded asset which also satisfies (74) and (77). (For example, in the Black–Scholes option model, $x = S$, the stock price which is a perpetual option with a zero exercise price.) If $\hat{F} = x$ does satisfy (77), then because $\hat{F}_{xx} = \hat{F}_t = 0$ and $\hat{F}_x = 1$ we get

$$\mu - \lambda - rx = 0. \tag{78}$$

Since λ is the same for all of the claims, we can substitute (78) into (77) to get

$$\tfrac{1}{2}\sigma^2 F_{xx} + rxF_x + F_t - rF = 0, \tag{79}$$

which is the Black–Scholes option equation. (Recall that in this case σ^2 represents the absolute variance.)

If x is not itself a price, but there is some asset whose value is a known function of x and t, then λ can still be eliminated from (77). Let $f(x, t)$ denote the value of this asset; then solving (77) gives

$$\mu - \lambda = \frac{rf - f_t - \tfrac{1}{2}\sigma^2 f_{xx}}{f_x} \tag{80}$$

This function can now be substituted into (77) to eliminate $\mu - \lambda$.

As an example of this type of problem consider an option on a stock price index. The so-called Standard and Poor's 100 Index option is currently the most actively traded option. This index is the value-weighted (arithmetic) average of 100 of the most actively traded stocks. Apart from a dividend correction, then, the S & P 100 index measures the value of a portfolio of common stocks. As such its value is a "price variable," and the standard option methods already described can be used. The Value Line Index, on the other hand, is constructed as a *geometric* average of the prices of around 1500 stocks. Since it is a geometric average, it does *not* measure the price of an asset which could actually be purchased. Value Line Index options are traded on the Kansas City Board of Trade.

To see the type of adjustment that must be made in cases like this, consider a simple case of a two-stock geometric index. Let $x \equiv \sqrt{S_1 S_2}$ be the geometric index. By Ito's lemma x evolves according to

$$\begin{aligned} dx &\equiv \mu\, dt + \sigma\, d\omega \\ &= [\tfrac{1}{2}(\alpha_1 + \alpha_2) - \delta]x\, dt + \tfrac{1}{2}\sigma_1 x\, d\omega_1 + \tfrac{1}{2}\sigma_2 x\, d\omega_2, \end{aligned} \tag{81}$$

where $\delta \equiv (\sigma_1^2 + \sigma_2^2 - 2\rho\sigma_1\sigma_2)/8$.

Now consider the portfolio of these two stocks which is constantly rebalanced to keep an equal dollar amount in each. The value of this portfolio evolves according to

$$\frac{dP}{P} = \tfrac{1}{2}(\alpha_1 + \alpha_2)\, dt + \tfrac{1}{2}\sigma_1\, d\omega_1 + \tfrac{1}{2}\sigma_2\, d\omega_2. \tag{82}$$

It is clear that x is perfectly correlated with this portfolio, and that $dx/x - dP/P = -\delta\, dt$. In other words, if $x(0) = P(0)$, then $x(t) = e^{-\delta t}P(t)$. Therefore, this portfolio's value is a "price" which is a known function of the state variable with properties $P_x = e^{\delta t}$, $P_{xx} = 0$, and $P_t = \delta e^{\delta t}x$. Substituting these derivatives into (80) gives

$$\mu - \lambda = (r - \delta)x. \tag{83}$$

So the option differential equation for this geometric index is

$$\tfrac{1}{2}\sigma^2 F_{xx} + (r - \delta)xF_x + F_t - rF = 0. \tag{84}$$

Note that this "correction" has the appearance of a dividend. Therefore, it might be optimal to exercise an American call option on the Value Line Index even if no stocks in the Index actually paid dividends. A European call option on the Value Line Index would have a price as given in Equation (24).

This technique is very useful for eliminating interest rate risk premiums in bond-pricing models. This is discussed in more detail in Chapter 18.

When the state variable x is not an asset price or a known function of a price, then this simplification cannot be done. In such cases it is tempting to conjecture a simple functional form for $\lambda(\cdot)$ and to proceed from there. This will usually work, but some care must be exercised. The assumed functional form might be inconsistent with any equilibrium. Then the valuation method, which is based ostensibly on the absence of arbitrage, will in fact guarantee the existence of arbitrage opportunities, at least under some conditions. An example of the type of problem that can arise is given in the next chapter.

PERMITTED STOCHASTIC PROCESSES

A natural question that might arise is, Are there any types of diffusion processes that are not allowed as price processes for primitive assets? The answer to this question is yes. This can be most easily illustrated by means of an example.

Assume that the diffusion process for some asset price is

$$dS = \mu(S)\,dt + \sigma|(A - S)|\,d\omega. \tag{85}$$

The "option" pricing equation for any derivative asset F is

$$\tfrac{1}{2}\sigma^2(A - S)^2 F_{SS} + rSF_S - rF + F_t = 0. \tag{86}$$

Now consider a particular contingent claim that will pay S^2 at time T. It can be easily verified that the solution to (86), and therefore the apparent value of this asset, has a quadratic form $f_1(t)S^2 + f_2(t)S + f_3(t)$. Substituting this guess into (86) gives three ordinary differential equations:

$$S^2[\sigma^2 f_1(t) + rf_1(t) - f_1'(t)] = 0, \tag{87a}$$

$$S[-2\sigma^2 A f_1(t) - f_2'(t)] = 0, \tag{87b}$$

$$\sigma^2 A^2 f_1(t) - rf_3(t) - f_3'(t) = 0 \tag{87c}$$

with boundary conditions $f_1(T) = 1$, $f_2(T) = f_3(T) = 0$.

After solving the set of equations in (87), the entire solution can be written as

$$\begin{aligned} F(S, t) = {} & e^{(\sigma^2+r)\tau} S^2 + \frac{2\sigma^2 A}{\sigma^2 + r}[1 - e^{(\sigma^2+r)\tau}]S \\ & + \frac{\sigma^2 A^2}{\sigma^2 + 2r}[e^{(\sigma^2+r)\tau} - e^{-r\tau}], \end{aligned} \tag{88}$$

where $\tau \equiv T - t$ is the time until maturity.

Now suppose that the actual drift is $\mu(S) = 0$. In this case if the asset's price ever happens to reach A, it will be trapped there forever because at that point the drift and variance are both zero. If this occurs, the derivative asset should obviously have a value of $A^2 e^{-r\tau}$, because it will with certainty be worth A^2 after τ more units of time. Unfortunately, the solution in (88) does not give this answer. In fact, it is easy to prove that the answer is greater than this for any positive interest rate. In addition, whenever $S_t < A$, the price is forever bounded below A, so the derivative asset's value should be less than $A^2 e^{-r\tau}$. But again this is not the case with (88).

The problem here is not one in the mathematics of the solution, but one in the economics of the assumptions. The computed answer is larger than the obvious one because under the risk-neutralized process, the asset price is *not* trapped at A once it reaches there. Under the risk-neutralized process the drift is positive, so the asset price is "sure" to end *above* A if it ever gets there.

The reason the no arbitrage solution has failed is that the original process admits to arbitrage in itself. The simplest arbitrage to spot occurs when the asset price is equal to A. In this case the asset becomes riskless, but its expected rate of return is less than the riskless rate of interest. In addition, there are arbitrage opportunities available whenever $S_t \leqslant A$. Since the price is bounded below A, the maximum realized return over the period from t to T is A/S_t. For T sufficiently far away this is less than $e^{r(T-t)}$, so the asset is a dominated one.

Although it is beyond the scope of this book to prove it, a necessary condition for the risk-neutralized pricing method to work is that the original process and the risk-neutralized one must have the same support. In other words, the asset's price must have the same set of possible outcomes under both stochastic processes. (The probabilities of the outcomes need not be the same, of course.) In the example above, this is not true. Fortunately, problems of this type will not often arise. The two processes will not have the same support only if the drift of the original process has a singularity (an "infinity") or the local variances of the two process have zeros at a point where the true and risk-neutralized drifts have different signs.

ARBITRAGE "DOUBLING" STRATEGIES IN CONTINUOUS TIME

There is a troublesome and potentially serious problem inherent in continuous rebalancing strategies which affects the derivations of the option model presented both here and in Chapter 14 as well as the continuous-time portfolio selection model. If markets are perfect so that unlimited borrowing is permitted and no restrictions on portfolio strategies are imposed, then it will always be possible, through continuous trading, to guarantee unlimited profits. First we show how it is possible to earn one dollar in one unit of time with no initial investment.

Define $t_0 = 0,\ t_1 = \frac{1}{2},\ \ldots,\ t_n = 2^{-n},\ \ldots$; W_n the net profit as of t_n ($W_0 = 0$); $\tilde{y}_n \equiv \ln[\tilde{S}(t_n)/S(t_{n-1})]$ the logarithmic return over the nth period; $\mu \equiv \alpha - \sigma^2/2$ the median logarithmic return per unit time on the stock to be used.

The trading strategy to be followed is this: If a one-dollar profit has been earned by t_{n-1}, invest it in the safe asset. If one dollar has not yet been realized,

$$\frac{\$1 - W_{n-1}}{\exp(2^{-n}\mu) - \exp(2^{-n}r)} \tag{89}$$

is borrowed and invested in the stock. (We assume for the remaidner of the discussion that $\mu > r$. Similar reasoning is valid for $\mu < r$, indicating lending and a short sale in (89).) With probability $\frac{1}{2}$, $\tilde{y}_n$ will be bigger than its median value $2^{-n}\mu \equiv \Delta\mu$, so in these cases

$$W_n = W_{n-1} + \frac{(1 - W_{n-1})(e^{\tilde{y}} - e^{r\Delta})}{e^{\mu\Delta} - e^{r\Delta}} > 1, \tag{90}$$

and the one-dollar profit has been made. Thus, the conditional probability of being up at least one dollar at t_n after $n - 1$ previous failures is $\frac{1}{2}$. The unconditional probability of having a profit of one dollar or more by t_n is $1 - 2^{-n}$, and the probability of earning at least one dollar by $t = 1$ is unity.

There is no hidden "cheating" in this strategy. It breaks none of the rules previously established for any of the models. Furthermore, since it could be carried out at any scale, it represents a true arbitrage opportunity.

Three questions naturally arise: What damage does this arbitrage do to the continuous-time models? How can it be minimized? Why did the portfolio selection problem not arrive at such a solution as optimal? If there is no way to remove the arbitrage, then the answer to the first question is that the damage is fatal. The answers to the last two questions are related.

One way to eliminate the arbitrage opportunity is to admit as feasible only those portfolios with bounded weights. The portfolio selection model implicitly does this because it considers only "interior" optimums. Clearly, the quantity in Equation (89) can become unboundedly large, so such a prohibition would eliminate this strategy.

A second correction would be to impose the restriction that each investor's wealth be nonnegative at all times. Again, this restriction is implicit in those cases for the portfolio selection model in which the derived utility of wealth function is defined only for positive levels of wealth (for example, power utility). The strategy outlined heretofore does not meet this requirement because it leads to negative wealth with positive probability from any initial level.

Both of these restrictions have some merit in their own right. The first is reasonable if the investor is to continue to act as a price taker. The second is reasonable because negative wealth is, at best, a poorly defined concept, and an investor with negative wealth would be better off to "default" and "restart" with a wealth of zero.

18

The Term Structure of Interest Rates

Most of the multiperiod models in finance assume that discount rates are constant over time. For example, this is true in the simple present-value formulas and in the continuous-time version of the CAPM. The term structure of interest rates is a subject that takes the change in discount rates into consideration explicitly.

Most of the literature on the term structure deals with riskless (in terms of default) bonds. As we have seen in Chapter 10, however, by using a martingale pricing process, the problem of valuing risky assets can be reduced to one of discounting at the riskless rate.

Terminology

Much of the difficulty with the term structure of interest rates is caused by the cumbersome notation often used. To a lesser extent, confusion is also caused by an inconsistent use of terminology. To minimize this problem, we shall keep notation to the minimum required.

We will denote the *spot (interest) rate*, the one-period riskless rate prevailing at time t for repayment at time $t + 1$, by $r_t = R_t - 1$. The price or present value at time t of one dollar at time T is denoted by $P(t, T)$. The $T - t$ period interest rate prevailing at time t is $Y(t, T)$. It is stated on a per period basis and compounded once per period. Often these functions will have other arguments as well which describe the state of nature. An *(implied) forward rate* is the interest rate embodied in current prices for some period in the future. The one-period forward rate (which corresponds to the interest rate that will, or may, prevail at time T for payment at time $T + 1$) which is implied in the time t prices is $f(t, T)$.

Often $P(t, T)$ is also called the price of a *pure discount* or *zero coupon* bond. $Y(t, T)$ is the *yield-to-maturity* on this bond.

The relations among these concepts are

$$P(t, T) \equiv [1 + Y(t, T)]^{t - T}, \qquad t \leq T, \tag{1a}$$

$$f(t, T) \equiv \frac{P(t, T)}{P(t, T+1)} - 1, \qquad t \leq T, \tag{1b}$$

$$f(t, t) \equiv Y(t, t+1) \equiv r_t \equiv R_t - 1, \tag{1c}$$

$$P(t, T) = \frac{1}{[1 + r_t]\,[1 + f(t, t+1)]\ldots[1 + f(t, T-1)]}. \tag{1d}$$

It should be noted that the second argument of $Y(\cdot)$ refers to the end of the period over which this long-term rate prevails, whereas the second argument in $f(\cdot)$ refers to the start of the single period for which this forward rate is relevant.

Relations (1a)–(1c) are definitions. They are not a result of a particular equilibrium which has been reached in the economy. In fact they do not even depend on the existence of an equilibrium. Equation (1d) follows by applying (1b) recursively.

In our study of the term structure we will concentrate on determining how zero coupon bonds are priced. Any other asset with known payments can be considered a portfolio of zero coupon bonds. For example, a bond with a face value of B that receives a coupon of C once per period and matures at time T must be worth $CP(t, t+1) + CP(t, t+2) + \ldots + (C + B)P(t, T)$. Unfortunately, more complex assets with payments that are uncertain, like callable bonds or bonds with optional sinking funds, cannot be priced this way. Some examples of this latter type will also be considered.

THE TERM STRUCTURE IN A CERTAIN ECONOMY

If the economy has no risk, or, more precisely, if all future interest rates are known with certainty, then any equilibrium must be characterized by the no arbitrage condition

$$f(t, T) = r_T \qquad \text{for all } t \leq T. \tag{2}$$

If this condition were not met, then an investor could realize an arbitrage profit through trading in T and $T + 1$ period bonds. For example, if $f(t, T) \geq r_T$, then an investor could sell short one bond maturing at time T and buy $1 + f(t, T)$ bonds maturing at time $T + 1$. From the definition in (1b) the net cost of this portfolio is zero. At time T the investor would owe one dollar on the maturing bond, but the bond maturing in the next period would be worth $1/[1 + r_T]$, so the net position would be worth $[1 + f(t, T)]/[1 + r_T] - 1 \geq 0$. If Equation (2) held with a less than inequality, then reversing this portfolio would also create an arbitrage profit.

Using the no arbitrage condition in (2) and applying (1b) recursively give the equivalent no arbitrage condition

$$\frac{1}{P(t, T)} = [1 + r_t][1 + r_{t+1}]\ldots[1 + r_{T-1}] \\ = R_t R_{t+1}\ldots R_{T-1}. \tag{3}$$

Equation (3) says that the sure return of holding a T maturity bond until it matures is equal to the total return on a series of one-period bonds over the same period. Equation (3) will also be recognized as the reciprocal of the standard present-value calculation with a changing, but known, discount rate. Similarly, using yields-to-maturity, we have

$$1 + Y(t, T) = [R_t R_{t+1}\ldots R_{T-1}]^{1/(T-t)}. \tag{4}$$

Finally, (3) can be used to evaluate the single-period return on a long-term bond to get

$$\frac{P(t+1, T)}{P(t, T)} = R_t. \tag{5}$$

That is, the return realized on every bond over any period is equal to the prevailing sure rate of interest plus 1.

All of these propositions may appear trivially obvious. They are nonetheless important because they serve as the basis for our understanding of the term structure of interest rates under uncertainty as well.

THE EXPECTATIONS HYPOTHESIS

In an economy in which future interest rates are not known with certainty, the given arbitrage relations need not hold. Many theories have been presented to explain the relation among interest rates on bonds of various maturities in an uncertain economy. One of the earliest theories to be developed has come to be known as the *expectations hypothesis*. Actually, the expectations hypothesis is not a single theory but rather a set of related (and often confused) theories.

The expectations hypothesis is not the only theory about the relation among interest rates of distinct maturities, but it does play a central role to all the other theories. The *liquidity preference theory* and the *preferred habitat theory*, for example, accept that expectations about future interest rates play a predominant role in the determination of long-term bond yields, but each theory ascribes a different roll to risk and the resulting premiums that different bonds earn. In addition, in continuous-time models, the expectations hypothesis plays the same pivotal role that risk neutrality does for option pricing. We shall consider other equilibrium conditions after we have developed the continuous-time model.

We shall examine four common versions of the expectations hypothesis. As we shall see, not only are the different versions of the theory distinct, but each of them is incompatible with the others.

Basically, the various forms of the expectations hypothesis were developed from the arbitrage relations in the previous section by using expectations of uncertaion quantities. To distinguish these various theories, we shall give each a name. No names have been universally or even commonly accepted; therefore, anyone studying the term structure should always be sure of precisely what a particular theory means.

If Equation (2) is used as the basis of the expectations theory, we get the *unbiased expectations hypothesis*, $E[\tilde{r}_T] = f(t, T)$, for all $t \leq T$. Applying (1d), we find that bond prices in an economy characterized by the unbiased expectations hypothesis are given by

$$P(t, T) = \frac{1}{R_t E[\tilde{R}_{t+1}]\ldots E[\tilde{R}_{T-1}]}. \tag{6}$$

The *return-to-maturity expectations hypothesis* is based on (3). For it, bond prices are given by

$$\frac{1}{P(t, T)} = E\left(R_t\tilde{R}_{t+1}\ldots\tilde{R}_{T-1}\right). \tag{7}$$

Under this version of the expectations hypothesis an investor would on average earn the same return by rolling over a series of one-period bonds and by buying a $(T-t)$–period bond and holding it until it matured.

In comparing (6) and (7) it should be clear that the unbiased expectations hypothesis and the return-to-maturity expectations hypothesis are incompatible unless the levels of future interest rates are mutually uncorrelated. Although it is certainly possible, and perhaps even interesting, to postulate and study such an economy, this is clearly not a true description of our own economy in which interest rate levels are highly autocorrelated. When interest rates are positively correlated over time, then bonds with maturities in excess of two periods will have higher prices under the unbiased expectations hypothesis than under the return-to-maturity expectations hypothesis. Two-period bonds will have the same price under both theories since there is no uncertain cross-product term.

Given this conflict, it might appear that the return-to-maturity expectations hypothesis would be the preferred theory. The unbiased expectations hypothesis is rather mechanical. On the other hand, the return-to-maturity expectations hypothesis resembles an equilibrium condition in which expected holding period returns are equated.

Actually, this resemblance to an equilibrium is not as strong as it might at first appear. The return-to-maturity expectations hypothesis does not state that the expected holding period return on all bond strategies must be equal. To see this, consider holding a bond maturing at s and, when it matures, buying a $(T - s)$-period bond. The expected return on this portfolio over the entire holding period is

$$\frac{1}{P(t, s)} E\left(\frac{1}{\tilde{P}(s, T)}\right) = E\left(R_t \tilde{R}_{t+1} \ldots \tilde{R}_{s-1}\right) E\left(\tilde{R}_s \tilde{R}_{s+1} \ldots \tilde{R}_{T-1}\right). \quad (8)$$

The return to holding a T maturity bond until it matures is given in (7). These will not be equal for all s unless future interest rate levels are uncorrelated.

To discuss the two other forms of the expectations hypothesis, it is useful for us to define the random variable

$$\tilde{X} \equiv (R_t \tilde{R}_{t+1} \ \ldots \ \tilde{R}_{T-1})^{-1}. \quad (9)$$

The return-to-maturity expectations hypothesis is then

$$[P(t, T)]^{-1} = E[\tilde{X}^{-1}]. \quad (10)$$

The yield-to-maturity expectations hypothesis is based on (4). Under this hypothesis the expected holding period yield on rolling over a series of short-term bonds equals the guaranteed yield from holding a long-term bond until maturity; that is,

$$[P(t, T)]^{-1/(T-t)} = E[\tilde{X}^{-1/(T-t)}]. \quad (11)$$

The local expectations hypothesis is based on (5). Under this hypothesis the expected rate of return on any bond over a single period is equal to the prevailing spot rate of interest. Using (5) recursively gives

$$\begin{aligned} P(t, T) &= \frac{E[\tilde{P}(t+1, \mathrm{I})]}{R_t} = \frac{1}{R_t} E\left(\frac{\tilde{P}(t+2, T)}{\tilde{R}_{t+1}}\right) \\ &= E\left([R_t \tilde{R}_{t+1} \ldots \tilde{R}_{T-1}]^{-1}\right) = E[\tilde{X}]. \end{aligned} \quad (12)$$

Because the expected rates of returns on all bonds are equal to the riskless rate of interest under the local expectations hypothesis, it has also been called the *risk-neutral* expectations hypothesis. This name is reminiscent of the Cox–Ross–Merton pricing methodology for options. As we shall see, however, universal risk neutrality does not lead to this form of the expectations hypothesis. To avoid confusion, therefore, this name will not be used.

One purely technical advantage of the local expectations hypothesis is that the expectation in (12) must always exist if interest rates are positive. In this case $R_t > 1$, and the random variable $\tilde{X}$ only takes on values in the bounded range 0 to 1, so its expectation is finite. The random variables in (10) and (11) are unbounded, however, so their expectations might be infinite. If the interest rate is bounded above, then this problem cannot arise, but many stochastic processes which might be used for interest rate modeling are not bounded. As a result, some care must be taken when constructing models based on the other three forms of the expectations hypothesis.

Jensen's inequality assures us that at most one of the relations (10)–(12) can be true if interest rates are uncertain. If the local expectations hypothesis is valid, then the return- and yield-to-maturity expectations hypotheses give bond prices which are too small. On the other hand, if the return-to-maturity expectations hypothesis is valid, then the local and yield-to-maturity expectations hypotheses give bond prices which are too large. Finally, if the yield-to-maturity expectations hypothesis is correct, then bond prices will be greater than predicted by the return-to-maturity expectations hypothesis but less than predicted by the local expectations hypothesis.

We can summarize these results as

$$P_{\mathrm{L}} > P_{\mathrm{YTM}} > P_{\mathrm{RTM}}, \tag{13a}$$

$$P_{\mathrm{U}} > P_{\mathrm{RTM}} \qquad \text{(for positive autocorrelation).} \tag{13b}$$

We cannot as yet sign the relation between the unbiased expectations hypothesis and the other two forms.

A SIMPLE MODEL OF THE YIELD CURVE

To begin our study of the yield curve, we postulate the following simple model for the evolution of the economy. At any point of time everything which is relevant for the determination of current and future interest rates is summarized in a single state variable.

For simplicity and concreteness, we assume that this single variable of importance is the spot rate of interest which evolves according to

$$\tilde{R}_t = R^{\gamma}_{t-1}\tilde{\varepsilon}_t. \tag{14}$$

We will assume that the parameter γ is in the range from 0 to 1 and that the random variables $\tilde{\varepsilon}_t$ are independent and identically distributed over time with a truncated geometric distribution whose density function is

$$g(\varepsilon) = a\varepsilon^{-a-1}, \qquad \varepsilon \geqslant 1. \tag{15}$$

If $R_{t-1} > 1$ (that is, the interest rate is positive), then R_t will be greater than 1 as well because both factors in (14) exceed unity. Thus, this stochastic process guarantees that the interest rate will remain positive.

The (defined) moments of the distribution in (15) are

$$E[\tilde{\varepsilon}^b] = \frac{a}{a-b}, \qquad b \leqslant a. \tag{16}$$

Combining (14) and (16) we see that for $a > 1$,

$$E[\tilde{R}_{t+1}|R_t] = R_t^{\gamma} \frac{a}{a-1} \equiv R_t^{\gamma} \mu^{1-\gamma}, \tag{17}$$

the last equality serving to define μ as $[a/(a-1)]^{1/(1-\gamma)}$, where μ is a stationary point of (17), so that if R_t is currently equal to μ, there is no expected change. If R_t is not equal to μ, then the expected value of R_{t+1} is between R_t and μ. Thus, there is a tendency for the interest rate to remain near this central point.

The interest factor at time T is related to that at time t by

$$\begin{aligned} R_T &= R_{T-1}^{\gamma}\,\tilde{\varepsilon}_T = R_{T-2}^{\gamma^2}\,\tilde{\varepsilon}_{T-1}^{\gamma}\,\tilde{\varepsilon}_T = \dots \\ &= R_t^{\gamma^{T-t}}\,\tilde{\varepsilon}_{t+1}^{\gamma^{T-t-1}}\,\tilde{\varepsilon}_{t+2}^{\gamma^{T-t-2}} \dots \tilde{\varepsilon}_{T-1}^{\gamma}\,\tilde{\varepsilon}_T. \end{aligned} \tag{18}$$

Using (18), we can compare the prices of bonds under the various forms of the expectations hypothesis. For example, if the current interest factor is R, then prices of two-period bonds are

$$P_{\mathrm{U}} = P_{\mathrm{RTM}} = \left(RE[R^{\gamma}\tilde{\varepsilon}]\right)^{-1} = R^{-(1+\gamma)}\,\frac{a-1}{a}, \tag{19a}$$

$$P_{\mathrm{YTM}} = \left(E[(RR^{\gamma}\tilde{\varepsilon})^{1/2}]\right)^{-2} = R^{-(1+\gamma)}\left(\frac{a-.5}{a}\right)^2, \tag{19b}$$

$$P_{\mathrm{L}} = E[(RR^{\gamma}\tilde{\varepsilon})^{-1}] = R^{-(1+\gamma)}\frac{a}{a+1}. \tag{19c}$$

This confirms the ordering $P_{\mathrm{L}} > P_{\mathrm{YTM}} > P_{\mathrm{U}} = P_{\mathrm{RTM}}$ as given in (13). It also illustrates the problem that can arise with unbounded interest rates that was mentioned earlier. For the yield-to-maturity expectations hypothesis the expectation in (19b) does not exist for $a \geqslant .5$. Similarly, for $a > 1$ the expectation in (19a) is undefined.

TERM STRUCTURE NOTATION IN CONTINUOUS TIME

We will often find it convenient to work in continuous time. In such cases a single period will be an instant, and interest rates will be compounded continuously. The definitions analogous to Equation (1) are

$$P(t, T) \equiv e^{-Y(t,\,T)(T\,-\,t)}, \qquad t \leqslant T, \tag{1a$'$}$$

$$f(t, T) \equiv -\frac{\partial P(t, T)/\partial T}{P(t, T)}, \qquad t \leqslant T, \tag{1b$'$}$$

$$f(t, t) \equiv r_t \equiv \lim_{T \to t} Y(t, T), \tag{1c$'$}$$

$$P(t, T) = \exp\left(-\int_t^T f(t, s)\, ds\right). \tag{1d'}$$

The unbiased expectations hypothesis is

$$P(t, T) = \exp\left(-\int_t^T E[\tilde{r}_s]\, ds\right). \tag{6'}$$

The local and return-to-maturity expectations hypotheses are as given in (10) and (12), where the random variable $\tilde{X}$ is now defined as

$$\tilde{X} = -\int_t^T \tilde{r}_s\, ds. \tag{9'}$$

The yield-to-maturity expectations hypothesis is

$$\log[P(t, T)] = E[\log(\tilde{X})]. \tag{11'}$$

Comparing (6′) and (11′), we see that in continuous-time models the unbiased and yield-to-maturity expectations hypotheses are equivalent.

Actually, for continuous-time models only the local expectations hypothesis is acceptable as a statement of equilibrium. The other three versions of the expectations hypothesis lead to arbitrage opportunities. This issue will be discussed later.

TERM STRUCTURE MODELING IN CONTINUOUS TIME

For the time being we will continue our practice of assuming that the spot rate of interest is the only variable of importance in bond pricing. In this case we need only model the diffusion process for the interest rate

$$dr = b(r, t)\, dt + a(r, t)\, d\tilde{\omega}. \tag{20}$$

The price of a zero coupon bond will evolve according to

$$\frac{dP(r, t, T)}{P(r, t, T)} = \alpha(r, t, T)\, dt + \delta(r, t, T)\, d\tilde{\omega}, \tag{21}$$

where $\alpha(\cdot)$ is the bond's expected instantaneous rate of return, and $\delta^2(\cdot)$ is its instantaneous variance.

By Ito's lemma

$$\alpha(r, t, T)P = \tfrac{1}{2}a^2(r, t)P_{rr} + b(r, t)P_r + P_t, \tag{22a}$$

$$\delta(r, t, T)P = a(r, t)P_r \tag{22b}$$

Since the price changes on all bonds are perfectly correlated, their risk premiums must be proportional to their standard deviations of returns. Thus, as in Chapter 17 we can substitute for $\alpha(r, t, T) = r + \lambda(r, t)P_r/P$, and (22a) becomes our basic bond-pricing equation

$$\tfrac{1}{2}a^2(r, t)P_{rr} + [b(r, t) - \lambda(r, t)]P_r + P_t - rP = 0. \qquad (23)$$

The appropriate boundary condition is $P(r, T, T) = 1$. Since the state variable in this model, the interest rate, is not itself a price, we can go no further in our simplification of (23) in terms of replacing $\lambda(\cdot)$ as explained in Chapter 17.

The writing of the risk premium as $\lambda(r, t)P_r/P$ has reduced the problem of determining a function of three variables $\alpha(r, t, T)$ to that of determining a function of only two variables $\lambda(r, t)$. Since the returns on all bonds are perfectly correlated, the maturity dependence of the risk premium must be determined endogenously within the model. If the interest rate process is time homogeneous—that is, $a(\cdot)$ and $b(\cdot)$ do not depend on time—then the expected rate of return on each bond will not depend on calendar time explicitly, although it will depend on the time left until maturity $\tau \equiv T - t$. In this case the risk-premium function will only depend on the interest rate.

Equation (23) is the same one that would result for the modified stochastic process

$$dr = [b(r, t) - \lambda(r, t)]\,dt + a(r, t)\,d\tilde{\omega} \qquad (24)$$

if the local expectations hypothesis held. Therefore, by (12) and (9′), the formal solution is

$$P(r, t, T) = \hat{E}\left[\exp\left(-\int_t^T \tilde{r}_s\,ds\right)\middle|\, r_t\right], \qquad (25)$$

where the expectation is taken with respect to the modified stochastic process in (24). In other words, for interest rate risk, the local expectations hypothesis assumes the role of the Cox-Ross-Merton risk-neutral pricing methodology.

This expectations hypothesis pricing method in (25) does not imply that the expectations hypothesis must hold. It is only a convenience, much as the risk-neutral method is for option pricing. The local expectations hypothesis actually holds only if $\lambda(r, t) \equiv 0$. Before examining the various forms of the expectations hypothesis and other equilibrium conditions, we shall solve the bond-pricing problem for some simple models of interest rate movements.

SOME SIMPLE CONTINUOUS-TIME MODELS

The simplest model of interest rate movement is the random walk with $a(r, t) = \sigma$ and $b(r, t) = \mu$, both constants. We shall also assume that the local expectations hypothesis holds. [Note that this is equivalent to using any stochastic process and risk adjustment for which $b(r, t) - \lambda(r, t) = \mu$, a constant in (23).] The bond-pricing equation is then

$$\tfrac{1}{2}\sigma^2 P_{rr} + \mu P_r + P_t - rP = 0. \tag{26}$$

To determine a solution to (26), let $\tau \equiv T - t$ and $P(r, t, T) = \exp[-r\tau + F(\tau)]$. Then $P_r = -\tau P$, $P_{rr} = \tau^2 P$, and $P_t = [r - F'(\tau)]P$. Substituting these derivatives into (26) leaves

$$(\tfrac{1}{2}\sigma^2\tau^2 - \mu\tau - r + r - F'(\tau))P = 0. \tag{26$'$}$$

Therefore, $F(\tau) = \sigma^2\tau^3/6 - \mu\tau^2/2$, and

$$P(r, t, T) = \exp(-r\tau - \tfrac{1}{2}\mu\tau^2 + \tfrac{1}{6}\sigma^2\tau^3). \tag{27}$$

This simple model gives a quantitative illustration of the differences among the expectations hypotheses. The yield-to-maturity and the forward rates are

$$Y(r, t, T) = r + \tfrac{1}{2}\mu\tau - \tfrac{1}{6}\sigma^2\tau^2, \tag{28a}$$

$$f(r, t, T) = r + \mu\tau - \tfrac{1}{2}\sigma^2\tau^2. \tag{28b}$$

The expected value of r_T conditional on $r_t = r$ is $r + \mu\tau$. Thus, the forward rate is biased low by the last term in (28b). Of course, for a certain economy this bias disappears. The expected average level of the interest rate over the period from t to T is

$$\frac{1}{T - t}\int_t^T (r + \mu s)\, ds = r + \tfrac{1}{2}\mu\tau, \tag{29}$$

so the yield-to-maturity is biased low by the final term in (28a). Again this bias disappears in a certain economy.

For $\mu \leqslant 0$, the interest rate is expected to decrease and both the yield curve and the forward rate curve are monotone declining in maturity. For $\mu > 0$, they first increase and then decline as the uncertainty effect begins to dominate. In either case both curves always keep the same basic shape over time. Only their levels change as the interest rate moves. The limiting behavior is $Y(r, t, T) \to -\infty$ and $f(r, t, T) \to -\infty$ as $T \to \infty$.

For short maturities, the bond price is declining in T as it should be; however, at beyond the point that the forward rate becomes negative, $\tau = (\mu + \sqrt{\mu^2 + 2\sigma^2 r})/\sigma^2$, the derivative $\partial P/\partial T$ becomes positive. Furthermore, for reasonable values of the parameters, the minimum bond price is reached at maturities short enough to be of concern. For example, if $\mu = 0$, $\sigma = .02$, and $r = 10\%$, then the minimum occurs between 22 and 23 years. In the limit, $P(r, t, T) \to \infty$.

These are clearly undesirable properties which are a result of the random walk assumption. Under a random walk the variance of r_T increases without limit; hence, very large negative and positive interest rates become more and more likely. Interest rates have an exponential effect on the bond-pricing function. Interest rate evolutions with predominantly large positive values contribute zero to the discount function, whereas evolutions with large negative rates contribute ∞ to the discount function.

To avoid this problem, we use a process for the interest rate that does not permit negative values: for example, a variance of $a^2(r, t) = \sigma^2 r$ and a drift term of $b(r, t) \equiv \kappa(\mu - r)$. Since the sample path of a diffusion is continuous, the interest rate cannot become negative without passing through zero. For this process $a(0, t) = 0$ and $b(0, t) > 0$. Thus, whenever the interest rate reaches zero, it is certain to become positive immediately.

This process also displays mean reversion. When $r > \mu$, $b(r, t) < 0$, and the interest rate tends to decrease, whereas for $r < \mu$, $b(r, t) > 0$, and the interest rate tends to increase. For a mean reverting process, the interest rate will tend to stay around a particular level as in the discrete-time model we examined earlier.

For this process the bond-pricing equation is

$$\tfrac{1}{2}\sigma^2 r P_{rr} + \kappa(\mu - r)P_r + P_t - rP = 0. \tag{30}$$

We now guess a solution of the form $P(\cdot) = \exp[A(\tau) + B(\tau)r]$. Substituting this into (30), we have

$$(\tfrac{1}{2}\sigma^2 r B^2(\tau) + \kappa(\mu - r)B(\tau) - r - A'(\tau) - rB'(\tau))P = 0. \tag{31}$$

For (31) to be satisfied for all values of r, the terms multiplying r and those independent of r must each be identically zero. Thus,

$$\tfrac{1}{2}\sigma^2 B^2(\tau) - \kappa B(\tau) - 1 - B'(\tau) = 0, \tag{32a}$$

$$\kappa\mu B(\tau) - A'(\tau) = 0. \tag{32b}$$

In each case we have $A(0) = B(0) = 0$ since $P(r, T, T) = 1$.

To solve (32a), we can rewrite it as

$$\frac{dB}{\tfrac{1}{2}\sigma^2 B^2 - \kappa B - 1} = d\tau. \tag{33}$$

Then integrating and applying the initial condition gives

$$B(\tau) = \frac{-2(1 - e^{-\gamma\tau})}{2\gamma + (\kappa - \gamma)(1 - e^{-\gamma\tau})}, \quad \text{where } \gamma \equiv \sqrt{\kappa^2 + 2\sigma^2}. \tag{34}$$

To solve (32b), we must integrate $B(\tau)$. This can be done most easily as follows. Define $g(\tau)$ to be the denominator of $B(\tau)$. The since $(\gamma - \kappa)(\gamma + \kappa) = 2\sigma^2$,

$$
\begin{aligned}
B(\tau) &= -\frac{\gamma-\kappa}{\sigma^2}\left(\frac{(\gamma+\kappa)(1-e^{-\gamma\tau})}{g(\tau)}\right) \\
&= -\frac{\gamma-\kappa}{\sigma^2}\left(\frac{g(\tau)-2\gamma e^{-\gamma\tau}}{g(\tau)}\right) \\
&= -\frac{\gamma-\kappa}{\sigma^2}\left(1-\frac{2g'(\tau)/(\kappa-\gamma)}{g(\gamma)}\right) \\
&= \frac{\kappa-\gamma}{\sigma^2}-\frac{2}{\sigma^2}\frac{g'(\tau)}{g(\tau)}.
\end{aligned}
\tag{35}
$$

And as $g(0) = 2\gamma$,

$$
\begin{aligned}
A(\tau) &= \frac{\kappa\mu}{\sigma^2}\int_0^\tau \frac{(\kappa-\gamma)-2g'(s)}{g(s)}\,ds \\
&= \frac{\kappa\mu}{\sigma^2}\left[(\kappa-\gamma)\tau - 2\log\frac{g(\tau)}{2\gamma}\right] \\
&= \frac{2\kappa\mu}{\sigma^2}\log\left(\frac{2\gamma e^{(\kappa-\gamma)\tau/2}}{g(\tau)}\right).
\end{aligned}
\tag{36}
$$

Combining (35) and (36), we can express the price of a zero coupon bond as

$$
P(r, t, T) = \left(\frac{2\gamma e^{(\kappa-\gamma)\tau/2}}{g(\tau)}\right)^{2\kappa\mu/\sigma^2}\exp[B(\tau)r]. \tag{37}
$$

For this interest rate process the yield and forward rate curves are

$$
Y(r, t, T) = \frac{-rB(\tau)+A(\tau)}{\tau}, \tag{38a}
$$

$$
\begin{aligned}
f(r, t, T) &= -rB'(\tau) - A'(\tau) \\
&= r + \kappa B(\tau)(r-\mu) - \tfrac{1}{2}\sigma^2 B^2(\tau).
\end{aligned}
\tag{38b}
$$

The second line of (38b) is obtained by substituting (32a) and (32b) into the first line.

The yield-to-maturity and the forward rate are both biased low. However, in this case they each approach the same finite limit of $Y_\infty \equiv 2\kappa\mu/(\gamma + \kappa)$. This value is somewhat smaller than μ, the stationary point of the distribution.

For this model of interest rate movements the yield curve and forward rate curve are not fixed in shape. If $r \geqslant \mu$, then the curves are downward sloping. If $r \leqslant Y_\infty$, then they are upward sloping. For intermediate values, the curves have a single hump. Examples of yield curves are plotted in Figure 18.1.

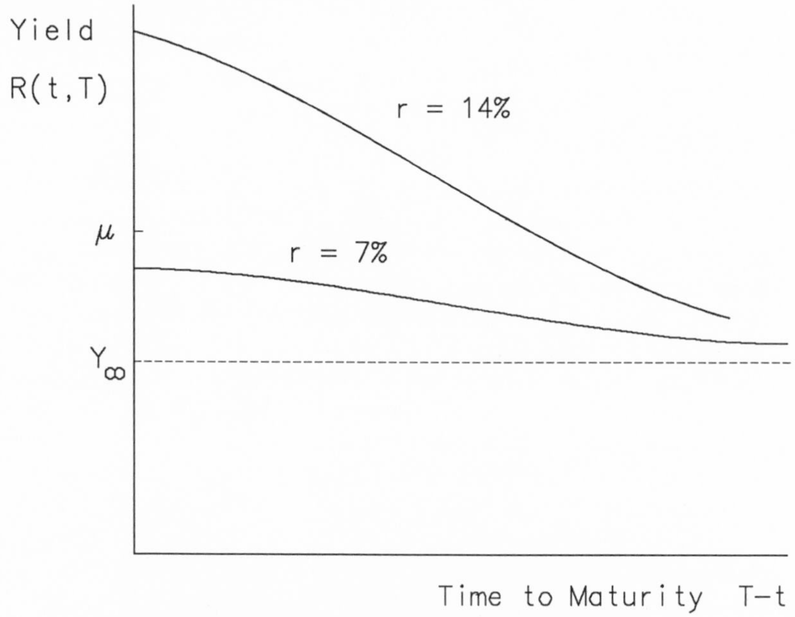

Figure 18.1 Illustration of Yield Curves

PERMISSIBLE EQUILIBRIUM SPECIFICATIONS

The local expectations hypothesis corresponds to the case when $\lambda(r, t) = 0$ and is clearly a permissible form of equilibrium since on arbitrage opportunities are available. In fact, we will construct a model in which this hypothesis is true. The other forms of the expectations hypothesis are not valid equilibrium conditions in continuous time.

For the return-to-maturity expectations hypothesis we have, from (10) and (9′),

$$[P(r, t, T)]^{-1} = E\left[\exp\left(\int_t^T \tilde{r}_s\, ds\right)\middle| r_t\right]. \tag{39}$$

Therefore, $E[d(1/P)/(1/P)] = -r\,dt$. But applying Ito's lemma to the general equation (21), we have for any equilibrium

$$d\left(\frac{1}{P}\right) = (-\alpha + \delta^2)\left(\frac{1}{P}\right)dt - \left(\frac{1}{P}\right)\delta\, d\tilde{\omega}. \tag{40}$$

In other words, for the return-to-maturity expectations hypothesis in continuous time $\alpha(, t, T) - r = \delta^2(r, t, T)$. That is, with Ito's lemma we can determine exactly how large the Jensen's inequality bias is.

The general no arbitrage condition is that the risk premium can be expressed as $\lambda(r, t)P_r/P$, so equating terms and using (22b) we have

$$\begin{aligned}\delta^2(r, t, T) &= \lambda(r, t)a(r, t)\delta(r, t, T), \\ \delta(r, t, T) &= \lambda(r, t)a(r, t).\end{aligned} \tag{41}$$

But the right-hand side of the second line in (41) does not depend on T, so the left-hand side cannot either. Since a bond becomes riskless the instant before it matures, $\delta(\cdot)$ must be identically zero if it is to be independent of T. This can be true only if there is no interest rate uncertainty. Our conclusion is that the return-to-maturity expectations hypothesis can hold only in a certain economy.

To illustrate further, suppose that the return-to-maturity expectations hypothesis did hold. Choose any two bonds of different maturities with standard deviations δ_1 and δ_2 and form the portfolio $w_1 = \delta_2/(\delta_2 - \delta_1)$ and $w_2 = -\delta_1/(\delta_2 - \delta_1)$. This portfolio has no risk and an expected (and therefore guaranteed) return of

$$\alpha_p = r + w_1\delta_1^2 + w_2\delta_2^2 = r + \delta_1\delta_2 \neq r. \tag{42}$$

Since the portfolio is riskless, this nonzero "risk" premium represents an arbitrage opportunity.

The yield-to-maturity and unbiased expectations hypotheses are also invalid equilibrium specifications. In these theories $\log[P(r, t, T)] = E[\log(\tilde{X})]$, so $E[d \log[P(r, t, T)]] = r\,dt$. By Ito's lemma the expected change in the logarithm of the stock price is $E[\mathrm{d} \log[P(r, t, T)]] = [\alpha(\cdot) - .5\delta^2(\cdot)]\,dt$ for any equilibrium. Thus, for these two versions of the expectations hypothesis, $\alpha(\cdot) - r = .5\delta^2(\cdot)$. The remainder of the proof is identical.

Multiple sources of uncertainty cannot salvage these other versions of the expectations hypothesis. The details of the proof need not concern us here. Briefly, with more than one state variable, (41) becomes a vector equation which imposes a constraint on the realizations of the Wiener processes governing the evolution of the state variables. But since it is always possible to construct the governing Wiener processes as independent (even if the state variables are correlated), no additional constraint can be imposed on their evolutions.

The problem with these versions of the expectations hypothesis is that they force the risk-premium factor $\lambda(\cdot)$ to be a function of the maturity of the bond—something which is not allowed by the no arbitrage condition.

Even in cases when $\lambda(\cdot)$ does not depend on maturity, there can be problems. For example, consider the second interest rate process given and assume that $\lambda(r, t) = \lambda_0 + \lambda_1 r$. In this case the pricing equation (31) is

$$\tfrac{1}{2}\sigma^2 r P_{rr} + [\kappa(\mu - r) - \lambda_0 - \lambda_1 r]P_r + P_t - rP = 0. \tag{43}$$

This can be rewritten as

$$\tfrac{1}{2}\sigma^2 r P_{rr} + \hat{\kappa}(\hat{\mu} - r)P_r + P_t - rP = 0, \quad \text{where } \hat{\kappa} \equiv \kappa + \lambda_1, \qquad \hat{\mu} \equiv \frac{\kappa\mu - \lambda_0}{\kappa + \lambda_1}. \tag{44}$$

Now the previous solution can be applied with $\hat{\kappa}$ and $\hat{\mu}$ used in place of κ and μ.

From (22) and (44) the risk premium and standard deviation of return on the bond are

$$\alpha(r, t, T) - r = (\lambda_0 + \lambda_1 r)\, B(\tau; \hat{\kappa}), \tag{45a}$$

$$\delta(r, t, T) = \sigma\sqrt{r}B(\tau; \hat{\kappa}). \tag{45b}$$

When the interest rate equals zero

$$\alpha(0, t, T) = \lambda_0 B(\tau; \hat{\kappa}), \tag{46a}$$

$$\delta(0, t, T) = 0, \tag{46b}$$

and we have a locally riskless bond earning interest at a rate different from the prevailing spot rate ($r = 0$) unless $\lambda_0 = 0$. Thus, only for $\lambda_0 = 0$ is this linear specification valid.

Note that there is nothing wrong with the mathematical analysis of this model. Nor are any of the assumptions when considered alone unreasonable. In fact, the resulting "equilibrium" is one in which all yields are linear in the spot rate of interest—certanly a useful empirical property. Nevertheless, they lead together to a no arbitrage model which permits arbitrage.

LIQUIDITY PREFERENCE AND PREFERRED HABITATS

The liquidity preference and preferred habitat theories explain the difference among expected rates of return on bonds of different maturities by risk arguments. The preferred habitat theory argues that we cannot determine which bonds are riskier until we know the investment horizons of investors. For example, an investor who wishes to have a certain sum of money in 15 years will view a zero coupon bond with a maturity of 15 years as the safest asset. Under the preferred habitat theory he or she would demand a higher expected rate of return on both 10- and 20-year bonds.

The liquidity preference theory is the older of the two. Rather than treat it separately, however, we can consider it to be a special case of the preferred habitat theory. In this theory it is argued that investors demand a risk premium as compensation for holding long-term bonds. Furthermore, since the variability of bond prices increases with maturity, the demanded risk premium does as well. That is, in terms of the preferred habitat theory, all investors have a habitat of a single period, so that the shortest-term bond is the safest.

As we have seen in earlier chapters, not all variability in price is risk. In fact, in some cases an increase in variability can lead to a reduced expected rate of return. (An asset with a negative beta in the CAPM is one example.) Nowhere has the investment horizon been a relevant concern before. The interval of time between trades has been important but not the investors' lifetimes.

To examine the predictions of the preferred habitat and liquidity preference theories, we will use a simple example. To highlight the effect of habitats, we assume that each investor desires to consume only at a particular point of time $\hat{T}$. Utility of consumption at this point is state independent and isoelastic in form. Thus, the utility of consumption function is

$$U(C, t) = 0, \quad t \neq \hat{T}, \qquad U(C, \hat{T}) = \frac{C^\gamma}{\gamma}. \tag{47}$$

As investors have no desire to consume prior to $\hat{T}$, they will invest all their wealth. The only primitive asset for this is a single physical production process which has locally riskless output. The rate of return on this process changes stochastically over time, however. Investors may also trade financial contracts among themselves. These assets are all in zero net supply. Since investors are all identical, the financial assets will be in zero gross supply as well. However, we can still compute their shadow prices and thereby examine their behavior.

Assuming that the only primitive asset is riskless will assure that the market portfolio is not risky. This will guarantee that any risk premium we observe is not of the standard systematic risk type found, for example, in the CAPM. The risk premiums that we will find are associated with a hedge portfolio as described in Chapter 13. In this case the state variable that the portfolio is hedging is the interest rate.

The predictions of the preferred habitat theory are clear for this simple economy. Each investor has a habitat of $\hat{T}$. The bond maturing at this time is the "safest," so if the expected rates of return on all bonds were equal, investors would demand more of this bond than any other. Of course, the net supply of all bonds is zero, so the bond market can be equilibrated only if the expected rate of return on the bond maturing at $\hat{T}$ is lower than that on any other bond. For the liquidity preference theory the expected rate of return on bonds should be an increasing function of maturity as always.

The state of this simple economy is completely described by three variables: per capita wealth, time, and the interest rate. Knowledge of the distribution of wealth among investors is not required because there are no wealth effects with power utility. The dynamics of the economy are

$$dW = r\,dt, \qquad dr = \sigma\, d\tilde{\omega}. \tag{48}$$

Here we have assumed that the interest rate follows a simple form of the random walk process used in the first example for simplicity. None of the following qualitative results depend in any way on the undesirable properties of this process.

Although changes in aggregate wealth are certain, any investor is free to hold risky financial assets, so each investor faces a portfolio problem of the type in Chapter 13. The differential equation for the derived utility of wealth function of a typical investor is

$$\begin{aligned} 0 = {} & \tfrac{1}{2}W^2 J_{WW}\textstyle\sum\sum w_i w_j \delta_i \delta_j + WJ_W\,(r + \textstyle\sum w_i(\alpha_i - r)) \\ & + \tfrac{1}{2}\sigma^2 J_{rr} + WJ_{Wr}\textstyle\sum w_i \delta_i \sigma + J_t. \end{aligned} \tag{49}$$

(Note that all correlations in (49) are perfect since there is but one source of uncertainty; therefore, covariances are just plus or minus the product of the standard deviations. δ_i is actually the negative of the bond's standard deviation.)

The first-order condition for the derivative with respect to w_i is

$$WJ_{WW}\sum_j w_j \delta_i \delta_j + J_W(\alpha_i - r) + J_{Wr}\delta_i \sigma. \tag{50}$$

A very similar problem was analyzed in Chapter 13. There we were concerned about investors' portfolio choices, so we determined the optimal portfolio for an exogenously specified value of α_i. Here we are concerned about the equilibrium expected rates of return on bonds, so the optimal portfolio (for the representative investor) is specified exogenously as $w_i^* = 0$. Then (50) can be used to solve for the expected rates of return for each bond. These are

$$\alpha_i = r - \frac{J_{Wr}}{J_W}\sigma\delta_i. \tag{51}$$

Once the derived utility function has determined, (51) will give the risk premiums on all bonds.

To solve for the derived utility function we substitute the optimal (zero) portfolio weights into (49), leaving

$$0 = \tfrac{1}{2}\sigma^2 J_{rr} + rWJ_W + J_t. \tag{52}$$

To solve (52) let $J(W, r, t) = Q(r, t)W^\gamma/\gamma$. Substituting into (52) leaves

$$0 = \frac{1}{\gamma}\left(\frac{1}{2}\sigma^2 Q_{rr} + \gamma r Q + Q_t\right)W^\gamma. \tag{53}$$

The terminal condition is $J(W, r, \hat{T}) = U(C, \hat{T}) = C^\gamma/\gamma$, which will be satisfied if $Q(r, \hat{T}) = 1$. This equation is almost the same as (26), and its solution can be determined in the same manner:

$$Q(r, t) = \exp\left(\gamma r(\hat{T} - t) + \gamma^2 \frac{\sigma^2(\hat{T} - t)^3}{6}\right). \tag{54}$$

Thus, from (51) and (54) the expected rates of returns on bonds are

$$\alpha_i = r - \gamma(\hat{T} - t)\delta_i. \tag{55}$$

Bond prices in this model can be determined by substituting (55) into the bond-pricing equation. Solving this gives

$$P(r, t, T) = \exp\left(-r(T-t) + \frac{(\sigma^2 + 2\gamma\sigma)(T - t)^3}{6} + \frac{\gamma\sigma(\hat{T}-T)(T-t)^2}{2}\right). \tag{56}$$

Therefore, $\delta_i = -(T - t)\sigma$ and

$$\alpha_i = r + \gamma\sigma(\hat{T} - t)(T - t). \tag{57}$$

Note that Equations (54)–(57) are also true for $T > \hat{T}$ (that is, for bonds which mature after the economy comes to an end), provided that an open short position in any bond at time $\hat{T}$ is considered a liability which must be settled at the price $P(r, \hat{T}, T)$ as given in (56).

Clearly, the term premiums on all bonds have the same sign as γ and are monotonic in maturity T. Thus, for this simple model the bond maturing at $\hat{T}$ can never have the lowest expected rate of return as predicted by the preferred habitat theory. The liquidity preference theory can be true for this simple economy, but only if $\gamma > 0$.

An explanation of this finding was given in Chapter 13 in a different context. Basically, interest rate risk is not like the risk of securities in portfolios. Security risk is the contemporaneous resolution of returns. Interest rate risk, on the other hand, is inherently intertemporal. An unexpected change in the interest rate now affects all future returns, so interest rate risk "compounds" over time.

The utility function which is neutral about compound (or exponential risks) is the logarithmic utility function. Thus, the expectations hypothesis obtains for logarithmic utility and not for risk neutrality ($\gamma = 1$). For risk-neutral investors, premiums are not zero but positive.

The traditional notion of a preferred habitat is partially true. Suppose that all investors have the same habitat $\hat{T}$ and are more risk averse than log ($\gamma < 0$). Then from (57) in a cross section of economies a given short-term bond will have a higher expected rate of return in an economy with a longer natural habitat. This result is as predicted by the traditional theory, since in the "longer" economy a given short-term bond is further from the "naturally" desired holding.

The traditional notion of a preferred habitat misses the importance of risk aversion, however. From this analysis we see that a habitat should reflect not only a propensity to consume at a particular point in time but also a stronger or weaker desire to hedge against changes in the interest rate. Furthermore, this latter effect can actually reverse the sign of the traditional effect. With multiple state variables, of course, we will measure habitats along more than one dimension, a desire to hedge against each of the state variables.

With a more complicated interest rate model like that in (30), a similar result holds. For these models an unexpected change in the interest rate will not change the entire future path of interest rates uniformly, but it will have a monotone effect for any diffusion process. Logarithmic utility investors will be indifferent about any pure interest rate change. Investors with utility functions that are more risk tolerant than log will prefer to face such risks.

If the return on aggregate wealth is not certain and changes in the interest rate are correlated with this return, then bond returns will also be correlated with returns on aggregate wealth. An investor with logarithmic utility or any other risk-averse investor will not be indifferent about this type of risk, and bonds will earn a standard "beta" or market risk premium.

DETERMINANTS OF THE INTEREST RATE

Up to this point we have simply assumed that the interest rate was the sole state variable affecting the prices of bonds, and we have taken its movement as exogenous. In this section we examine the underlying economic factors that influence the interest rate.

Aggregate wealth, the distribution of wealth among investors, the expected rates of return on physical investment, and the relations among the various investment opportunities are obvious factors that might be important. In addition, taxes, government policy, and inflation—things often ignored in financial models—probably also influence the behavior of interest rates.

To see how aggregate wealth affects the interest rate, consider a "representative investor" economy with a single risky primitive investment opportunity whose return is identically distributed over time. The representative investor must, by definition, invest only in the primitive investment opportunity. Demand for the risky asset as a proportion of the investor's wealth is, from Equation (12) of Chapter 13,

$$w^* = -\frac{J_W}{WJ_{WW}}\frac{\alpha - r}{\sigma^2}. \tag{58}$$

In equilibrium demand as given in (58) must be unity, so we can solve for the interest rate

$$r(W) = \alpha - R(W)\sigma^2, \tag{59}$$

where $R(W) \equiv -J_{WW}/WJ_W$ is the relative risk-aversion function of the representative investor.

From (59) it is obvious that the interest rate depends only on wealth. For example, if the derived utility function is exponential, $J(W) = -e^{-aW}$, then

$$r(W) = \alpha - \frac{a}{W}\sigma^2. \tag{60}$$

Thus, we have a Markov model for the interest rate with aggregate or per capita wealth as the driving factor.

Similarly, if the single risky investment opportunity does not have stochastic constant returns to scale, (59) remains valid, but α and σ are functions of aggregate wealth, so that the interest rate is as well.

It is also clear from (59) how the distribution of wealth among investors affects interest rates. If there are two classes of investors each with power utility, then aggregate wealth will be immaterial in determining the interest rate. The relative risk aversion of the representative investor, however, will depend on how much wealth each class has. (The actual determination of the interest rate in this case is more complicated since the class wealth percentage must be treated as a state variable.)

To examine how the distribution of returns affects the interest rate, we add one state variable to our economy. In this case the demand for the risky asset is, from Equation (47) of Chapter 13,

$$w^* = -\frac{J_W}{WJ_{WW}}\frac{\alpha - r}{\sigma^2} - \frac{J_{Wx}}{WJ_{WW}}\frac{\rho s}{\sigma}, \tag{61}$$

where ρ is the correlation coefficient between returns on the asset and changes in the single state variable, and s is the standard deviaton of changes in the state variable.

Solving for the interest rate gives

$$r(W, x) = \alpha(x) R(W, x)\sigma^2(x) - H(W, x)\rho(x)s(x)\sigma(x), \tag{62}$$

where $H(W, x) \equiv -J_{WW}/WJ_{Wx}$ is a measure of aversion to changes in the state variable. In general, the interest rate now depends on wealth and the state variable x. If utility is power, then both risk measures are independent of wealth, and only the state variable x matters.

The model of Cox, Ingersoll, and Ross, for example, assumes that investors have log utility (so that $R(W, x) = 1$ and $H(W, x) = 0$) and that α and σ^2 are each proportional to a single Markov state variable. In this case r is also proportional to this state variable and is therefore Markov.

BOND PRICING WITH MULTIPLE STATE VARIABLES

As we have seen, there are many factors or state variables which might affect interest rates. In applications it will be more convenient to use different interest rates as instrumental variables for these state variables. This is permissible if the functions which determine the interest rates from the state variables are globally invertible.

To illustrate how this works, suppose that there are two state variables governing bond prices and that we may use as instruments the spot rate r and a long-term rate L, the yield-to-maturity on some bond. The dynamics of these two instrumental variables are

$$dr = b_1(r, L, t)\,dt + a_1(r, L, t)\,d\tilde{\omega}_1, \tag{63a}$$

$$dL = b_2(r, L, t)\,dt + a_2(r, L, t)\,d\tilde{\omega}_2. \tag{63b}$$

As shown in Chapter 17, the resulting valuation equation for bond prices is

$$\begin{aligned} &\tfrac{1}{2}a_1^2(\cdot)P_{rr} + [b_1(\cdot) - \lambda_1(\cdot)]P_r + \rho a_1(\cdot)a_2(\cdot)P_{rL} \\ &+\tfrac{1}{2}a_2^2(\cdot)P_{LL} + [b_2(\cdot) - \lambda_2(\cdot)]P_L + P_t - rP = 0, \end{aligned} \tag{64}$$

where $\lambda_1(\cdot)$ and $\lambda_2(\cdot)$ are the risk-premium terms for the spot rate and long rate, respectively.

Since L is the yield-to-maturity on a particular bond, it is a known function of that bond's price, and we can use the method developed in the previous chapter to eliminate the second drift and risk-premium term. Denote the price and maturity date of the bond for which L is the yield-to-maturity by P^* and T^*, respectively. Then $P^* \equiv \exp[-L(T^*-t)]$, and its partial derivatives are $P_L = -(T^* - t)P^*$, $P_{LL} = (T^* - t)^2P^*$, $P_t = LP^*$, and $P_r = P_{rr} = P_{rL} = 0$. Substituting these into (64) and solving for $b_2 - \lambda_2$ give

$$b_2(\cdot) - \lambda(\cdot) = \frac{r - L - \frac{1}{2}a_2^2(\cdot)(T^* - t)^2}{t - T^*}. \tag{65}$$

Another useful type of two-factor model is standardly used in forecasting. In these models the expected change in the interest rate might be as given in the foregoing second example. The central tendency μ, however, is not a constant but varies over time.

For example, μ might be an exponentially weighted average of the past interest rates:

$$\mu_t = \beta \int_0^\infty e^{-\beta s} r_{t-s}\,ds. \tag{66}$$

This will be recognized as the continuous-time equivalent of the commonly used average of past interest rates with a geometrically declining weighting.

In differential form the state variable dynamics can be expressed as

$$dr_t = \kappa(\mu_t - r_t)\,\mathrm{dt} + b(r_t, \mu_t, t)\, d\tilde{\omega}_t, \tag{67a}$$

$$d\mu_t = \beta(r_t - \mu_t)\,\mathrm{dt}. \tag{67b}$$

Equation (67b) is the differential form of (66). Despite being a state variable, it is clear from (67b) that μ has *locally* deterministic movements. It is not globally deterministic, however, nor is it simply a function of the contemporaneous interest rate. To determine what μ_T is from μ_t, we must know r_s for the entire interval $[t, T]$.

If the variance term and the interest rate risk-premium factor are proportional to the interest rate, then the bond-pricing equation for this model is

$$\tfrac{1}{2}\sigma^2 rP_{rr} + [\kappa\mu - (\kappa + \lambda)r]P_r + \beta(r - \mu)P_\mu + P_t - rP = 0. \tag{68}$$

Note that there is no risk premium associated with μ since it is locally deterministic.

To solve this equation, we guess a solution of the form $P(\cdot) = \exp[A(\tau)\mu + B(\tau)r]$. Substituting this into (67) and collecting terms in r and μ, we have

$$\tfrac{1}{2}\sigma^2 B^2(\tau) - (\kappa + \lambda)B(\tau) - 1 + \beta A(\tau) - B'(\tau) = 0, \tag{69a}$$

$$\kappa B(\tau) - \beta A(\tau) - A'(\tau) = 0. \tag{69b}$$

The equations in (69) verify that this functional form of the solution is correct. Unfortunately, these two equations do not have known closed from solutions, they will yield easily to numerical methods, however.

To illustrate further the properties of this model and indicate how it might be estimated, define the new state variable $u \equiv \mathrm{r} - \mu$. Then by Ito's lemma

$$\begin{aligned} du_t &= dr_t - d\mu_t = (\kappa - \beta)(r_t - \mu_t)\,dt + \sigma\sqrt{r_t}\,d\tilde{\omega}_t \\ &= (\kappa - \beta)u_t dt + \sigma\sqrt{r_t}\,d\tilde{\omega}_t \qquad (70) \\ dr_t &= -\kappa u_t dt + \sigma\sqrt{r_t}\,d\tilde{\omega}_t. \end{aligned}$$

In this form it is clear that κ governs the short-term behavior of the interest rate. The state variable u measures the difference between the current interest rate and its past average. Thus, if κ is positive, then the interest rate tends to return to its recent levels. On the othe hand, if κ is negative, then the interest rate is extrapolative and tends to continue in the direction that it has been moving. By using more than one state variable of this type, both tendencies can be modeled.

To illustrate the estimation of this model, simplify the notation by defining $K \equiv \kappa\, dt$, $B \equiv \beta\, dt$, and $\tilde{\varepsilon}_t \equiv \sigma\sqrt{r_t}\, d\tilde{\omega}_t$. Then (70) is

$$du_t = (K - B)\mu_t + \tilde{\varepsilon}_t, \tag{71a}$$

$$dr_t = -Ku_t + \tilde{\varepsilon}_t. \tag{71b}$$

Now take the first difference in (71b) and substitute for the first difference in μ from (71a), giving

$$\begin{aligned} dr_{t+dt} - dr_t &= -K(u_{t+dt} - u_t + \tilde{\varepsilon}_{t+dt} - \tilde{\varepsilon}_t \\ &= -K(K - B)\mu_t - K\tilde{\varepsilon}_t + \tilde{\varepsilon}_{t+dt} - \tilde{\varepsilon}_t. \end{aligned} \tag{72}$$

Finally, we can substitute for $-Ku_t$ from (71b) and collect terms:

$$dr_{t+dt} = (1 + K - B)dr_t + \tilde{\varepsilon}_{t+dt} - (1 + 2K - B)\tilde{\varepsilon}_t. \tag{73}$$

This stochastic model is a first-order autoregressive, first-order moving average process in first differences; that is, a Box–Jenkins ARIMA (1,1,1) process and can be estimated by standard methods.

19

Pricing the Capital Structure of the Firm

The contingent claims analysis developed in Chapters 14, 17, and 18 can be used to value the component parts of a firm's liability mix. In general, the value of each component will depend upon the stochastic variables which determine the evolution of the firm's asset value, the evolution of the interest rate, the payouts (dividends, coupons, etc.) to the various claimants, and the division of the firm at any point of reorganization (e.g., bankruptcy). To take all of these factors into consideration would require a complete general equilibrium model. However, if we abstract from some of these risks, a much simpler partial equilibrium analysis can yield useful insights.

THE MODIGLIANI–MILLER IRRELEVANCY THEOREM

The Modigliani–Miller theorem states that the value of a firm is independent of its capital structure in the absence of taxes and bankruptcy costs. It has been demonstrated true in four cases: (a) The returns on the underlying assets are certain and investors can borrow at the risk free rate. (b) The firm is part of an effectively complete market with Arrow–Debreu state securities for each relevant outcome. (c) There are two or more firms with different leverage in the same "risk class" (firms whose returns are perfectly correlated), and this firm will no go bankrupt with probability 1. (d) Investors can arrange "no recourse" loans with the stock as collateral. In each of these cases any investment opportunity that could be created by a change in leverage or the creation of an identical firm with a different leverage is already spanned by the existing securities.

We demonstrate that if markets are always open for trading and asset prices have continuous sample paths, then the M–M theorem can hold even in the presence of bankruptcy, risk, and incomplete markets. These two conditions are sufficient for investors to create implicit "no recourse" loans. We also consider situations in which it is not valid. Since the proof is very similar to the alternative derivation of the option pricing equation given in Chapter 17, many of the details are omitted.

As in the original Modigliani–Miller presentation, we assume that there are no differential taxes or bankruptcy costs. We also assume that the interest rate is constant. For simplicity we consider a levered firm with only a single debt contract, with value F, calling for continuous coupons at the constant rate C_F and a final payment of B at time T. If the firm fails to live up to this indenture, the bondholders immediately take over the firm. Clearly, the company will pay the coupons as long as the assets have positive value. Dividends are paid at the rate C_f.

There is an identical unlevered firm paying aggregate dividends of $C = C_F + C_f$ and following the same investment policy. Let V denote the asset value and V_L and V_U the values of the levered and unlevered firms. With perfect markets $V_U = V$. We now want to prove that $V_L = V_U = V$. Clearly, if $V = 0$, then $V_L = V_U = 0$. Also at time T^- just before the debt is paid off, $V_L = V_U$, since momentarily the firm will be all equity financed with either the former equity owners or debtholders owning the entire firm. (If there are costs of bankruptcy, this condition may be violated.)

The value of both firms' assets V (and V_U) evolve over time according to

$$dV = (\alpha V - C)\, dt + \delta V d\tilde{\omega}, \tag{1}$$

with δ and C deterministic functions of V and t.

Consider the formal solution to the equation

$$\tfrac{1}{2}\sigma^2 V^2 Q_{VV} + (rV - C)Q_V - rQ + Q_t + C_F = 0 \tag{2a}$$

subject to

$$Q(V, T) = \text{Min}\,(V, B), \tag{2b}$$

$$Q(0, t) \quad = 0, \tag{2c}$$

$$Q(V, t) \quad \leqslant V. \tag{2d}$$

We construct a portfolio worth P dollars by investing VQ_V dollars in the unlevered firm and $P - VQ_V$ dollars lent at rate r. From this portfolio we make withdrawals at the rate C_F per unit time. Then

$$dP = [VQ_V\,(\alpha - r) + rP - C_F]\, dt + VQ_V\, \sigma\, d\tilde{\omega}. \tag{3}$$

But since Q is a function of V, by Ito's lemma

$$dQ = [\tfrac{1}{2}\, \delta^2 V^2 Q_{VV} + (\alpha V - C)Q_V + Q_t]\, dt + Q_V\, V\sigma\, d\tilde{\omega}. \tag{4}$$

Using (2a) we can rewrite (4) as

$$dQ = [(\alpha - r)VQ_V + rQ - C_F]\, dt + vQ_V\sigma\, d\tilde{\omega}, \tag{5}$$

and from (3) and (5)

$$dP - dQ = r(P - Q)\,dt. \tag{6}$$

If we select $P(0) = Q(V, 0)$, then $P(t) \equiv Q(V, t)$. But the portfolio P has cash flows C_F, is worth 0 if V is worth 0, and at T is worth Min $[V(T), B]$ = Min$[V_L(T), B]$, so the bond on the levered firm must be worth $F(V_L, t) = P(t) = Q(V, t)$.

Thus far we have seen the following:

1. If there are additional sources of uncertainty in the economy, they can affect the value of a contingent claim and the levered firm only through the variance of the asset value, r, the payouts C and C_F, and the contractual boundary conditions (6b)–(6d). Note that the value cannot be affected through α.

2. If there is a solution to (2a) subject to the appropriate boundary conditions, then it gives the price of the contingent claim. Using the same reasoning, we can show that the value of the equity, f, must satisfy Equation (2a), with C_f replacing C_F. $Q(V, T) = \text{Max}[V - B, 0]$, (2c), and (2d). Now consider the value of the levered firm $V_L = F + f$. Clearly, it is the solution to

$$\tfrac{1}{2}\sigma^2 V^2 Q_{VV} + (rV - C)\,Q_V - rQ + Q_t + C_F + C_f = 0 \tag{7a}$$

subject to

$$Q\,(V, T) = \text{Min}\,[V, B] + \text{Max}\,[V - B, 0] = V, \tag{7b}$$

(2c), and (2d). But this solution obviously is $V_L = V = V_U$, and the first proposition of the M–M theorem is proved. Furthermore, if there currently is no levered firm, the same steps could be used to show that the prices derived here would have to prevail if one were created.

FAILURE OF THE M–M THEOREM

Suppose there is an additional source of uncertainty which may affect the pricing of the contingent claims on a firm. Denote the state variable measuring this uncertainty by x and assume that

$$dx = \mu\,dt + s\,d\tilde{\omega}_2. \tag{8}$$

The value of the unlevered firm still moves according to (1), but C and σ may depend upon x. Suppose for the moment that the M–M theorem holds and $V_L = V$.

We write the value of a contingent claim as $F(V, x, t)$. By Ito's lemma

$$\frac{dF}{F} = \left(\alpha_F - \frac{C_F}{F}\right)dt + \frac{VF_V}{F}\,\sigma\,d\tilde{\omega}_1 + \frac{F_x}{F}s\,d\tilde{\omega}_2 \tag{9}$$

with $\alpha_F - C_F/F$, the expected capital gains rate composed of the expected rate of return less the rate of payout.

Consider a portfolio investing the fraction w_1 in F and $1 - w_1$ in the firm as a whole V; then

$$\frac{dP_1}{P_1} = w_1 \frac{dF + C_F dt}{F} + (1 - w_1) \frac{dV + C\,dt}{V} \tag{10}$$

$$= [w_1(\alpha_F - \alpha) + \alpha]\,dt +$$

$$\left[w_1\left(\frac{F_V V}{F} - 1\right) + 1\right]\sigma V\,d\tilde{\omega}_1 + w_1 \frac{F_x}{F} s\,d\tilde{\omega}_2.$$

If we select $w_1 = F/(F - VF_V)$, then $d\tilde{\omega}_2$ is the only remaining source of uncertainty. Consider a second portfolio with fraction w_2 invested in f and $1 - w_2$ invested in V with $w_2 = f/(f - Vf_V)$, so that it too has only the single source of uncertainty $d\omega_2$. Since these two portfolios are perfectly correlated, each must have an expected excess rate of return proportional to its standard deviation

$$\frac{w_1(\alpha_F - \alpha) + \alpha - r}{w_1 F_x/F} = \frac{w_2(\alpha_f - \alpha) + \alpha - r}{w_2 f_x/f} = \lambda(V, x, t), \tag{11}$$

where λ, the "price of risk" associated with x, does not depend upon the claim in question. In many cases when x is a macroeconomic state variable λ will not depend upon V. Rearranging terms in (11) gives

$$\alpha_F = r + \frac{VF_V}{F}(\alpha - r) + \frac{F_x}{F}\lambda. \tag{12}$$

Combining (9) and (12) yields the valuation equation

$$\tfrac{1}{2}\sigma^2 V^2 F_{VV} + (rV - C)F_V - rF + F_t + C_F + \tfrac{1}{2}s^2 F_{xx} \tag{13}$$
$$+ \rho s\sigma\, VF_{xV} + (\mu - \lambda)F_x = 0.$$

Instead of this hedging argument, we could have postulated a solution to the general equation (13) subject to certain boundary constraints and then proved that its solutions gave the prices of contingent claims and also that M–M proposition obtained. We can do all of the above if the equation is identifiable. This will be the case if we can observe λ. Clearly, if the levered firm exists and F is known, then λ can be determined by taking empirical derivatives and substituting into (13). So if both firms exist, $V_L = V_U$. If two levered firms, but no unlevered firm, exist, then $V_L = V'_L$. If a single levered firm exists, then V_L is also the value that an unlevered firm would have were it to be created.

Suppose only an unlevered firm(s) exists but that there is another asset whose price is a known function of x and t alone. Denote the value of this asset by G. From (11) $\alpha_G = r + \lambda$. By Ito's lemma

$$\tfrac{1}{2}s^2 G_{xx} + \mu G_x + G_t = \alpha_G G - C_G. \tag{14}$$

Combining equations gives

$$\frac{1}{G_x}\left[\tfrac{1}{2}s^2 G_{xx} + \mu G_x + G_t + C_G - rG\right] = \lambda. \tag{15}$$

Again λ is "observable," and the M–M proposition holds. If a levered firm were to be created, it would sell for V_U.

The Modigliani–Miller theorem will hold whenever a change in leverage by the firm does not cause the price of x-type risk to change. In addition to the case discussed above, this will be true if a perfect hedging portfolio for the state variable x (as discussed in Chapter 13) already exists. If the state variable is uncorrelated with returns on the market portfolio, then λ will be equal to the reward-to-risk ratio $(\alpha_h - r)/\sigma_h$ on the hedge portfolio. Alternatively, if logarithmic utility prevails in the market, then the excess rate of return on the hedge portfolio, $\alpha_h - r$, and therefore the price of risk λ, will be zero regardless of how good a hedge is available. However, if utility is not logarithmic and a perfect hedge does not already exist, then the portfolio described in (10) will be the new hedging portfolio. In general, the entire equilibrium will change.

The same general results obtain if there are multiple additional sources of uncertainty — x is a vector. If any of the hedging opportunities are improved by the introduction of debt, the firm value will be increased, and the M–M theorem will not hold.

In spirit this proof is similar to the earlier proofs of the M–M theorem. Corporate leverage is irrelevant unless the investors' opportunity set can be expanded.

PRICING THE CAPITAL STRUCTURE: AN INTRODUCTION

In this and the following sections we show how contingent claims analysis can be used to value typical contracts. The examples we consider here are all "discount" securities, that is, assets whose values arise from a single payment in the future. We have picked contracts that illustrate particular points of interest rather than the most realistic examples. In general, the valuation of contracts calling for interim payments will require numerical methods.

We assume that the firm makes no cash payouts prior to the maturity of the contract and that its value evolves according to the dynamics in (1):

$$\frac{dV}{V} = \alpha\, dt + \sigma\, d\tilde{\omega} \tag{16}$$

with σ a constant. The contract payoff at maturity is a deterministic function of the value of the firm at that time. If the firm's value achieves either of the two values $V(t)$ or $\bar{V}(t)$, the company is immediately reorganized, and contractually specified amounts are paid. These conditions can be stated as

$$F(V, T) = F_0(V), \tag{17a}$$

$$F(\bar{V}(t), t) = \bar{F}(t), \tag{17b}$$

$$F(\underline{V}(t), t) = \underline{F}(t). \tag{17c}$$

In the absence of explicit boundary conditions, the limited liability of the contract and the remaining claims guarantees that

$$F(V, t) \leq V, \tag{17b'}$$

$$F(0, t) = 0. \tag{17c'}$$

Under these conditions and the assumption of a constant interest rate, the Modigliani – Miller theorem holds, and the value of the contract is the solution to

$$\tfrac{1}{2}\sigma^2 V^2 F_{VV} + rVF_V - rF + F_t = 0 \tag{18}$$

subject to (17a) – (17c) as demonstrated previously. The solution to (18) is given formally in Equation (36) of Chapter 17.

Many of the contracts considered here have option-like features and can be priced in terms of options. Throughout the remainder of this chapter we shall use $W(S, \tau; X)$ to represent the Black – Scholes solution for a call option with time to maturity $\tau \equiv T - t$ and exercise price X on a stock with price S.

WARRANTS AND RIGHTS

In most respects warrants are identical to call options; they evidence the right to buy shares of stock in a particular company at a fixed price on or before a set date. The only important distinction between options and warrants is that the latter are issued by the corporation whose stock is to be purchased.

When a warrant is exercised, new shares of stock are issued, and the cash payment that is made increases the assets of the issuing firm. Options, on the other hand, are created by individuals (or other corporations). When they are exercised, already existing shares must be delivered, and the cash payment does not go to the corporation whose stock is delivered but to the party who wrote the option. Because of these differences, the Black – Scholes call option model cannot be used directly to value warrants, although as shown before the same basic method is applicable. Another difference between warrants and calls is that warrants are typically issued with maturities of several years rather than nine months or less, but this is only a quantitative difference and does not affect the choice of model.

Because of this difference, it will be optimal at some times to exercise warrants sequentially rather than simultaneously. Fortunately this does not affect the pricing, so we will ignore this feature for now and assume that all warrants are exercised at the same time. Sequential exercise is discussed later.

Suppose that a company has N shares of common stock and n warrants outstanding. Each warrant entitles the owner to receive one share of stock upon the payment of X dollars. These two forms of financing are the only ones that the company is using.

If the company's assets are worth V and all the warrants are exercised, then the company will be worth $V + nX$. Since there are now $N + n$ shares of stock outstanding, each is worth $1/(N + n)$ of this amount. Thus, just before this exercise each warrant must be worth

$$\frac{1}{N + n}(V + nX) - X. \tag{19}$$

Clearly, exercise will occur only if this quantity is nonnegative; that is, if $V \geqslant NX$. If it is known that the warrants will be exercised, then each share of stock is worth $S = (V + nX)/(N + n)$. At the point where the warrant owners are indifferent about exercising ($V = NX$), each share is worth X, so the warrants are exercised only if $S \geqslant X$, just as with call options. If the warrant owners strictly prefer exercising ($V > NX$), then the common equity is worth less than the value of the firm's assets. This shortfall has not vanished, of course; it simply measures the value of the warrants.

The same is generally true prior to the maturity of the warrants. The value of the equity is less than the value of the assets. If we think of the assets as being primitive, it is natural to price the warrants as contingent claims not on the stock but on the firm as a whole.

Let $w(V, \tau)$ denote the value of each warrant on a firm of value V when the time to maturity is τ. From (19) the maturity condition for the warrants is

$$w(V, 0) = \begin{cases} \lambda(V + nX) - X, & V > NX, \\ 0, & V \leqslant NX, \end{cases} \tag{20}$$

where $\lambda \equiv 1/(N + n)$ is the fraction of the firm to which each warrant is entitled (if all the warrants are exercised). This condition can be expressed as

$$w(V, 0) = \text{Max}\,[\lambda V - X(1 - n\lambda), 0] = \lambda\,\text{Max}[V - X(1 - n\lambda)/\lambda, 0].$$

Thus, if the Black – Scholes assumptions are satisfied, we can immediately write the value of the warrants as

$$w(V, \tau; \lambda, X) = \lambda W\left(V, \tau; \frac{X(1 - n\lambda)}{\lambda}\right) = W\Big(\lambda V, \tau; X(1 - n\lambda)\Big). \quad (21)$$

The last equality follows from the homogeneity of the option function.

Intuitively, this is the solution because the warrant is like a call on stock worth λV. The exercise price is lowered from its nominal value of X becuase only the fraction $1 - \lambda$ of it goes to the original stockholders; the rest reverts to the warrant holder through his proportionate claim on the whole firm.

One caution is in order. The quantity λV is (21) is *not* the current value of one share of common stock to which the warrant entitles its owner. In this regard the formula in (21) is different from the formula for valuing a call option. On the other hand, the use of the Black – Scholes formula in (21) disguises some of the similarity between pricing call options and warrants. If the firm dynamics are not lognormal but follow from some other diffusion or binomial process, then (21) is still valid, provided that $W(\cdot)$ is the call option valuation formula for this other process.

Now let us compare the value of a warrant to that of a call option on the stock of an otherwise identical firm without warrants. For a firm with no warrants and N shares of stock worth $\hat{S}_t$, n call options will be worth $W(n\hat{S}_t, \tau; nX)$. Now suppose that an identical firm has issued n warrants at w_t dollars. To keep the companies "otherwise identical," we must have $NS_t + nw_t = NS_t$. When the warrants expire, $\hat{V}_T = N\hat{S}_T$ and $V_T = \hat{V}_T$ if the warrants are not exercised or $V_T = \hat{V}_T + nX$ if they are exercised. In the former case, the warrants are worth zero. In the latter case, each is worth

$$\begin{aligned} w_T &= \frac{1}{N+n}V_T - X = \frac{1}{N+n}\hat{V}_T - X\left(1 - \frac{n}{N+n}\right) \\ &= \frac{N}{N+n}(\hat{S}_T - X) = (1 - n\lambda)(\hat{S}_T - X). \end{aligned} \quad (22)$$

This is exactly the payoff on $1 - n\lambda$ call options.

Thus, from (21) a warrant is worth more than a call option on an otherwise identical all-equity firm with the same stock price. From (22) a warrant is worth less than a call option on an otherwise identical all-equity firm with the same asset value.

The formula in (21) can be used to value warrants. The formula implied by (22) could not be so used unless we were lucky enough to have the otherwise identical firm. If the dilution factor is not too big, just valuing warrants as if they were calls will be approximately correct, however.

If there are more than just warrants and common stock in the capital structure of the firm, then the formula in (21) can still be used to price the warrants if V is the market value of just these two components. If the value of these two components has a lognormal distribution, then $W(\cdot)$ is the Black – Scholes function.

Rights offerings and executive stock options, which do create new shares when exercised, can also be priced by this model. Like warrants, these are also issued by a firm. Rights are given to existing shareholders in proportion to the number of shares that they own, like dividends. They usually have very short maturities and, when issued, are substantially in-the-money to assure that they will be exercised. Rights offerings are used by firms as a way to issue additional equity capital while letting each existing owner keep his proportionate share in the firm. Any owner who does not wish to exercise his rights can sell them in the secondary market. Executive stock options are just like warrants except that they usually have restricted marketability.

RISKY DISCOUNT BONDS

Pricing risky discount or zero coupon bonds issued by a firm is a second easy application of the Black – Scholes model. Consider a company which has issued a bond promising to pay B dollars at time T. We will ignore bankruptcy costs and assume that if the company fails to live up to this promise, then the firm is declared bankrupt, and the bondholders receive all the assets of the firm.

Suppose for the moment that just before time T the firm's operations will cease, and all of its fixed assets will be sold. At time T its assets will be entirely cash. The company will obviously pay off the bondholders if $V_T \geqslant B$. Doing so will leave $V_T - B \geqslant 0$ for the owners of the firm, whereas if they declared bankruptcy, they would have nothing, by the terms of the contract. If $V_T < B$, then the bondholders can be paid off entirely only if some new capital is raised. If new capital could be raised, the value of the firm after paying off the bondholders would be less than the amount raised; that is, if K $(> B - V_T)$ dollars of new capital is raised, then after paying the bondholders B the firm will be worth $V_T + K - B$ $(< K)$ dollars. Clearly, investors would not be willing to pay K dollars and receive a claim to less than K dollars.

In this case then the value of the bond at maturity is Min (V_T, B). The value of the equity is, therefore, $V_T - \text{Min}(V_T, B) = \text{Max}\ (V_T - B, 0)$. It is clear that the owners or equity holders of the firm have a claim on the firm assets which is like a call option. That is, they can reacquire full control of the assets and the right to receive all future cash flows resulting from them by paying an "exercise price" of B dollars.

The value of a risky zero coupon bond with τ periods to go before maturity is

$$D(V, \tau; B) = V - W(V, \tau; B) \qquad (23)$$
$$= VN(h_1) + Be^{-r\tau} N(h_2),$$

where

$$h_1 \equiv \frac{\log (Be^{-r\tau}/V) - .5\sigma^2\tau}{\sigma\sqrt{\tau}}, \qquad h_2 \equiv -h_1 - \sigma\sqrt{\tau}.$$

As in option pricing, a risk-neutral interpretation of (23) can be given. $N(d_2)$ is the probability, under the risk-neutral process, that the firm will be solvent when the bond matures. Thus, the second term in (23) is the riskless discounted expected value of receiving the promised payment B in full. The first term is the present value of receiving all the assets of the firm conditional on their being worth less than B.

Even if all of the firm's assets will not be cash at time T, the same analysis applies. The company will sell assets or issue new shares or bonds to raise the cash to repay the bondholders. They will be able to do this only if the value of the assets of the firm exceeds the payment promised on the debt so that the new claimants receive full value for the amount of their purchase.

A natural question at this point is, if the firm is bankrupt at time T, why would the bondholders not renegotiate the contract in hopes that subsequent good fortune would allow the firm to pay them in full? The answer should be clear. Under the current contract they have the right to receive all the assets of the firm. Why should they settle for less? If the firm is fortunate, they can have all of the profits rather than sharing them. Of course, they would renegotiate if the shareholders made the right concession — adding more money to the firm. However, they would have to add enough to make up the bankruptcy shortfall plus an amount equal to whatever claim on the refinanced firm they would like to own. But again, why should they do that? It would cost more than the value they would receive in return.

Before proceeding with our analysis, it should be pointed out that risky coupon bonds *cannot* be priced as if they were a portfolio of risky pure discount bonds. With default-free bonds that are subject only to interest rate risk, this portfolio treatment is valid. It cannot be used for risky bonds because the payment of one coupon lowers the value of the firm's assets and so affects the probability of future default.

All of the comparative statics for the bond function can be determined from those of options. A zero coupon bond is an increasing, concave function of the value of the firm's assets. Like default-free bonds, a risky, zero coupon bond is a decreaseing function of the interest rate and the time to maturity and an increasing function of the promised payment. The bond function is also a decreasing function of the variance of the firm's assets. Further effects of risk are considered in detail in the next section.

Another distinction between options and corporate securities should be made at this point. Typically, neither the buyer nor the writer of an option has any control over the underlying asset. However, the management of a company, which represents the shareholders, does have a certain amount of control over the assets of the firm, and this may affect the valuation of the bonds. For example, by changing the investment policy, the management could change the risk of the firm's assets. Since the risk of the assets directly affects the value of the debt, the claims of the bondholders and the stockholders will not be invariant to investment decisions even if the projects considered all have zero net present value.

As an extreme case suppose that a firm owes \$1000 in one year. Currently its assets are worth \$900 and are invested in Treasury bills paying 10% interest. In one year the firm will have \$990, so it will definitely be bankrupt. If nothing is going to change, the bonds should be selling for \$900, and the equity should be worthless. The company is considering a project which would either increase the assets by 120% or lose everything. The risk-neutral probabilities of these two outcomes are both $\frac{1}{2}$. If it takes the project, the firm will be worth either \$1980 or zero. The net present value of the project is $.5 \times 1980/1.1 + .5 \times 0 - 900 = 0$. The firm value will remain \$900 if it takes the project since the net present value is zero. However, the bonds will sell for $.5 \times \$1000/1.1 = \$454.55$, and the equity will be worth $.5 \times \$980/1.1 = \$445.45$. This investment would obviously be favored by the owners but be disliked by the creditors.

The owners would even like some projects with negative net present values. For example, suppose the good outcome only doubled the value of the assets. In this case, the net present value of the project is $-\$81.81$, and undertaking the project decreases the value of the firm from \$900 to \$818.19. The debt would be worth \$454.55 as before. The equity would be worth only $.5 \times \$800/1.1 = \$363.64$. Nevertheless, the owners would favor its adoption over keeping T-bills.

THE RISK STRUCTURE OF INTEREST RATES

It is common in dealing with bonds to discuss them in terms of yields rather than prices. The yield-to-maturity of a discount bond is the solution to $D = Be^{-Y\tau}$. The yield spread s or "risk premium" is the difference between the yield and the riskless rate. For the risky discount bond in (23) we have

$$Y(d, \tau; r, \sigma) = r - \frac{1}{\tau} \log \left(N(h_2) + \frac{1}{d} N(h_1) \right), \tag{24a}$$

$$s(d, \tau; \sigma) \equiv Y(d, \tau; r, \sigma) - r = -\frac{1}{\tau} \log \left(N(h_2) + \frac{1}{d} N(h_1) \right), \tag{24b}$$

where $d \equiv Be^{-r\tau}/V$ is the *quasi debt-to-firm-value ratio*. This is the leverage or fraction of the firm financed by debt when the debt is assigned its riskless value. The actual leverage of the firm measured at the market value of the debt will be smaller. Note that since h_1 and h_2 depend on V and B only through the ratio d, the yield does as well. The yield spread on the bond depends on only three variables: d, τ, and σ.

Another natural way to measure the bond's risk is by its instantaneous standard deviation of returns. By Ito's lemma this is

$$\sigma_D(d, \tau; \sigma) = \frac{VD_V}{D} \sigma = \eta(d, \sigma^2\tau)\, \sigma, \tag{25}$$

where

$$\eta(d, \sigma^2\tau) \equiv \frac{V(\partial D/\partial V)}{D(\cdot)} = \frac{N(h_1)}{N(h_1) + dN(h_2)},$$

and $N(\cdot)$ is the standard cumulative normal function. Like the spread, the instantaneous standard deviation is a function of only d, τ, and σ. $\eta(\cdot)$ is the elasticity of the bond price with respect to firm value. It measures the risk of the bond relative to that of the firm as a whole. Since the bond's elasticity is always less than 1, the bond is always less risky than the firm. The equity, which corresponds to a call option, is always more risky than the firm as a whole.

The bond's standard deviation measures the risk over the next instant. The yield spread, on the other hand, is the promised risk premium over the remaining life of the bond. There is no necessity that these two risk measures be equivalent, but they should be comparable in some respects.

The comparative statics of the yield spread and the bond's instantaneous standard deviation are

$$\frac{\partial s}{\partial d} = \frac{1}{\tau d} \eta(\cdot) > 0, \tag{26a}$$

$$\frac{\partial s}{\partial \sigma} = \frac{1}{\sqrt{\tau}} \eta(\cdot) \frac{n(h_1)}{N(h_1)} > 0, \tag{26b}$$

$$\frac{\partial s}{\partial \tau} = \frac{1}{\tau} \left(\frac{\sigma}{2\sqrt{\tau}} \eta(\cdot) \frac{n(h_1)}{N(h_1)} - s(\cdot) \right) \lesseqgtr 0, \tag{26c}$$

$$\frac{\partial \sigma_D}{\partial d} = \frac{\eta^2(\cdot)}{\sqrt{\tau}} \frac{N(h_2)}{N(h_1)} \left(\frac{n(h_2)}{N(h_2)} + h_2 + \frac{n(h_1)}{N(h_1)} + h_1 \right) > 0, \tag{26d}$$

$$\frac{\partial \sigma_D}{\partial \sigma} = \eta(\cdot)\left[1 - \frac{n(h_1)}{N(h_1)}\left(\frac{1}{2} - \eta(\cdot) + \frac{\log(d)}{\sigma^2 \tau}\right)\right] > 0, \tag{26e}$$

$$\frac{\partial \sigma_D}{\partial \tau} = \frac{\sigma^2}{\sqrt{\tau}}\left(\frac{\partial \sigma_D}{\partial \sigma} - \eta(\cdot)\right) \gtrless 0 \qquad \text{as } d \lesseqgtr 1, \tag{26f}$$

where $n(\cdot)$ is the standard normal density function.

It is clear that both the instantaneous risk and the spread are larger if the firm is riskier or if it is more levered. Both of these results are in accord with the intuition that when the debt is riskier, the yield spread should be larger. The effect of a longer maturity is not clear; the risk and yield spread can either rise or fall. Figures 19.1 and 19.2 show the yield spread and bond risk for bonds on a firm with an asset risk of 30% per year. As seen there, the spread and the risk are decreasing in maturity if $d \geqslant 1$. (The risk is constant for $d = 1$.) For $d < 1$, the spread first rises and then falls while the risk is rising.

This last result may at first seem counterintuitive — longer maturity debt "should" be riskier and command a larger premium. Recall that in this comparison we are holding constant not the ratio of the promised payment to the value of the firm but the ratio of the riskless discounted value of the promised payment to the firm value.

If $d > 1$, then the firm is "technically insolvent" in the risk–neutral economy since its assets are not expected to earn enough to pay off the debt. That is, to avoid bankruptcy it will need to have pleasant earnings

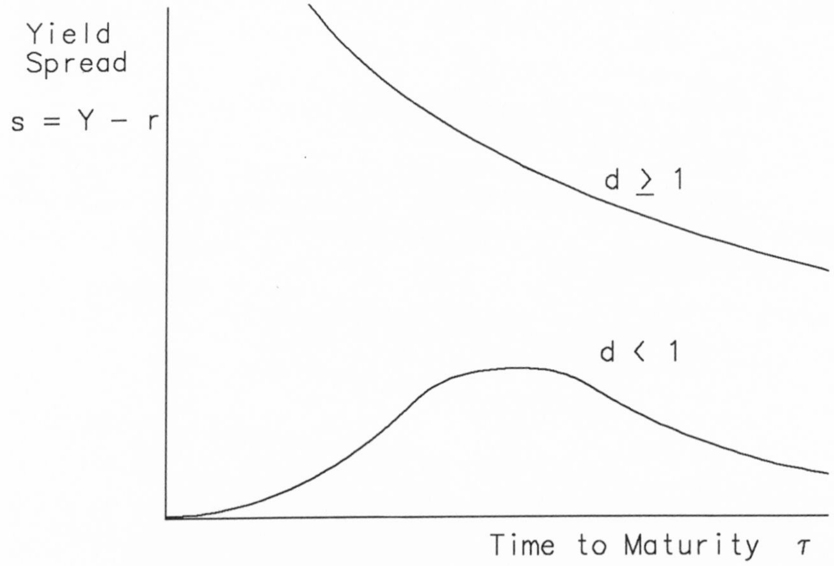

Figure 19.1 Yield Spread on Default-Free Bonds

surprises. The longer the maturity of the debt, the greater is the chance that this can happen so the larger will be the value of the debt (for a fixed payment in present value terms). On the other hand, lengthening the term of the debt does not hurt the bondholders because they are entitled to all the assets of the firm in the event of a bankruptcy, and their present value is V regardless of the debt's maturity. Since both the risk of the debt and the yield spread are measured on a percentage basis, they both decrease. As $\tau \to \infty$, the instantaneous risk approaches the limit $\sigma_D \to \sigma/2$. However, since there can never be a default on a perpetual discount bond, the yield spread vanishes.

When $d < 1$ and the bond has only a short time to go before maturity, it is unlikely that there will be a default on the bond. Thus, there is very little risk, and the yield need be little larger than the interest rate. At first, as the maturity is increased, the likelihood of a default increases, and the yield spread must widen with the increasing risk. For continued increases in maturity, the instantaneous risk continues to rise to its limit $\sigma_D \to \sigma/2$. The yield spread, on the other hand, begins to fall – again since there can never be a default on a perpetual bond, $s \to 0$.

We can conclude from our analysis that when comparing bonds of different maturities, the yield spread will not accurately reflect the relative bankruptcy risks. The yield spread can be a valid measure of the relative default risk of two bonds of the same maturity if we control for the different proportions of systematic and nonsystematic risk.

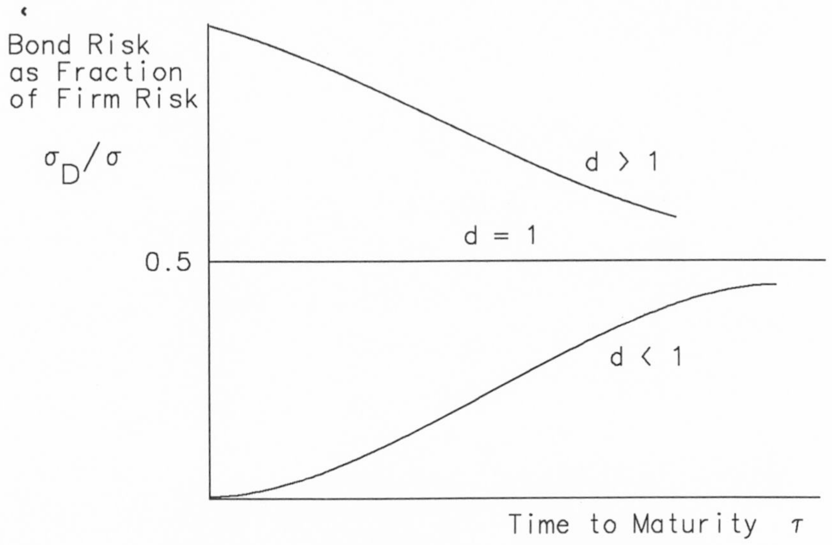

Figure 19.2 Bond Risk as Percent of Firm Risk

THE WEIGHTED AVERAGE COST OF CAPITAL

The second Modigliani–Miller proposition assures us that the weighted average cost of capital, or the expected rate of return on the firm as a whole, is independent of the capital structure. To keep the cost of capital constant as the leverage is changed requires that either the cost of debt or the cost of equity or both change with the capital structure.

From the no arbitrage condition in Equation (76) of Chapter 17, the expected excess rates of return on the debt and equity are proportional to their elasticities:

$$\alpha_D - r = \eta(d, \tau; \sigma)\,(\alpha - r), \tag{27a}$$

$$\alpha_E - r = \left(1 + \frac{D}{E}\,[1 - \eta(\cdot)]\right)(\alpha - r). \tag{27b}$$

The second result uses the fact that the weighted average of the debt and equity elasticities is 1. D/E is the market (not quasi) debt-to-equity ratio.

For the standard textbook case in which the debt is assumed to be riskless, the cost of debt capital is constant, and the cost of equity capital is linear in the market debt-to-equity ratio. But we can see from (27) that this is true *in general only* when the debt is riskless: that is $\eta(\cdot)$ is zero.

When default risk is explicitly considered, the cost of equity capital is

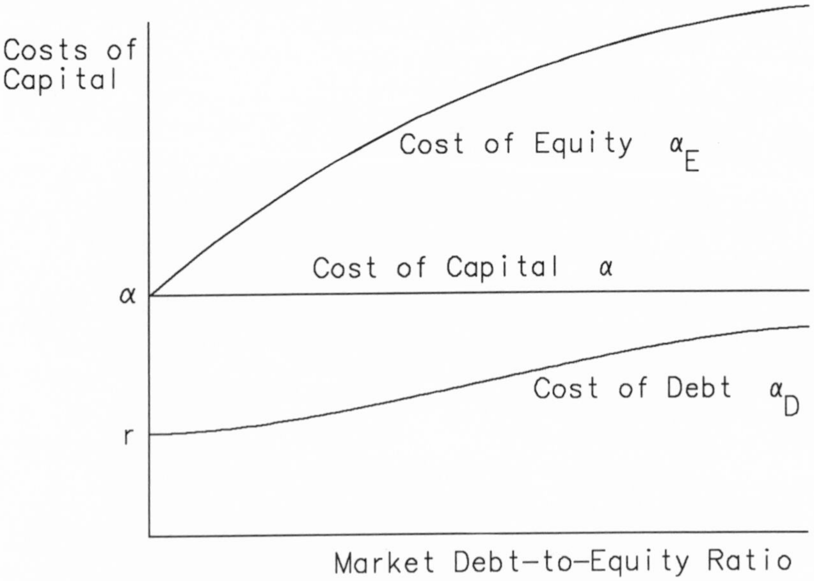

Figure 19.3 Costs of Capital

Table 19.1 Payoffs to Junior and Senior Debt Issues with the Same Maturity

Outcome	Senior Debt	Junior Debt	Equity
$B + b < V_T$	B	b	$V_T - B - b$
$B < V_T \leqslant B + b$	B	$V_T - B$	0
$V_T \leqslant B$	V_T	0	0

an increasing, concave, unbounded function of the market debt-to-equity ratio of the firm. At a debt-to-equity ratio of zero, the cost of equity capital is equal to the firm's cost of capital, α. For a small addition of debt, the debt will be almost riskless, so the equity risk and, therefore, the premium on the cost of equity capital will be increases in proportion to the debt-to-equity ratio. In other words, just as in the textbook case, the slope of the equity cost of capital curve at a debt-to-equity ratio of zero is $\alpha - r$, the risk premium on the firm.

The cost of debt capital is an increasing, S-shaped function of the market debt-to-equity ratio of the firm. At a debt-to-equity ratio of zero, the cost of debt capital is equal to the interest rate, and it has a slope of zero. It is bounded above by the firm's cost of capital. These curves are illustrated in Figure 19.3 for a firm with an asset risk of 50% and bonds maturing in one year.

SUBORDINATED DEBT

It is uncommon for firms to have only a single issue of debt. When they do have more than one, priority rights to the assets become important. Suppose that a firm has two outstanding zero coupon bonds maturing at the same time T. B dollars are promised on the senior debt, and b dollars are promised on the junior or subordinated debt. If both payments cannot be made, then the senior debt has absolute priority to all the assets of the firm. The payoff to the senior debt is $\text{Min}(V_T, B)$ just as before. The payoff to the junior debt is

$$J(V_T, 0) = \begin{cases} b, & B + b \leqslant V_T, \\ V_T - B, & B < V_T < B + b, \\ 0, & V_T \leqslant B, \end{cases} \tag{28}$$

or $\text{Min}(V_T, B + b) - \text{Min}(V_T, B)$. This is illustrated in Table 19.1.

From Table 19.1 and Equation (28) it is clear that the value of the junior bond and the senior bond together is equal to that of a single bond with a face value of $B + b$. Since the value of the senior bond is still $D(V, \tau; B)$, the junior bond is equal in value to the difference between two discount bond functions.

$$J(V, \tau; B, b) = D(V, \tau; B + b) - D(V, \tau; B), \tag{29}$$

where $D(\cdot)$ is the risky debt function defined in (23).

Another way to derive this result is to set the value of the junior debt equal to the value of the firm less the value of the senior debt less the value of the equity, $W(V, \tau; B + b)$. Since the first term in (29) is equal to $V - W(\cdot; B + b)$, these two methods give the same result.

The comparative statics of the junior debt can be determined from those of the option and debt functions. Since it is the difference between two debt functions, it is similar to a mixture of debt and equity. Its value does increase with its face value or the value of the firm, but the rest of its partial derivatives are indeterminant. When the value of the firm is low and it is likely to default, then the equity has very little value, and the junior debt behaves like equity. When the value of the firm is high so there is little chance of default on the senior debt, the junior debt has more pronounced debt characteristics.

SUBORDINATION AND ABSOLUTE PRIORITY

When the senior debt matures before the junior debt, it is clear that the former has first claim on the assets and, therefore, absolute priority. On the other hand, when the junior debt matures first, then additional complications can arise. If no provisions have been made for the satisfaction of the senior debt, then the earlier maturing junior debt must be paid in full even if this bankrupts the firm and leaves no assets to cover the senior debt. In this case the "junior" debt is effectively senior.

One common way to maintain some priority for the senior debt is an indenture in its contract providing that it becomes due and payable in full upon the failure to meet the payment due on any junior issue. To illustrate, suppose that the junior debt is due b dollars at T and the senior debt is due B dollars at T' with $T < T'$. Then at time T the junior debt will get b dollars if $V_T \geqslant b$. However, if $V < b$, the company will be in default, and the junior debt will be paid off only to the extent that money remains after repaying the senior debt. Thus, at T,

$$J(V_T, 0) = \begin{cases} b, & b \leqslant V_T, \\ V_T - B, & B < V_T < b, \\ 0, & V_T \leqslant B \text{ and } V_T < b. \end{cases} \tag{30}$$

The two cases when $B > b$ and $b > B$ are illustrated in Tables 19.2 and

Table 19.2 Payoffs to Junior and Senior Debt Issues when Junior Debt Matures First and $B \geqslant b$

Outcome	Senior Debt	Junior Debt	Equity
$B + b < V_T$	B	b	$V_T - B - b$
$B < V_T \leqslant B + b$	$V_T - b$	b	0
$V_T \leqslant b$	V_T	0	0

19.3. In these two tables the payoff to the senior bond is also given, assuming that it matures immediately after the junior bond. This column will be used later.

Note that if the promised payment to the senior debt exceeds that to the junior debt, then the second outcome in (30) is impossible. In this case the junior debt receives b if $V_T \geqslant b$; otherwise it receives nothing. Using the risk-neutral method gives that the value of this claim is equal to the "probability" that $V_T \geqslant b$ times the riskless present value of b. This is just the second term of the standard bond-pricing function (23). Thus, for $b \leqslant B$,

$$J(V, \tau; b, B | b \leqslant B) = be^{-r\tau}N\left(-\frac{\log(be^{-r\tau}/V) + .5\sigma^2\tau}{\sigma\sqrt{\tau}}\right). \tag{31}$$

If the promised payment to the junior debt exceeds the promise to the senior debt, it is possible in a bankruptcy to have money left to repay a portion of the junior debt. In this case, in addition to the term given in (31), the junior debt also have a claim against $V_T - B$ dollars when $B < V_T < b$.

In examining Table 19.3 it is clear that the junior debt can be separated

Table 19.3 Payoffs to Junior and Senior Debt Issues when Junior Debt Matures First and $b > B$

Outcome	Senior Debt	Junior Debt	Equity
$b + B < V_T$	B	b	$V_T - B - b$
$b < V_T \leqslant b + B$	$V_T - b$	b	0
$B < V_T \leqslant b$	B	$V_T - B$	0
$V_T \leqslant B$	V_T	0	0

into two claims: The first is a similar issue of junior debt with a face value of $b - B$ maturing *simultaneously* with an issue of senior debt with a face value of B. The second is a promise of B if and only if $V_T > b$. The former will be worth nothing if $V_T < B$, will be worth $V_T - B$ if $B < V_T < B + (b - B) = b$, and will be worth $b - B$ otherwise. The latter will increase the total payoff to b if $V_T > b$. Thus, combining (30) and (31), we have for $b > B$,

$$J(V, \tau; b, B|b > B) = D(V, \tau; b) - D(V, \tau; B) + Be^{-r\tau}N\left(-\frac{\log(be^{-r\tau}/V) + .5\sigma^2\tau}{\sigma\sqrt{\tau}}\right). \quad (32)$$

The indenture provision we have been examining, which accelerates the due date of the senior debt in the case of bankruptcy, provides only a partial protection of the absolute priority of the senior debt. This point can be most clearly illustrated if we assume that the senior debt matures immediately after the junior debt.

The payment to the senior debt in this case is given in the second column of Tables 19.2 and 19.3. It is clear that, whenever $b \leqslant V_T < B + b$, the senior debt does not receive the full payment that absolute priority would confer.

One other interesting feature of a shorter maturity, junior bond with this partial protection provision is that its value is not monotone in its promised payment b. The reason for this seeming paradox is that the payoff function is not monotone in b. If $b \leqslant V_T$, then the junior bondholders are paid in full. However, if V_T is less than b by a small amount, then the junior bondholders get either $V_T - B$ (if positive) or nothing.

Two problems arise because of this feature. First, it may be difficult to issue very risky junior debt since raising the promised interest rate (i.e., the promised payment) may not increase, and in some cases might actually decrease, the value of the bond.

Second, and of more interest, it may be to the benefit of the junior bondholders to forgive a portion of their debt rather than force a bankruptcy. In particular, if they can act unilaterally, they would be willing to forgive $b - V_T$ dollars. This would assure that the company does not have to declare bankruptcy although the senior debtholders and the owners will be left with valueless claims. Of course, the owners of the junior debt will not forgive any amounts that can be paid. In this case, the payoff to the junior bondholders is $\text{Min}(V, b)$. That is, the junior bondholders have established effective seniority despite the indenture in the senior debt contract designed to prevent this.

On the other hand, since the senior bondholders and the owners are left with nothing, they might try to reach some bargain between themselves. For example, if the company can refuse the offer of the junior bondholders to forgive a portion of the debt, it will still be in default. The senior bondholders will be due B, and they can make some side promise to the shareholders about splitting this. To add complications, the junior bondholders might be willing to forgive a larger portion of the debt or to make a side payment of their own to the shareholders. These bargaining tactics and their legal aspects are beyond the scope of this book.

SECURED DEBT

Another way in which priority issues can be resolved is through the use of secured debt. In addition to a general claim against the assets of a firm, secured debt has a first claim or mortgage against a specific asset.

To illustrate the use of secured debt, consider a firm with both junior and senior bonds which mature at the same time. The junior bond is secured by one of the firm's assets. We denote the value of this asset by S and the value of the firm including this asset by V. As before, the face values of the junior and senior bonds are b and B. At the maturity of both bonds, the payoff to the junior bond is

$$J(V_T, S_T, 0) = \begin{cases} b, & B + b \leqslant V_T \text{ or } b \leqslant S_T, \\ V_T - B, & S_T \leqslant V_T - B \leqslant b, \\ S_T, & V_T - B \leqslant S_T \leqslant b. \end{cases} \tag{33}$$

Comparing (33) to (28), we see that the secured junior bond is equal in value to an unsecured junior bond plus a full claim against S_T whenever $V_T - B < S_T < b$. Thus, not surprisingly, the secured junior bond is more valuable than an unsecured junior bond. This payoff is also equal to $\text{Min}(S_T, b)$ plus $V_T - S_T - B$ whenever $S_T \leqslant V_T - B < b$. That is, the subordinated secured bond is equal in value to a senior bond on the asset whose pirice is S_t plus this extra claim.

Senior debt with a shorter maturity than all junior issues would not be increased in value if it were secured by a specific asset of the firm. (Security which was not a part of the firm's assets would increase its value, of course.) However, a secured mortgage on some asset of the firm would help maintain its priority if a junior issue of debt matured first. Securing the senior debt puts the mortgaged asset out of the grasp of the junior debt whether or not it is also protected by a due-on-bankruptcy clause.

CONVERTIBLE SECURITIES

A convertible security is one that can be exchanged for another with different characteristics. Warrants and put and call options are examples of convertible securities. But the most common types of convertible securities issued by corporations are convertible bonds and convertible preferred stock. A typical convertible bond has one or more fixed payments like a regular bond and, in addition, may be exchanged for a certain number of shares of common stock of the company.

Continuing our earlier examples, suppose that a firm has a capital structure with a single convertible bond issue and common equity. At time T the bondholders are entitled to receive B dollars or all the assets of the firm if default occurs. Alternatively, they may exchange their bonds for n new shares of common stock. There are currently N shares of common stock outstanding. We define $\gamma \equiv n/(N + n)$.

If the bondholders choose not to convert, then they will receive $\text{Min}(V_T, B)$, just as with a regular bond. If they choose to convert, they will get stock worth γV_T. Therefore, at maturity

$$C(V_T, 0) = \begin{cases} \gamma V_T, & B \leqslant \gamma V_T, \\ B & B \leqslant V_T < B/\gamma, \\ V_T & V_T < B. \end{cases} \tag{34}$$

This may be expressed as $C(V_T, 0) = \text{Min}(V_T, B) + \text{Max}\,(\gamma V_T - B, 0)$, which is the sum of a bond payoff and a warrant payoff. Therefore, if it is never optimal for the bondholders to convert except at maturity,

$$C(V, \tau; B, \gamma) = D(V, \tau; B) + W(\gamma V, \tau; B). \tag{35}$$

Might it ever be optimal for the bondholders to convert prior to T? By analyzing (35) we can show that $C(V, \tau) > \gamma V$ *for* $\tau > 0$, so early conversion is never optimal. However, this proposition can also be proved in general without assuming diffusion or the other Black–Scholes conditions.

If the bondholders do convert at any time before T, they will receive shares representing an ownership of the fraction γ of the firm. Therefore, at time T they will have a claim worth γV_T. If they do not convert, their claim will be worth $\text{Min}(V_T, B) + \text{Max}(\gamma V_T - B, 0)$, which is at least as large as γV_T and is strictly greater whenever $V_T < B/\gamma$. Thus, the policy of not converting prior to maturity strictly dominates converting.

The intuition for this result is that the conversion option is like any other call option which is best to hold as long as possible. Of course, if the stock paid dividends, then it might pay to exchange the convertible bond for stock, just as it might be worthwhile exercising an option.

If we compare (34) and (35) to (21) and (22), it is clear that a convertible bond is similar to a regular bond plus a warrant whose exercise price is equal to the face value of the bond. The only difference is that the aggregate exercise price is not adjusted for dilution in (35) as it was in (22). The reason for this difference is that when the convertible is viewed as a bond plus a warrant, none of the exercise price reverts to the "warrant holders" — it all goes to pay off the "bondholders."

This general relation remains true even if the debt receives coupon payments. A convertible bond is equal in value to a regular bond plus a warrant with an exercise price equal to the bond's face value. If the common stock is paying dividends, this relatin is no longer necessarily true. Now it might pay to exercise the warrant and/or convert the bond prior to maturity. If these decisions do not always coincide, the value of the convertible will typically differ from that of a straight bond plus a warrant. Since the decision to convert depends on the level of both the dividends and the coupons and the decision to exercise depends only on the level of the dividends, this is usually the case.

A closely related contract is a warrant with a *usable bond*. With this pair of instruments, the investor either can pay cash to exercise his warrant or may use his bond as script at face value. A usable bond–warrant pair is obviously worth at least as much as a convertible bond because of the investor's exchange option. What makes this contract interesting is that one or the other of the two instruments is typically in excess supply. Usually there are more bonds than are needed to exercise all of the warrants, but the opposite is sometimes true.

As is always the case in competitive markets, the economic rent accrues to, and is reflected in, the price of the scarce asset. In this context, the "option" premium associated with using the pair together increases the value of the relatively scarce asset.

CALLABLE BONDS

Most bonds that are issued are callable. That is, the company retains the right to retire the bond upon the payment of a call price K. For typical coupon bonds issued by corporations the bonds are not callable for the first 5 or 10 years. After that they can be called at a price which declines over time until it reaches the face value at maturity (at which point all the bonds are "called" unless the firm is bankrupt).

The call option on a bond is just the same as any other call option. It confers the right to buy an asset at a specified price. We know that call options on assets which do not pay distributions are never used prior to maturity; therefore, a callable zero coupon bond will never be called prior to maturity (unless the call price is increasing over time). If the call price is greater than the face value, it will not be called at maturity either since the bond can be worth no more than its face value at maturity. (If the call price is less than the face value, it will always be called at maturity, unless the firm is bankrupt. In either case the bondholders do not receive the face value, so it is not really defined.)

Call provisions on convertible bonds are different. When a convertible is called, the bondholders can accept the cash payment offered or choose to convert instead. At maturity the call option is not of any value. The bondholder is already faced with the choice of converting or accepting a cash payment of B. Assuming $K \geqslant B$, exercising the option to call will simply increase the cash offered to K. Since a zero coupon convertible also has no distributions, it might appear that the call should not be used prior to maturity. However, this reasoning is wrong.

Exercising the call option on the convertible has value prior to maturity. If a convertible is called when its conversion value exceeds the call price, bondholders will obviously choose to convert. This is called a forced conversion. If the call price is larger, bondholders will choose to be paid in cash. In essence, then, a call shortens the maturity of the "warrant" held by the bondholders by forcing them to choose whether or not to convert earlier than they otherwise would need to. This is what makes the call feature have value to the firm.

For a zero coupon convertible with a constant call price equal to or greater than its face value, the proper call policy is to force conversion as soon as possible. On the other hand, the bond should never be called when bondholders will take the cash payment. This policy can be proved optimal by using dominance arguments like those in Chapter 14.

Suppose that the optimal policy where to call sometime after conversion could have been forced that is, when $V_t = V^* > K/\gamma$. Consider the value of the convertible when $V^* < V_t < K/\gamma$. If (in violation of the *assumed* optimal policy) the bond were to be called immediately, bondholders would convert and receive stock worth γV_t. At time T this stock would be worth γV_T, as illustrated in the last column of Table 19.4. If the presumed "optimal" policy were followed and bond remained uncalled, two futures would be possible. Either the value of the firm would rise to V^* before the bond matured and it would be called then, or the bond would not be called. In the former case the bondholders would convert and at the maturity of the bond would have stock worth γV_T. In the latter

Table 19.4 Illustration of Optimal Call Policy on Convertible Bonds

Event	Value of bond at T^* under	
	V* policy	Immediate call
Call sometimes in future	γV_T	γV_T
No call in future, $V_T < B$	V_T	γV_T
" $B < V_T < B/\gamma$	B	γV_T
" $B/\gamma < V_T$	γV_T	γV_G

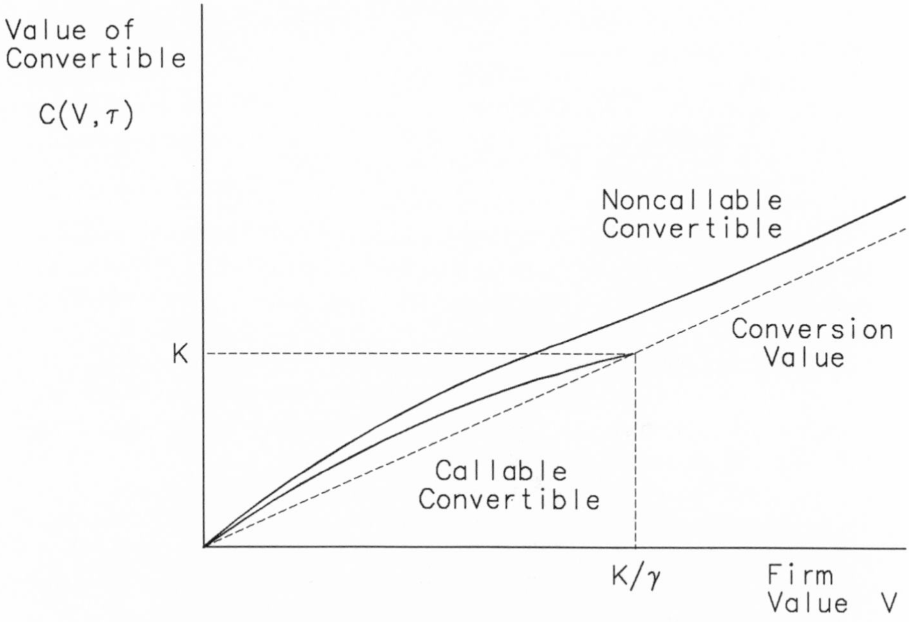

Figure 19.4 Callable and Noncallable Convertibles

case the bondholders might or might not convert. At maturity they would have an asset worth at least γV_T, as illustrated in the middle column of Table 19.4. Calling the bond immediately leads to a lower value to the bondholders at time T. Thus, the V^* policy cannot be optimal.

In addition, the optimal policy could never be to call when $\gamma V_t < K$. This policy is dominated by never calling. If the bonds remain uncalled, then at maturity the bondholders would get either B or γV_T. The present value of the former is less than B, which is no larger than K. The current value of the latter is γV_t, which is also less than K. Calling when $\gamma V_t < K$ is like giving the bondholders money. Clearly, it would be better not to call.

The optimal call policy is, therefore, to call when $V_t = K/\gamma$; that is, a call is made just as soon as conversion can be forced. It can be shown that a similar rule applies for coupon-bearing convertibles as well. A call should never be delayed past the point where conversion can be forced. A call might be made before this time, however, if interest rates drop or the fortunes of the firm improve so that the convertible bond can be replaced with lower interest debt.

With the optimal call policy established, the convertible can now be valued as outlined in Equation (36) of Chapter 17. The standard partial differential valuation equation applies with boundary and terminal conditions $C(0, \tau) = 0$, $C(B/\gamma, \tau) = B$, $C(V, 0) = \text{Min}\,(V, B) + \text{Max}\,(\gamma V - B, 0)$. The solution to this problem is

$$C(V, \tau; B, \gamma) = D(V, \tau; B) + W(\gamma V, \tau; B)$$
$$-\left(\frac{K}{\gamma V}\right)^{2r/\sigma^2}\left[W(\gamma V e^{-r\tau}, \tau; Ke^{r\tau}) - W\left(\gamma V e^{-r\tau}, \tau; \frac{Ke^{r\tau}}{\gamma}\right)\right] \quad (36)$$

The first two terms in (36) give the value of a noncallable convertible, so the last term is the discount for the call feature. In other words, the last term is the negative of the value of the call feature to the company's owners.

Callable and noncallable convertible pricing functions are plotted in Figure 19.4 for typical values. A noncallable convertible is, of course, always worth at least as much as the same convertible when callable. Both functions are increasing in the value of the company, but they are neither convex nor concave, so they have both debt and equity characteristics. The debt characteristics are more pronounced when the value of the firm is low, so that the probability of eventual conversion is low. When V is high, the equity characteristics are more pronounced. This is just the opposite of junior debt.

Another type of call on a bond issue is a call for a *sinking fund*. A sinking fund is a method of providing for the periodic retirement of a debt issue. Typically, a sinking fund will require that a certain fraction of the bond issue be paid off each year.

Sometimes an actual escrow fund is established. Each year the company will pay a set sum to the bond's trustees, who will deposit the funds in a bank account or buy government debt. By the time that the bond matures, the escrow fund will be worth enough to retire the debt.

More commonly, a sinking fund provides for bonds to be retired via purchase on the open market or by a special call. Each year the company must retire a certain amount of the outstanding debt. They can do this either by giving the bond trustees bonds that they have repurchased or by giving them cash to call in some bonds. Usually a sinking fund call is at the bond's face value, and the bonds to be called are determined by lot.

It is commonly held that a sinking fund is good for the bondholders because it reduces the risk they face by shortening the maturity of the bond. It is also assumed that the company's forced repurchase of bonds will provide some additional liquidity to the market. Of course, the option that the company has of buying bonds at the lower of the market price or par is also typically quite valuable. This is detrimental to the bondholders. In addition, sinking funds often provide the company the option of accelerating the sinking fund by calling more than the required amount. Again this option is only to the detriment of the bondholders.

OPTIMAL SEQUENTIAL EXERCISE: EXTERNALITIES AND MONOPOLY POWER

Unlike call options, warrants and convertibles are issued by companies, and when they are exercised new shares are created with the money paid increasing the firm's assets. We have already examined the effect that this dilution causes in the valuation. Now we will consider its effect on exercise. As we shall see, it is no longer necessarily the case that all warrants or convertibles are optimally exercised at the same time. Because they are the simpler instrument, we choose to look at warrants; however, all of the qualitative features apply to convertibles as well.

Under certain conditions, the exercise of a warrant can increase the value of the warrants that remain outstanding. Of course, in the absence of dividends a warrant is always worth more alive than exercised. Thus, no investor would be willing to make the sacrifice of exercising some warrants for "the public good" of all warrant owners without compensation. One obvious method of compensation is through the increased value of the other warrants held.

As a simple example to illustrate this point, consider a firm with $5000 in assets. Over the next period the firm's assets will either double or halve in value. The interest rate is zero. The firm is financed by 100 shares of

Table 19.5 Illustration of Monopoly Power in Warrant Holdings

	Value of			
Number of Warrants Exercised	Live Warrant	Exercised Warrant	Stock	All Warrants
0	22.73		47.73	227.27
1	22.80	22.72	47.72	227.95
2	22.88	22.72	47.72	228.46
3	22.95	22.71	47.71	228.82
4	23.03	22.71	47.71	229.02
5	23.11	22.71	47.71	229.08
6	23.18	22.71	47.71	228.99
7	23.26	22.71	47.71	228.76
8	23.33	22.72	47.72	228.40
9	23.41	22.72	47.72	227.90
10		22.73	47.73	227.27

stock and 10 warrants each with an exercise price of 25. The warrants can be exercised immediately or at the end of the period at which time they expire.

Suppose that no warrants are exercised now. In this case, the warrants can be valued by the binomial method developed in Chapter 14. The parameters are $h = 2$, $k = .5$, and $R = 1$. The risk-neutralized probability of a doubling of the asset value is $q = (R - k)/(h - k) = \frac{1}{3}$. If the firm doubles in value, the warrants will be exercised. If not, they will expire worthless. Thus, if no warrants are exercised, then each is worth

$$w(0) = R^{-1}q\left(\frac{Vh + nX}{N + n} - X\right) + R^{-1}(1 - q)\cdot 0 = 22.73. \tag{37}$$

Each share of stock is worth

$$S(0) = \frac{V - nw(0)}{N} = 47.73. \tag{38}$$

Now suppose that m of the warrants are exercised immediately. The current value of the assets will increase by mX. The remainder of the warrants will be exercised only if the firm's assets double in value, so they are worth

$$w(m) = R^{-1}q\left(\frac{(V + mX)h + (n - m)X}{N + n} - X\right). \tag{39}$$

Each share of stock is now worth

$$S(m) = \frac{V + mx - (n - m)w(m)}{N + m}. \tag{40}$$

The net value of an exercised warrant is, of course, $S(m) - X$.

These values are given in Table 19.5. It is clear that regardless of the number of warrants exercised, the value of a single warrant is always worth more than its intrinsic or "when exercised" value, $S(m) - X$. (Note that the intrinsic value changes as more warrants are exercised because $S(m)$ changes.) Thus, no one who holds a single warrant would exercise.

The table also shows that the value of each unexercised warrant increases as more warrants are exercised. Now consider an investor who owns two warrants. If neither is exercised (and no one else exercises any), they will be worth \$45.46. If one is exercised, they will be worth \$22.72 + \$22.80 = \$45.52. If both are exercised, they will be worth 2 × \$22.72 = \$45.44. Clearly, just one will be exercised. The warrant holder who owns two warrants captures enough of the externality created by exercising one warrant to justify giving up the option value.

The policy that gives the highest aggregate value to all the warrants, the "Pareto" exercise policy (ignoring the "cost" to the common stock owners), is to exercise five of them. However, without side payments, this will not occur unless there is some concentration of holdings. For example, if one investor holds only nine warrants, his best policy is to exercise four. This gives a total value of 4 × \$22.71 + 5 × \$23.03 = \$205.99. Exercising five would give a value of 5 × \$22.71 + 4 × \$23.11 = \$205.97.

Aside: If five investors each held two warrants, then each would exercise one, so a total of five warrants would be exercised in this case as well. However, this result is due to the indivisibility of the warrants. If a fraction of a warrant could be exercised to buy a fraction of a share, then each investor would choose to exercise less than one full warrant. The "Pareto" exercise policy would result only if one investor held all the warrants.

Two interesting questions to consider are, How might a monopoly position arise, and what might happen when one does? We shall answer the second question first.

If an investor has acquired sufficient warrants to achieve some monopoly power (in the foregoing example two warrants are sufficient), he or she will not voluntarily sell any warrants except at a price which includes this additional value. Likely, only another investor who had or was acquiring even greater monopoly power would pay this amount.

To illustrate, suppose that an investor has four warrants, and all other warrants are held individually. This investor will optimally exercise two warrants, and no other warrants will be exercised, so the investor's total position is worth 2 × \$22.88 + 2 × \$22.72 = \$91.20. Were the investor to sell one warrant to a new holder, then it would be correct to exercise only one and live warrants would then be worth only \$22.80. This is the highest sales price that could be realized. The three remaining warrants would be worth 2 × \$22.80 + \$22.72 = \$68.32; so the portfolio, including cash, would be worth \$91.12. This is a loss of eight cents, so the investor would not sell.

Now let us turn to the question of how someone might acquire a monopoly position with or without a competitive fringe. One way this might happen is through an original private placement. This situation has little interest. Could an investor buy up warrants in a competitive market place to achieve a monopoly position?

To examine this question suppose that originally 10 different investors each hold one warrant. If it were known that none would be exercised now, then they would be selling for \$22.73. If an investor who already owns one buys another at this price, the two warrants will be worth \$22.80 + \$22.72 = \$45.52, which is more than the original cost of 2 × \$22.73 = \$45.46. But if the market for warrants is strongly informationally efficient, any potential seller will know all this. He or she will reason that if this investor can acquire a second warrant and exercise one, then the warrants of all other investors will be worth \$22.80. Therefore, the seller will not part with a warrant for less than this amount. Of course, if an investor has to pay this much for a second warrant, it will not be worth the price.

The general rule is that no investor can accumulate a monopoly position because each potential seller will demand a full pro rata share of the externality created by the "premature" exercise. The buyer will not be willing to pay this much because he or she bears all the costs of creating the externality but shares in it only in proportion to the fraction of the live warrants owned. The only way over this hurdle is for the buyer to acquire all the warrants so that he captures all the externality to compensate for the cost of creating it.

The average value of the warrants if one investor acquires them all is \$22.91. An investor making an "all-or-nothing" tender offer for the warrants at this price should get them. Obviously, no higher tender offer will be made. A tender offer at any lower price should be met by a counter tender at this price in a competitive market, so this is the only possible tender price. Also, the tender must be of the all-or-nothing type since otherwise there is an incentive to hold out. For example, if nine investors tender and one refrains, then four warrants will be exercised, so the last warrant will be worth \$23.03. This is more than the tender price, so each investor has an incentive to refuse the tender offer.

To this point we have considered only the warrant holders' behavior. Because monpolist (or oligopolist) holders of warrants can follow exercise policies which increase the value of all warrants at the expense of the common stock, we should expect that the shareholders would take actions to minimize this damage.

The company could explicitly restrict exercise of the warrants, but this is seldomly done. It could also reduce or eliminate the monopoly power by changing its dividend or investment policies. Increasing dividends will accelerate warrant exercise. Cutting dividends will slow exercise. Adopting a dividend payment that is conditional on the number of warrants exercised can also be effective. For example, the policy of paying a huge dividend if just some of the warrants are exercised will force all warrants to be exercised at the same time since any warrant left outstanding would forfeit its share of the large dividend.

Conditional investment policies can also be effective in eliminating monopoly power. For instance, if the firm in the first example of this section were to invest the proceeds from the exercise of warrants in a riskless asset rather than in expanding the scale of the firm, then there would be no incentive to exercise warrants early since doing so would no longer increase risk.

Certain investment and dividend policies can also make obligopolist warrant holders worse off than competitors. The adoption of such policies would severely hamper the acquisition of a monopoly position because of the risk that some of the warrants could not be purchased.

OPTIMAL SEQUENTIAL EXERCISE: COMPETITIVE AND BLOCK STRATEGIES

Even if no investor has or might acquire a monopoly position in warrants, sequential exercise still must be taken into consideration. If the firm pays no dividends, then no (competitive) investor will wish to exercise prior to maturity. At maturity all investors will make the same decision. If the firm does pay dividends, however, it is possible that only some of the investors should exercise in a competitive equilibrium.

To illustrate this point, consider the same two-period model examined in the previous section with one change. The firm is paying a dividend of D in aggregate. If no warrants are exercised, this will be a dividend per share of D/N. However, any warrant holder who exercises shares in this dividend, and the per share dividend is correspondingly lower: $D/(N + m)$. If m warrants are exercised, the value of a warrant kept alive is

$$w(m) = R^{-1}q\left(\frac{(V - D + mX)h + (n - m)X}{N + n} - X\right). \quad (41)$$

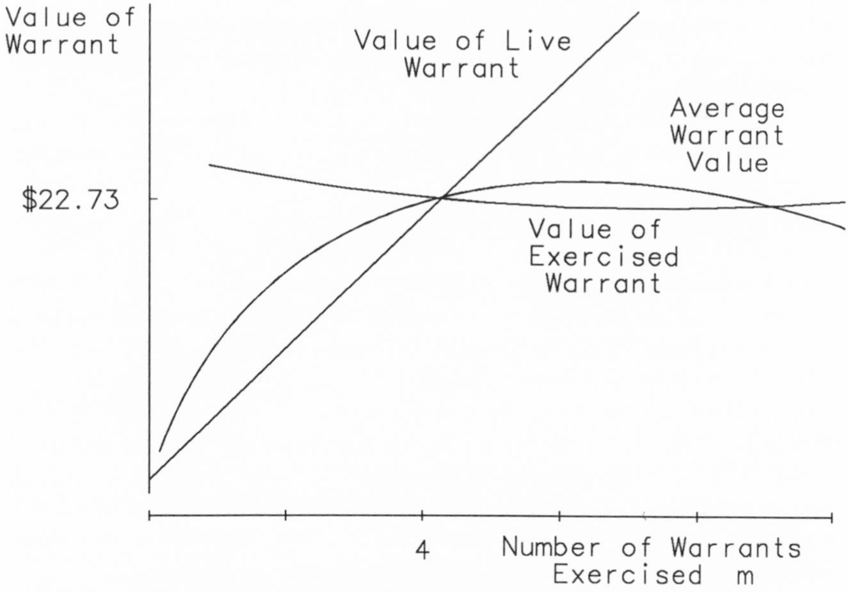

Figure 19.5 Illustration of Sequential Exercise

Table 19.6 Illustration of Competitive Equilibrium among Warrant Holders

	Value of			
Number of Warrants Exercised	Live Warrant	Exercised Warrant	Stock	All Warrants
0	22.42		47.76	224.24
1	22.50	22.75	47.75	225.25
2	22.58	22.74	47.74	226.08
3	22.65	22.73	47.73	226.76
4	22.73	22.73	47.73	227.27
5	22.80	22.72	47.72	227.63
6	22.88	22.72	47.72	227.84
7	22.96	22.72	47.72	227.91
8	23.03	22.72	47.72	227.83
9	23.10	22.72	47.73	227.62
10		22.73		227.27

The price of a share of stock is given by the formula in (40), where (41) is used to compute $w(m)$. Thus, the net value of an exercised warrant (cum the dividend it will receive) is

$$\frac{V + mX - (n - m)w(m)}{N + m} - X. \tag{42}$$

This example is illustrated in Figure 19.5 and Table 19.6 for an aggregate dividend of $50.

In a competitive (Nash) equilibrium each warrant holder chooses whether or not to exercise a warrant, assuming that other investors will not be influenced by this decision. In our example, suppose that an investor thought that three other warrant owners would exercise. If our investor exercises, too, then four warrants will be exercised, and each will be worth $22.73. If our investor chooses not to exercise the warrant it will be worth $22.65. The former is better, so four warrants are exercised. Suppose that four other investors will exercise. If our investor exercises, too, then each exercised warrant will be worth $22.72. Keeping the warrant alive is worth $22.73, so he will choose the latter.

In this example the competitive Nash equilibrium is to have four warrants exercised. Every investor is indifferent about whether or not they exercise because, in either case, their warrants are worth $22.73.

The monopolist solution in this example is to exercise seven (or if they are perfectly divisible, approximately 6.96) warrants because this maximizes the total value of all the warrants. More warrants are exercised than under a competitive solution because the monopolist keeps all of the positive externality created by the exercise of the warrants and takes this into consideration. (More warrants are exercised than in the previous monopolist example because the dividend makes waiting more costly.)

Suppose now that the warrants are all held by one investor, but that they must be exercised in a block. (In practice, there could be a single warrant entitling the holder to buy 10 shares of stock.) In this case the optimal solution is to exercise, and the 10 warrants are worth \$227.27. Note that this is the same value per warrant that arises in the competitive equilibrium even though a different number of warrants are exercised.

This feature is not a coincidence of this example. The value of warrants under a block exercise constraint is always equal to that which arises in a competitive equilibrium. This result is a fortunate one because it means that, in a competitive market, warrants can be valued, ignoring the sequential exercise that often arises in practice. The prices that we computed in our earlier examples all assumed block exercise. The proposition justifying this method of valuation can be stated as follows:

THEOREM 1 *Assume that the Modigliani–Miller capital structure irrelevancy proposition is true. Assume also that the warrants are infinitely divisible and the market for them is competitive. That is, each investor acts as a price taker and assumes that the decision to exercise has no affect on other investors. Then if each warrant holder is indifferent about exercising a warrant at time t or strictly prefers to do so, the warrants have the same value that they would have if all were exercised at time t.*

Proof. If each warrant holder strictly prefers to exercise a warrant, then the theorem is obviously true since all warrants will be exercised in either case. If each warrant holder is indifferent about exercising, the theorem is no longer obviously true.

Let N, n, and m denote the number of shares, number of warrants, and number of warrants exercised. Let $S(m)$, $w(m)$, and V be the cum dividend stock price, the live warrant price, and the value of the firm before the dividend is paid and the proceeds of exercise are received. The following two conditions are equivalent for all $m\,(0 \leqslant m \leqslant n)$:

$$w(m) \lesseqgtr S(m) - X, \tag{43a}$$

$$w(m) \lesseqgtr \frac{V + nX}{N + n} - X. \tag{43b}$$

Either equality (or inequality) can be verified by substituting the Modigliani–Miller proposition $V = (N + m)S(m) + (n - m)w(m)$ into the other equality (or inequality).

The remainder of the proof now follows immediately from (43). If investors are indifferent about exercising, then (43a) holds as an equality; so (43b) holds as an equality as well. But (43b) is the value of a warrant if all are exercised. Q.E.D.

As stated previously, the same result applies to the exercise of convertible bonds. A sample problem illustrating sequential exercise and the use of a block exercise fiction is illustrated in the next section of this chapter.

One final caution is in order concerning a competitive market for warrants or convertibles — the previously described equilibrium which matches the block exercise market in price is not necessarily unique. To illustrate this feature, we use the same example with an interest factor of 1.02 and a dividend policy of paying all of the proceeds from warrant exercsie but nothing more. The original stock holders and the warrant owners who receive new shares receive a dividend. The warrant owners who do not exercise receive no dividend.

Equations (41) and (42) remain valid, although now the dividend D depends on the number of warrants exercised. The warrant values are given in Table 19.7. Now there are two equilibria. If a warrant owner

Table 19.7 Illustration of Multiple Competitive Equilibria with Warrants

	Value of			
Number of Warrants Exercised	Live Warrant	Exercised Warrant	Stock	All Warrants
0	23.17		47.68	231.73
1	23.10	22.69	47.69	230.56
2	23.02	22.70	47.70	229.56
3	22.94	22.71	47.71	228.73
4	22.86	22.72	47.72	228.06
5	22.79	22.72	47.72	227.56
6	22.71	22.73	47.73	227.21
7	22.63	22.73	47.73	227.01
8	22.55	22.73	47.73	226.95
9	22.48	22.73	47.73	227.04
10		22.73	47.73	227.27

thinks that no others will exercise, a warrant will be worth \$23.17 alive but only \$22.69 if exercised. On the other hand, if the owner believes that all of the other nine warrants will be exercised, then a warrant is worth \$22.73 if exercised but only \$22.48 alive.

In general, if six or more of the other nine warrants will be exercised, it is better to exercise as well. If less than six of the others will be exercised, it is better to hold. Thus, the two equilibria are no warrants exercised or all warrants exercised. The two equilibria come from the conflict between the two goals of each investor. First, there is a desire to keep a warrant alive as long as possible to extract its full option value. On the other hand, if just one a warrant is exercised now, then the dividend which is financed by the payment is split among fewer shares.

This result is true in general. If there are multiple competitive equilibria, then at least one of them matches the "block exercise" equilibrium in price. The time of block exercise is also the first time that any competitively held warrants are exercised. This result follows immediately from Theorem 1.

SEQUENTIAL AND BLOCK EXERCISE: AN EXAMPLE

To illustrate valuation and sequential exercise, we use a perpetual warrant. To assure that it will be optimal to exercise at all, the firm must pay a dividend. For simplicity we assume that the firm's policy is to pay aggregate dividends proportional in size to the firm's value $D = \delta V$. At the start there are N_0 shares of stock and n_0 warrants. As in the problem given in Equation (50)–(53) of Chapter 17, the warrant is the solution to

$$\tfrac{1}{2}\sigma^2 V^2 w'' + (r - \delta)Vw' - rw = 0 \tag{44a}$$

subject to

$$w(0) = 0, \tag{44b}$$

$$w(\bar{V}) = \frac{1}{N_0 + n_0}(\bar{V} + nX) - X = \lambda(\bar{V} + nX) - X \tag{44c}$$

with the optimal exercise policy, $\bar{V}$, chosen to maximize the value of a warrant, $w(V)$. Note that the boundary condition (44c) makes use of Theorem 1 by assuming a block exercise when $V_t = \bar{V}$.

There are two solutions to (44a) of the form $w(V) = AV^{\upsilon}$ for two different values of υ. If we substitute this functional form into (44a), we get a quadratic equation for υ:

$$\tfrac{1}{2}\sigma^2\upsilon(\upsilon - 1) + (r - \delta)\upsilon - r = 0. \tag{45}$$

The two solutions are

$$\upsilon = \frac{\sigma^2 - 2(r - \delta) \pm \sqrt{[\sigma^2 - 2(r - \delta)]^2 + 8r\sigma^2}}{2\sigma^2}. \tag{46}$$

Of these two values, one is negative and the other is greater than one. The solution with the negative value for υ can satisfy (44b) only if its constant is set to zero. Then (44c) is satisfied for $A \equiv [\lambda\bar{V} - X(1 - \lambda n_0)]\bar{V}^{-\upsilon}$. Thus,

$$w(V) = \frac{1}{N_0 + n_0}\left(\bar{V} - N_0 X\right)\bar{V}^{-\upsilon}V^{\upsilon}. \tag{47}$$

The block exercise policy that maximizes $w(V)$ is

$$\bar{V} = \frac{\upsilon}{\upsilon - 1}N_0 X. \tag{48}$$

Equation (47) with $\bar{V}$ given in (48) correctly values the warrants until the first time that the value of the firm rises to $\bar{V}$. However, all of the warrants are not exercised at this point in a competitive market. When V first hits $\bar{V}$, all warrant holders are indifferent about exercise or retention of their warrants. One warrant will be exercised, but this changes the "block exercise" problem to one where there are $N_0 + 1$ shares of stock and $n_0 - 1$ warrants. The next warrant will not be exercised until the firm value grows to $\upsilon(N_0 + 1)X/(\upsilon - 1)$. The last warrant will not be exercised until the firm's value grows to $\upsilon\,(N_0 + n_0 - 1)X/(\upsilon - 1)$.

The formulas in (47) and (48) remain valid during the period of warrant exercise, provided we use the current number of outstanding warrants and shares of stock. Combining (47) and (48), we have

$$w(V;\, n,\, N) = \frac{1}{\upsilon - 1}\left(\frac{\upsilon}{\upsilon - 1}NX\right)^{-\upsilon}XV^{\upsilon}. \tag{49}$$

The length of time over which warrants are being exercised is random and can be quite long. To examine this problem, we first consider the case when the firm has no risk, $\sigma = 0$, and each warrant is infinitely divisible for the purpose of exercise.

The dynamics of the firm's value are

$$dV = (r - \delta)\,V\,dt - X\,dn. \tag{50}$$

The last term is the cash inflow from warrant exercise. (*Note*: dn is negative.) Throughout the period of exercise the warrant holders must remain indifferent about exercise, so $w_t = S_t - X$. In addition, since the firm and, therefore, the warrant has no risk, the latter's price must grow at the interest rate. Finally, the Modigliani–Miller proposition must hold. Combining all these equations, noting that $\upsilon = r/(r - \delta)$ when $\sigma = 0$, gives

$$n(t) = N_0 + n_0 - N_0 e^{r(t-\bar{t})}, \tag{51}$$

where $\bar{t}$ is the time at which V_t reaches $\bar{V}$ and the exercise of warrants begins.

The total length of time between the exercise of the first and last warrants is $\log(1 + n_0/N_0)r$. Thus, if the interest rate is 10%, and warrants representing a potential claim against one-quarter of the firm are outstanding, it will take more than two years for all the warrants to be exercised.

When the firm is risky, the total length of time between the exercise of the first and last warrants is random because the firm value can decline as well as increase. Its expected duration is

$$\frac{\log\,(1 + n_0/N_0)}{(\alpha - \delta - \sigma^2/2)\upsilon}. \tag{52}$$

PRICING CORPORATE SECURITIES WITH INTEREST RATE RISK

Uncertain interest rates are probably the next most important state variables in valuing most debt-like contingent contracts. Indeed, in some cases basis risk is probably more important than default risk. If the stochastic nature of the term structure can be explained by a few state variables, then equations like (13) are appropriate for valuing contingent claims.

Suppose that the term structure is fully explained by the instantaneous interest rate and, for simplicity, that it follows a random walk as in the first example in Chapter 18. In this case Equation (13) is

$$\begin{aligned} 0 = \tfrac{1}{2}\sigma^2 V^2 F_{VV} + rVF_V - rF + F_t + \tfrac{1}{2}s^2 F_{rr} + (\mu - \lambda)F_r \\ + \rho\sigma V s F_{Vr}. \end{aligned} \tag{53}$$

Recall that if the price of risk λ is constant, then a default-free zero coupon bond maturing in τ periods is worth

$$P(r, t, T) = \exp\left[-r\tau - \frac{(\mu - \lambda)\tau^2}{2} + \frac{s^2\tau^3}{6},\right] \tag{54}$$

from Equation (27) of Chapter 18. Now make the substitutions $X \equiv V/P(r, \tau)$ and $F(V, r, t) \equiv P(r, \tau)G(X, \tau)$. Using

$$F_V = G_X, \tag{55a}$$

$$F_{VV} = \frac{G_{XX}}{P}, \tag{55b}$$

$$F_r = P_r G + P G_X \tau X, \tag{55c}$$

$$F_{rr} = P_{rr} G + 2P_r G_X \tau X + P G_{XX} \tau^2 X^2 + P G_X \tau^2 X, \tag{55d}$$

$$F_{Vr} = G_{XX} \tau X, \tag{55e}$$

$$F_t = -P_\tau G - PG_\tau - PG_X X\left[r + (\mu - \lambda)\tau - \frac{s^2\tau^2}{2}\right], \quad (55f)$$

gives for Equation (54)

$$\begin{aligned} 0 = P\ &[(\tfrac{1}{2}\sigma^2 + \tfrac{1}{2}\tau^2 s^2 + \rho\sigma s\tau)X^2 G - G_\tau] \\ &+ G(\tfrac{1}{2}s^2 P_{rr} + (\mu - \lambda)P_r - rP - P_\tau) \\ &+ G_X(rX + \tfrac{1}{2}s^2 X\tau^2 - s^2\tau^2 X + (\mu - \lambda)\tau X - X_\tau). \end{aligned} \quad (56)$$

The second line in (56) is zero since the term in brackets is the bond-pricing equation. The third line is also zero from the definition of X_τ in (55f). This leaves a valuation equation of

$$0 = \tfrac{1}{2}(\sigma^2 + 2\rho\sigma s\tau + \tau^2 s^2 X)\ G_{XX} - G_\tau. \quad (57)$$

A final substitution of $v \equiv \sigma^2\tau + \rho\sigma s\tau + s^2\tau^2/3$ and $H(X, v) \equiv G(x, \tau)$ gives

$$0 = \tfrac{1}{2}X^2 H_{XX} - H_v. \quad (58)$$

This is the Black–Scholes option–pricing equation with an interest rate of 0 and a standard deviation of 1. Thus, the price of a risky zero coupon bond with a face value of B is

$$F(V, r, t; T) = P(r, \tau)D\left(\frac{V}{P(r, \tau)}, v; B\right), \quad (59)$$

where $D(\cdot)$ is the debt function introduced in (23) with a standard deviation of 1 and an interest rate of 0.

Other contracts can be similarly valued. If the interest rate process has some other forms, then this homogeneity property is lost. Nevertheless, the same basic principle applies.

CONTINGENT CONTRACTING

In addition to pricing contracts, contingent claims analysis can be used to design new contracts with certain desirable properties. For example, there has recently been great interest in floating rate or variable rate bonds. Floating rate bonds are debt contracts whose coupon payments are adjusted periodically. Ideally, the adjustment creates a contract whose value is not affected by changes in interest rates. We will show how such a contract could be created.

For a coupon-bearing bond issued by a company paying no dividends and a general interest rate process, the valuation equation is

$$\begin{aligned} 0 = &\tfrac{1}{2}\sigma^2 V^2 F_{VV} + (rV - C)F_V - rF + F_t + C \\ &+\tfrac{1}{2}b^2(r)F_{rr} + (b(r) - \lambda(r))F_r + \rho\sigma V s F_{Vr}, \end{aligned} \quad (60)$$

with $F(V, T) = \text{Min}(V, B)$. If the bond's value is to be unaffected by changes in the interest rate, all of the partial derivatives in the second line of (60) are zero. Therefore, (60) becomes

$$0 = \tfrac{1}{2}\sigma^2 V^2 F_{VV} + (rV - C)F_V - rF + F_t + C. \tag{61}$$

The valuation equation for the equity is the same, except that the inhomogeneous term is absent since the owners are receiving no payments:

$$\tfrac{1}{2}\sigma^2 V^2 f_{VV} + (rV - C)f_V - rf + f_t, \tag{62}$$

with $f(V, T) = \text{Max}\,(V - B, 0)$.

These same equations obtain even if there are many state variables which determine the term structure of interest rates. The original partial differential equations will have many terms, but the partial derivatives with respect to the state variables determining interest rates are all zero.

For (61) to be valid, the coupon payment C must depend on the interest rate. In particular, C must be linear in r since only first-degree terms appear in (61).

$$C(r, V, t) = h(V, t) + rH(V, t). \tag{63}$$

Substituting (63) into (62) and collecting terms give

$$0 = \tfrac{1}{2}\sigma^2 V^2 f_{VV} - h(\cdot)f_V + f_t, \tag{64a}$$

$$0 = r[(V - H(\cdot))f_V - f]. \tag{64b}$$

There are many ways to select $H(\cdot)$ and $h(\cdot)$ to satisfy the requirements of this problem. Once $h(\cdot)$ is chosen, (64a) will value of the equity, and then (64b) will determine the choice for $H(\cdot)$.

For example, suppose we select $h(V, t) = 0$. In this case the variable coupon payment will be proportional to the prevailing spot rate of interest. For this choice (64a) is the Black–Scholes option–pricing equation when the interest rate is zero. Its solution is

$$\begin{aligned} f(V, t) &= VN(x_1) - BN(x_2), \\ &\text{where } x_1 \equiv [\log(V/B) + .5\sigma^2\tau]/\sigma\sqrt{\tau}, \\ &x_2 \equiv x_1 - \sigma\sqrt{\tau}. \end{aligned} \tag{65}$$

Solving (64b) gives

$$H(V, t; h) = \frac{Vf_V - f}{f_V} = \frac{BN(x_2)}{N(x_1)}. \tag{66}$$

The function $H(V, \tau)$ depends only on the ratio of the book value of the debt, B, to the market value of the firm, V, and on the total remaining uncertainty, $\sigma^2\tau$.

Bibliography

A complete bibliography of the theoretical work in financial economics would consume a book by itself. The following bibliography is an attempt to highlight and expand upon the various topics covered in this book and to place them in perspective.

CHAPTER 1 UTILITY THEORY

Bergman, Yaacov A. 1985. "Time Preference and Capital Asset Pricing Models." *Journal of Financial Economics* 14: 145–59.

Diamond, Peter, and Joseph Stiglitz. 1974. "Increases in Risk and in Risk Aversion." *Journal of Economic Theory* 8: 605–20.

Dybvig, Philip H., and Steven A. Lippman. 1983. "An Alternative Characterization of Decreasing Absolute Risk Aversion." *Econometrica* 51: 223–24.

Fishburn, P. C. 1969. "A General Theory of Subjective Probabilities and Expected Utilities." *Annals of Mathematical Statistics* 40: 1419–29.

Hernstein, I., and J. Milnor. 1953. "An Axiomatic Approach to Measurable Utility." *Econometrica* 21: 291–97.

Karady, Gyorgy. 1982. "The Effect of Temporal Risk Aversion on Liquidity Preference." *Journal of Financial Economics* 10: 467–83.

Machina, Mark. 1982. "'Expected Utility' Analysis Without the Independence Axiom." *Econometrica* 50: 277–323.

Pratt, John W. 1964. "Risk-Aversion in the Small and in the Large." *Econometrica* 32: 122–36.

Richard, Scott F. 1975. "Multivariate Risk Aversion, Utility Independence, and Separable Utility Functions." *Management Science* 22: 12–21.

Ross, Stephen A. 1981. "Some Stronger Measures of Risk Aversion in the Small and the Large with Applications." *Econometrica* 49: 621–38.

Samuelson, Paul A. 1952. "Probability, Utility, and the Independence Axiom." *Econometrica* 20: 670–78.

———. 1977. "St. Petersburg Paradoxes: Defanged, Dissected, and Historically Described." *Journal of Economic Literature* 15: 24–55.

von Neumann, John, and Oskar Morgenstern. 1944. *Theory of Games and Economic Behavior*. Princeton, N.J.: Princeton University Press.

CHAPTER 2 ARBITRAGE AND PRICING: THE BASICS

Harrison, J. Michael, and David Kreps. 1979. "Martingales and Arbitrage in Multiperiod Securities Markets." *Journal of Economic Theory* 20: 381–408.

Protopapadakis, Aris, and Hans R. Stoll. 1983. "Spot and Futures Prices and the Law of One Price." *Journal of Finance* 38: 1431–55.

Ross, Stephen A. 1975. "Return, Risk and Arbitrage." In Irwin Friend and J. Bicksler, eds., *Studies in Risk and Return*. Cambridge, Mass.: Ballinger Publishing Co.

———. 1978. "A Simple Approach to the Valuation of Risky Streams." *Journal of Business* 51: 453–75.

CHAPTER 3 THE PORTFOLIO PROBLEM

Elton, Edwin J., and Martin J. Gruber. 1977. "Risk Reduction and Portfolio Size: An Analytical Solution." *Journal of Business* 50: 415–77.

Fishburn, Peter, and Burr Porter. 1976. "Optimal Portfolios with One Safe and One Risky Asset: Effects of Change in Rate of Return and Risk." *Management Science* 22: 1064–73.

Grossman, Sanford J. 1976. "On the Efficiency of Competitive Stock Markets Where Traders Have Diverse Information." *Journal of Finance* 31: 573–85.

Merton, Robert C. 1982. "On the Microeconomic Theory of Investment under Uncertainty." In Kenneth J. Arrow and Michael D. Intriligator, eds., *Handbook of Mathematical Economics*. New York: North-Holland Publishing Co.

Milgrom, Paul, and Nancy Stokey. 1982. "Information, Trade and Common Knowledge." *Journal of Economic Theory* 26: 17–27.

Roll, Richard, and Stephen A. Ross. 1977. "Comments on Qualitative Results for Investment Proportions." *Journal of Financial Economics* 5: 265–68.

Samuelson, Paul A. 1967. "General Proof That Diversification Pays." *Journal of Financial and Quantitative Analysis* 2: 1–13.

CHAPTER 4 MEAN-VARIANCE PORTFOLIO ANALYSIS

Baron, David P. 1977. "On the Utility Theoretic Foundations of Mean-Variance Analysis." *Journal of Finance* 32: 1683–97.

Black, Fischer. 1972. "Capital Market Equilibrium with Restricted Borrowing." *Journal of Business* 45: 444–54.

Brennan, Michael J. 1971. "Capital Market Equilibrium with Divergent Borrowing and Lending Rates." *Journal of Financial and Quantitative Analysis* 6: 1197–1205.

Chamberlain, Gary. 1983. "A Characterization of the Distributions that Imply Mean-Variance Utility Functions." *Journal of Economic Theory* 29: 185–201.

Dybvig, Philip H. 1984. "Short Sales Restrictions and Kinks of the Mean Variance Frontier." *Journal of Finance* 39: 239–44.

Fama, Eugene F. 1968. "Risk, Return and Equilibrium: Some Clarifying Comments." *Journal of Finance* 23: 29–40.

———. 1971. "Risk, Return and Equilibrium." *Journal of Political Economy* 71: 30–55.

Jensen, Michael. 1972. "Capital Markets: Theory and Evidence." *Bell Journal of Economics and Management Science* 3: 357–98.

Lintner, John. 1965. "The Valuation of Risk Assets and the Selection of Risky Investments in Stock Portfolios and Capital Budgets." *Review of Economics and Statistics* 47: 13–37.

———. 1965. "Security Prices, Risk, and Maximal Gains from Diversification." *Journal of Finance* 20: 587–615.

Markowitz, Harry, 1952. "Portfolio Selection." *Journal of Finance* 7: 77–91.

———. 1959. *Portfolio Selection: Efficient Diversification of Investment.* New York: John Wiley & Sons.

Mayers, David, and Edward M. Rice. 1979. "Measuring Portfolio Performance and the Empirical Content of Asset Pricing Models." *Journal of Financial Economics* 7: 3–28.

Merton, Robert C. 1972. "An Analytical Derivation of the Efficient Portfolio Frontier." *Journal of Financial and Quantitative Analysis* 7: 1851–72.

Mossin, Jan. 1966. "Equilibrium in a Capital Asset Market." *Econometrica* 34: 261–76.

Owen, Joel, and Ramon Rabinovitch. 1983. "On the Class of Elliptical Distributions and Their Applications to the Theory Portfolio Choice." *Journal of Finance* 38: 745–52.

Roll, Richard. 1977. "A Critique of the Asset Pricing Theory's Tests; Part 1: On Past and Potential Testability of the Theory." *Journal of Financial Economics* 4: 129–76.

———. 1978. "Ambiguity When Performance Is Measured by the Securities Market Line." *Journal of Finance* 33: 1051–69.

———. 1979. "A Reply to Mayers and Rice (1979)." *Journal of Financial Economics* 7: 391–400.

———. 1980. "Orthogonal Portfolios." *Journal of Financial and Quantitative Analysis* 15: 1005–23.

Ross, Stephen A. 1978. "The Current Status of the Capital Asset Pricing Model." *Journal of Finance* 33: 885–901.

Sharpe, William F. 1963. "A Simplified Model for Portfolio Analysis." *Management Science* 9: 277–93.

———. 1964. "Capital Asset Prices: A Theory of Market Equilibrium under Conditions of Risk." *Journal of Finance* 19: 425–42.

———. 1970. *Portfolio Theory and Capital Markets.* New York: McGraw-Hill.

Verrecchia, Robert E. 1980. "The Mayers-Rice Conjecture: A Counterexample." *Journal of Financial Economics* 8: 87–100.

Williams, Joseph. 1977. "A Note on Indifference Curves in the Mean-Variance Models." *Journal of Financial and Quantitative Analysis* 12: 121–26.

CHAPTER 5 GENERALIZED RISK, PORTFOLIO SELECTION, AND ASSET PRICING

Ai, Mukhatar M. 1975. "Stochastic Dominance and Portfolio Analysis." *Journal of Financial Economics* 2: 205–29.

Hadar, J., and W. R. Russell, 1969. "Rules for Ordering Uncertain Prospects." *American Economic Review* 59: 25–34.

Kroll, Yoram, and Haim Levy. 1979. "Stochastic Dominance with a Riskless Asset: An Imperfect Market." *Journal of Financial and Quantitative Analysis* 14: 179–204.

Levy, Haim. 1977. "The Definition of Risk: An Extension." *Journal of Economic Theory* 14: 232–34.

Levy, Haim, and Yoram Kroll. 1978. "Ordering Uncertain Options with Borrowing and Lending." *Journal of Finance* 33: 553–74.

Rothschild, Michael, and Joseph Stiglitz. 1970. "Increasing Risk I: A Definition." *Journal of Economic Theory* 2: 225–43.

———. 1971. "Increasing Risk II: Its Economic Consequences." *Journal of Economic Theory* 3: 66–84.

Scott, Robert C., and Philip A. Horvath. 1980. "On the Direction of Preference for Moments of Higher Order than the Variance." *Journal of Finance* 35: 915–19.

Whitmore, G. A. 1970. "Third Degree Stochastic Dominance." *American Economic Review* 60: 457–59.

CHAPTER 6 PORTFOLIO SEPARATION THEOREMS

Brennan, Michael J., and Alan Kraus. 1976. "The Geometry of Separation and Myopia." *Journal of Financial and Quantitative Analysis* 11: 171–93.

———. 1978. "Necessary Conditions for Aggregation in Securities Markets." *Journal of Financial and Quantitative Analysis* 13: 407–18.

Cass, David, and Joseph Stiglitz. 1970. "The Structure of Investor Preferences and Asset Returns, and Separability in Portfolio Allocation." *Journal of Economic Theory* 2: 122–60.

Dybvig, Philip H., and Stephen A. Ross. 1982. "Portfolio Efficient Sets." *Econometrica* 50: 1525–46.

Hakansson, Nils H. 1969. "Risk Disposition and the Separation Property in Portfolio Selection." *Journal of Financial and Quantitative Analysis* 4: 401–16.

Ingersoll, Jonathan E., Jr. 1975. "Multidimensional Security Pricing." *Journal of Financial and Quantitative Analysis* 10: 785–98.

Kraus, Alan, and Robert H. Litzenberger. 1976. "Skewness Preference and the Valuation of Risk Assets." *Journal of Finance* 31: 1085–1100.

Lintner, John. 1969. "The Aggregation of Investors' Diverse Judgments and Preferences in Purely Competitive Security Markets." *Journal of Financial and Quantitative Analysis* 4: 347–400.

Ross, Stephen A. 1978. "Mutual Fund Separation and Financial Theory — The Separating Distributions." *Journal of Economic Theory* 17: 254–86.

Rubinstein, Mark E. 1973. "The Fundamental Theorem of Parameter Preference Security Valuation." *Journal of Financial and Quantitative Analysis* 8: 61–69.

Vickson, R. G. 1975. "Separation in Portfolio Analysis." In W. T. Ziemba and R. G. Vickson, eds., *Stochastic Optimization Models in Finance*. New York: Academic Press.

CHAPTER 7 THE LINEAR FACTOR MODEL: ARBITRAGE PRICING THEORY

Admati, Anat R., and Paul Pfleiderer. 1985. "Interpreting the Factor Risk Premia in the Arbitrage Pricing Theory." *Journal of Economic Theory* 35: 191–95.

Chamberlain, Gary. 1983. "Funds, Factors, and Diversification in Arbitrage Pricing Models." *Econometrica* 51: 1305–23.

Chamberlain, Gary, and Michael Rothschild. 1983. "Arbitrage, Factor Structure, and Mean-Variance Analysis on Large Asset Markets." *Econometrica* 51: 1281–1304.

Chen, Nai-fu, and Jonathan E. Ingersoll, Jr. 1983. "Exact Pricing in Linear Factor Models with Finitely Many Assets." *Journal of Finance* 38: 985–88.

Connor, Gregory. 1982. "A Factor Pricing Theory for Capital Markets." Unpublished working paper.

———. 1984. "A Unified Beta Pricing Theory." *Journal of Economic Theory* 34: 13–31.

Dybvig, Philip H. 1983. "An Explicit Bound on Individual Assets' Deviations from APT Pricing in a Finite Economy." *Journal of Financial Economics* 12: 483–96.

Grinblatt, Mark, and Sheridan Titman. 1983. "Factor Pricing in a Finite Economy." *Journal of Financial Economics* 12: 497–507.

Huberman, Gur. 1982. "A Simple Approach to Arbitrage Pricing Theory." *Journal of Economic Theory* 28: 183–91.

Ingersoll, Jonathan E., Jr. 1984. "Some Results in the Theory of Arbitrage Pricing" Journal of Finance 39, 1021–1039.

Ross, Stephen A. 1975. "Return, Risk and Arbitrage." In Irwin Friend and J. Bicksler, eds., *Studies in Risk and Return.* Cambridge, Mass.: Ballinger Publishing Co.

———. 1976. "The Arbitrage Theory of Capital Asset Pricing" *Journal of Economic Theory* 13: 341–60.

———. 1978. "The Current Status of the Capital Asset Pricing Model." *Journal of Finance* 33: 885–901.

———. 1982. "On the General Validity of the Mean-Variance Approach in Large Markets." In William Sharpe and Cathryn Cootner, eds., *Financial Economics: Essays in Honor of Paul Cootner*. Englewood Cliffs, N.J.: Prentice-Hall.

Shanken, Jay, 1982. "The Arbitrage Pricing Theory: Is It Testable?" *Journal of Finance* 37: 1129–40.

Stambaugh, Robert. 1983. "Arbitrage Pricing with Information." *Journal of Financial Economics* 12: 357–69.

CHAPTER 8 EQUILIBRIUM MODELS WITH COMPLETE MARKETS

Arditti, Fred, and Kose John. 1980. "Spanning the State Space with Options." *Journal of Financial and Quantitative Analysis* 15: 1–9.

Arrow, Kenneth. 1964. "The Role of Securities in the Optimal Allocation of Risk Bearing." *Review of Economic Studies* 31: 91–96.

Banz, Rolf, and Merton Miller. 1978. "Prices for State-Contingent Claims: Some Estimates and Applications." *Journal of Business* 51: 653–72.

Breeden, Douglas, and Robert Litzenberger. 1978. "Prices of State Contingent Claims Implicit in Options Prices." *Journal of Business* 51: 621–52.
Debreu, Gerald. 1959. *Theory of Value*. New York: John Wiley & Sons.
Friesen, Peter H. 1979. "The Arrow-Debreu Model Extended to Financial Markets." *Econometrica* 47: 689–707.
Hirshleifer, Jack. 1970. *Investment, Interest and Capital.* Englewood Cliffs, N.J.: Prentice-Hall.
Myers, Stewart C. 1968. "A Time-State-Preference Model of Security Valuation." *Journal of Financial and Quantitative Analysis* 3: 1–33.
Ross, Stephen A. 1976. "Options and Efficiency." *Quarterly Journal of Economics* 90: 75–89.

CHAPTER 9 GENERAL EQUILIBRIUM CONSIDERATIONS IN ASSET PRICING

Arrow, Kenneth J. *Essays in the Theory of Risk Bearing*. Chicago: Markham Publishing Co.
Cootner, Paul. 1977. "The Theorems of Modern Finance in a General Equilibrium Setting: Paradoxes Resolved." *Journal of Financial and Quantitative Analysis* 12: 553–62.
Dybvig, Philip H., and Jonathan E. Ingersoll, Jr. 1982. "Mean-Variance Theory in Complete Markets." *Journal of Business* 55: 233–51.
John, Kose. 1984. "Market Resolution and Valuation in Incomplete Markets." *Journal of Financial and Quantitative Analysis* 19: 29–44.
Varian, Hal. 1985. "Divergence of Opinion in Complete Markets: A Note." *Journal of Finance* 40: 309–17.

CHAPTER 10 INTERTEMPORAL MODELS IN FINANCE

Fama, Eugene F. 1970. "Efficient Capital Markets: A Review of Theory and Empirical Work." *Journal of Finance* 25: 383–417.
Hakansson, Nils. 1969. "On the Dividend Capitalization Model Under Uncertainty." *Journal of Financial and Quantitative Analysis* 4: 65–87.
Jordan, J. S. 1983. "On the Efficient Markets Hypothesis." *Econometrica* 51: 1325–43.
LeRoy, Stephen F. 1976. "Efficient Capital Markets: Comment." *Journal of Finance* 31: 139–41.
———. 1982. "Expectations Models of Asset Prices: A Survey of Theory." *Journal of Finance* 37: 185–217.
Magill, Michael. 1981. "Infinite Horizon Programs." *Econometrica* 49: 679–711.
Ross, Stephen A. 1978. "A Simple Approach to the Valuation of Risky Streams." *Journal of Business* 51: 453–75.
Rubinstein, Mark. 1975. "Security Market Efficiency in an Arrow-Debreu Economy." *American Economic Review* 65: 812–24.
Samuelson, Paul A. 1965. "Proof That Properly Anticipated Prices Fluctuate Randomly." *Industrial Management Review* 6: 41–49.
———. 1973. "Proof That Properly Discounted Present Values of Assets Vibrate Randomly." *Bell Journal of Economics and Management Science* 4: 369–74.

Stone, Bernell. 1975. "The Conformity of Stock Values Based on Discounted Dividends to a Fair-Return Process." *Bell Journal of Economics* 6: 698–702.
Tirole, Jean. 1982. "On the Possibility of Speculation Under Rational Expectations." *Econometrica* 50: 1163–81.
Verrecchia, Robert E. 1979. "A Proof Concerning the Existence of Fama-Rubinstein Efficiency." *Journal of Finance* 34: 957–63.

CHAPTER 11 DISCRETE TIME INTERTEMPORAL PORTFOLIO SELECTION

Fama, Eugene F. 1970. "Multiperiod Consumption-Investment Decisions." *American Economic Review* 60: 163–74.
Goldman, M. Barry. 1974. "A Negative Report on the 'Near-Optimality' of the Max-Expected-Log Policy as Applied to Bounded Utilities for Long-Lived Programs." *Journal of Financial Economics* 1: 97–103.
Hakansson, Nils H. 1970. "Optimal Investment and Consumption Strategies under Risk for a Class of Utility Functions." *Econometrica* 38: 587–607.
———. 1971. "Capital Growth and the Mean-Variance Approach to Portfolio Selection." *Journal of Financial and Quantitative Analysis* 6: 517–57.
———. 1971. "On Optimal Myopic Portfolio Policies with and without Serial Correlation of Yields." *Journal of Business* 44: 324–34.
Huberman, Gur, and Stephen A. Ross. 1983. "Portfolio Turnpike Theorems, Risk Aversion, and Regularly Varying Utility Functions." *Econometrica* 51: 1345–61.
Markowitz, Harry. 1976. "Investment for the Long-Run: New Evidence for an Old Rule." *Journal of Finance* 31: 1273–86.
Merton, Robert C. 1975. "A Reexamination of the Capital Asset Pricing Model." In Irwin Friend and J. Bicksler, eds., *Studies in Risk and Return*. Cambridge, Mass.: Ballinger Publishing Co.
Merton, Robert C., and Paul A. Samuelson. 1974. "Fallacy of the Log-Normal Approximation to Optimal Portfolio Decision-Making over Many Periods." *Journal of Financial Economics* 1: 67–94.
Pye, Gordon. 1972. "Lifetime Portfolio Selection with Age Dependent Risk Aversion." In G. P. Szego and K. Shell, eds., *Mathematical Methods in Investment and Finance*. New York: North-Holland Publishing Co.
Rubinstein, Mark. 1976. "The Strong Case for the Generalized Logarithmic Utility Model as the Premier Model of Financial Markets." *Journal of Finance* 31: 551–71.
———. 1976. "The Valuation of Uncertain Income Streams and the Pricing of Options." *Bell Journal of Economics* 7: 407–25.
Samuelson, Paul A. 1969. "Lifetime Portfolio Selection by Dynamic Stochastic Programming." *Review of Economics and Statistics* 51: 239–46.

CHAPTER 12 AN INTORDUCTION TO THE DISTRIBUTIONS OF CONTINUOUS-TIME FINANCE

Malliaris, A. G., and W. A. Brock. 1982. *Stochastic Methods in Economics and Finance*. New York: North-Holland Publishing Co.

Merton, Robert C. 1982. "On the Mathematics and Economic Assumptions of the Continuous-Time Models." In William Sharpe and Cathryn Cootner, eds., *Financial Economics: Essays in Honor of Paul Cootner*. Englewood Cliffs, N.J.: Prentice-Hall.

Ohlson, James A. 1975. "The Asymptotic Validity of Quadratic Utility as the Trading Interval Approaches Zero." In W. T. Ziemba and R. G. Vickson, eds., *Stochastic Optimization Models in Finance*. New York: Academic Press.

Samuelson, Paul A. 1970. "The Fundamental Approximation Theorem of Portfolio Analysis in Terms of Means, Variances, and Higher Moments." *Review of Economic Studies* 37: 537–42.

CHAPTER 13 CONTINUOUS-TIME PORTFOLIO SELECTION

Breeden, Douglas. 1979. "An Intertemporal Asset Pricing Model with Stochastic Consumption and Investment Opportunities." *Journal of Financial Economics* 7: 265–96.

Merton, Robert C. 1969. "Lifetime Portfolio Selection under Uncertainty: The Continuous-Time Case." *Review of Economics and Statistics* 51: 247–57.

———. 1971. "Optimum Consumption and Portfolio Rules in a Continuous-Time Model." *Journal of Economic Theory* 3: 373–413.

———. 1973. "An Intertemporal Capital Asset Pricing Model." *Econometrica* 41: 867–80.

———. 1975. "Theory of Finance from the Perspective of Continuous Time." *Journal of Financial and Quantitative Analysis* 10: 659–74.

Richard, Scott F. 1975. "Optimal Consumption, Portfolio and Life Insurance Rules for an Uncertain Lived Individual in a Continuous Time Model." *Journal of Financial Economics* 2: 187–203.

Ross, Stephen A. 1975. "Uncertainty and the Heterogeneous Capital Goods Model." *Review of Economic Studies* 42: 133–46.

Williams, Joseph. 1977. "Capital Asset Prices with Heterogeneous Beliefs." *Journal of Financial Economics* 5: 219–39.

CHAPTER 14 THE PRICING OF OPTIONS

Black, Fischer. 1975. "Fact and Fantasy in the Use of Options." *Financial Analysts Journal* 31: 36–41 and 61–72.

Black, Fischer, and Myron Scholes. 1973. "The Pricing of Options and Corporate Liabilities." *Journal of Political Economy* 81: 637–54.

Boyle, Phelim P. 1977. "Options: A Monte Carlo Approach." *Journal of Financial Economics* 4: 323–38.

Brennan, Michael J. 1979. "The Pricing of Contingent Claims in Discrete Time Models." *Journal of Finance* 34: 53–68.

Cox, John C., Stephen A. Ross, and Mark Rubinstein. 1979. "Option Pricing: A Simplified Approach." *Journal of Financial Economics* 7: 229–63.

Cox, John C., and Mark Rubinstein. 1985. *Options Markets*. New York: Prentice-Hall.

Galai, Dan. 1978. "On the Boness and Black-Scholes Models for Valuation of Call Options." *Journal of Financial and Quantitative Analysis* 13: 15–27.

Garman, Mark B. 1976. "An Algebra for Evaluating Hedge Portfolios." *Journal of Financial Economics* 3: 403–27.

Jagannathan, Ravi. 1984. "Call Options and the Risk of Underlying Securities." *Journal of Financial Economics* 13: 425–34.

Jarrow, Robert A., and Andrew Rudd. 1982. "'Approximate Option Valuation for Arbitrary Stochastic Processes." *Journal of Financial Economics* 10: 347–69.

Merton, Robert C. 1973. "The Relationship Between Put and Call Option Prices: Comment." *Journal of Finance* 28: 32–39.

———. 1973. "Theory of Rational Option Pricing." *Bell Journal of Economics and Management Science* 4: 141–83.

Perrakis, Stylianos, and Peter J. Ryan. 1984. "Option Pricing Bounds in Discrete Time." *Journal of Finance* 39: 519–25.

Rendlemen, Richard J., Jr., and Brit J. Bartter. 1979. "Two-State Option Pricing." *Journal of Finance* 34: 1093–1110.

Rubinstein, Mark. 1976. "The Valuation of Uncertain Income Streams and the Pricing of Options." *Bell Journal of Economics* 7: 407–25.

———. 1983. "Displaced Diffusion Option Pricing." *Journal of Finance* 38: 213–17.

Smith, Clifford W., Jr. 1976. "Option Pricing: A Review." *Journal of Financial Economics* 3: 3–51.

Stapleton, R. C., and M. G. Subrahmanyam. 1984. "The Valuation of Multivariate Contingent Claims in Discrete Time Models." *Journal of Finance* 39: 207–28.

———. 1984. "The Valuation of Options When Asset Returns Are Generated by a Binomial Process." *Journal of Finance* 39: 1525–39.

Stoll, Hans R. 1969. "The Relationship Between Put and Call Option Prices." *Journal of Finance* 24: 802–24.

CHAPTER 15 REVIEW OF MULTIPERIOD MODELS

Bhattacharya, Sudipto. 1981. "Notes on Multiperiod Valuation and the Pricing of Options." *Journal of Finance* 36: 163–80.

Breeden, Douglas. 1979. "An Intertemporal Asset Pricing Model with Stochastic Consumption and Investment Opportunities." *Journal of Financial Economics* 7: 265–96.

———. 1980. "Consumption Risk in Futures Markets." *Journal of Finance* 35: 503–20.

Brennan, Michael J. 1979. "The Pricing of Contingent Claims in Discrete Time Models." *Journal of Finance* 34: 53–68.

Constantinides, George M. 1980. "Admissible Uncertainty in the Intertemporal Asset Pricing Model." *Journal of Financial Economics* 8: 71–86.

———. 1982. "Intertemporal Asset Pricing with Heterogeneous Consumers and without Demand Aggregation." *Journal of Business* 55: 253–67.

Cootner, Paul. 1977. "The Theorems of Modern Finance in a General Equilibrium Setting: Paradoxes Resolved." *Journal of Financial and Quantitative Analysis* 12: 553–62.

Cornell, Bradford. 1981. "The Consumption Based Asset Pricing Model: A Note on Potential Tests and Applications." *Journal of Financial Economics* 9: 103–8.

Cox, John C. 1984. "Optimal Consumption and Portfolio Policies When Asset Returns Follow a Diffusion Process." Unpublished working paper.

Cox, John C., Jonathan E. Ingersoll, Jr., and Stephen A. Ross. 1985. "An Intertemporal Asset Pricing Model with Rational Expectations." *Econometrica* 53: 363–84.

Cox, John C., and Hayne Leland. 1982. "On Dynamic Investment Strategies." *Proceedings, Seminar on the Analysis of Security Prices*, vol. 26, no. 2. Center for Research in Security Prices, (Graduate School of Business, University of Chicago).

Duffie, Darrell, and Chi-fu Huang. 1985. "Implementing Arrow-Debreu Equilibria by Continuous Trading of Few Long-Lived Securities." *Econometrica* 53: 1337–56.

Dybvig, Philip H., Jonathan E. Ingersoll, Jr., and Stephen A. Ross. 1986. "Martingales and Arbitrage." Unpublished working paper.

Grossman, Sanford J., and Robert J. Shiller. 1982. "Consumption Correlatedness and Risk Measurement in Economies with Non-traded Assets and Heterogeneous Information." *Journal of Financial Economics* 10: 195–210.

Hakansson, Nils H. 1978. "Welfare Aspects of Options and Supershares." *Journal of Finance* 33: 759–76.

Hansen, Lars P., and Kenneth Singleton. 1983. "Stochastic Consumption, Risk Aversion, and the Temporal Behavior of Asset Returns." *Journal of Political Economy* 91: 249–65.

Harrison, J. Michael, and David Kreps. 1979. "Martingales and Arbitrage in Multiperiod Securities Markets." *Journal of Economic Theory* 20: 381–408.

LeRoy, Stephen. 1973. "Risk Aversion and the Martingale Property of Stock Prices." *International Economic Review* 14: 436–46.

Lucas, Robert. 1978. "Asset Prices in an Exchange Economy." *Econometrica* 46: 1429–45.

Merton, Robert C. 1970. "A Dynamic General Equilibrium Model of the Asset Market and Its Application to the Pricing of the Capital Structure of the Firm." Unpublished working paper.

———. 1975. "A Reexamination of the Capital Asset Pricing Model." In Irwin Friend and J. Bicksler, eds., *Studies in Risk and Return*. Cambridge, Mass.: Ballinger Publishing Co.

———. 1975. "Theory of Finance from the Perspective of Continuous Time." *Journal of Financial and Quantitative Analysis* 10: 659–74.

Rosenberg, Barr, and James Ohlson. 1976. "The Stationary Distribution of Returns and Portfolio Separation in Capital Markets: A Fundamental Contradiction." *Journal of Financial and Quantitative Analysis* 11: 393–402.

Rubinstein, Mark. 1976. "The Strong Case for the Generalized Logarithmic Utility Model as the Premier Model of Financial Markets." *Journal of Finance* 31: 551–71.

CHAPTER 16 AN INTRODUCTION TO STOCHASTIC CALCULUS

Beckers, Stan. 1983. "Variances of Security Price Returns Based on High, Low, and Closing Prices." *Journal of Business* 56: 97–112.

Fischer, Stan. 1975. Appendix to "The Demand for Index Bonds." *Journal of Political Economy* 83: 509–34.

Garman, Mark B., and Michael J. Klass. 1980. "On the Estimation of Security Price Volatilities from Historical Data." *Journal of Business* 53: 67–78.

Karlin, S., and H. M. Taylor. 1975. *A First Course in Stochastic Processes*. New York: Academic Press.
———. 1981. *A Second Course in Stochastic Processes*. New York: Academic Press.
Malliaris, A. G., and W. A. Brock. 1982. *Stochastic Methods in Economics and Finance*. New York: North-Holland Publishing Co.
Merton, Robert C. 1975. Appendices to "An Asymptotic Theory of Growth under Uncertainty." *Review of Economic Studies* 42: 375–93.
Parkinson, Michael. 1980. "The Extreme Value Method for Estimating the Variance of the Rate of Return." *Journal of Business* 53: 61–65.
Smith, Clifford W., Jr. 1979. Appendix to "Applications of Option Pricing Analysis." In James L. Bicksler, ed., *Handbook of Financial Economics*. New York: North Holland Publishing Co.

CHAPTER 17 ADVANCED TOPICS IN OPTION PRICING

Bick, Avi. 1982. "Comments on the Valuation of Derivative Assets." *Journal of Financial Economics* 10: 331–45.
Brennan, Michael J., and Eduardo S. Schwartz. 1977. "The Valuation of American Put Options." *Journal of Finance* 32: 449–62.
———. 1978. "Finite Difference Methods and Jump Processes Arising in the Pricing of Contingent Claims: A Synthesis." *Journal of Financial and Quantitative Analysis* 13: 461–74.
Cox, John C., Jonathan E. Ingersoll, Jr., and Stephen A. Ross. 1981. "The Relation Between Forward Prices and Futures Prices." *Journal of Financial Economics* 9: 321–46.
Cox, John C., and Stephen A. Ross. 1976. "A Survey of Some New Results in Financial Option Pricing Theory." *Journal of Finance* 31: 383–402.
———. 1976. "The Valuation of Options for Alternative Stochastic Processes." *Journal of Financial Economics* 3: 145–66.
Cox, John C., and Mark Rubinstein. 1983. "A Survey of Alternative Option Pricing Models." In Menachem Brenner, ed., *Option Pricing*. Lexington, Mass.: D. C. Heath.
Fischer, Stan. 1978. "Call Option Pricing When the Exercise Price Is Uncertain, and the Valuation of Index Bonds." *Journal of Finance* 33: 169–76.
Geit, Alan. 1978. "Valuation of General Contingent Claims: Existence, Uniqueness, and Comparisons of Solutions." *Journal of Financial Economics* 6: 71–87.
Geske, Robert. 1978. "Pricing of Options with Stochastic Dividend Yields." *Journal of Finance* 33: 617–25.
———. 1979. "A Note on an Analytical Valuation Formula for Unprotected American Call Options on Stocks with Known Dividends." *Journal of Financial Economics* 7: 375–80.
———. 1979. "The Valuation of Compound Options." *Journal of Financial Economics* 7: 63–81.
Geske, Robert, and Herbert Johnson. 1984. "The American Put Option Valued Analytically." *Journal of Finance* 39: 1511–24.
Geske, Robert, and Richard Roll. 1984. "On Valuing American Call Options with the Black-Scholes European Formula." *Journal of Finance* 39: 443–55.
Goldman, M. Barry, Howard B. Sosin, and Mary Ann Gatto. 1979. "Path Dependent Options: 'Buy at the Low, Sell at the High.'" *Journal of Finance*

34: 1111–27.
Goldman, M. Barry, Howard B. Sosin, and Lawrence A. Shepp. 1979. "On Contingent Claims That Insure Ex-Post Optimal Stock Market Timing." *Journal of Finance* 34: 401–14.
Jones, E. Philip. 1984. "Arbitrage Pricing of Options for Mixed Diffusion-Jump Processes." *Journal of Financial Economics* 13: 91–113.
Margrabe, William. 1978. "The Value of an Option to Exchange One Asset for Another." *Journal of Finance* 33: 177–98.
Merton, Robert C. 1976. "The Impact on Option Pricing of Specification Error in the Underlying Stock Price Returns." *Journal of Finance* 31: 333–50.
———. 1976. "Option Pricing When Underlying Stock Returns Are Discontinuous." *Journal of Financial Economics* 3: 125–44.
———. 1977. "On the Pricing of Contingent Claims and the Modigliani-Miller Theorem." *Journal of Financial Economics* 5: 241–50.
Parkinson, Michael. 1977. "Option Pricing: The American Put." *Journal of Business* 50: 21–36.
Roll, Richard. 1977. "An Analytic Valuation Formula for Unprotected American Call Options on Stocks with Known Dividends." *Journal of Financial Economics* 5: 251–58.
Smith, Clifford W., Jr. 1976. "Option Pricing: A Review." *Journal of Financial Economics* 3: 3–51.
Stulz, Rene M. 1982. "Options on the Minimum or the Maximum of Two Risky Assets: Analysis and Applications." *Journal of Financial Economics* 10: 161–85.
Whaley, Robert E. 1981. "On the Valuation of American Call Options on Stocks with Known Dividends." *Journal of Financial Economics* 9: 207–11.

CHAPTER 18 THE TERM STRUCTURE OF INTEREST RATES

Brennan, Michael J., and Eduardo S. Schwartz. 1977. "Savings Bonds, Retractable Bonds and Callable Bonds." *Journal of Financial Economics* 5: 67–88.
———. 1979. "A Continuous Time Approach to the Pricing of Bonds." *Journal of Banking and Finance* 3: 133–55.
———. 1980. "Conditional Predictions of Bond Prices and Returns." *Journal of Finance* 35: 405–17.
———. 1982. "An Equilibrium Model of Bond Pricing and a Test of Market Efficiency." *Journal of Financial and Quantitative Analysis* 17: 301–29.
Constantinides, George M., and Jonathan E. Ingersoll, Jr. 1984. "Optimal Bond Trading with Personal Taxes." *Journal of Financial Economics* 13: 299–335.
Cox, John C., Jonathan E. Ingersoll. Jr., and Stephen A. Ross. 1979. "Duration and the Measurement of Basis Risk." *Journal of Business* 52: 51–61.
———. 1980. "An Analysis of Variable Rate Loan Contracts." *Journal of Finance* 35: 389–403.
———. 1981. "A Re-examination of Traditional Hypotheses about the Term Structure of Interest Rates." *Journal of Finance* 36: 769–99.
———. 1985. "A Theory of the Term Structure of Interest Rates." *Econometrica* 53: 385–407.
Dothan, L. Uri. 1978. "On the Term Structure of Interest Rates." *Journal of Financial Economics* 6: 59–69.
Dothan L. Uri, and Joseph Williams. 1980. "Term-Risk Structures and the

Valuation of Projects." *Journal of Financial and Quantitative Analysis* 15: 875–905.
Dybvig, Philip H., Jonathan E. Ingersoll, Jr., and Stephen A. Ross. 1986. "Long Forward Rates Can Never Fall" Unpublished working paper.
Ingersoll, Jonathan E., Jr., Jeffery Skelton, and Roman Weil. 1978. "Duration Forty Years Later." *Journal of Financial and Quantitative Analysis* 13: 627–50.
Langetieg, Terence. 1980. "A Multivariate Model of the Term Structure." *Journal of Finance* 35: 71–97.
Long, John B., Jr. 1974. "Stock Prices, Inflation, and the Term Structure of Interest Rates." *Journal of Financial Economics* 1: 131–70.
Malkiel, Burton G. 1962. "Expectations, Bond Prices, and the Term Structure of Interest Rates." *Quarterly Journal of Economics* 76: 197–218.
Richard, Scott F. 1978. "An Arbitrage Model of the Term Structure of Interest Rates." *Journal of Financial Economics* 6: 33–57.
Schaefer, Stephen, and Eduardo S. Schwartz. 1984. "A Two-Factor Model of the Term Structure: An Approximate Analytical Solution." *Journal of Financial and Quantitative Analysis* 19: 413–24.
Sundaresan, M. 1984. "Consumption and Equilibrium Interest Rates in Stochastic Production Economies." *Journal of Finance* 39: 77–92.
Van Horne, James. 1965. "Interest-Rate Risk and the Term Structure of Interest Rates." *Journal of Political Economy* 73: 344–51.
Vasicek, Oldrich. 1977. "An Equilibrium Characterization of the Term Structure." *Journal of Financial Economics* 5: 177–88.

CHAPTER 19 PRICING THE CAPITAL STRUCTURE OF THE FIRM

Black, Fischer, and John C. Cox. 1976. "Valuing Corporate Securities: Some Effects of Bond Indenture Provisions." *Journal of Finance* 31: 351–67.
Black, Fischer, and Myron Scholes. 1973. "The Pricing of Options and Corporate Liabilities." *Journal of Political Economy* 81: 637–54.
Brennan, Michael J., and Eduardo S. Schwartz. 1977. "Convertible Bonds: Valuation and Optimal Strategies for Call and Conversion." *Journal of Finance* 32: 1699–1715.
———. 1978. "Corporate Income Taxes, Valuation, and the Problem of Optimal Capital Structure." *Journal of Business* 51: 103–14.
———. 1980. "Analyzing Convertible Bonds." *Journal of Financial and Quantitative Analysis* 15: 907–29.
———. 1984. "Optimal Financial Policy and Firm Valuation." *Journal of Finance* 39: 593–606.
Chen, Andrew H., and E. Han Kim. 1979. "Theories of Corporate Debt Policy: A Synthesis." *Journal of Finance* 34: 371–84.
Constantinides, George M. 1984. "Warrant Exercise and Bond Conversion in Competitive Markets." *Journal of Financial Economics* 13: 371–97.
Constantinides, George M., and Robert W. Rosenthal. 1984. "Strategic Analysis of the Competitive Exercise of Certain Financial Options." *Journal of Economic Theory* 32: 128–38.
Cox, John C, Jonathan E. Ingersoll, Jr., and Stephen A. Ross. 1980. "An Analysis of Variable Rate Loan Contracts." *Journal of Finance* 35: 389–403.
Dunn, Kenneth B., and Chester S. Spatt. 1984. "A Strategic Analysis of Sinking Fund Bonds." *Journal of Financial Economics* 13: 399–423.

Dyl, Edward A., and Michael D. Joehnk. 1979. "Sinking Funds and the Cost of Corporate Debt." *Journal of Finance* 34: 887–93.

Emanuel, David C. 1983. "A Theoretical Model for Valuing Preferred Stock." *Journal of Finance* 38: 1133–55.

———. 1983. "Warrant Valuation and Exercise Strategy." *Journal of Financial Economics* 12: 211–35.

———. 1984. "Discussion of 'Optimal Financial Policy and Firm Valuation.'" *Journal of Finance* 39: 607–9.

Galai, Dan, and Ronald W. Masulis. 1976. "The Option Pricing Model and the Risk Factor of Stock." *Journal of Financial Economics* 3: 53–81.

Galai, Dan, and Mier I. Schneller. 1978. "Pricing of Warrants and the Value of the Firm." *Journal of Finance* 33: 1333–42.

Geske, Robert. 1977. "The Valuation of Corporate Liabilities as Compound Options." *Journal of Financial and Quantitative Analysis* 12: 541–52.

Geske, Robert, and Herbert Johnson. 1984. "The Valuation of Corporate Liabilities as Compound Options: A Correction." *Journal of Financial and Quantitative Analysis* 19: 231–32.

Ho, Thomas S. Y., and Ronald F. Singer. 1982. "Bond Indenture Provisions and the Risk of Corporate Debt." *Journal of Financial Economics* 10: 375–406.

———. 1984. "The Value of Corporate Debt with a Sinking-Fund Provision." *Journal of Business* 57: 315–36.

Ingersoll, Jonathan E., Jr. 1976. "A Theoretical and Empirical Investigation of the Dual Purpose Funds: An Application of Contingent-Claims Analysis." *Journal of Financial Economics* 3: 83–123.

———. 1976. "Using the Black-Scholes Option Model in Investment Decision Making: Designing a Convertible Preferred Issue." *Proceedings: Seminar on the Analysis of Security Prices*, vol. 20 no. 1. Center for Research in Security Prices, (Graduate School of Business, University of Chicago).

———. 1977. "A Contingent-Claims Valuation of Convertible Securities." *Journal of Financial Economics* 4: 289–321.

———. 1977. "An Examination of Corporate Call Policies on Convertible Securities." *Journal of Finance* 32: 463–78.

Kim, E. Han, John J. McConnell, and Paul R. Greenwood. 1977. "Capital Structure Rearrangements and Me-First Rules in an Efficient Capital Market." *Journal of Finance* 32: 789–810.

Mason, Scott P., and Sudipto Bhattacharya. 1981. "Risky Debt, Jump Processes, and Safety Covenants." *Journal of Financial Economics* 9: 281–307.

Merton, Robert C. 1970. "A Dynamic General Equilibrium Model of the Asset Market and Its Application to the Pricing of the Capital Structure of the Firm." Unpublished working paper.

———. 1974. "On the Pricing of Corporate Debt: The Risk Structure of Interest Rates." *Journal of Finance* 29: 449–70.

———. 1977. "On the Pricing of Contingent Claims and the Modigliani-Miller Theorem." *Journal of Financial Economics* 5: 241–50.

Miller, Merton H. 1977. "Debt and Taxes." *Journal of Finance* 32: 261–75.

Modigliani, Franco, and Merton H. Miller. 1958. "The Cost of Capital, Corporation Finance and the Theory of Investment." *American Economic Review* 48: 261–97.

———. 1963. "Corporate Income Taxes and the Cost of Capital: A Correction." *American Economic Review* 53: 433–43.

Schwartz, Eduardo S. 1977. "The Valuation of Warrants: Implementing a New Approach." *Journal of Financial Economics* 4: 79–93.

———. 1982. "The Pricing of Commodity-Linked Bonds." *Journal of Finance* 37: 525–41.

Smith, Clifford W., Jr. 1977. "Alternative Methods for Raising Capital: Rights versus Underwritten Offerings." *Journal of Financial Economics* 5: 273–307.

———. 1979. "Applications of Option Pricing Analysis." In James L. Bicksler, ed., *Handbook of Financial Economics*, New York: North Holland Publishing Co.

Smith, Clifford W., Jr., and Jerold B. Warner. 1979. "On Financial Contracting: An Analysis of Bond Covenants." *Journal of Financial Economics* 7: 117–61.

Warner, Jerold B. 1977. "'Bankruptcy, Absolute Priority, and the Pricing of Risky Debt Claims." *Journal of Financial Economics* 4: 239–76.

———. 1977. "Bankruptcy Costs: Some Evidence." *Journal of Finance* 32: 337–47.

Weinstein, Mark I. 1983. "Bond Systematic Risk and the Option Pricing Model." *Journal of Finance* 38: 1415–30.

Index

D

E